PRIVATE LAW DICTIONARY

and

BILINGUAL LEXICONS

OBLIGATIONS

Editorial Committee

France ALLARD

Jean-Maurice BRISSON

Paul-A. CRÉPEAU, President

Yaëll EMERICH

Nicholas KASIRER, Secretary

Marie-France BICH

Élise CHARPENTIER

Mathieu DEVINAT

Patrick FORGET

Centre de recherche en droit privé et comparé du Québec

Quebec Research Centre of Private & Comparative Law

ÉDITIONS YVON BLAIS

A THOMSON COMPANY

National Library of Canada cataloguing in publication

Main entry under title:

Private law dictionary and bilingual lexicons: obligations

Issued also in French under title: Dictionnaire de droit privé et lexiques bilingues : les obligations.

Includes some text in French.

ISBN 2-89451-680-0

1. Obligations (Law) – Quebec (Province) – Dictionaries. I. Quebec Research Centre of Private & Comparative Law.

KEQ365.A57D5213   2003   346.71402'03   C2003-941777-8

We acknowledge the financial support of the Government of Canada through the Book Publishing Industry Development Program (BPIDP) for our publishing activities.

© Les Éditions Yvon Blais Inc., 2003
C.P. 180 Cowansville (Québec) Canada
Tel.: (450) 266-1086   Fax: (450) 263-9256
Website: www.editionsyvonblais.qc.ca

Legal Deposit: 4th trimester 2003
National Library of Canada
Bibliothèque nationale du Québec
ISBN: 2-89451-680-0

CONTRIBUTORS

PRIVATE LAW DICTIONARY OF OBLIGATIONS AND BILINGUAL LEXICONS AND THE FORTHCOMING THIRD EDITION OF THE PRIVATE LAW DICTIONARY

Editorial Committee
France ALLARD, Advocate; Marie-France BICH, Professor of Law, University of Montreal; Jean-Maurice BRISSON, Professor of Law, University of Montreal; Élise CHARPENTIER, Professor of Law, University of Montreal; Paul-A. CRÉPEAU, Emeritus Professor, McGill University; Mathieu DEVINAT, Assistant Director, Quebec Research Centre of Private & Comparative Law; Patrick FORGET, Project Director (Jurilinguistics), Quebec Research Centre of Private & Comparative Law; Yaëll EMERICH, Project Director (Property Law), Quebec Research Centre of Private & Comparative Law; Nicholas KASIRER, Director, Quebec Research Centre of Private & Comparative Law, James McGill Professor of Law, McGill University

The following persons also participated as members of the Editorial Committee to the preparation of the third edition of the forthcoming dictionary:
Lise I. BEAUDOIN, Advocate; Maryse BEAULIEU, Advocate; John E.C. BRIERLEY, Wainwright Professor of Civil Law, McGill University; Madeleine CANTIN CUMYN, Professor of Law, McGill University; Nadia CHAMMAS, Law Clerk, Quebec Court of Appeal; Évelyne CÔTÉ, Advocate; Philippe DENAULT, Advocate; Mylène DESCHENES, Researcher, Centre de recherche en droit public, University of Montreal; Véronique HIVON, Advocate; Robert P. KOURI, Professor of Law, University of Sherbrooke; Roderick A. MACDONALD, F.R. Scott Professor of Public and Constitutional Law, McGill University; Pierre MARTINEAU, Emeritus Professor, University of Montreal; Albert MAYRAND, Justice of the Court of Appeal (retired)

Ad Hoc Consultants
Jean-Guy BELLEY, Sir William Macdonald Professor of Law, McGill University; Gérard CORNU, Emeritus Professor, Université de Paris II; Vincent GAUTRAIS, Professor of Law, University of Montreal; Roderick A. MACDONALD, F.R. Scott Professor of Public and Constitutional Law, McGill University; Luc PLAMONDON, Advocate; William TETLEY, Professor of Law, McGill University

Coordination
Mathieu DEVINAT

Research
Farida ABBADI, Charles C. ALLEN, Mischa AUERBACH-ZIOGAS, Sophie BARABÉ, Luisa BIASUTTI, Horia BUNDARU, Patrick CALLAGHAN, Emmanuelle CARTIER, Maryse CHOUINARD, Daphney COLIN, Geneviève COUTLÉE, Aileen DOETSCH, Caroline DESCHÊNES, Marie-Andrée DORAIS, Angela FERNANDEZ, L. Clair FITZGERALD, Véronique FORTIN, Catherine GALARDO, Isabelle GAUTHIER, Louis GRATTON, Elizabeth HUNTER, Azim HUSSAIN, Martine LACHANCE, Jodi LACKMAN, Dominique LAPIERRE, Pierre-Olivier LAPORTE, Manon LAVOIE, Nathalie LECOQ, Mathieu LEGRIS, Danielle MACKINNON, Annie MAILHOT-GAMELIN, Catherine McKENZIE, Shalini MELWANI, Eric

The editors wish to express sincere thanks to their colleagues for the contribution they made to the deliberations of the Editorial Committee. Responsibility for errors and omissions of course falls to members of the Committee at the time of publication.

CONTRIBUTORS

PRIVATE LAW DICTIONARY AND BILINGUAL LEXICONS

SECOND EDITION
(1988-1991)

Editorial Committee
John E.C. BRIERLEY, Sir William Macdonald Professor of Law, McGill University;
Paul-A. CRÉPEAU, Wainwright Professor of Civil Law, McGill University; Peter P.C.
HAANAPPEL, Professor of Law, McGill University; Nicholas KASIRER, Professor
of Law, McGill University; Robert P. KOURI, Professor of Law, University of
Sherbrooke

Joint Editorial Committee
John E.C. BRIERLEY, Sir William Macdonald Professor of Law, McGill University;
Paul-A. CRÉPEAU, Wainwright Professor of Civil Law, McGill University; Peter P.C.
HAANAPPEL, Professor of Law, McGill University; Nicholas KASIRER, Professor
of Law, McGill University; Robert P. KOURI, Professor of Law, University of
Sherbrooke; Lucie LAGUË, Advocate; Pierre MARTINEAU, Emeritus Professor,
University of Montreal; Albert MAYRAND, Legal counsel with Leduc, LeBel

Revision
France ALLARD, Luisa BIASUTTI, Lucie LAGUË

Coordination
France ALLARD, Lucie LAGUË, Geneviève REEVES

Research
Charles C. ALLEN, Myriam BARON, Guylaine BEAUCHAMP, Luisa BIASUTTI,
Denis BOULIANNE, Isabelle BRAULT, Claudette COMTOIS, Eric H. McDEVITT-
DAVID, Marie-Andrée DORAIS, Marcelle FIORENTINI, Ysolde GENDREAU,
Gérald GOLDSTEIN, Martine HÉBERT, Gaytri KACHROO, Gisèle LAPRISE,
Christiane LAVALLÉE, Ghislaine MONTPETIT, Mario PROVOST, Yolanda
RANGEL, Geneviève REEVES, Marie-Claude ROY, Mathieu SAVARIS

Administrative and Technical Supervision
Alice ARCHAMBAULT-ROBACZEWSKA

Typography
Manon BERTHIAUME

Word Processing
Manon BERTHIAUME, Liesbeth BUITING, Francine CADIEUX, Carole
CARRIÈRE, Marie-Claude de BROUWER, Dimitra KAZIANIS, Warren NEILL,
Marie POTHIER, Marisa ROSSI, Lisa SHAW

CONTRIBUTORS

PRIVATE LAW DICTIONARY AND BILINGUAL LEXICONS

FIRST EDITION
(1984-1988)

Editorial Committee
John E.C. BRIERLEY, Sir William Macdonald Professor of Law, McGill University; Paul-A. CRÉPEAU, Wainwright Professor of Civil Law, McGill University; Peter P.C. HAANAPPEL, Professor of Law, McGill University; Robert P. KOURI, Professor of Law, University of Sherbrooke

Joint Editorial Committee
John E.C. BRIERLEY, Sir William Macdonald Professor of Law, McGill University; Paul-A. CRÉPEAU, Wainwright Professor of Civil Law, McGill University; Antoni DANDONNEAU, Chef du service de conseil juridique, Commission des valeurs mobilières du Québec; Peter P.C. HAANAPPEL, Professor of Law, McGill University; Robert P. KOURI, Professor of Law, University of Sherbrooke; Lucie LAGUË, Research Associate, Q.R.C.P.C.L.; Pierre MARTINEAU, Emeritus Professor, University of Montreal; Albert MAYRAND, Wainwright Senior Fellow, McGill University

Revision
Lucie LAGUË

Coordination
Lucie LAGUË

Research
Michelle BEAUCHAMP, Dougall CLARK, Ginette COLLIN, Judith CUMMINGS, Walter ELMORE, Dominique FARIBAULT, Roland-Yves GAGNÉ, Michèle GRANJON-LEGENDRE, William D. HART, Suzy KUCER, Mario LAGACÉ, Pierre LANG, Catherine LAPOINTE, Gisèle LAPRISE, Pierre LAROSE, Patricia LAWSON, Louise LUSSIER, Lois McDONALD, Brigitte MORNEAULT, Pierre NORMANDIN, Ghislain OTIS, Manon POMERLEAU, Yolanda RANGEL, David G. REED, Elayne ROMOFF, Danielle SAINT-AUBIN, Anouk VIOLETTE, Martine WALLIMANN

Consultants
Michael BRIDGE, John W. DURNFORD, Yoine GOLDSTEIN, The Honourable George OWEN

Administrative and Technical Supervision
Alice ARCHAMBAULT-ROBACZEWSKA

In memory of John E.C. Brierley

Wainwright Professor of Civil Law in the Faculty of Law, McGill University, and a founding member of the Editorial Committee of the *Private Law Dictionary* at the Quebec Research Centre for Private & Comparative Law

A desire for concision and an effort to reduce the substance of a legal concept to its essence, while avoiding at the same time those legal definitions of the French Code which he often regarded as "truisms" or "tautologies", characterize most of the portions of the Code for which [Charles Dewey] Day was responsible. ... Some of his remarks in his first *cahier* devoted to Obligations merit full reproduction, for they contain the philosophy of codification upon which his drafting was animated ... . With respect to his rejection of the series of definitions of different kinds of contracts contained in articles 1101 to 1107 of the French Code, he remarked:

> Every Code of Laws however full & complete it may be necessarily presupposes not only the existence but also the knowledge ... of certain fundamental principles. There are laws of God, of Nature and of common sense which must underlie and sustain all legislation. ...

There are few better testimonies to the fact that the Civil Code of Lower Canada was not conceived in a spirit of legal positivism, or in the belief that law cannot be laid down exclusively in a series of legal rules amounting to no more than a system of legal norms.

John E.C. Brierley, "Quebec's Civil Law Codification Viewed and Reviewed" (1968) 14 *McGill L.J.* 521, pp. 564-565.

TABLE OF CONTENTS

ACKNOWLEDGMENTS

What an immense ENTREPRISE[1]! *Tout un BAIL* / LEASE[2]! Fraught with *ALÉAS* / RISKS, the task of preparing a *Private Law Dictionary of Obligations* in French and English has been an *ACTE COLLECTIF* / COLLECTIVE ACT involving the energy and *DISCERNEMENT* / DISCERNMENT of a great many people of whom all are deserving of our thanks.

The Centre wishes to record its sincere gratitude to the Ministry of Canadian Heritage which sponsors, together with the Department of Justice of the Government of Canada, the National Program for the Integration of Both Official Languages in the Administration of Justice. *PAJLO* / POLAJ has provided generous and sustained financial support to the Centre's research on the *Private Law Dictionary* project. Thanks are also extended to the Social Science and Research Council of Canada which, through a major grant, made possible much of the jurilinguistic research undertaken by scholars at McGill. Publishing this dictionary is more than the *RÉALISATION D'UNE CONDITION* / FULFILLMENT OF A CONDITION in respect of the agencies offering financial support to the Centre, it has been the *EXÉCUTION* / PERFORMANCE of an *ENGAGEMENT D'HONNEUR* / HONOUR-ONLY AGREEMENT. We thank Andrée Duchesne, the National Coordinator of POLAJ, and its presidents Mario Dion and Lionel Levert, for their wise counsel over the past several years. We are grateful to the whole of the POLAJ community, including Monique Albert, Liliane Lê, and Guylain Thorne of Heritage Canada, Marc Dubois of Justice Canada and, in particular, the dean of jurilinguists in Canada, Gérard Snow, Director of the Centre de traduction et de terminologie juridiques of the Université de Moncton for his MORAL support and intellectual encouragement.

The Chambre des notaires offered its financial help, with the utmost *BONNE FOI* / GOOD FAITH, to assist the advancement of Civil law research, and we extend thanks to the Fondation du Notariat, and to the Board's president, Mtre Denis Marsolais, a loyal friend of the Centre. Other members of the legal community have shown support for this study of civilian legal vocabulary. We thank especially Mtre Louis Fortier – who has such a keen eye for legal bilingualism –, Mtre Yoine Goldstein – an expert, of course, in the law of Obligations in his own right –, and Mtre Arthur Holden – a steady and generous source of advice in many matters – for the various expressions of

---

1. *Sic*! given that the definition of ENTERPRISE, *infra*, suggests an organized "economic" activity, which the *Private Law Dictionary* is not. On the care with which common parlance and legal terminology should be distinguished, see, by a former member of the Editorial Committee, Jean-Claude Gémar, "Les fondements du langage du droit comme langue de spécialité", (1990) 21 *R.G.D.* 756.
2. Watch out for *faux amis*! See, by another friend of the Centre's dictionary project, Denis Tallon, "Les faux amis en droit comparé", in J. Basedow *et al.*, eds., *Festschrift für Ulrich Drobnig* (Tübingen: Mohr Siebek, 1998) 677.

SOLIDARITÉ / SOLIDARITY they have shown over the years for the work carried out here and for the Centre's Director.

Thanks are due to the many colleagues who, through *DONS* / GIFTS of ideas and time, have contributed to the success of this venture. Mtre Luc Plamondon provided much needed periodic PRESTATIONS, fittingly, in respect of the law of Insurance and Annuities. Professors Jean-Guy Belley, Daniel Jutras, Roderick Macdonald, Stephen Scott, Lionel Smith and William Tetley of the Faculty of Law at McGill University and Professors Claude Fabien, Vincent Gautrais, Ejan Mackaay and Pierre Noreau of the Université de Montréal, all responded generously to appeals for assistance and have shown patience in light of repeated *TROUBLES DE VOISINAGE* / NEIGH-BOURHOOD DISTURBANCES. Visitors to the Centre, including Dr Isabelle de Lamberterie of the Centre national de recherche scientifique in Paris, Professor Gérard Cornu of the Université de Paris II and Professor Jean-Claude Gémar of the Université de Genève, have followed the dictionary project with interest and understanding; their contributions have plainly been a source of *ENRICHISSEMENT INJUSTIFIÉ* / UNJUSTIFIED ENRICHMENT for which we can only offer our thanks. Special mention should be made to Dean Peter Leuprecht of the Faculty of Law at McGill for support to the Centre which is the CONDITION *SINE QUA NON* of the project. The Wainwright Trust in the Faculty of Law and the Young Canada Works Program of the Government of Canada provided assistance enabling us to enter into *CONTRATS DE LOUAGE DE SERVICES* / CONTRACTS OF LEASE AND HIRE OF SERVICES with several research students for which we offer thanks. Our publisher the Éditions Yvon Blais Inc. has demonstrated much more than a concern for the *QUALITÉ MARCHANDE* / MERCHANTABLE QUALITY of the dictionaries. Thanks to Mtre Yvon Blais for his unflagging interest in the many Centre activities, to Mtre Louis Bossé for his intelligence and good cheer as a collaborator, and to their skilled group of editors who helped ensure that the work is free from *VICES APPARENTS* / APPARENT DEFECTS.

Last but not least, as a grateful Director of the Centre, I offer personal thanks to the team of research scholars and members of the Editorial Committee who have contributed to the success of this *SUI GENERIS* intellectual endeavour. In a manner of speaking, this volume of the dictionary, bearing as it does on the law of Obligations, is an *ACTION PAULIENNE* / PAULIAN ACTION. Professor Paul-André Crépeau, who has chaired the Editorial Committee since the inception of the project, was not so much the *MAÎTRE DE L'AFFAIRE* / PRINCIPAL or the *MAÎTRE DE L'OUVRAGE* / CLIENT, but more of a *BONUS PATER FAMILIAS* for the Committee, offering all of his time, energy and rich understanding of the law of Contract and Delict to the *Private Law Dictionary of Obligations*. Other members of the Committee, present and past, understood that their contributions were *ACTES À TITRE GRATUIT* / ACTS BY GRATUITOUS TITLE and yet cheerfully and collegially worked many hours on the dictionaries, notwithstanding the plain *PERTE D'UNE CHANCE* / LOSS OF A CHANCE in respect of their other work. Preparing definitions in the collegial context of the Committee is a challenge – in some measure a scholar must be content to *RENONCER* / RENOUNCE part of his or her academic *AUTONOMIE DE LA VOLONTÉ* / AUTONOMY OF THE WILL in service of the venture. France Allard, who has a patient understanding of the dictionaries as a *CONTRAT À EXÉCUTION SUCCESSIVE* / CONTRACT OF SUCCESSIVE PERFORMANCE, has regularly showed her sense of the *OBLIGATION DE SECOURS ET D'ASSISTANCE* / OBLI-GATION OF SUCCOUR AND ASSISTANCE (see *Private Law Dictionary of the*

Family) to the Committee. Marie-France Bich, one of the newest members of the Committee, has demonstrated herself worthy of a *CLAUSE D'OR* / GOLD CLAUSE in exchange for her keen insight and gentle encouragement. Jean-Maurice Brisson, whose *savoir* and *savoir vivre* means that he often helps us achieve an *ACCORD DE VOLONTÉS* / MEETING OF THE MINDS, has offered support to the present Director of the Centre over the years which can only be described as *INCONDITIONNEL* / UNCONDITIONAL. Élise Charpentier, who left the Centre's permanent staff to take up a teaching position, has kindly *CONSENTI* / CONSENTED to remain on the Editorial Committee, favouring us with intelligence and her sense of JUSTICE, *CONTRACTUELLE* / CONTRACTUAL or otherwise, in our deliberations. Thanks are warmly extended as well to all past members of the Committee – their names are gratefully recorded, *supra*, – whose *APPORT* / CONTRIBUTION, always generously offered, has no *PRIX* / PRICE. (While we are most grateful to them, past members are, of course, *EXONÉRÉS* / EXEMPT from liability!)

Professional and student research scholars – their names figure as well, with our thanks, in the previous pages – offered the hard work that is the veritable *CAUTION* / GUARANTEE of the scientific virtues of the dictionaries. Every researcher who has worked at the Centre over the years deserves our thanks. The success of the dictionary is that of an *ACTE COMPLEXE* / COMPLEX ACT, in both time and space, predicated on a group *RESPONSABILITÉ* / RESPONSIBILITY for the whole, responsibility that is, for current researchers at least, felt *CONJOINTEMENT ET SOLIDAIREMENT* / JOINT AND SEVERAL with members of the Committee. I allow myself to make special mention of current senior research scholars who worked on this project. Mathieu Devinat, the Assistant Director of the Centre, has had the *GARDE DE LA STRUCTURE* / CUSTODY OF THE STRUCTURE of the manuscript, and has acquitted his responsibilities admirably. Yaëll Emerich, with her expertise in Property law, has had ownership of the *CRÉANCES* / CLAIMS in the text, so to speak, bringing the insights from her doctoral research to our deliberations. Patrick Forget is the senior researcher in the group, a model of collegiality and FAIR DEALING (see *BONNE FOI*), with a gifted pen filled with much-appreciated ink. Martine Lachance, who has recently joined the group with the advantage of her acquired notarial science, has shown her work to be *SOLENNEL* / SOLEMN without being *FORMALISTE* / FORMALISTIC. Manon Lavoie and Eric Reiter, graduate students in the Faculty, deserve special mention too. Dr Reiter has done yeoman SERVICE in his careful proof-reading of the manuscript and no *VICE CACHÉ* / LATENT DEFECT could survive Ms Lavoie's critical eye. Finally, in an undertaking *À DURÉE INDÉTERMINÉE* / WITH AN INDETERMINATE TERM such as the on-going *Private Law Dictionary*, the personnel inevitably changes. But one member of the team, the Centre's Administrative Assistant Manon Berthiaume, has faithfully and cheerfully provided the project with the stability it so badly needs. Her keen judgment and hard work on the dictionaries is plainly above and beyond the call of *DEVOIR* / DUTY.

Readers inevitably agree to a measure of *ACCEPTATION DES RISQUES* / ASSUMPTION OF RISKS in the ACQUISITION of the present work. It is in the nature of academic work – an obvious instance of an activity characterized by an *OBLIGATION DE MOYENS* / OBLIGATION OF MEANS – that some *ERREURS* / MISTAKES will be made, whether they be *ERREURS MATÉRIELLES* / CLERICAL ERRORS or *ERREURS DE DROIT* / ERRORS OF LAW. We say this not as an *EXCLUSION DE RESPONSABILITÉ* / EXCLUSION OF LIABILITY for work that we anticipate to be deficient, but instead because we know the *PRODUIT* / PRODUCT can be improved. The dictionary is a sort of lexical *ANATOCISME* / ANATOCISM: future contributions will compound with the capital established in this dictionary to make up the complete *Private Law Dictionary* / *Dictionnaire de droit privé* to be published at a later date. Editors in future years will attempt to improve on existing terms in later editions (in this sense, we are less *AUTEURS* than PREDECESSORS IN TITLE of future dictionaries to be published at the Centre). We earnestly invite readers to write the Editorial Committee, care of its Secretary, at the Quebec Research Centre for Private & Comparative Law, McGill University, 3644 Peel Street, Montreal, Quebec H3A 1W9, if they have suggestions for improvement. Whereof QUIT.

Nicholas Kasirer, Director
Quebec Research Centre of Private & Comparative Law
June 30, 2003

GUIDE TO THE USE OF THE DICTIONARY

GUIDE TO THE USE OF THE DICTIONARY

In anticipation of the eventual publication of a comprehensive edition of the *Private Law Dictionary and Bilingual Lexicons*, the Quebec Research Centre of Private and Comparative Law has prepared the *Private Law Dictionary of Obligations and Bilingual Lexicons* which presents the fundamental private law terminology of Quebec's law of Obligations. The work takes into account the changes introduced by the *Civil Code of Québec* (S.Q. 1991, c. 64) and by other changes to the law that have occurred since the second edition of the *Private Law Dictionary* (1991), including those pertaining to federal legislation. An effort has been made to situate the law in view of the relationship between the *Civil Code of Québec* and the *Civil Code of Lower Canada*, as that relationship reflects both the continuity and renewal of the general law of Obligations.

The *Private Law Dictionary of Obligations and Bilingual Lexicons* is divided into two parts. The first part, the *Dictionary* proper, contains more than 2,400 terms and expressions taken from the vocabulary used in the legislative sources of the law of Obligations (codes, statutes and regulations), in doctrinal writings of legal scholars, in judgments of the courts and, to a certain extent, in the language used in dealings between individuals (e.g. contracts, wills) and ordinary usage. An English-French lexicon has been appended to the articles of the *Dictionary* at the end of each given entry. The second part consists of the French-English lexicon which, with the lexicon integrated in each entry, forms the other half of the *Bilingual Lexicons*. The entries which make up the two bilingual lexicons are drawn from those terms defined in the *Private Law Dictionary of Obligations* and the *Dictionnaire de droit privé des obligations*, published with this work by the same Editorial Committee.

In order to facilitate the use of the *Dictionary*, these explanatory notes present the principles that have guided the elaboration of the entries (I), the various elements that compose the structure of the articles (II) and, lastly, a description of the content of the bilingual lexicons (III).

I.   ENTRIES

The entries, whether they are composed of single or multiple words, form the nomenclature of the *Dictionary*. They are arranged in absolute alphabetical order, so that hyphens and spaces between the words of an entry have been discounted. Thus, the expression **ACT OF ANOTHER** comes directly after **ACT OF AN ANIMAL** and precedes **ACT OF A THING**. The entries include not only nouns and nominal phrases, as is usual in specialized dictionaries, but also terms belonging to other grammatical categories as, for example, adjectives (e.g. **CONTRACTUAL**) and verbs (e.g. **CONTRACT**).

Since it covers a specialized body of terminology, the *Dictionary* does not include words of ordinary parlance unless they have a distinct juridical meaning (e.g. **DAM-**

AGE or **RECEPTION**). However, discussion of the ordinary usage of a legal term may be included when confusion with its legal acceptation is likely. In these cases, the *Dictionary* may include a separate definition for each meaning (e.g. **DIVISIBILITY¹** and **DIVISIBILITY²**) or indicate their presence through an observation (e.g. **PAYMENT¹**).

The Editorial Committee wishes to acknowledge the following dictionaries, both legal and general, as important research tools in the preparation of entries: *Black's Law Dictionary*, B.A. Garner ed., 7th ed. (St. Paul: West Group, 1999); G. Cornu, *Vocabulaire juridique*, 4th ed. (Paris: P.U.F., 2003); *Dictionnaire historique de la langue française*, A. Rey, ed. (Paris: Dictionnaire Le Robert, 1992); *Le Grand Robert de la langue française*, 2nd ed., A. Rey, ed. (Paris: Le Robert, 2001); *Oxford English Dictionary* (Oxford: O.U.P., 1989).

A. Presentation of Entries

In principle, entries are presented in the singular, except when usage indicates that the plural form is preferred. Parts of certain entries are placed within parentheses, either in a multiple word entry or at the end thereof. In some cases, parentheses serve to indicate two possible versions of a term. For example, the word **QUIT(S)** may be written in the singular or in the plural; **CONTRACT FOR (OF) SERVICES** may be written as either **CONTRACT FOR SERVICES** or **CONTRACT OF SERVICES**. In other instances, the parentheses serve to modify the order of presentation of a word in an entry, most frequently for an entry beginning with a preposition (e.g. **AUTONOMY OF WILL (THEORY OF THE)**). These entries are listed alphabetically, according to the principal word.

B. Special Types of Entries

1. Entries in Languages other than English

Given the importance of Latin expressions in the Civil law terminology, the nomenclature includes a number of Latin terms (e.g. ***CAUSA CAUSANS***). Certain French-language terms also appear (e.g. ***CLAUSE COMPROMISSOIRE***). These entries are accompanied by an indication of their language of origin (e.g. (Latin), (French)) and are generally presented in italics, unless when they are considered as fully integrated in the English-language juridical vocabulary (e.g. **ANATOCISM**).

2. Controversial Usage

English Civil law parlance in Quebec contains examples of what some experts see as dubious or controversial usage. Many of these instances are borrowings from Anglo-American legal terminology. The circumstances of borrowing terms vary widely, and in many cases the terminology is not at all controversial. In other cases, terms have been criticized in that they promote confusion with Anglo-American legal ideas. There are also instances of gallicisms which have, in the opinion of some, been unduly relied upon in the English-language civilian lexicon. Many of these matters are subject to disagreement among jurilinguists.[1] The Editorial Committee has chosen, in the main, to alert readers as to the terms which are controversial by way of observations rather than formal indications that the term not be used (e.g. the observations under the entry **CONSIDERATION[3]**).

3. Cross-references

Certain entries are not defined where the Editorial Committee felt that a full treatment of the term was not necessary. In these cases, a reference is made to a relevant entry by the indication "See" which may contain information concerning the use of the undefined term (e.g. **CORRELATION** refers to **CAUSATION[1]**).

II. ARTICLES

The whole of the information provided in relation to a given entry constitutes an *article* of the *Dictionary*. The central element of the entry is the definition itself, but an article comprises of many other elements that, although they are accessory to the definition, serve to complete, clarify, situate or elaborate upon the term as defined.

Before describing these different elements, the typographical features of the *Dictionary* call for some comment.

In the lexicographical portion of the *Dictionary*, information relating to the term is divided into separate sections, each of which is listed in order and preceded by an abbreviation. For example, the list of occurrences for a given term is preceded by the abbreviation "**Occ.**". Observations bearing on usage and treatment of the term in different legal sources (**Obs.**), cross-references to synonyms (**Syn.**) and analogous terms (**See also**) are indicated in the same fashion. Italics serve to identify all those features of the term which pertain to the following considerations: linguistic form and function, such as grammatical category, and linguistic examples that draw attention to certain terms.

English-French equivalents are included with each English article so as to provide the reader with the French-language partner terms for any given entry. These are placed at the end of each article, preceded by the abbreviation "**Fr.**".

---

1. For an illustration, see Nicholas Kasirer, "Le *real estate* existe-t-il en droit civil ?", (1998) 29 *R.G.D.* 465.

There follows an explanation of the various elements which may form part of any given entry:

SCHEMA

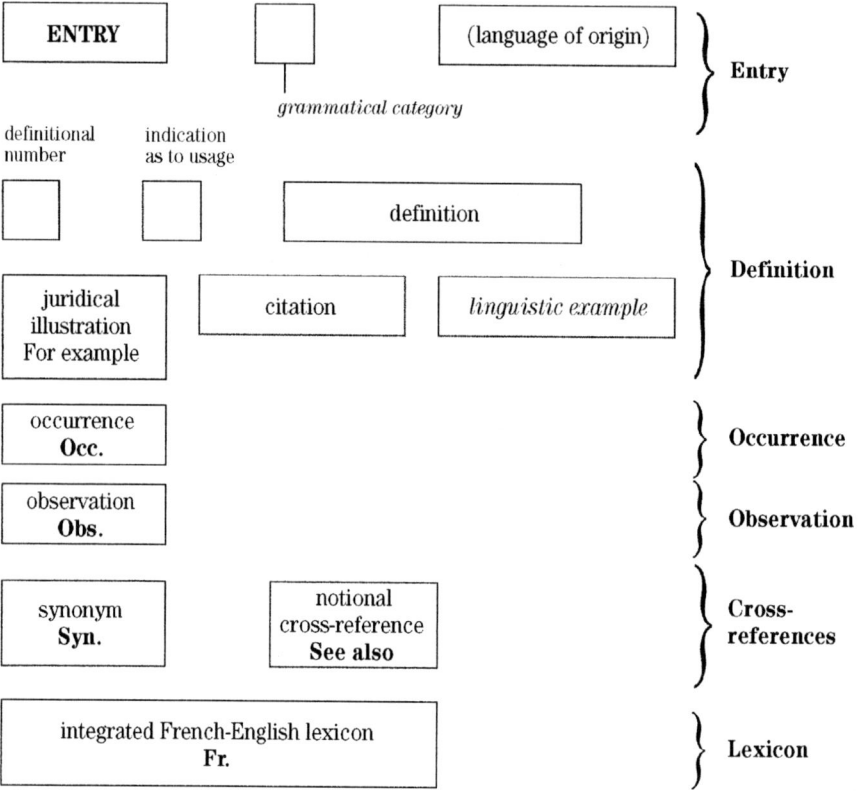

A. Definition

The purpose of the definition is to provide, in a single sentence or phrase, the essential elements of the meaning of a given juridical term. The definitions are built on basic terms which, within the hierarchical structure of the *Dictionary*, refer to the notion closest to the defined term. Thus, the definition of the **FAULT¹** reads "Transgression of an obligatory juridical rule of conduct"; **CIVIL FAULT** builds on the latter with its definition "Fault¹ susceptible of engaging a person's civil liability". To the root term (i.e. **FAULT¹**), information is added that qualifies and distinguishes a term from concepts to which it is related.

Where applicable, the text of the definition includes the technical designations of the actors encountered in a given juridical situation or transaction. For example, in the definition of the term **SALE**, the terms *seller* and *buyer* appear, which are themselves defined elsewhere in the *Dictionary*.

1. Definitions of Polysemous Terms

A term may have multiple meanings that vary according to context (e.g. **CONDITION**[1,2,3]). In order to distinguish those different meanings, each of them are sorted and numbered according to their importance. These numbers latter serve to precise the exact acceptation that is referred to (e.g. the definition of **CONDITIONAL OBLIGATION** refers to **CONDITION**[1]).

2. Synonymous Definitions

Some entries are defined as synonyms of another term. In these cases, the definition refers to another term or expression that is considered interchangeable with the entry. This may be tempered or qualified by an indication as to usage or by an observation (e.g. **IMPERFECT SOLIDARITY** is sometimes used as a synonym of **OBLIGATION *IN SOLIDUM***, but it is mainly used in contrast to **PERFECT SOLIDARITY**).

While some scholars have argued that there are few perfect synonyms in legal terminology, the Editorial Committee of the *Dictionary* has come to the view that there are in fact numerous synonyms in the law of Obligations. These synonyms reflect, in our estimation, the richness of vocabulary used by doctrinal writing and in decided cases in this field of the law. Moreover, multiple-word entries often have numerous synonyms because the combinations increase when one or more words of the compound term have their own synonyms. For example, the expression **CONTRACT FOR THE CARRIAGE OF PROPERTY** is an illustration of this latter situation. In this multiple-word entry, **GOODS** may replace **PROPERTY**.

Within any group of synonyms, only one is designated as a preferred term, i.e. the one under which the definition, illustrations in law, observations and cross-references will appear in the *Dictionary*. This choice of the preferred synonym is determined by various factors: the frequency of its use (e.g. **CONTRACTUAL** occurs more frequently than **CONVENTIONAL**); the precision of a certain form (e.g. **POTESTATIVE CONDITION** is preferred to **FACULTATIVE CONDITION**), and, when the synonyms are perfectly equivalent, one preferred form has been chosen by the Editorial Committee according to their appreciation of felicitous usage.

With a view to promoting English-language civilian parlance, the Editorial Committee generally refers to the English-language equivalents of Latin or French-language entries as the preferred term (e.g. **GIVING IN PAYMENT** preferred over its synonym ***DATION EN PAIEMENT***). In the absence of an English-language equivalent, the Latin term will receive a complete lexical consideration (e.g. ***ACCIPIENS***).

B. Elements Accessory to the Definition

The elements accessory to a definition include the grammatical category, the language of origin, indications as to usage, illustrations in law, quotations, linguistic examples, occurrences, observations and cross-references.

1. Grammatical Category

Single-word entries are followed by a reference to a grammatical category: noun, adjective, verb or adverb (e.g. **CONTRACT** *n.*). There is no such reference for multiple word entries, except with respect to nominal, adjectival or adverbial phrases (e.g. **SUBJECT OF LAW** *nom.ph.*).

2. Language of Origin

The language of origin is provided in the case of entries in languages other than English. These entries are usually in Latin (e.g. ***ERGA OMNES***) and, occasionally, in French (e.g. ***CLAUSE COMPROMISSOIRE***). If a part of a multiple-word entry is in a language other than English, the non-English origin is recorded (e.g. **ACTION *EN PASSATION DE TITRE*** (French); ***AD LITEM* MANDATE** (Latin)).

3. Indications as to Usage

Indications as to usage may either precede the definition or be included in the observations under a defined term. Where the Editorial Committee is of the view that a particular indication as to usage might become the object of disagreements between scholars, a critical note is included in the observations. Examples include accepted language viewed as imprecise (e.g. **UNDISPOSABILITY**) or considered to be inopportune for some reason (e.g. **JOINTLY AND SEVERALLY**). In these circumstances, the Editorial Committee has chosen to explain its view on usage rather than merely designating it as a faulty form. This represents a change from the practice followed in the second edition of the *Private Law Dictionary*.

4. Illustrations in Law

Illustrations in law are placed immediately after the definition of a term. Thus, *mandate* and *sale* serve as examples for the expression **NOMINATE CONTRACT**.

5. Quotations

Quotations serve to clarify or make concrete the definition, both as a matter of law and linguistically. The quotations can either clarify certain aspects of the definition or even repeat it, albeit using another formulation. As well, they may articulate certain rules that govern the application of the term, criticize the understanding others may have of the term, or even provide a further classification relevant to the term being defined.

Quotations are generally drawn from Quebec jurisprudence and scholarly writing. However, scholarly writings from other jurisdictions are also used, notably from France and Louisiana.

References as to the place of publication of these quotations are presented in an abbreviated form. Complete references are provided in the *List of Authors and Publications Quoted in Abbreviated Form* found at the end of the *Dictionary*.

6. Linguistic Examples

Linguistic examples are intended to offer models for the proper usage of a term in legal discourse. Their purpose is to show how terms and expressions are used in their particular legal context (e.g. *To accept an offer* is given as a linguistic example for **OFFER**).

7. Occurrences

Numerous references taken from provincial and federal legislation illustrate an occurrence of a term in statutory and codal texts. These occurrences are introduced by the abbreviation "**Occ.**". An occurrence found in a legislative text which is no longer in force is preceded by the indication *former* (e.g. former art. 1767 C.C.Q. at **SALE OF AN ENTREPRISE**).

8. Observations

Observations may focus upon either the legal, or more narrowly, linguistic aspects of an entry. The purpose of an observation of a juridical nature is to complete the definition by pointing out a characteristic feature of the legal regime in question or to draw attention to a possible confusion with related concepts (e.g. **CAUSE¹, CAUSE²**). Observations may also upon occasion refer to a source, usually legislative, in which the notion in question is explained, but where the term is not actually used (e.g. **FEAR** which refers to arts. 1402, 1403 C.C.Q.).

The observation may also provide information of a linguistic nature. For example, it may draw attention to the usage of a term in certain statutes or identify a problematic usage (e.g. **JOINT AND SEVERAL**).

Finally, the observation occasionally provides an etymological treatment of a term. It generally includes its word (the etymon) and language of origin.

9. Cross-references

Cross-references, found at the end of each entry, are intended to provide a comprehensive semantic treatment of a term. These include synonyms and notional cross-references.

a) Synonyms

Synonyms, or terms expressing exactly the same legal notion, are discussed above.

Within a series of terms regarded as synonyms, one is designated as the preferred term, under which the definition, the illustration in law, the observations and cross-references are found: the principal synonym (e.g. **OBLIGATION TO INFORM**). The other terms are understood as subsidiary ones, in that a reference to the principal synonym stands in place of an independent definition (e.g. **DUTY TO INFORM**).

b) Notional Cross-references

Notional cross-references, introduced by the words "**See also**", draw attention to a series of closely-related terms. The terms may be associated through a logical relationship of cause and effect (e.g. **RELATIVE NULLITY** and **ACTION IN NULLITY**), or of a part in relation to the whole (e.g. **LEGAL ORDER** and **REGIME**). The cross-references may also indicate a close notional proximity to a related term, as is the case for **GAMING CONTRACT** and **WAGERING CONTRACT**. The cross-references also refer to terms the meanings of which are either in relationships of opposition (e.g. **VOLUNTARY RESILIATION, FORCED RESILIATION**), of complementarity (e.g. **ADEQUATE CAUSE, DETERMINING CAUSE, MATERIAL CAUSE**) or of reciprocity (e.g. **BUYER, SELLER**). By cross-referencing closely related terms, the reader may more accurately grasp the nuances and limits of a particular concept.

III. BILINGUAL LEXICONS

Initially undertaken in the first and second editions of the *Private Law Dictionary* and the *Dictionnaire de droit privé*, the English-French and French-English lexicons seek to provide the most appropriate equivalents in the target language for a concept in the source language. English-French lexical entries have been appended to the English entries of the *Private Law Dictionary of Obligations*, and are placed at the end of each given entry, preceded by the abbreviation "**Fr.**". These terms appear in the target language in the French-English lexicon, which forms the second part of the *Dictionary*. This second lexicon is made up of terms which correspond to the entries in the *Dictionnaire de droit privé des obligations* and which are followed by one or more English equivalents defined in the *Private Law Dictionary of Obligations*.

In both the integrated lexical entries and the French-English lexicon, the designated equivalents are accompanied by various editorial symbols:

(>) (<)   These mathematical symbols, encountered exclusively in the *Lexicons*, are used occasionally to indicate a divergence of meaning between English and French terminology, involving either a wider (>) or a narrower (<) connotation in relation to the entry in the other language. As an illustration, compare **FACT**[1] to one of its French-language equivalents, **FAIT**[1]. The definition of the English term **FACT**[1] is more restricted. Thus, at the entry for the term **FACT**[1] in the *English-French Lexicon*, the French equivalent is followed by the symbol (>) to indicate that it has a wider meaning than that of its English equivalent. Conversely, in the *French-English Lexicon*, the entry **FAIT**[1] refers to **FACT**[1] as the English equivalent, followed by the symbol (<) to indicate that the latter is narrower in scope.

+   In the *Lexicons*, when the target language has several synonyms for an entry in the source language, the symbol (+) is placed alongside the preferred expression. This term, as the principal synonym, is the entry under which the corresponding definition will be found in either the *Private Law Dictionary of Obligations* or the *Dictionnaire de droit privé des obligations* as the case may be. For example, at the entry **CIVIL FAULT**, the "+" which follows **FAUTE CIVILE** in the lexical entry indicates that the definition in the *Dictionnaire de droit privé des obligations* will be found at that term and not at **FAUTE²**. Conversely, at the entry **FAUTE²** in the lexicon part of the *Dictionary*, the "+" which follows **CIVIL FAULT** indicates that the definition in the *Private Law Dictionary of Obligations* will be found at that term and not at **FAULT²**.

[*]   This symbol indicates the rare instance in which a term or expression has no equivalent in the target language.

LIST OF ABBREVIATIONS
AND LEXICOGRAPHIC SYMBOLS

[term]^2	The number in superscript refers to a specific meaning of a polysemous term.
+	Used in the lexicons, this symbol indicates which of the equivalents in the other language has been designated as the principal term under which the corresponding definition is to be found.
[*]	Used in the lexicons, this symbol indicates a term for which there is no equivalent term or expression in the target language.
(>) and (<)	Used in the lexicons, these symbols accompany equivalent terms in the target language. They indicate that the word is either more extensive (>) or narrower (<) in meaning than the term in the source language.
[ ]	Square brackets indicate an addition to the text of a quotation.
[...]	An ellipsis between square brackets indicates an omission in the text of a quotation. An ellipsis without brackets is part of the original passage quoted.
adj.	adjective
adj.ph.	adjectival phrase
adv.	adverb
adv.ph.	adverbial phrase
App.	Appendice
art. (arts.)	article(s)
Bk	Book
c.	chapter
ed. (eds.)	edition/editor(s)
e.g.	*exempli gratia* (for example)
esp.	especially
et al.	*et alter* (and others)
et seq.	*et sequential* (and following)
former art.	former article
Fr.	French: this abbreviation is placed at the end of the article of definition. It precedes the French-language equivalents and, together with the entry, constitutes the integrated English-French lexicon.
i.e.	*id est* (that is to say)
J.	Justice
Leg.	Legislature
n.	noun
n^o	number

Neol.	Neologism
nom.ph.	nominal phrase
Obs.	Observation: introduces observations of a juridical, linguistic or etymological nature.
Occ.	Occurrence
p. (pp.)	page(s)
para. (paras.)	paragraph(s)
pl.n.	plural noun
p.p.adj.	past participle used as an adjective
prep.ph.	prepositional phrase
s. (ss.)	section(s)
Sch.	Schedule
See	Refers to the multiple-word entry which includes this term.
See also	Introduces analogous cross-references to terms in a relation of cause and effect, or of a part to the whole or simply a close notional relationship.
Sess.	Session
Supp.	Supplement
Syn.	Synonym: when the abbreviation is not in bold, the term stands in for an independent definition.
t.	tome
U.K.	United Kingdom
v.	verb
v.	*versus*
verb.ph.	verbal phrase
30 & 31 Vict.	Regnal Year
vol.	volume

LIST OF ABBREVIATIONS OF
LEGAL DOCUMENTS AND PUBLICATIONS

A.C.	Appeal Cases (U.K.)
A.P.D.	Archives de philosophie du droit
Am. J. Comp. L.	American Journal of Comparative Law
B.R.	Banc de la Reine ou du Roi Recueils de jurisprudence du Québec, Cour du Banc de la Reine/du Roi (1942-1969) Rapports judiciaires officiels de Québec, Cour du Banc de la Reine/du Roi (1892-1941)
C.A.	Court of Appeal Recueils de jurisprudence du Québec, Cour d'appel (1970-1985)
C.C.L.C.	Civil Code of Lower Canada
C.C.P.	Code of Civil Procedure
C.C.Q.	Civil Code of Québec
C.C.Q. (1981)	*An Act to establish a new Civil Code and to* *reform family law*, S.Q. 1980, c. 39
C.C.R.O.	Civil Code Revision Office
C. de D.	Cahiers de Droit
C.F.L.Q.	Canadian Family Law Quarterly
C.J.	Chief Justice
C.P.A.	*Consumer Protection Act*, R.S.Q., c. P-40.1
C.S.	Cour supérieure Recueils de jurisprudence du Québec, Cour supérieure (1967-1985) Rapports judiciaires officiels de Québec, Cour supérieure (1942-1966) Rapports judiciaires officiels de Québec, Cour supérieure (1892-1941)
Can. Bar Rev.	Canadian Bar Review
Can. T.S.	Canada Treaty Series
Constitution Act, 1867	*Constitution Act, 1867* (U.K.), 30 & 31 Vict., c. 3, reprinted in R.S.C. 1985, App. II, No. 5
Constitution Act, 1982	*Constitution Act, 1982*, being Schedule B of the *Canada Act 1982* (U.K.), 1982, c. 11
Dig.	Digest
G.A.	General Assembly (United Nations)

G.O.Q.	Gazette officielle du Québec
Int'l J. L. & Psychiatry	International Journal of Law & Psychiatry
K.B.	Court of King's Bench
La. L. Rev.	Louisiana Law Review
Leg.	Legislature
Loyola L. Rev.	Loyola Law Review
Man. L.J.	Manitoba Law Journal
McGill L.J.	McGill Law Journal
Meredith Lect.	Meredith Memorial Lectures
M.O.	Ministerial Order
O.C.	Order in Council
O.R.	Ontario Reports
Osgoode Hall L.J.	Osgoode Hall Law Journal
P.C.	Privy Council
r.	regulation
R. du B.	Revue du Barreau
R. du N.	Revue du Notariat
R.D.U.S.	Revue de droit de l'Université de Sherbrooke
R.F.L.	Reports of Family Law
R.G.D.	Revue générale de droit
R.J.Q.	Recueils de jurisprudence du Québec
R.J.T.	Revue juridique Thémis
R.R.Q.	Revised Regulations of Québec
R.S.C.	Revised Statutes of Canada
R.S.O.	Revised Statutes of Ontario
R.S.Q.	Revised Statutes of Québec
S.C.	Statutes of Canada
S.C.C.	Supreme Court of Canada
S.C.L.R.	Supreme Court Law Reports
S.C.R.	Canadian Supreme Court Reports (1876-to date)
S.O.R.	Statutory Orders and Regulations
S.Q.	Statutes of Québec
Sask. Q.B.	Saskatchewan Queen's Bench
Sess.	Session
Sup. Ct.	Superior Court
Thémis	Thémis
Tul. L. Rev.	Tulane Law Review
U.T.L.J.	University of Toronto Law Journal

A

ABANDONMENT *n.*

1. Abdicative act bearing, in particular, on a real right, the possession of a thing or a juridical claim. For example, act of throwing away an object of slight value, the abandonment of the *mitoyenneté*. "The question in this case is as to whether the plaintiff having made an abandonment of his property prior to the institution of this action, defendant may demand that all proceedings herein be suspended until the curator of said abandonment has taken up the instance" (*Gauthier* v. *Rousseau* (1911), 15 Q.P.R. 36 (Sup. Ct.), J.C. McCorkill, J.).
Occ. Arts. 1208, 1804, 1915 C.C.Q.
Obs. 1° As a kind of abdicative act, abandonment is a unilateral juridical act which provokes the extinction of a right as it concerns the person exercising it. It may bear on movables or immovables. **2°** The faculty of abandonment is traditionally understood in connection with the *right of ownership* and is founded on the *abusus*, attribute that confers upon the owner the power to dispose juridically and materially of the property owned. Its application to other real rights proceeds by analogy to ownership. **3°** Whether it is possible to abandon the right of ownership on an immovable remains an open question. In certain cases, the law provides expressly for the abandonment of right of ownership in favor of a specified beneficiary (e.g. the abandonment of a part of servient land to the benefit of the owner of the dominant land (art. 1185 C.C.Q.)). **4°** The term *abandonment* broadly understood is synonymous with renunciation. On occasion, one finds reference to the abandonment of a personal right as, for example, in the case of the abandonment of the dwelling by the lessee (art. 1915 C.C.Q.). It is more usual, however, to refer to the *renunciation* of personal rights.
See also abdicative act, renunciation².
Fr. abandon.

2. Syn. renunciation².
Fr. renonciation.

ABDICATION *n.*

Rare. Syn. renunciation¹.
Fr. abdication, acte abdicatif⁺.

ABDICATIVE *adj.*

See abdicative act, abdicative effect.
Fr. abdicatif.

ABDICATIVE ACT

Rare. Syn. renunciation¹.
Fr. abdication, acte abdicatif⁺.

ABDICATIVE EFFECT

Syn. renunciatory effect.
Fr. effet abdicatif.

ABILITY *n.*

Syn. *de facto* capacity.
Occ. Arts. 29, 258 C.C.Q.; arts. 327, 1731.2 C.C.L.C.
Fr. aptitude⁺, capacité², capacité de fait, capacité naturelle.

ABLE *adj.*

Syn. capable².
Occ. Arts. 19.2, 335, 1731.8 C.C.L.C.
Obs. 1° This term is also used to describe the quality of a person who has the potential to enjoy or to exercise civil rights at law (e.g. art. 4 C.C.Q.; art. 56 C.C.P.). **2°** Another use of the term corresponds to having the necessary qualities, power or possibility to undertake a certain activity or fulfill a charge (e.g. art. 179 C.C.Q.).
Fr. apte⁺, capable².

ABSOLUTE *adj.*

See absolute error, absolute liability, absolute nullity, absolute obligation, absolute presumption, absolute public order.
Fr. absolu.

ABSOLUTE ERROR

Error preventing the meeting of minds.
Obs. 1° The notion of *absolute error* has been developed by scholars as a category to include error as to the nature of the juridical act, error as to the identity of the object and error as to the cause of the obligation. **2**° The distinction between absolute error, which leads to absolute nullity, and error constituting a defect of consent, which leads to relative nullity, is not explicitly drawn in the Civil Code.
See also error constituting a defect of consent.
Fr. erreur-obstacle.

ABSOLUTE LIABILITY

Syn. strict liability. "As to the contention that, without proof of fault or negligence, absolute liability of the company is established under article 1054 C.C.[L.C.] upon its being proved that the damage sued for was caused by a 'thing which it had under its care' or because, as contended, the company failed to prove that it was unable to prevent the act which caused the damage, I am in full accord with the judgment of the court of appeal [...]" (*Vandry* v. *Quebec Railway, Light, Heat and Power Co.* (1915-16), 53 S.C.R. 72, p. 75, L.H. Davies, J.).
Occ. S. 42(4), *Fisheries Act*, R.S.C. 1985, c. F-14.
Fr. responsabilité absolue, responsabilité causale, responsabilité de plein droit, responsabilité objective+, responsabilité sans faute, responsabilité stricte.

ABSOLUTE NULLITY

Nullity arising in the formation of a juridical act which sanctions the violation of a rule designed to protect the public interest. For example, the nullity of procreation or gestation agreements on behalf of another (art. 541 C.C.Q.), the nullity of the gift of an immovable which is not expressed in notarial form (art. 1824 C.C.Q.). "[...] art. 1265 [C.C.L.C.] prohibited husband and wife from conferring benefits on each other *inter vivos*, and this prohibition, which was intended to ensure that the then immutable nature of matrimonial regimes was preserved, was regarded as being of public order and resulted in the absolute nullity of any agreement contravening it" (*Royal Trust Co.* v. *Tucker*, [1982] 1 S.C.R. 250, p. 274, J. Beetz, J.). *On pain of absolute nullity.*
Occ. Arts. 440, 1418, 2692 C.C.Q.
Obs. 1° Absolute nullity may be invoked by any interested party or pronounced by the court of its own motion (art. 1418 C.C.Q.). **2**° In principle, a juridical act which is absolutely null is not susceptible of confirmation (art. 1418 C.C.Q.). However, marriages which are absolutely null may be confirmed, except where public order is concerned (art. 380 C.C.Q.). **3**° Sometimes, the terms *nullity ab initio*, *nullity pleno jure*, *radical nullity*, are used as synonyms of absolute nullity.
See also annulability, general interest, good morals, public order, relative nullity.
Fr. nullité absolue.

ABSOLUTE OBLIGATION

Syn. obligation of result.
Obs. According to some scholars, the term *absolute obligation* also includes the *obligation of warranty*.
Fr. obligation absolue, obligation de résultat+, obligation déterminée.

ABSOLUTE PUBLIC ORDER

Syn. public order of direction.
Fr. ordre public absolu, ordre public de direction+.

ABSOLUTE RIGHT

Syn. pure and simple right. "I must note that the contract regarding the rights of the bank to realize its securities stipulates, in paragraph 4, that it can do so without notice. Nonetheless, this seemingly absolute right must be tempered by the principle of reasonable delay, and what constitutes the abuse of contractual rights in this case is the absence of such reasonable delay to allow the company to pay after it was put in default" (*Houle* v. *Canadian National Bank*, [1990] 3 S.C.R. 122, p. 177, C. L'Heureux-Dubé, J.).
Fr. droit pur et simple.

ABSTRACT CAUSE

Syn. cause[1].
Fr. cause[1]+, cause abstraite, cause de l'obligation, cause finale, cause objective, considération[1].

ABUSE OF RIGHT(S)

Malevolent, excessive or unreasonable exercise of a right. "In a 1905 essay, Josserand defended the thesis that rights could be abused, and that such abuses could give rise to liability. For him, the notion of abuse of rights was already part of French law [...]" (Jutras, in *Tort Law*, 317, p. 330). *Doctrine of abuse of rights.*

Obs. 1° Once established, an abuse of right may give rise to civil liability when it causes prejudice to a victim. **2°** An abuse of right may result from the malicious exercise of a right with intention to harm or from the exercise of a right in an excessive and unreasonable manner, in violation of the requirements of good faith (arts. 6, 7 C.C.Q.). **3°** The mere exercise of one's rights does not, in principle, result in liability: *Qui suo jure utitur neminem lædit* (Gaius, *Dig*.L.17, 55). The idea that one must avoid exercising a right with the sole purpose of harming another was also expressed in the Digest: *malitiis non est indulgendum* (Celsius, *Dig*.VI.1, 38), and was applied in various situations in old French law. The general theory of abuse of right took shape only at the beginning of the twentieth century. It is now applied in both extra-contractual and contractual matters.
See also bad faith[1], good faith[1], intentional fault, neighbourhood disturbance.
Fr. abus de(s) droit(s).

ABUSIVE *adj.*

See abusive clause.
Fr. abusif.

ABUSIVE CLAUSE

Clause in a contract conferring an excessive advantage upon one party.
Occ. Art. 1437 C.C.Q.
Obs. 1° Article 1437 C.C.Q. defines the abusive clause as one "which is excessively and unreasonably detrimental to the consumer or the adhering party and is therefore not in good faith". **2°** In consumer contracts and contracts of adhesion, abusive clauses are null, or the obligation arising therefrom may be reduced. Abusive penal clauses may also be reduced (art. 1623 C.C.Q.). **3°** In matters relating to leases of dwellings, clauses stipulating penalties which exceed the damage actually suffered are considered abusive (art. 1901 C.C.Q.).
See also good faith[1], leonine clause, lesion, penal clause[1], usury.
Fr. clause abusive.

ACCEPT *v.*

1. To effect an acceptance[1,2].
Fr. accepter[1].

2. To effect an acceptance[3].
Occ. Arts. 2110, 2115 C.C.Q.; arts. 1093, 1165 C.C.L.C.
Obs. Both the verbs *to accept* and *to receive* may be used to designate the reception of a payment as well as the acknowledgment that the property delivered conforms to what which was agreed upon.
Syn. receive.
Fr. accepter[2], recevoir[+].

ACCEPTANCE *n.*

1. Assent of a person in response to an offer to contract. "To make a contract the law requires communication of offer and acceptance alike [...] to the person for whom each is respectively intended [...]" (*Charlebois* v. *Baril*, [1928] S.C.R. 88, p. 89, F.A. Anglin, J.).
Occ. Arts. 1387, 1390, 1392 C.C.Q.; s. 71, *An Act respecting the National Assembly*, R.S.Q. c. A-23.1; s. 20, *Consumer Protection Act*, R.S.Q. c. P-40.1; s. 54.7, *An Act respecting the Régie du logement*, R.S.Q. c. R-8.1; s. 12 (schedule), *International Sale of Goods Contracts Convention Act*, S.C. 1991 c. 13.
Obs. 1° Acceptance is understood to be an expression of consent in the theory of formation of contracts. Article 1386 C.C.Q. designates it as a "manifestation of the will" in respect of the exchange of consent in contract. **2°** In order to constitute an acceptance, assent must correspond substantially to the offer. When it does not, it may be considered as a new offer (art. 1393 C.C.Q.). **3°** Mere silence does not imply acceptance. The law and particular circumstances, such as usage or prior business relations, may give that effect to silence (art. 1394 C.C.Q.). The parties may also decide that silence will have this effect. **4°** The codal regime relating to offer and acceptance is set forth at articles 1388 *et seq.* of the *Civil Code of Québec*. The *Civil Code of Lower Canada* did not contain a comparably explicit treatment of the matter.
See also consent[1], express acceptance, tacit acceptance, theory of reception.
Fr. acceptation[1+], agrément[1].

2. Unilateral expression of intent by which a person, through his or her assent, agrees to certain juridical effects. "Once a person of full age has accepted a succession either expressly or tacitly, he cannot impugn his acceptance, unless it has been the result of fraud, fear or violence" (Marler, *Real Property*, p. 147). *Acceptance of a succession*; *acceptance of a stipulation for the benefit of another*.
Fr. acceptation[2].

3. Act by which the creditor accepts the property remitted on performance of the contract. "A major problem under our laws of construction [...] is the uncertainty as to when the work is completed (*fin des travaux*), which

marks the starting points for several delays (such as the commencement of the delay for registration of legal hypothecs and for the five-year guaranty). As the one-year guaranty runs from acceptance of the work by the owner which requires a positive act or a declaration from the owner, the starting point of that delay can be determined with greater ease" (Kauffman, (1997) 57 *R. du B.* 589, p. 628). *Acceptance of delivery.*
Occ. Arts. 2110, 2114, 2120 C.C.Q.
Obs. 1° In principle, the acceptance of the property by the creditor indicates that he or she acknowledges that the property remitted conforms to that which was agreed upon. Alternatively, the creditor may receive the property subject to reservation in respect of its conformity. **2°** *Acceptance* is most often used in this sense in respect of contracts of sale and contracts of enterprise. Used in this sense, the term applies, for example, to property purchased by catalogue, according to plans, or on the basis of a sample. It also applies when the contractor's work is completed. **3°** Juridical effects of acceptance vary according to circumstances. For example, acceptance of a work discharges the contractor from liability for apparent defects. However, the client retains the right to seek remedies in case of latent defects (art. 2113 C.C.Q.). **4°** The codal regime respecting acceptance by the client of the work of the contractor is set forth at articles 2110 *et seq.* C.C.Q.
Syn. reception[2].
Fr. acceptation[3], réception[2+].

ACCEPTOR *n.*

Author of an acceptance.
See also offeree, offeror, promisee.
Fr. acceptant.

ACCESSORY *adj.*

Character of that which, by reason of its relationship of dependence to something, is subordinated to it. For example, an accessory real right. "Hypothec is an immovable real right, accessory to the obligation of which it secures the fulfilment, and indivisible of its nature" (Marler, *Real Property*, n° 827, p. 384).
Occ. Arts. 1414, 1442, 1976, 2103, 2394 C.C.Q.; arts. 817, 817.3 C.C.P.; title preceding s. 206, *Consumer Protection Act*, R.S.Q. c. P-40.1.
See also principal.
Fr. accessoire.

ACCESSORY *n.*

That which, by reason of its relationship of dependence to something, is subordinated to it. "The warranty against latent defects, like the warranty against eviction, is clearly an accessory of the thing sold" (*General Motors Products of Canada Ltd.* v. *Kravitz*, [1979] 1 S.C.R. 790, p. 809, Y. Pratte, J.). *The accessory follows the principal.*
Occ. Arts. 455, 1124, 1178, 1442, 1638, 1718, 1892, 2344 C.C.Q.; s. 161, *Consumer Protection Act*, R.S.Q. c. P-40.1; s. 45, *An Act respecting the Régie du logement*, R.S.Q. c. R-8.1.
Obs. 1° As a general rule, the accessory is subject to the same legal regime as the principal (*accessorium sequitur principale*). Its juridical nature may be dictated by that of the principal (e.g. movables that are immobilized) and it can be subject to the same legal rules as the principal (e.g. the obligation to deliver all the accessories of the property sold). **2°** In the relationship between accessory and principal, the accessory may be joined to the principal for its service (e.g. the hypothec granted for the performance of an obligation), or its very existence may derive from the principal (e.g. the fruits periodically produced by a property). **3°** The term *accessory* is sometimes used to designate that which is secondary or negligible (art. 2103 C.C.Q.). Thus, that which in relation to other property is considered less valuable may be deemed accessory (arts. 971 *et seq.* C.C.Q. and art. 433 C.C.L.C.). **4°** From the Latin *accessorius*: that which is added.
See also doctrine of accession, principal[1].
Fr. accessoire.

ACCESSORY CONTRACT

Contract the existence of which depends on a principal contract to which it is attached or whose performance it ensures. For example, a suretyship. "Principal contracts are those which exist in an isolated state and accessory contracts are those which cannot exist without being attached to a principal contract. Contracts for the most part are principal; suretyship and the constitution of a mortgage are accessory" (Planiol & Ripert, *Treatise*, vol. 2, n° 959, p. 555).
Occ. Title preceding s. 206, *Consumer Protection Act*, R.S.Q. c. P-40.1.
See also accessory, principal contract.
Fr. contrat accessoire.

ACCESSORY REAL RIGHT

Real right, accessory to a claim, the purpose of which is to provide security in order to render

performance of the claim more certain. "Its status as an *accessory* real right signifies that, unlike ownership, a *principal* real right [...], the hypothec is ancillary to a principal obligation" (Pierre, (1997) 28 *R.G.D.* 235, p. 264).
Obs. 1° Within the category of real rights, a distinction is generally made between principal real rights and accessory real rights. However, the accessory real right is different in character from the principal real right in that it constitutes security which is necessarily attached to a claim for which it guarantees performance. **2°** In general, an accessory real right confers upon its holder neither the use nor the enjoyment of the property. It does confer, however, a right to follow and a right of preference. **3°** An accessory real right may exist with or without dispossession of the property upon which it bears. **4°** The *Civil Code of Québec* defines the hypothec as an accessory real right (arts. 2660, 2661 C.C.Q.).
See also principal real right, real right, right of preference[2], right to follow.
Fr. droit réel accessoire[+], droit réel de garantie.

ACCIDENTAL *adj.*

See conventional indivisibility.
Fr. accidentel.

ACCIDENTAL INDIVISIBILITY

Syn. conventional indivisibility.
Fr. indivisibilité accidentelle, indivisibilité artificielle, indivisibilité conventionnelle[+], indivisibilité de paiement, indivisibilité subjective.

ACCIPIENS n. (Latin)

Person who receives payment.
Obs. From the Latin *accipio*: to accept, to receive.
Syn. payee, *recipiens.*
Fr. *accipiens*[+], payé, *recipiens.*

ACCOMPLISHED CONDITION

Syn. fulfilled condition.
Fr. condition accomplie.

ACCOMPLISHMENT OF THE CONDITION

Syn. fulfilment of the condition. "If the conditional creditor dies before the accomplishment of the condition, it may be realized to the profit of his heirs [...]" (Planiol & Ripert, *Treatise*, vol. 2, n° 381, p. 218).

Fr. accomplissement de la condition, arrivée de la condition, réalisation de la condition[+].

ACCOUNTING *n.*

Rendering of an account to a person of the management of his or her affairs. "Defendant's failure to divulge any consideration for the transfer of these policies, [defendant's] contradictory testimony as to the application of the cash surrender values – let alone the basis of the assignments themselves – demonstrate the necessity of an accounting as ordered by the Court below" (*Evaco Ltée* v. *Lacroix-Bussières*, [1971] C.A. 785, p. 792, G.M. Hyde, J.).
Occ. Title preceding art. 532 C.C.P.
Obs. Accounting must be made by the administrator of property of another (art. 1351 C.C.Q.).
Fr. reddition de compte.

ACCRUED INTEREST

Interest, the payment of which has become exigible.
Occ. S. 42(6), *Public Service Superannuation Act*, R.S.C. 1985, c. P-36; s. 17, *Canada Student Loans Act*, R.S.C. 1985, c. S-23.
Obs. 1° Accrued interest does not, in principle, bear interest, except when there is an agreement or a legislative provision to that effect, or when it is expressly demanded for in a lawsuit (art. 1620 C.C.Q.). **2°** The expression "interest accrued" is also encountered (arts. 1620, 2667 C.C.Q.; art. 1078 C.C.L.C.; s. 39(3), *Canada Cooperatives Act*, S.C. 1998, c. 1).
Syn. interest owing. **See also** accrue interest (to), arrears[1,2].
Fr. intérêt échu.

ACCRUE INTEREST (TO)

Interest, the payment of which is not yet exigible.
See also accrued interest.
Fr. intérêt à échoir.

ACCUMULATED DEBT

Syn. arrears[2].
Fr. arrérages[2], arriéré[+].

ACKNOWLEDGMENT OF DEBT

Act by which a person recognizes that he or she is the debtor of another.
Fr. reconnaissance de dette.

ACQUIRE *v.*

1. To effect the acquisition of a patrimonial right. "By occupation a person acquires a thing belonging to no one by taking possession of it, that is by actually taking hold of it with the intention of keeping it as his own" (Marler, *Real Property*, n° 351, p. 141).
Occ. Arts. 325, 453, 936, 2730 C.C.Q.; arts. 766, 2203 C.C.L.C.
Fr. acquérir[1].

2. To take on a particular quality or status. *To acquire force of law.*
Fr. acquérir[2].

ACQUIRER *n.*

Person who makes an acquisition.
Occ. Arts. 405, 1082, 1453, 2760 C.C.Q.; arts. 1663.5, 2098 C.C.L.C.
Obs. Specific terms are sometimes used, according to circumstances, to designate the acquirer (e.g. the *assignee*, the *buyer*, the *donee*, the *heir*, the *legatee*).
See also alienee, author, joint acquirer, successor.
Fr. acquéreur.

ACQUISITION *n.*

1. Operation by which a person obtains entitlement to a patrimonial right, especially a right of ownership. "Prescription is a mode of acquisition of immoveable property and of extinction of charges on the same" (Durnford, (1964-65) 67 *R. du N.* 559, p. 590).
Occ. Arts. 416, 1004, 1612, 2209 C.C.Q.; arts. 366, 2027, 2190 C.C.L.C.
Obs. 1° Contract, succession, acquisitive prescription, accession and occupation are said to be the main modes of acquisition of property (art. 916 C.C.Q.). **2°** A distinction is drawn between modes of acquisition resulting from the transfer of a patrimonial right (e.g. contract and succession) and those which do not imply such transmission (e.g. occupation and accession). **3°** Book third of the *Civil Code of Lower Canada* was entitled "Of the Acquisition and Exercise of Rights of Property" (in "des droits de propriété"), which book included Title Third "Of Obligations". This arrangement was often criticized as unduly emphasizing the acquisition of ownership in the theory of obligations.
See also acquirer, alienation, assignment[1], capacity to enjoy (rights), gift[1], sale, subsequent acquisition, transmission.
Fr. acquisition[1].

2. Patrimonial right that has been the object of an acquisition[1].

Obs. When used in this sense, the term *acquisition* generally refers to corporeal property.
Fr. acquisition[2].

ACQUIT *v.*

1. Syn. pay. "It is to the debtor to whom the law accords the first right to make the imputation: he is free, when he pays, to declare which debt he intends to acquit" (Planiol & Ripert, *Treatise*, vol. 2, n° 442, p. 258). *To acquit a debt; to acquit oneself of an obligation.*
Fr. acquitter, payer[+], régler.

2. To give an acquittance.
Fr. quittancer.

ACQUITTANCE *n.*

1. Writing by which a creditor acknowledges having received payment of a claim. *To give an acquittance.*
Occ. Arts. 1568, 1571, 1609, 1697, 3065 C.C.Q.; arts. 953a(4), 1786 C.C.L.C.; s. 10(4), *Winding-up Act*, R.S.Q. c. L-4.
Obs. 1° Article 1568 C.C.Q. provides that the debtor has a right to obtain an acquittance once the payment is performed. This provision is drawn from article 220 of Book V of the *Draft Civil Code* (C.C.R.O.) and section 101 of the *Consumer Protection Act* (R.S.Q. c. P-40.1). **2°** An acquittance is the best proof of payment (art. 2860 C.C.Q.). **3°** An acquittance in connection with bodily or moral injury is without effect when obtained within thirty days of the incident which caused injuries and if it is damaging to the creditor (art. 1609 C.C.Q.). **4°** The debtor has the right to obtain an acquittance from a prior or hypothecary creditor who acquires the property on which he has a claim as a result of a judicial sale, a sale by the creditor or a sale by judicial authority (art. 1697 C.C.Q.). **5°** A distinction is sometimes drawn between a partial acquittance and a total acquittance (e.g. art. 3065 C.C.Q.). Whereas a total acquittance discharges the debtor and obliges the return of the original title, a partial payment only serves to recognize that the debtor has partly performed the obligation. **6°** In the *Civil Code of Québec*, the French term *quittance* and the English term *acquittance* appear as equivalents, except at article 2331 C.C.Q. where *discharge* is used. However, in article 1786 C.C.L.C., which corresponds to article 2331 C.C.Q. in the *Civil Code of Lower Canada*, *quittance* and *acquittance* appear as equivalents. **7°** In practice, acquittance is also used to record the fact of renouncing a right. For example, in an acquittance record-

ing a transaction, the party who obtains compensation generally acknowledges having received the amount of money agreed upon and renounces the right to any further legal proceedings for the same events.
Syn. discharge[6], quittance. **See also** discharge[3], paid, payment[2], partial payment, receipt[1], title of payment.
Fr. quittance[1].

2. Syn. payment[2]. "In order to protect those debtors who have simply failed to consult the registry office, the Code currently provides that payment or other mode of discharge made to the assignor following registration but prior to publication acts as due acquittance of the debt" (Miller & Sarna, (1981) 59 *Can. Bar Rev.* 638, p. 642).
Fr. acquittement, paiement[2+], payement, règlement.

ACT *n.*

1. Syn. juridical act.
Occ. Arts. 172, 319, 334, 1372 C.C.Q.
Obs. 1° An act that entails juridical consequences is said to be a *juridical act* when its consequences were intended. When such consequences were not intended, it is said to be a *juridical fact.* **2°** From the Latin *actum*, from *agere*: to act, to do.
Fr. acte[1], acte juridique[+], *negotium*, titre[2].

2. Syn. attesting deed. "[...] the written act, drawn up to attest the sale, is but a precaution taken in order to have at hand a means of proof, sure and easy, and in order to obviate recantations and denials" (Planiol & Ripert, *Treatise*, vol. 1, n° 285, p. 196).
Fr. acte[2], acte instrumentaire[+], *instrumentum*, titre[2].

3. Syn. juridical fact[1]. "The act may constitute an offence (or delict) or a quasi-offence (or quasi-delict). These are distinguished according to the intention of their author [...] This distinction is unimportant in civil law, since the person who is responsible for the act must in either case repair the damage" (Goldenberg, *Law of Delicts*, p. 2). *Illicit act.*
Fr. acte[3], fait juridique[1+].

ACT BY GRATUITOUS TITLE

Juridical act by which a person, prompted by a liberal intent, procures, without a counter-prestation, an advantage to another. For example, a gift, a legacy, a gratuitous release of debt.
Obs. 1° Scholars draw a distinction between *acts by gratuitous title* and *acts by onerous*

title. **2°** Scholars sometimes limit the meaning of this term to liberalities by gift or will.
See also act by onerous title.
Fr. acte à titre gratuit.

ACT BY ONEROUS TITLE

Juridical act by which each party derives an advantage in exchange for that which is supplied. For example, a bilateral or unilateral onerous contract, a loan bearing interest.
Occ. Arts. 402, 447, 1707, 2961 C.C.Q.
Obs. Scholars draw a distinction between *acts by onerous title* and *acts by gratuitous title.*
See also act by gratuitous title.
Fr. acte à titre onéreux.

ACTE n. (French)

Syn. attesting deed.
Fr. acte[2], acte instrumentaire[+], *instrumentum*, titre[3].

ACT *EN BREVET* (French)

Syn. notarial act *en brevet.*
Occ. Ss. 38, 39, *Notaries Act*, R.S.Q. c. N-3.
Fr. acte en brevet, acte notarié en brevet[+].

ACT *EN MINUTE* (French)

Syn. notarial act *en minute.*
Occ. S. 36, *Notaries Act*, R.S.Q. c. N-3.
Fr. acte en minute, acte notarié en minute[+], minute.

ACT *INTER VIVOS* (Latin)

Juridical act which produces its effects during the lifetime of its author. For example, a gift *inter vivos*, a sale.
Occ. Arts. 687, 689, 1841 C.C.Q.; arts. 778, 975, 2098 C.C.L.C.
Obs. A distinction is drawn between *acts* inter vivos and *acts* mortis causa.
See also contemplation of death (in), *inter vivos.*
Fr. acte entre vifs.

ACTION *n.*

Act by which a person submits his or her claim or requests to a court in order to obtain a judgment. *To take legal action (against another); abandon a legal action.*
Obs. An action is personal, real or mixed according to the nature of the claim in respect of which enforcement is sought; it is movable

or immovable according to the object of the claim.

Syn. judicial action, judicial demand, law suit, suit. **See also** right of action.

Fr. action+, action en justice, demande en justice.

ACTION IN INOPPOSABILITY

Syn. Paulian action.

Obs. 1° The English text of the Civil Code refers to the *Paulian action*, while the French text uses *action en inopposabilité*. **2°** This action is traditionally linked to the work of the Roman jurisconsult Paul (fl. c.190–c.AD 225).

Fr. action en inopposabilité+, action paulienne, action révocatoire.

ACTIVE *adj.*

See active indivisibility, active solidarity.
Fr. actif.

ACTIVE INDIVISIBILITY

Indivisibility among creditors. "Active indivisibility is a very rare thing. The fact that it enables one obligee to receive the entire performance from the obligor creates a risk that the other co-obligees may not receive their share of the performance [...]" (Levasseur, *Obligations*, p. 114).

See also active solidarity, indivisibility, passive indivisibility.
Fr. indivisibilité active.

ACTIVE SOLIDARITY

Solidarity among creditors.
Obs. 1° Payment made to one of the solidary creditors discharges the debtor with respect to all of the other creditors (art. 1542 C.C.Q.). **2°** Active solidarity can only be contractual in origin (art. 1541 C.C.Q.). **3°** The codal regime respecting active solidarity is set forth at articles 1541 to 1543 C.C.Q.

See also active indivisibility, passive solidarity, solidarity.
Fr. solidarité active.

ACT OF ADMINISTRATION

Act performed with a view to the preservation, enhancement or normal exploitation of property[1].
Occ. Arts. 1002, 1703 C.C.L.C.
Obs. 1° The act of administration cannot affect the capital nor impose a significant risk upon the patrimony; furthermore, it cannot, in principle, change the destination of the patrimony. Maintenance, deposit of property and disposition of ordinary fruits and income of property are examples of acts of administration. **2°** In principle, the act of administration is a juridical act; however, some scholars consider that certain material acts may also qualify as acts of administration (e.g. to repair the roof of a house). **3°** The act of administration is traditionally distinguished from the act of disposition (act compromising the substance of a patrimony) and the conservatory act (act intended to protect a property from an imminent risk). **4°** As regards the administration of the property of others, this traditional classification may be understood to be modified by the *Civil Code of Québec* in that the latter draws a distinction between simple administration, the purpose of which is the protection and preservation of property, and full administration, the purpose of which is not only to preserve the property to make it productive, but to enhance administered property[1] or to appropriate it to a determined purpose.

See also act of alienation, act of disposition, administration of the property of others, conservatory act.
Fr. acte d'administration.

ACT OF ALIENATION

Juridical act that results in an alienation of property[1].
Occ. Arts. 405, 1097, 1707 C.C.Q.; art. 442*f*(5) C.C.L.C.
Obs. 1° Depending on the object of the alienation and the context in which the alienation takes place, it may be characterized as an act of disposition (e.g. alienation of capital), as an act of administration (e.g. alienation of the interests produced by capital) or as a conservatory act (e.g. alienation of perishable property). **2°** Although article 900 C.C.Q. uses the term *act of alienation* as the equivalent for *acte de disposition*, the act of alienation must not be confused with the act of disposition.

See also act of administration, act of disposition, alienation, contract of alienation.
Fr. acte d'aliénation.

ACT OF AN ANIMAL

Behaviour of an animal which, when it causes damage, is susceptible of engaging the civil liability of the owner or keeper of the animal. "As far as the 'act' of an animal is concerned [...] the damaging act of any animal whatever, wild or tame, small or big, be it the sting of a bee, the kicking of a horse, or the biting of a dog or of a lion, provided of course that [...] the damage be caused by the animal without the

direct intervention of a human agency" (Crépeau, (1962) 40 *Can. Bar Rev.* 222, p. 237).
See also act of a thing, liability for damage caused by animals, personal act or omission.
Fr. fait de l'animal.

ACT OF ANOTHER

Act or omission of a person which, when it causes damage, is susceptible of engaging the civil liability of a distinct person.
Obs. Often used as an equivalent to the French expression *fait d'autrui* in the law of civil liability, the expression *act of another* should be understood to include omissions.
See also act of a thing, liability for damage caused by another, personal act or omission.
Fr. fait d'autrui.

ACT OF A THING

Action of a thing which, when it causes damage, is susceptible of engaging the civil liability of the thing's custodian or owner.
Obs. The expressions *fait de la chose* and *fait des biens* are used as equivalents for *act of a thing*.
See also act of an animal, act of another, autonomous act of a thing, liability for damage caused by things, personal act or omission.
Fr. fait de la chose+, fait des biens.

ACT OF CONSERVATION

Syn. conservatory act.
Fr. acte conservatoire+, acte de conservation.

ACT OF DISPOSITION

Act that reduces, compromises or exhausts the substance of either property[1] or patrimony.
Obs. 1° The act of disposition may be *inter vivos* or *mortis causa*, by gratuitous title or by onerous title; it may be universal, by universal title or by particular title. The alienation of capital, the constitution of a real right and abandonment are examples of acts of disposition. **2**° In principle, an act of disposition is a juridical act; however, some scholars consider that certain material acts may also qualify as acts of disposition (e.g. to destroy or to consume property). **3**° The act of disposition is traditionally distinguished from the act of administration (act of common preservation or exploitation of a patrimony) and the conservatory act (act intended to protect a property against an imminent risk).

See also act of administration, act of alienation, act of simple administration, disposition[1].
Fr. acte de disposition.

ACT OF FULL ADMINISTRATION

See full administration.
Fr. acte de pleine administration.

ACT OF MERE ADMINISTRATION

Act of administration of a common nature involving no patrimonial risk. For example, to collect income, to repair an immovable.
Occ. Art. 319 C.C.L.C.
Syn. act of simple administration[2]. **See also** act of administration.
Fr. acte de pure administration+, acte de simple administration[2].

ACT OF RENUNCIATION

Syn. renunciation[1].
Fr. abdication, acte abdicatif+.

ACT OF SIMPLE ADMINISTRATION

1. See simple administration.
Fr. acte de simple administration[1].

2. Syn. act of mere administration.
Fr. acte de pure administration+, acte de simple administration[2].

ACT OF STATE

Act under the authority of the State which renders the performance of an obligation impossible. For example, embargo, expropriation, war.
Syn. *fait du prince*. **See also** superior force[1].
Fr. fait du prince.

ACTUAL DAMAGE

Syn. certain damage.
Obs. Since the terms *damage* and *injury* are synonymous, the expression *actual injury* may also be used.
Fr. préjudice certain+, préjudice réel.

ACTUAL TENDER

Syn. tender.
Occ. Arts. 1162, 1164 C.C.L.C.
Fr. offre réelle.

ACTUAL TRADITION

Tradition which is carried out by the handing over of the thing.
Syn. effective tradition, real tradition. **See also** fictitious tradition, symbolic tradition, tradition by interversion of title.
Fr. tradition réelle.

ACTUAL VALUE

Value corresponding to the price a person would be willing to sell or pay for things or services under normal market conditions.
Occ. Art. 2623 C.C.Q.
Syn. market value, real value.
Fr. valeur marchande, valeur réelle+, valeur vénale.

ACT UNDER PRIVATE SIGNATURE

Syn. private writing.
Occ. S. 15(2), *Notaries Act*, R.S.Q. c. N-3.
Fr. acte sous seing privé.

ACT UNDER PRIVATE WRITING

Syn. private writing.
Fr. acte sous seing privé.

ADDITIONAL DAMAGES

1. Damages granted, in addition to the interest payable, by reason of the late performance of an obligation to pay a sum of money.
Occ. Arts. 1527, 1617, 2198 C.C.Q.
Obs. Article 1617 para. 3 C.C.Q. allows for the awarding of additional damages. Two conditions must, however, be met, namely a stipulation to that effect by the creditor and that he or she justify the additional damages.
Syn. additional indemnity[2]. **See also** additional indemnity[1].
Fr. dommages-intérêts additionnels[1+], indemnité additionnelle[2].

2. Damages granted to the creditor by reason of the deterioration of his or her physical condition subsequent to a first judgment.
Occ. Art. 1615 C.C.Q.; arts. 26.1, 71.1, 469.1, 510.1 C.C.P.
Obs. 1° Where it is impossible to determine the progression of the victim's physical condition, the court may reserve, for a maximum period of three years, the victim's right to apply for additional damages resulting from the aggravation of bodily injury (art. 1615 C.C.Q.). **2°** This rule serves to avoid a stringent application of the *res judicata* principle, which would preclude the granting of additional damages after the initial judgment, but only to the benefit of the creditor. It is an exception to the general law of civil liability and may be explained by the concern with protecting the integrity of the human person, as a preeminent legislative value.
See also bodily injury.
Fr. dommages-intérêts additionnels[2].

ADDITIONAL INDEMNITY

1. Indemnity added by the court to the amount of damages granted, representing a percentage of such amount, as determined by law.
Obs. 1° In an attempt to correct the insufficiency of the five percent legal interest rate (s. 3, *Interest Act*, R.S.C., c. I-15), by comparison to the interest rate of the market, the Quebec legislature added the additional indemnity at the second paragraph of art. 1056c C.C.L.C. in 1971. **2°** The additional indemnity is calculated by applying to the amount of damages "a percentage equal to the excess of the rate of interest fixed for claims of the State under Section 28 of the *Act respecting the Ministère du Revenu* over the rate of interest agreed by the parties or, in the absence of agreement, over the legal rate" (art. 1619 C.C.Q.). **3°** The *dies a quo* for the calculation of the additional indemnity is fixed at the day of default, or at any subsequent date considered to be more appropriate (arts. 1617 and 1618 C.C.Q.). **4°** The additional indemnity serves to prevent the unjust enrichment of the debtor at the expense of the creditor, as well as an incentive for settlement of the suit by the parties at an earlier stage of the dispute. **5°** The court has the discretion to grant or refuse the additional indemnity. However, its allocation should remain the rule rather than the exception according to jurisprudence. **6°** The court may, nonetheless, refuse to grant the additional indemnity where the plaintiff has, for example, sued for an excessive amount or in a manner which constitutes an abuse of procedure. **7°** Courts have recognized that the creation of the additional indemnity is *intra vires* of the provincial legislature and does not interfere with the federal parliament's power over interest (s. 91(19), *Constitution Act, 1867*).
See also additional damages[2], anatocism, interest, interest rate, legal interest rate.
Fr. indemnité additionnelle[1].

2. Syn. additional damages[1].
Fr. dommages-intérêts additionnels[1+], indemnité additionnelle[2].

ADDRESSEE *n.*

Syn. consignee.
Fr. consignataire, destinataire[2+].

ADEQUATE CAUSATION

Doctrine of causality that selects, among all the facts involved in the damage, only the acts or omissions that are susceptible of producing the damage by themselves. *Doctrine of adequate causation.*
Obs. 1° Alongside the theories of proximate causation and equivalence of conditions, the doctrine of adequate causation provides another conception of the cause of the damage. It is often described as the doctrine according to which, from among all the acts or omissions partaking in the occurrence of the injury, the court may retain only those that produce the damage in the normal course of events or those that increase the risks that it takes place. **2**° Unlike the theory of equivalence of conditions, the doctrine of adequate causation imposes a choice by the court of one or more act or omission from among all factors that may have contributed to the occurrence of the damage. **3**° Courts have generally preferred the doctrine of adequate causation to competing theories in establishing causation in matters of civil liability.
See also adequate cause, determining cause, equivalence of conditions, material causation, partial causation, proximate causation.
Fr. causalité adéquate.

ADEQUATE CAUSE

Cause[3] which, in the normal course of events, produces the damage.
See also adequate causation, determining cause, equivalence of conditions, material cause, proximate cause[1,2].
Fr. cause adéquate.

ADHERING PARTY

Party who, in an adhesion contract, has no opportunity to negotiate the terms thereof.
Occ. Arts. 1432, 1435 C.C.Q.
Fr. adhérent[1].

ADHESION *n.*

See adhesion contract, contract of adhesion.
Fr. adhésion.

ADHESION CONTRACT

Contract whose terms are predetermined by one party and accepted by the other party without allowing for the opportunity to negotiate them.
Obs. 1° Article 1379 C.C.Q. defines an adhesion contract as a contract "in which the essential stipulations were imposed or drawn up by one of the parties, on his behalf or upon his instructions, and were not negotiable". **2**° The validity of external, abusive, illegible or incomprehensible clauses contained in adhesion contracts is limited by articles 1435 to 1437 C.C.Q. **3**° Section 55 of the *Charter of the French Language* (R.S.Q. c. C-11) provides that "[c]ontracts pre-determined by one party, contracts containing printed standard clauses, and the related documents, must be drawn up in French. They may be drawn up in another language as well at the express wish of the parties".
Syn. contract of adhesion. **See also** consumer contract, contract by negotiation, general conditions, special terms, standard-form contract.
Fr. contrat d'adhésion.

***AD LITEM* MANDATE** (Latin)

Mandate[1] in which a person confers upon an advocate the power to represent him or her in legal proceedings.
Obs. From the Latin *litem*, accusative of *lis*: trial.
Fr. mandat *ad litem*.

ADMINISTRATION OF THE PROPERTY OF ANOTHER

Syn. administration of the property of others.
Fr. administration du bien d'autrui.

ADMINISTRATION OF THE PROPERTY OF OTHERS

Regime for the exercise of powers by a person, the *administrator*, over property[1] that is not his or her own.
Occ. Title seven of Book four of the C.C.Q.
Obs. 1° The administration of the property of others may bear on property, a mass of property, a fraction of universality, an universality or the whole patrimony. **2**° The title respecting the administration of the property of others applies, *inter alia*, to tutors (arts. 208, 286 C.C.Q.), curators (art. 282 C.C.Q.), liquidators of successions (art. 802 C.C.Q.), managers of divided or undivided property (arts. 1029, 1085 C.C.Q.), trustees (art. 1278 C.C.Q.), sequestrators (art. 2308 C.C.Q.) and creditors who have obtained the surrender of property (art. 2768 C.C.Q.). **3**° Some scholars argue that the title respecting the adminis-

tration of the property of others provides for a general suppletive regime applicable to all persons charged with the administration of property or patrimony that is not his or her own, including, for example, the administrator of a legal person, the mandatary and the manager of the business of another. **4°** Acts of administration of the property of another are traditionally divided into three categories: conservatory acts, acts of administration and acts of disposition. According to the traditional *summa divisio*, the act of mere or simple administration is a kind of act of administration that entails no risk for the patrimony being administered (e.g. to collect revenues). **5°** In the codal regime respecting the administration of the property of others (arts. 1299 *et seq.* C.C.Q.), the *Civil Code of Québec* no longer distinguishes between three different kinds of act of administration. Instead, it distinguishes between acts of simple administration, which aim at the protection and the preservation of property, and acts of full administration, which aim to increase property, or to appropriate a patrimony to a determined purpose in addition to its protection and preservation. Whether the two part division of the Civil Code replaces or precises the traditional three part division remains an open question.
Syn. administration of the property of another. **See also** act of administration, administrator of the property of others, full administration, power[2], simple administration.
Fr. administration du bien d'autrui.

ADMINISTRATOR OF THE PROPERTY OF ANOTHER

Syn. administrator of the property of others.
Fr. administrateur du bien d'autrui.

ADMINISTRATOR OF THE PROPERTY OF OTHERS

Person exercising powers over property[1] that is not his or her own.
Occ. Art. 1299 C.C.Q.
Syn. administrator of the property of another. **See also** administration of the property of others.
Fr. administrateur du bien d'autrui.

AD SOLEMNITATEM *adv.ph.* (Latin)

Said of a formality required for the formation of a juridical act.

Syn. *ad validitatem.* **See also** essential formality, evidentiary formality.
Fr. *ad solemnitatem*[+], *ad validitatem.*

AD VALIDITATEM *adv.ph.* (Latin)

Syn. *ad solemnitatem.*
Fr. *ad solemnitatem*[+], *ad validitatem.*

ADVANCE PAYMENT

Payment effected before the obligation is due. "With respect, we are unable to find in the transaction thus made an agreement whereby the respondent bound herself ('se serait obligée'), either with or for her husband. No new obligation was assumed by either of the parties in the 'Special contract'. The respondent did not, by that document, or on that date, or in respect of the advance payment made to her, bind herself to anything to which she was not already subject by having accepted the appropriation of the policy" (*Equitable Life Assurance Society of the United States* v. *Larocque*, [1942] S.C.R. 205, p. 234, T. Rinfret, J.).
Occ. Art. 1874 C.C.Q.
Syn. payment in advance.
Fr. paiement anticipé, paiement par anticipation[+].

ADVANCE UPON SUCCESSION

Gift made in favour of an abintestate heir, which is presumed to be made in anticipation of the share of the succession which that heir may be called to receive from the donor.
Obs. The advance upon succession is an application of the principle according to which the *de cujus* is presumed to have intended to benefit the abintestate heirs equally.
Syn. *avancement d'hoirie.*
Fr. avancement d'hoirie.

AESTHETIC DAMAGE

Moral damage related to the physical appearance of a person. For example, the mental suffering resulting from a facial scar.
Obs. 1° Aesthetic damage is non-pecuniary. Harm to the physical appearance of a person that bears on ability to earn income is characterized as a pecuniary damage, rather than æsthetic damage. **2°** Since the terms *damage* and *injury* are synonymous, the expression *æsthetic injury* may also be used.
Fr. préjudice esthétique.

AFFREIGHT *v.*

Syn. charter.
Fr. affréter.

AFFREIGHTMENT *n.*

Syn. contract of affreightment.
Occ. Art. 2001 C.C.Q.
Fr. affrètement, contrat d'affrètement[+].

AGENT *n.*

See agent and servant.
Obs. The use of the terms *principal*, *agent* and *servants* in article 1463 C.C.Q. as equivalents of *commettant* and *préposés* should not be taken as a reference to mandate relationships or to the Common law doctrine of agency.
Fr. préposé.

AGENT AND SERVANT

Person who exercises duties entrusted to him or to her by another person, *the principal*, who has authority and control over the former.
Obs. 1° The damage caused by the fault of an agent or servant in the performance of his or her duties engenders not only personal liability, but also that of the principal (arts. 1457, 1458, 1463 C.C.Q.). **2°** The use of the terms *principal*, *agent* and *servants* in article 1463 C.C.Q. as equivalents of *commettant* and *préposés* should not be taken as a reference to mandate relationships or to the Common law doctrine of agency.
See also employee[1], habitual employee, liability of the principal, subordination (relationship of), temporary employee.
Fr. préposé.

AGREEMENT *n.*

1. Syn. contract[1]. "Placing the topic of arbitration within the Civil Code, rather than elsewhere, is a formal indication that arbitration agreements as an object of legislative regulation are an integral part of Quebec's most fundamental enactment on private law" (Brierley, (1987-88) 13 *Can. Bus. L.J.* 58, p. 59).
Occ. Arts. 2638, 2639, 2642 C.C.Q.
Fr. contrat[1+], convention, pacte.

2. Syn. contract[2]. *Memorandum of agreement.*
Fr. contrat[2].

AGREEMENT FOR EARNEST

See stipulation as to earnest.
Fr. convention d'arrhes.

AGREEMENT IN PRINCIPLE

Contract by which the parties undertake to continue negotiations with a view to the formation of the projected final contract between them.
Obs. 1° The principal obligation contained in an agreement in principle is the obligation to negotiate in good faith. **2°** An agreement in principle may also reflect an agreement on the essential features of the projected contract. If, however, the parties agree on all the essential terms, the projected contract is formed notwithstanding any reserve as to their agreement on the secondary terms of the contract (art. 1387 C.C.Q.). **3°** The letter of intention may be distinguished from the agreement in principle in that it creates no binding obligations and, consequently, does not qualify as a contract.
Syn. letter of understanding, memorandum of understanding, preliminary agreement.
See also gentlemen's agreement, letter of intention.
Fr. accord de principe[+], accord préliminaire, protocole d'entente.

AGREEMENT TO ACT AS NOMINEE

Syn. contract of *prête-nom*. "In Quebec law, as in French law, an agreement to act as nominee (*prête-nom*) is a lawful form of the contract of mandate" (*Victuni* v. *Minister of Revenue of Quebec*, [1980] 1 S.C.R. 580, p. 584, L.-P. Pigeon, J.").
Fr. contrat de prête-nom[+], mandat clandestin, mandat dissimulé, prête-nom[2].

ALEATORY *adj.*

See aleatory contract.
Fr. aléatoire.

ALEATORY CONTRACT

Onerous contract in which the chance of gain or loss depends on the uncertain nature of one of the prestations' scope or existence. For example, an insurance contract, a gaming contract, a sale of an immovable in return for a life rent.
Occ. Art. 1378 C.C.Q.
Obs. In an aleatory contract, the contingency is the chance of gain or of loss.
See also betting, commutative contract, gaming contract, insurance contract.
Fr. contrat aléatoire.

ALIENABILITY *n.*

Attribute of property[1] that is susceptible of alienation.
Obs. Alienability is, in principle, a characteristic of all patrimonial rights. It may only be restricted by law or by a valid stipulation of inalienability.
See also assignability, inalienability, stipulation of inalienability, transmissibility.
Fr. aliénabilité.

ALIENABLE *adj.*

Susceptible of alienation.
Fr. aliénable.

ALIENATE *v.*

To transfer a patrimonial right by alienation.
Occ. Arts. 19, 401, 1015 C.C.Q.; arts. 358, 2186 C.C.L.C.
Fr. aliéner.

ALIENATION *n.*

Inter vivos transfer of a patrimonial right.
Occ. Arts. 427, 909, 1937 C.C.Q.; arts. 399, 441*p* C.C.L.C.
Obs. 1° Alienation is generally used to designate a consensual *inter vivos* transfer of assets. The term does not typically describe the transfer of debts. **2**° Alienation is by universal title or by particular title. It may also be made by gratuitous title (e.g. donation) or by onerous title (e.g. sale and exchange). **3**° The person who alienates is known as the *alienator*; the beneficiary of the alienation may be referred to as the *alienee*, but this usage is more rare in Quebec law. It is more common, however, to designate the parties to a patrimonial transfer by more specific terms depending on the nature of the juridical act that serves as vehicle for the alienation (e.g. in a sale, the alienator is referred to as *seller* and the alienee as *purchaser*). **4**° Article 25 C.C.Q. provides that "alienation by a person of a part or product of his body shall be gratuitous." Some commentators have criticized this usage of *alienation*, given that, from their view, body parts are not property and, being so, cannot be alienated. **5**° From the Middle French *alienation*, a derivative of the Latin *alienare* (root *alienus*: another, stranger): to detach, to sell.
See also acquisition[1], act of alienation, alienator, alienee, assignment[1], contract of alienation, disposition[2], mutation, transmission.
Fr. aliénation.

ALIENATION FOR RENT

Contract by which a person, the *lessor*, transfers to another, the *lessee*, the ownership of an immovable in return for an annuity which the latter undertakes to pay. "[...] in sale the price must be in money, in alienation for rent, the rent may be payable in money or in kind [...]" (Marler, *Real Property*, n° 733, p. 339).
Occ. Arts. 1802, 2368 C.C.Q.; title preceding art. 1593 C.C.L.C.
Obs. 1° When the capital is constituted from anything other than the transfer of ownership of an immovable, it is characterized as an annuity contract rather than an alienation for rent (arts. 1802, 2368 C.C.Q.). **2**° While the Civil Code does not explicitly treat the matter, the transfer of any movable other than money could also logically constitute an alienation for rent. **3**° The provisions respecting annuity (arts. 2366 to 2388 C.C.Q.) also apply to alienation for rent; however, this contract is principally governed by the rules respecting sale (art. 2368 C.C.Q.). **4**° The codal regime respecting the alienation for rent is set forth at articles 1802 to 1805 C.C.Q.
See also annuity[1], annuity contract, lessee[2], lessor[3].
Fr. bail à rente.

ALIENATOR *n.*

Rare. Person who alienates a patrimonial right.
Obs. Specific terms are generally used depending on the nature of the juridical act that effects the alienation (e.g. in a trust, the alienator is referred to as the *settlor*).
See also alienee, alienation.
Fr. aliénateur.

ALIENEE *n.*

Rare. Person to whom a patrimonial right is transferred by alienation.
Obs. 1° Specific terminology is generally used depending on the nature of the juridical act that serves as vehicle for the alienation (e.g. in a sale, the alienee is referred to as the *purchaser*). **2**° Although the term *acquirer* has a wider meaning than alienee, it is more frequently encountered, especially in the context of contract by onerous title.
See also alienator, alienation.
Fr. aliénataire.

ALIMENTARY CLAIM

Syn. alimentary right. "[...] the claim of any creditor for *support* from the estate of a deceased is an alimentary claim and not merely a claim for reserved portion or share of the estate. Article 686 [C.C.Q.] makes it plain that, in fixing the amount of the contribution for support, the needs, means and circumstances of the claimant or creditor must be taken into account" (*Droit de la famille – 2310*, [1997] R.J.Q. 859 (C.A.), p. 863, M.L. Rothman, J.).
Obs. Notwithstanding its procedural connotation, the expression *alimentary claim* is often used as a synonym for alimentary right.
Fr. créance alimentaire+, droit alimentaire.

ALIMENTARY CREANCE

Neol. Syn. alimentary right.
Obs. Because English Civilian vocabulary has used the same word *debt* to describe both the active and passive facets of the object of an obligation, the expression *alimentary creance* is suggested as a clear English-language equivalent to the French expression *créance alimentaire*.
Fr. créance alimentaire+, droit alimentaire.

ALIMENTARY RIGHT

Obligation of support[1] viewed from the perspective of the creditor. "The *Divorce Act* does not deal with the alimentary rights and obligations of children and grand-parents. Nor is this ancillary to the power to legislate on divorce. In my view, it is purely a matter of civil law and thus within the legislative competence of the Province of Quebec" (*Droit de la famille – 211*, [1985] C.A. 332, pp. 333-334, M.L. Rothman, J.).
Syn. alimentary claim, alimentary creance, claim for support.
Fr. créance alimentaire+, droit alimentaire.

ALTERNATE CUSTODY

Custody of a thing which passes temporarily from one person to another. For example, the owner may cease to be responsible for a thing when a borrower assumes control and supervision over it.
Obs. 1° Custody is more usually alternate than cumulative, since the liability of a custodian ceases when he or she is replaced by a second custodian. **2°** Alternate custody of the owner and of the person making use of an animal, however, does not necessarily entail the owner's exoneration from his or her liability for damage caused by the animal (art. 1466 C.C.Q.).
See also cumulative custody, liability for damage caused by things.
Fr. garde alternative.

ALTERNATIVE *adj.*

See alternative obligation.
Fr. alternatif.

ALTERNATIVE OBLIGATION

Obligation[2] comprising several prestations, the performance of any one of which releases the debtor. "[...] an obligation may have a plurality of objects: if the debtor has the option to choose to execute one or another obligation, the obligation is an alternative obligation [...]" (Brierley & Macdonald (eds.), *Quebec Civil Law*, n° 538, p. 489).
Occ. Title preceding art. 1545 C.C.Q.; arts. 1093, 1096, 1099 C.C.L.C.
Obs. 1° There is a plurality of objects in an alternative obligation. Unlike a conjunctive obligation, the debtor is not bound to perform all of the prestations, as the performance of any one prestation will put an end to his or her obligation. **2°** In principle, the choice as to the prestation to be performed is left to the debtor (art. 1546 C.C.Q.). **3°** The codal regime respecting alternative obligations is set forth at articles 1545 to 1551 C.C.Q.
See also conjunctive obligation, facultative obligation, obligation with a complex modality.
Fr. obligation alternative.

AMICABLE RESILIATION

Syn. bilateral resiliation.
Obs. The expressions *amicable resiliation* and *conventional resiliation* are used where there are more than two contracting parties.
Fr. résiliation amiable, résiliation bilatérale+, résiliation conventionnelle, révocation[2].

ANATOCISM *n.*

Integration of interest due with the capital of a debt so that the capital, now increased by the amount of the interest, in turn yields interest.
Obs. 1° Interest accrued on the principal itself bears interest when there is an agreement or a legislative direction to that effect, or when interest is expressly demanded in a lawsuit (art. 1620 C.C.Q.). **2°** From the Latin

anatocismus: compound interest, from the Greek *ana*: again, and *tokos*: interest.
See also compound interest.
Fr. anatocisme.

ANATOCISM AGREEMENT

Syn. compound interest contract.
Fr. convention d'anatocisme.

ANIMUS n. (Latin)

Intentional element. "[...] possession comprises two elements: *corpus* and *animus*. The intentional element, *animus*, consists of the will of the holder to perform certain acts of physical control as a titulary of the real right to which these acts correspond. The material element, *corpus*, consists of these acts themselves" (Macdonald, (1986) 31 *McGill L.J.* 573, p. 591). *Animus domini*; *animus donandi*; *animus novandi*.
Obs. This term is often used in situations where both material and intentional elements are required as the basis of a legal concept or status. Thus, it is notably employed in matters of domicile, gifts and possession.
See also *animus novandi*.
Fr. *animus*.

ANIMUS NOVANDI nom.ph. (Latin)

Intention to effect novation.
Obs. Article 1661 C.C.Q. provides that: "novation is not presumed; it is effected only where the intention to effect it is evident".
Syn. novatory intention.
Fr. *animus novandi*, intention novatoire+.

ANNUITANT n.

Creditor of an annuity. "[...] payments are made into the plan by the annuitant or the annuitant's spouse in order to provide the annuitant in due course with an annuity or registered retirement income fund" (*M. (M.)* v. *M. (L.L.)*, (1993) 49 E.T.R. 90 (C.A.), p. 95, M. Fish, J.A.).
Occ. Arts. 2367, 2369 C.C.Q.
Obs. The annuitant need not be the person who constitutes the annuity, since it is possible to constitute it for the benefit of a person other than the person who furnishes the capital (art. 2369 C.C.Q.).
See also annuity[1], dues.
Fr. crédirentier.

ANNUITY n.

1. Dues that a person, the *debtor of the annuity*, undertakes to pay to another, the *annuitant*, gratuitously or in exchange for the alienation of capital.
Occ. Arts. 2368, 2378 C.C.Q.
Obs. 1° Annuity, like a salary, is an income periodically paid; however, the two are distinguishable in that an annuity is not paid in exchange for work. **2°** Although the capital is generally a sum of money, it may also comprise any movable or immovable property. **3°** The dues payable under an annuity may also be called *arrears*, which must not be confused with another meaning of *arrears*, debts whose due date has expired.
Syn. rent[2]. **See also** alienation for rent, dues, periodic payment.
Fr. rente[1].

2. Personal right enabling a person, the *annuitant*, to demand from another, the *debtor of the annuity*, the payment of dues. "Broadly speaking, there are two types of [registered retirement plan], the first involves the purchase of an annuity from an insurance company, while the second contemplates an agreement between an annuitant and a trust company (or other eligible institution)" (*M. (M.)* v. *M. (L.L.)*, (1993) 49 E.T.R. 90 (C.A.), p. 95, M. Fish, J.A.). *Constitution of an annuity.*
Occ. Arts. 695, 1162 para. 4, 2369, 2393 C.C.Q.; arts. 777, 2473 C.C.L.C.; s. 178, *An Act respecting trust companies and savings companies*, R.S.Q. c. S-29.01.
Obs. 1° An annuity may be constituted by contract, judgment, will or law (art. 2370 C.C.Q.). **2°** The debtor of the annuity may undertake gratuitously to pay an annuity. Such a contract is assimilated to a gift (art. 1811 C.C.Q.). **3°** In general, the debtor of the annuity undertakes to pay the annuity in exchange for the alienation of capital, in money, for his or her benefit. If he or she undertakes to pay the annuity in exchange for the alienation of the ownership of an immovable for his or her benefit, the contract is called *alienation for rent* (arts. 1802 and 2368 C.C.Q.). While the Civil Code does not explicitly treat the matter, the transfer of any movable other than money could also logically constitute an alienation for rent. **4°** A distinction is drawn between life annuities, which are constituted for the lifetime of one or several persons, and fixed term annuities, which are constituted for any other term permitted by law (arts. 2371, 2376 C.C.Q.). **5°** In the *Civil Code of Lower Canada*, the term *rent* was used more often than *annuity* as the equivalent of the French term *rente*. However, in the *Civil Code of Québec*, *annuity* is the preferred term. **6°** In the *Civil Code of Lower Canada*, a distinction was drawn between constituted rents (art. 388 C.C.L.C.),

created by the alienation of a sum of money, and ground-rents (art. 391 C.C.L.C.), created by the alienation of an immovable. This distinction does not appear in the *Civil Code of Québec*. **7°** The codal regime respecting annuities is set forth at articles 2367 to 2388 C.C.Q.
Syn. pension, rent[3]. **See also** alienation for rent, annuity contract.
Fr. rente[2].

3. Syn. annuity contract.
Fr. contrat de rente+, rente[3].

4. Amount paid annually.
Occ. Art. 544 C.C.L.C.
See also monthly payment, periodic payment.
Fr. annuité.

ANNUITY CONTRACT

Contract by which a person, the *debtor of the annuity*, undertakes, gratuitously or in exchange for the alienation of capital, to pay dues for a determinate period to another person, the *annuitant*.
Occ. Art. 415 C.C.Q.
Obs. 1° An annuity may be instituted by contract, will, judgment or law (art. 2370 C.C.Q.). **2°** An annuity contract by gratuitous title is assimilated to a gift (art. 1811 C.C.Q.). **3°** Although the capital is generally a sum of money, it may also be constituted of any movable or immovable property. **4°** When the annuitant transfers the ownership of an immovable rather than alienating capital in return for the annuity, the contract is called *alienation for rent* (arts. 1802 and 2368 C.C.Q.). **5°** The codal regime respecting annuity is set forth at articles 2367 to 2388 C.C.Q.
Syn. annuity[3]. **See also** alienation for rent, annuity[1], arrears[1].
Fr. contrat de rente+, rente[3].

ANNUL *v.*

To pronounce an annulment. "[...] courts have sometimes been reluctant to annul a contract where the party seeking nullity was the source of the illegality or immorality, although when a breach of the criminal law is in issue, nullity is invariably pronounced" (Brierley & Macdonald (eds.), *Quebec Civil Law*, n° 442, p. 412). *To annul a contract; to annul a loan; to annul a disposition.*
Occ. Arts. 135, 390, 1416, 1417, 1418, 1419, 1421, 1422 C.C.Q.
Obs. The term *avoid* is also used, although some scholars see it as a Common law term.
See also invalidate, rescind, resiliate[1], resolve, set aside.
Fr. annuler.

ANNULABILITY *n.*

Characteristic of a juridical act that is susceptible of being annulled. "[...] all the legal systems derived from the Roman law admit [...] a simple annulability, which can destroy [an act] after it has produced effects during a more or less long period of time. The contract is not immediately null; it becomes so later when the action of nullity is brought against it and a judgment of nullity is rendered, if the action is successful" (Planiol & Ripert, *Treatise*, vol. 2, n° 1271, p. 725).
Obs. 1° The term *annulability* was traditionally reserved for juridical acts susceptible of a declaration of relative nullity rather than absolute nullity. **2°** The notion of *non-existence* of a juridical act is sometimes contrasted with that of *annulability*. Some scholars believe that certain juridical acts need not be annulled since they never existed. Others, basing their opinion in part on articles 1416 and 1422 C.C.Q., are of the view that the appearance of validity of a juridical act precludes its being considered non-existent. **3°** Even though one of the obligations of a juridical act may be annulled, the act itself remains valid except if it is considered to be an indivisible whole (art. 1438 C.C.Q.).
See also inopposability, invalidity, non-existence, nullity.
Fr. annulabilité.

ANNULLABLE *adj.*

Susceptible of annulment. *Annullable clause; annullable gift; annullable obligation.*
Obs. The term *voidable* is also used, although some scholars see it as a Common law term.
Fr. annulable.

ANNULMENT *n.*

Retroactive termination, by the court, of a juridical act tainted by nullity. For example, annulment of a contract due to a defect of consent. "It appears to me that it is at the time of dissolution of a marriage for nullity, when all rights, especially future rights, are to be affected, that the claims of the past, which the Civil Code [of Lower Canada] allows in certain circumstances of good faith, should be considered [...] in mitigation of the consequences of annulment" (*Montmigny* v. *Lelièvre* (1939), 67 B.R. 197, p. 207, J.C. Walsh, J.). *Annulment of marriage; subject to annulment.*
Occ. Arts. 2261.1, 2512 C.C.L.C.
Obs. The term *avoidance* is also used, although some scholars see it as a Common law term.
See also resiliation[1], resolution[1].
Fr. annulation.

ANONYMOUS PARTNERSHIP

Commercial partnership having no collective or firm name and in which the partners are solidarily liable for the obligations of the partnership.
Occ. Title preceding art. 1870 C.C.L.C.
Obs. 1° The distinction between civil and commercial partnerships established by the *Civil Code of Lower Canada* (arts. 1863 *et seq.* C.C.L.C.) is not made in the *Civil Code of Québec*. **2°** The anonymous partnership of the *Civil Code of Lower Canada* is similar to the undeclared partnership of the *Civil Code of Québec* (arts. 2250 *et seq.* C.C.Q.).
See also commercial partnership, contract of partnership, partnership, undeclared partnership.
Fr. société anonyme.

APPARENT *adj.*

That which is ostensible, easily perceived. "The seller is not bound for defects which are apparent and which the buyer might have known of himself" (Marler, *Real Property*, n° 531, p. 251).
Occ. Arts. 1438, 1726, 2050, 2104 C.C.Q.
See also apparent act, apparent defect, apparent right.
Fr. apparent.

APPARENT ACT

Attesting deed which, in connection with a simulation, ostensibly exhibits the features of an agreement between parties that does not correspond to a juridical reality that remains concealed. For example, a sale concealing a donation. "Where there is a conflict between third parties – some who benefit from the apparent act, and some from the counter-letter – it appears that the apparent act will be enforced against everyone" (Brierley & Macdonald (eds.), *Quebec Civil Law*, n° 458, p. 425).
Obs. Fictitious acts and acts involving an interposition of persons are apparent acts.
Syn. ostensible act, simulated act. **See also** apparent contract, concealed act, counter letter, fictitious act, simulation.
Fr. acte apparent[+], acte ostensible, acte simulé.

APPARENT CONTRACT

Contract constituting the apparent act in a simulation.
Occ. Arts. 1451, 1452 C.C.Q.

See also simulation.
Fr. contrat apparent.

APPARENT DEFECT

Defect in property[2] that a reasonable person would detect upon examination. "In such cases where there is an apparent defect or bad workmanship which does not entail the solidity of the building, the acceptance of the latter by the owner without reservation discharges the seller, builder, architect or engineer" (Brien, in *Meredith Lectures (1983-84)*, 1, pp. 16-17).
Occ. Art. 1726 C.C.Q.
Obs. The concept of *apparent defect* is generally contrasted with latent defect. In many settings, the law requires a person to warrant against latent defects, for example, although generally speaking warranties against apparent defects are not required.
Syn. patent defect. **See also** latent defect.
Fr. défaut apparent, vice apparent[+].

APPARENT MANDATE

Fictitious mandate which arises when a person allows it to be believed that a person is his or her mandatary when in fact this is not the case.
Obs. 1° Rules relating to the apparent mandate are designed to protect third persons in good faith. **2°** The apparent mandate results from the exercise of a power that either does not exist or no longer exists. **3°** When the apparent mandate results from the exercise of a power that does not exist, the apparent mandator will, in principle, be liable to third persons for acts performed by the apparent mandatary. However, in circumstances in which the error was foreseeable, the apparent mandator will not be liable if he or she has taken appropriate measures to prevent the error (art. 2163 C.C.Q.). **4°** When the apparent mandate results from the exercise of a power that no longer exists, the mandator may only be liable to third persons for acts performed by the mandatary, if the mandate was terminated or revoked without the knowledge of the third person (arts. 2162, 2181 C.C.Q.). **5°** The tacit mandate (e.g. art. 2132 C.C.Q.) is often confused with the apparent mandate. Tacit mandate depends on the form of consent given, which may be express or tacit. In an apparent mandate, no consent was ever given, thus no contractual connection exists between the apparent mandator and the apparent mandatary.
Fr. mandat apparent.

APPARENT RIGHT

Right that evinces the characteristics of probability associated with an appearance of right.
See also appearance of right.
Fr. droit apparent.

APPEARANCE *n.*

External aspect inducing a belief in the existence of a situation or a juridical quality that does not conform to reality. "Simulation is pretense or semblance; it connotes an unreal appearance" (Lemann, (1954) 29 *Tul. L. Rev.* 22, p. 22)
See also simulation.
Fr. apparence.

APPEARANCE OF RIGHT

Plausible quality of a right, resulting from sufficiently convincing *prima facie* proof, which allows an action to proceed in its initial stages without the right claimed being conclusively established.
Obs. 1° In certain circumstances, an appearance of right allows legal proceedings to go forward in the absence of definitive evidence of the right alleged. **2°** The application of appearance of right is limited to certain contexts, e.g. in interlocutory injunctions (art. 752 C.C.P.) and in class actions (art. 1003 C.C.P.; s. 23, *An Act respecting the class action*, R.S.Q. c. R-2.1). **3°** Courts sometimes add the qualifying adjective "strong" or "good" to the notion of *appearance of right*.
Syn. colour of right. **See also** apparent right, theory of appearance.
Fr. apparence de droit.

APPLICANT

Syn. client[1]. "The information insurance applicants have to declare is to be relevant to the risk against which they are insured. Insurers must demonstrate, through the use of actuarial tables, reasonable grounds for using this type of information in the calculation of a particular premium" (Lemmens, (2002) 45 *McGill L.J* 347, p. 401).
Occ. Ss. 24, 219, 424, *An Act respecting insurance*, R.S.Q. c. A-32; ss. 79, 200, *An Act respecting the distribution of financial products and services*, R.S.Q. c. D-9.2.
Fr. preneur[1+], souscripteur.

APPOINTMENT OF (AN) HEIR

Designation of a person as heir.
Occ. Art. 830 C.C.L.C.
Fr. institution d'héritier.

APPROVAL CLAUSE

Clause that precludes a party from undertaking a juridical or material act without the prior agreement of his or her co-contractant. For example, a clause in a partnership agreement forbidding a partner from disposing of his or her share without the prior agreement of the other partners.
See also first refusal agreement, preemption clause.
Fr. clause d'agrément.

APTITUDE *n.*

Syn. *de facto* capacity.
Fr. aptitude[+], capacité[2], capacité de fait, capacité naturelle.

ARBITRATE *v.*

1. To agree to the presentation of a dispute to arbitration.
Fr. compromettre.

2. To settle a dispute through arbitration.
Fr. arbitrer.

ARBITRATION *n.*

1. Mode of settlement that consists of referring a dispute to one or more persons not involved in the dispute, called *arbitrators*, to the exclusion of civil actions before a court. "Agreements providing for resort to arbitration are fully contractual in nature but put into operation a process that is more 'judicial' in nature than anything else" (Brierley, (1970) 30 *R. du B.* 473, p. 488).
Occ. Arts. 2638, 2892, 2895, 3133 C.C.Q.; arts. 1926.2, 2587 C.C.L.C.; arts. 382, 940, 950 C.C.P.
Obs. 1° A distinction is drawn between conventional arbitration, which has its source in the parties' common will, and arbitration imposed by law (e.g. grievance arbitrations in labour law). **2°** By way of the arbitration clause, parties can decide that the arbitrator will rule in *amiable composition*. Released from the obligation to apply rules of law, the arbitrator may then settle the dispute according to equity. **3°** Parties may provide for the intervention of a third person in order to determine an element of the contract (e.g. the value of a set of goods according to market value). Depending on the circumstances, this intervention may be by way of expertise or arbitration. It is an arbitration when the need to refer to a third person arises from a dispute between the parties and reflects their

intention to submit the dispute to the juris-dictional authority of an arbitrator.
See also arbitration agreement, submission (to arbitration), undertaking to arbitrate.
Fr. arbitrage.

ARBITRATION AGREEMENT

Contract by which the parties agree to submit a present or future dispute to arbitration, to the exclusion of the courts. "The arbitration agreement in Quebec has [...] been placed upon an entirely new footing by reason of the insertion of the principle of its validity in the Civil Code itself" (Brierley, (1987-88) 13 *Can. Bus. L.J.* 58, p. 61).
Occ. Arts. 2638, 3121 C.C.Q.; art. 1926.1 C.C.L.C.; arts. 940.1, 950 C.C.P.
Obs. 1° Generally, an arbitration agreement takes the form of an arbitration clause insert-ed in a contract. **2°** Since the reform of the law of arbitration in 1986 (*An Act to amend the Civil Code and the Code of Civil Procedure in respect of arbitration*, S.Q. 1986, c. 73), undertakings to arbitrate and submissions are understood as different forms that can take an arbitration agreement. Undertak-ings to arbitrate relate to future disputes, whereas submissions relate to present dis-putes. **3°** Parties may not submit disputes over matters of public order to arbitration (e.g. disputes over the status and capacity of persons (art. 2639 C.C.Q.)). **4°** The presence of a third person, the arbitrator, who is called upon to decide the dispute between the par-ties, is one of the attributes of the arbitration agreement that distinguishes it from a trans-action. **5°** The arbitration agreement is to be distinguished from expertise insofar as it implies the existence of a dispute and an intention of the parties to submit their dis-pute to arbitration. **6°** The codal regime respecting arbitration agreements is set forth at articles 2638 to 2643 C.C.Q.
Syn. contract of arbitration. **See also** arbi-tration[1], submission (to arbitration), transac-tion[1].
Fr. convention d'arbitrage.

ARBITRATION CLAUSE

See arbitration agreement. "An arbitration clause is merely a jurisdiction clause which specifies the place of settling a dispute *and* stipulates that the hearing will be before arbi-trators" (Tetley, (1994) 39 *McGill L.J.* 303, p. 324).
Occ. Art. 2587 C.C.L.C.

Obs. Generally, an arbitration agreement takes the form of an arbitration clause inserted in a contract.
Fr. clause d'arbitrage.

ARBITRATOR *n.*

Person designated by parties to settle a dis-pute between them.
Occ. Arts. 2638, 2895, 3148, 3165 C.C.Q.; art. 1926.1 C.C.L.C.; arts. 234, 382, 390, 940.2, 950 C.C.P.
See also arbitration[1], arbitration agreement.
Fr. arbitre.

ARREARS *pl.n.*

1. Periodic payments of an annuity[1].
Occ. Art. 2960 C.C.Q.; art. 1907 C.C.L.C.
Obs. In practice, *periodic payment* is more commonly used than *arrears* to designate the payment of the dues owed to the annuitant.
See also annuity, dues, interest, periodic payment.
Fr. arrérages[1].

2. Payment for which the due date has expired. *To accumulate arrears.*
Occ. Arts. 596, 1953 C.C.Q.; arts. 580, 1658.20 C.C.L.C.
Obs. 1° According to a maxim of old French law, *les aliments ne s'arréragent point* (arrears of alimentary or support payments may not be accumulated). The principle remained of gen-eral application until the reform of family law in 1981 (arts. 595 and 596 C.C.Q.). **2°** The dues payable under an annuity may also be called *arrears*, which must not be confused with another meaning of *arrears*, debts whose due date has expired.
Syn. accumulated debt.
Fr. arriéré.

ARREARS (IN) *adv.ph.*

Said of a debt for which the date of exigibility has passed. *To be in arrears.*
Fr. arriéré.

ARRIVAL OF THE TERM

Syn. expiration. "Prior to the arrival of the term, the creditor cannot demand perfor-mance, subject to a stipulation accelerating the performance of the obligation upon the occurrence of specified events" (Brierley & Macdonald (eds.), *Quebec Civil Law*, n° 533, p. 484).
Fr. arrivée du terme, avènement du terme, échéance+, échéance du terme.

ARTIFICIAL INDIVISIBILITY

Syn. conventional indivisibility. "By their contract, parties may provide for an *artificial* indivisibility of an obligation which, otherwise, would be naturally divisible" (Levasseur, *Obligations*, p. 131).

Fr. indivisibilité accidentelle, indivisibilité artificielle, indivisibilité conventionnelle[+], indivisibilité de paiement, indivisibilité subjective.

ASSENT *n.*

Approval, by the author of the invitation to enter into a contract, required for the formation of the contract. "If a foetus were subjected to experimentation from which harm resulted, it is doubtful that the assent of the mother to this research would provide the researcher with immunity from an action in damages brought on behalf of the newborn child" (Kouri, (1991) 22 *R.D.U.S.* 77, p. 91).
See also right of refusal.
Fr. agrément[3].

ASSENT *v.*

To give assent.
Fr. agréer.

ASSIGN *v.*

To effect an assignment[1]. "Any right of action in general may be assigned. The debt may be present or future, exigible or executory, conditional or subject to a term, as long as it is licit and not purely personal to the debtor; for example, an alimentary debt cannot be assigned" (Miller & Sarna, (1981) 59 *Can. Bar Rev.* 638, p. 639).
Occ. Arts. 1637, 1701, 2529 C.C.Q.; arts. 494, 1201, 1619 C.C.L.C.
Syn. cede.
Fr. céder[+], transporter[2].

ASSIGNABILITY *n.*

Attribute of a right susceptible of assignment[1]. "The assignability of the obligation and the existence of circumstances necessary to support an action upon it are distinct things" (*Maloney* v. *Campbell* (1897), 28 S.C.R. 228, p. 233, G.E. King, J.).
Occ. Art. 3120 C.C.Q.
See also non-assignability, transmissibility.
Fr. cessibilité.

ASSIGNABLE *adj.*

Susceptible of assignment[1]. "Moral rights, inspired by the continental civil law concept of *droit d'auteur*, are concerned primarily with protecting the integrity and paternity of the work [...], which is then regarded as an extension of the author's personality. These are extra-patrimonial rights, which, by definition, are not assignable [...]" (*Théberge* v. *Galerie d'Art du Petit Champlain inc.*, [2002] 2 R.C.S. 336, p. 389, C.D. Gonthier, J.).
See also non-assignable, transmissible.
Fr. cessible.

ASSIGNED DEBTOR

Debtor of a claim which is the object of an assignment[1]. "Whether the assignment is given in sale but not as security, or as a security by way of mere pledge, the assignee maintains a right to sue the assigned debtor without interference from or the impleading of the assignor" (Sarna, (1978) 56 *Can. Bar Rev.* 626, p. 644).
Occ. Art. 3120 C.C.Q.
Fr. cédé, débiteur cédé[+].

ASSIGNEE *n.*

Person in whose favour an assignment[1] is made. "The principal effect of the assignment is to transfer the assignor's title to the 'assignee'" (Miller & Sarna, (1981) 59 *Can. Bar Rev.* 638, p. 639).
Occ. Arts. 1639, 2462 C.C.Q.; art. 1192 C.C.L.C.
See also assignor.
Fr. cessionnaire.

ASSIGNMENT *n.*

Inter vivos transfer of a right. For example, an assignment of book debts.
Occ. Arts. 1637, 1680, 2476, C.C.Q.; art. 1192 C.C.L.C.; s. 63, *An Act respecting the lands in the public domain*, R.S.Q. c. T-8.1; s. 13(4), *Copyright Act*, R.S.C., c. C-30.
Obs. 1° Assignment may occur by gratuitous or onerous title. **2°** The term *assignment* is used in particular with regard to a claim, but it may also be used with regard to a debt or a contract. **3°** The parties to an assignment are known as the *assignor*, the *assignee* and, as the case may be, the *assigned debtor* and the *assigned creditor*.
Syn. cession, conveyance[3]. **See also** disposition[2], transfer, transmission.
Fr. cession[+], transport[3].

ASSIGNMENT OF CLAIM(S)

Assignment by which a creditor transfers to an assignee his or her rights against the debtor. "Although the *Barreau du Québec* had suggested that Article 1642 of the *Civil Code [of Québec]* be modified in order to address the difficulties of rendering certain assignments of claims opposable to third parties, the legislator did not take this suggestion into account in Bill 181. Practitioners will continue to be faced with difficult issues respecting assignments of claims and universalities" (Dietze, (1999) 59 *R. du B.* 1, p. 43). **Occ.** Title preceding art. 1637 C.C.Q.; arts. 888, 1638 C.C.Q.; s. 22, *An Act respecting collective agreement decrees*, R.S.Q. c. D-2; s. 81, *An Act respecting labour relations, vocational training and manpower management in the construction industry*, R.S.Q. c. R-20. **Obs. 1°** Rights attached exclusively to the creditor's person (e.g. alimentary claims), as well as certain claims specified by law, may not be the object of an assignment of claims (art. 1610 C.C.Q.). **2°** The assignment is formed upon the agreement between the creditor and the assignee. However, it may only be set up against the debtor and third parties if the debtor has given his or her assent or has been informed (art. 1641 C.C.Q.). **3°** While assignment of claims may be by gratuitous or onerous title, it may be noted that the *Civil Code of Lower Canada* used the term *sale of debts*, since assignment generally occurs by onerous title (art. 1570 C.C.L.C.). **4°** The term *assignment of debts* is sometimes used as a synonym for *assignment of claims* (art. 888 C.C.Q.). **5°** In practice, the term *assignment of contract* is sometimes used for what is merely an assignment of debt or claim. **6°** The codal regime respecting assignment of claims is set forth at articles 1637 to 1650 C.C.Q. **Syn.** assignment of creance, transfer of claim, transfer of debt. **See also** novation by change of creditor, sale of claims, warranty of payment. **Fr.** cession de créance+, cession-transport, transport-cession, transport de créance.

ASSIGNMENT OF CONTRACT

Assignment of the rights and obligations arising from a contract. **Obs. 1°** Obligations are not, in principle, transmissible *inter vivos* (arts. 1441, 1442 C.C.Q.). Consequently, an assignment of contract is possible only when expressly provided for by law (e.g. the assignment of insurance of persons (art. 2463 C.C.Q.); the assignment of lease (art. 1870 C.C.Q.)). **2°** In practice, the term *assignment of contract* is sometimes used for what is merely an assignment of debt or claim. **Fr.** cession de contrat.

ASSIGNMENT OF CREANCE

Syn. assignment of claim(s). **Fr.** cession de créance+, cession-transport, transport-cession, transport de créance.

ASSIGNMENT OF DEBT

Assignment in which an assigning debtor transfers to an assignee a debt[1] owed to the assigned creditor. **Obs. 1°** The assignment of debt does not discharge the assigning debtor unless the creditor has expressly consented to it. However, assignment of contract, which is the conjunction of an assignment of debt and an assignment of claims, is permitted only in exceptional circumstances (e.g. the assignment of insurance of persons (art. 2463 C.C.Q.); the assignment of lease (art. 1870 C.C.Q.)). **2°** From the assignee's point of view, the transaction may be styled as an *assumption of debt*. **3°** The term *assignment of debt* is sometimes used as a synonym for *assignment of claim* (art. 888 C.C.Q.). **See also** assignment of contract, assumption of debt, novation by change of debtor. **Fr.** cession de dette+, transport de dette.

ASSIGNMENT OF HEREDITARY RIGHTS

Syn. assignment of successional rights. **Fr.** cession de(s) droits héréditaires, cession de(s) droits successifs+, cession d'hérédité.

ASSIGNMENT OF INHERITANCE

Syn. assignment of successional rights. **Fr.** cession de(s) droits héréditaires, cession de(s) droits successifs+, cession d'hérédité.

ASSIGNMENT OF LITIGIOUS RIGHTS

Assignment of a right, most often a claim, the existence or the scope of which gives rise or may give rise to litigation. **Obs.** As with assignment of claims, assignment of litigious rights ordinarily refers to a sale. Indeed, the Civil Code speaks of the *sale of litigious rights* (title preceding art. 1782 C.C.Q.). **See also** litigious personal right, redemption of litigious rights, sale of litigious rights. **Fr.** cession de droits litigieux.

ASSIGNMENT OF RIGHTS OF INHERITANCE

Syn. assignment of successional rights.
Fr. cession de(s) droits héréditaires, cession de(s) droits successifs+, cession d'hérédité.

ASSIGNMENT OF RIGHTS OF SUCCESSION

Syn. assignment of successional rights. "The assignment of rights of succession is the contract whereby a person called to receive a succession, transfers to another all the rights which he may have to the property of the deceased on condition that the assignee acquits in his place, all the charges to which he is bound in his capacity as heir" (Planiol & Ripert, *Treatise*, vol. 2, n° 1639, p. 908).
Fr. cession de(s) droits héréditaires, cession de(s) droits successifs+, cession d'hérédité.

ASSIGNMENT OF SUCCESSIONAL RIGHTS

Assignment by which an heir transfers to a coheir or to another person the rights he or she has in the succession.
Obs. 1° By assignment, the heir transfers only the rights and obligations resulting from the opening of the succession. The capacity of the heir in itself is personal and thus non-assignable. **2°** The assignment of successional rights can occur only if the succession is open. Pacts on future successions are prohibited by article 631 C.C.Q. **3°** An assignment granted to a person, other than an heir, often called "stranger to the succession", gives the coheirs of the assignor the option to exercise a right of successional redemption (art. 848 C.C.Q.). **4°** As with the assignment of litigious rights, the operation is usually designated as a sale. Indeed, the Civil Code refers to the *sale of rights of succession* (title preceding art. 1779 C.C.Q.).
Syn. assignment of hereditary rights, assignment of inheritance, assignment of rights of inheritance, assignment of rights of succession. **See also** sale of successional rights.
Fr. cession de(s) droits héréditaires, cession de(s) droits successifs+, cession d'hérédité.

ASSIGNOR *n.*

Person who transfers a right by assignment[1]. "The creditors of the assignor are entitled to satisfy their claims out of all his property, moveable and immoveable, present and future" (Miller & Sarna, (1981) 59 *Can. Bar Rev.* 638, p. 649).

Occ. Arts. 1646, 2462 C.C.Q.; arts. 1192, 2558 C.C.L.C.
See also assignee, seller.
Fr. cédant.

ASSOCIATION *n.*

Group of persons who, in a spirit of cooperation, carry on a joint activity devoted to a purpose other than the realization of financial gain to be shared between them. "The association is the contract by which several persons put in common their activity and in case of need, revenue or capital with a purpose other than to share in the benefits [...] This contract permits the attainment of a purpose or the exercise of influence, which for individual persons acting alone would be more difficult or even impossible" (Planiol & Ripert, *Treatise*, vol. 2, part. 2, n° 1988, p. 184).
Occ. Arts. 2186, 2187, 2267 C.C.Q.
Obs. 1° Associations are established by contract. **2°** A distinction is drawn between associations created under the Civil Code, which are not endowed with juridical personality, and other associations which, because they have been incorporated pursuant to special statutes, such as the *Companies Act*, R.S.Q. c. C-38, are legal persons. **3°** Although associations created under the Civil Code are not endowed with juridical personality, they are similar to legal persons in some respects (e.g. the directors of an association may sue to assert its rights and interests (art. 2271 C.C.Q.)). **4°** The absence of the purpose of realizing a financial gain to be shared between the members distinguishes associations from partnerships. **5°** Associations are distinguished from foundations in that associations are groups of persons whereas foundations are understood to be a universality of property dedicated to the fulfilment of a socially beneficial purpose (art. 1256 C.C.Q.).
See also contract of association, contract of partnership, member[1], partnership[1].
Fr. association.

ASSUMPTION OF DEBT

Contract by which a person assumes liability for a debt[1] for which he or she is not otherwise responsible.
Obs. 1° An assumption of debt does not release the original debtor unless the creditor expressly consents to the release. **2°** From the point of view of the original debtor, the transaction is called an *assignment of debt*.
See also assignment of debt.
Fr. reprise de dette.

ASSUMPTION OF RISK(S)

Act or omission whereby a person voluntarily accepts exposure to a danger that he or she knows or should know about.
Obs. The assumption of risk, although it may be considered imprudent, does not necessarily imply renunciation of a remedy (art. 1477 C.C.Q.).
Fr. acceptation de(s) risque(s).

AT FAULT *adj.ph.*

Said of a person who has committed a fault.
Occ. Arts. 1465, 1861, 2154, 2229 C.C.Q.; art. 1636 C.C.L.C.
See also wrongful.
Fr. fautif[1].

ATTESTING DEED

Document which records a juridical act or a juridical fact. For example, act of civil status, authentic deed, minutes of a meeting.
Obs. See articles 1824, 2818, 2826 C.C.Q.
Syn. act[2], *acte*, deed[1], *instrumentum*, title[3].
See also authentic act, formalism, juridical act, juridical fact[1,2], notarial act, private writing, semi-authentic act, technology-based document.
Fr. acte[2], acte instrumentaire[+], *instrumentum*, titre[3].

ATTORNEY *n.*

Syn. mandatary.
Occ. Arts. 87, 442*i* (5) C.C.L.C.; art. 62 C.C.P.
Obs. In Quebec law, the term *attorney* applies to advocates and notaries who act as representatives of persons within defined spheres of competence.
See also mandate[1], power of attorney[1].
Fr. mandataire[+], procureur.

ATTRIBUTIVE *adj.*

Conferring a right upon a person.
See also attributive act.
Fr. attributif.

ATTRIBUTIVE ACT

Juridical act which confers a right upon a person.
Obs. An attributive act may be constitutive or translatory.
See also constitutive title, declaratory act, renunciation[1], translatory act.
Fr. acte attributif.

AUCTION (SALE)

Sale by which property is offered to several persons through the intermediary of a third person, the *auctioneer*, and declared sold to the highest and last bidder.
Occ. Arts. 945, 1757, 3001 C.C.Q.; arts. 594, 900 C.C.P.
Obs. 1° The auction may be either voluntary or forced (art. 1758 C.C.Q.). **2°** In the case of a forced sale by auction, the rules of the *Code of Civil Procedure* (see arts. 605 *et seq.* and arts. 683 *et seq.* C.C.P.) take precedence over the rules in the Civil Code with respect to auction sales in the event of a conflict (art. 1758 C.C.Q.). **3°** The term *auction* is used alone to designate *auction sale*. **4°** The codal regime respecting auction sale is set forth at articles 1757 to 1766 C.C.Q.
Syn. sale by auction.
Fr. vente aux enchères.

AUTHENTIC ACT

Attesting deed received or certified by a competent public officer according to the requisite legal formalities. For example, a notarial act, an act of civil status.
Occ. Arts. 2813, 2815, 2821 C.C.Q.; art. 871.1 C.C.P.
Obs. The notion of *authentic act* is closely associated with the codal regime related to evidence (see arts. 2803 *et seq.* C.C.Q.).
Syn. authentic deed, authentic document, authentic instrument, authentic writing.
See also notarial act, private writing, semi-authentic act.
Fr. acte authentique.

AUTHENTIC DEED

Syn. authentic act.
Occ. Art. 2133 C.C.L.C.; art. 870 C.C.P.
Fr. acte authentique.

AUTHENTIC DOCUMENT

Syn. authentic act.
Occ. Arts. 1218, 2178 C.C.L.C.
Fr. acte authentique.

AUTHENTIC INSTRUMENT

Syn. authentic act.
Occ. Art. 1225 C.C.L.C.
Fr. acte authentique.

AUTHENTIC WRITING

Syn. authentic act. "Art. 1207, of the Civil Code, says that letters patent, issued by the Government of Quebec, are authentic writings, and art. 1210 adds that 'an authentic writing makes complete proof between the parties to it', of the obligation expressed in it [...]" (*A.G. Quebec* v. *Fraser*, (1906) 37 S.C.R. 577, p. 590, D. Girouard, J.).
Occ. Arts. 1210, 1211 C.C.L.C.; arts. 223, 311 C.C.P.
Fr. acte authentique.

AUTHOR *n.*

Person from whom a successor in title acquires a right or an obligation. For example, the vendor of a thing is the author of the purchaser, who is, in turn, the vendor's successor in title.
Occ. Art. 2200 C.C.L.C.
Obs. From the Latin *auctor*: one who makes a thing grow (root *augere*: to make, to grow, to originate).
Syn. predecessor (in title). **See also** assignor, coauthor, seller, successor, transmission.
Fr. auteur+, prédécesseur en droit, prédécesseur en titre.

AUTONOMOUS ACT OF A THING

Action of a thing, without direct human intervention which, when it causes damage, is susceptible of engaging the civil liability of the thing's custodian or owner. For example, the spontaneous explosion of a furnace boiler or of a bottle. "What then is the 'autonomous act' of a thing causing damage? [...] It would seem that such an act can be described both in negative and in positive terms. In negative terms, it would mean that paragraph 1 of article 1054 [C.C.L.C.] cannot be applied if, at the moment of the accident, the thing was in a state of inertia, of complete passivity. The damage then was not caused by a thing and liability must be proved under article 1053 [C.C.L.C.]. [...] In positive terms, the application of paragraph 1 of article 1054 [C.C.L.C.] requires that a thing have actively caused the damage as a result of its own dynamism, of its own motion, without the direct intervention of man" (Crépeau, (1962) 40 *Can. Bar Rev.* 222, pp. 234-235).
Obs. 1° It is recognized that this fiction, which consists in speaking of the *act* of an inanimate object, is a device to link the damage caused by a thing to the person responsible for it. **2°** In French law, it is not necessary that the act of the thing be autonomous to give rise to the custodian's liability.
See also act of an animal, act of a thing, liability for damage caused by things.
Fr. fait autonome de la chose.

AUTONOMY OF THE WILL (THEORY OF THE)

Theory according to which intention is considered to be the source of contractual obligations. "It is one thing to recognize that will has a role in contract [...] It is quite another thing to postulate will as an a priori and exclusive basis from which are deduced in rigorous fashion the consequences which it implies. Only the second attitude belongs to an adherence to the theory of the autonomy of the will" (Rouhette, in *Contract Law Today*, 38, p. 47).
Obs. 1° The genius of the theory of the autonomy of the will is that it explains the contractual obligation by reference to individual will. At the end of the nineteenth century, scholars applied the philosophical doctrine of the autonomy of the will to law on the basis of four concepts: the will creates the contract; the contract is the law of the parties; the contract must be interpreted in conformity with the intention of the parties; and the contract is necessarily fair since it was voluntarily undertaken. Therefore, a valid obligation which conforms to public order may be thought of as valid and just because it reflects a free expression of will. **2°** The theory of the autonomy of the will was developed on the basis of principles predating the theory of obligations, notably freedom of contract, consensualism and the binding force of contract. At a technical level, each of these principles is subject to numerous restrictions in addition to those related to the requirements of public order. It is therefore important to remember that these principles are not, by their very nature, absolute. Some provisions are indeed so essential that they cannot be dismissed as simple exceptions limiting the will of the parties (e.g. arts. 1375, 1434 C.C.Q. and the *Consumer Protection Act*, R.S.Q. c. P-40.1). **3°** Two main criticisms have been raised against the theory of the autonomy of the will. The first questions the very foundation of the theory by adopting a conception of contract based on the preeminence of law rather than intention. The second concerns contractual justice. While recognizing intention as the source of contractual obligations, this perspective calls into question the idea that the concurrence of free will inherently produces just outcomes.

See also binding force of contract, consensualism, consent[1], contract[1], formalism, freedom of contract.
Fr. autonomie de la volonté (théorie de l').

AVANT-CONTRAT n. (French)

Syn. pre-contract.
Fr. avant-contrat.

AVOID *v.*

See annul.
Occ. Art. 1009 C.C.L.C.
Fr. annuler.

AVOIDANCE *n.*

See annulment.
Occ. Art. 1592 C.C.L.C.
Fr. annulation.

B

BAD FAITH

1. Dishonesty or lack of loyalty in the exercise of civil rights. "[...] any slight proof of bad faith usually suffices to shift the burden upon the person claiming good faith to establish it" (Rosenberg, (1960-61) 7 *McGill L.J.* 2, p. 12).
Occ. Arts. 621, 651, 1397 C.C.Q.
See also abuse of right(s), defect of consent, good faith[1].
Fr. mauvaise foi[1].

2. Knowledge of the fact that one is acting contrary to law. For example, the bad faith of a possessor who has made useful disbursements on land that he or she knows to be the property of another (art. 959 C.C.Q.); the bad faith of a spouse regarding the nullity of his or her marriage (art. 383 C.C.Q.). "It was open to the learned trial judge to refuse to believe [the defendant] and had he based his decision that [the defendant] was in bad faith on his disbelief of this testimony, it might have been difficult to set it aside" (*Grossman* v. *Barrett*, [1926] S.C.R. 129, pp. 133-134, P.-B. Mignault, J.).
Occ. Arts. 383, 931 C.C.Q.; arts. 1516, 2202 C.C.L.C.
See also good faith[2], Paulian fraud.
Fr. mauvaise foi[2].

BALANCE *n.*

Sum of money that, in a partition, compensates the inequality of value of the shares or, in a contract of exchange, compensates for the imbalance in value of the things exchanged.
Fr. soulte.

BARGAIN *n.*

See contract[1].
Fr. entente.

BARTER *n.*

Syn. exchange. "[...] the object of such a voyage [a trading voyage] [...] being for trade and barter, that is, the exchange from time to time, and from place to place during the continuance of the voyage, of the delivered cargo for a return cargo" (*Merchants' Marine Insurance Co.* v. *Rumsey*, (1884) 9 S.C.R. 577, p. 582, J.W. Ritchie, J.).
Fr. contrat d'échange, échange[+], troc.

BARTER *v.*

Syn. exchange.
Fr. échanger[+], troquer.

BENEFICIARY *n.*

1. Person advantaged by a liberality[1]. For example, the substitute, the institute, the donee, the legatee.
Fr. bénéficiaire[1].

2. Person, other than the client or the participant, designated in a contract of insurance to receive the payment from the insurer in the event of the occurrence of the risk. "The Quebec legislature maintained the unseizable class of family life insurance policies defined *vis-à-vis* the beneficiary's relationship to the policyholder, not the life insured" (*Perron-Malenfant* v. *Malenfant (Trustee of)*, [1999] 3 S.C.R. 375, p. 406, C.D. Gonthier, J.).
Occ. Arts. 2414, 2445, 2447 C.C.Q.; arts. 2500, 2540, 2550 C.C.L.C.; ss. 238, 424, *Insurance Act*, R.S.Q. c. A-32; ss. 102, 243, *An Act respecting the distribution of financial products and services*, R.S.Q. c. D-9.2.
Obs. 1° Although they often refer to the same person, the terms *insured*, *client* and *beneficiary* must be distinguished. Life insurance best illustrates the difference between them: the *insured* is the person whose death triggers the payment by the insurer; the *client*, who may or may not be the person insured, subscribes to the contract with the insurer; the *beneficiary* is the person who receives the payment at the death of the insured. **2°** According to article 2445 of the Civil Code, the beneficiary is distinct from the client or the participant, but the word is nevertheless commonly used to designate clients and participants when they are entitled to receive the insured capital themselves.
See also client[1], insurance contract, insured, insurer.
Fr. bénéficiaire[2].

BENEFICIARY OF A PROMISE

Syn. promisee.
Fr. bénéficiaire d'une promesse.

BENEFIT OF DISCUSSION *nom.ph.*

Right of the surety and of a third-party holder of property serving as security, to demand that the creditor suing for payment seize and sell the principal debtor's property before their own.
Occ. Arts. 1766, 2347, 2348, 2352 C.C.Q.; art. 1941 C.C.L.C.
Obs. 1° The exercise of the benefit of discussion suspends proceedings taken against the surety or third-party holder. Proceedings continue if the sale of the debtor's property does not generate funds sufficient to extinguish the debt. **2°** The judicial surety and the solidary surety may not invoke the benefit of discussion (arts. 2347, 2352 C.C.Q.).
Syn. right of discussion. **See also** benefit of division, suretyship.
Fr. bénéfice de discussion+, droit de discussion.

BENEFIT OF DIVISION *nom.ph.*

Right of the cosurety sued for the whole of a debt to demand that the creditor divide the claim and reduce it to the surety's share of the debt.
Occ. Arts. 1528, 2349 C.C.Q.; arts. 1946, 2585 C.C.L.C.
Obs. 1° Where there is more than one surety, each may renounce the benefit of division. **2°** A solidary surety may not invoke the benefit of division (art. 2352 C.C.Q.).
Syn. right of division. **See also** benefit of discussion, suretyship.
Fr. bénéfice de division+, droit de division.

BENEFIT OF SUBROGATION

Right conferred by law upon a surety or a third party holder to oppose the action[1] of a creditor who by his or her behaviour has rendered subrogation in the latter's rights and recourses impossible.
Occ. Art. 2355 C.C.Q.
Obs. 1° The law confers the benefit of subrogation on the solidary debtor (art. 1531 C.C.Q.). **2°** The surety may not renounce the benefit of subrogation in advance (art. 2355 C.C.Q.).
See also personal subrogation.
Fr. bénéfice de cession d'actions, bénéfice de subrogation+.

BENEVOLENT CONTRACT

Gratuitous contract the purpose of which is to provide services to one of the parties rather than to transfer property[1]. For example, a deposit, a gratuitous mandate.
Obs. On the basis of article 1105 *C.civ.fr.*, some writers consider this term to be synonymous with *gratuitous contract.*
See also liberality[1], onerous contract.
Fr. contrat de bénévolat, contrat de bienfaisance+, contrat désintéressé.

BET *n.*

Syn. wagering contract.
Occ. Art. 1927 C.C.L.C.
Fr. contrat de pari+, pari.

BETTING *n.*

Syn. wagering contract.
Fr. contrat de pari+, pari.

BILATERAL *adj.*

Syn. synallagmatic.
Fr. synallagmatique+, bilatéral.

BILATERAL ACT

Juridical act entered into by two parties.
Obs. 1° A distinction is drawn between *bilateral acts* and *unilateral acts.* **2°** The bilateral act should not be confused with the bilateral contract (generally designated as a *synallagmatic contract*) which is a species of bilateral act producing reciprocal obligations for both parties.
See also multilateral act, unilateral act.
Fr. acte bilatéral.

BILATERAL CONTRACT

Contract in which the parties have reciprocal and interdependent obligations. For example, a sale, a lease. "The contract of employment, like all bilateral contracts, creates mutual rights and obligations between the parties" (Charlap, in *Livre-Souvenir* 417, p. 448).
Occ. Art. 1380 C.C.Q.
Obs. 1° The bilateral contract is a species of bilateral act producing reciprocal obligations for both parties. **2°** The term *bilateral* reflects the reciprocal character of the obligations, so that a contract that reciprocally binds two or more persons is said to be bilateral.

Syn. synallagmatic contract. **See also** imperfect bilateral contract, unilateral contract.
Fr. contrat bilatéral, contrat synallagmatique+.

BILATERAL PROMISE OF SALE

Bilateral promise to enter into a contract of sale. "A bilateral promise of sale or accepted option is a contract that obliges the parties to enter into a contract of sale at a later date" (Brierley & Macdonald (eds.), *Quebec Civil Law*, n° 574, p. 515).
Syn. synallagmatic promise of sale. **See also** bilateral promise (to contract), unilateral promise of sale.
Fr. promesse bilatérale de vente+, promesse synallagmatique de vente.

BILATERAL PROMISE (TO CONTRACT)

Promise to contract by which both parties undertake to enter into a contract at a later date, the essential terms of which are determined immediately.
Obs. The bilateral promise to contract may result from an agreement between the parties or from the acceptance of a unilateral promise (art. 1396 C.C.Q.).
Syn. synallagmatic promise to contract. **See also** unilateral promise (to contract).
Fr. promesse bilatérale (de contrat), promesse synallagmatique (de contrat)+.

BILATERAL RESILIATION

Voluntary resiliation resulting from an agreement between the contracting parties.
Obs. Where there are more than two contracting parties, the expressions *amicable resiliation* or *conventional resiliation* are more generally used.
Syn. amicable resiliation, conventional resiliation, revocation[2].
Fr. résiliation amiable, résiliation bilatérale+, résiliation conventionnelle, révocation[2].

BILL OF LADING *nom.ph.*

Writing evidencing all or part of a contract for the carriage of goods.
Occ. Arts. 2041, 2043 C.C.Q.; s. 2, *Bill of Lading Act*, R.S.C. 1985, c. B-5.
Obs. 1° The Civil Code enunciates certain elements that usually appear on a bill of lading (art. 2041 C.C.Q.). **2** The bill of lading

may constitute a negotiable title when the negotiability of the bill of lading is provided for by law or by contract (art. 2043 C.C.Q.).
See also acquittance, attesting deed, contract for the carriage of goods, receipt[2].
Fr. connaissement.

BIND *v.*

To oblige someone morally or at law. "When in one document a party binds himself to do more acts than one, some of which are legal and some illegal, the question whether the agreement to do the legal acts is severable and so enforceable is one of construction of the document" (*Pauze* v. *Gauvin*, [1954] S.C.R. 15, p. 27, J.R. Cartwright, J.).
Occ. Arts. 309, 1062, 1434, 2130, 2336 C.C.Q.; arts. 1028, 1600 C.C.L.C.; s. 260.6, *Consumer Protection Act*, R.S.Q. c. P-40.1.
Syn. obligate, oblige.
Fr. engager, obliger+.

BINDING *adj.*

That which has the attributes of a legal obligation. "[...] to say that contracts are binding upon parties is merely a shorthand for a number of related ideas. It means first, that parties are bound, under compulsion of law, to perform the prestations that they have agreed to [...] Second, the notion means that contracts are, in principle, irrevocable [...] Third, the notion signifies that not only the courts, but also the parties, are bound by the parties' self-made law such that, subject to explicit exceptions [...] judicial revision or modification of contracts is generally unavailable" (Brierley & Macdonald (eds.), *Quebec Civil Law*, n° 453, p. 420).
Occ. Arts. 215, 1395, 1435, 2097, 3145 C.C.Q.; ss. 18, 42, 234, *Consumer Protection Act*, R.S.Q. c. P-40.1; s. 3, *An Act respecting the Régie du logement*, R.S.Q. c. R-8.1.
Obs. The expression *binding in conscience* is used in the positivist tradition to refer to *moral* as opposed to *legal* obligations.
Syn. obligatory. **See also** obligational.
Fr. obligatoire.

BINDING FORCE OF CONTRACT

Obligatory character conferred by law[1] upon a valid contract.
Obs. 1° Some scholars argue that the binding force of contract draws its justification directly from the meeting of the minds, while others contend that this obligational character actually originates in law. Article 1372

C.C.Q. provides that "an obligation arises from a contract", in contrast to obligations that arise from any act or fact to which the effects of an obligation are attached. The text of the Code may thus be said to suggest that contract is at least a source of obligations distinct from law. **2°** From the perspective of its obligational content, a contract is not limited to what the parties have expressly stipulated, but is understood to include also "what is incident to it according to its nature and in conformity with usage, equity or law" (art. 1434 C.C.Q.).
See also autonomy of will, consensualism, contract[1], formalism, relativity of contract, third person.
Fr. force obligatoire du contrat.

BODILY INJURY

Damage relating to the physical integrity of a person. For example, the loss of a body part resulting from a violation of one's right to integrity of the person. "The words in art. 2262(2) [C.C.L.C.] 'for bodily injuries' cannot [...] be read literally as they stand. There is no action *for* bodily injuries in the literal sense of those words. A man sues for his wages, but he does not sue for bodily injuries; he sues to recover the damages which he has sustained from the wrongful infliction of bodily injuries" (*Regent Taxi and Transport Co.* v. *Congrégation des Petits Frères de Marie*, [1932] A.C. 295 (P.C.), p. 302, Lord Russell of Killowen).
Occ. Arts. 1474, 1615, 1609 C.C.Q.; arts. 1056*b*, 2262 C.C.L.C.
Obs. 1° Bodily injury is one of the few types of injury recognized by the Civil Code, the others being material and moral damage (art. 1607 C.C.Q.). **2°** The *Civil Code of Québec* gives the human person a more visible and central place than did the *Civil Code of Lower Canada*. This finds expression in many of the Civil Code's provisions including, for example, the regime of compensation for bodily or moral damage, comprised of rules aimed at providing greater protection to the human person (e.g. arts. 1474, 1609, 1615 C.C.Q.). **3°** Some statutes adopt a different meaning of *bodily injury* (e.g. *Automobile Insurance Act*, R.S.Q. c. A-25, which provides that *bodily injury* includes damage to the clothing worn by the victim). **4°** The expression *personal injury* is sometimes used as a synonym for *bodily injury* although they do not share the same meaning.
Syn. corporal damage. **See also** æsthetic damage, injury, loss[1], material damage, moral damage.
Fr. préjudice corporel.

BONA FIDES (Latin)

See good faith.
Fr. *bona fides.*

BON PÈRE DE FAMILLE
nom.ph. (French)

Syn. reasonable person. "Until delivery the debtor is obliged to keep the thing with the care of a prudent administrator (*bon père de famille*)" (Le Dain, (1952-55) 1 *McGill L.J.* 237, p. 239).
Obs. 1° The expression *bon père de famille*, which no doubt reflects the idea that prudence and diligence are the hallmarks of a responsible parent, has fallen from favour because many regarded it as outdated and, given that it consecrates a model of behaviour reflecting a male perspective, imprecise and perhaps even sexist. The expression *reasonable person* is used more frequently. **2°** This expression may be traced to Roman law (*bonus pater familias*).
Fr. bon père de famille, *bonus pater familias*, personne raisonnable[+].

BONUS PATER FAMILIAS
nom.ph. (Latin)

Syn. reasonable person. "To determine whether a particular conduct measures up to the requisite standard, the courts compare it to what they suppose would be under similar circumstances, the behaviour of a reasonably prudent man, and the requisite care is called the care of a 'bon père de famille', the Latin bonus pater familias" (Brossard, (1955) 16 *Thémis* 239, p. 240).
Fr. bon père de famille, *bonus pater familias*, personne raisonnable[+].

BORROW *v.*

To contract a loan, from the perspective of the borrower.
Occ. Art. 2326 C.C.Q.; arts. 297, 1772 C.C.L.C.
See also lend.
Fr. emprunter.

BORROWER *n.*

Person who contracts a loan.
Occ. Arts. 1756, 2313, 2317, 2322, 2327, C.C.Q.; arts. 1763, 1766 C.C.L.C.
Obs. In a simple loan, the borrower becomes owner of the property loaned, subject to the obligation to return a property of like quantity and of the same kind and quality. The

borrower consequently bears the risk of loss (art. 2327 C.C.Q.). In a loan for use, the borrower does not, in principle, bear this risk, since the lender remains owner of the property (art. 2322 C.C.Q.). However, he is bound to act with prudence and diligence in the safekeeping and preservation of the property (arts. 2317, 2318 C.C.Q.).
See also lender, loan for use, simple loan.
Fr. emprunteur.

BREVI MANU TRADITION (Latin)

Syn. tradition by interversion of title.
Fr. *traditio brevi manu*, tradition de brève main, tradition par interversion de titre+.

BULK SALE

Sale by which a merchant, outside the ordinary course of that merchant's commercial activities, transfers the whole or a substantial portion of his or her stock in trade or an interest in the business.
Occ. Art. 1569a C.C.L.C.
Obs. 1° The term *bulk sale* designates a sale or any other transfer by onerous title of the stock in trade, whether by way of exchange, by giving in payment or in connection with a partnership. **2°** In 1994, the legislature replaced the bulk sale, which included only the sale of a stock in trade and of merchandise (arts. 1569a to 1569e C.C.L.C.), by the sale of an enterprise (arts. 1767 to 1778 C.C.Q.). The articles relating to the sale of an enterprise were later repealed (s. 8, S.Q. 2002, c. 50).
Fr. vente en bloc.

BUY *v.*

To enter into a sale, from the perspective of the buyer. "The promise of sale is a contract by which one person engages himself to sell a thing to another person, without the latter immediately consenting to buy" (Planiol & Ripert, *Treatise*, vol. 2, part. 1, n° 1398, p. 788).

Occ. Art. 1785 C.C.Q.; arts. 290, 1482 C.C.L.C.
Syn. purchase. **See also** acquire[1], sell.
Fr. acheter.

BUYER *n.*

Person who, by contract of sale, acquires property. "It is the duty of the seller to give adequate information; it is not the obligation of the buyer to ascertain for himself the true facts. Any other interpretation of art. 1519 C.C.[L.C.] would nullify its effect" (*Forget* v. *Gohier*, [1945] B.R. 437, p. 451, G. Barclay, J.).
Occ. Arts. 1734, 1736 C.C.Q.; arts. 1532, 1706 C.C.L.C.
Obs. Although the term *purchaser* does not appear in the chapter on sale, it is generally preferred to *buyer* in Book Six of the Civil Code on prior claims and hypothecs.
Syn. purchaser. **See also** property[1], seller.
Fr. acheteur.

BUYER SUBJECT TO RIGHT OF REDEMPTION

Buyer who, in a contract of sale, grants the vendor a right of redemption.
See also sale with right of redemption.
Fr. acheteur à réméré.

BY GRATUITOUS TITLE *adj.ph.*

See act by gratuitous title.
Fr. à titre gratuit.

BY ONEROUS TITLE *adj.ph.*

See act by onerous title.
Occ. Arts. 213, 1640, 2961 C.C.Q.; arts. 441x, 823, 978 C.C.L.C.; s. 120, *An Act respecting the implementation of the reform of the Civil Code*, S.Q. 1992, c. 57; s. 150.31, *Consumer Protection Act*, R.S.Q. c. P-40.1.
Fr. à titre onéreux.

C

CANCEL *v.*

To effect a cancellation. "[...] the appellant admitted that under art. 1691 of the Civil Code [of Lower Canada] the respondent was entitled to cancel the agreement, and this point of view was accepted by the learned trial judge who pronounced the agreement duly cancelled" (*Tidewater Shipbuilders Ltd.* v. *Société Naphtes Transports*, [1927] S.C.R. 20, p. 24, P.B. Mignault, J.).

Occ. Arts. 135, 364, 2477, 3071 C.C.Q.

Fr. annuler(<)[+], résilier[2](<)[+], résoudre(<)[+], révoquer(<)[+].

CANCELLATION *n.*

Setting aside of a juridical act. "[...] article 1691 of the Civil Code [of Lower Canada][...] clearly did not apply to this case for there was no cancellation of the contract within the meaning of that article which plainly means an entire cancellation of the whole contract" (*Maisonneuve (Ville de)* v. *Banque Provinciale du Canada* (1903), 33 S.C.R. 418, p. 429, J.D. Armour, J.).

Occ. Arts. 98, 439, 2443, 3075 C.C.Q.

See also annulment, resiliation[1,2], resolution, revocation.

Fr. annulation(<)[+], résiliation(<)[1,2+], résolution(<)[+], révocation(<)[1+].

CAPABLE *adj.*

1. Said of a person having legal capacity. "All persons are capable in law, except where some incapacity is expressly declared. This principle, originally stated explicitly only in relation to contract [...] has nonetheless always been of general application" (Brierley & Macdonald (eds.), *Quebec Civil Law*, n° 173, p. 213). *Fully capable of exercising his or her civil rights; capable of contracting.*

Occ. Arts. 179, 783, 1323, 1398, 3086 C.C.Q.; arts. 324, 352, 985, 1010 C.C.L.C.; art. 558 C.C.P.

See also able, incapable[1], legal capacity.

Fr. capable[1].

2. Said of a person who has sufficient physical or mental disposition to formulate an opinion, to make a decision or to express his or her will.

Occ. Arts. 19, 20, 291, 1398, 2167, 2172 C.C.Q.; art. 776 C.C.P.

Obs. The term is often used in its ordinary sense of having the necessary qualities to do a certain thing or to fulfill a charge.

Syn. able. **See also** capable[1], *de facto* capacity, endowed with reason, incapable[2].

Fr. apte[+], capable[2].

CAPACITY *n.*

1. Syn. legal capacity.

Occ. Arts. 154, 1409, 2681, 2991 C.C.Q.; arts. 6, 759 C.C.L.C.; title II, *An Act to secure the carrying out of the Entente between France and Québec respecting mutual aid in judicial matters*, R.S.Q. c. A-20.1; s. 46(1), *Bills of Exchange Act*, R.S.C. 1985, c. B-4; s. 15(1), *Bank Act*, S.C. 1991, c. 46.

Fr. capacité[1], capacité juridique[+], capacité légale.

2. Syn. *de facto* capacity.

Obs. In matters of capacity to contract, capacity is ascertained in legal or factual terms, depending on the context.

Fr. aptitude[+], capacité[2], capacité de fait, capacité naturelle.

CAPACITY OF DISCERNMENT

See discernment.

Fr. capacité de discernement.

CAPACITY OF FACT

Syn. *de facto* capacity.

Fr. aptitude[+], capacité[2], capacité de fait, capacité naturelle.

CAPACITY TO ACQUIRE (RIGHTS)

Syn. capacity to enjoy (rights).

Fr. capacité d'acquisition, capacité de jouissance[+].

CAPACITY TO ENJOY (RIGHTS)

Legal vocation to hold rights.
Obs. 1° The capacity to enjoy rights and the capacity to exercise rights together constitute legal capacity. **2°** Although the capacity to enjoy rights was traditionally conceived of in the context of subjective rights, it also extends to the possibility of being subjected to obligations. **3°** A complete denial of the capacity to enjoy rights would be equivalent to the negation of legal personality. **4°** The capacity to exercise rights presupposes the capacity to enjoy. Indeed, for a person to exercise a right, he or she must have the enjoyment of that right. However, the capacity to enjoy rights does not necessarily entail the capacity to exercise them. In some cases, such as that of a minor, a person may have the enjoyment of a right but not the capacity to exercise such right. **5°** A difference between article 18 C.C.L.C. and article 1 C.C.Q, is that the former states that the enjoyment of civil rights could only be limited by express provision of law, whereas the latter does not. **6°** See also article 301 C.C.Q. concerning the capacity to enjoy rights of legal persons.
Syn. capacity to acquire (rights). **See also** capacity to exercise (rights), incapacity to enjoy (rights), legal capacity.
Fr. capacité d'acquisition, capacité de jouissance[+].

CAPACITY TO EXERCISE (RIGHTS)

Legal vocation to exercise the rights that one holds.
Occ. Art. 303 C.C.Q.
Obs. 1° The capacity to enjoy and the capacity to exercise rights together constitute legal capacity. **2°** The capacity to exercise rights presupposes the capacity to enjoy. Indeed, for a person to exercise a right, he or she must have the enjoyment of that right. The capacity to enjoy rights does not, however, necessarily entail the capacity to exercise them. For example, a minor may have the enjoyment of a right but not the capacity to exercise it. **3°** See also article 303 C.C.Q. concerning the capacity to exercise rights of legal persons.
See also aptitude, capacity to enjoy (rights), discernment, incapacity to exercise (rights), legal capacity.
Fr. capacité d'exercice.

CAPITAL *n.*

Sum of money owed, as opposed to the interest this sum may generate.
Occ. Arts. 1570, 1616 C.C.Q.; arts. 1159, 1974 C.C.L.C.
Obs. In the *Consumer protection Act* (R.S.Q. c. P-40.1), the capital is designated by the expression *net capital* (s. 68).
Syn. capital sum, principal[2]. **See also** interest.
Fr. capital[+], principal[2].

CAPITAL SUM

Syn. capital.
Occ. Art. 947 C.C.L.C.
Fr. capital[+], principal[2].

CARE *n.*

Syn. custody.
Fr. garde[+], garde juridique[2].

CARRIAGE *n.*

1. Act of taking a person or of conveying property from one place to another.
Occ. Arts. 2031, 2039, 2049, 2056, 2070 C.C.Q.
Obs. Carriage of persons or property does not necessarily entail a contractual relationship.
Syn. conveyance[1], transport[1], transportation. **See also** contract for the carriage of persons, contract for the carriage of goods.
Fr. transport[1].

2. Syn. contract of carriage.
Fr. contrat de transport[+], transport[2].

CARRIAGE OF GOODS

Act of conveying property from one place to another.
Obs. 1° Carriage of goods does not necessarily entail a contractual relationship. **2°** The prevalence of the term *goods*, which is unusual in Quebec civil law parlance as a synonym for movable property may be explained by the influence of Common law terminology in transportation law. Often associated with the sale of movables in commercial law outside Quebec, the term is also encountered in international commercial law. **3°** In the expression *carriage of goods*, the term *carriage* is interchangeable with *transport* or *transportation*.
Syn. carriage of merchandise, carriage of property. **See also** contract for the carriage of goods.
Fr. transport de biens[+], transport de choses, transport de marchandises.

CARRIAGE OF MERCHANDISE

Syn. carriage of goods.
Fr. transport de biens[+], transport de choses, transport de marchandises.

CARRIAGE OF PERSONS

Act of taking a person from one place to another.
Obs. 1° Carriage of persons does not necessarily entail a contractual relation. **2**° In the expression *carriage of persons*, the term *carriage* is interchangeable with *transport* or *transportation*.
See also contract for the carriage of persons.
Fr. transport de personnes.

CARRIAGE OF PROPERTY

Syn. carriage of goods.
Fr. transport de biens[+], transport de choses, transport de marchandises.

CARRIER *n.*

Person who undertakes to take a person or to convey property from one place to another. "A letter of indemnity, then, which could establish that the goods in question were damaged before receipt by the carrier, cannot be invoked against consignees or third parties" (Tetley, (1977) 23 *McGill L.J.* 668, p. 669).
Occ. Arts. 2030, 2037, 2044, 2063 C.C.Q.; arts. 1666 para. 2, 1672, 1678 C.C.L.C.; ss. 1(*d*), 36, *Transport Act*, R.S.Q. c. T-12; s. 2(1), *Carriage by Air Act*, R.S.C. 1985, c. C-26; s. 6, *Canada Transportation Act*, S.C. 1996, c. 10.
See also consignee, contract of carriage, passenger, property[2], shipper.
Fr. transporteur[+], voiturier.

CARRY *v.*

To effect the carriage of a person or property.
Occ. Arts. 2030, 2038, 2049 C.C.Q.
Syn. convey[1], transport.
Fr. transporter.

CASE LAW

1. Syn. jurisprudence[1]. "The *Civil Code* does not contain the whole of civil law. It is based on principles that are not all expressed there, which it is up to case law and doctrine to develop" (*Lauréat Giguère Inc.* v. *Cie. Immobilière Viger*, [1977] 2 S.C.R. 67, p. 76, J. Beetz, J.). *Quebec case law*.
Obs. Because the expression suggests there is an inherent authority in decided cases (i.e.

that cases make law), some civilians see *case law* as inappropriate to the theory of the sources in private law, preferring expressions such as *decided cases, jurisprudence* or *established jurisprudence*.
Fr. jurisprudence[1].

2. Syn. jurisprudence[2]. *Contradictory case law; established case law; governing case law.*
Fr. jurisprudence[2].

CASH *n.* and *adj.*

Money, in paper or coin, that is legal tender. "All of this leads one to conclude that 'bonds or other titles of indebtedness' involve documentary titles that are issued or delivered and are of the nature of 'securities' as known to securities law. They are usually sold for cash, but this is not an essential feature of their nature" (Claxton, (1999) 44 *McGill L.J.* 665, p. 696). *Cash purchase; to pay cash.*
Occ. Arts. 909, 1127, 1326, 1579 C.C.Q.; arts. 1163(4), 1569*b* C.C.L.C.
Obs. Only those bills and coins issued by the Bank of Canada are legal tender (see ss. 8, 13, *Currency Act*, R.S.C. 1985, c. C-52).
Syn. *specie.* **See also** payment in cash.
Fr. argent, espèces[+], numéraire.

CASH (IN) *n.*

With regard to a payment which must be made without delay.
Occ. Arts. 427, 685, 1616, 1770, 2367 C.C.Q.
See also payment in cash, term (with a).
Fr. comptant (au).

CASH PAYMENT

1. Syn. payment in cash. "The respondent maintains that he was entitled as a matter of law to force the appellant to take back the new car, to keep the two old cars that he had turned in, and to pay him with interest not only the amount of the cash payment that he had made ($1,400) but also the amount of the credit allowance he had been given on the two old cars ($1,160)" (*Touchette* v. *Pizzagalli*, [1938] S.C.R., 433, p. 445, H.H. Davis, J.).
Fr. paiement en espèces.

2. Payment required to be made without delay.
Obs. Not to be confused with payment in cash[1], which is only a form of cash payment.
See also payment with (a) term.
Fr. paiement (au) comptant.

CASUAL *adj.*

Resulting from chance; accidental. *Casual event.*
Occ. Art. 1004 C.C.L.C.
Fr. casuel.

CASUAL CONDITION

Condition[1] resulting solely from chance and in no way from the will of the parties. For example, if a given person dies before another. "The polar opposite of the purely potestative condition is the 'casual condition' [...] The contract of insurance against rain [...] provides an example: the condition 'if it rains' is casual in this sense" (Nicholas, *Contract*, p. 160).
See also mixed condition, potestative condition.
Fr. condition casuelle.

CAUSA CAUSANS nom.ph. (Latin)

Syn. determining cause. "The fault must be the proximate cause – the causa causans – of the damage. It is insufficient to prove that it was merely an incidental or indirect cause. There must be no doubt that it was the determining cause of the accident" (Goldenberg, *Law of Delicts*, p. 15).
Fr. *causa causans*, cause déterminante+, cause efficiente, cause génératrice.

CAUSAL FAULT

Civil fault that is the cause[3] of damage.
Obs. Courts have generally used the doctrine of adequate causation, as opposed to other theories, to establish causation in matters of civil liability. Adequate causation is often described as a theory according to which, from among all the acts or omissions contributing to the occurrence of the damage, only those that would be susceptible of producing the damage by themselves are considered to be the cause of the damage.
See also adequate causation, simultaneous faults.
Fr. faute causale.

CAUSALITY

1. Syn. causation[1].
Fr. causalité[1].

2. Syn. causation[2].
Fr. causalité[2+], causalité juridique, lien de causalité.

CAUSAL RELATION

Syn. causation[2].
Fr. causalité[2+], lien de causalité.

CAUSA PROXIMA nom.ph. (Latin)

Syn. proximate cause[1].
Fr. *causa proxima*, cause immédiate+.

CAUSA SINE QUA NON nom.ph. (Latin)

Syn. condition *sine qua non*.
Fr. *causa sine qua non*, cause *sine qua non*, condition *sine qua non*+.

CAUSATION *n.*

1. Relation of cause and effect which is susceptible of having consequences in law.
Obs. Causation is relevant in matters such as unjustified enrichment or compensatory allowance. It is, however, a much more flexible concept than causation in matters of civil liability. Hence, to avoid any confusion, the Civil Code uses the term *correlation* rather than *causation* in the chapter on unjustified enrichment (e.g. art. 1493 C.C.Q.), although the idea of correlation refers to a relation of reciprocity.
Syn. causality[1]. **See also** material causation.
Fr. causalité[1].

2. Causation[1] between an act or omission of a person or the act of a thing and the damage suffered, susceptible of bringing about civil liability. "The fault of the victim may enable the keeper of the thing to escape liability, partially or completely, for his proven or presumed fault. The question is one of causation: either there is a single cause of the damage, and it is to be found entirely in the victim's actions, in which case the keeper is completely exonerated, though he may have committed a fault, since the latter did not contribute to the damage; or there are two causes of the damage, the fault of the victim and the fault of the keeper, in which case the responsibility is shared" (*Hamel* v. *Chartré*, [1976] 2 S.C.R. 680, p. 687, J. Beetz, J.).
Obs. 1° Causation is, along with fault and damage, one of the three traditional requirements to establish civil liability. **2°** Causation does not include all of the factors that may have contributed to the damage. Causation requires a direct and immediate connection between an act or omission imputed to the defendant and the damage suffered (art. 1607 C.C.Q.). **3°** To identify the cause of the

damage, courts have recourse to various theories of causation, notably proximate causation, adequate causation and equivalence of conditions. **4°** Civil liability may be shared when the damage results from the behaviour of several actors, including the conduct of the victim. **5°** Causation must be proved to the satisfaction of the court on the balance of probabilities. It may be established by direct proof or, in the absence of such proof, by presumptions that are serious, precise and concordant (art. 2849 C.C.Q.).
Syn. causality[2], causal relation, causation in law, juridical causation. **See also** adequate causation, causal fault, cause[3], civil liability, damage, equivalence of the conditions, imputability[2], material causation, *novus actus interveniens*, partial causation, proximate causation.
Fr. causalité[2+], causalité juridique, lien de causalité.

CAUSATION IN FACT

Syn. material causation.
Fr. causalité matérielle.

CAUSATION IN LAW

Syn. causation[2].
Obs. The expression *causation in law* is used when a distinction needs to be drawn between causation *per se* and material causation or cause in fact.
Fr. causalité[2+], causalité juridique, lien de causalité.

CAUSE *n.*

1. Objective reason of the obligation which results from a juridical act. "Thus, in his [Domat] conception, cause could easily be thought of as an invariable abstraction, always the same for a given kind of contract" (Litvinoff, in *Treatise*, vol. 6, n° 213, p. 381).
Occ. Art. 1371 C.C.Q.
Obs. 1° In this sense, the cause is said to be the *cause of the obligation* rather than *cause of the contract* (arts. 1371 and 1385 C.C.Q.). **2°** For a given category of juridical acts, the cause of an obligation is always the same, and is thus considered *objective*. For example, in a bilateral contract, the cause of the obligation of one party is the prestation of the other. In a lease, the lessor's obligation to provide for the peaceful enjoyment of the thing has as its cause the paying of the rent.
Syn. abstract cause, cause of the obligation, consideration[1], final cause, objective cause.
See also unjust enrichment.

Fr. cause[1+], cause abstraite, cause de l'obligation, cause finale, cause objective, considération[1].

2. Subjective reason to conclude a contract. "[...] like the codal regulation of the object of a contract, subjective cause is a concept by which the licit and moral character of an agreement may be policed by courts" (Brierley & Macdonald (eds.), *Quebec Civil Law*, n° 439, p. 409-10).
Occ. Arts. 1385, 1410, 1411 C.C.Q.
Obs. 1° Used in this sense, cause is said to be the *cause of the contract* rather than the *cause of the obligation*. The cause of the contract differs from the cause of the obligation. Far from being objective and abstract, the cause of the contract is *subjective* in that it differs for each contract and for each party. **2°** Cause is one of the four conditions for the formation of contracts, along with capacity, consent and object (art. 1385 C.C.Q.). **3°** Article 1411 C.C.Q. states that "[a] contract whose cause is prohibited by law or contrary to public order is null". It was generally recognized under the former law that the nullity of the contract whose cause is illicit could only be pronounced if the cause was known to all the parties. The issue of whether or not the law has changed remains uncertain. **4°** The usefulness of the notions of *object of the contract* and *cause of the contract* has been called into question by certain scholars. They argue that the notion of *public order* is sufficient to cover the two others.
Syn. cause of the contract, concrete cause, consideration[2], motive, principal consideration, subjective cause. **See also** contract[1], illicit cause, licit cause.
Fr. cause[2+], cause concrète, cause du contrat, cause impulsive et déterminante, cause subjective, considération[2], considération principale, mobile, motif.

3. Act or omission which produces the damage. "In the circumstances as revealed by the evidence, one must necessarily conclude that the appellant notary's opinion was the direct, immediate, and logical cause of the respondents' decision not to purchase the property" (*Roberge* v. *Bolduc*, [1991] 1 S.C.R. 374, p. 443, C. L'Heureux-Dubé, J.).
Obs. Damage may, in fact, materially result from a wide range of factors in given circumstances. In the law of civil liability, however, cause is understood to be limited to those acts or omissions which, by reason of their direct and immediate connection, have produced the damage (art. 1607 C.C.Q.). The requirement of immediate damage does not necessarily designate a cause that immediately pre-

cedes the loss in time and space, to the exclusion of any other cause. It is generally understood to refer to the relationship between the loss and the cause whereby the loss must not only be the direct consequence of the act or omission but must also be so connected thereto, but for the debtor's default, the loss would not have occurred.
See also adequate cause, causation[2], determining cause, immediate cause, material cause.
Fr. cause[3].

CAUSE OF ACTION

Fact or set of facts that gives rise to a right of action.
Occ. Arts. 1078, 2257 C.C.Q.; arts. 442, 1836, 2190 C.C.L.C.; arts. 66, 130, 957, 970 C.C.P.
Obs. If certain conditions are satisfied, it is possible for several causes of action to be joined in the same suit (art. 66 C.C.P.).
Fr. cause d'action.

CAUSE OF THE CONTRACT

Syn. cause[2].
Fr. cause[2+], cause concrète, cause du contrat, cause impulsive et déterminante, cause subjective, considération[2], considération principale, mobile, motif.

CAUSE OF THE OBLIGATION

Syn. cause[1]. "Thus the cause of the obligation of the buyer to pay the price is found in the obligation of the seller to deliver the thing sold, or, as they also put it, the cause of the one obligation is the object or content of the other" (Lee, (1915-16) 25 *Yale L.J.* 536, p. 538).
Fr. cause[1+], cause abstraite, cause de l'obligation, cause finale, cause objective, considération[1].

CAUSE *SINE QUA NON* (Latin)

Syn. condition *sine qua non*.
Fr. *causa sine qua non*, cause *sine qua non*, condition *sine qua non*[+].

CEDE *v.*

Syn. assign. "Our legal subrogation comes from the Roman law. Under varied circumstances the ancient jurisconsults admitted that the person whose debt was paid by another was bound to cede him his action" (Planiol & Ripert, *Treatise*, vol. 2, n° 492, p. 278).
Fr. céder[+], transporter[2].

CERTAIN CLAIM

Claim the existence or validity of which cannot reasonably be disputed.
Obs. 1° Litigious claims are not certain. **2°** Under the *Civil Code of Lower Canada*, a liquid claim was considered to be certain. The fact that the *Civil Code of Québec* refers to both attributes at article 1673 C.C.Q. suggests that a distinction may be drawn between liquid claims and certain claims, thereby detracting from the significance of the notion of *liquidity*. This view, which is difficult to reconcile with the wording of article 966 C.C.P., suggests that the notion of *liquidity* relates only to the fixed character of the monetary value of a claim.
Syn. certain creance. **See also** certain debt, exigibility, liquidity, litigious personal right, litigious right, oblique action, suspensive condition, uncertain claim.
Fr. créance certaine.

CERTAIN CREANCE

Syn. certain claim.
Fr. créance certaine.

CERTAIN DAMAGE

Damage the occurrence of which leaves no doubt.
Obs. 1° Damage must be certain in order to be compensated (art. 1611 C.C.Q.). **2°** Certain damage can be either present or future. **3°** Since the terms *damage* and *injury* are synonymous, the expression *certain injury* may also be used.
Syn. actual damage. **See also** future damage, possible damage, present damage.
Fr. préjudice certain[+], préjudice réel.

CERTAIN DEBT

Debt[1] the existence or validity of which cannot reasonably be disputed.
Obs. 1° Litigious debts are not certain. **2°** Only certain, liquid and exigible debts whose object is either a sum of money or fungible property identical in kind are susceptible of compensation (art. 1673 C.C.Q.). **3°** Under the *Civil Code of Lower Canada*, a liquid debt was considered to be certain. The fact that the *Civil Code of Québec* refers to both attributes at article 1673 C.C.Q. suggests that a distinction may be drawn between liquid debts and certain debts, thereby detracting from the significance of the notion of *liquidity*. This view, which is difficult to reconcile with the wording of article 966 C.C.P., suggests that the notion of *liquidity* relates only to the

fixed character of the monetary value of a debt.
See also certain claim, compensation, exigibility, liquidity, litigious personal right, litigious right, suspensive condition, uncertain debt.
Fr. dette certaine.

CERTAIN TERM

Term[1] whose date of arrival is specified at the time of the inception of a right or obligation. "A term is certain whenever the period of time preceding the occurrence of the event has been fixed. [...] One can select as a certain term, a religious event (Christmas day), a personal event (a birthday) or a set period of time (the 25th of this month, one month, a calendar year...)" (Levasseur, *Obligations*, p. 37).
Obs. 1° The term is always certain in the sense that, unlike the condition, it will necessarily come to pass. The certainty of a term depends therefore on whether one knows when the event will occur (e.g. "August 25th", "six months from [...]"). **2°** Most scholars consider that it is preferable to speak of a *known term*, a *determinate term* or a *fixed term*.
Syn. determinate term, fixed term, known term. **See also** uncertain term.
Fr. terme certain+, terme connu.

CESSION *n*.

Syn. assignment[1].
Occ. Arts. 2956, 3042 C.C.Q.
Fr. cession+, transport[3].

CHARGE *n*.

Syn. obligation[3]. "The existence of a right of credit [...] always becomes a special charge for the debtor, an element of liability in his patrimony [...]" (Planiol & Ripert, *Treatise*, vol. 1, n° 2163, p. 274).
Occ. Arts. 1154, 1226, 1821 C.C.Q.
Fr. charge, dette, devoir juridique, engagement[2], obligation[3]+, obligation juridique[2].

CHARTER *v*.

To place at the disposal of a person all or part of a means of transportation for transport.
Syn. affreight.
Fr. affréter.

CHARTERER *n*.

Person who, pursuant to a contract of affreightment, has at his or her disposal all or part of a means of transportation. "The char-

terer must generally give advance notice of the expected time and place of redelivery [of the vessel]" (Tetley, in *Int. Enc. Comp. L.*, vol. XII, c. 4, p. 47).
Occ. Arts. 2001, 2013 C.C.Q.
Fr. affréteur.

CHIROGRAPHIC CREDITOR

Syn. unsecured creditor. "*Chirographic creditors* are all on the same footing, and, when the proceeds of the judicial sale of any of their debtor's property is to be distributed, they are paid rateably out of such proceeds, without regard to the date of creation of their several claims, the older debt having no preference over that subsequently contracted, but after the privileged and hypothecary claims against such property have been satisfied" (Marler, *Real Property*, n° 745, p. 342).
Obs. From Latin *chirographarius*, derived from ancient Greek: written by one own hand.
Fr. créancier chirographaire, créancier ordinaire+.

CIVIL *adj*.

See civil act, civil capacity, civil code, civil fault, civil law, civil obligation, civil liability.
Fr. civil.

CIVIL ACT

Juridical act which is not effected with a view to speculation. For example, a loan between two non-traders, a will.
Obs. 1° The *Civil Code of Lower Canada* established different juridical regimes for civil acts and commercial acts. **2°** In the *Civil Code of Québec*, the notion of *enterprise* has replaced the notions of *commerce* and *commercial acts* (arts. 457, 1384, 1714, 1842, 2186, 2221, 2254, 2683 to 2685, 2830, 2831, 2862, 2870 C.C.Q.). The concept of *enterprise* is broader than that of *commercial activity*, in that it includes crafts, agriculture and professional activities, as well as those based on cooperation, with or without the objective of profit.
See also commercial act, enterprise[1].
Fr. acte civil.

CIVIL CAPACITY

Legal capacity in respect of civil rights.
Occ. Former art. 1755(4) C.C.L.C.
Obs. 1° Invested with the full enjoyment of civil rights (arts. 1, 301 C.C.Q.) and the capacity to exercise such rights (arts. 4, 303 C.C.Q.), every person, physical or legal, has civil capacity. **2°** Political capacity (the voca-

tion to enjoy political rights) is to be distinguished from civil capacity which has an independent content and character.
See also political capacity.
Fr. capacité civile.

CIVIL CODE

Code the purpose of which is to regulate generally all matters within the purview of the civil law[1]. "[...] a Civil Code can only contain rules of general application, with some degree of stability, reflecting an overall legislative policy. It is not intended to regulate every situation to the last detail nor tackle merely passing problems; this is left to statutory legislation" (C.C.R.O., *Commentaries*, vol. II, t. 2, p. 552).
Obs. 1° In jurisdictions where the law has been codified, the Civil Code is often seen as a foundation of the law that serves as an expression of the general law in private law and even sometimes in public law. **2°** A number of Civil law jurisdictions – Scotland and South Africa for example – do not have a civil code. **3°** Notwithstanding the ambition of a civil code to cover all matters pertaining to private law, it generally contains only substantive rules relegating the law of procedure to separate codes. **4°** The contents of a civil code and its mode of expression may vary according to place and time. Although they are very different, the French *Code civil* of 1804 and the German Code of 1900 (*Bürgerliches Gesetzbuch*) have been viewed in different contexts, as archetypes of the genre.
See also *Civil Code of Lower Canada, Civil Code of Québec*, code, *Code Napoléon*.
Fr. code civil.

CIVIL CODE OF QUÉBEC

1. Civil Code enacted by the Quebec National Assembly on December 18, 1991 and declared in force as of January 1st, 1994. "The two linguistic texts are forced together in a system of interpretation for which the metaphor of dialogue has been advanced as one basis for understanding how they interact to produce meaning. Dialogue throws the texts into a living relationship for the *Civil Code of Québec*, the vigour of which the Supreme Court of Canada recently saw fit to reaffirm as a tenet of constitutional law relevant to that enactment" (Brisson & Kasirer, in *Civil Code of Québec* (1997) ix, p. xiii).
Obs. 1° On January 1st, 1994, the Civil Code replaced both the *Civil Code of Lower Canada* and the *Civil Code of Québec*, which had come into force in August 1st, 1866 and April 2, 1981 respectively (see the Final Provisions of

the Code). In principle, with the coming into force of the Code, both its predecessors ceased to have any effect in law, subject to the application of transitional rules and s. 129 of the *Constitution Act, 1867*. **2°** The Civil Code is the culmination of a process of revision that began formally in 1955 and which led to the submission of the final report of the Civil Code Revision Office in 1977, including the *Draft Civil Code*. **3°** Like the 1866 Code at the time it was promulgated, the *Civil Code of Québec* seeks to provide a statement of the fundamental rules of law for those subject matters falling within its purview. To this end, the Civil Code contains a Preliminary Provision, itself having force of law, that explicitly confers this role on the Code. This provision also states that "[t]he Civil Code of Québec, in harmony with the *Charter of Human Rights and Freedoms* and the general principles of law, governs persons, relations between persons, and property". **4°** One of the salient features of the *Civil Code of Québec* is that it is composed of parallel French and English texts. Both texts aspire to express legislative intent completely; moreover, both are understood as having, as a matter of constitutional law, equal weight in the interpretation of the Civil Code. **5°** Although it was adopted as a statute (S.Q. 1991, c. 64), it is common to characterize the *Civil Code of Québec* as an "enactment" rather than as a "statute". This characterization serves to differentiate the code from ordinary legislation. **6°** Unlike the 1866 Code, however, the 1994 Code does not include a distinct book on commercial law, the general regulation of which appears to have been blended into the corpus of the civil law. **7°** Used alone, the expression *Civil Code* is generally understood to refer to the code presently in force. The abbreviation "C.C." is then sometimes used although the designation "C.C.Q." is also prevalent. **8°** The following abbreviations are used for the *Civil Code of Québec*, depending on whether one refers to the year a code was adopted or that of its coming into force: C.C.Q. (1991); C.C.Q. (1994). **9°** It was not uncommon for jurists and non-jurists to refer informally to the *Civil Code of Lower Canada* as the "Civil Code of Quebec" or the "Civil Code of the Province of Quebec". **10°** In its formal English language title, the Civil Code presents the word *Québec* with an accent (i.e. *Civil Code of Québec*).
See also *Civil Code of Lower Canada*, code[1], *Code Napoléon*, general principles of law.
Fr. Code civil du Québec[1].

2. Civil Code enacted by the Quebec National Assembly that was declared in force on April

2, 1981 and replaced, as of January 1st, 1994 by the *Civil Code of Québec*[1]. "Quebec may well be in the unique position in the world of having two Civil Codes: the *Civil Code of Lower Canada* which dates back to August 1st, 1866 and the *Civil Code of Québec* which came into force on 2 April 1981" (Crépeau, in *Civil Codes* (1993) xi, p. xii).

Obs. 1° Beginning in 1955, a process of revision of the *Civil Code of Lower Canada* was undertaken which led to the adoption of this Civil Code designed to replace the *Civil Code of Lower Canada* in planned stages. Within their respective spheres of application, the *Civil Code of Lower Canada* and the *Civil Code of Québec* co-existed until January 1st, 1994, at which time the new *Civil Code of Québec* came into force. **2°** From the time of its initial enactment and including amendments adopted in 1989, this Civil Code applied only to family law, both in respect to the patrimonial (e.g. matrimonial regimes) and the extrapatrimonial aspects of the law (e.g. rights and obligations of the spouses as between themselves). Certain provisions dealing with marriage and divorce never came into force, as the division of powers between the provincial and federal legislatures made their constitutionality questionable. **3°** In 1987, the *Act to Add the Reformed Law of Persons, Successions and Property to the Civil Code of Québec* (S.Q. 1987, c. 18) was to add provisions relating to the law of Persons, Successions and Property to this Civil Code. This statute was enacted but never came into force. **4°** For the most part, the provisions of the 1981 Code were carried forward in the 1994 Code which, from a technical point of view, replaced its predecessor (see the Final Provisions of the 1994 *Civil Code of Québec*). **5°** The following abbreviations may be used for the earlier enactment of the *Civil Code of Québec*, depending on whether one refers to the year a code was adopted or that of its coming into force: C.C.Q. (1980); C.C.Q. (1981).

See also *Civil Code of Lower Canada*, code[1], *Code Napoléon*.

Fr. Code civil du Québec[2].

CIVIL CODE OF LOWER CANADA

Civil Code applicable in Quebec as of August 1st, 1866 until January 1st, 1994, at which time it was replaced by the *Civil Code of Québec*.

Obs. 1° As indicated by its title, the *Civil Code of Lower Canada* was promulgated and came into force prior to the Confederation of Canada on July 1st, 1867. It applied initially to the territory of Lower Canada, then part of the British colony of United Canada. After July 1st, 1867, this territory became the Province of Quebec. **2°** The advent of a code in the Civilian tradition in Quebec can be explained on the basis of the historical sources of the law, in particular, the reception of civil law connected with the colonization of the territory by France. After the cession to Great Britain in 1763, the *Quebec Act* of 1774 (*An Act for making more effectual Provision for the Government of the Province of Quebec in North America*, 14 George III, c. 83 (U.K.)) re-established the civil law that had been in force prior to 1763 in respect of "property and civil rights" (which is subject to provincial jurisdiction under s. 92 (13) of the *Constitution Act, 1867*). **3°** In 1857, *An Act to provide for the Codification of the Laws of Lower Canada relative to Civil matters and Procedure* (S.C. 1857, c. 43) was enacted, giving formal expression to the decision to codify the laws of Lower Canada in civil matters and procedure. This led to the adoption in 1865 of the *Civil Code of Lower Canada* and, in 1866, of the *Code of Civil Procedure*. **4°** The *Civil Code of Lower Canada* treated all of the fundamental aspects of the law relating to civil matters. Unlike the French *Code civil* of 1804, however, the *Civil Code of Lower Canada* also included a significant section relating to commercial law. **5°** It is generally said that the main objective of the codification process of 1857 and the codes that followed therefrom was to maintain rather than reform the existing law. **6°** From the time of its enactment, the *Civil Code of Lower Canada* has been considered as foundational for Quebec, not only because of its sweeping expression of the general law but also because it was perceived as a symbol of the survival of the Civilian tradition in Canada. **7°** It is in part due to this exceptional status of the Code that the civil law was often modernized, notably through statute law. Since the statutes were separate from the Code, there grew a perception that the Code was inadequate for contemporary needs. The Code's revision was thus undertaken in 1955, leading to the adoption in 1991 of a new Civil Code with a similar role that came into force January 1st, 1994. The *Civil Code of Lower Canada* then ceased to have legal effect, subject to the application of transitional rules and of s. 129 of the *Constitution Act, 1867*. **8°** One of the distinguishing features of the *Civil Code of Lower Canada* is its bilingualism. Originally printed side by side as dictated by the 1857 codification statute, the French and English texts have been understood to have equal status in the interpretation of the Code. **9°** The abbreviation C.C.L.C., rather than C.C., is used for the

41

Civil Code of Lower Canada in order to distinguish it from the *Civil Code of Québec*, although formerly C.C. was the most common abbreviation.
See also Civil Code, *Civil Code of Québec*, code[1], *Code Napoléon*, general law.
Fr. Code civil du Bas Canada.

CIVIL FAULT

Fault[1] susceptible of engaging a person's civil liability. "In considering the scheme of delictual civil liability under general civil law, reference must be made to the traditional rules derived from art. 1053 C.C.L.C. to determine whether the respondents' acts constitute civil fault resulting in liability for the damage caused" (*Rocois Construction Inc.* v. *Quebec Ready Mix Inc.*, [1990] 2 S.C.R. 440, p. 460, C.D. Gonthier, J.).
Obs. 1° Civil fault constitutes, along with causality and damage, one of the three traditional requirements to establish civil liability. **2°** Civil fault may be said to have both an objective and a subjective dimension. It is subjective in that it depends on the imputability of behaviour to a given individual as well as the circumstances of those persons involved; it is objective in that it reflects conduct measured against that of a reasonable person. **3°** The existence of fault depends upon the nature, extent and intensity of the obligation breached. The analysis of fault thus requires the identification of the conduct expected of the debtor in order to fulfil the obligation, as well as the determination of the intensity of the obligation which the debtor is required to meet. This may be either via a contractual obligation established by the parties or via an extracontractual obligation arising "according to the circumstances, usage or law" (art. 1457 C.C.Q.). **4°** Civil fault should be distinguished from simple error, though the latter may be relevant to establish the existence of a fault. **5°** Civil fault comprises contractual (art. 1458 C.C.Q.) and extracontractual fault (art. 1457 C.C.Q.). **6°** A distinction is drawn between civil fault and penal fault. Civil fault is relevant to the determination of civil liability in a dispute between private law actors. Conversely, fault in criminal law is relevant to the determination of the guilt or innocence of a person in connection with criminal proceedings opposing an individual and the State. **7°** The codal regime respecting civil fault is set forth at articles 1457 *et seq.* C.C.Q. in the chapter on civil liability.
Syn. fault[2]. **See also** civil liability, contractual fault, delict, delictual fault, duty, error, extracontractual fault, imprudence, imputa-
bility[1], imputable[1], negligence, obligation[1,2], obligation of means, obligation of result, obligation of warranty, quasi-delict, quasi-delictual fault, strict liability.
Fr. faute[2], faute civile[+].

CIVIL LAW

1. Law[1] whose origin and inspiration are largely drawn from Roman law. For example, The Civil law of France, of Quebec, of Louisiana and of countries of South America. "The Civil Law is not simply a collection of rules drawn from Roman, ecclesiastical or customary law, and handed down to us in a solidified form. The Civil Law, as it was so aptly described by Professor René David [...] consists essentially of a 'style': it is a particular mode of conception, expression and application of the law, and transcends legislative policies that change with the times in the various periods of the history of a people" (Crépeau, in *Draft*, vol. I, xxiii, pp. xxvii-xxviii).
Obs. 1° Civil law has spread widely throughout the world, albeit in differing configurations, and is at present one of the most prevalent legal traditions (along with the Common law). **2°** Quebec private law is regulated by the Civil law, whereas English law has served, since the 18th century, as the basis of its public law. Elsewhere in Canada, English law has been received and constitutes the fundamental law in all matters. **3°** The Civil law constitutes the general law in matters relating to property and civil rights in Quebec. The fundamental rules that make up Civil law are set forth principally in the Civil Code, as mentioned in the Preliminary Provision of the Code. **4°** The coming into force of the *Civil Code of Québec* in 1994 was perceived to have rendered necessary an effort to harmonize federal legislation and the Civil law, given that the Code is also the expression of the general law in private law of federal origin when it is applied in Quebec (*Civil Law Harmonization Act*, S.C. 2001, c. 4). A similar effort was undertaken in Quebec law to harmonize public statutes with the *Civil Code of Québec*, at the conceptual, terminological and technical levels alike (*An Act to harmonize public statutes with the Civil Code*, S.Q. 1999, c. 40).
See also Common law[2], general law, legal order.
Fr. droit civil[1].

2. Syn. private law.
Occ. Art. 356 C.C.L.C.
Obs. Used in this sense, the term *civil law* refers to private law without reference to the civil law tradition. In order to mark the con-

trast, some scholars capitalize Civil law when referring to the Romanist legal tradition.
Fr. droit civil[2], droit privé[1+].

3. Branch of private law which covers those rules that apply to relationships civil as opposed to commercial in nature and to civil procedure insofar as the latter is connected to private law.
Obs. 1° Used in this sense, civil law includes, in addition to rules of the general law, those rules in ordinary legislation that are civil in character. In federal legislation, for example, the *Divorce Act* (R.S.C. 1985, c. 3 (2nd Supp.)) falls into this category and, in provincial law, certain portions of the *Consumer Protection Act* (R.S.Q. c. P-40.1). **2°** Scholars have criticized the traditional division between civil law and commercial law, in particular because the basic legal regimes associated with each of these sectors now appear to run together in many circumstances (art. 1377 C.C.Q.).
See also private law.
Fr. droit civil[3].

CIVIL LIABILITY

Juridical responsibility entailing the obligation to repair harm caused to another person. "[...] the possibility of the rifle being fired in an unlocked position, when to the ordinary and even cautious user the bolt action would appear to be locked, is a latent defect of the Ross rifle entailing the civil liability of the appellant as its manufacturer for the damages incurred by the respondents" (*Ross* v. *Dunstall* (1921), 62 S.C.R. 393, p. 420, P.B. Mignault, J.).
Occ. Title preceding art. 1457 C.C.Q.; arts. 2498, 3129 C.C.Q.; art. 2600 C.C.L.C.; s. 85, *An Act respecting the implementation of the reform of the Civil Code*, S.Q. 1992, c. C-57; s. 438, *An Act respecting industrial accidents and occupational diseases*, R.S.Q. c. A-3.001; s. 85, *Automobile Insurance Act*, R.S.Q. c. A-25.
Obs. 1° Civil liability has two regimes: contractual liability and extracontractual liability. **2°** The constituent elements of civil liability are traditionally considered to be fault, damage and causation. One may be held liable for a personal fault and, in certain instances, for the act or fault of another or for the act of a thing. **3°** Civil liability confers upon the victim the right to claim compensation for the harm suffered. However, in certain instances, other remedies may be obtained, such as the cessation of harm or even the prevention of an anticipated injury.

4° Damages obtained through the application of the rules of civil liability are in principle purely compensatory. However, in certain circumstances they may be of a punitive nature. This is the case when such damages are provided for by law (see art. 1621 C.C.Q. and, by way of example, s. 49 para. 2, *Charter of Human Rights and Freedoms*, R.S.Q. c. C-12) or by a penal clause (art. 1622 C.C.Q.). **5°** The establishment of parallel regimes of indemnification based upon legal liability without regard to fault has altered the application of the traditional principles of the general regime of civil liability (e.g. *An Act respecting industrial accidents and occupational diseases*, R.S.Q. c. A-3.001; *Automobile Insurance Act*, R.S.Q. c. A-25). **6°** The codal regime respecting civil liability is set forth at articles 1457 to 1481 C.C.Q.
Syn. civil responsibility. **See also** causation[1,2], civil fault, compensatory damages[1,2], contractual liability, damage, extracontractual liability, imputability[1], imputable[1], juridical responsibility, liability for damage caused by another, liability for damage caused by things, no-fault liability, obligation[2], personal liability[2], punitive damages, reparation[1], strict liability.
Fr. responsabilité civile.

CIVIL OBLIGATION

Obligation[2] susceptible of compulsory performance. For example, the obligation of support between spouses. "Civil obligations are those which are fully enforceable by means of *an action, i.e.*, a right accorded to a creditor to obtain satisfaction by means of legal proceedings and under the protection of the state" (Aubry & Rau, *Civil Law*, vol. 4, n° 297, p. 3).
Obs. Unlike a natural obligation, which is only susceptible of voluntary performance, a civil obligation is susceptible of compulsory execution in the case of non-performance.
See also moral obligation, natural obligation.
Fr. obligation civile.

CIVIL PARTNERSHIP

Partnership the principal purpose of which is to accomplish civil acts. "Since codification, the use of the partnership vehicle has evolved considerably so that today, apart from professional, agricultural, and artisanal endeavours, few civil partnerships are of great significance" (Brierley & Macdonald (eds.), *Quebec Civil Law*, n° 801, p. 667).

Obs. The distinction between civil and commercial partnerships established under the *Civil Code of Lower Canada* (arts. 1863 *et seq.* C.C.L.C.) is not made under the *Civil Code of Québec*.
See also civil act, commercial act, commercial partnership, partnership.
Fr. société civile.

CIVIL RESPONSIBILITY

Syn. civil liability. "[...] there are in Quebec [...] two regimes of civil responsibility: one, *ex contractu*, applying when the defendant has violated a contractual obligation; the other, *ex delicto*, when the defendant has violated a legal or extra-contractual duty" (Crépeau, (1962) 40 *Can. Bar Rev.* 222, p. 225).
Occ. Art. 2494 C.C.L.C.
Fr. responsabilité civile.

CLAIM *n.*

Syn. personal right. "Thus, the usufruct over a claim or other incorporeal cannot be a true usufruct since it does not bear upon a thing. Similarly, the usufruct over a consumable, such as a sum of money, is dematerialized into value. Doctrinally these are characterized as quasi-usufructs, under which title to the claim or the money is transferred to the usufructuary subject to an obligation to repay the capital upon the expiration of the usufruct" (Macdonald, (1994) 39 *McGill L.J.* 761, p. 791).
Occ. Arts. 484, 590, 1592 C.C.Q.
Obs. English civilian vocabulary generally uses the same word *debt* to describe the object of an obligation from the perspective of both the debtor and creditor. The term *claim* is often used to describe the interest of the creditor and is so employed in various instances in the *Civil Code of Québec* (e.g. arts. 888, 1656, 2651, 2724 C.C.Q.).
Fr. créance, dette active, droit de créance, droit personnel+, *jus in personam*, obligation[4].

CLAIM FOR SUPPORT

Syn. alimentary right. "Although the claim for support will depend on the needs, means and other circumstances of the parties, Art. 688 [C.C.Q.] provides a formula for establishing the maximum contribution that can be granted by an estate to a spouse or child or other descendant, however great their needs may be. But there is no doubt [...] that the granting of the maximum under that formula will be conditional upon proof by the claimant of needs that are at least equal to the maximum calculated under the formula" (*Droit de la famille – 2310*, [1997] R.J.Q. 859 (C.A.), pp. 864-865, M.L. Rothman, J.).
Occ. Art. 553.2(2) C.C.P.
Fr. créance alimentaire+, droit alimentaire.

CLANDESTINE MANDATE

Syn. contract of *prête-nom*.
Fr. contrat de prête-nom+, mandat clandestin, mandat dissimulé, prête-nom[2].

CLAUSE *n.*

Particular provision of a juridical act. "Clauses susceptible of two meanings must be understood in the sense in which they have some effect rather than in that according to which they would be completely ineffective" (Aubry & Rau, *Civil Law*, vol. 4, n° 347, p. 350). *Contractual clause.*
Occ. Arts. 1427, 1428, 1435, 1436 C.C.Q.; arts. 1014, 1018 C.C.L.C.; s. 13, *Charter of Human Rights and Freedoms*, R.S.Q. c. C-12; s. 130, *Consumer Protection Act*, R.S.Q. c. P-40.1.
Syn. stipulation[1]. **See also** condition[2], provision.
Fr. clause+, stipulation[1].

CLAUSE COMPROMISSOIRE (French)

Syn. undertaking to arbitrate. "The *clause compromissoire* is a clause inserted in a contract, by which the parties agree to adjust all future difficulties, disputes or claims arising out of the contract, by means of arbitration" (Johnson, *Clause Compromissoire*, p. 18).
Fr. clause compromissoire.

CLAUSE DE STYLE *nom.ph.* (French)

Clause ordinarily inserted in juridical acts which might be held to be inapplicable by the courts for the reason that it does not represent the intention of the parties. "[...] the Court is of the opinion that the clause invoked by the defendant '*de prendre ledit immeuble dans l'état où il se trouve actuellement*' is one which is often referred to as a *clause de style* and that it should not be considered as specifically revoking the warranty referred to elsewhere in the contract and created by law; an effective revocation would have to be in much more specific terms" (*Tellier* v. *Proulx*, [1954] C.S. 180, p. 182, H. Batshaw, J.).
See also customary clause.
Fr. clause de style[1].

CLAUSE EXCLUDING WARRANTY

Clause in a contract whereby a warranty is excluded.
Obs. See articles 1732 and 1733 C.C.Q.
See also conventional warranty, legal warranty, warranty clause.
Fr. clause de non-garantie.

CLAUSE IN RESTRAINT OF TRADE

See exclusivity clause, non-competition clause.
Fr. clause restrictive de commerce.

CLAUSE NOT TO COMPETE

Syn. non-competition clause.
Fr. clause de non-concurrence.

CLAUSE OF *DATION EN PAIEMENT* (French)

Syn. giving in payment clause.
Fr. clause de dation en paiement.

CLAUSE OF *FOURNIR ET FAIRE VALOIR* (French)

Syn. warranty of payment clause.
Fr. clause de fournir et faire valoir.

CLAUSE OF GIVING IN PAYMENT

Syn. giving in payment clause.
Occ. Art. 1646 C.C.L.C.; s. 102, *An Act respecting the implementation of the reform of the Civil Code*, S.Q. 1992, c. 57.
Fr. clause de dation en paiement.

CLAUSE OF LIMITATION OF LIABILITY

Syn. limitation of liability clause.
Fr. clause de limitation de responsabilité, clause de responsabilité atténuée, clause de responsabilité limitée, clause limitative de responsabilité[+].

CLAUSE OF RESOLUTION

Syn. resolutory clause[1].
Fr. clause de résolution, clause résolutoire[1+].

CLAUSE OF RESOLUTION OF RIGHT

Syn. resolutory clause of right.
Fr. clause de résolution de plein droit, clause expresse de résolution, clause résolutoire de plein droit[+], clause résolutoire expresse, pacte commissoire.

CLEAR *adj.*

Said of property released from all charges. For example, an immovable clear of all hypothecs.
Fr. quitte[2].

CLERICAL ERROR

Error in writing or transcription of a document that records an otherwise valid juridical act. For example, error of calculation or designation.
Obs. An error of form does not affect consent, but rather affects only its manifestation. Thus, when the courts correct the error, they do not change the juridical act itself.
Syn. error of form, error as to (of) form. **See also** defect of form.
Fr. erreur de forme, erreur matérielle[+].

CLIENT *n.*

1. Person who subscribes to a contract of insurance for his or her own benefit or for the benefit of another person.
Occ. Arts. 2389, 2398, 2400 C.C.Q.; ss. 19, 408, 430, *An Act respecting the distribution of financial products and services*, R.S.Q. c. D-9.2.
Obs. 1° Although they often refer to the same person, the insured, the client, the titulary, and the beneficiary must be distinguished. Life insurance best illustrates the difference between these terms: the insured is the person whose death triggers the payment by the insurer; the client, who may or may not be the person insured, subscribes to the contract with the insurer; the titulary is the person who may, with respect to the insurer, exercise the rights that derive from the contract, the client being the initial titulary; the beneficiary is the person who receives the payment upon the death of the insured. **2°** In group insurance, a distinction must be drawn between the client and the participant. The client is the contracting party, who is bound to make the payment of the premium, whereas the participant is the person who, by way of his or her participation in a specified group, benefits for himself or herself or for another, from the protection which is provided for in the master policy. **3°** In the *Civil Code of Lower Canada*, the term *policyholder* was used as the equivalent of *preneur*.
Syn. applicant. **See also** beneficiary[1], contracting party, insurance contract, insurance policy, insured, participant, premium.
Fr. preneur[1+], souscripteur.

2. Person for whom the contractor or the provider of services produces a work or provides services in return for remuneration. "Arts. 2125 and 2129 [C.C.Q.] permit the client under a contract of services to resiliate it, subject to its obligation to compensate the service provider for the loss suffered by such resiliation" (*Phoenix Flight Operation Ltd.* v. *Royal Aviation*, [2000] Q.J. No. 761 (Sup. Ct.), para. 116 (Q.L.), J. Bishop, J.).
Occ. Art. 2098 C.C.Q.; s. 60.4, *Professional Code*, R.S.Q. c. C.-26.
Obs. 1° The term *client* is used in this sense in the context of a contract of enterprise or for services. **2°** In construction law, the generic term *owner* is often used to designate the client.
See also contract for (of) services, contract of enterprise, employer[1], principal[3].
Fr. client+, donneur d'ouvrage, maître de l'ouvrage.

COAUTHOR *n.*

One of several authors in relation to a common successor.
Obs. The written form *co-author* is also encountered.
Fr. coauteur.

COCONTRACTING PARTY

Contracting party from the point of view of the other contracting party or parties.
Fr. cocontractant.

CO-CREDITOR *n.*

One of several creditors of a common debt. "The creditor who has received payment of the whole must share that payment with his co-creditors according to their respective rights" (Levasseur, *Conventional Obligations*, p. 16).
Occ. Arts. 1666, 1678, 1685 C.C.Q.
Obs. The written form *cocreditor* is also encountered.
See also co-debtor.
Fr. cocréancier.

CODE *n.*

1. Corpus of fundamental legislative provisions designed to present the different subject matters of an important branch of law in a systematic and coherent manner. For example, the Civil Code, the *Code of Civil Procedure*. "The function of a code, in the view of the French draftsmen, was to trace the leading principles of law in general terms, which judge and jurist would then direct in their detailed application [...]" (Brierley, (1968) 14 *McGill L.J.* 521, p. 562).
Obs. 1° The concept of a code has changed substantially over time and even today the term is used to refer to widely different ideas. It is, however, most generally understood within this meaning, at least in countries sharing the Civil law tradition. **2°** There is a tendency to treat law expressed in a code as the *embodiment* of the general law or *droit commun*, such that the latter is sometimes used as a synonym. This said, the idea that a code might perfectly express the general law is, at best, an aspiration for codification. **3°** Although the first codes of this type appeared at the end of the 17th century, the French codification of the beginning of the 19th century produced what has long been considered the archetype of the genre, the *Code civil* of 1804. **4°** The majority of countries within the civilian tradition adopted codes for the Civil law – the fundamental private law, civil procedure and commercial law. Public law seems to be excluded from this mode of legislative expression. **5°** From the Latin *codex*: tablet, book.
See also Civil Code, *Civil Code of Lower Canada*, *Civil Code of Québec*, *Code Napoléon*, law[2], statute.
Fr. code[1].

2. Name given to a statute or to designated legislative provisions in order to highlight their importance within a particular branch of law. For example, the *Criminal Code*, the *Labour Code*, the *Municipal Code*, the *Professional Code*. "Over the years all manner of statutes have been dubbed codes in Canada, both formally and informally, and it seems fair to suspect that, at the very least, Quebeckers and non-Quebeckers use the term differently" (Kasirer, (1990) 35 *McGill L.J.* 841, pp. 867-868). *Complete Code.*
Occ. *Code of Civil Procedure*, R.S.Q. c. C-25; *Code of Penal Procedure*, R.S.Q. c. C-25.1; *Highway Safety Code*, R.S.Q. c. C-24.2; *Municipal Code of Quebec*, R.S.Q. c. C-27.1; *Professional Code*, R.S.Q. c. C-26; *Criminal Code*, R.S.C. 1985, c. C-46.
Fr. code[2].

3. Compendium of statutory or regulatory materials relating to a particular branch of law. For example, the *Annotated Criminal Code*.
Fr. code[3].

4. Corpus of rules or values that are considered fundamental in a given community. For example, a code of ethics, a code of conduct, a code of honour. "The Barreau has also adopted a code of ethics governing the general and special duties of the professional towards

the public, his client and his profession, particularly the duties to discharge his professional obligations with integrity, refrain from acts that are derogatory to the dignity of the profession, refrain from incompatible responsibilities and avoid conflict of interest, and respect professional secrecy (s. 87 P.C. and Code of ethics of advocates, R.R.Q. 1981, c. B-1, r. 1)" (*Fortin* v. *Chrétien*, [2001] 2 S.C.R. 500, pp. 513-514, C.D. Gonthier, J.).
Fr. code[4].

CO-DEBTOR *n.*

One of several debtors of a common debt.
Occ. Arts. 1538, 1585, 1690, 2352 C.C.Q.; arts. 1103, 1104, 2229 C.C.L.C.
Obs. The written form *codebtor* is also encountered.
See also co-creditor.
Fr. codébiteur[+], coobligé.

CODE NAPOLÉON (French)

Name attributed to the French *Code civil* of 1804.
Obs. 1° The French *Code civil*, adopted in 1804, was designated as the *Code Napoléon* from 1807 to 1816, and from 1852 to 1870, i.e. under the First and the Second Empire. This name is sometimes used today to describe the *Code Civil* as it was in 1804. **2°** By common but mistaken belief, the *Civil Code of Lower Canada* is often thought to be a simple copy of the *Code Napoléon*. The codifiers did receive the mandate to cast the law then in force in Lower Canada in the form of a code but the French code was only a model for the general plan and, according to the terms of the 1857 act respecting codification (*An Act to provide for the Codification of the Laws of Lower Canada relative to Civil matters and Procedure* (S.C. 1857, c. 43)), the codifiers were to provide "the like amount of detail on each subject".
See also Civil Code.
Fr. *Code Napoléon.*

COLLECTIVE *adj.*

See collective act, collective contract, cumulative custody, collective fault, collective injury, collective liability.
Fr. collectif.

COLLECTIVE ACT

Act jointly undertaken by a group of persons pursuing a common interest or a common purpose.

Obs. 1° A collective act may be unilateral (e.g. a strike), bilateral (e.g. the formation of a partnership), or even multilateral (e.g. the sale of property by co-owners). **2°** The term *collective act* is most often used to describe a collective unilateral act.
See also bilateral act, collective contract, individual act, unilateral act.
Fr. acte collectif.

COLLECTIVE CONTRACT

Contract that binds a person or a group of persons who have not individually endorsed it. For example, a collective labour agreement, a group insurance contract. "Certainly to the extent of the matters covered by the collective agreement, freedom of contract between master and individual servant is abrogated. The collective agreement tells the employer on what terms he must in the future conduct his master and servant relations" (*Syndicat Catholique des Employés de Magasins de Québec Inc.* v. *Cie Paquet*, [1959] S.C.R. 206, p. 212, W. Judson, J.).
Obs. A distinction is drawn between *collective contracts* and *individual contracts*.
See also collective act, individual contract.
Fr. contrat collectif.

COLLECTIVE CUSTODY

Syn. cumulative custody.
Fr. garde collective, garde conjointe, garde cumulative[+].

COLLECTIVE FAULT

Civil fault resulting from the behaviour jointly undertaken by two or more persons in circumstances where it is impossible to determine which of them caused the damage.
Obs. 1° Collective fault, like common fault, is the result of the behaviour of more than one person. This term, rather than *common fault*, is used when it is difficult to identify the author of the damage. **2°** Article 1480 C.C.Q. distinguishes the situation where "several persons have jointly taken part in a wrongful act" from where several persons "have committed separate faults". The former situation describes collective fault, the latter describes contributory fault. In both instances, the members of the group are solidarily liable for the damage.
See also collective liability, common fault, contributory fault, individual fault.
Fr. faute collective.

COLLECTIVE INJURY

Damage suffered by an indeterminate number of people by reason of their inclusion in a given group. For example, hate propaganda directed against a particular social group.
Obs. 1° Collective damage may give rise to either an individual action or to a class action. **2**° The concept of collective damage is different from the cumulation of individual damage claims. It should not be confused with a simultaneous action brought by co-plaintiffs for various distinct individual damage claims, nor with joinder of actions (arts. 271 to 273 C.C.P.). **3**° Since the terms *damage* and *injury* are synonymous, the expression *collective damage* may also be used.
Fr. préjudice collectif.

COLLECTIVE LIABILITY

Civil liability incurred by members of a group as the result of the commission of a collective or common fault.
See also collective fault, common fault, contributory fault.
Fr. responsabilité collective.

COLOUR OF RIGHT

Syn. appearance of right. "The legislator intended the Courts to reject entirely any frivolous or manifestly improper action, and authorize only those in which the facts alleged disclose a good colour of right" (*Comité regional des usagers* v. *Commission des transports de la Communauté urbaine de Québec*, [1981] 1 S.C.R. 424, p. 429, J. Chouinard, J.).
Fr. apparence de droit.

COMMERCE *n.*

1. Economic activities, carried out with a view of profit or speculation, that contribute to the production and circulation of property or the provision of services. *Out of commerce.*
Occ. Art. 1978 C.C.L.C.
Obs. Under the *Civil Code of Lower Canada*, the term *commerce* did not include the activities of persons such as artisans, farmers or professionals. Under the *Civil Code of Québec*, the notion of *enterprise*, which replaces those of commerce and commercial acts (arts. 457, 1384, 1714, 1842, 2186, 2221, 2254, 2683 to 2685, 2830, 2831, 2862, 2870 C.C.Q.), includes, not merely commercial activities, but also skilled, agricultural or professional activities.
See also commercial act, enterprise[1], merchant.
Fr. commerce[1].

2. See object not in commerce, object of commerce.
Fr. commerce[2].

COMMERCIAL *adj.*

Pertaining to commerce. *Commercial activities*; *commercial matter*.
See also commercial act.
Fr. commercial.

COMMERCIAL ACT

Act by onerous title undertaken with a view to speculation.
Obs. 1° Commercial acts and civil acts were not governed by the same rules in the *Civil Code of Lower Canada*. **2**° In the *Civil Code of Québec*, the notion of *enterprise* has replaced the notions of *trade*, *commerce* and *commercial acts* (arts. 457, 1384, 1714, 1842, 2186, 2221, 2254, 2683 to 2685, 2830, 2831, 2862, 2870 C.C.Q.). The notion of *enterprise* is broader than that of *commercial activity*. An enterprise may include skilled, agricultural or professional activities or those based on cooperation, with or without profit-making objectives. **3**° Under the *Civil Code of Lower Canada*, an act could be considered a commercial act for both parties or for only one of them; in the latter case, one spoke of a mixed act. **4**° A juridical act undertaken by a trader in the ordinary course of his or her business was necessarily, for that trader, a commercial act. An act could also be commercial even if the person effecting it was not a trader.
See also civil act, commerce, enterprise[1].
Fr. acte de commerce.

COMMERCIALITY *n.*

Quality of that which concerns commerce. *Commerciality of a contract*; *commerciality of a claim*; *commerciality of a debt*.
Fr. commercialité.

COMMERCIAL PARTNERSHIP

Partnership the principal purpose of which is to accomplish commercial acts. "While a partnership does not have the same distinct legal personality as a corporation, it is [...] well established that the patrimony of a commercial partnership is distinct from the patrimonies of the individual partners" (*Lalumière* v. *Moquin*, J.E. 95-909 (C.A.), M.L. Rothman, J.).
Occ. Arts. 1854, 1863, 1892 C.C.L.C.
Obs. The distinction between civil and commercial partnerships established by the *Civil Code of Lower Canada* (arts. 1863 *et seq.*

C.C.L.C.) is not made under the *Civil Code of Québec*.
See also civil act, civil partnership, commercial act, partnership[1].
Fr. société commerciale.

COMMINATORY CLAUSE

Clause in a juridical act containing the threat of a sanction in the event of the non-performance of an obligation.
Syn. penal clause[2]. **See also** penal clause[1].
Fr. clause comminatoire+, clause pénale[2].

COMMISSION *n.*

Remuneration paid to an intermediary which consists of a percentage of the amount generated by the conclusion of a matter with which he or she was entrusted. For example, payment of a commission to a real estate agent.
Occ. Art. 2506 C.C.Q.; arts. 1149, 1569*d*, 1736 C.C.L.C.
See also salary.
Fr. commission.

COMMITMENT *n.*

Syn. undertaking.
Fr. engagement[1].

COMMITTENT *n*

Neol. Syn. principal[3].
Obs. 1° The term *committent* is suggested as a more accurate equivalent of the French term *committant* than *principal*, which appears in art. 1463 C.C.Q., since it avoids the confusion with regards to the contract of agency that principal may create. **2**° From the Latin *committere*: to entrust, to consign, to commit.
Fr. committant.

COMMODATUM *n.* (Latin)

Syn. loan for use.
Occ. Art. 1762 C.C.L.C.
Fr. commodat, prêt à usage+.

COMMON INTENTION

That which is wanted by the parties.
Occ. Art. 1425 C.C.Q.
Obs. When interpreting a contract, the search for the common intention of the parties is preferred to a literal interpretation of the terms of the contract (art. 1425 C.C.Q.).
See also declared will, internal will.
Fr. intention commune.

COMMON FAULT

Civil fault to which several persons jointly contributed. For example, the illegal sale of a firearm by co-owners. "A common fault occurs when several persons join in committing the same fault, but the doctrine is applied to cases where several persons commit different faults which combine to cause damages" (Watt, (1947) 7 *R. du B.* 226, p. 226).
Obs. 1° The obligation to provide compensation for the damage resulting from a common fault is solidary (art. 1526 C.C.Q.). **2**° The victim may have contributed to the realization of the common fault, as he or she may have committed a contributory fault. In this case, the fault of the victim is taken into account in the apportionment of liability (art. 1478 C.C.Q.). **3**° Collective fault, like common fault, is the result of the behaviour of a group. *Collective fault*, rather than that of *common fault*, is used when it is difficult to identify the author of the damage. **4**° Article 1480 C.C.Q. distinguishes two situations: where "several persons have jointly taken part in a wrongful act" and where several persons "have committed separate faults". The former situation describes collective fault, the latter describes contributory fault. In both instances, the members of the group are solidarily liable for the damage. **5**° The expression *contributory fault* is sometimes used as synonym of *common fault*.
Syn. common offence. **See also** collective fault, collective liability, contributory fault, fault of the victim, individual fault, joint liability.
Fr. faute commune.

COMMON LAW

1. Syn. general law. "[The private law's] origins lie in the seventeenth century when Louis XIV adopted measures by which the colony of New France was provided with the first elements of an organized legal system and, more lasting in importance, an initial body of customary but written law in the form of the *Coutume de Paris*, the 'common law' (*droit commun coutumier*) of northern France, upon which many of the Quebec Civil Code's provisions were subsequently to be based" (Brierley, (1968) 14 *McGill L.J.* 521, p. 522).
Occ. Art. 366 C.C.L.C.
Fr. droit commun[1]+, *jus commune*, loi générale.

2. Legal system of England and of those countries that have received English law, as opposed to other legal systems, especially those evolved from Roman law. "The common law is not a written code. It is unlike the civil law of Rome as set forth in Justinian's *Corpus Juris Civilis*, which for the Middle Ages in western Europe was the great example of written law. The principles of common law have always eluded complete embodiment in any code or collection of writings" (Hogue, *Common Law*, p. 186).

Obs. 1° While Roman law was not formally received in England, it is generally agreed that Roman law exercised an indirect influence on the development of the Common law. **2°** The Common law provides the basis for private law in all Canadian provinces and territories except Quebec which, after the Conquest and notwithstanding the transfer of New France to the British Crown by the *Treaty of Paris* in 1763, has retained private law in the French tradition in matters of "property and civil rights", pursuant to the terms of the *Quebec Act* of 1774 (*An Act for making more effectual Provision for the Government of the Province of Quebec in North America*, 14 George III, c. 83 (U.K.)). It is thus only in private law that Quebec is a Civil law province. **3°** One of the special features of the Common law tradition in Canada is that it is expressed in both English and French.
See also Civil law[1].
Fr. common law[1].

3. English law of judicial origin, as opposed to statutory law.
Fr. common law[2].

4. Corpus of rules of law developed and applied in England by the Courts of King's Bench, Common Pleas and Exchequer, as opposed to the rules of Equity applied by the Court of Chancery. "In England the rigidity of the Common law, a system of positive law linked to procedural considerations, made necessary the elaboration of other rules, called *rules of equity*, intended to complete and correct the Common law. Such a need was never felt in the Romano-Germanic family and, as a result, its member-countries knew nothing of the fundamental English distinction between Common law and Equity" (David & Brierley, *Major Legal Systems*, p. 45).

Obs. 1° This corpus of rules developed progressively since the Norman conquest of England in 1066 through the decisions of the royal courts, which decisions sought to standardize the law throughout the kingdom. **2°** In England, the duality of Common law and Equity was formally abolished by the *Judicature Acts* of 1873-1875 which created a new jurisdiction: the High Court of Justice. This juris-diction was made up of three divisions: Queen's Bench, Chancery and Probate (the latter previously known as Probate, Divorce and Admiralty). In the Canadian Common law provinces, where comparable divisions existed, they were progressively integrated into a unified judicial system. **3°** Notwithstanding the merging of the jurisdictions, the two systems of rules remain distinct; even though all courts can apply both Common law rules and those of Equity, the equitable remedies (e.g. injunction) are distinguished from the Common law remedies (e.g. damages). **4°** It is generally understood that the Common law constitutes the general law in matters falling within the realm of public law in Quebec.
See also custom[2], Equity[3], general law.
Fr. common law[3].

COMMON OFFENCE

Syn. common fault. "Under article 1106 C.C.[L.C.] an innocent party sustaining damage through the common offence or quasi-offence of two or more persons has a joint and several claim against each and all of them and is entitled to recover the full amount of his damages from any one of them" (Meredith, (1948) 26 *Can. Bar Rev.* 95, p. 103).
Occ. Art. 1106 C.C.L.C.
Obs. 1° This use of the term *offence*, which is increasingly rare, was no doubt reinforced at one time by its use in the title preceding article 1053 C.C.L.C. **2°** Used in this context, offence should not be confused with the term as it is employed in criminal law.
Fr. faute commune.

COMMON PLEDGE OF CREDITORS

See patrimony.
Fr. gage commun des créanciers.

COMMUTATIVE CONTRACT

Contract by onerous title in which the prestations are certain and determined at the time of its formation. For example, the sale of a thing for a specific price.
See also aleatory contract.
Fr. contrat commutatif.

COMPENSABLE *adj.*

Susceptible of compensation[1]. *Compensable debt*; *compensable damage*.
Fr. compensable.

COMPENSATE v.

To extinguish an obligation by compensation[1]. "[...] if parties to reciprocal obligations, consisting one in a sum of money and the other in the delivery of a corporeal movable, wish to compensate their obligations they may do so even though the requirements for a compensation by operation of law are not met" (Levasseur, *Obligations*, p. 231).

Syn. set off.

Fr. compenser.

COMPENSATION n.

1. Extinction of obligations between persons who are mutually debtor and creditor. "Compensation can be defined as the simultaneous, reciprocal extinction by the sole force of law of two debts of money (or quantities of identical things) which are due and exigible, whatever the cause or consideration of the debts" (Tetley, (1987) 47 *R. du B.* 237, p. 239). Extinction by *compensation*.

Occ. Arts. 748, 959, 1670, 1672 C.C.Q.; art. 1187 C.C.L.C.; s. 207, *An Act respecting industrial accidents and occupational diseases*, R.S.Q. c. A-3.001; s. 15, *Savings and Credit Unions Act*, R.S.Q. c. C-4; s. 28, *Cooperatives Act*, R.S.Q. c. C-67.2.

Obs. 1° Compensation is a means of extinction of obligations. **2°** Articles 1672 and 1673 C.C.Q. set forth the conditions under which debts may be extinguished by compensation. The conditions are reciprocity, exigibility, certitude, liquidity and fungibility. **3°** Reciprocity implies that the persons are mutually debtor and creditor and that they are obliged in the same quality (e.g. the debtor of the representative cannot compensate his debt with the person represented). **4°** The debts must be exigible, i.e. the obligations from which they follow are civil, not natural, and they are not subject to terms or conditions. **5°** Debts are certain and liquid when their existence is not contested and their amount is determined. **6°** The object of the prestations must be a sum of money or fungible property identical in kind (art. 1673 C.C.Q.). **7°** Compensation extinguishes the debts up to the amount of the lesser debt (art. 1672 C.C.Q.). **8°** The codal regime respecting compensation is set forth at articles 1672 to 1682 C.C.Q.

Syn. set-off. **See also** confusion, conventional compensation, discharge[2], extinction, extinctive term, impossibility of performance, judicial compensation, legal compensation, novation, payment[1,2], reciprocal obligation, release[1].

Fr. compensation[1].

2. Syn. reparation by equivalence. "Under our laws, parties to a contract are free to insert into such agreements modifications to the rules of compensation usual in cases of breach of contract" (Blumenstein, in *Meredith Lectures (1964)*, 57, p. 59).

Occ. Arts. 1680, 2612 C.C.Q.

Fr. compensation[2], indemnisation, réparation par équivalent[+].

3. See counterprestation. "Consequently, the debtor if he has not accepted the assignment, may plead compensation against the assignee respecting debts due by the assignor prior to publication and possibly raise all other grounds of extinction of debt mentioned in article 1138 [C.C.L.C.] occurring prior to publication" (Miller & Sarna, (1981) 59 *Can. Bar Rev.* 638, p. 642).

Occ. Art. 1736 C.C.L.C.

Fr. [*].

4. Syn. indemnity.

Occ. S. 579, *An Act respecting industrial accidents and occupational diseases*, R.S.Q. c. A-3.001.

Fr. compensation[3], indemnité[+].

COMPENSATORY adj.

Serving to compensate. "The lack of a relationship between monetary awards and the non-pecuniary losses they were meant to compensate made it difficult to fit moral damages within the compensatory framework thought to underlie the Code" (Brierley & Macdonald (eds.), *Quebec Civil Law*, n° 472, p. 435). *Compensatory payment.*

Occ. Arts. 430, 3100 C.C.Q.

See also compensatory damages[1,2], indemnificatory.

Fr. compensatoire.

COMPENSATORY DAMAGES

1. Damages the main purpose of which is to make good the harm suffered by the victim.

Obs. 1° All damages are, in principle, compensatory, except punitive or exemplary damages. **2°** In certain cases, however, the harm suffered is not fully compensated. Damages may, for example, be limited by a provision of law (legal damages) or by agreement of the parties (contractual damages).

See also full reparation, full reparation, punitive damages.

Fr. dommages-intérêts compensatoires[1].

2. Damages granted as compensation for harm resulting from the unjustified non-performance of an obligation other than harm associated with late performance. "Although

the nature of the harm that gives rise to damages and its evaluation are identical for both compensatory and moratory damages, whenever the obligation is not for the payment of money, the present doctrinal position is to reserve the expression 'moratory damages' for all those cases when the damage results from the late performance [...]" (Brierley & Macdonald (eds.), *Quebec Civil Law*, n° 521, p. 474).
Obs. 1° Although moratory damages are compensatory in nature in that they offer compensation for the harm resulting from late performance of the obligation, scholars have drawn a distinction between *moratory damages* and *compensatory damages*. This distinction serves a practical purpose, particularly where the issue is to remedy the debtor's tardiness to perform a pecuniary obligation. Article 1617 C.C.Q. provides that the creditor is entitled, in such a case, to damages without having to prove that he or she has sustained any injury. **2°** Damages that may be claimed in contractual matters are generally assessed using the criteria used in extracontractual matters, except for the foreseeability of the harm which is a criteria imposed in contractual matters only.
See also conventional damages, contractual damages[2], judicial damages, moratory damages.
Fr. dommages-intérêts compensatoires[2].

COMPETENCE n.

Syn. *de facto* capacity. "Since *competence* as a legal concept refers to 'fitness' to perform an act or choose in a certain situation, its connotation is operational, relating to the specific task to be accomplished or decision to be made" (Cranley Glass, (1997) 20 *Int'l J. L. & Psychiatry* 5, p. 6).
Fr. aptitude[+], capacité[2], capacité de fait, capacité naturelle.

COMPETENCY n.

(*Pers.*) Syn. *de facto* capacity.
Fr. aptitude[+], capacité[2], capacité de fait, capacité naturelle.

COMPLEX adj.

See complex obligation, obligation with a complex modality.
Fr. complexe.

COMPLEX CONTRACT

Syn. mixed contract.
Fr. contrat complexe[+], contrat mixte.

COMPLEX OBLIGATION

Obligation[2] subject to a modality.
Obs. Complex obligations are subject to a modality which may itself be simple (conditional obligation or obligation with a term) or complex (alternative, conjunctive, divisible, facultative, indivisible, joint or solidary obligation) (arts. 1497 to 1552 C.C.Q.).
Syn. obligation with a modality. **See also** obligation with a complex modality, obligation with a simple modality, pure and simple obligation.
Fr. obligation à modalité, obligation complexe[+], obligation modale.

COMPOUND adj.

See compound interest, compound interest contract.
Fr. composé.

COMPOUND INTEREST

Interest calculated on the basis of the capital and the unpaid interest that it has already produced.
Occ. S. 124.1, *Excise Tax Act*, R.S.C., c. E-15.
Obs. In principle, accrued interest does not bear interest, except when there is an agreement or a legislative provision to that effect, or when it is expressly claimed in a lawsuit (art. 1620 C.C.Q.).
See also anatocism, interest, simple interest.
Fr. intérêt composé.

COMPOUND INTEREST CONTRACT

Contract whereby the parties agree that the interest accrued, once added to the capital, will itself bear interest.
Obs. Interest accrued on the principal itself bears interest only when there is an agreement or a legislative direction to that effect, or when interest is expressly demanded in a lawsuit (art. 1620 C.C.Q.).
Syn. anatocism agreement, contract of capitalization of interest. **See also** anatocism, compound interest.
Fr. convention d'anatocisme.

COMPROMIS n. (French)

Syn. submission (to arbitration). "Apart from mere form, and fundamental to the existence of a *compromis*, as in the case of other contracts, the parties must have capacity [...]" (Johnson, *Clause Compromissoire*, p. 15).
Fr. compromis.

COMPULSORY EXECUTION

Performance of an obligation exacted from the debtor pursuant to a court order.
Occ. Art. 2633 C.C.Q.
Obs. Compulsory execution is achieved through specific performance or by equivalence (arts. 1590, 1607 C.C.Q.).
See also performance by equivalence, specific performance, voluntary performance.
Fr. exécution forcée.

CONCEALED ACT

Act containing the true agreement between the parties, but which is concealed by an apparent act. For example, a donation disguised as a sale, a sale price different from the one that appears in the apparent act. "There are a few cases where the simulation itself causes nullity of the concealed act, which would have been valid if done openly" (Lemann, (1954) 29 *Tul. L. Rev.* 22, p. 29).
Obs. A concealed act is one of the ways in which simulation may arise.
Syn. disguised act. **See also** apparent act, counter letter, fictitious act, interposition of persons, simulation.
Fr. acte déguisé.

CONCEALMENT *n.*

Act of a person who voluntarily remains silent regarding facts that another person would have an interest in knowing.
Occ. Arts. 1401, 2410 C.C.Q.
Obs. 1° Concealment constitutes a fraud when it provokes an error relating to the nature of a juridical act, the object of a prestation, or something that is essential in determining consent (arts. 1400 and 1401 C.C.Q.). **2°** The act of a person who voluntarily remains silent can, in certain circumstances, be viewed as a breach of the obligation to inform. That obligation is designed to protect the enlightened nature of consent by making a person aware of all that might be susceptible of influencing his or her decision.
See also *dolus bonus*, error, fraud[1], fraudulent artifices, obligation to inform.
Fr. réticence.

CONCRETE CAUSE

Syn. cause[2].
Fr. cause[2+], cause concrète, cause du contrat, cause impulsive et déterminante, cause sub-jective, considération[2], considération principale, mobile, motif.

CONDITION *n.*

1. Future and uncertain event upon which the existence of a right or an obligation depends. "[...] a conditional obligation fails when the condition itself fails [...]" (*Colonial Real Estate Co.* v. *Communauté des Soeurs de la Charité de l'Hôpital Général de Montréal* (1919), 57 S.C.R. 585, p. 602, P.B. Mignault, J.). *An obligation subject to a condition.*
Occ. Arts. 1499, 1504 C.C.Q.; arts. 1080, 1083 C.C.L.C.
Obs. 1° Conditions, like terms, are modalities of an obligation. While terms affect the exigibility or extinction of the obligation, conditions affect its existence (arts. 1497, 1508 C.C.Q.). In addition, whereas a term is characterized by the certainty of its eventuality, the advent of a condition is uncertain. **2°** Resolutory and suspensive conditions are retroactive in that their effect begins the day the contract was entered into (art. 1506 C.C.Q.). **3°** The codal regime respecting conditions is set forth at articles 1497 to 1517 C.C.Q.
See also failure of the condition, fulfilment of the condition, illicit condition, impossible condition, modality of the obligation, resolutory condition, retroactivity of a condition, suspensive condition, term[1].
Fr. condition[1].

2. Part of the content of a juridical act. "The policy of the code is the freedom of contract and it was open to the parties to stipulate the conditions upon which they agreed, provided they were not prohibited by law, or contrary to good morals or public order (Art. 990 C.C.Q.)" (*Consumers Cordage Co. Ltd.* v. *St. Gabriel Land & Hydraulic Co. Ltd.*, [1945] S.C.R. 158, p. 166, T. Rinfret, C.J.). *Terms and conditions of the contract; conditions of a will.*
Occ. Arts. 411, 694, 1118 C.C.Q.; arts. 1029, 1658.1, 2693 C.C.L.C.; ss. 107, 144, 150.13, *Consumer Protection Act*, R.S.Q. c. P-40.1.
Syn. term[2]. **See also** clause, provision, stipulation[1].
Fr. condition[2].

3. Element required for the existence of a juridical act, fact or situation. *Condition for the exercise of an action; condition of admissibility; condition of validity of a contract.*
Occ. Art. 1385 C.C.Q.
See also condition as to form, equivalence of conditions, substantive condition.
Fr. condition[3].

CONDITIONAL *adj.*

Subject to a condition[1]. *Conditional creditor*; *conditional gift*; *conditional right*; *conditional sale*.
Occ. Arts. 1498, 1524, 1808, 2682 C.C.Q.; arts. 392, 760 C.C.L.C.
See also conditional obligation, conditional right, conditional sale[1], modal, term (with a).
Fr. conditionnel.

CONDITIONAL CONTRACT OF SALE

Syn. instalment sale. "Long before the provisions of the *Consumer Protection Act*, R.S.Q. c. P-40.1, came into force, it was recognized that there is no public policy objection to a conditional contract of sale allowing a seller to repossess goods sold without judicial authorization if the buyer does not pay the price" (*National Bank of Canada* v. *Atomic Slipper Co*, [1991] 1 S.C.R. 1059, p. 1080, C.D. Gonthier, J.).
Fr. vente à tempérament.

CONDITIONAL OBLIGATION

Obligation[2] subject to a condition[1]. "A conditional obligation is an obligation whose very existence is made to depend on a future, uncertain event [...]" (Brierley & Macdonald (eds.), *Quebec Civil Law*, n° 529, p. 481).
Occ. Title preceding art. 1497 C.C.Q.; title preceding art. 1079 C.C.L.C.; art. 1084 C.C.L.C.
Obs. 1° The retroactivity of a condition serves to date back the effects of the condition to the time the contract was entered into (art. 1506 C.C.Q.). **2°** A condition is a modality of the obligation relevant to its existence. In order to be valid, the condition must be licit and possible (art. 1499 C.C.Q.).
See also complex obligation, condition[1], conditional right, illicit condition, impossible condition, obligation with a simple modality, obligation with a term, resolutory condition, suspensive condition.
Fr. obligation conditionnelle+, obligation sous condition.

CONDITIONAL RIGHT

Right subject to a condition[1]. "Again, no real right can bear on a future thing and, in principle, no real right may be claimed on another real right. Finally, the right itself must be existing and actual. An indeterminate future right or a conditional right cannot be a real right because, whatever its vocation, it does not directly lie in a thing" (Macdonald, (1994) 39 *McGill L.J.* 761, p. 788).

Occ. Arts. 392, 2081(2) C.C.L.C.
Obs. A conditional right has all the necessary elements to render it a perfect right except that it is subject to a modality, i.e. the condition.
See also conditional obligation, eventual right[1], qualified right, unconditional right[1,2].
Fr. droit conditionnel.

CONDITIONAL SALE

1. Sale whose existence is subject to a condition.
Obs. The sale may be made subject to a suspensive condition, as is presumed to be the case in trial sales (art. 1744 C.C.Q.). It can also be made subject to a resolutory condition, as in sales with a right of redemption (art. 1750 C.C.Q.).
See also condition[1].
Fr. vente conditionnelle[1].

2. Syn. instalment sale. "Reduced to its simplest terms, the purpose of a conditional sale is to enable a vendor to make a sale on credit to a purchaser who cannot, or chooses not to, pay the entire sale price at the time of purchase. To reduce the risk of a loss on the transaction, the vendor reserves title to the property in question until the final payment is made by the purchaser" (Pound, (1970) 16 *McGill L.J.* 312, p. 317).
Fr. vente à tempérament.

CONDITIONAL SALES CONTRACT

Syn. instalment sale.
Fr. vente à tempérament.

CONDITION AS TO FORM

Formality relating to the exterior aspect of a juridical act.
Obs. The term *condition of form* is sometimes used as a synonym for *condition as to form*.
See also defect of form, formalism, formalistic contract, substantive condition.
Fr. condition de forme.

CONDITION OF PAYMENT

Syn. modality of payment. "The risk, the event which triggers payment by the insurer, is determined and described contractually by the parties. The insurance contract is an aleatory contract, that is, when it is signed, as Baudouin says in *Les obligations* (3rd ed. 1989), at p. 57, 'the parties' benefits are not yet determined, in terms of their extent or measure". It is a condition of payment that the risk have occurred" (*Caisse populaire de*

Maniwaki v. *Giroux*, [1993] 1 S.C.R. 282, p. 292, C.D. Gonthier, J.). *To fix conditions of payment.*
Occ. Arts. 482, 2416 C.C.Q.
Fr. condition de paiement, modalité de paiement[+].

CONDITION *SINE QUA NON* (Latin)

Condition[3] without which the damage would not have occurred.
Syn. *causa sine qua non*, cause *sine qua non*.
See also adequate causation, determining cause, equivalence of conditions, material causation, proximate causation.
Fr. *causa sine qua non*, cause *sine qua non*, condition *sine qua non*[+].

CONFIRM *v.*

To effect confirmation. "[...] only a contract struck with a relative nullity may be ratified or confirmed by the parties to it" (Brierley & Macdonald (eds.), *Quebec Civil Law*, n° 441, p. 412). *To confirm a contract.*
Occ. Art. 1423 C.C.Q.
Syn. ratify[2].
Fr. confirmer[+], ratifier[2].

CONFIRMATION *n.*

Unilateral juridical act by which a person, in renouncing the right to invoke the relative nullity of an antecedent act, retroactively validates it. "It is further necessary to distinguish confirmation from transaction, because they are subject to different systems. Transaction is a contract. Confirmation is a unilateral legal act" (*Denis-Cossette* v. *Germain*, [1982] 1 S.C.R. 751, p. 798, J. Beetz, J.).
Occ. Title preceding art. 1423 C.C.Q.
Obs. 1° Even though confirmation may be tacit, the will to confirm must be unequivocal and manifest. Voluntary performance is a means of tacit confirmation. **2°** Confirmation by one of the parties to a juridical act does not prevent the others from invoking the nullity of the act (arts. 1420, 1424 C.C.Q.). **3°** A juridical act that is absolutely null is not susceptible of confirmation (art. 1418 C.C.Q.).
Syn. ratification[2]. **See also** transaction[1].
Fr. confirmation[+], ratification[2].

CONFUSION *n.*

Reunion in the same person of the qualities of debtor and creditor. "Although confusion normally occurs in successions, it may also arise in situations involving hypothecary creditors who have taken an immoveable in payment [...], or holders who are evicted by an hypothecary action [...], or in cases of servitudes existing between lots owned by the same person [...]" (Brierley & Macdonald (eds.), *Quebec Civil Law*, n° 554, p. 501). *Extinction by confusion.*
Occ. Arts. 1671, 1683 to 1686 C.C.Q.
Obs. 1° Confusion is a means of extinction of obligations. **2°** The codal regime respecting confusion is set forth at articles 1683 to 1686 C.C.Q.
See also compensation[1], discharge[3], extinction, extinctive term, impossibility of performance, novation, payment[1], release[1].
Fr. confusion.

CONJUNCTION *n.*

Accretion resulting from the lapse of a joint legacy or from the non-acceptance of a joint gift in favour of the joint legatee or donee.
Obs 1° It is generally admitted that conjunction may arise in respect of all types of legacies even though articles 755 and 756 C.C.Q. seemed to contemplate only the case of the particular legacy. **2°** The rules relating to conjunction may be set aside by the testator or the donor.
See also joint gift.
Fr. conjonction.

CONJUNCTIVE OBLIGATION

Obligation[2] in which the debtor undertakes to perform several prestations, all of which must be performed in order for him or her to be released.
Obs. The conjunctive obligation may involve a single obligation having several objects, e.g. the obligation of a travel agent to provide a client with transportation, food, and accommodation, or it may involve several distinct obligations, e.g. the obligation to deliver an automobile and to pay a sum of money.
See also alternative obligation, facultative obligation, obligation with a complex modality.
Fr. obligation conjonctive.

CONSENSUAL *adj.*

Resulting from consent alone.
See also consensual act, consensual contract, consensualism, formalistic, real, solemn.
Fr. consensuel.

CONSENSUAL ACT

Juridical act formed by the sole manifestation of the will.
See also consensual contract, consensualism, formalistic act, solemn act.
Fr. acte consensuel.

CONSENSUAL CONTRACT

Contract formed by the meeting of the minds, without any formalities. "But modern civilians depart from the analogy of the Roman law by inventing a 'cause' for the consensual contracts as well. This they find not in a necessary antecedent, but in an invariable concomitant" (Lee, (1915-16) 25 *Yale L.J.* 536, p. 538).
Obs. 1° Contracts are, in principle, consensual (arts. 1385, 1386 C.C.Q.). **2**° A distinction is drawn between *consensual contracts* and *formalistic contracts*.
See also consensualism, formalistic contract, real contract, solemn contract.
Fr. contrat consensuel.

CONSENSUALISM *n.*

Principle according to which the meeting of the minds is sufficient to produce juridical effects without resorting to particular formalities. "The dichotomy between the transfer of ownership as an effect as opposed to an obligation results from the post-codification principle of consensualism in sale. Contrary to Roman law and the *ancien droit français*, the transfer of ownership under the *Civil Code of Lower Canada* of 1866 was not dependent upon the performance of the parties' obligations, *i.e.* delivery by a seller and payment of the price by a buyer" (Boodman, in *Mélanges Crépeau*, 75, pp. 80-81).
Obs. 1° The meeting of the minds may not only create, modify or extinguish obligations, but might also constitute, transfer, modify or extinguish real rights (art. 1433 C.C.Q.). However, certain requirements may be necessary to ensure enforceability or opposability of the contract as, for example, the rules applicable to publicity or proof (e.g. in the sale of immovable property). **2**° The formation of consensual juridical acts results from the meeting of the minds which may, notably, be oral or in writing, express or tacit, provided the will to be bound is certain (arts. 1385, 1386 C.C.Q.). **3**° Consensualism is opposed to formalism, which requires the respect of certain formalities as conditions for the validity of the act: such is the case with solemn contracts and real contracts.

See also autonomy of the will (theory of the), binding force of contract, formalism, freedom of contract.
Fr. consensualisme.

CONSENT *n.*

1. Meeting of the minds of two or more persons upon a projected contract. "[...] consent between contracting parties suffices to create a contract, provided that parties are capable of contracting and that the contract has an object and a lawful cause" (Haanappel, (1982) 60 *Can. Bar Rev.* 393, p. 402).
Occ. Arts. 2211, 2231 C.C.Q.
Syn. meeting of the minds. **See also** acceptance[1], consensualism, declared will, doctrine of undertaking by unilateral will, internal will, offer, theory of reception.
Fr. accord de(s) volonté(s), consentement[1+].

2. Manifestation of a person's willingness to enter into a juridical act. "In another and more restricted sense, consent means *each party's individual acquiescence* to the conditions of the projected contract, given with the intent of creating binding legal effects" (Litvinoff, in *Treatise*, vol. 6, n° 129, p. 210).
Occ. Arts. 1385, 1386, 1398 C.C.Q.
Obs. 1° An *offer* is said to express the consent of the offeror, and the *acceptance* of the offer is said to express the consent of the offeree (arts. 1386, 1388 C.C.Q.). **2**° Consent must, in principle, be both free and enlightened. It may be vitiated by error, fear or lesion (art. 1399 C.C.Q.).
See also consent freely given, declaration of will, defect of consent, enlightened consent, express consent, integrity of consent, tacit consent.
Fr. consentement[2].

3. Assent of a person to an act that another cannot accomplish without this formality. For example, the consent of a parent to the marriage of a minor. "[...] in the event of the absence, refusal, or withdrawal of parental consent or its substitute [to the marriage of a minor child], no jurisdiction to supply the authorization is vested in any court" (Brierley, in *Canadian Family Law*, vol. 2, 795, p. 802).
Occ. Arts. 120, 401, 462, 1870, 2209 C.C.Q.
Fr. agrément[2], consentement[3+].

CONSENT *v.*

To give one's consent. "According to etymology, to consent means to will the same thing that another wills and wishes us to will" (Litvinoff, in *Treatise*, vol. 6, n° 129, p. 210).

Obs. From the Latin *consentire*: to agree, to share an opinion.
Occ. Arts. 403, 495, 583 C.C.Q.
Fr. consentir.

CONSENT FREELY GIVEN

Consent given without constraint.
Obs. The consent must, in principle, be both free and enlightened to produce effects in law (art. 1399 C.C.Q.).
See also defect of consent, enlightened consent, integrity of consent.
Fr. consentement libre.

CONSERVATORY ACT

Act necessary for the preservation of a property[1] threatened by an imminent risk.
Occ. Arts. 341, 1235, 1333 C.C.Q.; art. 646 C.C.L.C.
Obs. 1° Examples of conservatory acts include the sale of perishables, the publicity of rights, the interruption of prescription and the determination of boundaries. 2° Conservatory acts are generally understood to be juridical; some scholars consider that certain material acts may also qualify as conservatory acts (e.g. reinforcing the structure of a building that is about to collapse). 3° The conservatory act is traditionally distinguished from the act of administration (act of common preservation or exploitation of a patrimony) and the act of disposition (act compromising the substance of a patrimony).
Syn. act of conservation. **See also** act of administration, act of disposition.
Fr. acte conservatoire+, acte de conservation.

CONSIDERATION *n.*

1. Syn. cause[1]. "At the outset, it must be said that the words 'cause' and 'consideration', in the law of Quebec, are synonymous. 'Cause' comes from the old French law, 'consideration' from the Common law. The commissioners charged with the preparation of the Code [C.C.L.C.] used both terms, but it is admitted by all commentators that the provisions of the Code take their inspiration from the Civil law alone" (Newman, (1952) 30 *Can. Bar Rev.* 662, p. 664).
Occ. Arts. 989, 990 C.C.L.C.
Fr. cause[1]+, cause abstraite, cause de l'obligation, cause finale, cause objective, considération[1].

2. Syn. cause[2].
Occ. Art. 510 C.C.Q.

Fr. cause[2]+, cause concrète, cause du contrat, cause impulsive et déterminante, cause subjective, considération[2], considération principale, mobile, motif.

3. See counterprestation. "When the Commissioners charged with the duty of drafting the Civil Code of Lower Canada reached the subject of 'Contracts', they departed slightly from the model of the Code Napoleon, and introduced into the fourth requisite of the validity of a contract the word 'consideration', which was a term unknown to the Roman law, and to the civil law which had been introduced into Canada" (Hall, (1945) 23 *Can. Bar Rev.* 831, p. 831).
Occ. Art. 1600 C.C.L.C.
Obs. Used in this sense, *consideration* refers to the Common law notion of *consideration*, although it does not share all of its characteristics. In civil law, the idea of counterprestation plays a less significant role in the theory of contracts and *consideration* is more generally recognized as a synonym for cause. Some scholars are of the view that to use it in this second sense is an inappropriate borrowing from the Common law that courts confusion.
Fr. considération[3].

CONSIGN *v.*

Syn. deposit[2]. "The law [...] puts at the disposition of the debtor the special procedure of tender and consignment which permits him to triumph over the bad will of the creditor. The debtor commences by tendering to the creditor the object due, and after his refusal is established, he consigns the object due in a designated place" (Planiol & Ripert, *Treatise*, vol. 2, n° 446, p. 260).
Occ. Art. 1748 C.C.L.C.
Fr. consigner.

CONSIGNEE *n.*

Person to whom the carrier must deliver property.
Occ. Arts. 1740(2), 2420, 2454 C.C.L.C.; s. 4, *Bills of Lading Act*, R.S.C. 1985, c. B-5; s. 2(1), *Carriage by Air Act*, R.S.C. 1985, c. C-26.
Obs. The term *receiver* is preferred in the *Civil Code of Québec* (art. 2030 C.C.Q.).
Syn. addressee, receiver. **See also** bill of lading, contract for the carriage of goods, contract of carriage, shipper.
Fr. consignataire, destinataire[2]+.

CONSIGNMENT *n.*

Syn. deposit[3]. "[...] the consignment does not transfer to the creditor the ownership of the object consigned which continues vested in the debtor. It follows that the debtor may unilaterally withdraw this object so long as the consignment has not yet been accepted by the creditor or has not yet been declared good and valid by a judgment with the force of *res judiciata*" (Aubry & Rau, *Civil Law*, vol. 4, n° 322, p. 217).
Occ. Art. 2526 C.C.Q.
Fr. consignation.

CONSIGNOR *n.*

Syn. shipper.
Fr. chargeur, expéditeur+.

CONSOLIDATION OF DEBTS

Operation by which several debts are replaced by a single debt.
Occ. S. 99, *Consumer Protection Act*, R.S.Q. c. P-40.1.
Obs. A consolidation of debts constitutes a form of novation.
Syn. consolidation of indebtedness. **See also** novation by change of debt.
Fr. consolidation de dettes.

CONSOLIDATION OF INDEBTEDNESS

Syn. consolidation of debts.
Fr. consolidation de dettes.

CONSTITUTING ACT

Syn. constitutive act. "Where the trustee has the control and exclusive administration of the trust patrimony, and where the titles of which it is composed are drawn up in his or her name, the trustee acts as the administrator of the property of another, although the trustee's powers may be substantially varied in the constituting act" (Macdonald, (1994) 39 *McGill L.J.* 761, p. 782).
Occ. Arts. 312, 355, 1280, 1308, 1345, 2717 C.C.Q.
Fr. acte constitutif.

CONSTITUTIVE *adj.*

See constitutive effect, constitutive title.
Fr. constitutif.

CONSTITUTIVE ACT

Juridical act, the object of which is to create a new right. *Constitutive act of usufruct; constitutive act of servitude; constitutive act of hypothec.*
Obs. 1° Whereas translatory acts transfer existing rights, constitutive acts create new rights. **2°** See article 1433 C.C.Q.
Syn. constituting act. **See also** attributive act, constitutive effect, declaratory act, renunciation[1], translatory title.
Fr. acte constitutif.

CONSTITUTIVE EFFECT

Effect of that which creates a new right. For example, filiation resulting from adoption is constitutive of rights and obligations founded upon a bond of kinship.
Obs. The constitutive effect of the contract is expressly stated at art. 1433 C.C.Q. This article is in apparent contradiction with the definition of the contract (art. 1378 C.C.Q.) which, by characterizing the contract as a mere instrument for the creation of obligations, excludes from its scope numerous contracts.
See also constitutive title, extinctive effect, renunciatory effect, translatory effect.
Fr. effet constitutif.

CONSTITUTIVE TITLE

Title[1], the legal basis of which is a constitutive act.
See also translatory title.
Fr. titre constitutif.

CONSUMER *n.*

Physical person who obtains property or services for his or her personal benefit from a merchant.
Occ. Art. 1384 C.C.Q.; ss. 1(e), 8, 9, *Consumer Protection Act*, R.S.Q. c. P-40.1.
Obs. 1° A corporate entity can never be a consumer under the *Consumer Protection Act* (s. 1e), R.S.Q. c. P-40.1). **2°** A physical person who carries on an organized economic activity and who obtains property or services for reasons unrelated to the business is a consumer.
Fr. consommateur.

CONSUMER CONTRACT

Contract by which a consumer obtains property or services for his or her personal benefit from a person carrying on an organized economic activity.
Occ. Arts. 1384, 1435, 1436, 1437, 1746, 3117 C.C.Q.
Obs. 1° When the consumer contract bears on property or services, it is subject to the general law of obligations of the Civil Code, in particular, the provisions relating to the validity of external, abusive, illegible and incomprehensible clauses (arts. 1435 to 1437 C.C.Q.). **2°** Where the object of the contract is movable property, the consumer contract is also subject to the *Consumer Protection Act* (R.S.Q. c. P-40.1).
See also adhesion contract.
Fr. contrat de consommation.

CONSUMER CREDIT

Credit[1] granted by a merchant to a consumer.
Obs. The *Consumer Protection Act* regulates consumer credit arising not only in sales and loans, but in other arrangements as well (s. 1*f*), *Consumer Protection Act*, R.S.Q. c. P-40.1).
Fr. crédit à la consommation.

CONSUMPTION *n.*

See simple loan.
Fr. consommation.

CONTEMPLATION OF DEATH (IN)
adv.ph.

In view of the death of a person. *Gift made in contemplation of death.*
Occ. Arts. 706 C.C.Q.; arts. 597, 756, 778, 807, 824, 898, 941, 975 C.C.L.C.
Syn. *mortis causa.* **See also** act *inter vivos.*
Fr. cause de mort (à)+, *mortis causa.*

CONTINGENCIES OF LIFE

Events which may affect the life expectancy or the earning capacity of an individual.
Obs. Contingencies of life, considered prospectively, are often taken into account by courts when fixing awards for damages in actions in civil liability. In their calculation of the indemnity due to a victim, which is often done on the basis of actuarial tables, the courts have tended to reduce the award by a certain arbitrary percentage in order to take into account the contingencies the victim might have suffered in his or her lifetime, thereby avoiding, in theory at least, awards exceeding the amount necessary for compensation. The validity of this practice is questionable (see *Lignes Aériennes Canadien Pacifique Ltée* v. *Gendron*, [1983] C.A. 596), and some scholars criticize it as inherently arbitrary and difficult to justify in view of the principle of *restitutio in integrum.*
Fr. aléas de la vie.

CONTINGENCY *n.*

1. Uncertain event, chance.
Fr. aléa[1].

2. Factor of uncertainty in respect of the anticipated results of an activity.
Obs. Some have argued that this notion of *contingency* is a criterion that distinguishes obligations of means from obligations of result. The presence of a contingency renders the result uncertain so that the debtor can only be held to a standard of due diligence.
Fr. aléa[2].

CONTINGENT RIGHT

1. Syn. eventual right[2].
Occ. Art. 658 C.C.L.C.
Fr. droit éventuel[2].

2. See eventual right[1]. "The right of the fiduciary substitute prior to the opening of the substitution (even where the underlying substituted right is ownership) is another example of a contingent right, characterized as 'eventual' so as to acknowledge the ambiguity arising from its uncertainty" (Macdonald, (1994) 39 *McGill L.J.* 761, p. 768).
Obs. While *contingent right* is occasionally encountered as a synonym for *eventual right*[1], this usage is to be discouraged in order to avoid confusion with the term as it is most often used, as a synonym for the broader eventual right[2].
Fr. [*].

CONTINUOUS *adj.*

See continuous damage, continuous obligation.
Fr. continu.

CONTINUOUS DAMAGE

Damage which manifests itself in an uninterrupted manner.
Obs. Since the terms *damage* and *injury* are synonymous, the expression *continuous injury* may also be used.
See also gradual damage, periodic damage, recurrent damage.
Fr. préjudice continu.

CONTINUOUS OBLIGATION

Obligation[3] for which the prestation must be performed in a continuous or repeated manner. For example, the obligation of a lessor to provide the enjoyment of the property leased, the obligation of an employee to perform the work agreed upon.
Syn. obligation of successive performance, successive obligation. **See also** contract of successive performance, instantaneous obligation.
Fr. obligation continue+, obligation (à exécution) successive.

CONTRACT *n.*

1. Juridical act resulting from a concurrence of wills between two or more persons with a view to producing effects in law. For example, a sale, a gift, a mandate. "To make a contract the law requires communication of offer and acceptance alike either to the person for whom each is respectively intended, or to his authorized agent" (*Charlebois* v. *Baril*, [1928] S.C.R. 88, p. 89, F.A. Anglin, J.). *The contract is the law unto the parties.*
Occ. Arts. 1378, 1385, 1433 C.C.Q.
Obs. 1° Article 1378 C.C.Q. defines a contract as an "agreement of wills by which one or several persons obligate themselves to one or several other persons to perform a prestation". By reducing the contract to an instrument that creates obligations, the legislature appears to have underestimated the full breadth of the notion, thereby excluding numerous contracts from the definition. Article 1378 C.C.Q. also appears to contradict article 1433 C.C.Q. which, keeping with the substance of the former law, provides that a contract can create, modify or extinguish obligations, and that it can also constitute, transfer, modify or extinguish real rights. It would therefore seem preferable to define the contract so as to include all the effects in law that it may produce. **2°** The four conditions of formation of contracts are capacity, cause, consent and object (see art. 1385 C.C.Q.). **3°** The civilian tradition formerly distinguished a contract from an agreement (in French, *convention*). While an agreement could create, modify or extinguish juridical relations, a contract was said to be a type of agreement designed only to create juridical effects. Today the distinction has no practical significance and the terms are used interchangeably. **4°** From the Latin *contrahere:* to draw together.
Syn. agreement[1], covenant[1], pact, transaction[2]. **See also** cause[2], consensualism, consent[1], delict, formalism, object of the contract, quasi-contract, quasi-delict.
Fr. contrat[1+], convention, pacte.

2. Writing that records a contract[1].
Syn. agreement[2], deed[2].
Fr. contrat[2].

CONTRACT *v.*

1. To enter into a contract. *To contract marriage*; *to contract insurance*; *to contract before a notary.*
Occ. Arts. 372, 1386, 1401, 1409 C.C.Q.
Fr. contracter[1].

2. To become obligated by contract. "The notion of *pacta sunt servanda* requires a contracting party to be bound by his voluntarily assumed obligations. By removing a recourse against a defaulting party when he contracts an obligation detrimental to his business interests would offend that notion" (Jukier, (1987) 47 *R. du B.* 47, p. 66). *To contract a debt*; *to contract an obligation.*
Occ. Arts. 213, 1613, 2221, 2254 C.C.Q.
Fr. contracter[2].

CONTRACT BETWEEN ABSENTS

Syn. contract *inter absentes.* "[...] if the [...] manufacturer was to send an illustrated catalogue of his merchandise giving price and all other relevant details, or a letter offering a certain specific item, and the [...] merchant was to mail, or telegraph or telephone his acceptance, there would be a contract between absents [...]" (Kahn, (1959-60) 6 *McGill L.J.* 98, p. 100).
Fr. contrat à distance, contrat entre absents, contrat entre non-présents+.

CONTRACT BETWEEN PERSONS PRESENT

Contract formed while the parties are in the presence of one another.
See also contract *inter absentes.*
Fr. contrat entre présents.

CONTRACT BY CORRESPONDENCE

Contract *inter absentes* formed as a result of an acceptance transmitted in writing. "[...] the parties may be in different places, so that it takes some time for them to communicate with each other. Their declarations of will must be conveyed by some means of communication such as a messenger, or a letter or a telegram. Contracts formed in this way between parties at a distance are called contract by correspondence" (Walton, *Obligations*, vol. 1, p. 187).

Obs. 1° Article 1387 C.C.Q. provides that the contract is formed when and where the offeror receives acceptance. **2°** The offeree can transmit his or her acceptance by mail, telegram, electronic mail, messenger or other like means.

See also contract *inter absentes*, theory of reception.

Fr. contrat par correspondance.

CONTRACT BY GRATUITOUS TITLE

Syn. gratuitous contract.
Fr. contrat à titre gratuit.

CONTRACT BY MUTUAL AGREEMENT

Syn. contract by negotiation.
Occ. Art. 1379 C.C.Q.
Fr. contrat de gré à gré+, contrat de libre discussion, contrat négocié.

CONTRACT BY NEGOTIATION

Contract the terms of which are freely discussed by the parties and thus can be the object of reciprocal concessions.

Syn. contract by mutual agreement, contract *de gré à gré*, negotiated contract. **See also** adhesion contract, special terms.

Fr. contrat de gré à gré+, contrat de libre discussion, contrat négocié.

CONTRACT BY ONEROUS TITLE

Syn. onerous contract.
Occ. Art. 1262 C.C.Q.; arts. 774, 1035 C.C.L.C.
Fr. contrat à titre onéreux+, contrat intéressé, contrat onéreux.

CONTRACT BY TELEPHONE

Contract *inter absentes* formed as a result of an acceptance transmitted by telephone.

Obs. Article 1387 C.C.Q. provides that the contract is formed when and where the offeror receives acceptance.

See also contract *inter absentes*, theory of reception.

Fr. contrat par téléphone.

CONTRACT *DE GRÉ À GRÉ* (French)

Syn. contract by negotiation.
Fr. contrat de gré à gré+, contrat de libre discussion, contrat négocié.

CONTRACT FAULT COMMITTED FRAUDULENTLY

See fraud[2].
Fr. faute dolosive.

CONTRACT FOR (OF) SERVICES

Contract by which a person, the *provider of services*, undertakes, without subordination, to provide services for another person, the *client*, in return for remuneration.

Obs. 1° The contract for services is characterized by the absence of subordination of the provider of services towards the client, and in this sense is different from a contract of employment where the employee is subordinated to the employer. **2°** Article 2100 C.C.Q. provides that the intensity of the obligations arising from contracts of enterprise and for services depends on the circumstances of each case. It is generally understood that an obligation of means arises from contracts for services, whereas the contractor is bound by an obligation of result. **3°** The notion of *lease and hire of work* in the *Civil Code of Lower Canada* included what is designated in the *Civil Code of Québec*, depending on the context, as the contract of employment, the contract of enterprise, the contract for services or the contract of carriage. It bears mention that under the *Civil Code of Québec* only property can be leased. **4°** The same codal regime governs both the contract for services and the contract of enterprise, except that some specific provisions concerning works (arts. 2110 to 2124 C.C.Q.) apply only to contracts of enterprise. **5°** The codal regime respecting the contract for services is set forth at articles 2098 to 2109 and 2125 to 2129 C.C.Q.

Syn. contract of lease (and hire) of services[2], contract of service(s). **See also** contract of carriage, contract of employment, contract of enterprise, lease and hire of work, service(s)[2].

Fr. contrat de louage de services[2], contrat de service(s)+.

CONTRACT FOR THE CARRIAGE OF GOODS

Contract of carriage by which a person, the *carrier*, undertakes to transport property from one place to another for a price called *freight*.
Obs. 1° Except when the shipper and consignee are the same person, the contract for the carriage of goods is characterized as a stipulation for another. In this case, the shipper is the stipulator, the carrier is the promisor, and the consignee is the third party beneficiary. **2°** The carrier is released from his or her obligation of result by the delivery of the goods to the designated person, who may be the shipper or the consignee. **3°** The contract for the carriage of goods is often evidenced in a document called a *bill of lading* (art. 2041 C.C.Q.). **4°** The term *goods*, which is unusual in Quebec civil law parlance as a synonym for movable property in a commercial setting, likely appears in transportation law under the influence of common law terminology in this field. It may be observed that the term is also encountered in international commercial law. **5°** The expression *contract for the carriage of property* is preferred in the *Civil Code of Québec* (art. 2041 C.C.Q.). **6°** In the expression *contract for the carriage of goods*, the term *carriage* may be replaced by *transport* or *transportation*. **7°** The codal regime respecting the contract for the carriage of goods services is set forth at articles 2040 to 2084 C.C.Q.
Syn. contract for the carriage of property.
See also bill of lading, carriage of goods, consignee, contract of affreightment, contract of carriage, freight[1], property[2], shipper, stipulation for another.
Fr. contrat de transport de biens+.

CONTRACT FOR THE CARRIAGE OF PERSONS

Contract of carriage by which a person, the *carrier*, undertakes to take another person, the *passenger*, from one place to another for a price.
Obs. 1° The obligation to carry a person implies for the carrier the obligation to ensure the security of the passenger. **2°** In the expression *contract for the carriage of persons*, the term *carriage* may be replaced by *transport* or *transportation*. **3°** The codal regime respecting contracts for the carriage of persons is set forth at articles 2036 to 2039 C.C.Q.
See also carrier, contract of carriage, passenger.
Fr. contrat de transport de personnes+.

CONTRACT FOR THE CARRIAGE OF PROPERTY

Syn. contract for the carriage of goods.
Occ. Art. 2041 C.C.Q.
Fr. contrat de transport de biens+.

CONTRACT FOR WORK

Syn. contract of enterprise.
Occ. Art. 1794 C.C.Q.
Fr. contrat d'entreprise.

CONTRACTING PARTY

Person who has entered into a contract. "For a third party, both the existence of a contractual obligation and the failure to perform that obligation are juridical facts, which do not, as such, entitle it to assert any claim. These juridical facts must further fulfil the conditions of delictual liability, in the circumstances, in order that such liability may be asserted against the contracting party which has failed to perform its contractual duties" (*Bank of Montreal* v. *Bail Ltée*, [1992] 2 S.C.R. 554, p. 581, C.D. Gonthier, J.).
Occ. Arts. 999, 1404, 1440, 1443, 1458 C.C.Q.
See also cocontracting party.
Fr. contractant+, partie contractante.

CONTRACT *INTER ABSENTES* (Latin)

Contract formed while the parties are not in each other's presence.
Obs. 1° For a contract to qualify as a contract *inter absentes*, the parties must not have been in each other's presence at the time the acceptance was given. It does not matter, however, if they were in each other's presence prior to that time, whether at the time of the offer or during negotiations. **2°** The notion of *contract* inter absentes includes both the contract by correspondence and the contract by other modes of communication. **3°** Traditionally, contracts *inter absentes* gave rise to the problem of determining the place and time of formation of the contract. The issue as to the determination of the place of formation still remains problematic. Various theories – generally designated as declaration, emission, expedition, reception and information theories of contractual formation – have been advanced in order to solve these problems. The legislature has adopted the reception theory at article 1387 C.C.Q., according to which the contract is formed when and where the offeror receives acceptance. **4°** The parties may stipulate that the formation of the contract is suspended until the moment when the offeree receives an acknowledgment of

receipt or confirmation of the reception of his or her acceptance. Such clauses are frequently encountered in electronic contracts.
5° In matters relating to consumer protection, the contract is considered to have been formed at the consumer's address if he or she did not solicit the offer (s. 21, *Consumer Protection Act*, R.S.Q. c. P-40.1).
Syn. contract between absents, remote-parties contract. **See also** contract between persons present, contract by correspondence, contract by telephone, theory of reception.
Fr. contrat à distance, contrat entre absents, contrat entre non-présents[+].

CONTRACT OF ADHESION

Syn. adhesion contract.
Occ. Art. 1379 C.C.Q.
Fr. contrat d'adhésion.

CONTRACT OF AFFREIGHTMENT

Contract by which a person, the *lessor*, undertakes, in return for a price called *freight*, to place all or part of a means of transportation at the disposal of another person, the *charterer*, for transport. "When a shipowner, or person having for the time being as against the shipowner the right to make such an agreement, agrees [...] to furnish a ship for the purpose of so carrying goods, in return of a sum of money to be paid to him, such a contract is called a *contract of affreightment* and the sum to be paid is called a *freight*" (Scrutton, *Affreightment*, p. 1).
Occ. Arts. 2006, 2574 C.C.Q.
Obs. 1° Although the contract of affreightment originated in maritime law, it is now also associated with other means of transportation such as aircraft, rail and trucking.
2° In the *Civil Code of Québec*, the chapter respecting affreightment applies only to affreightment of ships. **3°** Generally, and especially in maritime matters, the relationships between the lessor and the charterer are governed by standard-form contracts, called *charterparty* or *charter-party*, used and acknowledged internationally. **4°** One might question the applicability of the provisions in the Civil Code pertaining to affreightment of ships since maritime law falls under federal jurisdiction as Navigation and Shipping (*Constitution Act, 1867*, s. 91(10)) and Admiralty, as defined by section 2 of the *Federal Court Act* (R.S.C. 1985, c. F-7). Thus, Canadian courts have developed federal law of general application in maritime matters. **5°** The codal regime respecting the contract of affreightment is set forth at articles 2001 to 2029 C.C.Q.

Syn. affreightment. **See also** contract for (of) services, contract of carriage, freight[2], lessor[2].
Fr. affrètement, contrat d'affrètement[+].

CONTRACT OF ALIENATION

Contract effecting an alienation of a patrimonial right. "A contract of alienation [...] transfers from the one party to the other the ownership of the thing which is the object of the contract, when it is certain and determinate, although no delivery is made [...]" (Marler, *Real Property*, n° 410, p. 179).
See also alienation.
Fr. contrat d'aliénation.

CONTRACT OF ARBITRATION

Syn. arbitration agreement.
Fr. convention d'arbitrage.

CONTRACT OF ASSOCIATION

Contract by which two or more persons establish an association.
Occ. Arts. 2186, 2268 C.C.Q.
Obs. 1° The contract of association is consensual and collective in character. **2°** Parties to a contract of association become *members*[1] of the association. Parties are, in general, physical or legal persons. Associations may, however, be established by actors without legal personality, such as general and limited partnerships as well as trusts. **3°** The codal regime respecting the contract of association is set forth at articles 2186, 2187 and 2267 to 2279 C.C.Q.
See also association, contract of partnership, member[1], partnership[1].
Fr. contrat d'association.

CONTRACT OF CAPITALIZATION OF INTEREST

Syn. compound interest contract.
Fr. convention d'anatocisme.

CONTRACT OF CARRIAGE

Contract by which a person, the *carrier*, undertakes, for remuneration, to take a person or to convey property from one place to another. "In addition to serving as evidence of a contract of carriage, the bill of lading is also a receipt issued by the carrier, the terms of which describe the condition of the goods received" (Tetley, (1977) 23 *McGill L.J.* 668, p. 668).
Occ. Art. 2030 C.C.Q.

Obs. 1° The parties to a contract for the carriage of persons are, in general, the carrier and the passenger. The parties to a contract for the carriage of goods are the carrier, the shipper and the consignee; the shipper and the consignee may be the same person. **2°** In the *Civil Code of Québec*, the provisions respecting the contract of carriage apply only to contracts of carriage by onerous title (compare art. 606, Bk V, *Draft Civil Code,* C.C.R.O.). **3°** Contracts of transport by onerous title give rise to an obligation of result (arts. 2037 and 2049 C.C.Q.). By contrast, the gratuitous carrier is, in principle, only bound by an obligation of means (art. 2032 C.C.Q.). **4°** The carrier may not exclude or limit his or her liability for bodily or moral injury caused to another, nor for material injury caused to another through an intentional fault or gross negligence (arts. 1474, 1475, 2034 C.C.Q.). **5°** The codal regime respecting the contract of carriage governs carriages by onerous title to be performed inside Quebec (s. 92(10), *Constitution Act, 1867*). According to some scholars, the provisions of the Civil Code may also apply as suppletive law to interprovincial carriages, although, in principle, these fall under the exclusive jurisdiction of the federal Parliament (ss. 92(10)(a), 91(29), *Constitution Act, 1867*). **6°** One might question the applicability of the provisions in the Civil Code pertaining to maritime transport since maritime law falls under federal jurisdiction as Navigation and Shipping (*Constitution Act, 1867*, s. 91(10)) and Admiralty, as defined by section 2 of the *Federal Court Act* (R.S.C. 1985, c. F-7). Thus, Canadian courts have developed federal law of general application in maritime matters. **7°** The codal regime respecting the contract of carriage is set forth at articles 2030 to 2084 C.C.Q.
Syn. carriage[2], contract of transport, contract of transportation, transport[2]. **See also** carrier, consignee, contract of affreightment, freight[1], mixed contract, passenger, property[2], shipper.
Fr. contrat de transport[+], transport[2].

CONTRACT OF CREDIT

Contract in which one party grants credit[1] to another. For example, a loan of money.
Occ. S. 66, *Consumer Protection Act*, R.S.Q. c. P-40.1.
Syn. credit contract.
Fr. contrat de crédit.

CONTRACT OF DEPOSIT

Syn. deposit[1].
Occ. Art. 2281 C.C.Q.; art. 1797 C.C.L.C.
Fr. contrat de dépôt, dépôt[1+].

CONTRACT OF EMPLOYMENT

Contract by which a physical person, the *employee*, undertakes, against remuneration and for a limited time, to perform work on the behalf of and under the direction or control of another person, the *employer*. "Where an employer decides unilaterally to make substantial changes to the essential terms of an employee's contract of employment and the employee does not agree to the changes and leaves his or her job, the employee has not resigned, but has been dismissed" (*Farber* v. *Royal Trust Co.*, [1997] 1 S.C.R. 846, p. 850, C.D. Gonthier, J.).
Occ. Arts. 1976, 2085 C.C.Q.; ss. 234, 237, *An Act respecting industrial accidents and occupational diseases*, R.S.Q. c. A-3.001.
Obs. 1° The subordination of the employee to the employer is said to be of the essence of a contract of employment. Its presence serves to distinguish the contract of employment from the contract of enterprise and the contract for services. **2°** Subordination implies an element of control, which the employer may exercise strictly (e.g. by providing precise instructions as to the performance) or with flexibility (e.g. by providing a general framework to the employee). **3°** Unlike the French text of article 2085 of the Civil Code, the English text refers explicitly to the instructions given by the employer to the employee. This discrepancy did not appear in the recommendations of the C.C.R.O. (art. 667, Bk V, *Draft Civil Code*, C.C.R.O.). **4°** The contract of employment may be for a fixed or an indeterminate term (art. 2086 C.C.Q.). **5°** The employment contract is not subject to any requirements of form. A non-competition clause contained in a contract of employment must, however, be stipulated in writing (art. 2089 C.C.Q.). **6°** Although the expression *contract of employment* refers, in general, only to the individual contract of employment, it is sometimes used to designate collective agreements. **7°** The lease and hire of personal services, which was a kind of lease and hire of work under the *Civil Code of Lower Canada*, corresponds to the contract of employment under the *Civil Code of Québec* (arts. 1665a, 1667 C.C.L.C.). **8°** The codal regime respecting the contract of employment is set forth at articles 2085 to 2097 C.C.Q.
Syn. contract of lease and hire of personal services, contract of lease (and hire) of services[1], employment contract, individual contract of employment, work contract. **See also** contract for (of) services, contract of enterprise, employee[1], employer[1], mandate[1].
Fr. contrat d'emploi, contrat de louage de services[1], contrat de louage de service(s)

personel(s), contrat de travail[+], contrat individuel de travail, louage de service(s) personel(s).

CONTRACT OF ENTERPRISE

Contract by which a person, the *contractor*, undertakes towards another, the *client*, to produce a work of an intellectual or material nature in return for remuneration, without subordination. "The fact that the owner has the right to give general instructions as to how the work requires to be carried out or that the owner reserves a right of inspection and supervision that the work is properly done does not convert a contract of enterprise into a lease and hire of services [...]" (*Drouin* v. *Desautels*, [1955] C.S. 123, pp. 128-129, G.S. Challies, J.).
Occ. Art. 2098 C.C.Q.
Obs. 1° The contract of enterprise is characterized by the absence of subordination of the contractor towards the client, as opposed to the contract of employment where the employee is subordinated to the employer. **2°** Article 2100 C.C.Q. provides that the intensity of the obligations arising from contracts of enterprise and for services depends on the circumstances of each case. It is generally understood to be the case that an obligation of result arises from contracts of enterprise whereas the provider of services is bound by an obligation of means. **3°** A *work* (in French *un ouvrage*) is understood as a product rather than as labour or services. It may be observed that articles 2098 *et seq.* C.C.Q. are inconsistent in their references to a work, referring on occasion to *work* without a definite or indefinite article, which might be confused with services. **4°** The term *enterprise* as used in the expression *contract of enterprise* should not be confused with the concept of enterprise understood as the carrying on of an organized economic activity at article 1525 para. 3 C.C.Q. **5°** The notion of *lease and hire of work* in the *Civil Code of Lower Canada* included what is designated in the *Civil Code of Québec*, depending on the context, as the contract of employment, the contract of enterprise, the contract for services or the contract of carriage. It bears mention that under the *Civil Code of Québec* only property can be leased. **6°** Except for some specific provisions respecting works (arts. 2110 to 2124 C.C.Q.), which apply only to contracts of enterprise, the contract of enterprise and the contract for services are governed by the same provisions. **7°** The codal regime respecting the contract of enterprise is set forth at articles 2098 to 2129 C.C.Q.

Syn. contract for work. **See also** contract for (of) services, contract of carriage, contract of employment, lease and hire of work, service(s)[1].
Fr. contrat d'entreprise.

CONTRACT OF GIFT

Syn. gift[1]. "The first paradox is that the apparent commonality between contracts of gift and legacies has been diminished in so far as gifts are regulated in the title of nominate contracts (at arts. 1806 *et seq.* C.C.Q.) and legacies are integrated into the book on successions (at arts. 703 *et seq.* C.C.Q.)" (Brierley, in *Mélanges Crépeau*, 119, p. 125).
Fr. contrat de donation, don[1], donation[+].

CONTRACT OF INSTANTANEOUS EXECUTION

Syn. contract of instantaneous performance.
Fr. contrat à exécution instantanée[+], contrat instantané.

CONTRACT OF INSTANTANEOUS PERFORMANCE

Contract for which the prestations, by their very nature, are susceptible of being performed at a single moment in time. For example, a sale.
Occ. Arts. 1378, 1383 C.C.Q.
Obs. 1° The performance of the prestations may occur either immediately or at the expiration of a term. **2°** According to most scholars, a contract is not considered to be a successive performance simply because its performance is spread out over time (e.g. a sale with payment by instalments, a sale with successive deliveries).
Syn. contract of instantaneous execution, instantaneous contract. **See also** contract of successive performance, instantaneous obligation, resolution[1].
Fr. contrat à exécution instantanée[+], contrat instantané.

CONTRACT OF INSURANCE

Syn. insurance contract. "[B]oth parties are required by law to treat the contract of insurance as an *uberrimæ fidei* contract. The insured will disclose fully and fairly or face the annulment of the contract, and the prudent insurer will ensure that it acquires a good knowledge of the industry in which it insures or fail to do so at its peril" (*Canadian Indemnity Co.* v. *Canadian Johns-Mansville Co.*, [1990] 2 S.C.R. 549, pp. 620-621, C.D. Gonthier, J.).

Occ. Arts. 691, 2379, 2389, 2398, 2399 C.C.Q.; arts. 607.8, 2468 C.C.L.C.; art. 69 C.C.P.; s. 11, *An Act respecting insurance*, R.S.Q. c. A-32.
Fr. assurance, contrat d'assurance+.

CONTRACT OF LEASE

Syn. lease[1].
Occ. Arts. 1667, 1692, 1765, 1822 C.C.L.C.; s. 166, *Consumer Protection Act*, R.S.Q. c. P-40.1; s. 46, *An Act respecting the Régie du logement*, R.S.Q. c. R-8.1.
Fr. bail[1], contrat de bail, contrat de location, contrat de louage, location[2], louage+, louage de choses.

CONTRACT OF LEASE AND HIRE

Syn. lease and hire.
Fr. louage(<).

CONTRACT OF LEASE AND HIRE OF PERSONAL SERVICE(S)

Syn. contract of employment. "In contracts of lease and hire of personal services, the obligations of loyalty and trust are implied conditions of the contract" (*Montour Ltée* v. *Jolicoeur*, [1988] R.J.Q. 1323 (Sup.Ct.), p. 1329, A.D. Guthrie, J.).
Occ. Art. 1667 C.C.L.C.
Obs. 1° The lease and hire of personal services, which was a kind of lease and hire of work under the *Civil Code of Lower Canada*, corresponds to the contract of employment under the *Civil Code of Québec* (arts. 1665a, 1667 C.C.L.C.). **2°** The term *lease and hire of personal services* may be a calque from the Common law[2] expression *letting of personal service*.
Fr. contrat d'emploi, contrat de louage de services[1], contrat de louage de service(s) personel(s), contrat de travail+, contrat individuel de travail, louage de service(s) personel(s).

CONTRACT OF LEASE (AND HIRE) OF SERVICES

1. Syn. contract of employment.
Obs. The expression *lease and hire of services* in the sense of contract of employment is rarely encountered. Even under the *Civil Code of Lower Canada*, the expressions *lease and hire of personal services* or *contract of employment* were preferred.
Fr. contrat d'emploi, contrat de louage de services[1], contrat de louage de service(s) personel(s), contrat de travail+, contrat indivi-

duel de travail, louage de service(s) personel(s).

2. Syn. contract for (of) services.
Fr. contrat de louage de services[2], contrat de service(s)+.

CONTRACT OF LEASING

Syn. leasing.
Occ. Art. 1844 C.C.Q.
Fr. contrat de crédit-bail, crédit-bail+.

CONTRACT OF LOAN

Syn. loan.
Fr. contrat de prêt, prêt+.

CONTRACT OF MANDATE

Syn. mandate[1]. "The substantive and formal requirements of a mandate are minimal. Where there are two adults capable of consenting who agree that one of them, the mandatary, shall perform a legal act with a third party on the mandator's behalf, it can be concluded that there is an implied contract of mandate" (*Caisse populaire des Deux Rives* v. *Société mutuelle d'assurance contre l'incendie de la Vallée du Richelieu*, [1990] 2 S.C.R. 995, p. 1007, C. L'Heureux-Dubé, J.).
Fr. contrat de mandat, mandat[1]+.

CONTRACT OF PARTNERSHIP

Contract by which two or more persons, the *partners*, establish a partnership[1]. "[...] partners are presumed to act by majority vote, although changes to the contract of partnership continue to require unanimity (article 2216(2) [C.C.Q.])" (Wilhelmson, (1992) 37 *McGill L.J.* 995, p. 1014).
Occ. Art. 2186 C.C.Q.; art. 1830 C.C.L.C.
Obs. 1° The contract of partnership is consensual, collective and onerous in character. **2°** Partners are, in general, physical or legal persons. Partnerships may, however, be established by actors having no legal personality themselves, such as general and limited partnerships as well as trusts. **3°** General and limited partnerships are commonly understood to operate as if they have a patrimony distinct from those of the partners, notwithstanding that the partners may be bound to fulfill the obligations of the partnership according to the rules applicable to the type of partnership in question (arts. 2199, 2208, 2221, 2249 C.C.Q.). For undeclared partnerships, each partner remains, in respect of third persons, owner of the property he or she

has contributed to the partnership (art. 2252 C.C.Q.) and is personally liable for the obligations he or she contracts (arts. 2253, 2254 C.C.Q.). **4°** In return for their contribution to the partnership, each partner receives a share (or shares), which is characterized as a claim over the patrimony of the partnership. **5°** General and limited partnerships must be declared within the time period and in the manner prescribed by the *Act respecting the legal publicity of sole proprietorships, partnerships and legal persons* (R.S.Q c. P-45). In the absence of declaration, such partnerships are deemed to be undeclared (arts. 2189, 2190 C.C.Q.). **6°** The codal regime respecting the contract of partnership is set forth at articles 2186 to 2266 C.C.Q.
Syn. partnership[2], partnership agreement.
See also contract of association, general partnership, limited partnership, partner, partnership[1], undeclared partnership.
Fr. contrat de société+, société[2].

CONTRACT OF *PRÊTE-NOM* (French)

Mandate[1] in which the mandatary agrees to act in his or her own name for the mandator without revealing his or her status as mandatary.
Obs. 1° The mandatary acting in his or her name is liable to the third person, subject to any rights that the latter may have against the mandator (art. 2157 C.C.Q.). **2°** Article 2159 C.C.Q. introduces a variation to the contract of *prête-nom* in providing for the possibility that the mandatary agree with a third party to disclose the identity of the mandator within a fixed period. This implies that even if the mandatary reveals his or her representative quality, he or she still conceals the identity of the mandator. In such case, the mandatary will be held personally liable if he or she fails to reveal the identity of the mandator once the fixed time period has expired. Such an agreement has been characterized as *semi-clandestine mandate*.
Syn. agreement to act as nominee, clandestine mandate, *prête-nom[2]*, secret mandate.
See also apparent contract, counter letter, fictitious contract, imperfect representation, interposition of persons, simulation.
Fr. contrat de prête-nom+, mandat clandestin, mandat dissimulé, prête-nom[2].

CONTRACT OF SALE

Syn. sale. "In a contract of sale, the seller has two principal obligations: the delivery and the warranty of the thing sold (art. 1491 C.C.L.C.)" (*General Motors Products of Can-*

ada Ltd. v. *Kravitz*, [1979] 1 S.C.R. 790, p. 796, Y. Pratte, J.).
Obs. The term *sale* is sometimes used in the plural (e.g. in the expression *sales contract*), as in the law of Louisiana, although *sale* is generally used in the singular in Quebec civil law parlance.
Occ. Arts. 1708, 1798, 1800 C.C.Q.; s. 158, *Consumer Protection Act*, R.S.Q. c. P-40.1.
Fr. contrat de vente, vente+.

CONTRACT OF SERVICE(S)

Syn. contract for (or) services.
Occ. S. 34, *Consumer Protection Act*, R.S.Q. c. P-40.1.
Fr. contrat de louage de services[2], contrat de service(s)+.

CONTRACT OF SUCCESSIVE EXECUTION

Syn. contract of successive performance.
Fr. contrat à exécution successive+, contrat successif.

CONTRACT OF SUCCESSIVE PERFORMANCE

Contract in which at least one of the prestations must be performed in a continuous or repeated manner. For example, a contract of employment, a lease. "Where the contract is of successive performance and the obligations must be performed over a period of time (such as a lease), the effect of the judicial declaration setting aside the contract is to terminate the contract for the future only, a remedy sometimes called judicial resiliation" (Brierley & Macdonald (eds.), *Quebec Civil Law*, n° 460, p. 426).
Occ. Arts. 1378, 1383, 1604, 2931 C.C.Q.
Obs. The contract of successive performance may be stipulated for a determinate or an indeterminate term.
Syn. contract of successive execution, successive contract. **See also** continuous obligation, contract of instantaneous performance, contract with a determinate term, contract with an indeterminate term.
Fr. contrat à exécution successive+, contrat successif.

CONTRACT OF SURETYSHIP

Syn. suretyship. "If the surety is aware of the debtor's incapacity the contract of suretyship could still be valid. Thus a contract entered into by a minor or by a corporation without

capacity may still be guaranteed" (Claxton, *Security*, p. 302).
Fr. caution[2], cautionnement[+], contrat de cautionnement.

CONTRACT OF TRANSACTION

Syn. transaction[1].
Fr. contrat de transaction, règlement hors cour, transaction[+].

CONTRACT OF TRANSPORT

Syn. contract of carriage.
Fr. contrat de transport[+], transport[2].

CONTRACT OF TRANSPORTATION

Syn. contract of carriage.
Fr. contrat de transport[+], transport[2].

CONTRACTOR *n.*

Person who undertakes to produce a work pursuant to a contract of enterprise for another person, the *client*, in return for remuneration and without subordination. "The three Courts were thus unanimous in their opinion that the subsequent purchaser of a building had a right of action against the contractor, under art. 1688 C.C.[L.C.]" (Weber, (1960) 20 *R. du B.* 526, p. 528).
Occ. Arts. 1794, 2098 C.C.Q.; art. 1697 C.C.L.C.; s. 109.1*b*), *Labour Code*, R.S.Q. c. C-27; s. 117, *Consumer Protection Act*, R.S.Q. c. P-40.1.
Obs. 1° In principle, the contractor may delegate the performance of all or part of the work to a third party. In such cases, the work remains under his or her supervision and responsibility (art. 2101 C.C.Q.). **2**° Where the contractor retains subcontractors and suppliers, he or she is often called *general contractor*.
See also agent and servant, client[1], contract of enterprise, employee[1], principal[3].
Fr. entrepreneur.

CONTRACT TRANSLATORY OF OWNERSHIP

Contract, the object of which is to transfer a right of ownership from one contracting party to another.
Obs. In the context of translatory acts of ownership, delivery transfers neither the ownership nor the possession of the property, since both have been transferred, in principle, upon the conclusion of the contract (art. 1453 C.C.Q.).
See also translatory act of ownership.
Fr. contrat translatif de propriété.

CONTRACTUAL *adj.*

Resulting from or related to a contract. "[...] in order fully to appreciate the content of a contractual relationship, it is not sufficient to know how many obligations, either express or implied, have been undertaken by the parties. Also it is essential to determine the character or the 'intensity' of each of the duties arising out of a contract" (Crépeau, in *Essays on the Civil Law*, 83, p. 96). *Contractual appointment of an heir; contractual liability.*
Occ. Arts. 1458, 2498 C.C.Q.; s. 110, *Consumer Protection Act*, R.S.Q. c. P-40.1.
Syn. conventional. **See also** delictual, extra-contractual, legal[4], quasi-contractual, quasi-delictual.
Fr. contractuel[+], conventionnel.

CONTRACTUAL COMPENSATION

Syn. conventional compensation. "In *Nova Scotia Construction* v. *Quebec Streams Commission* [1933] 2 D.L.R. 593, at pp. 601-2, Cannon J. cited English legal theory and case law to the effect that the architect does not guarantee to the contractor the accuracy of his calculations. It is true that the action was against the owner, not the engineer who had prepared the plans for the dam. However, in holding that, with respect to the additional work required which was not provided for in the initial plans, the contractor could recover only the contractual compensation rather than all the expenses incurred, the Court undoubtedly applied the contractual rule" (*Vermont Construction* v. *Beatson*, [1977] 1 S.C.R. 758, p. 769, L.-P. Pigeon, J.).
Fr. compensation conventionnelle.

CONTRACTUAL DAMAGES

1. Syn. conventional damages.
Fr. dommages-intérêts conventionnels.

2. Damages granted as compensation for harm resulting from the non-performance, without justification, of a contractual obligation.
Obs. 1° In contractual matters, the debtor is only liable for those damages that were foreseen or foreseeable at the time the obligation was contracted (art. 1613 C.C.Q.), provided the obligation in question is licit. **2**° However, where non-performance results from an intentional or gross fault on the part of the debtor, he or she may be held liable for all damages, including those that were not foreseen or foreseeable. **3**° In all cases, contractual damages included only what is an immediate and direct consequence of the non-

performance. **4°** A distinction is drawn between *contractual damages* and *extracontractual damages*.

See also contractual liability, conventional damages, extracontractual damages, legal damages.

Fr. dommages-intérêts contractuels[1].

CONTRACTUAL FAULT

Civil fault resulting from the unjustified non-performance of a contractual obligation. "It is generally held that the fault which consists in exercising a contractual right in bad faith is delictual (extracontractual). However, it should be possible in many cases to consider it as a contractual fault. If one considers that the obligation to perform the contract in good faith is a condition implicitly agreed by the parties, the abuse of a contractual right is in itself a violation of the contract" (Mayrand, (1974) 34 *La. L. Rev.* 993, p. 1010).

Obs. 1° From the perspective of its obligational content, a contract is not limited to what the parties have expressly stipulated, but is understood to include also "what is incident to it according to its nature and in conformity with usage, equity or law" (art. 1434 C.C.Q.). **2°** When justified by law, the non-performance of the obligation by the debtor does not constitute a fault, as, for example, in the case of superior force (arts. 1470, 1693 C.C.Q.) or in the case of a corresponding non-performance on the side of the contracting party (art. 1591 C.C.Q.). **3°** Unlike extracontractual fault, proof of a contractual fault does not benefit from any regime of legal presumption. **4°** A distinction is drawn between *contractual fault* and *extracontractual fault*. However, non-performance of a contractual obligation that causes damage to a third party is considered an extracontractual fault.

See also abuse of right(s), contract[1], contractual liability, contractual obligation, extracontractual fault, fraud[2], non-performance, superior force[1].

Fr. faute contractuelle.

CONTRACTUAL FREEDOM

Syn. freedom of contract. "Inherent in the codal regime of contract, although for a long time unrecognized by jurists, are a number of substantive controls on contractual freedom. Predominant among these is the notion of public order and good morals" (Brierley & Macdonald (eds.), *Quebec Civil Law*, n° 415, p. 392).

Fr. liberté contractuelle.

CONTRACTUAL INDIVISIBILITY

Syn. conventional indivisibility. "Contractual indivisibility is presented in the Civil Code [*C. civ. fr.*] as a simple exception to the effects of the division of obligations" (Planiol & Ripert, *Treatise*, vol. 2, n° 787, p. 422).

Fr. indivisibilité accidentelle, indivisibilité artificielle, indivisibilité conventionnelle[+], indivisibilité de paiement, indivisibilité subjective.

CONTRACTUAL LIABILITY

Liability resulting from the unjustified violation of an obligation arising from a contract.

Occ. Art. 1458 C.C.Q.

Obs. 1° Civil liability comprises contractual liability and extracontractual liability. **2°** Contractual obligations must be performed in full, properly and without delay (art. 1590 C.C.Q.). Non-performance may therefore be complete or partial. Furthermore, improper performance is equivalent to absence of performance. **3°** The unjustified violation of any contractual obligation, including those expressly stated in the contract as well as those implicit therein, gives rise to contractual liability. However, non-performance of a contractual obligation that causes damage to a third party is considered an extracontractual fault.

Syn. contractual responsibility. **See also** contractual obligation, cumulation (of regimes), extracontracual liability, legal liability[2], non-performance, option (between regimes), quasi-contractual liability.

Fr. responsabilité contractuelle.

CONTRACTUAL OBLIGATION

Obligation[2] resulting from a contract.

Occ. Art. 3127 C.C.Q.

Obs. 1° The Civil Code distinguishes between two sources of obligations: contractual obligations and those arising from "any act or fact to which the effects of an obligation are attached by law" (art. 1372 C.C.Q.). **2°** Contractual obligations include not only that which is expressed in the contract, but also that which "is incident to it according to its nature and in conformity with equity, usage and the law" (art. 1434 C.C.Q.).

Syn. conventional obligation. **See also** contractual liability, extracontractual obligation, legal obligation[1,2], quasi-contractual obligation.

Fr. obligation contractuelle.

CONTRACTUAL REPRESENTATION

Syn. conventional representation.
Fr. représentation contractuelle, représentation conventionnelle+.

CONTRACTUAL RESPONSIBILITY

Syn. contractual liability.
Fr. responsabilité contractuelle.

CONTRACTUAL SOLIDARITY

Syn. conventional solidarity. "[...] contractual solidarity is never presumed; it must expressly result from the original title of the obligation or from a legal provision declaratory of the presumed intention of the parties" (Aubry & Rau, *Civil Law*, vol. 4, n° 298b, p. 23).
Fr. solidarité contractuelle, solidarité conventionnelle+.

CONTRACTUAL SUBROGATION

Syn. conventional subrogation.
Fr. subrogation conventionnelle.

CONTRACTUAL TERM

Syn. conventional term. "Ordinarily the contract from which the term is derived is express, and there is good reason for this: it is important to fix its duration by establishing a definite date. However, the contractual term can be tacit: that happens when the obligation is of such a nature that it cannot be exercised immediately, either because of the distance, or because it involves the accomplishment of work; the duration of the term is then determined by usage, or by the judge, based upon the circumstances" (Planiol & Ripert, *Treatise*, vol. 2, n° 349, p. 206).
Fr. terme contractuel, terme conventionnel+.

CONTRACT WITH A DETERMINATE TERM

Contract of successive performance the duration of which has been specified by the parties at the time of the formation of the contract.
See also contract of instantaneous performance, contract of successive performance, contract with an indeterminate term.
Fr. contrat à durée déterminée.

CONTRACT WITH AN INDETERMINATE TERM

Contract of successive performance the duration of which has not been specified by the parties at the time of the contract's formation.

Occ. Art. 2091 C.C.Q.
Obs. Contracts of employment with an indeterminate term may be unilaterally resiliated by either party (art. 2091 C.C.Q.).
See also contract of instantaneous performance, contract of successive performance, contract with a determinate term.
Fr. contrat à durée indéterminée.

CONTRA PROFERENTEM RULE (Latin)

Rule of interpretation designed to overcome a textual ambiguity according to which the contract is interpreted against the interests of the party who has prepared it.
Obs. In adhesion and consumer contracts, the contract is interpreted in favour of the adhering party or the consumer even in circumstances in which that person has drafted it in whole or in part (art. 1432 C.C.Q.).
See also adhesion contract, attesting deed, consent[1], consumer contract.
Fr. règle *contra proferentem*.

CONTRIBUTION (BY) *prep. ph.*

Syn. rateably.
Occ. Art. 1118 C.C.L.C.
Fr. marc la livre (au), par concurrence, par contribution+, *pro rata*.

CONTRIBUTION (TO THE PARTNERSHIP)

That which each partner brings into the partnership.
Occ. Arts. 2190, 2198, 2200, 2236, 2240, 2246, 2266 C.C.Q.; arts. 1839, 1873, 1881, 1885, 1893 C.C.L.C.
See also partnership[1].
Fr. apport (en société)+, mise commune, mise sociale.

CONTRIBUTION TO THE DEBT(S)

Final apportionment of a common debt among co-debtors.
Occ. Arts. 474, 880 C.C.L.C.
Obs. See article 1537 C.C.Q.
See also indivisibility, obligation for the debt, solidarity.
Fr. contribution à la dette.

CONTRIBUTORY FAULT

Civil fault which combines with one or more distinct civil faults to cause the damage.
Obs. 1° The obligation to compensate the damage resulting from a contributory fault is solidary (art. 1526 C.C.Q.). **2°** The victim

may have contributed to the realization of the common fault, as he or she may have committed a contributory fault. In this case, the fault of the victim is taken into account in the apportionment of liability (art. 1478 C.C.Q.). **3°** Article 1480 C.C.Q. distinguishes the situation where "several persons have jointly taken part in a wrongful act" from where several persons "have committed separate faults". The former situation describes collective fault, the latter describes contributory fault. **4°** The expression *contributory fault* is sometimes used as synonym of *common fault*.
See also collective fault, collective liability, common fault, fault of the victim.
Fr. faute contributoire.

CONVENTIONAL *adj.*

Syn. contractual. *Conventional damages*; *conventional hypothec*; *conventional interest*; *conventional obligation*.
Occ. Arts. 1652, 2004, 2664, 3122 C.C.Q.; ss. 44, 151, *Consumer Protection Act*, R.S.Q. c. P-40.1.
Fr. contractuel+, conventionnel.

CONVENTIONAL COMPENSATION

Compensation[1] resulting from an agreement between the parties in the absence of the prerequisites for legal compensation. "A conventional compensation is effective only from the time it is entered into; it can have no retroactive effect because it is the intent of the parties that brings about the compensation" (Levasseur, *Obligations*, pp. 231-232).
Obs. Conventional compensation may not make up for the absence of reciprocity of the debts, but it enables the parties to extinguish debts that do not meet the prerequisites relating to the exigibility, certainty, liquidity and fungibility of the debts.
Syn. contractual compensation. **See also** compensation[1], judicial compensation, legal compensation.
Fr. compensation conventionnelle.

CONVENTIONAL DAMAGES

Extrajudicial damages agreed upon by the parties.
Obs. 1° Contractual damages comprise damages granted in contractual matters and extracontractual damages. **2°** Although nothing prohibits the use of the French expression *dommages-intérêts contractuels* to describe conventional damages, this meaning of the term is not often encountered in common legal parlance.

Syn. contractual damages[1]. **See also** contractual damages[2], fixed price, legal damages, penal clause[1].
Fr. dommages-intérêts conventionnels.

CONVENTIONAL INDIVISIBILITY

Indivisibility established by agreement notwithstanding that the object of the obligation is, by its very nature, susceptible of division. "Conventional indivisibility strives to conceptually and artificially attach to an object a legal feature which only nature would normally impose. Regardless of the number of parties involved, the item of performance cannot be divided between them because their will has made it indivisible" (Levasseur, *Obligations*, p. 110).
Obs. 1° Conventional indivisibility necessarily applies to an obligation with an object that is susceptible of division by its very nature. **2°** A divisible obligation, such as an obligation for the payment of a sum of money, is divisible among the heirs of a deceased debtor even though the obligation is solidary. The purpose of conventional indivisibility is to prevent this situation from arising, thus allowing a creditor to obtain full payment from any one of the heirs. **3°** Indivisibility must be expressly stipulated unless it is natural (art. 1519 C.C.Q.).
Syn. accidental indivisibility, artificial indivisibility, contractual indivisibility, subjective indivisibility. **See also** natural indivisibility, indivisibility, indivisibility of payment.
Fr. indivisibilité accidentelle, indivisibilité artificielle, indivisibilité conventionnelle+, indivisibilité de paiement, indivisibilité subjective.

CONVENTIONAL INTEREST

See conventional interest rate.
Fr. intérêt conventionnel.

CONVENTIONAL INTEREST RATE

Interest rate fixed by the contracting parties.
Obs. Contractual freedom relating to the fixation of an interest rate is limited, notably in matters concerning loans of money. The borrower, when faced with behaviour by a lender that amounts to lesion, may obtain the annulment of the contract, the reduction of his or her obligations, or the revision of the terms and conditions of performance (art. 2332 C.C.Q.). Certain statutes establish maximum interest rates (e.g. *Small Loans Act*, R.S.C. 1970, c. S-11; *Pawnbrokers Act*, R.S.C. 1970, c. P-5). A contractual stipulation providing for a 60 percent interest rate consti-

tutes a criminal offence (s. 347(2), *Criminal Code*, R.S.C. 1985, c. C-46).
Syn. rate of conventional interest. **See also** interest, interest rate, legal interest rate, lesion, usurious interest rate.
Fr. taux d'intérêt conventionnel.

CONVENTIONAL MANDATE

Syn. power of attorney[1].
See also conventional representation, judicial mandate, legal mandate.
Fr. mandat conventionnel, procuration[1+].

CONVENTIONAL OBLIGATION

Syn. contractual obligation. "[...] certain scholars view each source of obligation [...] as giving rise to a distinctive regime of liability, enforcement, and remedy. The structure of the French *Code civil*, which elaborates contracts and other conventional obligations as a whole [...] prior to setting out rules relating to those obligations arising independently of agreements [...] seems to reflect this view" (Brierley & Macdonald (eds.), *Quebec Civil Law*, n° 403, p. 379).
Fr. obligation contractuelle.

CONVENTIONAL REPRESENTATION

Representation resulting from a contract of mandate.
Occ. Title preceding art. 3116 C.C.Q.
Syn. contractual representation. **See also** conventional mandate, judicial representation, legal representation, voluntary representation.
Fr. représentation contractuelle, représentation conventionnelle[+].

CONVENTIONAL RESILIATION

Syn. bilateral resiliation.
Obs. The expressions *amicable resiliation* and *conventional resiliation* are used where there are more than two contracting parties.
Fr. résiliation amiable, résiliation bilatérale[+], résiliation conventionnelle, révocation[2].

CONVENTIONAL SEQUESTRATION

Real contract of sequestration.
Occ. Arts. 1818, 1827 C.C.L.C.; art. 745 C.C.P.
Obs. 1° The decision of the parties to elect a sequestrator, when prompted by necessity, is called conventional sequestration. Even when the parties petition the court to choose the sequestrator or to determine the condi-

tions attached to his or her duties, he or she does not become a judicial sequestrator. **2°** The sequestration may be settled between the parties to the litigation and a third party or between each party to the litigation (art. 2307 C.C.Q.).
See also judicial sequestration.
Fr. séquestre conventionnel.

CONVENTIONAL SOLIDARITY

Solidarity established by a juridical act.
Obs. While passive solidarity can be either conventional or legal (art. 1525 C.C.Q.), active solidarity must be conventional (art. 1541 C.C.Q.).
Syn. contractual solidarity. **See also** legal solidarity.
Fr. solidarité contractuelle, solidarité conventionnelle[+].

CONVENTIONAL SUBROGATION

Subrogation resulting from a contract between a third person and the creditor or the debtor.
Occ. Art. 1653 C.C.Q.; art. 1155 C.C.L.C.
Obs. Conventional subrogation must be express and in writing (art. 1653 C.C.Q.).
Syn. contractual subrogation. **See also** legal subrogation.
Fr. subrogation conventionnelle.

CONVENTIONAL TERM

Term[1] established by the will of the parties. For example, in a contract of sale, the term granted to the purchaser for the payment of the price. "[...] a conventional term is a term expressly or implicitly agreed upon between the parties to a contract [...]" (Levasseur, *Conventional Obligations*, p. 8).
Syn. contractual term. **See also** judicial term, legal term, term of right.
Fr. terme contractuel, terme conventionnel[+].

CONVENTIONAL WARRANTY

Warranty established by contract.
Occ. Title preceding art. 1732 C.C.Q.; arts. 1506, 1511 C.C.L.C.; ss. 44, 49, 151, 260.6, *Consumer Protection Act*, R.S.Q. c. P-40.1.
Obs. 1° See articles 1716, 1723, 1732 and 1733 C.C.Q. **2°** The expression *contractual warranty* may also be used.
See also legal warranty, obligation of warranty.
Fr. garantie contractuelle, garantie conventionnelle[+].

CONVEY *v.*

1. Syn. carry.
Occ. Arts. 1673, 2419 C.C.L.C.
Fr. transporter[1].

2. Syn. transfer.
Occ. Arts. 981*a*, 981*b* C.C.L.C.
Fr. transférer.

CONVEYANCE *n.*

1. Syn. carriage[1].
Occ. Arts. 1666(2), 1681 C.C.L.C.
Fr. transport[1].

2. Syn. transfer. "[...] a written conveyance, executed with some solemnity, is not only extrinsic evidence that a proprietary transfer has taken place but also a conveyancing mechanism other than the contract itself" (Gow, (1967) 13 *McGill L.J.* 245, p. 248).
Fr. transfert[+], translation.

3. Syn. assignment[1]. "Or, insofar as concerns proof of 'intention to prefer', the trustee can establish a presumption in his favour providing he can prove that the conveyance, payment, etc., *in fact had the effect* of giving the creditor a preference over other creditors" (Gliserman, (1972) 32 *R. du B.* 498, p. 499).
Occ. Arts. 1603, 2127 C.C.L.C.
Fr. cession[+], transport[3].

4. Transfer of a right in immovable property.
Obs. This usage, encountered in certain notarial instruments for the transfer of land, may originate in the vocabulary of conveyancing in the Common law.
Fr. [*].

CORPORAL DAMAGE

Syn. bodily injury.
Occ. Art. 2926 C.C.Q.
Obs. Given that *damage* and *injury* are synonyms, the expression *corporal injury* may also be used to designate corporal damage.
Fr. préjudice corporel.

CORPOREAL DAMAGE

Syn. material damage.
Obs. 1° Care should be taken to avoid confusing *corporeal damage* and *corporal damage*.
2° Since the terms *damage* and *injury* are synonymous, the expression *corporeal injury* may also be used.
Fr. perte économique, préjudice économique, préjudice matériel[+], préjudice pécuniaire.

CORPOREAL PROPERTY

Syn. property[2]. "Corporeal property is that which has a *corpus* or substance, and is, therefore, perceptible by the senses, such as land, cattle, merchandise, gold and silver coin" (Marler, *Real Property*, p. 1).
Fr. bien[2+], bien corporel, bien matériel, chose appropriable.

CORPOREAL THING

Syn. thing[1]. "The practical significance of the [Roman Law] distinction between corporeals and incorporeals was that possession and modes of acquisition of ownership based on possession were applicable to corporeal things only" (Yiannopoulos, in *Treatise*, vol. 2, n° 25, p. 43).
Fr. chose[1+], chose corporelle, chose matérielle.

CORREALITY *n.*

Rare. Syn. solidarity.
Obs. The use of the term *correality* as a synonym for *solidarity* is inspired by Romanist legal terminology.
Fr. corréalité, solidarité[+], solidarité parfaite, solidité.

CORRECTIVE JUSTICE

See justice[1].
Fr. justice commutative, justice corrective.

CORRELATION *n.*

See causation[1].
Obs. Causation is relevant in matters such as unjustified enrichment or compensatory allowance. It is, however, a much more flexible concept than causation in matters of civil liability. Hence, to avoid any confusion, the Civil Code uses the term *correlation* rather than *causation* in the chapter on unjustified enrichment (e.g. art. 1493 C.C.Q.), although the idea of correlation refers to a relation of reciprocity.
Fr. corrélation.

CORRELATIVE OBLIGATION

Obligation of a party to a bilateral contract viewed from the perspective of the other party's corresponding obligation. For example, the obligation of a buyer to pay the price is correlative to the obligation of the vendor to deliver the thing sold. "Where a contract is dissolved as a consequence of the refusal of one party to perform an obligation due under

it, the dissolution has the effect of putting an end to it and liberating the creditor from the duty to perform the correlative obligation" (Brierley & Macdonald (eds.), *Quebec Civil Law*, n° 460, p. 426).
Occ. Art. 1694 C.C.Q.
See also reciprocal obligation.
Fr. obligation corrélative.

COSURETY *n.*

Person who, together with others, is bound as surety for a debt.
Occ. Title preceding art. 1955 C.C.L.C.
Obs. Cosureties need not necessarily share the same obligations with respect to the creditor. They may in fact be bound as sureties under different contracts.
Fr. co-caution, cofidéjusseur+.

COUNTER LETTER *n.*

Act made secretly by the parties that modifies or extinguishes the effects of an apparent act entered into for the purpose of concealing the true agreement. "If [the parties] intended to make a sale of the movables to the appellant, coupled with a promise to reconvey them to the respondent (which is the effect of what is called the counter-letter), then possession could remain with the respondent and the sale would nevertheless be perfect [...]" (*J. R. Booth Ltd.* v. *McLean*, [1927] S.C.R. 243, p. 245, P.B. Mignault, J.).
Occ. Arts. 1451, 1452 C.C.Q.
Obs. When counter letters are designed so as to defraud the law, they are viewed as contrary to public order and are therefore null.
Syn. real act, secret act, true act. **See also** apparent act, concealed act, contract of *prête-nom*, fictitious contract, secret contract, simulated contract, simulation.
Fr. acte réel, acte secret, acte véritable, contre-lettre+.

COUNTER-OFFER *n.*

Offer in which the recipient of a previous offer proposes substantial modifications to the latter.
Obs. An acceptance implies the offeree's adherence to all the essential elements of the offer. If, however, the offeree proposes substantial changes to the content of the offer, this counter-offer does not constitute acceptance but rather represents a new offer that has the effect of causing the initial offer to lapse (art. 1393 C.C.Q.).

Syn. counter-proposal. **See also** initial offer.
Fr. contre-offre, contre-proposition+.

COUNTERPRESTATION *n.*

Advantage received by a contracting party in exchange for a prestation.
See also bilateral contract, cause[1,2], onerous contract.
Fr. contrepartie+, contre-prestation.

COUNTER-PROPOSAL *n.*

Syn. counter-offer.
Fr. contre-offre, contre-proposition+.

COVENANT *n.*

1. *Rare.* Syn. contract[1].
Fr. contrat[1+], convention, pacte.

2. Syn. clause.
Fr. clause.

COVENANT IN RESTRAINT OF TRADE

See non-competition clause.
Fr. clause restrictive de commerce.

CREANCE *n.*

Neol. Syn. personal right. "[...] with regards to the unwed mother [...] she has no alimentary creance against the father of her baby" (Kouri, (1984) 9 *Jus Medicum* 71, p. 74).
Obs. 1° English Civilian vocabulary generally uses the same word *debt* to describe the object of an obligation from the standpoints of both the debtor and the creditor. The term *claim* is often used to describe the interest of the creditor, although for some it has a procedural connotation. The term *creance* is suggested as an alternative English-language equivalent to the French term *créance*. Among other possible terms, the word *credit*, although retained as a synonym, is seen as less useful than creance because of its multiple meanings. **2°** Even though the terms *creance* and *personal right* are synonyms, *personal right* is helpful since it makes clear the distinction with real rights. **3°** From the Middle English term, itself connected to the Old French *créance*, corresponding to the Latin *credentia*, a derivative of *credere*: to believe.
See also assignment of créance, sale of creance.
Fr. créance, dette active, droit de créance, droit personnel+, *jus in personam*, obligation[4].

CREDIT *n.*

1. Right granted by a creditor to a debtor to perform, within a given period of time, the obligation to pay a sum of money.
Occ. S. 72, *Consumer Protection Act*, R.S.Q. c. P-40.1.
Obs. Section 1*f*) of the *Consumer Protection Act* (R.S.Q. c. P-40.1) defines the term *credit* in the context of consumers and merchants, in which case one speaks of consumer credit.
See also credit rate.
Fr. crédit.

2. *Rare.* Syn. personal right.
Occ. Art. 703 C.C.L.C.
Obs. The term *credit* in this sense is encountered in Louisiana civilian parlance.
Fr. créance, dette active, droit de créance, droit personnel⁺, *jus in personam*, obligation⁴.

CREDIT CONTRACT

Syn. contract of credit.
Fr. contrat de crédit.

CREDITOR *n.*

Titulary of a personal right. "On a practical level, an order of specific performance will often be a better remedy for the creditor. A creditor taking an action in damages usually must wait a long time for his damage award, whereas an interlocutory injunction can produce fairly immediate results" (Jukier, (1987) 47 *R. du B.* 47, p. 71).
Occ. Arts. 87, 438, 512, 587, 684, 748, 781, 817 C.C.Q.; arts. 1032, 1065 C.C.L.C.; s. 149.5, *Automobile Insurance Act*, R.S.Q. c. A-25; s. 126, *Consumer Protection Act*, R.S.Q. c. P-40.1.; s. 427, *Bank Act*, S.C. 1991, c. 46.
Obs. 1° Titularies of extrapatrimonial rights are not generally called creditors, but more typically holders. Exceptionally, one speaks of the creditor of an alimentary claim. **2°** The term *obligee* is commonly used in Louisiana law.
Syn. obligee. **See also** debtor.
Fr. créancier.

CREDITOR OF SUPPORT

Creditor of an obligation of support.
Occ. Arts. 587, 588, 592, 684, 688 C.C.Q.; s. 31, *An Act respecting income support, employment assistance and social solidarity*, R.S.Q. c. S-32.001.
Obs. The obligation of support between married or civil union spouses and between relatives in the direct line in the first degree is

reciprocal and variable according to the needs and means of the parties (arts. 585, 587 C.C.Q.). Thus, not only might the amount of support change over time, but so might the status of creditor and debtor.
See also debtor of support.
Fr. créancier alimentaire⁺, créancier d'aliments.

CREDIT RATE

Annual percentage that allows one to determine the cost for credit¹.
Occ. S. 72, *Consumer Protection Act*, R.S.Q. c. P-40.1.
Fr. taux de crédit.

CULPA IN COMMITTENDO
nom.ph. (Latin)

Syn. fault of commission.
Fr. *culpa in committendo*, *culpa in faciendo*, faute d'action, faute de commission⁺.

CULPA IN CONTRAHENDO
nom.ph. (Latin)

1. Fault² of one who enters into a contract without disclosing to the other party the causes of nullity that the former should have known.
See also precontractual fault.
Fr. *culpa in contrahendo*¹.

2. Syn. precontractual fault.
Obs. The *culpa in contrahendo* includes the fault of one who undertakes negotiations for a contract without having the intention to enter into it. It also includes the fault of one who, without any valid reason, withdraws his or her offer to contract. In this respect, *culpa in contrahendo* approximates the notion of *precontractual fault*.
Fr. *culpa in contrahendo*², faute précontractuelle⁺.

CULPA IN FACIENDO *nom.ph.* (Latin)

Syn. fault of commission.
Fr. *culpa in committendo*, *culpa in faciendo*, faute d'action, faute de commission⁺.

CULPA IN NON FACIENDO
nom.ph. (Latin)

Syn. fault of omission.
Fr. *culpa in non faciendo*, *culpa in omittendo*, faute d'abstention, faute d'omission⁺.

CULPA IN OMITTENDO *nom.ph.* (Latin)

Syn. fault of omission.
Fr. *culpa in non faciendo, culpa in omittendo,* faute d'abstention, faute d'omission[+].

CULPA LATA *nom. ph.* (Latin)

Syn. gross fault. "Much may be said for the view that it is hardly fair to the defendant that he should pay heavy damages for a mere temporary and not very blameworthy aberration. [...] Why then should we not take the further step and make the damages to be paid commensurate with the gravity of the fault even when the whole of the damage has clearly been caused by the defendant? [...] Is it fair that a defendant who has not been guilty of *dolus* or *culpa lata* should be ruined by having to pay damages, or even put in a critical position financially?" (Lawson, *Negligence,* p. 64).
Obs. Prior to the codification of 1866, the law recognized a gradation in the degrees of fault, extending from *culpa levissima* to *culpa lata* (gross fault). These distinctions have lost their importance, although the term gross fault remains a relevant concept to which legal effect is attached. For instance, proof of gross fault is sometimes required to hold someone liable for their acts in prescribed circumstances (e.g. arts. 1461, 1474 C.C.Q.).
Fr. *culpa lata,* faute lourde[+].

CULPA LEVIS *nom.ph* (Latin)

Fault[2] that a normally prudent person would not commit, event though its objective gravity would otherwise be considered slight.
Obs. Prior to the codification of 1866, the law recognized a gradation in the degrees of fault, extending from *culpa levissima* to *culpa lata* (gross fault). These distinctions have lost their importance, although the term gross fault remains a relevant concept to which legal effect is attached. For instance, proof of gross fault is sometimes required to hold someone liable for their acts in prescribed circumstances (e.g. arts. 1461, 1474 C.C.Q.).
Syn. slight fault. **See also** *culpa levissima,* gross negligence, obligation of means.
Fr. *culpa levis,* faute légère[+].

CULPA LEVISSIMA *nom.ph.* (Latin)

Fault[2] that an especially prudent person would not commit.
Obs. Prior to the codification of 1866, the law recognized a gradation in the degrees of fault, extending from *culpa levissima* to *culpa lata*

(gross fault). These distinctions have lost their importance, although the term gross fault remains a relevant concept to which legal effect is attached. For instance, proof of gross fault is sometimes required to hold someone liable for their acts in prescribed circumstances (e.g. arts. 1461, 1474 C.C.Q.).
See also *culpa levis,* gross negligence.
Fr. *culpa levissima,* faute très légère[+].

CUMUL (OF REGIMES) (French)

Syn. cumulation (of regimes). "By Cumul of the regimes is meant the possibility for the plaintiff A. of invoking both regimes, but in such a way that he takes in both of them the technical rules that are most favourable to his claim" (Crépeau, in *Meredith Lectures (1964),* 1, p. 9).
Fr. cumul (des régimes).

CUMULATION (OF REGIMES)

Neol. Prerogative of the victim of a contractual fault to select the most favourable rules from among those of the regimes of contractual and extracontractual liability to obtain compensation.
Obs. 1° The Supreme Court of Canada in *Wabasso Ltd.* v. *National Drying Machinery Co.,* ([1981] 1 S.C.R. 578) allowed for option between liability regimes but not for cumulation of regimes. **2°** Cumulation of regimes, like option between regimes, is henceforth prohibited (art. 1458 para. 2 C.C.Q.).
Syn. *cumul* (of regimes). **See also** contractual liability, extracontractual liability, option (between regimes).
Fr. cumul (des régimes).

CUMULATIVE CUSTODY

Custody exercised by several persons simultaneously and in the same quality with regard to property. For example, co-owners, joint borrowers.
Obs. 1° Cumulative custody is exceptional since the power to control, supervise or direct a thing is rarely exercised by several persons simultaneously. **2°** Cumulative custody, in which the same power of control and supervision is exercised by several persons, should not to be confused with shared custody in which each custodian exercises a distinct power of control and supervision.
Syn. collective custody, joint custody. **See also** alternate custody, liability for damage caused by things, shared custody.
Fr. garde collective, garde conjointe, garde cumulative[+].

CUSTODIAL FAULT

Civil fault that consists in the non-performance of an obligation resulting from custody of a person or property.

Obs. 1° It is not necessary to be the owner of property in order to be held liable for a custodial fault. One need only be its custodian at the time the harm occurs. **2°** See articles 1459 *et seq.*, 1465 *et seq.* C.C.Q.

See also custody, fault in the education, fault of supervision, liability for damage caused by another, liability for damage caused by things.

Fr. faute dans la garde.

CUSTODIAN *n.*

(*Pers.*) Person who has the custody of a person or of a property.

Syn. guardian. **See also** keeper.
Fr. gardien.

CUSTODY *n.*

Power to control, supervise or direct a person or property, which obliges the custodian to see that the person or property does not suffer or cause any damage.

Occ. Arts. 83, 1054 para. 4 C.C.L.C.; s. 25, *Mental Patients Protection Act*, R.S.Q. c. P-41.
Obs. 1° Custody is a fact that does not necessarily correspond to a right. A thief has no right to the thing stolen, for example, although he or she has the custody of the thing in fact. **2°** Custody is not necessarily co-terminous with possession, notably in that the intention to act as the holder of the right is not necessary (compare art. 921 C.C.Q.). **3°** Custody may be exercised by more than one person. It is alternative when it passes temporarily from one person to another. It is cumulative when it is exercised by several persons simultaneously.

Syn. care, juridical custody[2], legal custody[2].
See also custodial fault, fault of supervision, liability for damage caused by another, liability for damage caused by things, material custody.
Fr. garde[+], garde juridique[2].

CUSTODY *DE FACTO* (Latin)

Syn. *de facto* custody.
Fr. garde de fait.

CUSTODY IN FACT

Syn. *de facto* custody.
Fr. garde de fait.

CUSTODY OF THE ACTIVITY (OF THE THING)

Custody that extends only to the functioning or operation of a thing.

Obs. 1° The theory of shared custody, developed in French law and which divides the notion of *custody* into custody of the activity and custody of the structure of the thing, has been invoked in a number of Quebec judicial decisions. **2°** The custodian of the activity is liable, in principle, for damage except that which is attributable to a defect in the thing. **3°** The French expression *garde du comportement* is often used in English to convey this meaning.

Syn. *garde du comportement.* **See also** custody of the structure (of the thing), liability for damage caused by things, shared liability[3].
Fr. garde du comportement.

CUSTODY OF THE STRUCTURE (OF THE THING)

Custody that extends only to the internal state or composition of the thing.

Obs. 1° The theory of shared custody, developed in French law and which divides the notion of *custody* into custody of the activity and custody of the structure of the thing, has been invoked in a number of Quebec judicial decisions. **2°** The custodian of the structure is, in principle, only liable for damage attributable to a defect in the thing. **3°** The French expression *garde de la structure* is often used in English to convey this meaning.

Syn. *garde de la structure.* **See also** custody of the activity (of the thing), liability for damage caused by things, shared custody.
Fr. garde de (la) structure.

CUSTOM *n.*

1. Constant and repeated practice that is recognized as legally binding in a given society. For example, the prohibition concerning the sale of religious objects. "Implicit formulaic norms, such as those constituted in and acted upon through custom or trade usage, are meant to describe practice so as to make it possible to engage in that practice. Here, language is not used to construct an authoritative text. The only 'text' is the practice itself" (Macdonald, (1997) 42 *McGill L.J.* 119, p. 145).

Occ. Art. 1139 C.C.Q.; s. VIII, *An Act for making more effectual Provision for the Government of the Province of Quebec in North America*, 14 George III, c. 83 (U.K.).
Obs. 1° Under its traditional conception, custom is comprised of two elements: the first is

material, a usage (*usus*), that determines a rule of conduct, and the second is psychological, a belief in its obligatory character (*opinio juris seu necessitatis*). Some customs are only applicable to a given community or territory (e.g. the *Coutume de Paris*), or to a category of persons (e.g. custom of the owners (art. 1139 C.C.Q.)). **2°** In its authentic form, custom must be an emanation of social activity alone, independent of any influences from the State. However, certain scholars enlarge the scope of custom by designating fundamental principles of law and maxims as *learned custom*. **3°** The distinction between *custom* and *usage* is difficult to delineate precisely, and the terms are sometimes used interchangeably even though they are not strictly speaking synonyms (e.g. arts. 976, 2004, 2526 C.C.Q. where the terms *custom* and *customary* are used as equivalents of the French term *usage*).
See also jurisprudence[2], usage.
Fr. coutume[1].

2. Law[1] established by custom[1]. "[...] justification for the recognition of custom is nowadays sought *within* a legislative framework, even if, in doing so, custom must be falsely presented as being in harmony with legislation when really it is either filling in the gaps of a text or is even contrary thereto" (David & Brierley, *Major Legal Systems*, p. 132).
Syn. customary law.
Fr. coutume[2+], droit coutumier[1].

CUSTOMARY CLAUSE

Clause ordinarily inserted which might reflect or give rise to a custom or usage.
Occ. Art. 1017 C.C.L.C.
See also *clause de style*.
Fr. clause de style[2].

CUSTOMARY LAW

Syn. custom[2].
Occ. Art. 2807 C.C.Q.
Fr. coutume[2+], droit coutumier[1].

D

DAMAGE *n*.

Injury suffered through the infringement of the rights or interests of a person. "Damage generally results from several sets of facts. Once the primary circumstances are established, the determination of a causal relation between one or more facts evincing fault and the damage presupposes a choice, an appraisal and a characterization of the facts" (*Morin* v. *Blais*, [1977] 1 S.C.R. 570, p. 578, J. Beetz, J.). *To incur damage*; *to repair the damage*.

Occ. Arts. 164, 1860, 2481, 3129 C.C.Q.; arts. 1053, 1054 C.C.L.C.; s. 278, *An Act respecting the implementation of the reform of the Civil Code*, S.Q. 1992, c. 57.

Obs. 1° Damage, fault and causation are the three traditional requirements to establish civil liability. **2°** Although damage is often defined by scholars as an infringement upon the rights or interests of a person, more than a mere infringement is required to establish damage. The infringement must be considered through its consequences, as these are suffered by the victim. In this respect, some scholars have defined damage as the consequence of an infringement upon the rights or interests of a person. **3°** The victim has a right to compensation if the damage suffered is the direct and immediate result of a wrongful act or omission. The damage must also be certain and constitute an infringement upon a licit interest. In contractual matters, the damage must be foreseeable at the time the obligation was contracted. **4°** There are three kinds of damage: bodily, moral and material (arts. 1457, 1607 C.C.Q.). These various types of damage may manifest themselves in pecuniary or non-pecuniary losses or by a lost profit. Any such loss may be compensated by damages (art. 1611 C.C.Q.). **5°** In the *Civil Code of Québec*, the legislature has preferred to use the word *injury* rather than *damage*, particularly in the chapter on civil liability. This terminological change may be explained, in part, as an effort to avoid the common confusion between *damage*, used in the sense of injury, and *damages*, used to designate the compensation owed to the victim. Nevertheless, the term *damage* is in current use in

Quebec legal language. **6°** From the Latin *damnum* and the Old French *damage*: loss.

Syn. harm, injury, loss[2], prejudice, wrong[2].
See also bodily injury, causation[2], certain damage, civil fault, civil liability, collective damage, continuous damage, damages, direct damage, foreseeable damage, future damage, indirect damage, initial damage, licit damage, loss[1], loss of chance, material damage, moral damage, possible damage, present damage, probable damage, profit deprived, rebounding damage, reparation[1], victim.
Fr. dommage, préjudice[+], tort[2].

DAMAGE INSURANCE

Contract of insurance that protects the insured against risks that could affect his or her patrimony.

Occ. Arts. 2391, 2395, 2411, 2463 C.C.Q.; arts. 2471, 2475, 2488, 2562 C.C.L.C.; ss. 1, 93.3, 203, *An Act respecting insurance*, R.S.Q. c. A-32; ss. 5, 38, 41, *An Act respecting the distribution of financial products*, R.S.Q. c. D-9.2.

Obs. 1° Damage insurance includes property insurance (arts. 2396, 2498 *et seq.* C.C.Q.) and liability insurance (arts. 2396, 2480 *et seq.* C.C.Q.). **2°** The object of property insurance is to indemnify the insured for material losses, for example, following a theft or robbery, whereas liability insurance protects the insured against pecuniary consequences of civil liability. **3°** The expression *P. & C. insurance* (which stands for *property and casualty insurance*) is frequently used in the insurance industry as a synonym for *property insurance*.
See also insurance of persons, non-marine insurance.
Fr. assurance de dommages.

DAMAGES *pl.n.*

Pecuniary indemnification granted to a creditor as compensation for harm resulting from the non-performance, without justification, of the debtor's obligation. "In theory, specific performance is the classic civil law remedy. In France, specific performance is seen to be the principal remedy by both doctrine and

jurisprudence; in Quebec, doctrinal writers assert that specific performance is to be treated as at least on par with damages" (Jukier, (1987) 47 *R. du B.* 47, p. 51). *Action in damages; to grant damages.*
Occ. Arts. 1397, 1604, 1607, 1608, 1610, 1611, 1622, 2316 and 2356 C.C.Q.; arts. 1065, 1070 C.C.L.C.; arts. 26.1, 75.2 C.C.P.; s. 123.87, *Companies Act*, R.S.Q. c. C-38.
Obs. 1° A creditor may, in a situation of unjustified non-performance by a debtor of an obligation and without prejudice to the right to obtain damages, either force specific performance of the obligation or demand, in the case of a contractual obligation, the resolution or resiliation of the contract or the reduction of a correlative obligation, or take any other measure provided by law to enforce his or her right to the performance of the obligation (art. 1590 C.C.Q.). **2°** Damages are, in principle, intended only to give full reparation of the injury suffered by the victim. **3°** Notwithstanding that the primary function of damages is to offer reparation for the harm suffered by the victim, punitive or exemplary damages are recognized in Quebec civil law. Although designated as damages, punitive or exemplary damages are characterized as a penalty of a private nature. They are awarded only by express provision of law and, as such, are of an exceptional nature (art. 1621 C.C.Q.). **4°** The term *damage*, used as a synonym for *harm* or *loss*, must not be confused with the term *damages* in the sense of pecuniary indemnification.
See also civil liability, compensation[1], compensatory damages, contractual damages, damage, extracontractual damages, extrajudicial damages, judicial damages, legal damages, liquidated damages, moratory damages, nominal damages, non-performance, performance by equivalence, punitive damages, specific performance.
Fr. dommages, dommages et intérêts, dommages-intérêts[+].

DAMNUM EMERGENS *nom.ph.* (Latin)

Syn. loss[1].
Obs. 1° Certain scholars have limited the use of the expression *damnum emergens* to cases involving pecuniary loss. **2°** A distinction is drawn between *damnum emergens* and *lucrum cessans.*
See also *lucrum cessans.*
Fr. *damnum emergens*, perte[+].

DATION *n.*

Rare. Transfer[1] of a real right.

See also giving in payment, giving in payment clause.
Fr. dation.

DATION EN PAIEMENT (French)

Syn. giving in payment. "In conclusion, it is submitted that a sufficiently strong line of jurisprudence has been developed for one to safely say that one of the effects of art. 1040b C.C.[L.C.] is to render inoperative an acceleration clause in a contract of loan where the creditor wishes to foreclose upon the debtor in default by exercising his *dation en paiement* rights" (Hoffman, (1974) 20 *McGill L.J.* 124, p. 129).
Fr. dation en paiement.

DATION EN PAIEMENT CLAUSE (French)

Syn. giving in payment clause[1]. "Although the concept of *dation en paiement* is an old one in the civil law, its use in deeds of loan was not common before 1930. As such clauses became more popular, they began to cause severe hardship among builders and other construction tradesmen who had previously found protection in the Civil Code under their respective privileges. They soon realized that this protection was at best precarious and could be lost entirely should the lender choose to exercise his right under the *dation en paiement* clause" (Hoffman, (1974) 20 *McGill L.J.* 124, p. 124).
Fr. clause de dation en paiement.

DEBT *n.*

1. Syn. obligation[3]. *Exigible debt; outstanding debt.*
Occ. Arts. 464, 823, 1569, 1691, 2358 C.C.Q.; art. 1158 C.C.L.C.; s. 83.50, *Automobile Insurance Act*, R.S.Q. c. A-25; s. 138, *Consumer Protection Act*, R.S.Q. c. P-40.1.; s. 428(7), *Bank Act*, S.C. 1991, c. 46.
Obs. In English, the word *debt* can be used to designate both the creance or claim and the obligation owed by the debtor. The latter notion is pinpointed more precisely by *dette* in French. Influence from English explains the questionable usage of *dette* in the French text of articles 1571a and 1571c of the *Civil Code of Lower Canada*, where the word *dette* is used in the sense of creance or claim. The *Civil Code of Québec* rectifies this.
Fr. charge, dette, devoir juridique, engagement[2], obligation[3+], obligation juridique[2].

2. Syn. personal right. "In New France, doubtless partly due to the practical limita-

tion posed by the lack of prisons, as well as to the socio-economic circumstances of a settlement colony in the early stages of development, creditors did not use imprisonment as a means of debt recovery" (Kolish, (1986-87) 32 *McGill L.J.* 602, p. 604).
Occ. Arts. 1339(7), 2462 C.C.Q.; art. 1570 C.C.L.C.
Fr. créance, dette active, droit de créance, droit personnel[+], *jus in personam*, obligation[4].

DEBT FALLEN DUE

Debt, the term of which has arrived.
Obs. A debt that falls due on a designated day becomes exigible the next day.
Syn. expired debt. **See also** exigibility, expiration.
Fr. dette échue.

DEBT FOR SUPPORT

Syn. obligation of support[2].
Occ. Art. 553(2) C.C.P.
Fr. dette alimentaire, obligation alimentaire[2+].

DEBTOR *n.*

Person obliged to perform a prestation. "It is a basic legal principle that a debtor must execute his obligations at the time and in the manner agreed upon. As a legal corollary to this statement one may add that a debtor who is tardy in fulfilling his obligations, or who does not execute them exposes himself to a recourse in damages" (Kouri, (1971) 2 *R.D.U.S.* 1, p. 3).
Occ. Arts. 420, 470, 484, 591, 652, 694, 1021 C.C.Q.; arts. 1162, 1981 C.C.L.C.
Obs. Since the word *debtor* has a monetary connotation, the term *obligor* is occasionally encountered as an English-language equivalent to the French term *débiteur*.
Syn. obligor. **See also** creditor.
Fr. débiteur[+], obligé.

DEBTOR OF AN ANNUITY

Person who undertakes, gratuitously or in exchange for the alienation of capital, to pay dues to the annuitant.
Syn. debtor of the rent. **See also** annuity[1], arrears[1].
Fr. débirentier.

DEBTOR OF SUPPORT

Debtor of an obligation of support.
Occ. Art. 593 C.C.Q.

Obs. The obligation of support between married or civil union spouses and between relatives in the direct line in the first degree is reciprocal and variable according to the needs and means of the parties (arts. 585, 587 C.C.Q.). Thus, not only is the amount of support susceptible to change over time, but so is the status of creditor and debtor.
See also creditor of support.
Fr. débiteur alimentaire[+], débiteur d'aliments.

DEBTOR OF THE RENT

Syn. debtor of an annuity.
Fr. débirentier.

DEBT PAYABLE (ON DEMAND)

Syn. exigible debt.
Fr. dette exigible.

DECEITFUL CONCEALMENT

Syn. fraudulent concealment.
Occ. Art. 2486 C.C.L.C.
Fr. réticence dolosive[+], réticence frauduleuse.

DECLARATION OF WILL

The expression of intention, in a manner perceptible to another, to enter into a juridical act.
Obs. The notion of *declaration of will*, which constitutes a step towards the formation of a contract, is distinct from the notions of *declared will* and *internal will* which are linked to the determination of the intention to enter into a juridical act.
See also declared will, doctrine of the declaration of will, offer.
Fr. déclaration de volonté.

DECLARATORY *adj.*

See declaratory act, declaratory effect.
Fr. déclaratif.

DECLARATORY ACT

Juridical act, the object of which is to recognize or specify a pre-existing right. For example, an admission, an acknowledgment of debt.
Obs. Partition is a declaratory act of ownership. The declaratory effect is a legal fiction that allows partition to operate retroactively (art. 884 C.C.Q.).
See also constitutive title, declaratory effect, renunciation[1], translatory title.
Fr. acte déclaratif.

DECLARATORY EFFECT

Effect of that which acknowledges or defines a pre-existing right. For example, individual ownership resulting from act of partition.
Occ. Art. 888 C.C.Q.
See also constitutive effect, declaratory act, extinctive effect, renunciatory effect, translatory effect.
Fr. effet déclaratif.

DECLARED WILL

Intention to enter into a juridical act, as disclosed to another.
Syn. externalized will. **See also** declaration of will, doctrine of the declaration of will, internal will.
Fr. volonté déclarée[+], volonté externe.

DEED *n.*

1. Syn. attesting deed. *Notarial deed.*
Fr. acte[2], acte instrumentaire[+], *instrumentum*, titre[3].

2. Syn. contract[2]. "[...] in construing a deed what must be sought is the intention of the parties; and however ambiguous may be the language they used may be, if that intention can be ascertained with reasonable certainty, then effect must be given to it" *(Quebec (City of)* v. *Lampson* (1918), 56 S.C.R. 288, p. 291, C. Fitzpatrick, C.J.). *Deed of sale; trust deed.*
Fr. contrat[2].

DEED UNDER PRIVATE WRITING

Syn. private writing.
Fr. acte sous seing privé.

DE FACTO CAPACITY (Latin)

Physical or mental ability of a person to formulate an opinion, to make a decision or to express his or her will.
Syn. ability, aptitude, capacity[2], capacity of fact, competence, competency. **See also** *de facto* incapacity, discernment, legal capacity.
Fr. aptitude[+], capacité[2], capacité de fait, capacité naturelle.

DE FACTO CUSTODY (Latin)

Custody that is not based on a right. For example, although a thief does not have any right to the thing stolen, he or she nonetheless has custody of it in fact.

Obs. *De facto* custody may or may not coincide with possession depending on whether the legal elements of possession set forth at art. 921 C.C.Q. are present.
Syn. custody *de facto*, custody in fact. **See also** legal custody[1].
Fr. garde de fait.

DE FACTO INCAPACITY (Latin)

Physical or mental disability precluding a person from making a decision or from expressing his or her will.
Occ. S. 423(7), *An Act respecting the implementation of the reform of the Civil Code*, S.Q. 1992, c. 57.
Obs. 1° *De facto* incapacity is considered in matters of consent to care and establishment of protective supervision of persons of full age. The criteria used in evaluating such incapacity and its legal consequences vary however according to the situation or decision in respect of which the issue arises. Thus, in matters pertaining to consent to care, once a person's *de facto* incapacity is observed, it may give rise to the exercise of substituted consent by another authorized by law (art. 11 para. 2 C.C.Q.). In matters of protective regimes, the degree of *de facto* incapacity of a person to care for himself or herself or to administer his or her property will determine the appropriate protective supervision (arts. 258, 259 C.C.Q.). **2°** In matters of capacity to contract, *de facto* capacity of the person is considered in addition to legal capacity. In the case of *de facto* incapacity, it is said that consent has not been given to the juridical act since the person can neither understand the consequences of his or her acts nor express his or her will. **3°** Section 423(7) of *An Act respecting the implementation of the reform of the Civil Code* (S.Q. 1992, c. 57) provides that the expression *physical or mental incapacity* must be replaced by de facto *incapacity* when used in statutes and other statutory instruments. **4°** The Civil Code does not make an explicit distinction between legal incapacity and *de facto* incapacity. Unlike the French text which generally uses the term *inaptitude* when referring to *de facto* incapacity, the English text uses the terms *incapacity* to refer to both notions (e.g. arts. 259, 270, 295, 2128, 2166 C.C.Q.). It is interesting to note that to highlight this distinction, the *Civil Code of Lower Canada* used the term *inability* when referring to inaptitude (e.g. arts. 19.2, 332.2, 1731.1 C.C.L.C.).
Syn. factual incapacity, inability, incapacity[2], natural incapacity. **See also** consent[2], *de facto* capacity, incapable[2], incapable person[2], legal incapacity, mandate[2], nullity.

Fr. inaptitude[+], incapacité[2], incapacité de fait, incapacité naturelle.

DEFAMATION *n.*

1. Civil fault that reflects the communication of remarks which damage the reputation of a person by provoking a loss of esteem in the eyes of others.
Obs. 1° Defamation can be either written or spoken. **2°** The defamatory nature of the communicated speech is evaluated objectively. **3°** Unlike the common law, Quebec civil law does not distinguish between defamation and libel, nor between defamation and slander, although the expressions *libel* and *slander* are encountered in Quebec legal parlance.
4° Because there is no formal distinction in Quebec civil law between defamation and slander, the notion of *defamation* is understood to extend to the communication of remarks that affect the honour of a person. In such cases, however, the evaluation of the effect of harmful remarks may be based upon considerations subjective to the victim since a person's honour is intimately linked to the perception a person has of himself or herself.
5° From the Latin *diffamatio*, derived from *fama*: renown.
Fr. diffamation[1].

2. Violation of a person's right to his or her reputation, which grounds an action in civil liability.
Obs. 1° Defamation gives rise to civil liability. **2°** Quebec civil law provides no specific remedies for defamation. Defamation is instead subjected to the general regime of extracontractual civil liability in article 1457 C.C.Q. **3°** It is generally considered that the fault in matters of defamation can be the result of two different types of acts: lack of precaution in divulging information or bad faith or intention to harm by the person attaking the reputation of another. **4°** The action in defamation is the object of a particular prescription (art. 2929 C.C.Q.).
Fr. diffamation[2].

DEFAULT *n.*

Legally recognized lateness in the performance of an obligation by a debtor. "One may be in default even during the time limit, if the work is not proceeding with adequate speed so as to be completed by the end of the period specified" (*Winer & Chazonoff (Ontario) Ltd.* v. *Thomas Fuller Construction Co. (1958) Ltd.*, [1980] C.S. 570, p. 581, O. Frenette, J.). *Notice of default; to be in default; to put the debtor in default.*

Occ. Title preceding art. 1594 C.C.Q.; arts. 1263, 1597, 1602 C.C.Q.; title preceding art. 1067 C.C.L.C.; art. 1068 C.C.L.C.; s. 2(2), *Advance Payments for Crops Act*, R.S.C. c. C-49; Schedule I, para. 6, *Bretton Woods and Related Agreements Act*, R.S.C., c. B-7.
Obs. 1° The debtor may be put in default either by a formal notice demanding the performance of the obligation (the putting in default), by the terms of a clause stipulating that the lapse of time will have this effect (art. 1594 C.C.Q.), or by sole operation of law (art. 1597 C.C.Q.). **2°** Putting in default is necessary when the debtor is late with the performance of the obligation. It serves to warn the debtor that if the obligation is not performed, the creditor will exercise his or her rights. The operation of law alone enables the creditor to exercise his or her rights without having to put the debtor in default when, for example, performance of the obligation is no longer possible or when the debtor has made it clear that he or she will not perform the obligation (art. 1597 C.C.Q.). **3°** In principle, the debtor in default is no longer able to invoke superior force as a basis for avoiding liability and must compensate for the damage caused to the creditor by the lateness (art. 1600 C.C.Q.). **4°** The codal regime respecting default is set forth at articles 1594 to 1600 C.C.Q.
See also moratory damages, non-performance, notice of default, putting in default.
Fr. défaut, demeure[+].

DEFAULT IN PERFORMANCE

Syn. non-performance.
Fr. défaut d'exécution, inexécution[+].

DEFECT OF CONSENT

Imperfection that undermines the integrity of consent.
Obs. 1° Defects of consent are error, fear and lesion (arts. 1399 to 1408 C.C.Q.). **2°** Contracts affected by a defect of consent are relatively null (arts. 1407, 1419 C.C.Q.). **3°** Although the defects of consent undermine the integrity of consent, they do not prevent the formation of a contract. In such a case the contract exists but is susceptible of annulment or confirmation.
See also bad faith[1], error, fear, inexcusable error, integrity of consent, lesion, nullity.
Fr. vice du consentement.

DEFECT OF FORM

Defect in a juridical act or in an attesting deed which fails to meet to the formal require-

ments of the law for its validity. For example, a gift *inter vivos* of an immovable which is not in notarial form (art. 1824 C.C.Q.), a holograph will which does not carry the testator's signature (art. 726 C.C.Q.).
Occ. Art. 1221 C.C.L.C.
Syn. formal defect. **See also** clerical error.
Fr. défaut de forme, vice de forme+.

DEFECT OF SUBSTANCE

Syn. substantive defect.
Fr. vice de fond.

DEFER *v.*

See deferred payment.
Fr. différer.

DEFERRED PAYMENT

Payment postponed to a date later than the one originally provided for.
See also conditional right, payment with (a) term.
Fr. paiement différé.

DEFINITIVE RIGHT

Present right that, in the context of the gradual creation of a right, exhibits all the intrinsic elements essential to its perfection. For example, right of the substitute to the property of a substitution that has become perfect upon the death of the institute.
See also eventual right[1].
Fr. droit définitif

DEFRAUD *v.*

To commit a fraud. "In order to impeach the acts of his debtor, the creditor must prove intent to defraud on part of the former" (Rosenberg, (1960-61) 7 *McGill L.J.* 2, p. 17). *Intention to defraud; to defraud creditors.*
Occ. Arts. 1033, 1035 C.C.L.C.
Fr. frauder.

DELAY OF GRACE

Syn. judicial term. "In some instances the judge has no discretionary power. Thus the debtor is unable to obtain a delay of grace" (Aubry & Rau, *Civil Law*, vol. 1, n° 319, p. 182).
Fr. délai de grâce, terme de grâce, terme judiciaire+.

DELEGATE *n.*

Person who, in a delegation and upon the request of the delegation, agrees to oblige himself or herself towards the delegatee.

Occ. Arts. 1667, 1669, 1670 C.C.Q.
See also delegatee, delegation, delegator.
Fr. délégué.

DELEGATE *v.*

To effect a delegation. "Delegation, therefore, requires the consent of three people, of the person who delegates another to be debtor or prevails upon another to accept the delegated debtor, of the person who accepts the delegated debtor to be his debtor, and of the delegated debtor himself" (Nicholls, (1938) 16 *Can. Bar Rev.* 602, p. 605).
Occ. Art. 1180 C.C.L.C.
Fr. déléguer.

DELEGATEE *n.*

Person who, in a delegation, accepts the obligation that the delegate makes towards him or her at the request of the delegator.
Occ. Arts. 1667 to 1670 C.C.Q.
See also delegate, delegation, delegator.
Fr. délégataire.

DELEGATION *n.*

Contract by which a person, the delegate, at the request of another, the delegator, obliges himself or herself towards a third person, the delegatee, to perform a prestation. "[...] I reach the conclusion [...] that the acknowledgment of such debt by the debtor and his acceptance of the delegation of payment by his creditor to the bank and the latter's acceptance thereof, did not indicate any intention on the part of the bank to release its primary debtor, and consequently no novation resulted [...]" (*Gaudreault* v. *Beauchamp* (1940), 68 B.R. 353, p. 361, W.-L. Bond, J.). *Delegation of payment.*
Occ. Title preceding art. 1667 C.C.Q.; arts. 1667, 1669 C.C.Q.; art. 1173 C.C.L.C.
Obs. 1° Delegation of payment is regulated by law as an instance of the mutation of the obligation. Delegation is distinguished from indication of payment in that the person designated by the debtor to pay has personally agreed to make the payment (art. 1667 C.C.Q.). **2°** In principle, the rights of the delegatee against the delegator remain even if he or she has accepted the delegation (art. 1668 C.C.Q.). **3°** The parties to a delegation are the new debtor or *delegate*, the initial debtor or *delegator* and the creditor or *delegatee*. **4°** The codal regime respecting delegation is set forth at articles 1667 to 1670 C.C.Q.
See also assignment of debt, imperfect delegation, indication of payment, novation, perfect delegation, subrogation.
Fr. délégation.

DELEGATOR n.

Person who, in a delegation, asks the delegate to oblige himself or herself towards the delegatee.
Occ. Arts. 1668, 1669, 1670 C.C.Q.
See also delegate, delegatee, delegation.
Fr. délégant.

DELICT n.

Juridical fact that constitutes an intentional fault in an extracontractual context. "A person injured as a result of the commission of a delict or quasi-delict acquires [...] as of that moment, against the author of his misfortune, a claim in damages for the loss sustained by him [...]" *(Driver* v. *Coca-Cola Ltd.,* [1961] S.C.R. 201, p. 220, D.C. Abbott, J.). *To commit a delict.*
Obs. 1° See article 1457 C.C.Q. **2**° The term *delict* and its synonym *offence*, which appeared at articles 983 and 1007 C.C.L.C., are no longer to be found in the Civil Code. However, as specified by s. 423 of *An Act respecting the implementation of the reform of the Civil Code* (S.Q. 1992, c. 57), the notion of *fault in the context of extra-contractual civil liability* corresponds to the notions of *offence* and *quasi-offence* in the C.C.L.C. (arts. 164, 1526, 2498 C.C.Q.). **3**° From the Latin *delictum*, from *delinquere*: to fail, to commit a fault.
Syn. offence. **See also** civil fault, contract[1], delictual fault, illicit, intentional fault, quasi-contract, quasi-delict.
Fr. délit.

DELICTUAL adj.

Resulting from or relating to a delict. "[...] the classical view in France at the turn of the century was to think of civil responsibility as applying only to cases in which there was a breach of an extracontractual duty [...] One of the most unfortunate consequences of such a view has been the identification, in the minds of generations of lawyers and judges alike, of the concept of 'fault' and of 'negligence' with delictual and quasi-delictual fault [...]" (Crépeau, in *Essays on the Civil Law,* 83, p. 84).
See also contractual, extracontractual, legal[4], quasi-contractual, quasi-delictual.
Fr. délictuel.

DELICTUAL FAULT

Intentional fault committed in extracontractual matters. "In Quebec the courts generally require evidence of behaviour which is a delictual fault in its own right, that is, negligent behaviour which stands apart from the contract" (Jutras, (1986-87) 12 *Can. Bus. L.J.* 295, p. 304).
Obs. According to the former classification of obligations established under article 983 C.C.L.C., offences (delicts) were opposed to quasi-offences (quasi-delicts). This distinction is not made in the *Civil Code of Québec,* which no longer uses these terms. A distinction between extracontractual fault and contractual fault now serves to classify obligations. Furthermore, section 423 of *An Act respecting the implementation of the reform of the Civil Code* (S.Q. 1992, c. 57) provides that the words *offences* and *quasi-offences* correspond to "fault in the context of extracontractual civil liability".
See also delict, delictual liability, extracontractual fault, intentional fault, quasi-delictual fault.
Fr. faute délictuelle.

DELICTUAL LIABILITY

Extracontractual liability resulting from an intentional fault.
Syn. delictual responsibility. **See also** contractual liability, delict, extracontractual liability, legal liability[2], quasi-contractual liability, quasi-delictual liability.
Fr. responsabilité délictuelle.

DELICTUAL OBLIGATION

Obligation to compensate for the harm caused by a delict.
Obs. Like contracts, delicts are traditionally considered as one of the sources of obligations. However, delicts are not the source of the obligation to not cause harm to others. It is the violation of that latter obligation that may constitute, strictly speaking, a delict. Therefore, it is preferable to characterize the obligation to not cause harm to others as *legal* rather than *delictual*.
See also delict, delictual liability, legal obligation[1], quasi-delictual obligation.
Fr. obligation délictuelle.

DELICTUAL OFFENCE

Syn. delictual fault. "As a mandatory or as a representative charged by law with the administration of the company, a director must act in its best interests and he commits a delictual offence if he disregards them" (Smith, (1973) 33 *R. du B.* 253, p. 255).
Obs. 1° This use of the term *offence*, which is increasingly rare, was no doubt reinforced by its use in the title preceding article 1053 C.C.L.C. **2**° Used in this context, offence

should not be confused with the term as it is employed in criminal law.
Fr. faute délictuelle.

DELICTUAL RESPONSIBILITY

Syn. delictual liability. "The idea of fault then is underlying the whole law of delictual responsibility in Quebec – and generally speaking damage caused by fault, actual or presumed, is actionable" (Brossard, (1945) 23 *Can. Bar Rev.* 1, p. 3).
Fr. responsabilité délictuelle.

DELIVER v.

1. To effect delivery[1]. "The first of the two principal obligations of the seller is to deliver the thing sold (art. 1491 [C.C.L.C.]) that is, to transfer the thing into the power and possession of the buyer [...]" (Brierley & Macdonald (eds.), *Quebec Civil Law*, n° 581, p. 520).
Occ. Arts. 1716, 1720, 1737 C.C.Q.; art. 1493 C.C.L.C.
Fr. délivrer.

2. To effect delivery[2].
Occ. Arts. 1027, 1063 C.C.L.C.; art. 68(3) C.C.P.; ss. 99, 121, *Bank* Act, S.C. 1991, c. 46.
Fr. livrer.

DELIVERY n.

1. Operation by which property is placed at the disposal of the person who is entitled to it. "The right of retention is intended to protect the seller by permitting him, under certain circumstances, to withhold delivery of goods to his buyer" (Boodman, (1988) 67 *Can. Bar Rev.* 658, p. 660).
Occ. Title preceding art. 1717 C.C.Q.; arts. 822, 1722, 1807, 2709 C.C.Q.; art. 1492 C.C.L.C.
Obs. 1° The obligation to deliver arises typically in respect of acts translatory of ownership as, for example, sale, gift and giving-in-payment. Such an obligation may also be encountered in the context of lease (art. 1854 C.C.Q.) and the contract for the carriage of goods (art. 2043 C.C.Q.), which are not translatory of the right of ownership. **2°** Delivery implies the transfer of physical control over the property. In certain cases, the obligation to deliver may be performed by the remittance of the title of ownership of property. **3°** In the context of translatory acts of ownership, delivery transfers neither the ownership nor the possession of the property, since both have been transferred, in principle, at the conclusion of the contract (art. 1453 C.C.Q.). **4°** Except when parties agree otherwise, the person alienating property assumes the risks of loss until its delivery, in keeping with the rule *res perit debitori* (art. 1456 C.C.Q.). This is an exception to the rule according to which the owner of the property assumes the risks of loss (art. 950 C.C.Q.). **5°** The confusion between the French terms *deliverance* (delivery[1]) and *livraison* (delivery[2]) is no doubt aggravated by the following facts: first, when there is a delivery[2], delivery[1] (act of placing property at the disposal of a person) and delivery[2] (remittance of property) are concomitant; second, the term *délivrance* is often used in French law to designate *livraison* (delivery[2]); and third, *délivrance* and *livraison* share the term *delivery* as English equivalent. It may be observed that the French expression *prendre livraison* is used in the context of a delivery[1] to describe the removal of the property (art. 1734 C.C.Q.). **6°** Specific provisions respecting delivery in the context of sale are set forth at articles 1717 to 1722 C.C.Q.
See also delivery[2], remittance, removal, sale, tradition.
Fr. délivrance[1].

2. Remittance of a corporeal movable to the person entitled to it.
Occ. Art. 1740 C.C.Q.; arts. 1063, 1530 C.C.L.C.; art. 140 C.C.P.; ss. 75, 150.24, 163, *Consumer Protection Act*, R.S.Q. c. P-40.1.
Obs. 1° Delivery in this sense is generally associated with the contract of sale or the contract for the carriage of goods. **2°** Delivery[2] is distinguished from delivery[1], which simply consists of placing property at the disposal of the person entitled to it. **3°** In the context of sale, the seller has the obligation to place the property at the disposal of the purchaser, although he or she need not necessarily remit it to the purchase. From that moment, the costs related to transportation, such as delivery fees and customs dues, are, in principle, payable by the purchaser. **4°** The confusion between the French terms *délivrance* and *livraison* no doubt is compounded by the following facts: first, when there is a delivery[2], delivery[1] (act of placing property at the disposal of a person) and delivery[2] (remittance of property) are concomitant; second, the term *délivrance* is often used in French law to designate *livraison* (delivery[2]); and third, *délivrance* and *livraison* share the term *delivery* as English equivalent. It may be observed that the French expression *prendre livraison* is used in the context of a delivery[1] to describe the removal of the property (art. 1734 C.C.Q.).
See also acceptance[3], contract for the carriage of goods, delivery[1], remittance, removal.
Fr. livraison.

DEMANDABLE *adj.*

Syn. exigible. "[...] the debtor cannot choose to extinguish a debt not yet demandable when the term is in favor of the creditor" (Levasseur, *Conventional Obligations*, p. 67).
Occ. Arts. 947, 1188 C.C.L.C.
Fr. exigible.

DEMANDABLE CLAIM

Syn. exigible claim.
Fr. créance exigible.

DEMANDABLE CREANCE

Syn. exigible claim.
Fr. créance exigible.

DEMANDABLE DEBT

Syn. exigible debt.
Fr. dette exigible.

DEMAND LETTER

Syn. notice of default.
Fr. mise en demeure[2].

DEPOSIT *n.*

1. Real contract by which a person, the *depositor*, remits a movable to another, the *depositary*, who is entrusted with its custody and who must restore it after a certain time. "The object of deposit is to keep the property safe, and this is what distinguishes it from other contracts where property changes hands but ownership does not" (Deschamps, in *Reform of the Civil Code*, 3, p. 3).
Occ. Arts. 2280, 2298, 2305 C.C.Q.; arts. 1794, 1814, 1818 C.C.L.C.
Obs. 1° In addition to the general rules of deposit, the *Civil Code of Québec* provides special rules for necessary deposit, deposit with an innkeeper and sequestration. Sequestration may, however, apply to immovables and may be established by the court (arts. 2305 *et seq.* C.C.Q.). Under the *Civil Code of Lower Canada*, only simple deposit and sequestration were explicitly recognized. **2°** Deposit is, in principle, a contract by gratuitous title, although it may be by onerous title where permitted by usage or specified by agreement (art. 2280 C.C.Q.). **3°** The depositary must safeguard the property with prudence and diligence. He or she must return the actual property received. Unlike the borrower in a loan for use, the depositary may not use the property without the permission of the depositor (art. 2283 C.C.Q.). **4°** A fictitious remittance is sufficient for the formation of the contract of deposit where the depositary already has detention of the property under another title (art. 2281 C.C.Q.). **5°** A bank deposit is not technically considered to be a contract of deposit. Instead, it is generally viewed as a contract of loan where the client lends money to the bank. **6°** The word *deposit* is also used to describe the delivery of a document to a public authority so as to ensure its custody or to effect the publication of a right. *Deposit* can also designate the handing over of a sum of money to a public authority in order for it to be delivered to a third person entitled to it. **7°** The codal regime respecting the deposit is set forth at articles 2280 to 2311 C.C.Q.
Syn. contract of deposit. **See also** custody, deposit with an innkeeper, irregular deposit, necessary deposit, sequestration, simple deposit.
Fr. contrat de dépôt, dépôt[1+].

2. Sum of money paid in advance in partial payment of the price. For example, the purchaser leaves a deposit and pays the balance at a later date. *To leave a deposit.*
Occ. Arts. 1711, 1904 C.C.Q.; art. 1665.2 C.C.L.C.
Obs. 1° Article 1711 C.C.Q. provides that "[a]ny amount paid on the occasion of a promise of sale is presumed to be a deposit on the price [...]". **2°** Unlike the giving of earnest, the deposit paid at the time of the formation of the contract does not include the faculty of withdrawal.
Syn. payment on account. **See also** deposit[3], earnest, withdrawal option.
Fr. acompte.

3. Deposit of a sum of money or of securities by the debtor who wishes to pay but is prevented from doing so. "In the event an obligee has, unequivocally and without apparent justification, refused to accept the performance offered by his obligor, the latter may, thereafter, make a tender followed by a deposit [...]" (Levasseur, *Obligations*, p. 186). *Tender and deposit.*
Occ. Arts. 1583, 1587 C.C.Q.; arts. 1166, 1167 C.C.L.C.; arts. 189, 191 C.C.P.; s. 8, *Deposit Act*, R.S.Q. c. D-5.
Obs. 1° The debtor may be prevented from effecting payment because of the refusal of the creditor to accept it. This may be due to the creditor's absence from the place where the debt is payable or other similar reasons (art. 1583 C.C.Q.). **2°** When a deposit has been made, the debtor is no longer liable for the payment of interest accruing thereafter (art. 1586 C.C.Q.). **3°** The codal regime

respecting tender and deposit is set forth at articles 1573 to 1589 C.C.Q. **4°** The procedure pertaining to deposit[3] is governed by articles 187 to 191 C.C.P. as well as by the *Deposit Act*, R.S.Q. c. D-5.
Syn. consignment. **See also** tender.
Fr. consignation.

DEPOSIT *v.*

1. To effect a deposit.
Occ. Art. 1341 C.C.Q.; arts. 296*a*, 981*r* C.C.L.C.
Fr. déposer.

2. To make a deposit[3].
Occ. Art. 1162 C.C.L.C.
Syn. consign.
Fr. consigner.

DEPOSITARY *n.*

Person who receives the property deposited. "[...] keepers of inns, boarding-houses and taverns [are] responsible as depositaries for things brought by travellers who lodge in their houses" (*Filteau* v. *Cardy*, [1957] C.S. 252, p. 255, G.S. Challies, J.).
Occ. Arts. 2280, 2283 C.C.Q.; title preceding art. 1802 C.C.L.C.; art. 744 C.C.P.
Obs. 1° The depositary must, in principle, return the property on demand even if a term has been fixed for restitution (art. 2285 C.C.Q.). Nevertheless, where the depositary is the sole beneficiary of the term, the depositor is bound to indemnify him or her for the loss resulting from the premature restitution (art. 2294 C.C.Q.). **2°** The depositary is entitled to retain the property deposited until the payment, by the depositor, of the sum of money he or she is owed (art. 2293 C.C.Q.). **3°** The depositary is not bound to collect the fruits and revenues received from the property deposited. However, if he or she does collect them, they must be restored to the depositor (art. 2287 C.C.Q.). **4°** Where the deposit is made by gratuitous title or where the depositor did not declare the nature or value of documents, money or other valuables at the time of their deposit, the court may reduce the damages payable by the depositary (art. 2290 C.C.Q.).
See also deposit with an innkeeper, depositor, sequestrator.
Fr. dépositaire.

DEPOSITOR *n.*

Person who effects a deposit.
Occ. Arts. 2280, 2290, 2293 C.C.Q.; arts. 1809, 1812 C.C.L.C.

Obs. The depositor must pay the depositary the agreed remuneration and, if it is necessary, indemnify him or her for any loss caused by the property. Moreover, if the depositary incurred expenses to preserve the property, the depositor must reimburse them (art. 2293 C.C.Q.).
See also depositary.
Fr. déposant.

DEPOSIT WITH AN INNKEEPER

Deposit[1] made with a person, called an *innkeeper*, who offers lodging to the public.
Occ. Title preceding art. 2298 C.C.Q.
Obs. 1° The innkeeper cannot refuse to receive documents, sums of money or other valuables brought by guests unless they are cumbersome, dangerous or of excessive value given the size and operating conditions of the hotel (art. 2299 C.C.Q.). **2°** The innkeeper is responsible, in the same manner as a depositary by onerous title, for the loss of property brought by guests even if they did not entrust the property to the innkeeper for deposit (art. 2298 C.C.Q.). **3°** A special regime of civil liability is established by the *Civil Code of Québec* whereby loss is fixed as a multiple of the cost of lodging (arts. 2298, 2301 C.C.Q.).
See also depositary.
Fr. dépôt hôtelier.

DETERMINABLE OBJECT

Object of the prestation not fixed as to quantity at the time of the formation of the contract, but for which the parties have agreed on a mode of determination.
Obs. It is not essential that the object be individualized at the time of formation of the contract. It is sufficient that it be determinate as to kind and determinable as to quantity (arts. 1373 and 1374 C.C.Q.).
See also determinate object.
Fr. objet déterminable.

DETERMINATE CLAIM

Syn. liquid claim.
Fr. créance déterminée, créance liquide[+].

DETERMINATE CREANCE

Syn. liquid claim.
Fr. créance déterminée, créance liquide[+].

DETERMINATE DEBT

Syn. liquid debt.
Fr. dette déterminée, dette liquide[+].

DETERMINATE OBJECT

Object of the prestation defined as to its kind at the time of formation of the contract. "While sale, as to a determinate object, is translatory of ownership, a sale by a non-owner is without effect, saving the right of the buyer to claim damages if he was ignorant of the lack of title of the seller" (*Grossman v. Barrett*, [1926] S.C.R. 129, p. 130, P.B. Mignault, J.).
Obs. It is not essential that the object be individualized at the time of formation of the contract. It is sufficient that it be determinate as to kind and determinable as to quantity (arts. 1373 and 1374 C.C.Q.).
See also determinable object.
Fr. objet déterminé.

DETERMINATE TERM

Syn. certain term.
Fr. terme certain[+], terme connu.

DETERMINING CAUSE

Cause[3] which has given rise to direct and immediate damage so as to engage the civil liability of a person. "The other theory [adequate causation] requires courts to determine which condition or conditions played the most important role in the realization of the damage: wrongful behaviour may only be regarded as a legal cause if it is found that it was a decisive condition, the *causa causans* or determining cause" (Brierley & Macdonald (eds.), *Quebec Civil Law*, n° 478, p. 441).
Obs. 1° When the legislature provides at article 1607 C.C.Q. that the damage must be "an immediate and direct consequence of the debtor's default" in order for the victim to obtain damages, it indicates that the default must be the determining cause of the loss suffered by the victim. **2°** Care should be taken to avoid confusion between the criteria established in article 1607 C.C.Q. and the notions of *proximate cause* or *immediate cause* used by scholars as one of the theories to establish causality. The requirement of immediate damage does not necessarily designate a cause that immediately precedes the loss in time and space, to the exclusion of any other cause. It is generally understood to refer to the relationship between the loss and the cause whereby the loss must not only be the direct consequence of the act or omission but must also be so connected thereto, but for the debtor's default, the loss would not have occurred.
Syn. *causa causans*, efficient cause, proximate cause[2]. **See also** adequate cause, causation[2], condition *sine qua non*, material cause, proximate cause.
Fr. *causa causans*, cause déterminante[+], cause efficiente, cause génératrice.

DILIGENCE *n.*

See negligence, obligation of means.
Fr. diligence.

DIRECT ACTION

1. Action taken by a creditor, in his or her personal capacity, against a debtor of his or her own debtor. For example, a consumer who purchases a thing with a latent defect has a direct action against the manufacturer (s. 53, *Consumer Protection Act*, R.S.Q. c. P-40.1). "In a direct action, the plaintiff is allowed to reach beyond his co-contractant and to invoke the terms of the contract between the co-contractant and the defendant" (Jutras, (1986-87) 12 *Can. Bus. L.J.* 295, p. 301).
Obs. 1° Because a direct action is a personal action brought by the creditor against a third party, the proceeds benefit the creditor exclusively, instead of devolving to the patrimony of the debtor, as is the case in an oblique action. **2°** Direct actions may be based on a legislative text expressly providing for an action against a third party or on the general law of obligations, in particular on articles 1441 and 1442 C.C.Q.
See also oblique action, relative effect of contract.
Fr. action directe[1].

2. Action exercised by the beneficiary of a stipulation in favour of a third party against the promisor[2].
Obs. See art. 1444 C.C.Q.; also *Hallé v. Canadian Indemnity Co.*, [1937] S.C.R. 368.
Fr. action directe[2].

3. Action brought against a third party by a principal for whom a representative has contracted, or by such third party against the principal. For example, the direct action by mandator in mandate or by the principal in the management of the business of another.
Occ. Art. 2141 C.C.Q.; art. 1711 C.C.L.C.
Obs. Said to be *direct*, this action is the normal consequence of representation (see, for example, art. 2160 C.C.Q.).
Fr. action directe[3].

DIRECT DAMAGE

Damage that has a causal relationship with the act or omission giving rise to liability.

Obs. 1° Damage must be direct in order to be compensated. **2°** Since the terms *damage* and *injury* are synonymous, the expression *direct injury* may also be used.
See also indirect damage, initial damage, personal damage, ricochet damage.
Fr. préjudice direct.

DISCERNMENT *n.*

De facto capacity of a person to judge the nature of his or her acts and to understand their consequences. "[...] discernment is a necessary condition for civil liability since it would be unjust to hold children of tender years, or adults temporarily or permanently unable to distinguish right from wrong, responsible for their mistakes" (Kasirer, (1992) 40 *Am. J. Comp. L.* 343, p. 345). *Capacity of discernment*; *power of discernment*.
Occ. Arts. 34, 157, 220 C.C.Q.; arts. 20, 21 C.C.L.C.
Obs. 1° Discernment is a manifestation in private law of the philosophical idea of *free agency*, understood in the liberal tradition to be the *sine qua non* of imputability. **2°** The notion of *discernment* is taken into account in matters respecting civil liability (art. 1457 C.C.Q.) and is relevant in different circumstances in the law of persons, particularly with respect to minors (arts. 34 and 157 C.C.Q.). It serves to evaluate the aptitude of a person to express consent or the possibility of being held liable for his or her own fault. However, with respect to civil liability, the legislature chose the expression "endowed with reason" (art. 1457 C.C.Q.) instead of the expression "capable of discerning right from wrong" (art. 1053 C.C.L.C.). **3°** Discernment is a question of fact to be determined by the court. **4°** Capacity of discernment should not be confused with juridical capacity, as the latter is a capacity of a legal rather than a factual nature.
See also civil fault, civil liability, *de facto* capacity, *de facto* incapacity, *doli capax*, endowed with reason, imputability[1], imputable[1], legal capacity.
Fr. discernement.

DISCHARGE *n.*

1. Fact of being released from an office.
Occ. Arts. 816, 819 C.C.Q.; arts. 679, 878 C.C.L.C.; art. 585 C.C.P.
Obs. The liquidation of the succession ends on the discharge of the liquidator once his or her final account has been accepted by the heirs.
Syn. quit.
Fr. décharge[1+], quitus.

2. Writing recording a discharge.
Occ. Art. 609 C.C.P.
Syn. receipt[3]. **See also** acquittance[1], receipt[1], title of payment.
Fr. décharge[2+], quittance[2].

3. Fact of being released from an obligation whatever the cause of extinction of the said obligation. For example, the discharge of a debtor by a remission of the debt (art. 1687 C.C.Q.). "Once an obligor has had his obligation remitted, he is discharged of any performance. The extinction of the primary obligation will carry with it the discharge of any accessory obligation by virtue of the principle 'accessorium sequitur principale'" (Levasseur, *Obligations*, p. 248).
Occ. Arts. 100, 1671, 1692 C.C.Q.; s. 27, *An Act respecting the Ministère du revenu*, R.S.Q. c. M-31; s. 62, *An Act respecting the Québec pension plan*, R.S.Q. c. R-9.
Obs. The discharge of the debtor results from the extinction of his or her obligation. Article 1671 C.C.Q. sets forth a list of the main causes of extinction of obligations: payment, expiry of an extinctive term, novation, prescription, compensation, confusion, release, impossibility of performance and acquisition by a prior or hypothecary creditor of the property on which he or she has a claim. The legislature designates this last cause of extinction by the expression *discharge of the debtor* (title preceding art. 1695 C.C.Q; arts. 1695, 1696 C.C.Q.).
Syn. release[2]. **See also** compensation[1], confusion, extinction, extinctive term, impossibility of performance, novation, payment[1], release[1], resolutory condition, superior force.
Fr. décharge[3], libération[1+].

4. Extinction of an obligation resulting from the acquisition by a prior or hypothecary creditor of the property on which he or she has a claim.
Occ. Title preceding art. 1695 C.C.Q.; art. 1671 C.C.Q.
Obs. 1° The discharge of the debtor is a cause of extinction of obligations according to articles 1695 and 1696 C.C.Q. **2°** The discharge of the debtor is determined by the market value of the property rather than by the price the creditor paid to acquire it (art. 1695 C.C.Q.). **3°** Since *discharge* also describes a consequence of the extinction of obligations, the use of the same term to designate a particular cause of extinction of obligations can be misleading. In this sense, the title of the corresponding section of the C.C.L.C., *Of the discharge of certain debtors*, was more precise. **4°** The codal regime respecting the discharge of the debtor is set forth at articles 1695 to 1698 C.C.Q.

See also discharge[3], extinction.
Fr. libération[2].

5. Fact, for a property, of being released from a charge. For example, the discharge of an immovable from a servitude or a hypothec.
Syn. release[3]. **See also** extinction, real right.
Fr. libération[3].

6. Syn. acquittance[1].
Occ. Arts. 656.3 para. 2 C.C.P.
Fr. quittance[1].

DISCHARGE v.

To effect a discharge[3,5]. "I think that in every case where the surety has been held to have been discharged, the decision was founded upon some act or omission of the creditor which was held to be a breach of obligation due by him to the surety" (*Trust and Loan Co. of Canada* v. *Würtele* (1905), 35 S.C.R. 663, p. 678, W. Nesbitt, J.). *To discharge debtors; to discharge land of an encumbrance.*
Occ. Arts. 1668, 2497 C.C.Q.; art. 1103 C.C.L.C.
Syn. relieve. **See also** obligate.
Fr. libérer.

DISCHARGED adj.

Released from an obligation[1]. *Debtor discharged from a contractual obligation.*
Occ. Arts. 579, 1690, 2567 C.C.Q.; s. 121, *Automobile Insurance Act*, R.S.Q. c. A-25.
Syn. freed. **See also** obliged.
Fr. affranchi, libéré+.

DISCHARGE OF THE DEBTOR

See discharge[3,4].
Fr. libération du débiteur.

DISCHARGING

Syn. liberating.
Fr. libératoire.

DISCOUNT n.

Reduction of the amount of a debt granted to a debtor who pays it without delay or in advance of the due date.
Occ. Art. 1614 C.C.Q.; art. 1149 C.C.L.C.
Fr. escompte.

DISCUSS v.

To implement a discussion of the property of a debtor.

Occ. Art. 2221 C.C.Q.; art. 1942 C.C.L.C.; art. 572 C.C.P.
Fr. discuter.

DISCUSSION n.

Seizure and judicial sale of certain property in preference to other property.
Occ. Arts. 484, 1233, 1766, 2347, 2352 C.C.Q.; arts. 1943, 2066 C.C.L.C.; arts. 168(2), 714(3) C.C.P.
Obs. 1° In conventional or legal suretyship, the property of the principal debtor must, in principle, be discussed before that of the surety (arts. 2346, 2347 C.C.Q., but see art. 2352 C.C.Q.). **2°** In the execution of judgments against a debtor, there is discussion of movables before immovables (art. 572 C.C.P.).
See also benefit of discussion, contract by negotiation.
Fr. discussion.

DISGUISED p.p.adj.

See concealed act.
Fr. déguisé.

DISGUISED ACT

Syn. concealed act.
Fr. acte déguisé.

DISPONIBLE RIGHT

Neol. Right that may be freely disposed of by its titulary.
Fr. droit disponible.

DISPOSAL n.

1. Syn. disposition[1].
Fr. disposition[1].

2. Syn. disposition[2]. *Disposal of capital.*
Occ. Art. 909 C.C.Q.
Fr. disposition[2].

3. Syn. disposition[3]. *To have the free disposal of property* (art. 569 C.C.L.C.).
Occ. Arts. 461, 486 C.C.Q.; art. 399 C.C.L.C.
Fr. disposition[3].

DISPOSE v.

1. To perform a material or juridical act that compromises or extinguishes a patrimonial right. For example, to transform, consume, destroy or alienate property. "It is that right [of ownership] which entitles the owner *to*

enjoy and to dispose of a thing in the most absolute manner, provided that no use be made of it which is prohibited by law or by regulations" (Marler, *Real Property*, n° 58, p. 31).
Occ. Arts. 406, 463, 1212 C.C.Q.; arts. 366*a*, 502, 545 C.C.L.C.
See also disposition[1].
Fr. disposer[1].

2. To transfer property[1] by disposition[2]. *To dispose of property.*
Occ. Art. 706 C.C.Q.; art. 831 C.C.L.C.
Obs. Specific terms are used for the verb *to dispose* as in, for example, sale, *to sell* (to sell property), and trust, *to settle* (to settle property by trust).
Syn. settle[3].
Fr. disposer[2].

DISPOSITION *n.*

1. Act, material or juridical in character, by which the holder of a patrimonial right compromises or extinguishes his or her right.
Obs. 1° Used in this sense, the term *disposition* is not restricted to the transfer of a patrimonial right, but extends to any juridical fact that compromises or extinguishes a right, whether or not the juridical fact involves a transfer (e.g. to dispose of property by abandonment or consumption). **2°** Abandonment and alienation are examples of disposition by juridical act, whereas destruction and consumption are instances of disposition by material act.
Syn. disposal[1]. **See also** act of alienation, act of disposition.
Fr. disposition[1].

2. *Inter vivos* or *mortis causa* transfer of a patrimonial right.
Occ. Art. 863 C.C.L.C.
Obs. A distinction is drawn between disposition by onerous title (e.g. sale or exchange) and disposition by gratuitous title (e.g. gift or legacy).
Syn. disposal[2]. **See also** acquisition[1], act of disposition, alienation, assignment[1], liberality[1], mutation, transfer, transmission.
Fr. disposition[2].

3. Prerogative of the holder of a patrimonial right to perform any juridical or material act that compromises or extinguishes his or her right.
Occ. S. 6, *Charter of Human Rights and Freedoms*, R.S.Q. c. C-12.
Obs. 1° The right to effect a disposition of property by juridical act, which in theory is enjoyed by holders of all holder patrimonial rights, must be distinguished from the right

to effect a disposition by material act, which, in principle, only belongs to the owner. Within the limits of his or her administration, the administrator of the property of another may also dispose juridically and materially of the property he or she administers. **2°** With respect to the right of ownership, which encompasses the Romanist prerogatives of *usus, fructus* and *abusus* over property, dispositions by material and juridical act correspond to the concept of *abusus*. Article 947 C.C.Q. refers to this prerogative by the expression "right [...] to dispose of property fully and freely". **3°** Disposition is not an absolute prerogative: it must be expressed in conformity to law and to the requirements of order and good faith (arts. 7 and 9 C.C.Q.).
Syn. disposal[3]. **See also** administration of the property of others, disposition (of property) by juridical act, disposition (of property) by material act.
Fr. disposition[3].

DISPOSITION BY GENERAL TITLE

Disposition[2] in favour of a person or a purpose of private or social utility of an aliquot share of a patrimony, a universality or an aliquot share of any such universality.
Obs. 1° A dispositon by general title may profit more than one person or purpose. **2°** For example, trusts allow for the disposal of property by general title in favour of purposes of private or social utility (arts. 1266, 1269, 1270 C.C.Q.). **3°** A distinction is drawn between dispositions by general title, universal dispositions and dispositions by particular title.
See also transmission by general title.
Fr. disposition à titre universel.

DISPOSITION BY GRATUITOUS TITLE

Disposition[2] by which a person, prompted by a liberal intent, procures, without a counterprestation, an advantage to another.
See also liberality[1].
Fr. disposition à titre gratuit.

DISPOSITION (OF PROPERTY) BY JURIDICAL ACT

Prerogative of the holder of a patrimonial right to perform any juridical act that compromises or extinguishes his or her right.
Obs. Abandonment, alienation and succesion are examples of disposition by juridical act.
See also disposition[3], disposition (of property) by material act, enjoyment.
Fr. disposition juridique.

DISPOSITION (OF PROPERTY) BY MATERIAL ACT

Prerogative of the owner of property to perform any material act that compromises or extinguishes his or her right of ownership.
Obs. 1° Destruction and consumption of property are examples of disposition by material act. **2°** The person entitled to a dismemberment of the right of ownership cannot, in principle, compromise the existence of the thing on which his or her right bears through its disposition by material act, because this would violate the underlying right of the owner. Exceptionally, the usufructuary of perishable or consumable property may dispose of it materially, subject to compensation (see arts. 1127, 1128 C.C.Q.).
See also disposition[3], disposition (of property) by juridical act, enjoyment.
Fr. disposition matérielle[+], disposition physique.

DISPOSITION BY ONEROUS TITLE

Disposition[2] by which a person derives an advantage in exchange for that which is provided.
Fr. disposition à titre onéreux.

DISPOSITION BY PARTICULAR TITLE

Disposition[2] of one or more specified items of property in favour of a person or a purpose of private or social utility.
Obs. 1° A dispositon by particular title may profit more than one person or purpose. **2°** Trusts allow for the disposal of property by particular title in favour of purposes of private or social utility (arts. 1266, 1269, 1270 C.C.Q.). **3°** A distinction is drawn between dispositions by particular title, universal dispositions and dispositions by general title.
See also transmission by (a) particular title.
Fr. disposition à titre particulier.

DISPOSITION IN CONTEMPLATION OF DEATH

Syn. disposition *mortis causa.*
Occ. Art. 840 C.C.L.C.
Fr. disposition à cause de mort[+], disposition *mortis causa.*

DISPOSITION *INTER VIVOS* (Latin)

Disposition[2] which takes effect during the life of the person making it.
Obs. 1° A distinction is drawn between dispositions *inter vivos* and dispositions *mortis*

causa, the latter relating to the law of successions in general. **2°** A disposition *inter vivos* may have as a term the death of the disposing party. Nevertheless, this kind of disposition takes effect during the life of the disposing party, even though the exigibility of the transferred right is postponed until the death of the disposing party. **3°** It may be observed that, in Quebec, the Latin expression appears to be preferred in English in legislative texts, private juridical acts and scholarly writing, whereas it is rarely encountered in French.
See also disposition *mortis causa.*
Fr. disposition entre vifs[+], disposition *inter vivos.*

DISPOSITION *MORTIS CAUSA* (Latin)

Disposition[2] which takes effect at the death of the person making it.
Obs. 1° A distinction is drawn between dispositions *mortis causa* and dispositions *inter vivos.* **2°** It may be observed that, in Quebec, the Latin expression appears to be preferred in English but is rarely encountered in French.
Syn. disposition in contemplation of death.
See also disposition *inter vivos.*
Fr. disposition à cause de mort[+], disposition *mortis causa.*

DISTRIBUTIVE JUSTICE

See justice[1]. "Distributive justice differs from the corrective variety in that it is not limited to just two parties in a correlative relation, but instead could involve an infinite number of parties. Distributive justice is also distinctive in that it involves the sharing of a benefit or burden according to some criteria of merit" (Neyers, (1998) 11 *Can.J.L. & Juris.* 311, p. 312).
Fr. justice distributive.

DISTURBANCE OF FACT

Interference with the exercise of a real right without the intention of claiming the right as titulary.
See also disturbance of law.
Fr. trouble de fait.

DISTURBANCE OF LAW

Interference with the exercise of a real right with an intention to claiming the right as titulary.
See also disturbance of fact.
Fr. trouble de droit.

DIVISIBILITY *n.*

1. Characteristic of that which may be divided. *Divisibility of the admission; divisibility of the obligation.*
Fr. divisibilité[1].

2. Characteristic of an obligation that may be performed in parts because its object is susceptible of division. *Divisibility of the debt; divisibility of an obligation.*
Occ. Art. 1122 C.C.L.C.
See also divisible obligation, indivisibility, modality of the obligation.
Fr. divisibilité[2].

DIVISIBLE *adj.*

See divisible claim, divisible debt, divisible obligation.
Fr. divisible.

DIVISIBLE CLAIM

Creance the payment of which may be demanded in parts.
Obs. The notion of *divisible claim* is most relevant in situations where there is more than one creditor, each of whom is entitled to only part of the claim (art. 1520 C.C.Q. *a contrario*).
Syn. divisible creance. **See also** divisibility[2], divisible debt, divisible obligation, indivisible claim.
Fr. créance divisible.

DIVISIBLE CREANCE

Syn. divisible claim.
Fr. créance divisible.

DIVISIBLE DEBT

Debt the payment of which may be made in parts.
Obs. In the presence of only one debtor and one creditor, a divisible debt must be performed in the same manner as would an indivisible debt (art. 1522 C.C.Q.). The notion is most relevant in situations where there is more than one debtor, each of whom is obliged to only part of the debt (art. 1520 C.C.Q. *a contrario*).
See also divisible creance, divisible obligation, indivisible debt, payment[1].
Fr. dette divisible.

DIVISIBLE OBLIGATION

Obligation that may be performed in parts because its object is susceptible of division.
Occ. Arts. 1040, 1522, 2901 C.C.Q.; art. 1122 C.C.L.C.

See also divisible creance, divisible debt, indivisible obligation, joint obligation, obligation with a complex modality.
Fr. obligation divisible.

DIVISION *n.*

See benefit of division.
Occ. Arts. 1528, 2349; arts. 889, 1946, 2585 C.C.L.C.
Fr. division.

DOCTRINE *n.*

1. Body of opinions expressed in legal writings, the purpose of which is to explain or to interpret the law.
Obs. 1° Though doctrine has not traditionally been seen as a formal source of law, it nevertheless exercises an influence on the interpretation and evolution of law. **2°** Sometimes the term *doctrine* is used to designate the scholars themselves rather than their opinions. **3°** Long influenced by scholarship imported from France and England, Quebec doctrine started to gain independence in the 1930s and reached its maturity with the expansion of legal academia in law faculties during the 1960s. **4°** There are different views of the role of doctrine. Some view its primary function as to describe the law[1], others see it as providing the basis for a systematization of law[1]. Doctrine has also been perceived as a means to adapt law to a given society or set of values. Doctrine can also be attributed a more speculative dimension extending to its own literary or philosophical ambitions.
Syn. scholarly writing, scholarship. **See also** custom[1], jurisprudence[1], law[2].
Fr. doctrine[1].

2. Opinion advanced by one or more scholars on a point of law. For example, the doctrine of Aubry and Rau on the notion of *patrimony*. "After hearing the reasons and opinions for and against the doctrine of irrevocability [of substitutions of art. 930 C.C.L.C.] of the most learned men in France of that time, Chancellor d'Aguesseau came to the conclusion that the doctrine of irrevocability was the soundest, the most rational, the most equitable one" (*Meloche* v. *Simpson* (1899), 29 S.C.R. 375, p. 390, H.E. Taschereau, J.). *Prevailing doctrine.*
Fr. doctrine[2].

DOCTRINE OF ADEQUATE CAUSATION

See adequate causation.
Fr. théorie de la causalité adéquate.

DOCTRINE OF *CAUSA PROXIMA*
(Latin)

See proximate causation.
Fr. théorie de la *causa proxima*.

DOCTRINE OF PARTIAL CAUSATION

See partial causation.
Fr. théorie de la causalité partielle.

DOCTRINE OF PROXIMATE CAUSATION

See proximate causation.
Fr. théorie de la causalité immédiate.

DOCTRINE OF RELATIONAL CONTRACT

See relational contract (doctrine of).
Fr. théorie du contrat relationnel.

DOCTRINE OF RISKS

1. Doctrine that determines which of the parties to a contract must assume the loss associated with the non-performance of an obligation due to superior force.
Obs. 1° The doctrine of risks was developed with respect to bilateral contracts. Where one of the contracting parties is prevented by superior force from performing the obligation, he or she is, in principle, relieved from performance (art. 1693 C.C.Q.). The doctrine of risks determines whether the cocontracting party is also freed from correlative obligation, or remains bound by it. **2°** In a synallagmatic contract that is not translatory of ownership, the risks are borne by the debtor of the obligation whose performance is rendered impossible by superior force. That party is relieved from his or her obligation and cannot require the cocontracting party to perform the correlative obligation (art. 1694 C.C.Q.). This is reflected by the Latin maxim *res perit debitori*, the thing perishes for the debtor. **3°** The same analysis applies to synallagmatic contracts transferring ownership. Article 1456 C.C.Q. provides that the risks are borne by the debtor of the obligation to deliver, even if he or she is no longer the owner when the superior force occurs (*res perit debitori*). This is an exception to the principle enunciated at article 950 C.C.Q. according to which the owner of the thing assumes the risks of loss. **4°** In instalment sales concluded with a consumer, the merchant assumes the risk of loss or deterioration of the goods by superior force until the title is transferred to the consumer (s. 133, *Consumer Protection Act*, R.S.Q. c. P-40.1). **5°** In a unilateral contract (e.g. loan for use, deposit), a single party is obligated. If, by superior force, that party is prevented from performing the obligation, he or she is relieved therefrom. The creditor assumes the loss of the thing that is the object of the contract (*res perit creditori*).
See also impossibility of performance, *res perit creditori*, *res perit debitori*, *res perit domino*, risk of the contract.
Fr. théorie des risques[1].

2. Doctrine according to which the extracontractual liability of a person rests not on fault, but on the causal relationship between a damage and the risk created by an activity from which that person gains a profit.
Obs. 1° Following this theoretical conception of civil liability, a person who benefits from an activity should bear the risks that flow from it and, accordingly, compensate the damage it causes to others, even in the absence of fault. Applied without restriction, the doctrine of risks would have the practical effect of establishing a strict liability regime. **2°** The doctrine of risks was advanced by scholars at the turn of the 20th century in various parts of the industrialized world as a new basis for civil liability to respond to perceived injustices associated with the application of the classical regime of civil liability in the context of industrial accidents. Because the cause of the accident and the employer's fault were both difficult to establish, workers who had suffered damage where often left to bear that loss, without remedy.
See also civil liability, material cause, strict liability.
Fr. théorie des risques[2].

DOCTRINE OF THE DECLARATION OF WILL

Doctrine according to which the declared will rather than the internal will prevails in the determination of the intention to enter into a juridical act.
Obs. This doctrine of German origin has not found favour in Quebec or in French civil law.
See also declared will, doctrine of the internal will, internal will.
Fr. théorie de la déclaration de volonté.

DOCTRINE OF THE EQUIVALENCE OF CONDITIONS

See equivalence of conditions.
Fr. théorie de l'équivalence des conditions.

DOCTRINE OF THE INTERNAL WILL

Doctrine according to which the internal will prevails over the declared will in the determination of the intention to enter into a juridical act.
See also declared will, doctrine of the declaration of will, internal will.
Fr. théorie de la volonté réelle.

DOCTRINE OF UNDERTAKING BY UNILATERAL WILL

Doctrine according to which one person can constitute himself or herself a debtor of another without the need for the latter's acceptance.
Obs. This doctrine recognizes a unilateral undertaking of will or an undertaking by unilateral will as a source of obligations. Scholars who reject this theory argue that undertakings by unilateral will only give rise to obligations in cases expressly specified by law and that, even in those circumstances, the source of the obligation is the law rather than the undertaking itself.
See also unilateral act, unilateral undertaking (of will).
Fr. théorie de l'engagement par volonté unilatérale.

DOCTRINE OF UNFORESEEN CIRCUMSTANCES

See unforeseeability[2].
Fr. théorie de l'imprévision.

DOCTRINE OF UNILATERAL UNDERTAKING

See doctrine of undertaking by unilateral will.
Fr. théorie de l'engagement unilatéral.

DOLI CAPAX adj.ph. (Latin)

Endowed with reason so as to be held liable for one's acts or omissions. "Hence, infants and insane persons, being unable to discern right from wrong, are incapable of committing fault and are not civilly liable for their acts. They are not 'doli capax'" (Goldenberg, *Law of Delicts*, p. 19).
Obs. This term may also be encountered in the plural: *doli capaces*.
See also discernment, imputability[1].
Fr. *doli capax*.

DOLUS BONUS nom.ph. (Latin)

Slight exaggeration by a contracting party of the qualities or the value of that which is offered. "One should distinguish, however, between dolus bonus and dolus malus [...] There are assertions which ought not deceive a reasonable man: example: puffing in advertisement. When the falsehood of the assertion can be easily ascertained one has only himself to blame" (Levasseur, *Conventional Obligations*, p. 38).
Obs. Unlike fraud[1], *dolus bonus* is not a cause of nullity of juridical acts (see *Lortie* v. *Bouchard*, [1952] 1 S.C.R. 508).
See also fraud[1].
Fr. bon dol[+], *dolus bonus*.

DOLUS MALUS nom.ph. (Latin)

Syn. fraud[1].
Fr. dol[1+], *dolus malus*, fraude[1].

DOMESTIC PUBLIC ORDER

Public order of national origin governing relations that fall within internal private law and private international law.
Obs. 1° Domestic public order governs either relations falling within internal law (internal public order) or those falling within private international law (international public order). **2°** Domestic public order may be of federal or provincial origin depending on the subject matter at issue.
See also internal public order, international public order[1].
Fr. ordre public national.

DONATION n.

Rare. Syn. gift[1].
Occ. Art. 941 C.C.L.C.
Fr. contrat de donation, don[1], donation[+].

DONEE n.

Person who receives a gift. "Domat [...] has been cited to prove the undeniable proposition that donations are revocable with the donee's consent" (*Meloche* v. *Simpson*, (1899) 29 S.C.R. 375, p. 383, H.E. Taschereau, J.).
Occ. Arts. 217, 1220, 1806 C.C.Q.; arts. 755, 771 C.C.L.C.; art. 234(6) C.C.P.
See also gift[2].
Fr. donataire.

DON MANUEL nom.ph. (French)

Gift of a corporeal movable effected by mere delivery. "[...] delivery is an essential element of the contract itself of *don manuel*: it is not only an obligation resulting from such contract. In other words, there is no *don manuel* if delivery does not accompany the consent"

(*Succession Meighen and Reford and Royal Trust*, [1972] C.S. 120, p. 125, L. Bélanger, J.).
Fr. don manuel.

DONOR *n.*

Person who makes a gift.
Occ. Arts. 217, 869, 1144, 1253, 1806 C.C.Q; arts. 755, 762 C.C.L.C.
Obs. When a person makes a gift in a will, he or she is most usually designated as a *testator* or *testatrix*. Where a gift results in the creation of a trust, the donor is also designated as a *settlor*.
See also gift[2].
Fr. donateur.

DOUBLE MANDATE

Juridical situation in which a person acts as a mandatary for both parties to a contract. For example, a person who, entrusted with the sale of an immovable by its owner, sells it to a buyer from whom he or she received the mandate to buy. "[T]he rule which has emerged from the jurisprudence is that the double mandate is not so inherently illegal and may be enforced by the courts in situations where the interests of the parties do not appear to be opposed, provided the broker has frankly disclosed his position to both parties and has acted fairly and honestly in the interest of both" (Le Dain, (1957) 4 *McGill L.J.* 219, p. 244).
Occ. Art. 2143 C.C.Q.
Obs. Double mandate consists of two contracts of mandate in which the same person plays the role of mandatary towards two distinct mandators.
Fr. double mandat.

DROIT COMMUN *nom.ph.* (French)

Syn. general law. "The Civil Code is a central institution of Quebec law. It is the principal statement on property and civil rights in the province and it constitutes the *droit commun* or 'common law' of citizens' interpersonal dealings" (Brierley, (1987-88) 13 *Can. Bus. L.J.* 58, p. 59).
Fr. droit commun[1+], *jus commune*, loi générale.

DROIT DE PRÉFÉRENCE *nom.ph.* (French)

Syn. right of preference[2]. "[The notion of *ownership*] is referred to as a real right, the consequences of which are that it is enforceable against all persons, and it accords among other benefits a *droit de suite* and a *droit de*

préférence to the holder" (Pierre, (1997) 28 *R.G.D.* 235, p. 251).
Fr. droit de préférence[2+], préférence.

DROIT DE SUITE *nom.ph.* (French)

Syn. right to follow.
Fr. droit de suite.

DUES *pl.n.*

Sum which must be paid at fixed intervals.
Occ. Art. 2210 para. 2 C.C.L.C.
See also arrears[1], periodic payment.
Fr. redevance.

DUTY *n.*

That which a person must do or refrain from doing. "There is [...] at the very heart of the notion of obligation the compelling belief of a duty" (Levasseur, *Conventional Obligations*, p. 1). *Duty of supervision*; *moral duty*.
Occ. Arts. 400, 599, 1457, 1458 C.C.Q.; s. 56, *Interpretation Act*, R.S.Q. c. I-16; s. 5, *Public Curator Act*, R.S.Q. c. C-81.
Obs. 1° A duty may be either moral or juridical. **2°** The notion of *duty* is rooted in a system of values that dictates conduct and fixes sanctions. **3°** According to some scholars, the legislature's occasional choice of the term *duty* rather than *obligation* emphasizes the moral foundation of these legal relations.
Syn. obligation[1]. **See also** interest, moral obligation, obligation[2], right.
Fr. devoir[+], obligation[1].

DUTY OF CONFIDENTIALITY

Obligation to keep certain information secret. "The legislator has envisaged various situations where a hospital may be relieved from its duty of confidentiality to give communication of the records of a beneficiary of services" (*Frenette* v. *Metropolitan Life Ins. Co.*, [1992] 1 S.C.R. 647, p. 677, C. L'Heureux-Dubé, J.).
Obs. 1° The information that is the object of the duty of confidentiality may be confidential by reason of its connection to a person or to the activities of a group or enterprise. **2°** The sources of the duty of confidentiality are generally seen to be the right to privacy and the duty of loyalty. **3°** The duty of confidentiality may arise, explicitly or implicitly, from law or contract. Confidentiality of personal information exists in both contractual settings (e.g. in professional relations between an advocate and his or her client) and in extracontractual settings (e.g. in family relations). **4°** While disclosure of confidential information may give rise to civil liability,

some exceptions are provided by law (for the case of trade secrets (art. 1612 C.C.Q.)). **5°** In principle, persons bound by a professional secret cannot disclose information, even in court, that has been revealed to them by reason of the functions they occupy (s. 9, *Charter of Human Rights and Freedoms*, R.S.Q. c. C-12). **6°** Many statutes expressly provide for an obligation of confidentiality (e.g. arts. 36, 37 C.C.Q.; s. 10, *An Act respecting the protection of personal information in the private sector*, R.S.Q. c. P-39.1; s. 7, 8, *Privacy Act*, R.S.C. 1985, c. P-21).
Syn. obligation of confidentiality. **See also** obligation of loyalty.
Fr. devoir de discrétion, obligation de confidentialité+.

DUTY OF CONSCIENCE

Syn. moral obligation.
Fr. devoir de conscience, devoir moral, obligation imparfaite, obligation morale+.

DUTY TO COLLABORATE

Syn. duty to cooperate.
Fr. devoir de collaboration, obligation de collaboration+, obligation de coopération.

DUTY TO COOPERATE

Obligation for the parties to a contract to assist one another in accordance with their legitimate expectations in the circumstances.
Obs. 1° The duty to cooperate reflects the application of the principle of good faith in the law of obligations (arts. 6, 7, 1375 C.C.Q.). The content of the duty varies according to the nature of the contract; it may or may not be made explicit therein. **2°** The duty to cooperate is generally a feature of contracts the performance of which requires close and sustained relations between the parties, as in the case of a contract of employment. **3°** The duty to cooperate may arise at the formation of the contract (e.g. the precontractual obligation to inform), as well as during its performance (e.g. the obligation of the franchisor to provide technical assistance to the franchisee). **4°** The insured person who suffers a loss has a duty to cooperate with the insurer. The failure of the insured to cooperate may cause the forfeiture of the right to indemnity (arts. 2470, 2471 C.C.Q.).
Syn. duty to collaborate. **See also** continuous obligation, good faith[1], implicit obligation, obligation of loyalty.
Fr. devoir de collaboration, obligation de collaboration+, obligation de coopération.

DUTY TO INFORM

Syn. obligation to inform. "The doctor owes a duty to inform the patient of all circumstances and possible risks of the treatment. Possessed of this knowledge of the patient, the doctor is under a duty to keep this information confidential" (Gonthier, (2000) 45 *McGill L.J.* 567, p. 580).
Fr. devoir de renseignement(s), obligation de renseigner, obligation d'information, obligation de renseignement(s)+.

E

EARNEST *n.*

Sum of money paid by one party to another, at the conclusion of a contract, in accordance with a stipulation as to earnest. For example, a person promising to purchase pays earnest money to the owner of the thing that he or she has promised to purchase. *Earnest money*; *payment in earnest.*
Occ. Art. 1477 C.C.L.C.
Obs. 1° Payment in earnest is distinguished from payment on account or deposit[2], since it is not merely a sum of money paid in advance on the sale price. It also represents a penalty attached to the exercise by the parties of the right of withdrawal provided for by a stipulation as to earnest. Such stipulation typically provides that the purchaser may withdraw from the contract subject to the loss of the monies paid. It also provides that the seller may exercise his or her right of withdrawal, on the condition that he or she pay the purchaser a sum traditionally fixed at double the amount received. **2°** Earnest is generally encountered in sales or promises of sale. **3°** From the Latin *arrhas*, shorter form of *arrhabo*: pledge.
See also deposit[2], penalty of withdrawal, promise of sale, stipulation as to earnest.
Fr. arrhes.

ECONOMIC *adj.*

See economic error, economic public order, material damage.
Fr. économique.

ECONOMIC AND SOCIAL PUBLIC ORDER

Syn. economic public order.
Fr. ordre public économique[+], ordre public économique et social.

ECONOMIC ERROR

Error relating to the value of the counter-prestation.
Syn. error as to the value. **See also** lesion.
Fr. erreur économique[+], erreur sur la valeur.

ECONOMIC LOSS

Syn. material damage.
Obs. This term is most often used to establish a comparison with the Common law category of pure economic loss. However, the expression *pure economic loss* does not have any designated substantive meaning in civil law. The civil law puts no special conditions on the right to compensation for material damage except that it be direct and certain.
Fr. perte économique, préjudice économique, préjudice matériel[+], préjudice pécuniaire.

ECONOMIC PUBLIC ORDER

Public order regulating the production and exchange of property and services.
Obs. 1° Scholars distinguish between two types of economic public order: public order of direction and public order of protection. **2°** Economic public order is largely of legislative origin, as in legislation governing the trading of securities, the contract of insurance, the protection of lessees and of consumers.
Syn. economic and social public order. **See also** moral public order, political public order.
Fr. ordre public économique[+], ordre public économique et social.

EFFECTIVE TRADITION

Syn. actual tradition.
Fr. tradition réelle.

EFFICIENT CAUSE

Syn. determining cause.
Fr. *causa causans*, cause déterminante[+], cause efficiente, cause génératrice.

ELECTRONIC CONTRACT

Contract *inter absentes* for which the offer or the acceptance is made manifest by means of a computer connected to an open or restricted network. For example, online sales, the contract of electronic data interchange (EDI). "Electronic contracts generally engage the same rules, and present the same risks, as contracts formed using other means of distant

communications, such as postal correspondence, telephones, telex and facsimile" (Freedman, (2000) 28 *Man. L.J.* 1, p. 10).
Obs. 1° The circumstances of negotiation and formation of electronic contracts are such that they are often adhesion or consumer contracts. **2°** The contracting party who offers the goods or services online must provide a mechanism to permit a person using the pre-programmed site to avoid or correct, as soon as possible, an error in the order (s. 35, *An Act to establish a legal framework of information technologies*, S.Q. 2001, c. 32). **3°** Contracts that are formed by telephone, telex or fax, where the offer or the acceptance has been conserved by electronic means, could be considered as electronic contracts broadly understood. In that broad sense, the concept of the *electronic contract* can also include those contracts for which the offer or the acceptance is transmitted by means of a message on a voicemail system or by electronic mail.
See also technology-based document, theory of reception.
Fr. contrat électronique.

ELECTRONIC DOCUMENT

Syn. technology-based document.
Occ. S. 31.8, *Canada Evidence Act*, R.S.C. 1985, c. C-5; s. 31(1), *Personal Information Protection and Electronic Documents Act*, S.C. 2000, c. 5.
Fr. document électronique, document technologique+.

EMPLOYEE *n.*

1. Physical person who performs work, in return for remuneration, under the direction or control of an employer. "Often expressed as an employee's obligation rather than as an employer's right, employees owe their employer a duty of loyalty" (Morgan, (1999) 44 *McGill L.J.* 849, p. 889).
Occ. Arts. 2085, 2090 C.C.Q.; s. 1(*l*), *Labour Code*, R.S.Q. c. C-27; s. 1(10), *An Act respecting labour standards*, R.S.Q. c. N-1.1; art. 3(1), *Canada Labour Code*, R.S.C. 1985, c. L-2.
Obs. Definitions of the term *employee*, encountered in certain laws relating to labour relations, such as the *Labour Code* (R.S.Q. c. C-27) and *An Act respecting labour standards* (R.S.Q. c. N-1.1), may add to or depart from the meaning of employee under of the general law.
See also agent and servant, contract of employment, contractor, employer[1], mandatary, provider of services, workman.
Fr. employé, salarié+.

2. See agent and servant.
Obs. The term *employee* as an equivalent of *préposé* is generally understood to include the *agents* and *servants* mentioned in article 1463 C.C.Q.
Fr. [*].

EMPLOYER *n.*

1. Person on whose behalf and under whose direction or control the employee performs work. "An employer must act toward his employee as a 'bon père de famille', must supply him with appropriate tools and equipment for the work he is to perform and must protect him not only against external dangers, but also against his own errors and imprudence" (*Poulet* v. *Hébert*, [1950] C.S. 315, p. 317, G.S. Challies, J.).
Occ. Arts. 2085, 2095 C.C.Q.; art. 1661.4 C.C.L.C.; s. 19, *Charter of Human Rights and Freedoms*, R.S.Q. c. C-12.; ss. 1(7), 41.1, 122, *An Act respecting labour standards*, R.S.Q. c. N-1.1; s. 3(1), *Canada Labour Code*, R.S.C. 1985, c. L-2.
See also client[2], contract of employment, employee[1], mandator, principal[3].
Fr. employeur.

2. See principal[3].
Occ. Art. 1054 C.C.L.C.
Obs. 1° The term *employer*, as used regarding the regime of civil liability established by article 1463 C.C.Q., has a wide meaning and does not refer to the more specialized sense in which the term is used in the context of employment contracts at articles 2085 to 2097 C.C.Q. and in various other statutes. **2°** The term *principal* has a particular meaning that is distinct from the meaning usually given to the term *employer*, but equivalent to the meaning given to the expression *masters and employers* in the interpretation of article 1054 para. 7 C.C.L.C.
Fr. [*].

EMPLOYER-EMPLOYEE RELATIONSHIP

See subordination. "A breach of the obligation of good faith can give rise, like a breach of any contractual obligation, to the employee's responsibility for damages caused to the employer by the breach. An employee who profits from breach of this obligation must turn over those profits to the employer. In the employer-employee relationship, the concept of breach of confidence does not lie in proprietary rights; it lies in the notion of an obligation of conscience and loyalty arising from the circumstances" (*Matrox Electronics Systems*

Ltd. v. *Gaudreau*, [1993] R.J.Q. 2429 (Sup. Ct.), p. 2466, A.D. Guthrie, J.).
Fr. [*].

EMPLOYMENT CONTRACT

Syn. contract of employment. "Article 2085 of the *Civil Code of Québec* sanctions, in the same manner as its predecessor, the essentially temporary character of the employment contract. In insisting on the fact that an employee cannot commit himself to an employer for life, the legislature has reiterated its desire to prevent any form of slavery" (Bonhomme, Gascon & Lesage, *Employment Contract*, p. 9).
Fr. contrat d'emploi, contrat de louage de services[1], contrat de louage de service(s) personel(s), contrat de travail[+], contrat individuel de travail, louage de service(s) personel(s).

ENABLING FORM

Syn. formality *ad habilitatem*. "Article 2692 as drafted should be interpreted restrictively for another reason: it is in neither declarative nor enabling form. It contains no express declaration of any principle of substantive law, nor does it enable any principle to be applied in a particular way" (Claxton, (1999) 44 *McGill L.J.* 665, p. 678).
Fr. formalité *ad habilitatem*, formalité habilitante[+], forme habilitante.

ENACTMENT

Syn. law[2]. "Within the inventory of legislative sources of law, the Code occupies a unique place. As an enactement of a legislature, its normative status is inferior to that of the constitution and to quasi-constitutional documents" (Brierley & Macdonald (eds.), *Quebec Civil Law*, n° 97, p. 116).
Fr. loi[1].

ENDOWED WITH REASON

Said of a person who has the power of discernment.
Occ. Arts. 1457, 1461, 1462 C.C.Q.
Obs. 1° The requirement that a person be endowed with reason is an application in private law of the philosophical idea of *free agency*, understood in the Judeo-Christian and liberal traditions to be the *sine qua non* of imputability. **2°** A person must be endowed with reason to be held civilly liable for his or her own act or omission. **3°** Whether a person is endowed with reason is a question of fact to be determined by the court. **4°** With respect

to civil liability, the legislature chose the expression "endowed with reason" (art. 1457 C.C.Q.) instead of the expression "capable of discerning right from wrong" (art. 1053 C.C.L.C.).
See also capable[2], civil fault, civil liability, discernment, imputability[1], incapable[2].
Fr. doué de raison.

ENGAGEMENT *n.*

Syn. undertaking.
Fr. engagement[1].

ENJOY *v.*

To have the enjoyment. "Some, such as intellectual property rights and personality rights, simply have no connection to the notion of personal or real rights. Others, such as the right of the lessee to enjoy the thing leased (often called a *jus ad rem trans personam*), seem to be partly real rights and partly personal rights" (Macdonald, (1994) 39 *McGill L.J.* 761, p. 768).
Occ. Art. 947 C.C.Q.
Fr. jouir.

ENJOYMENT *n.*

Right to make use of property[2] and, should the occasion arise, to receive the fruits and revenues of it. "It is [...] of the essence of a lease that enjoyment of the thing be granted and that grant of enjoyment must persist through the duration of the lease" (*Equilease Ltée* v. *Bouffard*, [1979] C.S. 191, p. 193, J.B. O'Connor, J.).
Occ. Arts. 1124, 1851 C.C.Q. *To provide enjoyment.*
Obs. 1° Enjoyment can result from a personal right, such as the right of a lessee (art. 1851 C.C.Q.). **2°** Enjoyment can also result from a real right, such as usufruct. It then corresponds to the first two attributes of the right of ownership: *usus* and *fructus* (arts. 1120, 1124 C.C.Q.).
Syn. right of enjoyment. **See also** disposition[3].
Fr. droit de jouissance, jouissance[+].

ENLIGHTENED CONSENT

Consent given knowingly. "Free and enlightened consent – It is trite to state that art. 19 C.C.L.C. allows for the infringement of a person's integrity as long as the individual concerned has been adequately informed of the nature and risks of the act contemplated and has expressed a valid consent thereto" (Kouri, (1991) 22 *R.D.U.S.* 77, p. 83).

Occ. Arts. 10, 365 C.C.Q.
Obs. 1° In principle, consent must be both free and enlightened in order to give rise to effects in law (art. 1399 C.C.Q.). **2°** The obligation to inform and the duty to enquire seek to protect the enlightened nature of consent in that they provide the person with the knowledge necessary to inform properly his or her decision.
Syn. informed consent. **See also** consent freely given, defect of consent, integrity of consent, obligation to inform.
Fr. consentement éclairé.

ENTERPRISE *n.*

1. Organized economic activity.
Obs. 1° According to article 1525 C.C.Q., the carrying on of an enterprise consists of an organized economic activity such as providing a service or producing, administering or alienating property. The carrying on of an enterprise can be undertaken by one or more persons. **2°** Solidarity is presumed between debtors of an obligation contracted for the service or carrying on of an enterprise (art. 1525 C.C.Q.). **3°** The notion of *enterprise* replaces *notions of commerce* and *commercial acts* (arts. 457, 1384, 1714, 1842, 2186, 2221, 2254, 2683 to 2685, 2830, 2831, 2862, 2870 C.C.Q.). The range of activities envisaged by the concept of *enterprise* is broader than the notion of *commercial activity*. It includes skilled, agricultural and professional activities as well as those based on cooperation, with or without profit-making objectives.
See also contract of enterprise, solidarity.
Fr. entreprise[1].

2. See contract of enterprise.
Fr. entreprise[2].

EQUIPOLLENT *adj.*

Rare. Equivalent.
Fr. équipollent.

EQUITABLE *adj.*

1. Acting in conformity with equity. *An equitable person; an equitable judge.*
Fr. équitable[1](<).

2. In conformity with equity[1]. *An equitable decision; equitable law; an equitable partition.*
Occ. Art. 1408 C.C.Q.
Syn. fair. **See also** legitimate[1].
Fr. équitable[2](<).

EQUITY *n.*

1. Type of justice that aspires to establish a measure of fairness in the presence of competing interests. *To decide in equity.*
Occ. Arts. 975, 1434 C.C.Q.; arts. 429, 1024 C.C.L.C.
Obs. 1° Whereas rules of equity were traditionally seen as opposed to positive law, the notion has achieved today the status of source of law, consecrated by enactment. In this way, article 1434 C.C.Q. envisages that a validly formed contract binds the parties not only to what is incident to its nature, but also to what is equitable in the circumstances. **2°** While courts are bound to decide according to law, they also may, when explicitly (e.g. art. 975 C.C.Q.) or implicitly authorized by law, have recourse to equity. Arbitrators may, with the consent of the parties to a dispute, disregard suppletive law and decide in equity (art. 944.10 C.C.P.). **3°** From the Latin *æquitas*, from *æquus*: equal.
See also justice[1], positive law.
Fr. équité.

2. Rules of law, initially developed in England from the fifteenth century by the Court of Chancery, and applied by courts in order to render more just the strict application of the Common law[2] in the English legal tradition. "It is characteristic of the flexibility of legal ideas in the Romano-Germanic family that the concept of equity (*équité*) has at all times been part of the law, and that there has never been any necessity of correcting legal solutions by means of autonomous rules or courts of equity" (David & Brierley, *Major Legal Systems*, p. 151).
Obs. 1° In England, the Judicature Acts of 1873-1875 effected a fusion of the Common law[2] and Equity, but only from the perspective of judicial organization: all superior courts may rule according to both the Common law[2] and Equity. Canadian Common law provinces have progressively done the same. **2°** Equity has never been perceived as a complete and autonomous system of law, but rather as a system parallel to the Common law[2] and destined to fill its gaps or to temper its effects. **3°** Despite the crystallization of the rules of Equity, equitable remedies stem from the discretionary power of the court, which can withhold them from a party who, given the circumstances, does not appear to merit the court's protection. **4°** The term *Equity* used in this sense should not be confused with *equity*[1] as understood in civil law.
See also Common law[4].
Fr. *Equity.*

EQUIVALENCE OF CONDITIONS

Theory that attributes an identical causal weight to all facts without which the damage would not have occurred.
Obs. Alongside the theories of proximate causation and adequate causation, equivalence of conditions is a means to determine the cause of the damage. In determining the cause of the damage, courts tends to prefer the theory of adequate causation.
See also adequate causation, condition *sine qua non*, determining cause, material causation, proximate causation.
Fr. équivalence des conditions.

ERGA OMNES adv. ph. (Latin)

With regard to all others. "If I am the owner of a house my right to the uninterrupted enjoyment of it is a right as against everybody - *erga omnes*" (Walton, *Obligations*, vol. 1, p. 6). *Opposable* erga omnes; *valid* erga omnes.
See also opposability.
Fr. *erga omnes.*

ERROR *n.*

Inaccurate understanding of a situation that impels a person to enter into a juridical act. "[...] to be a cause of nullity [...] error must have existed at the time of the making of the contract." (Baudouin, in *Essays on the Civil Law*, 151, p. 169).
Occ. Arts. 1399, 1400, 1401, 1407 C.C.Q.
Obs. 1° Error vitiates consent when it relates to the nature of the juridical act, the object of the prestation or something that is essential to the determination of consent (art. 1400 C.C.Q.). **2°** A person whose consent is vitiated by fear can apply for annulment. If the error results from fraud, the person can also apply for a reduction of the obligation and claim damages (art. 1407 C.C.Q.). Such nullity is relative since its role is the protection of an individual interest (arts. 1419, 1420 C.C.Q.).
See also absolute error, consent[1,2], defect of consent, error constituting a defect of consent, error of fact, error of law, fear, fraud[1], lesion.
Fr. erreur.

ERROR AS TO A PRINCIPAL CONSIDERATION

Error affecting the cause[2].
Obs. The notion of *error as to a principal consideration*, to which art. 992 C.C.L.C. referred, is no longer explicitly alluded to in the Civil Code. However, the notion of *error on something that is essential to the determination of consent*, to which article 1400 C.C.Q. refers, would appear to include both error as to a principal consideration and error as to substance.
See also error as to substance.
Fr. erreur sur la considération principale.

ERROR AS TO (OF) FORM

Syn. clerical error.
Fr. erreur de forme, erreur matérielle[+].

ERROR AS TO SUBSTANCE

Error on that which is essential to the determination of consent. For example, an error as to the authenticity of a work of art in the sale of an original painting, error as to the age of an object in the sale of an antique.
Obs. The notion of *error as to substance*, to which art. 992 C.C.L.C. referred, is no longer used in the Civil Code. However, the notion of *error on something that is essential in the determination of consent*, to which article 1400 C.C.Q. refers, would appear to include both the identity of the object of the contract, the essential qualities of the cocontracting party or the object of the prestation.
See also error as to a principal consideration.
Fr. erreur sur la substance.

ERROR AS TO THE PERSON

Error as to the identity or qualities of the cocontracting party. "[...] where a party has been induced into marriage through externally applied physical or psychological force or where one party was in 'error as to the person', that party may seek the nullity of the marriage" (Brierley & Macdonald (eds.), *Quebec Civil Law*, n° 208, p. 237).
Occ. Former art. 148 C.C.L.C. (1866-1981).
Obs. Error as to the person formed part of the notion of *error as to a principal consideration* to which article 992 C.C.L.C. referred. The Civil Code does not expressly use the notion of *error as to principal consideration*. However, the notion of *error on something that is essential in the determination of consent*, to which article 1400 C.C.Q. refers, appears to include error as to a principal consideration and, therefore, error as to the person.
Fr. erreur sur la personne.

ERROR AS TO VALUE

Syn. economic error. "This kind of error produces what is called a lesion. [...] [L]esion is not a cause of nullity except in certain contracts [...] The error as to the value of the

thing is therefore only rarely a cause of nullity" (Planiol & Ripert, *Treatise*, vol. 2, n° 1055, p. 606).
Fr. erreur sur la valeur.

ERROR CONSTITUTING A DEFECT OF CONSENT

Error that, without precluding the meeting of the minds, compromises the integrity of the consent[2] of one the parties.
Obs. The distinction between absolute error, which leads to absolute nullity, and error constituting a defect of consent, which leads to relative nullity, is not made explicitly in the Civil Code.
See also absolute error.
Fr. erreur-vice du consentement.

ERROR OF FACT

Error relating to the existence or the consequences of a fact. For example, an error as to the authenticity of a work of art in the sale of an original painting. "No importance is attached to the origin of the error, because no material distinction is drawn between errors of fact and errors of law" (Brierley & Macdonald (eds.), *Quebec Civil Law*, n° 430, p. 404).
Occ. Art. 2852 C.C.Q.
See also error of law.
Fr. erreur de fait.

ERROR OF FORM

Syn. clerical error.
Fr. erreur de forme[+], erreur matérielle.

ERROR OF LAW

Error relating to the existence or the interpretation of a rule of law. "To argue error of law is not to attempt to escape the application of law but to show that one was mistaken as to the existence, nature or extent of the rights and obligations which were the principal cause of the contract" (Levasseur, *Conventional Obligations*, p. 37).
Occ. Art. 2634 C.C.Q.
Obs. Error of law can vitiate consent except in the case of transactions and judicial oaths (arts. 1400, 2634, 2852 C.C.Q.)
See also error of fact.
Fr. erreur de droit.

ESCALATOR CLAUSE

Syn. sliding scale clause.
Fr. clause d'échelle mobile[+], clause d'indexation, clause indexée.

ESSENTIAL FORMALITY

Formality required for the formation of a valid juridical act. For example, the drawing up of a hypothec in notarial form. "The law, art. 843 C.C.[L.C.], determines that certain essential formalities shall replace the signature of a person physically unable to sign" (*Gendron* v. *Duranleau* (1941), 71 B.R. 243, p. 249, J.C. Walsh, J.).
Obs. The accomplishment of essential formalities is a condition of the formation of solemn acts, such as marriage contracts, and real contracts, such as deposits (arts. 440, 713, 2280, 2693 C.C.Q.).
Syn. formality *ad solemnitatem*, solemn form, solemnity. **See also** evidentiary formality, real contract, solemn act.
Fr. formalité *ad solemnitatem*, formalité substantielle[+], forme solennelle, solennité.

EVENTUAL DAMAGE

Syn. possible damage.
Obs. Since the terms *damage* and *injury* are synonymous, the expression *eventual injury* may also be used.
Fr. préjudice éventuel[+], préjudice hypothétique.

EVENTUAL RIGHT

1. Present, yet imperfect, right that will become definitive upon the realization of a future but uncertain intrinsic element necessary to its perfection. For example, right of a substitute to property of a substitution while it is in the possession of the institute (art. 1235 C.C.Q.), the rights set forth in a marriage contract signed before the celebration. "[...] some of the central institutions for the transfer of wealth presuppose the gradual acquisition of the economic value of the right (or of the thing) prior to its definitive vesting (conditional, future and eventual rights)" (Macdonald, (1994) 39 *McGill L.J.* 761, p. 792).
Occ. Art. 1235 C.C.Q.; art. 956 C.C.L.C.
Obs. 1° An eventual right, when considered in the context of the gradual creation of a right, is an intermediate stage between a mere hope and a definitive right. **2°** An eventual right is patrimonial in nature. It is susceptible of legal protection and, as such, is a present right. Thus, the titulary thereof can, as a matter of principle, renounce or dispose of it, and perform all conservatory acts (e.g. art. 1235 C.C.Q.). **3°** An eventual right and a right subject to a suspensive condition, while sharing some characteristics (the occurrence

of a future and uncertain event), are nonetheless distinguishable in other respects. The eventual right depends, for its formation, upon the occurrence of an intrinsic event essential to its perfection (e.g. the death of the institute causing the opening of the substitution). On the other hand, a right subject to a suspensive condition is dependent on the occurrence of an extrinsic event unnecessary for its creation (e.g. the sale of a house if the vendor is appointed to a foreign posting). Once the condition is fulfilled, in the case of a right subject to a suspensive condition, its effects are retroactive, whereas in the case of an eventual right, its effects begin only from the moment the event rendering the right definitive happens.
See also conditional right, contingent right[2], definitive right, mere expectancy.
Fr. droit éventuel[1].

2. Right that is susceptible of coming into existence.
Syn. contingent right[1].
Fr. droit éventuel[2].

EVIDENTIARY FORM

Syn. evidentiary formality.
Fr. formalité *ad probationem*, formalité probatoire+, forme probante, forme probatoire.

EVIDENTIARY FORMALITY

Formality required for proof of a juridical act. For example, preparation of an agreement in writing for a contract the value of which exceeds an amount determined by law.
Obs. Evidentiary formalities facilitate the enforceability of juridical acts (arts. 2860 and 2862 C.C.Q.).
Syn. evidentiary form, formality *ad probationem*, probative form, probatory form, probatory formality. **See also** essential formality, formality *ad habilitatem*, formality as to publicity.
Fr. formalité *ad probationem*, formalité probatoire+, forme probante, forme probatoire.

EX BONA FIDE (Latin)

See good faith.
Fr. *ex bona fide.*

EXCEPTION OF NON-PERFORMANCE

Exception that permits one party to a bilateral contract to refrain from performing an obligation thereunder until the other party performs or offers to perform his or her own obligation. "Because a buyer's obligation to pay the price is the direct counterpart to a

seller's delivery obligation, a buyer can invoke the exception of non-performance (*exceptio non adimpleti contractus*) and withhold payment if a seller does not perform the corresponding delivery obligation" (Brierley & Macdonald (eds.), *Quebec Civil Law,* n° 591, pp. 526-527).
Occ. Title preceding art. 1591 C.C.Q.
Obs. 1° The absence of performance of the obligation must be substantial in order to give rise to the exception (art. 1591 C.C.Q.). **2°** The exception of non-performance may not be invoked by the creditor who is bound to perform first (art. 1591 C.C.Q.).
Syn. *exceptio non adimpleti contractus.* **See also** bilateral contract, non-performance.
Fr. exception d'inexécution+, *exceptio non adimpleti contractus.*

EXCEPTIO NON ADIMPLETI CONTRACTUS *nom.ph.* (Latin)

Syn. exception of non-performance. "The seller's right of retention and rights of dissolution are respectively illustrations of the *exceptio non adimpleti contractus* and right of dissolution [...] as adapted to the contract of sale" (Boodman, (1987) 47 *R. du B.* 871, p. 920).
Fr. exception d'inexécution+, *exceptio non adimpleti contractus.*

EXCHANGE *n.*

Contract by which the parties reciprocally transfer property other than a sum of money. "Exchange is not the same as a sale, because in sale there is one seller and one buyer, one thing and one price. In exchange, each of the things is at the same time the thing and the price, each of the parties is at the same time seller and buyer [...]" (Marler, *Real Property,* p. 340). *To give in exchange; to receive in exchange.*
Occ. Arts. 769, 885, 1795, 2367 C.C.Q.; art. 1596 C.C.L.C.
Obs. 1° The Civil Code presents exchange as one of a series of contracts similar to sale (title preceding art. 1795 C.C.Q.). As article 1795 C.C.Q. suggests, the archetype for this contract is the exchange of the rights of ownership, but there is no reason, in theory, why exchange could not bear on another real right. **2°** In the case of an exchange of property of unequal value, the parties may provide for the payment of a balance. **3°** The codal regime respecting exchange is set forth at articles 1795 to 1798 C.C.Q.
Syn. barter. **See also** giving in payment, sale.
Fr. contrat d'échange, échange+, troc.

EXCHANGE *v.*

To effect an exchange.
Syn. barter.
Fr. échanger+, troquer.

EXCLUSION (OF LIABILITY) CLAUSE

Clause by which the parties agree in advance to exclude the debtor's liability resulting from the non-performance of an obligation. "Ultimately, *faute lourde* also preserves the sanctity of freedom of contract even when invalidating exclusion clauses. By ensuring a minimum standard of performance and a minimum of good faith the plaintiff does not feel totally cheated of his 'bargain'" (Crothers, (1985) 26 *C. de D.* 881, p. 920).
Obs. 1° Exclusion clauses may not exonerate the debtor from liability arising from an intentional or gross fault, nor that which is relative to bodily or moral injuries (art. 1474 C.C.Q.). **2°** Exclusion clauses are without effect in matters relating to leases of dwellings and to consumer protection (art. 1900 C.C.Q.; s. 10, *Consumer Protection Act*, R.S.Q. c. P-40.1).
Syn. exemption clause, exoneration clause[2], no liability clause[2], stipulation of non-liability. **See also** exoneration clause[1], limitation of liability clause, non-performance, notice of exoneration of liability.
Fr. clause de non-responsabilité[2], clause d'exclusion de responsabilité+, clause d'exonération de responsabilité[2], clause exonératoire de responsabilité, clause exonératrice de responsabilité.

EXCLUSIVE FAULT

Fault that is the sole cause of damage.
See also causal fault, common fault, contributory fault.
Fr. faute exclusive.

EXCLUSIVE OFFER

Offer made only to the person or group of persons to whom it was addressed.
Obs. An exclusive offer is one made only to a specified person or group of persons. However, the Civil Code Revision Office proposed that an offer to a specified person is not necessarily exclusive (art. 14, Bk V, *Draft Civil Code*, C.C.R.O.).
See also non-exclusive offer.
Fr. offre exclusive.

EXCLUSIVITY CLAUSE

Clause whereby a party, by undertaking not to enter into agreements of the same nature with others, provides his or her cocontracting party with the sole benefit of a prestation.
Obs. 1° Exclusivity clauses may be found in many types of contracts, such as in supply, employment and franchise contracts, as well as in subcontracting. An exclusivity clause may, for example, oblige a distributor to buy his or her supplies from one supplier only (e.g. an exclusivity of supply contract between a gas station and an oil company) or oblige a supplier to provide goods and services to one distributor only (e.g. a concession contract between a car manufacturer and a car dealer). **2°** Exclusivity to the profit of the cocontracting party is often limited to a particular territory.
See also non-competition clause, restrictive covenant.
Fr. clause d'exclusivité.

EX CONTRACTU adv.ph. (Latin)

Of contractual origin.
See also *ex delicto, ex lege, quasi ex contractu, quasi ex delicto.*
Fr. *ex contractu.*

EX DELICTO adv.ph. (Latin)

Of delictual origin.
See also *ex contractu, ex lege, quasi ex contractu, quasi ex delicto.*
Fr. *ex delicto.*

EXECUTE *v.*

Syn. perform.
Occ. Arts. 752, 1712, 1827 C.C.Q.
Fr. exécuter.

EXECUTION *n.*

Syn. performance. "[...] an obligation with a term is not an obligation which has been suspended, but only one whose execution has been delayed" (Pound, (1970) 16 *McGill L.J.* 312, p. 316).
Occ. Arts. 803, 1327, 3073 C.C.Q.
Fr. exécution.

EXECUTORY *adj.*

Having an executory effect. For example, an executory title, an executory transaction.
Occ. Art. 1078 C.C.Q.; art. 442 C.C.L.C.; arts. 469.1, 543, 651 C.C.P.
Fr. exécutoire.

EXECUTORY EFFECT

Quality granted by law to certain juridical acts allowing for the use of public constraint to obtain the forced performance of an obligation that is partially or totally unexecuted.
Obs. In Quebec, only judicial decisions are endowed with executory effect because of the power to command (*imperium*) that they express. Unlike French law, in Quebec the notarial act is not endowed with executory effect.
See also binding force of contract, compulsory execution, specific performance.
Fr. force exécutoire.

EXEMPLARY DAMAGES

Syn. punitive damages. "Despite these various special features, an action for exemplary damages based on the second paragraph of s. 49 of the *Charter* cannot be dissociated from the principles of civil liability. [...] The necessary connection with the wrongful conduct that gives rise to civil liability leads one to associate the remedy of exemplary damages with the principles of civil liability" (*Béliveau St-Jacques* v. *Fédération des employés et employées de services publics inc. (CSN)*, [1996] 2 S.C.R. 345, p. 409, C.D Gonthier, J.).
Fr. dommages-intérêts exemplaires, dommages-intérêts punitifs+.

EXEMPT FROM SEIZURE

Syn. unseizable.
Occ. Arts. 1676, 2457, 2645, 2668 C.C.Q.
Fr. insaisissable.

EXEMPTION CLAUSE

Syn. exclusion (of liability) clause. "The exclusion of *faute lourde* [...] seems to be a residue of the original dislike of exemption clauses, based on the fear that the removal of the risk of liability would encourage negligence or recklessness" (Nicholas, *Contract*, p. 233).
Fr. clause de non-responsabilité[2], clause d'exclusion de responsabilité+, clause d'exonération de responsabilité[2], clause exonératoire de responsabilité, clause exonératrice de responsabilité.

EXEMPTION FROM SEIZURE

Syn. unseizability. "[...] the exemption from seizure protects [the owner] from the acts of his creditors, and removes the property given from the mass which is their common pledge, but does not prevent the owner from alienating it" (Marler, *Real Property*, p. 836).
Occ. Art. 553.1 C.C.P.
Fr. insaisissabilité.

EXERCISE OF AN OPTION

Declaration of intent by the beneficiary of an option to enter into the proposed contract.
Obs. 1° The exercise of an option constitutes the acceptance of a unilateral promise which creates either the proposed contract or a bilateral promise (art. 1396 C.C.Q.). **2°** The expression *taking up an option* is also encountered.
See also option.
Fr. levée d'option+, lever une option.

EXIGIBILITY *n.*

Quality of a debt[2] whose creditor is entitled to demand its performance. "Where the time of exigibility is not indicated in the title, the creditor may sue the debtor for payment immediately, unless, according to its nature, the obligation can be discharged only after the lapse of a certain period of time" (Aubry & Rau, *Civil Law*, vol. 4, n° 319, p. 1791).
Occ. S. 322, *An Act respecting Industrial Accidents and Occupational Diseases*, R.S.Q. c. A-3.001.
Obs. 1° A pure and simple obligation is exigible in character. **2°** A debt that falls due on a designated day becomes exigible the next day. **3°** When the debtor loses or renounces the benefit of a term, the debt becomes exigible (art. 1515 C.C.Q.). **4°** Only certain, liquid and exigible debts whose objects are a sum of money or fungible property identical in kind are susceptible of compensation (art. 1673 C.C.Q.).
See also debt fallen due, exigible claim, exigible debt, expiration, forfeiture of (the) term, pure and simple obligation.
Fr. exigibilité.

EXIGIBLE *adj.*

Said of a debt[2] whose creditor is entitled to demand performance.
Occ. Art. 1515 C.C.Q.; art. 2058 C.C.L.C.
Syn. demandable, payable (on demand). **See also** exigibility.
Fr. exigible.

EXIGIBLE CLAIM

Claim, the holder of which is entitled to demand its performance.

Syn. demandable claim, demandable creance, exigible creance. **See also** debt fallen due, exigibility, exigible debt.
Fr. créance exigible.

EXIGIBLE CREANCE

Syn. exigible claim.
Fr. créance exigible.

EXIGIBLE DEBT

Debt[1] whose creditor is entitled to demand performance.
Obs. Only certain, liquid and exigible debts whose objects are a sum of money or fungible property identical in kind are susceptible of compensation (art. 1673 C.C.Q.).
Syn. debt payable (on demand), demandable debt. **See also** debt fallen due, exigibility, exigible claim.
Fr. dette exigible.

EX LEGE adv.ph. (Latin)

Of legal origin. "Most expositors contented themselves with rather adapting and adjusting the Justinianic system [...] Some added a fifth category [...] ('obligationes ex lege') in order to accommodate, for instance, the actio ad exhibendum [...] which had always fallen between the four stools of Justinian's scheme" (Zimmerman, *Obligations*, p. 19). Ex lege *claim*; ex lege *share*.
See also *ex contractu, ex delicto, quasi ex contractu, quasi ex delicto*.
Fr. *ex lege*.

EXONERATE *v.*

To discharge a person from an obligation[3] that he or she is bound to perform.
Occ. Art. 801 C.C.L.C.
Fr. exonérer.

EXONERATION *n.*

Discharge of a person from an obligation[3] that he or she is bound to perform. "The lessor, by contrast, is liable for damages if the object leased is not fit for its purpose, whether or not he had knowledge of the defect at the time of the contract. The drafters have removed the grounds of exoneration formerly available to the lessor under the second paragraph of article 1606 C.C.L.C., thereby improving the lessee's prospects of obtaining damages" (Olivier, (1995) 40 *McGill L.J.* 187, p. 197).
Occ. Art. 1664.4 C.C.L.C.

Obs. The term *exoneration* can also describe that which results from such discharge.
See also exclusion clause.
Fr. exonération.

EXONERATION CLAUSE

1. Clause by which the parties agree in advance to exclude or limit the debtor's liability resulting from the non-performance of an obligation. "Although exoneration clauses are not by definition contrary to public morals, they do not afford protection against what the writers and the courts call 'dol' and 'faute lourde', or intentional or gross fault" (Haanapel, (1982) 60 *Can. Bar Rev.* 393, p. 400).
Obs. 1° Exoneration clauses may not exclude or limit liability arising from an intentional or gross fault, nor that which is relative to bodily or moral harm (art. 1474 C.C.Q.). **2°** This clause may apply to both contractual and extracontractual liability. **3°** Exoneration clauses are without effect in matters relating to leases of dwellings and to consumers (art. 1900 C.C.Q.; s. 10, *Consumer Protection Act*, R.S.Q. c. P-40.1). **4°** In its generic sense, the term includes both exclusion clauses and limitation of liability clauses.
Syn. exoneration of liability clause, no liability clause[1]. **See also** abusive clause, exclusion (of liability) clause, limitation of liability clause, non-performance, notice of exoneration of liability, withdrawal option.
Fr. clause de non-responsabilité[1], clause d'exonération de responsabilité[1+].

2. Syn. exclusion (of liability) clause. "Although exoneration clauses are not by definition contrary to public order and good morals, they do not afford protection against what the writers and the courts call 'dol' and 'faute lourde', or intentional or gross fault" (Haanappel, (1982) 60 *Can. Bar Rev.* 393, p. 400).
Fr. clause de non-responsabilité[2], clause d'exclusion de responsabilité[+], clause d'exonération de responsabilité[2], clause exonératoire de responsabilité, clause exonératrice de responsabilité.

EXONERATION OF LIABILITY CLAUSE

Syn. exoneration clause[1]. "Traditionally, the judiciary has likened *faute lourde* to *dol* as regards both exoneration and limitation of liability clauses. [...] The courts have again resorted to the technique of severance, thus removing exoneration of liability clauses from

contracts without otherwise disturbing the agreements" (Legrand, (1988) 62 *Tul. L. Rev.* 963, p. 1013).
Obs. See article 1664.4 C.C.L.C.
Fr. clause de non-responsabilité[1], clause d'exonération de responsabilité[1+].

EXPECTANCY *n.*

Syn. mere expectancy.
Fr. droit virtuel, expectative, simple expectative[+].

EXPECTATION *n.*

Syn. mere expectancy.
Fr. droit virtuel, expectative, simple expectative[+].

EXPENDITURE *n.*

1. Syn. expense[1].
Fr. déboursé[1], dépense[1+].

2. Syn. expense[2].
Fr. déboursé[2], dépense[2+].

EXPENSE *n.*

1. Outlay of money, in particular as it relates to an enterprise. "Besides the expenses necessary to convert into money the debtor's property, there are those incurred in the interest of the mass of the creditors, which include such as have served for the preservation of their common pledge, C.C.[L.C.] 1996" (Marler, *Real Property*, n° 760, p. 347).
Occ. Arts. 1487, 2107, 2599, 2652 C.C.Q.
Obs. The *disbursement*, an expense made in respect of existing property, is a particular kind of expense. In some cases where the term *expense* is used, only the context may help to determine if, precisely, a disbursement is made (e.g. arts. 2215, 2320 C.C.Q.).
Syn. expenditure[1]. **See also** payment[2].
Fr. déboursé[1], dépense[1+].

2. The sum of money used.
Occ. Arts. 1022, 2129 C.C.Q.
Syn. expenditure[2].
Fr. déboursé[2], dépense[2+].

EXPIRATION *n.*

Moment in time at which the term[1] occurs. *Expiration of a debt*; *expiration of the obligation.*
Occ. Art. 1090 C.C.L.C.
Syn. arrival of the term, expiration of the term, expiry of the term. **See also** debt fallen due, forfeiture of the term.

Fr. arrivée du terme, avènement du terme, échéance[+], échéance du terme.

EXPIRATION OF THE TERM

Syn. expiration. For example, date of a lease's expiration. "In a similar way, under article 1667 C.C.[L.C.], will tacit renewal operate in the case of personal services (provided, of course, they were not leased for a determinate undertaking), if the lessor continues to give his services beyond the expiration of the term originally fixed, without any opposition or notice on the part of the lessee" (*Stewart* v. *Hanover Fire Insurance*, [1936] S.C.R. 177, p. 184, T. Rinfret, J.).
See also forfeiture of the term.
Fr. arrivée du terme, avènement du terme, échéance[+], échéance du terme.

EXPIRE (TO) *v.*

To fall due. *The term expired on March 15th.*
See also accrued interest, accrue interest (to).
Fr. échoir.

EXPIRED DEBT

Syn. debt fallen due.
Fr. dette échue.

EXPIRY OF THE TERM

Syn. expiration.
Occ. Arts. 1114, 1296, 1517, 2090 C.C.Q.
Fr. arrivée du terme, avènement du terme, échéance[+], échéance du terme.

EXPLICIT CONSENT

Syn. express consent.
Fr. consentement explicite, consentement exprès[+], manifestation de volonté expresse.

EXPLOITATION *n.*

Behaviour of one who takes unfair advantage of the weakness of another. "It will be noted that section 8 of the Quebec Act [*Consumer Protection Act*] appears to give two separate grounds of relief. The courts may grant relief, it appears, either where there is 'exploitation of the consumer' or where the obligation of the consumer is 'excessive, harsh or unconscionable'" (Waddams, in *Meredith Lectures (1979)*, 63, p. 65).
Occ. Art. 1406 C.C.Q.; s. 48, *Charter of Human Rights and Freedoms*, R.S.Q. c. C-12; s. 8, *Consumer Protection Act*, R.S.Q. c. P-40.1.

Obs. 1° Exploitation can be of a physical, psychological, social or moral nature (*Commission des droits de la personne du Québec* v. *Brzozowski*, [1994] R.J.Q. 1447, p. 1471 (Q.H.R.T.), M. Rivet, J.). **2**° Section 48 of the *Charter of Human Rights and Freedoms* states that "every aged person and every handicapped person has a right to protection against any form of exploitation". **3**° In contractual matters, exploitation of one of the parties resulting from a significant disproportion between their prestations constitutes mixed lesion. This represents one of the exceptional circumstances in which lesion entails the nullity of the contract (arts. 1405, 1406 C.C.Q.; s. 8, *Consumer Protection Act*, R.S.Q. c. P-40.1).
See also lesion, mixed lesion.
Fr. exploitation.

EXPRESS ACCEPTANCE

Acceptance[1] resulting from an explicit manifestation of intent. "In certain cases the law requires express acceptance communicated to the offeror. This is the case as to gifts" (Schlesinger, *Formation of Contracts*, p. 1314).
Occ. Art. 650 C.C.L.C.
See also acceptance[1], tacit acceptance.
Fr. acceptation expresse.

EXPRESS CLAUSE OF RESOLUTION

Syn. resolutory clause of right.
Fr. clause de résolution de plein droit, clause expresse de résolution, clause résolutoire de plein droit[+], clause résolutoire expresse, pacte commissoire.

EXPRESS CONSENT

Consent made known by conduct which clearly manifests the will to effect a juridical act.
Occ. Art. 338 C.C.Q.
Obs. Express consent may be communicated by means of an action (written, spoken or gesticular) intended to convey it to another.
Syn. explicit consent, express manifestation of intent, express manifestation of will. **See also** tacit consent.
Fr. consentement explicite, consentement exprès[+], manifestation de volonté expresse.

EXPRESS MANDATE

1. Mandate[1] in which the nature of the acts authorized is specified.
Obs. 1° The express mandate may be general or special, depending on whether it relates to all the affairs of the mandator or to a particular one. **2**° According to article 2135 C.C.Q., only an express mandate can confer upon the mandatary the power to perform acts of full administration, such as alienation by onerous title or granting of a hypothec. **3**° The *express mandate* is opposed to the *mandate expressed in general terms*.
See also general mandate, mandate expressed in general terms, special mandate.
Fr. mandat exprès[1].

2. Mandate[1] entered into explicitly, whether in written or oral form.
Occ. Art. 1043 C.C.L.C.
Obs. *Express mandate*[2] is opposed to *tacit mandate*.
Fr. mandat exprès[2].

EXPRESS MANIFESTATION OF INTENT

Syn. express consent.
Fr. consentement explicite, consentement exprès[+], manifestation de volonté expresse.

EXPRESS MANIFESTATION OF WILL

Syn. express consent.
Fr. consentement explicite, consentement exprès[+], manifestation de volonté expresse.

EXPRESS NULLITY

Syn. textual nullity.
Fr. nullité expresse, nullité textuelle[+].

EXPRESS OBLIGATION

Obligation that results from an explicit manifestation of intention.
Obs. 1° The explicit manifestation of intention that creates the express obligation may originate in a juridical act or in a legislative provision. **2**° The express obligation need not be in writing. It may arise through an oral agreement or by the effect of unspoken behaviour of the debtor and creditor. **3**° The expression *express obligation* is generally used to distinguish this kind of obligation from implicit obligations.
See also consensualism, declaration of will, formalism, implicit obligation.
Fr. obligation expresse.

EXPRESS OFFER

Offer resulting from an explicit manifestation of intent.
Obs. 1° In matters relating to consumer protection, the offer relative to a contract that

must be evinced in writing does not bind the consumer until it has been recorded in the contract (s. 24, *Consumer Protection Act*, R.S.Q. c. P-40.1). **2°** Some scholars limit the notion of *express offer* to that which is made known in written or verbal form.
See also implied offer.
Fr. offre expresse.

EXPRESS RELEASE

Release[1] resulting from an explicit manifestation of intent.
Occ. Arts. 1690, 1692 C.C.Q.
Obs. Art. 1688 C.C.Q. states that release may be express or tacit.
Fr. remise expresse.

EXPRESS RESOLUTORY CLAUSE

Syn. resolutory clause of right. "The rescinding *ab initio* of a contract for fraud has no doubt the same effect as would the rescinding of a contract under an express resolutory clause in the case provided for by article 1088 C.C.[L.C.]" (*Angers* v. *Mutual Reserve Fund Assn.* (1904), 35 S.C.R. 330, p. 339, H.E. Taschereau, C.J.).
Fr. clause de résolution de plein droit, clause expresse de résolution, clause résolutoire de plein droit[+], clause résolutoire expresse, pacte commissoire.

EXTEND *v.*

To effect prorogation.
Occ. Art. 2439 C.C.Q.
Syn. prorogue.
Fr. prolonger, proroger[+].

EXTENSION *n.*

1. Syn. prorogation[1].
Occ. Art. 2645 C.C.L.C.
Fr. prolongation[1], prorogation[1+].

2. Syn. prorogation[2].
Occ. Art. 1658.1 C.C.L.C.
Fr. prolongation[2], prorogation[2+].

EXTERNAL CAUSE

Event that is not imputable to the debtor of the non-performed obligation or to the author of the damage. "The maxim *contra non valentem agere*, on which the notion of *impossibility to act* is based, is thus distinct from superior force, which is a purely external cause that can be assessed objectively, and requires a subjective assessment of the impossibility to act based on the circum-

stances of the victim of the fault that caused it" (*Gauthier* v. *Brome Lake (Town)*, [1998] 2 S.C.R. 3, p. 46, C.D. Gonthier, J.).
Occ. Art. 1470 C.C.Q.
Obs. 1° In the Civil Code, "[a] superior force is an unforeseeable and irresistible event, including external causes with the same characteristics" (art. 1470 C.C.Q.). **2°** Three types of external causes are recognized: the fault of the victim, the act or omission of a third person and superior force[2].
See also imputability[2], superior force[1].
Fr. cause étrangère.

EXTERNAL CLAUSE

Clause, the text of which is not found in a written contract but which is nevertheless incorporated therein by way of a reference to it made within the contract.
Occ. Art. 1435 C.C.Q.
Obs. 1° An external clause in a consumer contract or contract of adhesion is null unless its existence was known by the consumer or the adhering party (art. 1435 C.C.Q.). **2°** The expression *incorporated by reference* is often used to describe the technique by which an external clause becomes part of the contract.
Fr. clause externe.

EXTERNALITY *n.*

Characteristic of an event that does not fall within the normal scope of activities of the debtor of the obligation who is at fault.
Obs. 1° Even though it is not mentioned at article 1470 C.C.Q., externality is sometimes listed, along with unforeseeability and irresistibility, as an element used to determine whether or not an event can be considered as a case of superior force with respect to the law of civil liability. For example, from this perspective, a strike, a failure of the equipment, or an automobile accident resulting from the state of health of the driver (s. 108, *Automobile Insurance Act*, R.S.Q. c. A-25), are not considered as external events. **2°** Superior force is a cause of extinction of obligations and of exemption from civil liability (arts. 1470, 1693 C.C.Q.).
See also damage, irresistibility, *novus actus interveniens*, superior force[1], unforeseeability[1].
Fr. extériorité.

EXTERNALIZED WILL

Syn. declared will.
Fr. volonté déclarée[+], volonté externe.

EXTINCTION *n.*

Termination of a real or personal right on one of the grounds provided for by law. For example, a usufruct is extinguished upon the death of the usufructuary (art. 1162 C.C.Q.), an obligation is extinguished by payment (art. 1671 C.C.Q.). "The mode of extinction of an obligation is as intimate a part of that obligation as is the mode of its creation; as much as the latter, the former must be contemplated, if at all possible, when an obligation is engendered" (Levasseur, *Obligations*, p. 171). *Mode of extinction.*
Occ. Title preceding arts. 1162, 1671 C.C.Q.; arts. 1168, 1671, 1937, 2385, 2797, 2939 C.C.Q.
Obs. 1° The principal causes of extinction of obligations are payment, novation, compensation, confusion, discharge, release, expiry of an extinctive term, impossibility of performance and extinctive prescription (art. 1671 C.C.Q.). **2°** Unlike other limited real rights, ownership is not extinguished by non-usage.
Syn. termination.
Fr. extinction.

EXTINCTIVE EFFECT

Effect of that which terminates a right. "Given the extinctive effect of novation, courts have shown reluctance to find tacit novation, an attitude also reflected in the codal rule that a mere indication of payment does not operate novation (art. 1174 [art. 1667 C.C.Q.])" (Brierley & Macdonald (eds.), *Quebec Civil Law*, n° 557, p. 503).
Obs. The possibility that a contract might have an extinctive effect is expressly provided for at art. 1433 C.C.Q. This article is in apparent contradiction with the definition of the contract (art. 1378 C.C.Q.) which, by characterizing the contract as a mere instrument for the creation of obligations, excludes from its scope numerous contracts, including those with an extinctive effect.
See also constitutive effect, declarative effect, extinction, renunciatory effect, translatory effect.
Fr. effet extinctif.

EXTINCTIVE TERM

Term[1] upon which depends the extinction of a right or obligation[2]. "An extinctive term is one which, when it occurs, extinguishes an existing obligation. Once the event selected as the term occurs, the obligation which existed until then ceases to exist *ex nunc*,

from then on. It is common, for example, for a lease to terminate after one year; thereafter, the lessor cannot demand payment of the rent since the lessee's obligation to pay has been terminated" (Levasseur, *Obligations*, p. 36).
Occ. Art. 1671 C.C.Q.
Obs. 1° The duration of an extinctive term is fixed by law or by the parties (art. 1517 C.C.Q.). **2°** An extinctive term, in contrast to a resolutory condition, has no retroactive effect.
See also resolutory condition, suspensive term.
Fr. terme extinctif.

EXTRACONTRACTUAL *adj.*

Resulting from a source other than a contract or from that which is unrelated to a contract. *In extracontractual matters.*
Obs. This term is also written *extra-contractual.*
Syn. legal[5]. **See also** contractual, delictual, legal[4], quasi-contractual, quasi-delictual.
Fr. extracontractuel+, légal[4].

EXTRACONTRACTUAL DAMAGES

Damages granted as compensation for harm resulting from non-performance, without justification, of an extracontractual obligation.
Obs. 1° Damages that may be claimed in extracontractual matters are generally assessed using the same criteria used in contractual matters, except for the criterion of the foreseeability of the harm which is only imposed in contractual matters. **2°** A distinction is drawn between *extracontractual damages* and *contractual damages.*
See also contractual damages[2], extracontractual liability.
Fr. dommages-intérêts extracontractuels.

EXTRACONTRACTUAL FAULT

Civil fault resulting from the unjustified non-performance of a duty originating in a source other than a contract. "[...] civil responsibility rests essentially on the violation of a juridical obligation, be it contractual or legal [...] Such was not, however, the accepted view among the nineteenth century French writers who insisted on trying to establish that there was a difference in kind between contractual and extracontractual fault" (Crépeau, in *Essays on the Civil Law*, 83, p. 87).
Obs. 1° Article 1457 C.C.Q. establishes a general duty upon every person to abide by

the rules of conduct that lie upon him or her, "according to the circumstances, usage or law", so as not to cause injury to another. **2°** Extracontractual fault is, in principle, evaluated *in abstracto*, that is from a purely objective point of view, by comparing the conduct of the person with that of a reasonable person placed in similar circumstances. **3°** Extracontractual fault may, in certain cases, be proven on the basis of legal presumptions (e.g. art. 1465 C.C.Q.). **4°** A distinction is made between *extracontractual fault* and *contractual fault*. However, non-performance of a contractual obligation that causes damage to a third party is considered an extracontractual fault.

See also abuse of right(s), contractual fault, delict, delictual fault, discernment, extracontractual liability, extracontractual obligation, imprudence, legal presumption, negligence, neighbourhood disturbance, quasi-delict, quasi-delictual fault, reasonable person, strict liability, superior force[1], unforeseeability[1].

Fr. faute extracontractuelle.

EXTRACONTRACTUAL LIABILITY

Civil liability based on a source other than contract.

Obs. 1° The Civil Code sets out certain legal presumptions of extracontractual liability (arts. 1463, 1466 C.C.Q.). **2°** The unjustified violation of any contractual obligation, whether expressly stated in the contract or implicit therein, gives rise to contractual liability. However, non-performance of a contractual obligation that causes damage to a third party is considered an extracontractual fault.

See also contractual liability, cumulation (of regimes), delictual liability, extracontractual obligation, legal liability[2], management of the business of another, option (between regimes), quasi-contractual liability, quasi-delictual liability, reception of a thing not due, unjust enrichment.

Fr. responsabilité extracontractuelle.

EXTRACONTRACTUAL OBLIGATION

Obligation[2] arising from a source other than contract.

Obs. Scholars traditionally view the expressions *extracontractual obligation* and *legal obligation* as synonymous.

Syn. non-consensual obligation. **See also** contractual obligation, legal obligation[1], extracontractual liability.

Fr. obligation extracontractuelle.

EXTRAJUDICIAL DAMAGES

Damages determined by a means other than by a judgment.

Obs. 1° Extrajudicial damages are determined by law or by agreement of the parties. **2°** A distinction is drawn between *extrajudicial damages* and *judicial damages*.

See also contractual damages[2], judicial damages, legal damages, penal clause.

Fr. dommages-intérêts extrajudiciaires.

EXTRAPATRIMONIAL *adj.*

See extrapatrimonial right.

Fr. extrapatrimonial.

EXTRAPATRIMONIAL RIGHT

Right that, because of its close association with the person who enjoys it, is not part of his or her patrimony. For example, the right to alimentary support, the right to vote, personality rights.

Obs. 1° Because they are imagined as the antithesis of property or patrimonial rights, extrapatrimonial rights are often defined as rights that are not susceptible of pecuniary evaluation. However, certain rights that are measured in financial terms are qualified as extrapatrimonial, such as the right to alimentary support. **2°** Extrapatrimonial rights are, in principle, inalienable, intransmissable, unseizable and imprescriptible, as they are not a part of the patrimony of a person. **3°** Some rights that do not have an inherent financial value because of their object are, in certain respects, susceptible of pecuniary evaluation. Personality rights are an example of this, since their infringement can give rise to compensable patrimonial loss and because this infringement may be waived or be consented to in the context of a contract. These rights remain extrapatrimonial as it is only the right to compensation for their infringement that becomes, as a claim, part of the patrimony. **4°** The *patrimonial right* is opposed to the *extrapatrimonial right*.

See also fundamental right, object not in commerce, patrimonial right.

Fr. droit extrapatrimonial.

F

FACT *n.*

Occurrence of whatever nature. For example, a natural phenomenon, an accident, an action, an abstention.

Obs. 1° Material fact[1] and juridical fact[2] are distinguished according to whether or not the fact is viewed independently of its juridical consequences. **2°** The French-language term *fait* has a wider application. For example, it is used in the law of civil liability to include both acts and omissions.

See also act[1], error of fact, juridical fact[1,2].

Fr. fait(>).

FACTUAL INCAPACITY

Syn. *de facto* incapacity.

Fr. inaptitude, incapacité[2], incapacité de fait[+], incapacité naturelle.

FACULTATIVE *adj.*

Syn. potestative.

Occ. Art. 2196 C.C.L.C.

Fr. facultatif, potestatif[+].

FACULTATIVE CONDITION

Syn. potestative condition.

Obs. 1° As a result of the use of the French expression *condition purement facultative* at article 1081 C.C.L.C., the adjective *facultative* was commonly preferred to *potestative* in Quebec Civil law. The expression *potestative condition* may be preferred to that of *facultative condition* in order to avoid confusion with *facultative obligation*, i.e. an obligation comprising a single prestation from which the debtor may be freed by performing another prestation.

Fr. condition facultative, condition potestative[+].

FACULTATIVE OBLIGATION

Obligation[2] comprising a single prestation from which the debtor may be freed by performing another prestation. For example, a testator bequeathing a house by particular title, while giving the heirs the power to free themselves of this obligation by paying a sum of money to the particular legatee. "The additional object, by means of which the debtor of the facultative obligation is entitled to a discharge cannot be considered as comprised in the obligation of which it is an adjunct merely for the purpose of facilitating payment" (Aubry & Rau, *Civil Law*, vol. 4, n° 300, p. 47).

Occ. Art. 1552 C.C.Q.

Obs. In the event that the debtor is prevented from performing his or her prestation as a result of a superior force, the obligation is extinguished, the debtor is released from the obligation and he or she is not obliged to perform the other prestation.

See also alternative obligation, conjunctive obligation, obligation with a complex modality.

Fr. obligation facultative.

FAIL *v.*

To be unfulfilled, with respect to a condition[1]. *The condition fails or is realized.*

Occ. Arts. 1501, 1514 C.C.Q.; art. 1082 C.C.L.C.

See also failed condition.

Fr. défaillir.

FAILED CONDITION

Condition[1] that has not been fulfilled and that is certain never to be fulfilled.

Obs. See article 1082 C.C.L.C.

See also failure of the condition, fulfilled condition, pending condition, retroactivity of the condition.

Fr. condition défaillie.

FAILURE OF THE CONDITION

State of a condition[1] that has not been fulfilled and that is certain never to be fulfilled. "[...] the condition is considered to have failed once it is certain that the event will not occur. The impact of the failure of the condition differs with the type of condition involved" (Levasseur, *Obligations*, p. 81).

Occ. Art. 910 C.C.L.C.

Obs. 1° Upon failure of a suspensive condition, the obligation is deemed never to have

existed and, by extension, the contract is treated as never having existed. Upon failure of the resolutory condition, however, the condition alone disappears, leaving only the obligation, which is deemed to have existed purely and simply from the day the contract was formed. **2°** Where the failure of the condition is attributable to the conduct of one of the parties, it is common to speak of a *breach of condition*.
See also forfeiture of (the) term, fulfilment of the condition, retroactivity of the condition.
Fr. défaillance de la condition.

FAIR *adj.*

Syn. equitable[2].
Occ. Arts. 650, 815.4 C.C.P.
Fr. équitable[2](<).

FAIR DEALING

Syn. good faith[1].
Fr. bonne foi[1].

FAIT DU PRINCE (French)

Syn. act of state. "The French jurisprudence offers innumerable instances where measures taken by the authorities, acting in the name of the State, were held to constitute 'le fait du prince', akin to *force majeure*, exonerating the debtor for inexecution of his contractual obligation" (Wasserman, (1952) 12 *R. du B.* 366, p. 382).
Fr. fait du prince.

FALSE *adj.*

See false cause.
Fr. faux.

FALSE CAUSE

Mistaken belief in the existence of a cause[1].
See also illicit cause, immoral cause.
Fr. cause fausse, fausse cause[+].

FAULT *n.*

1. Transgression of an obligatory juridical rule of conduct. "It should be understood that fault, in the civil-law meaning of the term, does not necessarily mean negligence, absence of reasonable care, or conduct not up to the standard of a 'bon père de famille'. It means simply any breach of *one's* duty, whatever the duty may be" (Crépeau, (1962) 40 *Can. Bar Rev.* 222, p. 223). *To commit a fault.*

Obs. 1° This notion of *fault* may, in certain of its manifestations, coincide with the notion of *moral fault*. Unlike the latter, however, a fault may bring about state-controlled sanctions. **2°** Conduct that may be perceived as wrongful at first blush will not always constitute a fault. There may be legitimate reasons preventing such conduct from being considered wrongful in given circumstances (e.g. superior force; the lack of discernment of the wrongdoer; the legitimate exercise of a concurrent right, such as the exercise of freedom of expression with respect to the right to privacy). **3°** The notion of *fault* comprises civil and penal fault, which are themselves distinct concepts. Civil fault is relevant to the determination of civil liability in a dispute between private law actors. Conversely, penal fault is relevant to the determination of the guilt or innocence of a person in connection with criminal proceedings opposing an individual and the State. **4°** From the Latin *fallere*: to deceive, to disappoint.
Syn. wrong[1]. **See also** civil fault, civil liability, duty, imputability[1,2], legal rule[1,2], obligation[1,2].
Fr. faute[1+], tort[1].

2. Syn. civil fault. "A fault may broadly be defined as a violation of one's pre-existing duty whether it be one voluntary assumed by contract (contractual obligation) or one imposed by law (legal or extracontractual obligation). Fault is, generally speaking, a necessary and essential ingredient of civil responsibility under the civil law of Quebec" (Crépeau, (1962) 40 *Can. Bar Rev.* 222, p. 223). *To be at fault.*
Occ. Arts. 164, 408, 1459, 1460, 1527, 1862, 2115, C.C.Q.; arts. 1053, 1054, 1072, 1087(4), 2390 C.C.L.C.
Fr. faute[2], faute civile[+].

FAULT IN THE EDUCATION

Civil fault in the moral, intellectual or social formation that a person is bound to impart to another.
Obs. See articles 1459 *et seq.* C.C.Q.
See also custodial fault, fault of supervision, liability for damage caused by another.
Fr. faute dans l'éducation.

FAULT OF COMMISSION

Civil fault consisting of doing that which one is obliged not to do.
Syn. *culpa in committendo, culpa in faciendo.*
See also fault of omission.
Fr. *culpa in committendo, culpa in faciendo,* faute d'action, faute de commission[+].

FAULT OF IMPRUDENCE

Syn. imprudence.
Fr. faute d'imprudence, imprudence[+].

FAULT OF NEGLIGENCE

Syn. negligence.
Fr. faute de négligence, négligence[+].

FAULT OF OMISSION

Civil fault consisting of not doing that which one is obliged to do. "Quebec civil law recognizes faults of omission whenever the fault is the failure to fulfill a duty owed, regardless of whether the duty arises from express statutory text, or simply is the duty to see to the security of others" (Rodgers Magnet, (1980) 40 *R. du B.* 373, p. 392).
Obs. 1° Scholars distinguish between an omission in action and a pure and simple omission. In the former case, the omission is within the scope of a given activity and is thus itself susceptible of being characterized as part of a positive act (e.g. the act of a cyclist speeding down a steep slope not to brake upon approaching an intersection). In the case of a pure and simple omission, the abstention is not linked to an activity and must be connected to a pre-existing duty to act in order to generate liability (e.g. the act of a passerby, able to save a drowning person, in refraining from throwing the latter a line). **2°** The violation of section 2 of the *Charter of Human Rights and Freedoms* (R.S.Q. c. C-12), which imposes an obligation to assist a "human being whose life is in peril", may constitute a fault of omission.
Syn. *culpa in non faciendo, culpa in omittendo*. **See also** fault of commission, negligence.
Fr. *culpa in non faciendo, culpa in omittendo*, faute d'abstention, faute d'omission[+].

FAULT OF SUPERVISION

Civil fault consisting in the non-performance of the obligation to supervise a person or a thing of which one has custody.
Obs. See articles 1459 *et seq.*, 1465 *et seq.* C.C.Q.
See also custodial fault, fault in the education, liability for damage caused by another, liability for damage caused by things.
Fr. faute dans la surveillance.

FAULT OF THE VICTIM

Fault committed by a person that causes, in whole or in part, the damage claimed by that person.

Occ. Ss. 108(1), 109, *Automobile Insurance Act*, R.S.Q. c. A-25.
Obs. The impact of the fault of the victim on civil liability varies according to the circumstances in which that fault occurs. When it occurs alone or in conjunction with a superior force, there is no civil liability, and the victim alone sustains the financial consequences. When it occurs together with the fault of another, civil liability is shared (art. 1478 C.C.Q.).
See also common fault, contributory fault.
Fr. faute de la victime.

FEAR *n.*

Feeling of apprehension which impels a person to enter into a juridical act. "Where the act of a contracting party or even of a third person engenders such fear in a co-contractant that there is only forced consent, a contract may be annulled" (Brierley & Macdonald (eds.), *Quebec Civil Law*, n° 432, p. 405).
Occ. Arts. 1399, 1402, 1403, 1404, 1407 C.C.Q.
Obs. 1° Fear can result from violence, threats, the abusive exercise of a right or power or the threat of such exercise (arts. 1402, 1403 C.C.Q.). **2°** Fear vitiates consent when it is induced by the other contracting party or is induced with his or her knowledge, and when the prejudice apprehended is serious. **3°** A person whose consent is vitiated by fear can apply for annulment or for a reduction of the obligation and claim damages (art. 1407 C.C.Q.). The nullity is relative since its role is the protection of an individual interest (art. 1419 C.C.Q.).
See also abuse of right(s), defect of consent, reverential fear, state of necessity[2], threat, violence.
Fr. crainte.

FEIGNED TRADITION

Syn. fictitious tradition.
Fr. tradition feinte[+], tradition fictive.

FICTITIOUS *adj.*

See fictitious act, fictitious contract, fictitious tradition.
Fr. fictif.

FICTITIOUS ACT

Apparent act intended to induce belief in the existence of an agreement the effects of which have in fact been destroyed by a counter letter between the parties. For example, in order to

avoid a seizure, a debtor pretends to sell his property to a third party but declares in a counter letter that he or she remains the owner. "The motive of simulation is [...] deception. The parties wish to expose a fictitious act to public view" (Lemann, (1954) 29 *Tul. L. Rev.* 22, p. 22).
Obs. A fictitious act is one of the forms by which simulation may arise.
See also concealed act, counter letter, interposition of persons, simulation.
Fr. acte fictif.

FICTITIOUS CONTRACT

Contract that constitutes the fictitious act in a simulation.
See also contract of *prête-nom*, counter letter, simulated contract, simulation.
Fr. contrat fictif.

FICTITIOUS TRADITION

Tradition carried out by the sole consent of the parties without dispossession by the person alienating.
Syn. feigned tradition. **See also** actual tradition, symbolic tradition, tradition by interversion of title.
Fr. tradition feinte[+], tradition fictive.

FINAL CAUSE

Syn. cause[1].
Fr. cause[1+], cause abstraite, cause de l'obligation, cause finale, cause objective, considération[1].

FINANCE LEASE

Syn. leasing.
Fr. contrat de crédit-bail, crédit-bail[+].

FINANCIAL LEASE

Syn. leasing. "It is the essence of a contract of lease that the lessor is the owner of the asset leased. However, in a financial lease the lessor retains only naked ownership and passes on to the lessee all other attributes thereof as well as all duties and obligations normally associated with ownership" (Smyth, in *Meredith Lectures (1981)*, 23, p. 29).
Fr. contrat de crédit bail, crédit-bail[+].

FINANCIAL LEASING

Syn. leasing.
Occ. Ss. 417, 464(1), *Bank Act*, S.C. 1991, c. 46.
Fr. contrat de crédit-bail, crédit-bail[+].

FIRST REFUSAL AGREEMENT

Agreement whereby a person undertakes to another that should the former enter into a particular contract, he or she will offer to enter into such contract with the latter first.
Occ. Arts. 1397, 2679 C.C.Q.
Obs. 1° While a first refusal agreement is necessarily established by contract, the right of preemption may also be provided by law. **2°** A contract entered into with a third party that is in violation of the first refusal agreement may be set up against the beneficiary of the latter. The beneficiary may not ask for the nullity of the contract; however, he or she could seek damages from the cocontracting party and the third party in bad faith (art. 1397 C.C.Q.). Nevertheless, in anticipatory breach of the first refusal agreement, the beneficiary may demand an injunction. **3°** A right to purchase land under a first refusal agreement does not, in principle, constitute a servitude even if the parties designate it as such in the agreement. Most experts are of the view that, unlike a servitude, the first refusal agreement does not represent an advantage to the land (art. 1177 C.C.Q.).
Syn promise of first option. **See also** approval clause, preemption clause, right of preemption, right of preference[1].
Fr. pacte de préférence[+], promesse d'offre préalable.

FIRST REFUSAL CLAUSE

See first refusal agreement.
Fr. clause de premier refus.

FIXED PRICE

Sum of money determined in advance.
Occ. Art. 2109 C.C.Q.; arts. 1690, 1691 C.C.L.C.
Obs. A fixed price may result either from the will of the parties (e.g. sums established in a penal clause), or from a schedule of payments established by public authorities (e.g. *Automobile Insurance Act*, R.S.Q. c. A-25).
See also fixed price contract, penal clause[1], predetermined reparation.
Fr. forfait.

FIXED PRICE CONTRACT

Contract in which one party undertakes to provide a prestation for a global price that is predetermined and invariable.
Obs. 1° The term is often used in construction contracts and in sub-contracting. **2°** The parties to a fixed price contract may not claim an increase or a reduction of the price, even

where the work or service required more or less effort or cost more or less than had been foreseen (art. 2109 C.C.Q.).
Syn. lump-sum contract.
Fr. contrat à forfait[+], marché à forfait.

FIXED TERM

Syn. certain term.
Fr. terme certain[+], terme connu.

FORCED REPOSSESSION

Repossession ordered by a court. "With every payment, the buyer's interest evolves into something closer to ownership, and the potential prejudice from a forced repossession becomes correspondingly greater" (Bridge *et al.*, (1999) 44 *McGill L.J.* 567, p. 591).
Occ. Ss. 141, 146, *Consumer Protection Act*, R.S.Q. c. P-40.1.
Fr. reprise forcée.

FORCED REPRESENTATION

Representation in which the representative's power is based on a source other than the will of the person represented. For example, tutorship granted by a court.
Obs. *Forced representation* is to be contrasted with *voluntary representation*.
See also judicial representation, legal representation.
Fr. représentation forcée.

FORCED RESILIATION

Resiliation brought about by operation of law.
Obs. 1° In exceptional cases, the law provides that a contract will be resiliated upon the death of one of the parties. This is the case for contracts *intuitu personæ* (e.g. contracts for services (art. 2128 C.C.Q.), contracts of partnership (art. 2259 C.C.Q.) and contracts of mandate (art. 2175 C.C.Q.)). **2°** The law also provides that expropriation terminates a lease (art. 1888 C.C.Q.).
See also voluntary resiliation.
Fr. résiliation forcée.

FORCE MAJEURE nom.ph. (French)

1. Syn. superior force[1]. "[...] the impossibility to execute a synallagmatic contract due to *force majeure*, puts an end to the correlative obligation [...]" (Kouri, (1971) 2 *R.D.U.S.* 1, p. 38).
Fr. force majeure[1].

2. Syn. superior force[2].
Fr. force majeure[2].

FORESEEABILITY *n.*

Characteristic of an event that a prudent and diligent person would normally have been able to anticipate.
See also foreseeable damage, foreseen damage, unforeseeability[1,2].
Fr. prévisibilité.

FORESEEABLE *adj.*

See foreseeable damage.
Fr. prévisible.

FORESEEABLE DAMAGE

Damage that a prudent and diligent debtor would normally have been able to anticipate as a result of the non-performance of his or her obligation.
Obs. Since the terms *damage* and *injury* are synonymous, the expression *foreseeable injury* may also be used.
See also foreseen damage, non-performance, unforeseeable damage, unforeseen damage.
Fr. préjudice prévisible.

FORESEEN DAMAGE

Damage anticipated by the debtor in the event of the non-performance of an obligation.
Obs. Since the terms *damage* and *injury* are synonymous, the expression *foreseen injury* may also be used.
See also foreseeable damage, non-performance, unforeseeable damage, unforeseen damage.
Fr. préjudice prévu.

FORFEIT CLAUSE

Syn. withdrawal clause. "[...] in opposition to a penal clause, a *dédit* or forfeit clause enables the debtor to free himself from his primary obligation by paying the stated liquidated damages" (Sheppard, (1963) 23 *R. du B.* 311, p. 350).
Fr. clause de dédit[+], stipulation de dédit.

FORFEITURE *n.*

Sanction consisting in the loss of a right. "These different causes of forfeiture entitle the creditor to pursue the debtor by all the legal means his title permits him to employ" (Aubry & Rau, *Civil Law*, vol. 1, n° 303, p. 90). *Under pain of forfeiture; on pain of forfeiture.*
Occ. Arts. 967, 1516, 1635, 2472 C.C.Q.; art. 1202*l* C.C.L.C.
Fr. déchéance.

FORFEITURE OF (THE) TERM

Loss, by way of sanction, of the benefit of a suspensive term granted to the debtor. For example, forfeiture of the term due to insolvency or bankruptcy of the debtor. "There is forfeiture of the term when the debtor is deprived of it contrary to his will. There is such forfeiture only where the term is for the benefit of the debtor; it does not exist against the creditor" (Planiol & Ripert, *Treatise*, vol. 2, n° 362, p. 211).

Obs. 1° Forfeiture of term renders the obligation immediately exigible (art. 1515 C.C.Q.). **2°** Forfeiture of term results from insolvency, bankruptcy, a reduction of security to guarantee performance and the failure to meet the conditions in exchange for which the term was granted (art. 1514 C.C.Q.).

See also expiration, failure of the condition, suspensive term.

Fr. déchéance du terme.

FORM *n.*

1. Syn. formality. For example, the marriage contract must be made by a notarial act *en minute* (art. 440 C.C.Q.).

Occ. Arts. 838, 2369, 2683 C.C.Q.; art. 708 C.C.L.C.

Fr. formalité+, forme1.

2. Means of externalizing intent in a juridical act. "If art. 714 and other rules announce a healthy suspicion of formalities for juridical acts, other texts confirm that the legislature continues to place faith in rules of form to meet the purposes and policies pursued in the determination of their validity" (Kasirer, (1996) 99 *R. du N.* 3, n° 18, p. 37). *Notarial form; standard form contract.*

Occ. Arts. 379, 704, 1414, 1415, 2986 C.C.Q.; ss. 2, 426(2), *Bank Act*, S.C. 1991, c. 46; s. 85, *An Act respecting the Régie du logement*, R.S.Q. c. R-8.1.; s. 323, *Consumer Protection Act*, R.S.Q. c. P-40.1.

Fr. forme2.

FORMAL CONTRACT

Syn. solemn contract.

Fr. contrat solennel.

FORMAL DEFECT

Syn. defect of form.

Fr. défaut de forme, vice de forme+.

FORMALISM *n.*

Principle according to which the formation, enforceability or opposability of a juridical act require the fulfilment of special formalities in addition to the manifestation of intent. "It is no doubt unfair to denounce formalism unthinkingly as a plague on the civilian house of liberalities. The better view is that recent trends to desolemnization heighten the need to understand the way in which rules of form satisfy what are, in many instances, their legitimate purposes" (Kasirer, (1996) 99 *R. du N.* 3, n° 18, p. 38).

Obs. 1° In the narrow sense, the term *formalism* refers to a condition of formation of the act: such is the case with solemn contracts and real contracts (arts. 440, 2280, 2693 C.C.Q.). In a wider sense, *formalism* refers to requirements sufficient to ensure enforceability or opposability of a juridical act, such as, for example, rules pertaining to publicity or proof (arts. 2860, 2862, 2941 C.C.Q.). Certain formalities, consisting of an authorization, are also imposed on minors, protected persons of full age or their legal representatives for the formation of specified juridical acts (arts. 211, 212, 213, 266, 293, 294 C.C.Q.). **2°** Since the manifestation of intent may be insufficient to produce juridical effects, formalities play a role in the protection of the parties. Certain formalities, such as publicity rules, are designed for the protection of third persons.

See also attesting deed, autonomy of the will (theory of the), binding force of contract, consensualism, essential formality, evidentiary formality, formality *ad habilitatem*, formality as to publicity, freedom of contract, solemn act, tradition.

Fr. formalisme.

FORMALISTIC *adj.*

Subject to formalities prescribed by law. "Article 713 C.C.Q. warns prospective testators that the will remains a formalistic juridical act, subject to what is, at least for their successors, the often agonizing 'pain of nullity' in the event of non-compliance with the rules of form" (Kasirer, (1996) 99 *R. du N.* 3, n° 1, p. 3).

See also consensual, real, solemn, solemn contract.

Fr. formaliste.

FORMALISTIC ACT

Juridical act the formation of which requires the fulfilment of formalities prescribed by law. For example, the creation of an immovable hypothec must be consigned in a notarial deed (art. 2693 C.C.Q.); or the formation of a contract of deposit requires delivery of the thing (art. 2280 C.C.Q.).

See also condition (as to) of form, consensual act, formalism, formalistic contract, solemn act.
Fr. acte formaliste.

FORMALISTIC CONTRACT

Contract the formation of which requires the fulfilment of formalities prescribed by law. For example, the creation of an immovable hypothec requires the drafting of a notarial deed (art. 2693 C.C.Q.); the formation of a contract of deposit requires delivery of the thing (art. 2280 C.C.Q.).
Obs. 1° Formalistic contracts can be of two types: solemn contracts (e.g. a contract of marriage) or real contracts (e.g. a deposit). **2°** A distinction is drawn between *formalistic contracts* and *consensual contracts*.
See also condition (as to) of form, consensual contract, formalism, real contract, solemn contract.
Fr. contrat formaliste.

FORMALITY *n.*

Operation prescribed by law to ensure the formation, opposability or proof of a juridical act. For example, marriage contracts must be consigned in a notarial act *en minute* (art. 440 C.C.Q.). "By requiring a certain formality to be fulfilled the moment of contracting is postponed from the moment of reaching consent to the moment of complying with the formality" (Haanappel, (1982) 60 *Can. Bar Rev.* 393, p. 403). *Essential formality.*
Occ. Arts. 166, 713, 1645, 2813 C.C.Q.; arts. 678, 792, 855 C.C.L.C.; s. 38, *Public Curator Act*, R.S.Q. c. C-81.
Syn. form[1]. **See also** condition (as to) of form, defect of form, essential formality, evidentiary formality, formality *ad habilitatem*, formality as to publicity.
Fr. formalité[+], forme[1].

FORMALITY *AD HABILITATEM* (Latin)

Formality consisting of an authorization that a person must obtain in order to enter into a juridical act.
Obs. 1° See articles 211, 212, 213, 266, 293, 294 C.C.Q. **2°** The expression *formality* ad habilitatem is generally used in relation to an incapable person or his or her legal representative.
Syn. enabling form. **See also** essential formality, evidentiary formality, formality as to publicity, incapable[1,2], mandatary.
Fr. formalité *ad habilitatem*, formalité habilitante[+], forme habilitante.

FORMALITY *AD PROBATIONEM* (Latin)

Syn. evidentiary formality.
Fr. formalité *ad probationem*, formalité probatoire[+], forme probante, forme probatoire.

FORMALITY *AD SOLEMNITATEM* (Latin)

Syn. essential formality.
Fr. formalité *ad solemnitatem*, formalité substantielle[+], forme solennelle, solennité.

FORMALITY AS TO PUBLICITY

Formality intended to inform third persons as to the existence of a juridical fact or juridical act. For example, the publication of real rights.
Obs. 1° Formalities as to publicity ensure the opposability of juridical acts. However, the absence of publication does not, in principle, prevent rights from producing effects between the parties (art. 2941 C.C.Q.). **2°** The codal regime respecting the publication of rights is set forth at articles 2934 to 3075.1 C.C.Q.
Syn. formality of publication, publication formality. **See also** essential formality, evidentiary formality, formality *ad habilitatem*.
Fr. formalité de publicité.

FORMALITY OF PUBLICATION

Syn. formality as to publicity.
Occ. S. 50, *An Act respecting the implementation of the reform of the Civil Code*, S.Q. 1992, c. 57.
Fr. formalité de publicité.

FORMAL NOTICE

Syn. notice of default.
Occ. S. 432, *An Act respecting industrial accidents and occupational diseases*, R.S.Q. c. A-3.001; s. 204, *Savings and Credit Unions Act*, R.S.Q. c. C-4.1.
Fr. mise en demeure[2].

FORSEEN *p.p.adj.*

See foreseen damage.
Fr. prévu.

FORTUITOUS EVENT

Superior force[1] resulting from the act or omission of a person. "Acts causing damage which are due to a fortuitous event [...] are not imputable to any person and do not give rise

to civil responsibility" (Goldenberg, *Law of Delicts*, pp. 20-21).
Occ. Art. 1072 C.C.L.C.; s. 423, *An Act respecting the implementation of the reform of the Civil Code*, S.Q. 1992, c. 57.
Obs. 1° The term *fortuitous event* is used in contradistinction to *superior force*[2], which results from the forces of nature. **2°** A fortuitous event cannot result from the act or omission of the person who invokes it.
See also superior force[1,2].
Fr. cas fortuit.

FOURNIR ET FAIRE VALOIR
nom.ph. (French)

See clause of *fournir et faire valoir.* "An assignment of book debts stipulating a warranty 'de fournir et faire valoir' imposes an obligation of suretyship upon the assignor for the debts ceded" (Sarna, (1978) 56 *Can. Bar Rev.* 626, p. 638).
Fr. fournir et faire valoir.

FRANC ET QUITTE *adj.ph.* (French)

See clear, contribution clause, quit(s).
Fr. franc et quitte.

FRAUD *n.*

1. Means used by a person to deceive another so as to impel the latter to enter into a juridical act or to enter into it on terms different than those that he or she would otherwise have accepted. "Fraud simultaneously excludes accident, inadvertence and ignorance: a person is only guilty of fraud if he acts knowingly, with the object of deceiving someone" (*Antoine Guertin Ltée* v. *Chamberland Co. Ltd.*, [1971] S.C.R. 385, p. 400, L.-P. Pigeon, J.). *Contract tainted by fraud.*
Occ. Art. 1401 C.C.Q.
Obs. 1° Error resulting from fraud vitiates consent when it relates to the nature of the juridical act, the object of the prestation or something that is essential in determining consent (arts. 1400 and 1401 C.C.Q.). **2°** The fraud has to be committed by the other contracting party or by a third party with his or her knowledge. **3°** Fraud can be, among other reasons, the result of lies, artifice, silence or concealment. **4°** The victim of fraud may apply for annulment and, in addition, claim damages or may prefer to apply for a reduction of the obligation (art. 1407 C.C.Q.). The nullity is relative since its role is the protection of individual interests (art. 1419 C.C.Q.). **5°** A fraud is said to be a *principal fraud* when, without it, the victim would never have entered into the juridical act. It is

said to be an *incidental fraud* when it impels the victim to enter into it on terms different than those he or she would otherwise have accepted. **6°** Fraud is to be distinguished from simple exaggeration, sometimes called *bluff* or *dolus bonus*, which does not result in nullity of the contract.
Syn. *dolus malus.* **See also** concealment, defect of consent, *dolus bonus*, error, fear, fraudulent artifices, incidental fraud, principal fraud.
Fr. dol[1+], *dolus malus*, fraude[1].

2. Fault of a debtor who, in bad faith and with deliberate intent, refuses to perform a contractual obligation. "Under [arts. 1073 to 1075 C.C.L.C.] more extensive damages may be granted in the case of fraud; whether or not there is fraud, damages claimed must be the immediate and direct consequence of the offence of the debtor [...]" (Brossard, (1945) 23 *Can. Bar Rev.* 1, p. 5).
Occ. Arts. 1074, 1075 C.C.L.C.
Obs. 1° Used in this sense, fraud is understood as a fault committed during the execution of the contract. It should not be confused with simple fraud, which misleads the cocontractant during the formation of the contract. **2°** In cases of fraud, a more extensive obligation of compensation is imposed on the wrongdoer than in cases of simple fault. He or she is not only liable for the damages that were foreseeable at the time the obligation was contracted but also for the damages that are "an immediate and direct consequence of the non-performance" (art. 1613 C.C.Q.). **3°** Fraud is an intentional fault. As such, exoneration clauses are of no effect (art. 1474 C.C.Q.). **4°** There is no exact English equivalent for the French expression *faute dolosive.* It may be translated as *contractual fault committed fraudulently.*
See also contractual fault, exclusion (of liability) clause, intentional fault.
Fr. dol[2], faute dolosive[+], fraude[2].

FRAUDULENT *adj.*

Tainted by fraud. "The attempt to give this transaction the colour of a sale by the respondent of its debt or claim to the appellant was just one of those fraudulent contrivances which so often recoil against those who resort to them. So far from helping the respondent's case it assists to prove the fraudulent character of the transaction as regards the general body of the creditors" (*Brigham* v. *Banque Jacques-Cartier*, (1900) 30 S.C.R. 429, p. 434, H. Strong, C.J.). *Fraudulent act*; *fraudulent alienation*; *fraudulent artifices*; *fraudulent concealment.*

Occ. Art. 1632 C.C.Q.; arts. 1569c, 2626 C.C.L.C.
Fr. frauduleux.

FRAUDULENT ARTIFICES

Scheme constituting a fraud[1] that is intended to deceive. For example, to falsify the odometer reading of an automobile prior to sale; to present false financial statements. "After having carefully read all the depositions I have, as a matter of inference from the facts in evidence, come to the conclusion that the natural affection of the deceased for his wife, the appellant, had been poisoned and his sense of right perverted by the fraudulent artifices practised upon him by the respondent" (*Mayrand* v. *Dussault* (1907), 38 S.C.R. 460, p. 462, C. Fitzpatrick, C.J.).
Obs. An artifice constitutes a fraud when it provokes an error relating to the nature of the juridical act, the object of the prestation or something that is essential in the determination of the consent (arts. 1400, 1401 C.C.Q.).
See also *dolus bonus*, error, fraud[1], concealment.
Fr. manoeuvre dolosive[+], manoeuvre frauduleuse.

FRAUDULENT CONCEALMENT

Concealment amounting to fraud[1].
Syn. deceitful concealment. **See also** obligation to inform.
Fr. réticence dolosive[+], réticence frauduleuse.

FRAUDULENTLY *adv.*

In a fraudulent manner. "[...] where both parties to an agreement act fraudulently or where one contracting party attempts to defraud the other, courts have tended to annul the contract" (Brierley & Macdonald (eds.), *Quebec Civil Law*, n° 155, p. 198). *To remove fraudulently.*
Occ. Art. 2638 C.C.L.C.
Fr. frauduleusement.

FREE AND CLEAR *adj.ph.*

See clear, contribution clause, free and clear clause, quit(s).
Fr. franc et quitte.

FREED *adj.*

Syn. discharged. *Debtor freed from a contractual obligation.*
Fr. affranchi, libéré[+].

FREEDOM OF CONTRACT

Freedom to bind oneself and to determine the scope, content, modalities and duration of an obligation. "The decline of will theory and the consequent nuancing of freedom of contract reflects the growing appreciation that the parties are rarely of equal bargaining power [...]" (Brierley & Macdonald (eds.), *Quebec Civil Law*, n° 413, pp. 390-391).
Syn. contractual freedom. **See also** autonomy of the will (theory of the), consensualism, contract[1], formalism, public order.
Fr. liberté contractuelle.

FREIGHT *n.*

1. Price agreed upon for the carriage of goods under a contract for the carriage of goods.
Occ. Arts. 2041, 2075 C.C.Q.; s. 3c, *Bills of Lading Act*, R.S.C. 1985, c. B-5; ss. 2(1), 12, *Marine Insurance Act*, S.C. 1993, c. 22.
Fr. fret[1].

2. Price agreed upon for placing a means of transportation at the disposal of the charterer under a contract of affreightment.
Occ. Arts. 2001, 2005, 2012, 2019, 2024 C.C.Q.
See also lessor[2].
Fr. fret[2].

3. Designated set of goods that are being carried or that are susceptible to be carried.
Obs. This meaning of the term *freight* refers, for example, to the cargo or the load of a ship, a plane, a train or a truck.
See also contract for the carriage of goods.
Fr. fret[3].

FREIGHTER *n.*

Syn. shipper.
Occ. Arts. 2410, 2420 C.C.L.C.
Fr. chargeur, expéditeur[+].

FULFILLED CONDITION

Condition[1] that has been realized.
Syn. accomplished condition. **See also** failed condition, fulfilment of the condition, pending condition, retroactivity of the condition.
Fr. condition accomplie.

FULFILMENT OF THE CONDITION

Occurrence of the condition[1]. "In the case [...] of a sale, if the thing perishes between the making of the contract and the fulfilment of the condition, the risk is on the seller in the sense that, though he is released by supervening impossibility from the obligation to

deliver the thing, he cannot claim the price from the buyer" (Nicholas, *Contract*, p. 158).
Occ. Arts. 1501, 1504, 1506 C.C.Q.; arts. 1082, 1086 C.C.L.C.; s. 56, *An Act respecting the implementation of the reform of the Civil Code*, S.Q. 1992, c. 57.
Obs. Upon fulfilment of a resolutory condition, the obligation is deemed never to have existed and, by extension, the contract is treated as never having existed. Conversely, upon fulfilment of the suspensive condition, the obligation is deemed to have existed purely and simply from the day the contract was entered into. In this case, it is as though no condition had ever existed (art. 1507 C.C.Q.).
Syn. accomplishment of the condition, realization of the condition. **See also** failure of the condition, fulfilled condition, retroactivity of the condition.
Fr. accomplissement de la condition, arrivée de la condition, réalisation de la condition[+].

FULL *adj.*

See full compensation, full payment, full reparation.
Fr. intégral.

FULL ADMINISTRATION

Regime of administration of the property of others that aims, in addition to the protection and preservation of property, to increase property[1] or to appropriate it to a determined purpose.
Occ. Arts. 1306, 2135 C.C.Q.
Obs. 1° Full administration may bear on property, a mass of property, a fraction of a universality, a universality or the whole patrimony. **2°** The curator (except with regard to the purchase of financial products for investment purposes (art. 282 C.C.Q.)), and the trustee (art. 1278 C.C.Q.) are endowed with the powers of the administrator charged with full administration. The Public Curator has the powers of the administrator charged with simple administration (art. 262 C.C.Q.; s. 30, *Public Curator Act*, R.S.Q. c. C-81).
See also act of administration, administration of the property of others, simple administration.
Fr. pleine administration.

FULL COMPENSATION

See full reparation.
Obs. The expression *full compensation* is often used as a synonym for *full reparation*. Strictly speaking, however, compensation refers only to reparation by equivalent (e.g. in money) rather than specific performance in kind.
Fr. réparation intégrale(>)[+], *restitutio in integrum*(>).

FULL PAYMENT

Payment of the whole of a debt. "It is particularly important to note that reservation of title in sales as a security mechanism has not necessarily been fully covered by Article 1745 of the *Civil Code*. The definition of an instalment sale in such article requires that the seller reserve ownership of the property until *full* payment of the sale price" (Dietze, (1999) 59 *R. du B.* 1, p. 9).
Occ. Art. 1202 C.C.Q.
Obs. In principle, full payment is the rule applicable to payment, because the creditor cannot be compelled to accept partial payment of the obligation (art. 1561 C.C.Q.).
See also partial payment.
Fr. paiement intégral.

FULL REPARATION

Reparation equal to the damage actually sustained. "In the context of bodily injuries, under the direction of the Supreme Court of Canada, the principle of full reparation has acquired a scientific aura: actuarial evidence is used to give a sense of precision and objectivity to the quantification of damage. Although the principle of full reparation is said by some to apply to non-pecuniary losses as well, the courts have, in practice, imposed ceilings on amounts that may be claimed under headings such as pain and suffering" (Brierley & Macdonald (eds.), *Quebec Civil Law*, n⁰ 519, p. 472).
Obs. 1° The principle of full reparation for the damage actually sustained partakes of corrective or commutative justice. It consists in making good the loss – no more, no less – thereby seeking to avoid, through its application, either an impoverishment or an enrichment of the creditor. **2°** The principle is said to apply notwithstanding inherent difficulties in assessing the quantum of certain types of loss, such as extrapatrimonial damage. **3°** There are both legal and contractual exceptions to this principle, such as punitive damages. **4°** The expression *full compensation* is often used as a synonym for *full reparation*. Stricly speaking, however, compensation refers only to reparation by equivalent (e.g. in money), rather than specific performance in kind.
Syn. *restitutio in integrum*. **See also** damages, predetermined reparation.
Fr. réparation intégrale[+], *restitutio in integrum*.

FUNDAMENTAL PRINCIPLES OF LAW

Syn. general principles of law.
Occ. Art. 3155 C.C.Q.
Obs. 1° The established expression is used in the plural but the singular form of the expression may also be used. **2°** In French law, one often distinguishes the general principles, to which statutes can go against, and the supereminent principles, which have a supra-legislative value.
Fr. principes fondamentaux de droit, principes généraux du droit+.

FUNDAMENTAL RIGHT

Right which, because it partakes of the essence of human dignity, cannot be violated in its totality or be the object of a complete renunciation under any circumstances.
Occ. Art. 72, *Geneva Conventions Act*, R.S.C., c. G-3; preamble, *Emergencies Act*, R.S.C., c. E-4.5.
Obs. 1° Used in this sense, the expression *fundamental right* reflects a vision of human rights developed in the international context according to which a right may only be said to be fundamental where its violation amounts to a negation of the inherent dignity of the human person. **2°** In private law, the notion of fundamental right is often understood by reference to the principles of public order (e.g. s. 9.1, *Charter of Human Rights and Freedoms*, R.S.Q. c. C-12).
See also duty, public order.
Fr. droit fondamental.

FUTURE DAMAGE

Damage that has not yet occurred at the time the claim for compensation is made, nor at the time the liability is assessed.

Obs. 1° Future damage may either be certain or possible, but is only susceptible of compensation in the former case, when it is susceptible of evaluation (art. 1611 C.C.Q.). **2°** Since the terms *damage* and *injury* are synonymous, the expression *future injury* may also be used.
See also certain damage, loss of (a) chance, present damage, possible damage.
Fr. préjudice futur.

FUTURE PROPERTY

Property[1] that is the object of a prestation although it has not yet come into existence. For example, a future harvest, rent from an immovable under construction.
Occ. Art. 1374 C.C.Q.
Obs. While the *Civil Code of Lower Canada* referred to *future thing*, the *Civil Code of Québec* now uses the expression *future property*.
Syn. future thing.
Fr. bien à venir+, chose future.

FUTURE THING

Syn. future property. "Strictly speaking, [...] one cannot own a future thing but can only be a creditor of a person who will procure or manufacture a thing in the future" (Yiannopoulos, in *Treatise*, vol. 2, n° 214, p. 397).
Occ. Art. 1061 C.C.L.C.
Obs. While the *Civil Code of Lower Canada* referred to *future thing*, the *Civil Code of Québec* now uses the expression *future property*.
Fr. bien à venir+, chose future.

G

GAMBLING DEBT

Debt resulting from a gaming or a wagering contract.
Obs. See articles 2629 and 2630 C.C.Q.
See also gaming contract, wagering contract.
Fr. dette de jeu (ou de pari).

GAMING CONTRACT

Aleatory contract by which the parties undertake to remit a sum of money or a specific thing to the one who attains a result, which depends on an event that can, to some extent, be controlled by the parties. For example, a gaming contract between card players; the contract between participants in a long-distance race or in a bingo game licensed by a state agency.
Occ. Arts. 2512, 2629 C.C.Q.; art. 1927 C.C.L.C.
Obs. 1° A gaming contract is valid where it is expressly authorized by law, in particular, if it bears on "lawful activities and games requiring only skills or bodily exercises on the part of the parties, unless the amount at stake is immoderate according to the circumstances and in view of the condition and means of the parties" (art. 2629 C.C.Q.). **2°** When the gaming contract is not authorized, the obligation that results from it is not susceptible to compulsory execution. However, if the losing party voluntarily pays the debt, what has been paid cannot be legally reclaimed, except if the claimant is a minor or a protected person of full age or a person of full age not endowed with reason (art. 2630 C.C.Q.). **3°** The legal regimes governing gaming and wagering contracts are the same. However, these contracts are distinguished in practice. In wagering contracts, the party whose opinion in respect of a given fact is found to be correct has the right to be paid. This fact, although it may bear on a past, present or future event, is beyond the control of the parties. By contrast, in gaming contracts, parties' participation in an event makes the payment due. **4°** The codal regime respecting gaming contracts is set forth at articles 2629 and 2630 C.C.Q.

See also contingency[1], gambling debt, natural obligation, wagering contract.
Fr. contrat de jeu[+], jeu.

GARDE DE LA STRUCTURE
nom.ph. (French)

Syn. custody of the structure (of the thing).
Fr. garde de (la) structure.

GARDE DU COMPORTEMENT
nom.ph. (French)

Syn. custody of the activity (of the thing).
Fr. garde du comportement.

GENERAL AUTHORIZATION

Syn. general power of attorney.
Occ. Art. 409 C.C.P.
Fr. procuration générale.

GENERAL CONDITIONS

Conditions[2] that are established beforehand in a standard-form contract. *General conditions of sale; general conditions of contract.*
See also adhesion contract, special terms, standard-form contract.
Fr. conditions générales.

GENERAL INCAPACITY

Legal incapacity relating to all juridical acts except those expressly authorized by law or by judicial decision.
Obs. The incapacity to enjoy rights can never be general; this would amount to the negation of legal personality. In matters of incapacity to exercise rights, however, there may be a general incapacity (e.g. the incapacity of an unemancipated minor, the incapacity of persons of full age under curatorship or under an equivalent regime resulting from a mandate given in anticipation of the mandator's incapacity).
Syn. total incapacity. **See also** incapacity to enjoy (rights), incapacity to exercise (rights), special incapacity.
Fr. incapacité générale[+], incapacité totale.

GENERAL INTEREST

That which is to the advantage of all. "For aught that appears to the contrary the use of the regulating valve, of which the plaintiff complains, may have been in the general interest of the municipality and its inhabitants. The curtailing of the water supply in a limited district may have been on the whole beneficial. Its purpose may have been to prevent a large majority of the inhabitants of the town being deprived to a great extent of their supply of water" (*Belanger* v. *Montreal Water and Power Co.* (1914), 50 S.C.R. 356, p. 373, F.A. Anglin, J.).
Occ. Art. 1417 C.C.Q.
Obs. Although the expression *general interest* is frequently used in the Civil Code (e.g. arts. 67, 1270, 1472 C.C.Q.), the notion of *general interest* has a particular meaning in contract law. The nullity of a juridical act is absolute when it is contrary to the general interest (art. 1417 C.C.Q.) and it is relative when it is contrary to an individual interest (art. 1419 C.C.Q.).
See also individual interest, nullity, public order.
Fr. intérêt général.

GENERAL LAW

Law[1] serving as a foundation for a legal system as a whole and, therefore, applicable in the absence of special rules. For example, the general theory of contract in the Civil Code, as opposed to the provisions of the *Consumer Protection Act* (R.S.Q. c. P-40.1); the Common law as opposed to the *Criminal Code*, in matters relating to defences.
Obs. 1° It is generally understood that there are two bodies of general law in Quebec. Despite the unsettled character of the categories *private law* and *public law*, the Civil law – the body of fundamental private law rules – is said to provide the general law in the realm of private law, whereas the Common law – the corpus of rules of law developed by courts, with the exception of the Courts of Chancery – is said to provide the general law in matters falling within the realm of public law. **2°** The explanation for the presence of two sets of general law in Quebec is historical. Initially a French colony having received the law of France in all matters, Quebec became a British colony by cession of the territory in 1763, after the Conquest. The English Common law applied fully to the new colony. With the *Quebec Act* of 1774 (*An Act for making more effectual Provision for the Government of the Province of Quebec in North America*, 14

George III, c. 83 (U.K.), the Civil law was re-established for private law, while English law was retained for all other matters. Since 1774, both legal traditions have formally coexisted in their respective spheres of Quebec law. **3°** Although the Civil Code does not contain all of the Civil law, the Preliminary Provision of the *Civil Code of Québec* states that the Code lays down the *jus commune* in matters falling within its scope. **4°** The Civil law is also considered to be the expression of the general law for federal legislation pertaining to private law matters to the extent that the legislation applies in Quebec. **5°** The English text of the Preliminary Provision of the *Civil Code of Québec* employs *jus commune* as a parallel term for *droit commun*, rather than general law, common law or ordinary law which are more often encountered in English. **6°** A distinction is drawn between *general law* and *special law*.
Syn. common law[1], *droit commun*, *jus commune*, ordinary law. **See also** civil law[3], legal rule[1], private law, public law.
Fr. droit commun[1+], *jus commune*, loi générale.

GENERAL MANDATE

Mandate[1] relating to all the affairs of the mandator.
Obs. 1° Article 2135 C.C.Q. expressly states that a mandate may be general. **2°** The general mandate can be expressed in general terms (e.g. management of the mandator's property or business and the performance of all necessary acts related thereto); or in express terms (e.g. to sell all of the mandator's property). **3°** The *general mandate* is opposed to the *special mandate*.
See also express mandate[1], general procuration, mandate expressed in general terms.
Fr. mandat général.

GENERAL OBLIGATION OF PRUDENCE AND DILIGENCE

Syn. obligation of means.
Fr. obligation de diligence, obligation de moyens[+], obligation générale de prudence et diligence, obligation relative.

GENERAL PARTNER

Partner of a limited partnership who, as well as being solidarily liable for the debts of the partnership, holds exclusive powers of administration of the partnership.
Occ. Arts. 2190, 2236 C.C.Q.; art. 1872 C.C.L.C.

Obs. 1° More than one general partner may be party to a contract establishing a limited partnership. **2°** In respect of the property of the partnership, general partners are considered as persons charged with full administration.
See also special partner.
Fr. commandité[+], gérant[2].

GENERAL PARTNERSHIP

Partnership carrying on business under a name common to the partners, in which the partners are solidarily liable for the debts of the partnership. "All partners of a general partnership have the power to bind the partnership in the ordinary course of its business; no stipulation to the contrary may be set up against third parties in good faith" (Fortin, in *Meredith Lectures (1997)*, 1, p. 7).
Occ. Art. 2238 C.C.Q.; arts. 1864, 1865 C.C.L.C.; s. 187.12, *Professional Code*, R.S.Q. c. C-26; s. 2(2), *An Act respecting the legal publicity of sole proprietorships, partnerships and legal persons*, R.S.Q. c. P-45.
Obs. 1° General partnerships must be declared within the time period and in the manner prescribed by the *Act respecting the legal publicity of sole proprietorships, partnerships and legal persons*. In the absence of a declaration, general partnerships are deemed to be undeclared ones (arts. 2189, 2190 C.C.Q.). **2°** Although general partnerships are not endowed with juridical personality, they are similar to legal persons in many ways. For example, they have a firm name and the power to sue in a civil action under this name (art. 2225 C.C.Q.); they also operate as if they have a patrimony distinct from those of the partners (arts. 2199, 2208, 2221 C.C.Q.). **3°** The partners are jointly liable for the obligations of the partnership not contracted for the service or operation of its enterprise (art. 2221 C.C.Q.). The codal regime relating to limited partnership does not draw a distinction between obligations that are contracted for the service or operation of an enterprise of the partnership and those that are not (art. 2246 C.C.Q.). **4°** A general partnership is often identified by the abbreviation *G.P.* (in French *S.N.E.C.*). **5°** The codal regime respecting general partnerships is set forth at articles 2186 to 2235 C.C.Q.
See also contract of partnership, limited partnership, partner, partnership[1], undeclared partnership.
Fr. société en nom collectif.

GENERAL POWER

Syn. general power of attorney.
Occ. Arts. 61, 629 C.C.P.
Fr. procuration générale.

GENERAL POWER OF ATTORNEY

Power of attorney relating to all the affairs of the mandator.
Obs. The *general power of attorney* is opposed to the *special power of attorney*.
Syn. general authorization, general power, general procuration. **See also** general mandate.
Fr. procuration générale.

GENERAL PRINCIPLES OF LAW

Foundational juridical precepts that constitute the basis of a legal system and express its animating values. For example, *audi alteram partem* or *fraus omnia corrumpit*. "'General principles of law,' or as the idea has been termed elsewhere, 'super-eminent principles,' have a double role. They are the foundational concepts of Codal rules that apply them or derogate from them; and, where the written law is silent or obscure, they justify not only the new interpretation of an existing rule, but also the discovery and application of a new rule" (Brierley, (1992) 42 *U. of T.L.J.* 484, p. 500).
Occ. Preliminary Provision of the *Civil Code of Québec*; s. 38(c), *Statute of the International Court of Justice*, [1945] *Can.T.S.*, n° 7.
Obs. 1° General principles of law, which are embedded in the heart of our law, have a dual role in positive law: on the one hand, they constitute the foundation of the juridical rules that follow or depart from them; on the other hand, where the law is silent or unclear, they justify the application of a new rule or the interpretation of an existing rule (see *Cie Immobilière Viger* v. *Lauréat Giguère Inc.*, [1977] 2 S.C.R. 67, J. Beetz, J.). **2°** Because of the variety of general principles of law, scholars have classified them in different ways, including classification as juridical or social principles (e.g. respect of the right of defence) and principles expressing moral values (e.g. the principle of good faith). **3°** Maxims which express a legal norm often reflect a general principle of law.
Syn. fundamental principles of law, super-eminent principles of law. **See also** legal rule[1].
Fr. principes généraux du droit.

GENERAL PROCURATION

Syn. general power of attorney.
Fr. procuration générale.

GENERAL TITLE (BY)

See transmission by general title, usufruct by general title.
Fr. titre universel (à).

GENTLEMEN'S AGREEMENT

Syn. honour-only agreement.
Fr. engagement d'honneur.

GIFT *n.*

1. Contract by gratuitous title that entails disposition[2] of property. "Article 1806 C.C.Q. views the gift as a translatory contract that transfers a right of ownership of a thing or some other real right in its regard, or again some other right, from the donor to the donee such that the donor is impoverished and the donee is enriched by virtue of the liberal intention of the former" (Brierley, in *Mélanges Crépeau*, 119, p. 133). *To transfer property by gift.*
Occ. Arts. 173, 211, 415, 613, 737, 867, 1212, 1240, 1258, 1279, 1806 C.C.Q.; arts. 754, 776 C.C.L.C.; art. 553 C.C.P.
Obs. 1° Gifts are formalistic contracts. In principle, gifts must be made by a notarial deed *en minute* and must be published. With regards to movable property, delivery, which is also a formality, may replace the notarial deed and publicity requirements (art. 1824 C.C.Q.). In this latter case, gifts are called *manual gifts.* **2°** Indirect gifts and disguised gifts are assimilated to gifts, except as to their form (art. 1811 C.C.Q.). **3°** The parties to a contract of gift are called the *donor* and the *donee.* However, where gifts are used for the establishment of a trust, it should be noted that the transfer of property is made to a patrimony by appropriation, not to a donee (art. 1260 C.C.Q.). **4°** Gifts *inter vivos*, by which the donor deprives himself or herself immediately of property (art. 1807 C.C.Q.), are to be distinguished from gifts *mortis causa* where the divestment is conditional upon and postponed until the donor's death (art. 1808 C.C.Q.). **5°** Gifts *inter vivos* are valid only as to present property, whereas gifts *mortis causa* may bear on future property (art. 1818 C.C.Q.). **6°** A gift *mortis causa* is null unless it is made by marriage contract or unless it may be upheld as a legacy (art. 1819 C.C.Q.). **7°** The codal regime respecting gifts is set forth at articles 1806 to 1841 C.C.Q.

Syn. contract of gift, donation. **See also** liberality[1].
Fr. contrat de donation, don[1], donation[+].

2. Object of a gift[1]. *To receive a gift.*
Occ. Art. 700 C.C.L.C.
Fr. don[2].

GIVE *v.*

1. To transfer a patrimonial right.
Occ. Art. 1556 C.C.Q.; arts. 1058, 1063 C.C.L.C.
Obs. 1° This notion of *giving* relates to the Latin word *dare* (dation) rather than *donare* (to make a gift). **2°** The expression *to give in payment* (art. 1556 C.C.Q.) means to hand over as payment, sometimes by means of a giving in payment (arts. 1799 *et seq.* C.C.Q.).
See also obligation to give.
Fr. donner[1].

2. To make a gift[1].
Occ. Arts. 644, 942, 1816 C.C.Q.; art. 771 C.C.L.C.
Fr. donner[2].

GIVING IN PAYMENT

Transfer of ownership of property by the debtor to the creditor, who accepts it as payment in lieu of the originally agreed upon prestation.
Occ. Arts. 419, 1799, 1800 C.C.Q.; art. 1592 C.C.L.C.
Obs. 1° Giving in payment is a contractual method of extinguishing an obligation. While taking in payment is a compulsory form of performance of an obligation, giving in payment is voluntary (art. 1799 C.C.Q.). **2°** A clause giving the creditor the right to become owner or to dispose of the property of the debtor, for the purpose of securing the performance of an obligation, is deemed not written (art. 1801 C.C.Q.). **3°** Giving in payment is subject to the rules relative to the contract of sale (art. 1800 C.C.Q.) and to arts. 1799 to 1801 C.C.Q.
Syn. *dation en paiement.* **See also** giving in payment clause, release of obligation.
Fr. dation en paiement.

GIVING IN PAYMENT CLAUSE

Clause in a contract whereby the creditor is given either the right to become owner of property, by way of payment and as a substitute to a previously agreed upon obligation, or the right to dispose of the debtor's property for the purpose of securing the performance of an obligation. "The loan with a giving-in-payment clause whereby on default the lender could take the property (with effect retroactive to the date of the loan) in repayment was sanctioned first by the courts and then by amendment to the CCLC in 1964" (Claxton, *Security*, p. 3).

Obs. 1° The giving in payment clause is deemed not written when it is made with a view to securing the performance of his debtor (art. 1801 C.C.Q.). Under the *Civil Code of Lower Canada*, such a clause was valid and was most often found in contracts of loan secured by hypothec or in sales of immovables (arts. 1040*a*, 1085 C.C.L.C.). **2°** The inefficacy of giving in payment clauses is limited to those that are designed to secure the performance of an obligation. Giving in payment, i.e. transfer of ownership of property to extinguish an obligation, remains possible (arts. 1799 to 1801 C.C.Q.).

Syn. clause of *dation en paiement*, clause of giving in payment, *dation en paiement* clause.
See also giving in payment.
Fr. clause de dation en paiement.

GOLD *n.*

See gold clause.
Fr. or.

GOLD CLAUSE

1. Monetary clause whereby a debtor undertakes to pay the debt by remitting a specified quantity of gold to the creditor.
See also sliding scale clause.
Fr. clause or.

2. Monetary clause whereby a debtor undertakes to pay in legal tender an amount calculated by reference to the value of gold on the day payment is due.
See also sliding scale clause.
Fr. clause valeur or.

GOOD FAITH

1. Loyalty and honesty in the exercise of civil rights. "In the spirit of our law, the general principle of good faith is of the essence, and much in the same way as in criminal law where every person is deemed innocent until found guilty, so too in civil law, every person is considered to be in good faith until proven otherwise" (Rosenberg, (1960-61) 7 *McGill L.J.* 2, p. 12). *Presumption of good faith.*
Occ. Arts. 6, 1375, 2545, 2805 C.C.Q.
Obs. 1° The principle according to which "[e]very person is bound to exercise his civil rights in good faith" stated at article 6 C.C.Q. is one of the fundamental notions of the civil

law. Notwithstanding its heightened visibility in the Civil Code, the principle is not new to the civil law. Formerly, article 1024 C.C.L.C. was interpreted so as to recognize the generality of the principle of good faith in contractual matters. **2°** Used in this sense, good faith is measured according to an objective criterion based on a reasonable standard of behaviour, notwithstanding the difference between the French and English texts of article 6 C.C.Q. (compare "selon les exigences de la bonne foi" with "in good faith"). **3°** Article 1375 C.C.Q. explicitly recognizes that good faith should govern the conduct of the parties at all times, not only at the time of the performance of contracts, but also at the time of their formation and extinction. **4°** The Civil Code establishes duties of loyalty and honesty in different sectors of the law that are in fact illustrations of the general principle of good faith applied to specific situations (e.g. arts. 322, 1309, 2138 C.C.Q.). **5°** Consumer contracts and contracts of adhesion (e.g. in the context of maritime insurance (art. 2545 C.C.Q.)) require that the party considered to be in a dominant position must demonstrate the "utmost good faith". The expression uberrima fides *contracts* is often used in these contexts.
Syn. fair dealing. **See also** abuse of right(s), bad faith[1], equity[1].
Fr. bonne foi[1].

2. Incorrect belief that one is acting in conformity with law. For example, the good faith of a possessor concerning the useful disbursements made on the land of another (art. 959 C.C.Q.); the good faith of a spouse as regards the nullity of his or her marriage (art. 382 C.C.Q.). "[...] good faith is defined as ignorance of the reason for the invalidity of the act" (*Paré* v. *Bonin*, [1977] 2 S.C.R. 342, p. 352, J. Beetz, J.). *Possession in good faith.*
Occ. Arts. 382, 959, 1454, 2919 C.C.Q.; arts. 1027, 2202 C.C.L.C.
Obs. Good faith may arise from the simple ignorance of an irregular juridical situation or on the basis of misleading appearances.
See also bad faith[2].
Fr. bonne foi[2].

GOOD MORALS

Body of moral rules considered to be important for the preservation of society and which are therefore imposed upon all jural relations. "[...] the notion of good morals (*bonnes mœurs*) had a particular referent that is not especially well captured in its English formulation. Good morals is to be understood as evoking the notion of right conduct as lived in a society

(social *mores*) and, however much influenced by religion, it is not a specifically religious notion (*la morale*)" (Brierley & Macdonald (eds.), *Quebec Civil Law*, n° 153, p. 194).
Occ. Arts. 13, 760, 831, 990, 1062, 1080 C.C.L.C.
Obs. 1° The expression *good morals* that was used at articles 13, 760, 990, 1080 C.C.L.C. is not used in the *Civil Code of Québec* (e.g. arts. 8, 757, 1411, 1412, 1499 C.C.Q.) Scholars generally consider that good morals are now included in the notion of *public order* (art. 9 C.C.Q.). The expression *moral public order* is used in this sense. **2°** Good morals are characterized by the specificity of their object, which is to ensure basic morality in juridical acts. The notion varies over time in a given society. **3°** Good morals often find their expression in various maxims, for example, *fraus omnia corrumpit* (fraud corrupts all).
See also general interest, public order.
Fr. bonnes mœurs.

GRADUAL DAMAGE

Damage that manifests itself over time.
Obs. Since the terms *damage* and *injury* are synonymous, the expression *gradual injury* may also be used.
See also continuous damage, periodic damage, recurrent damage.
Fr. préjudice graduel+, préjudice progressif.

GRATUITOUS CONTRACT

Contract by which one party confers a benefit upon another without receiving a benefit in return. For example, a gift. "When a contract is onerous, a debtor receives in the consideration the equivalent of the thing alienated; but when the contract is gratuitous, his patrimony is diminished and he must not so diminish it as to leave himself unable, by reason of the gift, to pay his debts in full" (Marler, *Real Property*, p. 544).
Occ. Art. 1034 C.C.L.C.
Obs. In general, a distinction is made between two types of gratuitous contracts: those in which property is transferred from one patrimony to another (e.g. gifts), and those that consist solely of services rendered, called *benevolent contracts* (e.g. a loan without interest, a gratuitous mandate).
Syn. contract by gratuitous title. **See also** benevolent contract, gift[1], onerous contract.
Fr. contrat à titre gratuit.

GRÉ À GRÉ (DE) *nom.ph.* (French)

See contract by negotiation.
Fr. gré à gré (de).

GROSS FAULT

Civil fault that even the least prudent person would not commit. "Gross fault (the Roman *culpa lata*) is not easy to define. It is neither the intention to cause damage, nor a lack of honesty; it suggests extreme carelessness or, at times, an absolute lack of a minimum skill. It is such fault that, though unintentional, it looks intentional – almost as if damage had been caused on purpose" (Litvinoff, in *Treatise*, vol. 7, Book 2, n° 185, p. 348).
Occ. Arts. 1461, 1471, 1474, 1613 C.C.Q.; art. 1054.1 C.C.L.C.; s. 20(b), *Crime Victims Compensation Act*, R.S.Q. c. I-6.
Obs. 1° Prior to the codification of 1866, the law recognized a gradation in the degrees of fault, extending from *culpa levissima* to *culpa lata* (gross fault). These distinctions have lost their importance, although the term gross fault remains a relevant concept to which legal effect is attached. For instance, proof of gross fault is sometimes required to hold someone liable for their acts in prescribed circumstances (e.g. arts. 1461, 1474 C.C.Q.). Furthermore, it generally prevents recourse to a limitation or exclusion of liability set in a clause or a legislative provision (e.g. arts. 1474, 2301 C.C.Q.). Proof of gross fault may also have an impact on the apportionment of liability (art. 1478 C.C.Q.) and on the establishment of a causal link. **2°** Article 1474 C.C.Q. defines gross fault as behaviour that shows gross recklessness, gross carelessness or gross negligence.
Syn. *culpa lata*. **See also** *culpa levis, culpa levissima*.
Fr. *culpa lata*, faute lourde+.

GROSS NEGLIGENCE

See gross fault. "[...] a clause contracting out of liability for negligence is ineffective with respect to gross negligence [...] on the ground that it is against public order" (*Ceres Stevedoring Co.* v. *Eisen und Metall A.G.*, [1977] C.A. 56, p. 63, G.R.W. Owen, J.).
Occ. Art. 1474 C.C.Q.; art. 2633 C.C.L.C.; s. 56, *Mining Duties Act*, R.S.Q. c. D-15; s. 15, *Pay Equity Act*, R.S.Q. c. E-12.001.
Fr. négligence grossière.

GUARANTEE OF PAYMENT

Syn. warranty of payment.
Occ. Art. 1646 C.C.Q.
Fr. garantie de fournir et faire valoir.

GUARANTEE OF PAYMENT CLAUSE

Syn. warranty of payment clause.
Fr. clause de fournir et faire valoir.

GUARANTOR *n.*

Syn. surety.
Fr. caution[1+], fidéjusseur.

GUARDIAN *n.*

Syn. custodian.
Fr. gardien.

H

HABILITATE *v.*

1. To confer legal capacity upon an incapable person.
Fr. habiliter[1].

2. To authorize a person to perform certain acts.
Fr. habiliter[2].

HABITUAL EMPLOYEE

Agent or servant who usually works under the authority of one principal, although he or she may be subject temporarily to the authority of another principal.
See also agent and servant, habitual employer, liability of the principal, temporary employee.
Fr. préposé habituel.

HABITUAL EMPLOYER

Principal who usually has authority over an employee, although he or she may also temporarily place the employee in the service of another principal.
See also habitual employee, liability of the principal, temporary employer.
Fr. commettant habituel.

HANDING OVER

Syn. remittance.
Occ. Arts. 694, 1562, 1889, 2281, 2704 C.C.Q.; art. 607.11 C.C.L.C.
Fr. remise[1].

HAND OVER *verb.ph.*

Syn. remit.
Occ. Arts. 1780, 2691 C.C.Q.
Fr. remettre.

HARM *n.*

Syn. damage. "[...] Article 1054 C.C.[L.C.] declares that where one person suffers harm from something in the care of another the law presumes that the harm is due to the fault of the person having care of the thing which has caused the harm [...]" (*Vandry* v. *Quebec Railway, Light, Heat and Power Co.* (1915-16), 53 S.C.R. 72, p. 105, L.P. Duff, J.).
Occ. Art. 272 C.C.Q.; art. 19 C.C.L.C.; art. 41 C.C.P.
Fr. dommage, préjudice[+], tort[2]

HIDDEN DEFECT

Syn. latent defect. "The responsibility of the manufacturer where he has himself sold to the plaintiff, either directly or through an agent, for injuries occasioned to the purchaser by hidden defects in the thing sold is clearly covered by Arts. 1522 and 1527 C.C.[L.C.]" (*Ross* v. *Dunstall*, (1921) 62 S.C.R. 393, p. 400, F.A. Anglin, J.).
Fr. défaut caché, vice caché[+], vice rédhibitoire.

HIRE *n.*

Syn. lease and hire.
Obs. In the *Civil Code of Lower Canada*, the terms *lease* and *hire* were used together (title preceding art. 1600 C.C.L.C.).
Fr. louage(<).

HONOUR-ONLY AGREEMENT

Agreement that cannot be enforced by the State. "These 'honour-only' agreements [...] seem to be confined to family or friendly relations. Nowadays, however, we see – especially in commerce and in international relations – numerous instances of 'honour-only' agreements [...] One discovers a set of situations in which, without binding themselves legally, the parties still intend to bind themselves, each being entitled to expect that the other will carry out the obligation to which they have consented" (Jauffret-Spinosi, in *Contract Law Today*, 113, n° 23, pp. 122-123).
Obs. The performance of honour-only agreements is generally viewed to depend solely on the will of the parties.
Syn. gentlemen's agreement. **See also** moral obligation, natural obligation.
Fr. engagement d'honneur.

HYPOTHETICAL LOSS

Syn. possible damage.
Obs. Since the terms *loss* and *injury* are synonymous, the expression *hypothetical injury* may also be used.
Fr. préjudice éventuel[+], préjudice hypothétique.

I

ILLEGAL *adj.*

1. Contrary to law[2]. *Illegal act*; *illegal exercise of a function*; *illegal regulation*; *illegal transaction.*
Occ. Art. 1464 C.C.Q.; art. 2611 C.C.L.C.
See also illegitimate[1,2], illicit, legal[3].
Fr. illégal[1].

2. Syn. illicit. *Illegal cause.*
Occ. Art. 998 C.C.L.C.
Fr. illégal[2], illicite[+].

ILLEGAL CAUSE

Syn. illicit cause.
Fr. cause illégale, cause illicite[+], considération illégale.

ILLEGAL CONDITION

Syn. illicit condition. "I am therefore to hold that the condition in question which was that if any difficulty should arise between the parties during marriage which would lead to an appearance in Court, that the gifts should be null even if the Court proceedings should have been initiated by the husband, is an illegal condition against public order and is to be considered as not written and the judgment of the Court below maintained" (*Weingart* v. *Stober*, [1922] 60 C.S. 55, p. 58, J.S. Archibald, J.).
Fr. condition illégale, condition illicite[+].

ILLEGALITY *n.*

1. Quality of that which is illegal[1]. *Illegality of a detention.*
Occ. Arts. 2538, 2539 C.C.Q.
See also illicitness, legality.
Fr. illégalité[1].

2. Syn. illicitness. *Exception of illegality*; *illegality of a cause*; *to commit an illegality.*
Fr. illégalité[2], illicéité[+].

ILLEGIBLE CLAUSE

Clause that, by reason of its material appearance, is unclear. For example, a clause in small print.

Obs. An illegible clause that forms part of a contract is null if the consumer or the adhering party suffers harm therefrom; the other party may avoid the annulment of the clause by proving that adequate explanations were given (art. 1436 C.C.Q.). Moreover, the *Consumer Protection Act* (R.S.Q. c. P-40.1) specifies that the contract must be drawn up clearly and legibly (s. 25). Furthermore, in respect of insurance contracts, the government may make regulations establishing standards relating to the presentation of the policy, including the printing type, and provide for the adoption by insurers of mandatory forms of insurance policies (s. 420, *An Act respecting insurance*, R.S.Q. c. A-32).
Fr. clause illisible.

ILLEGITIMACY *n.*

1. Quality of that which is in conformity with justice, equity, or fairness. *Illegitimacy of a situation.*
See also illicitness, legitimacy[1].
Fr. illégitimité[1].

2. Quality of that which is not grounded in or recognized by law[1]. *Illegitimacy of a cause*; *illegitimacy of a status.*
See also illegality[1], legitimacy[2].
Fr. illégitimité[2].

3. Quality of that which is not worthy of legal protection.
See also illegitimate[3], legitimate[3], legitimacy[3].
Fr. illégitimité[3].

ILLEGITIMATE *adj.*

1. Not based on justice, equity[1] or fairness. *Illegitimate claim*; *illegitimate purpose.*
See also illegal[1], illicit, legitimate[1].
Fr. illégitime[1].

2. Not grounded in law[1]; not recognized by law[1]. *Illegitimate force.*
Syn. unlawful[2]. **See also** illegal[1], illicit, legitimate[2].
Fr. illégitime[2].

3. Not worthy of legal protection.
See also illegitimacy[3], legitimacy[3], legitimate[3].
Fr. illégitime[3].

ILLICIT *adj.*

Contrary to law[1]. *Illicit cause; illicit condition; illicit consideration; illicit damage.*
Occ. S. 136, *An Act respecting the National Assembly*, R.S.Q. c. A-23.1.
Obs. 1° The term *illicit* includes non conformity with law[2], public order and with good morals. **2°** In connection with the *Civil Code of Lower Canada*, some scholars understood *illicit* more restrictively, to mean non conformity with a provision of law[2] or with public order. Used in this sense, *illicit* was opposed to *immoral*, signifying non conformity with *good morals*. It may be observed that the notion of *good morals* is no longer used in the *Civil Code of Québec*. **3°** When the same contract contains both licit and illicit clauses, the nullity of the whole contract may be avoided. In the case where illicit clauses do not bear upon an essential element of the contract, the invalid clauses may be severed from the portion that is licit.
Syn. illegal[2], unlawful[1]. **See also** illegal[1], illegitimate[1,2], illicit cause, illicit condition, illicit damage, illicit object[1,2], licit.
Fr. illégal[2], illicite[+].

ILLICIT CAUSE

Cause[2] that is contrary to law. "The obligation can have an illicit cause. If the contract by virtue of which the note was signed was prohibited by law, the debtor may refuse to pay it, by proving the cause of the nullity [...]" (Planiol & Ripert, *Treatise*, vol. 2, n° 1045, p. 600).
Obs. Since the law has formally abandoned the distinction between public order and good morals, the immoral cause is now included in the notion of *illicit cause*, and the latter is now included in the notion of *public order* (art. 9 C.C.Q.).The immoral cause may be assimilated with the illicit cause, insofar as the distinction between public order and good morals has been abandoned in the *Civil Code of Québec* (art. 9 C.C.Q.).
Syn. illegal cause, illicit consideration, unlawful cause, unlawful consideration. **See also** false cause, immoral cause, licit cause.
Fr. cause illégale, cause illicite[+], considération illégale.

ILLICIT CONDITION

Condition[1] whose object or consequences are contrary to a legal rule or to public order. For example, a condition limiting the rights of a surviving spouse in the event of a remarriage or new civil union (art. 757 C.C.Q.).
Obs. 1° A condition that depends on the performance of an illicit act, or a condition that is predicated on illicit results arising from the advent of an event that is itself licit, may qualify as *illicit*. **2°** In principle, an illicit condition is null and renders the obligation null. However, in matters relating to wills, an illicit condition is deemed unwritten (art. 747, 1499 C.C.Q.).
Syn. illegal condition, unlawful condition.
See also immoral condition, impossible condition.
Fr. condition illégale, condition illicite[+].

ILLICIT CONSIDERATION

Syn. illicit cause.
Fr. cause illégale, cause illicite[+], considération illégale.

ILLICIT DAMAGE

Damage that results from the interference with an activity or an interest that is contrary to law or to public order.
Obs. 1° Illicit damage does not give rise to compensation; only damage that constitutes an infringement upon a licit interest may be compensated. **2°** Since the terms *damage* and *injury* are synonymous, the expression *illicit injury* may also be used.
See also licit damage.
Fr. préjudice illicite.

ILLICITNESS *n.*

Quality of that which is illicit.
Obs. Some scholars have noted that illicitness may manifest itself in different ways: it may take the form of a violation of a subjective right (e.g. a violation of one's property), a violation of a legal or customary rule of conduct (e.g. the rule stated at art. 1375 C.C.Q., according to which good faith shall govern the parties), or a departure from an abstract model of good sense (e.g. the model of a reasonable person).
Syn. illegality[2]. **See also** illegality[1], illegitimacy[2], licitness.
Fr. illégalité[2], illicéité[+].

ILLICIT OBJECT

1. Juridical operation contrary to law[3].
Obs. An illicit object may bring about the nullity of a contract (art. 1413 C.C.Q.). In some cases, the nature of the nullity is expressly stated by law, as in the case of procreation or gestation agreements and contracts of marine insurance by way of gaming or wagering, all of which are absolutely null (arts. 541 and 2512 C.C.Q.). Where not specified by law, the nature of the nullity is determined by evaluating whether the remedy protects the general interest or an individual interest. In the former case, the contract is absolutely null (art. 1417 C.C.Q.); in the latter, it relatively null (art. 1419 C.C.Q.).
See also nullity, licit object[1].
Fr. objet illicite[1].

2. Prestation contrary to law[3].
Obs. An illicit prestation may bring about the nullity of the obligation of which it is the object (art. 1373 C.C.Q.). It can also entail the nullity of the contract when it is the principal prestation of the contract. For example, in the case of gestation agreement, the principal prestation (i.e. the obligation to bring the foetus to term) is null, as is the contract itself (art. 541 C.C.Q.). Where not specified by law, the nature of the nullity is determined by evaluating whether the remedy protects the general interest or an individual interest. In the former case, the contract is absolutely null (art. 1417 C.C.Q.); in the latter, it is relatively null (art. 1419 C.C.Q.).
See also impossible object, nullity, licit object[2].
Fr. objet illicite[2].

IMMEDIATE CAUSE

Syn. proximate cause[1].
Obs. The expression *immediate cause*, used as an equivalent for *proximate cause*, does not correspond to the Civil Code's requirement in article 1607 C.C.Q. that the damage must be "an immediate and direct consequence of the debtor's default" in order for the victim to obtain compensation. The requirement respecting the immediate character of the damage does not necessarily designate a cause that immediately precedes the loss in time and space, without the occurrence of any other cause. Rather. it generally refers to the relationship between the loss and the cause, whereby the loss must not only be the direct consequence of the act or omission, but must also be so connected that, but for the debtor's default, the loss would not have occurred. Care should be taken to avoid confusion between the criteria established at article 1607 C.C.Q. and the notions of *proximate cause* or *immediate cause* used by scholars as one of the theories to establish causality.
Fr. cause immédiate[+], *causa proxima*.

IMMEDIATE VICTIM

Victim who suffers harm which, because of a connection between the victim and another person, results in that other person suffering harm. For example, injury caused to a child has repercussions for the parents. "[...] any person, even if he or she is not the immediate victim, could claim against the party responsible for the accident, always subject to the condition that there is a direct causal relation between the fault of the author of the accident and the damages claimed" (*Gendron* v. *Lignes Aériennes Canadien Pacifique Ltée*, [1977] C.S. 606, p. 607, B.J. Greenberg, J.).
Obs. The *immediate victim* is contrasted with the *mediate victim*, also known as the *victim by ricochet* or *victim once removed*.
Syn. initial victim, principal victim. **See also** initial damage, mediate victim, personal damage.
Fr. victime immédiate, victime initiale[+], victime principale.

IMMORAL CAUSE

Cause[2] contrary to good morals.
Obs. The immoral cause may be assimilated with the illicit cause, insofar as the distinction between public order and good morals has been abandoned in the *Civil Code of Québec* (art. 9 C.C.Q.).
See also false cause, illicit cause.
Fr. cause immorale.

IMMORAL CONDITION

Condition[1] the fulfilment of which depends upon the performance of an act contrary to good morals. "With respect to testamentary dispositions and donations *inter vivos*, the law declares that impossible, illicit, and immoral conditions are regarded as not written *viz.*, they are ignored and the dispositions to which they are attached are to be performed as if they were unconditional" (Aubry & Rau, *Civil Law*, vol. 4, n° 302, p. 62).
Obs. The notion of *good morals*, to which article 1080 C.C.L.C. made reference, is not explicitly referred to in article 1499 C.C.Q.
See also illicit condition, impossible condition.
Fr. condition immorale.

IMPERATIVE LAW

Law[1] from which one cannot derogate, notably by private agreement. "Evasion/fraud may be the act of one person (e.g. in a contract of adhesion or standard form contract such as a bill of lading), of two persons (e.g. when both parties to a divorce travel to another jurisdiction to avoid the applicable imperative law), or of two parties against a third party (e.g. in the case of the shipper and carrier so contracting that the normal law of estoppel benefiting a third party consignee of a bill of lading is not applicable)" (Tetley, (1994) 39 *McGill L.J.* 303, p. 307).
Obs. 1° The law governing the status and the capacity of persons is an example of imperative law. **2**° Section 51 of the *Interpretation Act* (R.S.Q. c. I-16) provides that, when law uses the expressions *shall be done* or *must be done*, the obligation will be considered as imperative. When this is the case, it signals the presence of a provision that is part of *legislative* or *public order*.
Syn. *jus cogens.* **See also** legislative public order, suppletive law[1].
Fr. droit impératif+, *jus cogens.*

IMPERFECT *adj.*

See imperfect bilateral contract, imperfect delegation, imperfect representation, imperfect synallagmatic contract.
Fr. imparfait.

IMPERFECT BILATERAL CONTRACT

Unilateral contract in which the party who initially had no obligation becomes debtor of an obligation by reason of an event subsequent to its formation. For example, a gratuitous deposit obliging the depositor to reimburse the depositary for expenses relating to the preservation of the property on deposit (art. 2293 C.C.Q.).
Syn. imperfect synallagmatic contract. **See also** bilateral contract.
Fr. contrat synallagmatique imparfait.

IMPERFECT DELEGATION

Delegation that does not entail the discharge of the delegator with respect to his or her creditor. For example, an undertaking by the purchaser of an immovable to pay part of the price to the vendor's hypothecary creditor.
Obs. Article 1668 C.C.Q. provides that, in the absence of a clear intention of the delegatee to discharge the delegator, the delegation is to be considered imperfect since the rights of the delegatee against the delegator remain the same.
See also indication of payment, perfect delegation.
Fr. délégation imparfaite.

IMPERFECT OBLIGATION

Syn. moral obligation.
See also perfect obligation.
Fr. devoir de conscience, devoir moral, obligation imparfaite, obligation morale+.

IMPERFECT REPRESENTATION

Performance of a juridical act in one's own name, although on behalf of someone else, without disclosing one's representative quality. For example, the situation of the *prête-nom*[1].
Obs. 1° This situation, which is not representation in the proper sense of the word, may be encountered in matters of mandate where it is agreed that the mandatary will act in his or her own name, without revealing the identity of the mandator. The juridical act entered into by a third person and the mandatary produces its effects with respect to the mandatary and not the mandator. The same occurs if the mandatary acts in his or her own name and on his or her own initiative (art. 2157 C.C.Q.). **2**° The expression *imperfect representation* is used in contrast to *perfect representation*, which describes true representation.
See also contract of *prête-nom*.
Fr. représentation imparfaite+, représentation médiate.

IMPERFECT SOLIDARITY

Syn. obligation *in solidum*. "[...] a segment of Quebec jurisprudence and doctrine has applied a slightly different regime of joint liability, borrowed from France, called 'imperfect' solidarity. Where solidarity is imperfect, each debtor is liable for the whole obligation, and performance by one debtor discharges the others indirectly. But the secondary effects of solidarity, founded upon the representation among debtors, do not apply" (Brierley & Macdonald (eds.), *Quebec Civil Law*, n° 535, pp. 486-487).
Obs. Imperfect solidarity is not in fact a form of solidarity. The expression is used in contrast to *perfect solidarity*, which describes true solidarity.
Fr. obligation *in solidum*+, solidarité imparfaite.

IMPERFECT SYNALLAGMATIC CONTRACT

Syn. imperfect bilateral contract.
Fr. contrat synallagmatique imparfait.

IMPLICIT CONSENT

Syn. tacit consent. "The Civil Code provides that consent to a contract may arise by implication. It follows then that facts establishing a defendant's implicit consent to a synallagmatic contract which impoverishes the plaintiff through expenditure of professional skill and time, while also leading directly to the defendant's enrichment, would cause a court to declare the plaintiff's right to recover in contract" (Fine, (1973) 19 *McGill L.J.* 453, p. 458).
Obs. See article 988 C.C.L.C.
Fr. consentement implicite, consentement tacite+, manifestation de volonté tacite.

IMPLICIT OBLIGATION

Obligation that, without being expressed formally, arises from the law or a juridical act, according to its nature and in conformity with usage or equity. "[...] it seems indisputable that an implicit obligation of good faith exists in every contract in Quebec civil law. This obligation is derived from a long civil law tradition formulated in art. 1024 *C.C.L.C.* [art. 1434 C.C.Q.]; it mandates that rights be exercised in a spirit of fair play" (*Houle* v. *National Bank of Canada*, [1990] 3 S.C.R. 122, p. 158, C. L'Heureux-Dubé, J.).
Obs. 1° Good faith, which was rediscovered through the interpretation of article 1024 C.C.L.C. in the 1960s and is now generally acknowledged as a source of implicit obligations. Moreover, the *Civil Code of Québec*, at article 1434, which substantially reproduces the terms of article 1024 C.C.L.C., has codified the duty to respect the requirements of good faith in articles 6, 7, 1375 C.C.Q. **2°** Implicit obligations of security, of loyalty and to inform or to advise others arise from the nature of certain contracts (e.g. medical contract, contract of enterprise or for services and mandate). **3°** The expression *implicit obligation* is used in order to distinguish this kind of obligations from express obligations.
Syn. implied obligation. **See also** duty to cooperate, express obligation, good faith[1,2], legal obligation[1,2], obligation of loyalty, obligation to inform.
Fr. obligation implicite.

IMPLIED CONSENT

Syn. tacit consent.
Fr. consentement implicite, consentement tacite+, manifestation de volonté tacite.

IMPLIED OBLIGATION

Syn. implicit obligation. "It is true to say that in this day and age, contractual absolutism no longer exists. Parties have a positive implied obligation of fair play. Minimally, that means that one of the parties cannot squeeze out part of the market of the other in an attempt to secure better renegotiated terms of agreement" (*Louis Dreyfus Canada Ltd.* v. *Quebec Cartier Mining Co.*, [1992] Q.J. N° 1923 (Sup.Ct.), para. 27 (QL), N. Duval-Hesler, J.).
Fr. obligation implicite.

IMPLIED OFFER

Offer inferred from conduct of a person indicating an intention to enter into a contract. For example, the lessee who continues to occupy the premises after the expiration of the lease implicitly agrees to renew it.
Obs. Some scholars distinguish implied offers from tacit offers, limiting the former to offers manifested by actions and the latter to offers evidenced by silence or inaction.
Syn. tacit offer. **See also** express offer.
Fr. offre implicite, offre tacite+.

IMPOSSIBILITY OF PERFORMANCE

Situation in which the debtor cannot provide the agreed upon prestation due to superior force. "It is this ancient Roman maxim [*nemo tenetur ad impossibilia*, no one is bound to the impossible], also with the writings of Pothier on the subject, together with art. 1302 C.N., which are the basis of the Quebec Civil Law on impossibility of performance as a means of extinguishing an obligation" (Wasserman, (1952) 12 *R. du B.* 366, p. 366).
Occ. Title preceding art. 1693 C.C.Q.; arts. 1671, 1694 C.C.Q.
Obs. 1° Impossibility of performance entails extinction of the correlative obligation and, where the prestation has already been performed, restitution thereof (arts. 1693, 1694 C.C.Q.). **2°** Given that impossibility of performance is measured objectively, it may not result from an impossibility that is peculiar to the debtor, but rather reflects an impossibility for anyone in the debtor's circumstances. **3°** Extinction of an obligation based on impossibility of performance is drawn from two maxims of Roman origin: *nemo tenetur ad impossibilia* (no one is bound to the impossi-

ble) and *impossibilium nulla obligatio* (an impossibility creates no obligation).
See also doctrine of risks[1], superior force[1].
Fr. impossibilité d'exécution.

IMPOSSIBLE *adj.*

See impossible condition.
Fr. impossible.

IMPOSSIBLE CONDITION

Condition[1] consisting of an event that cannot happen either physically or juridically. "A juridical act subject to an affirmative impossible condition or to a condition contrary to law or to good morals should, in pure doctrine, be null and void. The law, however, has adopted this solution only with respect to onerous agreements, namely onerous contracts and agreements relating to such contracts" (Aubry & Rau, *Civil Law*, vol. 4, n° 302, p. 62).
Occ. Art. 760 C.C.L.C.
Obs. 1° The impossibility is physical when the condition conflicts with the laws of nature; it can be absolute (e.g. to reach out and touch the sky) or relative, when the realization of the event is beyond the capacity of the person concerned (e.g. to run a hundred meters in less than five seconds). **2°** The impossibility is juridical when a rule of law prevents the realization of the event (e.g. the gift of property on the condition that it be forever inalienable). The juridically impossible condition is closely related to the illicit condition. **3°** In principle, an impossible condition is null and renders the obligation null; however, in matters relating to wills, it is deemed unwritten (arts. 757, 1499 C.C.Q.).
See also illicit condition, immoral condition.
Fr. condition impossible.

IMPOSSIBLE OBJECT

Prestation that, by reason of a situation of fact, is not susceptible of performance.
Obs. 1° The impossibility may result from a fact unknown at the time of the formation of the contract, such as the destruction of the object of the prestation. It may also result from a pre-existing cause, as in the example traditionally offered of an obligation to reach up and touch the sky with one's hand. **2°** Only an absolute impossibility renders the contract null. If the impossibility is relative or subjective, i.e. if the prestation is impossible for a particular debtor but would be possible for another person, the obligation remains valid. **3°** The term *illicit object* is used to describe an impossibility that is juridical in origin. **4°** In principle, if the execution of a prestation is rendered impossible by reason of superior force, the contract is not null but the debtor is nevertheless released (art. 1693 C.C.Q.).
See also illicit object[2], possible object.
Fr. objet impossible.

IMPRÉVISION *n.* (French)

Syn. unforeseeability[2].
Fr. imprévision.

IMPRUDENCE *n.*

Unintentional fault consisting of the failure to conduct oneself with the prudence required of a reasonable person in the circumstances in order to avoid a foreseeable injury. "'*Imprudence*' is given a broad interpretation by the Courts. It has been held that although there may be no law or regulation to this effect, a person must take all means of precaution which prudence may suggest under the circumstances" (Goldenberg, *Law of Delicts*, p. 11).
Occ. Art. 1053 C.C.L.C.
Obs. 1° Imprudence is often linked to foolhardiness in the face of danger or risk endangering safety. The prudence demanded of a reasonable person requires one to consider the potential consequences of his or her conduct and undertake the necessary steps to avoid dangerous situations or to minimize the risk of foreseeable injury. **2°** Imprudence and negligence are both classes of unintentional fault and entail the same legal consequences. As legal terms, they are often employed together or interchangeably. However, a distinction may be drawn between the two notions. Negligence consists in the absence of diligence whereas imprudence consists in the absence of prudence. It is often said of imprudence that, unlike negligence, it presupposes a missed initiative. **3°** Unlike article 1053 C.C.L.C., article 1457 C.C.Q. does not specifically mention imprudence as an illustration of fault.
Syn. fault of imprudence. **See also** civil fault, negligence, non-intentional fault, obligation of means, quasi-delict, quasi delictual fault, reasonable person.
Fr. faute d'imprudence, imprudence+.

IMPRUDENT *adj.*

See imprudence.
Fr. imprudent.

IMPUTABILITY *n.*

1. Fact of attributing to a person a civil fault by reason of his or her capacity of discernment. "The child of tender years is capable of having acted in an illicit manner but incapable of fault. Fault and blameworthiness are linked through imputability, but behaving badly cannot amount to a fault unless the actor is capable of discerning right from wrong" (Kasirer, (1992) 40 *Am. J. Comp. L.* 343, p. 350).

Obs. The role of imputability in ascertaining civil liability is the subject of debate. Some scholars view imputability as intrinsic to civil fault or, at the very least, a prerequisite to its existence. Others consider imputability to be a factor distinct from fault and relevant only to the determination of liability of a person for harm caused through his or her own fault (compare arts. 1457 and 1462 C.C.Q.).

Syn. moral imputability, psychological imputability. **See also** civil fault, civil liability, discernment, *doli capax.*

Fr. imputabilité[1+], imputabilité morale, imputabilité psychologique.

2. Fact of establishing a causal link between an injury and the act or omission of a person that gave rise to it.

Obs. This sense of the term *imputability* only describes the relationship of cause and effect between the damage and its origin. It does not take into account the capacity of discernment of the person who may be held liable.

Syn. material imputability. **See also** causation[1,2], external cause.

Fr. imputabilité[2+], imputabilité matérielle.

IMPUTABLE *adj.*

1. Able to be attributed to the civil fault of a person by reason of his or her capacity of discernment. *Harmful act imputable to the fault of a person.*

See also civil fault, civil liability, discernment, *doli capax*, imputability[1].

Fr. imputable[1].

2. When speaking of an injury, able to be attributed to a person by reason of a causal factor. "For it may be said that in industry there are three kinds of damage: that resulting from the fault of the victim, that resulting from the fault of the employer or of someone for whom he is responsible and that imputable to neither, either because the cause of it was a fortuitous event or irresistible force, or was completely unknown" (Nicholls, *Offences and Quasi-Offences*, p. 85).

Occ. Arts. 2019, 2155 C.C.Q.; art. 1722 C.C.L.C.; s. 149.2, *Automobile Insurance Act*, R.S.Q. c. A-25.

See also imputability[2].

Fr. imputable[2].

IMPUTATION OF PAYMENT

Application of a payment when the sum paid by the debtor does not cover all the debt or debts owed to the same creditor. "Articles 1158 and 1160 [C.C.L.C.] authorize imputations of payment by the debtor or creditor or both, provided they are made at the moment of payment" (*R.* v. *Ogilvie* (1899), 29 S.C.R. 299, p. 330, D. Girouard, J.).

Occ. Title preceding art. 1569 C.C.Q.; art. 1677 C.C.Q.; title preceding art. 1158 C.C.L.C.

Obs. 1° The imputation of payment may be made by the debtor or creditor or it may arise by operation of law. **2°** In the absence of contrary stipulations, the Civil Code establishes the order of imputation of payments (art. 1572 C.C.Q.). **3°** The codal regime respecting imputation of payment is set forth at articles 1569 to 1572 C.C.Q.

See also compensation[1], payment[1].

Fr. imputation des paiements.

IMPUTE *v.*

1. See imputability[1].

Fr. imputer[1].

2. See imputability[2].

Fr. imputer[2].

3. To apply the payment to a particular debt when the sum paid by the debtor does not cover the whole of the debts owed to the creditor. "The enactment of this article [1160 C.C.L.C.] is not limited to the case where the debtor has omitted to make an imputation, but provides generally for the case where the debtor has accepted a receipt in which the creditor has imputed [...] by returning [the] receipt [...] as requested" (*R.* v. *Ogilvie* (1899), 29 S.C.R. 299, p. 324, D. Girouard, J.). *To impute the payment in discharge of the capital.*

Occ. Arts. 1569, 1570 C.C.Q.; arts. 1159, 1843 C.C.L.C.

Obs. From the Latin *imputare*: to bring into a reckoning, to enter into the account.

Fr. imputer[3].

INABILITY *n.*

Syn. *de facto* incapacity.

Occ. Arts. 19.2, 328, 332.2, 1054.1, 1731.1 C.C.L.C.; art. 884.2 C.C.P.; s. 14, *Public Cura-*

tor Act, R.S.Q. c. C-81; s. 22, *An Act respecting health services and social services*, R.S.Q. c. S-4.2; s. 105, *An Act respecting health services and social services for Cree native persons*, R.S.Q. c. S-5.

Obs. The *Civil Code of Lower Canada* used the term *inability* to make plain the distinction between legal incapacity and *de facto* incapacity (e.g. arts. 19.2, 332.2, 1731.1 C.C.L.C.). This term is replaced by *incapacity* in the corresponding provisions of the *Civil Code of Québec*, which does not make the distinction between legal incapacity and *de facto* incapacity clear. Unlike the French text, which uses the term *inaptitude* when referring generally to *de facto* incapacity, the English text invariably uses the term *incapacity* to refer to both notions (e.g. arts. 259, 270, 295, 2128, 2166 C.C.Q.).
Fr. inaptitude+, incapacité[2], incapacité de fait, incapacité naturelle.

IN ABSTRACTO (Latin)

See extracontractual fault, *in concreto*, objective fault, objective lesion, obligation of means, reasonable person.
Obs. This Latin maxim means *in the abstract*.
Fr. *in abstracto*.

IN ADVANCE

See advance payment.
Fr. anticipé.

INALIENABILITY *n.*

Attribute of property not susceptible of alienation.
Occ. Title preceding art. 1212 C.C.Q.; art. 1212 C.C.Q.
Obs. 1° Inalienability constitutes an exception to the principle of free circulation of property. Consequently, legal provisions that prescribe inalienability must be strictly interpreted (*Laframboise* v. *Vallière* [1927] S.C.R. 193). **2°** Inalienability may result from law[2] (e.g. inalienability of State property) or from a juridical act (e.g. by means of a stipulation of inalienability). **3°** Inalienability of property results in its unseizability (art. 1215 C.C.Q.), because seizure for debt entails the sale of the property, which is precluded by inalienability. **4°** While some scholars consider that inalienability has the same effects as undisponibility, these two notions are in fact different. *Undisponibility*, which precludes the disposal of property, is a broader term than *inalienability*, which only forbids its

alienation, while leaving a possibility of the material disposal of the thing. Moreover, undisponibility is often associated with rights attached to a person (e.g. the right to a name). **5°** The terms *inalienability* and *non-assignability* are not synonyms, the use of the term *non-assignability* being generally associated with incorporeal property or rights.
See also intransmissibility, non-assignability, stipulation of inalienability, undisposability.
Fr. inaliénabilité.

INALIENABLE *adj.*

Not susceptible of alienation by the effect of law[2] or a juridical act. *Inalienable right.*
Occ. Arts. 3, 1213, 1216, 2377 C.C.Q.
See also alienable, inalienability, intransmissible, non-assignable, stipulation of inalienability, undisposable.
Fr. inaliénable.

INCAPABLE *adj.*

1. Said of a person subject to a legal incapacity. For example, a person of full age under protective supervision. "The expression 'incapable' and 'incapacity' are ambiguous. They ordinarily are used in connection with persons, who, possessing all their rights, have not the free exercise of them, as minors and interdicts. They are incapables, properly so called [...] But the same expressions are also used to designate persons who are deprived, in substance and in reality, of one or several rights" (Planiol & Ripert, *Treatise*, vol. 1, n° 1610, p. 2).
Occ. Art. 3086 C.C.Q.; arts. 833, 986, 1042 C.C.L.C.; art. 165(2) C.C.P.
See also capable[1], legal incapacity.
Fr. incapable[1].

2. Said of a person who, by reason of a physical or mental disability, is precluded from formulating an opinion, making a decision or expressing his or her will. "Among the persons declared by the Civil Code to be incapable of contracting are those who 'by reason of weakness of understanding are unable to give a valid consent': Art. 986 [C.C.L.C.]" (*Mathieu* v. *Saint-Michel*, [1956] S.C.R. 477, p. 487, I.C. Rand, J.).
Occ. Arts. 11, 21, 31, 258, 2177 C.C.Q.; arts. 268, 917 C.C.L.C.; arts. 394.1, 478.1, 776 C.C.P.
Syn. unable. **See also** capable[2], *de facto* incapacity.
Fr. inapte+, incapable[2].

INCAPABLE PERSON

1. Person under a legal incapacity. For example, a person of full age under protective supervision.
Occ. Art. 774 C.C.L.C.; arts. 558, 872 C.C.P.
Obs. The expression *incapable person* is most often used to describe a person of full age under protective supervision. It is seldom used in the case of minors. In French, the term *inapte* used as a noun or the expressions *majeur inapte* or *majeur protégé* are used to describe a person of full age placed under protective supervision.
See also incapable[1].
Fr. incapable[1].

2. Person who, by reason of a physical or mental disability, is precluded from making a decision or from expressing his or her will.
Occ. Arts. 348*a*, 1800 C.C.L.C.; arts. 394.1, 878.1 C.C.P.
See also *de facto* incapacity, incapable[2].
Fr. inapte[+], incapable[2].

INCAPACITY *n.*

1. Syn. legal incapacity. "The three central themes of the *ancien droit* as it related to marriage – incapacity for married women and their relative powerlessness under the legal regime, a marked preference for sharing in society's prototype for marriage, and freedom of contract – were carried into the *Civil Code of Lower Canada*" (Brisson & Kasirer, (1996) 23 *Man. L.J.* 406, p. 410).
Occ. Arts. 160, 256, 2340, 3086 C.C.Q.; arts. 987, 1484 C.C.L.C.; s. 86(4), *Canada Corporations Act*, R.S.C. 1970, c. C-32;
Fr. incapacité[1], incapacité de droit, incapacité juridique[+], incapacité légale.

2. Syn. *de facto* incapacity.
Fr. inaptitude[+], incapacité[2], incapacité de fait, incapacité naturelle.

INCAPACITY OF PROTECTION

Legal incapacity imposed by law in order to protect the person subject to it. For example, the incapacity of a minor, the incapacity of persons of full age under protective supervision.
Obs. 1° Incapacities of protection are generally imposed as incapacities to exercise. However, there are incapacities to enjoy that are imposed in order to protect the incapacitated person (e.g. the incapacity of the minor to give valuable property *inter vivos* (art. 1813 C.C.Q.)). **2°** Notwithstanding an incapacity of protection, juridical acts that are entered into are in principle subject to relative nullity.
See also incapacity of public order, incapacity to enjoy (rights), incapacity to exercise (rights), relative nullity.
Fr. incapacité de protection.

INCAPACITY OF PUBLIC ORDER

Neol. Legal incapacity imposed by law in order to protect third parties or the general interest. For example, the incapacity of officers of justice to acquire litigious rights (art. 1783 C.C.Q.).
Obs. 1° Incapacities of public order are generally, in the public interest, incapacities to enjoy. **2°** Juridical acts entered into notwithstanding an incapacity of public order are, in principle, subject to absolute nullity.
See also absolute nullity, incapacity of protection, incapacity to enjoy (rights), public order.
Fr. incapacité de défiance[+], incapacité d'ordre public.

INCAPACITY RATE

See *quantum.*
Fr. taux d'incapacité.

INCAPACITY TO ACQUIRE (RIGHTS)

Syn. incapacity to enjoy (rights).
Fr. incapacité d'acquisition, incapacité de jouissance[+].

INCAPACITY TO ENJOY (RIGHTS)

Legal incapacity depriving a person of the ability to be the holder of a right.
Obs. 1° An incapacity to enjoy rights has the effect not only of depriving a person of the exercise of a right but of the possibility of holding the right itself. Such a person is therefore precluded from performing juridical acts either personally or through a representative. The traditional example is the incapacity of a minor to bequeath property by will (arts. 708, 711 C.C.Q.). **2°** Incapacity to enjoy rights is necessarily special in the sense that a person may only be deprived of specified rights. A general incapacity to enjoy would amount to a denial of legal personality. **3°** Article 18 C.C.L.C. clearly provided that the enjoyment of civil rights could only be limited by express provision of law whereas article 1 C.C.Q. does not expressly say so.
Syn. incapacity to acquire (rights). **See also** capacity to enjoy (rights), general incapacity, incapacity of public order, incapacity

of protection, incapacity to exercise (rights), nullity, special incapacity.
Fr. incapacité d'acquisition, incapacité de jouissance[+].

INCAPACITY TO EXERCISE (RIGHTS)

Legal incapacity depriving a person of the ability to exercise a right of which he or she is the holder. "Minority is a cause of incapacity [...] to exercise rights, which in practice means that a minor can validly enter into a contract provided that the tutor to the minor intervenes in the act [...]" (Brierley & Macdonald (eds.), *Quebec Civil Law*, n° 435, p. 407).
Obs. 1° Incapacity to exercise a right does not deprive the incapacitated person of the right itself. Such incapacity has the effect of depriving the person of the ability to act personally as regards that right, that is to say without assistance or representation (e.g. the incapacity of the minor who, in order to exercise his or her civil rights, must, in principle, be represented by a tutor (art. 158 C.C.Q.)).
2° In principle, incapacities to exercise rights are considered incapacities of protection established in the interest of the incapable person (arts. 177, 256 C.C.Q.). **3°** Minors and persons of full age under protective supervision are placed under an incapacity to exercise rights. In the case of unemancipated minors, the incapacity is general (arts. 155, 158 C.C.Q.). In the case of persons of full age, the extent of incapacity is determined by the judgment of the court establishing protective supervision (arts. 258, 268 C.C.Q.).
See also capacity to exercise (rights), general incapacity, incapacity of protection, incapacity to enjoy (rights), nullity.
Fr. incapacité d'exercice.

INCIDENTAL FRAUD

Fraud that has induced a person to accept different contractual terms than those he or she would otherwise have accepted.
Obs. 1° Article 993 C.C.L.C. only recognized fraud as a basis for an error vitiating consent when, but for the error, the party would not have contracted at all. Article 1401 C.C.Q. recognizes that consent is also vitiated when, but for the error, the party would have contracted on different terms. This solution, inspired by scholarly writing and jurisprudence, is based on a distinction between principal fraud – where the party would not have entered into the juridical act – and incidental fraud – where the party would have entered into the juridical act under different terms.

2° The remedies of the victim of fraud are however the same, since art. 1407 C.C.Q. does not make any reference to the distinction between principal and incidental fraud. Therefore, all victims may demand an annulment, a reduction of the obligation or an award of damages.
See also fraud[1], principal fraud.
Fr. dol incident.

IN CONCRETO (Latin)

See *in abstracto*, inexcusable error, obligation of means, subjective fault, subjective lesion.
Obs. This Latin maxim means *in context*.
Fr. *in concreto*.

INCORPORATED BY REFERENCE

See external clause.
Fr. clause externe.

IN CORPORE adv. ph. (Latin)

In kind, with regard to the performance of an obligation. For example, the debtor of a certain and determinate thing must return it *in corpore*, which is to say the object itself rather than a substitute or equivalent.
See also payment in kind[2], reparation in kind, specific performance.
Fr. *in corpore*.

INCORPOREAL PROPERTY

Syn. patrimonial right. "Incorporeal property has no substance, no physical existence; it can be perceived only by the intellect. It comprises rights of all kinds having property for their object, such as a debt, or a share in a commercial corporation" (Marler, *Real Property*, p. 1).
Fr. bien[1], bien incorporel, chose incorporelle, droit patrimonial[+].

INCORPOREAL THING

Syn. patrimonial right. "In Roman Law, distinction was drawn between *res corporales* and *res incorporales* [...] Incorporeal things were abstract conceptions, objects having no physical existence but having a pecuniary value. The illustrations given were rights of various kinds, including inheritance, obligations, and all real rights with the exception of ownership" (Yiannopoulos, in *Treatise*, vol. 2, n° 25, p. 43).
Fr. bien[1], bien incorporel, chose incorporelle, droit patrimonial[+].

INDEMNIFIABLE *adj.*

Susceptible of reparation by equivalence.
Indemnifiable damage.
Fr. indemnisable.

INDEMNIFICATION *n.*

Syn. reparation by equivalence. "[...] the hypothecary debtor took out an insurance policy containing a hypothecary clause, which sets out a separate insurance contract between the hypothecary creditor and the insurer. Since the hypothecary creditor and not the debtor is the insured under this separate second contract, indemnification of the hypothecary creditor for the loss caused by its debtor's intentional fault is not contrary to the prohibition of public order contained in art. 2563 C.C.L.C." (*Caisse populaire des Deux Rives* v. *Société mutuelle d'assurance contre l'incendie de la Vallée du Richelieu*, [1990] 2 S.C.R. 995, p. 1028., C. L'Heureux-Dubé, J.).
Occ. Art. 454 C.C.Q.; s. 350, *Consumer Protection Act*, R.S.Q. c. P-40.1.
Fr. compensation[2], indemnisation, réparation par équivalent[+].

INDEMNIFICATORY *adj.*

Having the characteristics of an indemnity.
See also compensatory
Fr. indemnitaire.

INDEMNIFY *v.*

To repair a loss by providing something equivalent to that which was lost. "Where the debtor is guilty of fraud he is bound to indemnify the creditor for the entire loss which he has suffered and for all gains of which he is deprived [...]" (Aubry & Rau, *Civil Law*, vol. 4, n° 308, p. 112). *To indemnify the victim.*
Occ. Arts. 892, 1493, 2517 C.C.Q.
Fr. indemniser.

INDEMNITY *n.*

Something serving as reparation for damage sustained, most often a sum of money. "After the properties in question were completely destroyed by arson on June 25, 1983, the respondents refused to pay the indemnity to the hypothecary creditors, alleging that the policy was void *ab initio* because of the misrepresentations by Katsikonouris at the time the policy was purchased. The appellants and the National Bank of Greece (Canada) brought actions against Katsikonouris' insurers to claim the indemnity" (*National Bank of*

Greece (Canada) v. *Katsikonouris*, [1990] 2 S.C.R. 1029, p. 1060, C. L'Heureux-Dubé, J.).
Occ. Arts. 1075, 1701, 3042 C.C.Q.
Syn. compensation[4], reparation[2]. **See also** damages, reparation[1].
Fr. compensation[3], indemnité[+].

INDEX *v.*

To determine the amount of a debt according to the fluctuation of a specific indicator. For example, to index a salary according to a measure of the cost of living.
Fr. indexer.

INDEXATION *n.*

Determination of the amount of a debt according to the fluctuation of a specific indicator.
Obs. The market value of a thing or a service, the cost of living index and variations in the municipal or school taxes, inter alia, may be used for indexation.
See also sliding scale clause.
Fr. indexation.

INDEXATION CLAUSE

Syn. sliding scale clause.
Fr. clause d'échelle mobile[+], clause d'indexation, clause indexée.

INDICATION OF PAYMENT

Act by which the debtor informs the creditor, or the creditor informs the debtor, of a mandate given to a third person to pay or to receive payment on his or her behalf.
Occ. Art. 1667 C.C.Q.
Obs. An indication of payment does not effect novation. It is distinguished from delegation in that the person to whom the debtor has given a mandate to pay is not personally obligated toward the creditor.
See also imperfect delegation, mandate[1], perfect delegation.
Fr. indication de paiement.

INDIRECT *adj.*

See indirect action, indirect damage, indirect liability, indirect responsibility.
Fr. indirect.

INDIRECT ACTION

Syn. oblique action.
Occ. Art. 1035 C.C.Q.
Fr. action indirecte, action oblique[+].

INDIRECT DAMAGE

Damage that has no causal relationship with the fact giving rise to liability. "As to what is 'indirect' damage not recoverable [...] It is damage of which the fault (fait) of the defendant has been merely the occasion, not the cause" (*Regent Taxi & Transport Co.* v. *Congrégation des Petits Frères de Marie*, [1929] S.C.R. 650, p. 663, F.A. Anglin, C.J.).
Obs. Since the terms *damage* and *injury* are synonymous, the expression *indirect injury* may also be used.
See also direct damage, initial damage, personal damage, ricochet damage.
Fr. préjudice indirect.

INDIRECT LIABILITY

Civil liability of a person who must answer for the damage caused by another or by a thing under his or her control.
Obs. 1° The liability under the applicable provisions of the Civil Code is said to be indirect in that the person held liable is not himself or herself the direct author of the damage (see arts. 1459 to 1469 C.C.Q.). **2°** There are two species of indirect liability: first, where the person is held to be at fault by reason of his or her failure to exercise proper supervision of the person or thing that causes damage; second, where the person is held vicariously liable for the fault of another person.
Syn. indirect responsibility. **See also** liability for damage caused by another, liability for damage caused by things, personal liability[2], vicarious liability.
Fr. responsabilité indirecte.

INDIRECT RESPONSIBILITY

Syn. indirect liability.
Fr. responsabilité indirecte.

INDIVIDUAL ACT

Act that emanates from a single person. For example, a will, a unilateral resiliation of a contract.
Obs. 1° The characterization of an act as an *individual act* is made in order to draw a distinction with the *collective act.* **2°** The expression *individual act* is most often used to designate *individual unilateral acts.*
See also collective act, individual contract, unilateral act.
Fr. acte individuel.

INDIVIDUAL CONTRACT

Contract that is binding only on those persons who have consented to it.

Obs. A distinction is drawn between *individual contracts* and *collective contracts.*
See also collective contract.
Fr. contrat individuel.

INDIVIDUAL CONTRACT OF EMPLOYMENT

Syn. contract of employment. "[...] the contractual theory consists of founding the exercise and existence of the employers disciplinary power in the contents of the individual contract of employment between the employer and employee and suppletively, in the rules governing contracts in the Civil Code" (Athanassidis, (1985) 5 *R.E.J.* 267, p. 273).
Fr. contrat d'emploi, contrat de louage de services[1], contrat de louage de service(s) personel(s), contrat de travail[+], contrat individuel de travail, louage de service(s) personel(s).

INDIVIDUAL FAULT

Civil fault that is attributable to a specific person rather than a group.
See also collective fault, common fault, personal fault.
Fr. faute individuelle.

INDIVIDUAL INTEREST

That which is to the advantage of a party to a juridical act.
Occ. Art. 1419 C.C.Q.
Obs. The notion of *individual interest* takes a particular colour in contract law. The nullity of a juridical act is relative when it is contrary to an individual interest (art. 1419 C.C.Q.), whereas it is absolute when it is contrary to the general interest (art. 1417 C.C.Q.).
See also general interest, nullity, public order.
Fr. intérêt particulier.

INDIVISIBILITY *n.*

Characteristic of an obligation the object of which is not susceptible of partial performance. "[...] indivisibility is a characteristic of an obligation and not, as in solidarity, a characteristic of the relationship between parties to it" (Brierley & Macdonald (eds.), *Quebec Civil Law,* n° 537, p. 488).
Occ. Art. 1125 C.C.L.C.
Obs. 1° Indivisibility with regard to several creditors is called *active indivisibility,* whereas indivisibility with regard to several debtors is called *passive indivisibility.* **2°** As to its sources, indivisibility may be either natural or conventional. **3°** When there are sev-

eral creditors, indivisibility allows any one of them to obtain full performance of the prestation. When there are several debtors, it allows the creditor to obtain full performance of the prestation from any one of them. 4° Indivisibility relates to the object of the obligation which, by reason of its nature or because of a fiction, is not susceptible of division. Solidarity, on the other hand, does not pertain to the object of the obligation, but rather to a plurality of titularies. In this case, the full performance of the obligation arises as a result of mutual representation or community of interests between them. 5° The codal regime respecting indivisibility is set forth at articles 1519 to 1522 C.C.Q.
See also active indivisibility, conventional indivisibility, divisibility[2], indivisibility of payment, indivisible obligation, modality of the obligation, natural indivisibility, passive indivisibility, solidarity.
Fr. indivisibilité.

INDIVISIBILITY OF PAYMENT

Character of payment that a debtor may not, in principle, force a creditor to receive in parts even though the debt is otherwise divisible.
Obs. See articles 1522 and 1561 C.C.Q.
See also conventional indivisibility, payment[1].
Fr. indivisibilité du paiement.

INDIVISIBLE *adj.*

See indivisible debt, indivisible obligation.
Fr. indivisible.

INDIVISIBLE CLAIM

Creance, the payment of which may not be demanded in parts.
Obs. The notion of *indivisible claim* takes on its full meaning in situations where there is more than one creditor, each of whom is entitled to the entire debt (art. 1520 C.C.Q.).
Syn. indivisible creance. **See also** divisible creance, indivisibility, indivisible debt, indivisible obligation, solidarity.
Fr. créance indivisible.

INDIVISIBLE CREANCE

Syn. indivisible claim.
Fr. créance indivisible.

INDIVISIBLE DEBT

Debt, the payment of which may not be made in parts.
Occ. Arts. 823, 827 C.C.Q.

Obs. The notion of *indivisible debt* takes on its full meaning in situations where there is more than one debtor, all of whom are obliged to pay the entire debt (art. 1520 C.C.Q.). By contrast with solidary debts, indivisible debts are passed to the debtors' heirs, each of which is held for the same debt.
See also divisible debt, indivisible claim, indivisible obligation, payment[1], solidarity.
Fr. dette indivisible.

INDIVISIBLE OBLIGATION

Obligation that may not be performed in parts because its object is not susceptible of division. For example, the obligation to deliver a certain and determinate thing. "The obligation to go or not to go to a certain town is an indivisible obligation by reason of the physical impossibility of division of its object" (Aubry & Rau, *Civil Law*, vol. 1, n° 301, pp. 49-50).
Occ. Arts. 1040, 1519 to 1522, 2900 C.C.Q.; arts. 1127 to 1130 C.C.L.C.
Obs. Indivisibility does not result from a stipulation of solidarity alone (art. 1521 C.C.Q.), because it may also depend on the nature of the object of the obligation or an express stipulation (art. 1519 C.C.Q.).
See also divisible obligation, indivisible claim, indivisible debt, obligation with a complex modality, solidary obligation.
Fr. obligation indivisible.

INEXCUSABLE ERROR

Error that, because it is wrongful, cannot constitute a defect of consent.
Occ. Art. 1400 C.C.Q.
Obs. The determination that an error is inexcusable is established *in concreto*, i.e. by taking into account the circumstances existing at the time of formation of the contract, in particular, the age, mental state, intelligence and financial position of the parties.
See also defect of consent.
Fr. erreur inexcusable.

INEXECUTION *n.*

Syn. non-performance. "Quebec courts have, in the past, been reluctant to grant injunctions to specifically enforce obligations, especially obligations to do. In this regard, there has been a considerable divergence between the availability of specific performance as a remedy for the inexecution of an obligation in theory and in practice" (Jukier, (1987) 47 *R. du B.* 47, p. 51).
Fr. défaut d'exécution, inexécution⁺.

INEXISTENCE n.

Syn. non-existence.
Fr. inexistence.

INFORMED CONSENT

Syn. enlightened consent. "One of the essential elements in a contract entered into between a patient and his physician for treatment is consent. [...] 'Informed consent' simply means that a patient is entitled to know the risks of the treatment or surgery proposed which are known to the physician or surgeon and unknown to the patient" (Paterson, (1980) 40 *R. du B.* 816, p. 816).
Obs. This expression is particularly current in medical law.
Fr. consentement éclairé.

INGRATITUDE n.

Serious fault resulting from a lack of gratitude of the beneficiary towards the author, which may give rise to a penalty as provided by law.
Occ. Art. 811(1) C.C.L.C.
Obs. 1° There are three cases of ingratitude: an attempt upon the life of the donor; acts that render the donee guilty of ill usage, crimes or grievous injuries upon the donor; and the refusal to provide maintenance. **2°** Ingratitude entails a sanction of a purely personal nature; it cannot, for example, be demanded by the donor against the heirs of the donee.
Fr. ingratitude.

IN INTEGRUM adj.ph. (Latin)

See full reparation.
Fr. in integrum.

INITIAL adj.

See initial damage, initial offer, initial victim.
Fr. initial.

INITIAL DAMAGE

Damage suffered by a person that, because of a connection between the victim and another person, results in that person suffering harm.
Obs. Since the terms *damage* and *injury* are synonymous, the expression *initial injury* may also be used.
See also direct damage, personal damage, ricochet damage.
Fr. préjudice initial.

INITIAL OFFER

Original offer to which the offeree proposes certain changes.
Obs. 1° An acceptance implies the offeree's adherence to the elements of the offer. If the offeree proposes substantial changes to the content of the offer, this counter-offer does not amount to acceptance, but may constitute a new offer that has the effect of causing the initial offer to lapse (art. 1393 C.C.Q.). **2°** This expression is generally used to describe the original offer in the context of offer and counter-offer.
See also counter-offer.
Fr. offre initiale.

INITIAL VICTIM

Syn. immediate victim.
Fr. victime immédiate, victime initiale[+], victime principale.

INJURY n.

Syn. damage. "However slight the fault may be, it engenders civil responsibility where it is productive of injury to another" (Goldenberg, *Law of Delicts*, p. 13). *To cause an injury*; *to redress an injury*.
Occ. Arts. 1457, 1458, 1607, 1609 C.C.Q.; art. 1776 C.C.L.C.; s. 278 *An Act respecting the implementation of the reform of the Civil Code*, S.Q. 1992, c. 57.
Obs. 1° In the *Civil Code of Québec*, the legislature appears to prefer the term *injury* to *damage*, particularly in the chapter on civil liability. This terminological change may be seen, in part, as an effort to avoid the common confusion between *damage*, used in the sense of injury, and *damages*, used to designate the compensation owed to the victim. **2°** Although the Civil Code uses the terms *injury* and *damage* synonymously in the context of *material* and *moral injury*, the term *injury* is more frequently used as a description of physical or bodily harm.
See also bodily injury.
Fr. dommage, préjudice[+], tort[2].

INJURY TO FEELINGS

Moral damage resulting from sentiments of affection having been hurt. For example, the grief caused by the death or the injury of a loved one. "In reality, one could say that aside from the Criminal law aspect, the law does not protect the [dead] body, but rather protects the members of the family from anguish

and other injury to their feelings occasioned by illicit acts upon their loved ones" (Kouri, (1970) 1 *R.D.U.S.* 77, p. 85).
Obs. This term is generally used to designate the injury to the feelings of a person for the victim of a wrong inflicted by a third person.
See also mediate victim, moral damage, *pretium affectionis*, *pretium doloris*, ricochet damage, *solatium doloris*.
Fr. préjudice d'affection.

INNOMINATE *adj.*

See innominate contract.
Fr. innommé.

INNOMINATE CONTRACT

Contract that is not specifically regulated. For example, contract for medical services, franchise. "The codes devote considerable space to the detailed regulation of the more important contractual types, and there is evidently a strong tendency to make the innominate contracts run in their channels" (Ryan, *Introduction*, p. 38).
Obs. 1° Innominate contracts are governed by the general rules of the Civil Code pertaining to contractual matters, both with respect to their formation and effects. **2°** A distinction is drawn between *innominate contracts* and *nominate contracts*.
Syn. *sui generis* contract. **See also** mixed contract, nominate contract.
Fr. contrat innommé+, contrat *sui generis*.

INOPPOSABILITY *n.*

Characteristic of a right or juridical act that prevents it from being raised against third persons. "The courts however have seemingly denied the hypothecary debtor this protection of inopposability by ruling in *Banque Canadienne Nationale* v. *Lachance* that such debtor who has received simple service of the transfer cannot invoke the failure to register the transfer and serve the registration certificate against the assignee when the latter seeks payment" (Miller & Sarna, (1981) 59 *Can. Bar Rev.* 638, p. 644). *Inopposability of the contract.*
Obs. 1° Inopposability is especially relevant with respect to the law relating to fraud, to simulation and to the publication of rights (arts. 1451 *et seq.*, 1631 *et seq.*, 2941 *et seq.* C.C.Q.). **2°** A right that is *inopposable* may also be described as one that *may not be set up against* another (e.g. art. 1631 C.C.Q.). **3°** This term is sometimes characterized as a calque from the French *inopposabilité*.

See also annulability, invalidity, non-existence, nullity, opposability, paulian action, relative effect of contract.
Fr. inopposabilité.

INOPPOSABLE *adj.*

Not able to be invoked against third persons. *Inopposable act*; *inopposable right*.
Obs. 1° The expression *set up against* is sometimes used in preference to *opposable*. Similarly, *not set up against* is sometimes preferred to *inopposable* and to *set up against* to the verb *oppose*. **2°** This term is sometimes characterized as a calque from the French *inopposable*.
See also opposable.
Fr. inopposable.

IN SOLIDUM *adj.ph.* (Latin)

See liability *in solidum*, obligation *in solidum*.
Fr. *in solidum*.

IN SOLIDUM LIABILITY (Latin)

Syn. liability *in solidum*.
Fr. responsabilité *in solidum*.

IN SOLIDUM OBLIGATION (Latin)

Syn. obligation *in solidum*.
Fr. obligation *in solidum*+, solidarité imparfaite.

INSTALMENTS *n.*

Syn. periodic payment. "[...] under our jurisprudence there may be as many actions as there are instalments of salary or wages falling due" (*Weiss* v. *Bruck Silk Mills Ltd.* (1928), 30 Q.P.R. 381 (Sup. Ct.), p. 383, W.L. Bond, J.).
Occ. Arts. 411, 2442 C.C.Q.; arts. 1149, 1651.5 C.C.L.C.
Fr. paiement échelonné, paiement périodique+.

INSTALMENT SALE

Sale with a term deferring the transfer of ownership of the property until the payment, by the purchaser, of the price in full. "The limits of the classical theory are also reached whenever a real right is only gradually perfected. For example, neither the purchaser under an instalment sale, nor the lessee with an option to purchase, nor the financial lessee, nor the owner under suspensive condition have a present real right in the thing

which is the object of their rights" (Macdonald, (1994) 39 *McGill L.J.* 761, p. 791).
Occ. Art. 1745 C.C.Q.; ss. 131, 135, 148, *Consumer Protection Act*, R.S.Q. c. P-40.1.
Obs. 1° In an instalment sale, the price is generally paid by way of periodic payments over a set period of time. **2°** Instalment sales are often used to secure the financing granted for the purchase of property with a high purchase price as, for example, an automobile. **3°** The codal regime respecting instalment sales is set forth at articles 1745 to 1749 C.C.Q. A special regime for movable instalment sales between a consumer and a merchant is set forth at sections 132 to 149 of the *Consumer Protection Act* (R.S.Q. c. P-40.1).
Syn. conditional contract of sale, conditional sale[2], conditional sales contract, sale by instalment. **See also** sale with a term.
Fr. vente à tempérament.

INSTANTANEOUS CONTRACT

Syn. contract of instantaneous performance.
Fr. contrat à exécution instantanée+, contrat instantané.

INSTANTANEOUS OBLIGATION

Obligation[3] whose prestation is susceptible of being performed in one stroke. For example, the obligation of a vendor to deliver the thing sold, the obligation of the buyer to pay the price agreed upon.
Syn. obligation of instantaneous performance. **See also** continuous obligation, contract of instantaneous performance.
Fr. obligation instantanée.

INSTRUMENTUM n. (Latin)

Syn. attesting deed. "Our old language had the word 'instrument' from the Latin instrumentum, which had the merit of avoiding all confusion between the fact proved and the means of its proof [...]" (Planiol & Ripert, *Treatise*, vol. 2, n° 56, p. 43).
Fr. acte[2], acte instrumentaire+, *instrumentum*, titre[3].

INSURANCE n.

Syn. insurance contract.
Occ. Arts. 2389, 2390, 2391 C.C.Q.; art. 2469 C.C.L.C.; art. 739 C.C.P.; ss. 1, 10, *An act respecting insurance*, R.S.Q. c. A-32; ss. 22, 76, *An Act respecting the distribution of financial products and services*, R.S.Q. c. D-9.2.
Fr. assurance, contrat d'assurance+.

INSURANCE CONTRACT

Contract whereby a person, the *insurer*, in exchange for a premium or assessment, undertakes to make a payment to another, the *client* or a *third person*, upon the occurrence of a specified event. "The insurance contract protects against the occurrence of the event that is the object of the risk. The contingent nature of that element makes the insurance transaction possible" (*Goulet* v. *Transamerica Life Insurance Co. of Canada*, [2002] 1 S.C.R. 719, p. 732, L. LeBel, J.).
Occ. Arts. 2414, 2433, 2440 C.C.Q.; arts. 2476, 2496, 2499 C.C.L.C.; ss. 1, 358, *An Act respecting insurance*, R.S.Q. c. A-32; ss. 18, 439, 463, *An Act respecting the distribution of financial products and services*, R.S.Q. c. D-9.2.
Obs. 1° Insurance is based on a principle of mutuality which involves the sharing of risks among the persons insured. **2°** The existence of an insurable interest, by the person who takes out the insurance, in the life or health of the person who is the object of the risk or in the insured property is of the essence of the contract of insurance. This condition, of public order (art. 2414 C.C.Q.), is justified by the purpose of insurance, which is to indemnify or compensate, not to enrich, a person, as well as by the concern to avoid speculation on the life, health or property of another. **3°** The contract of insurance is divided into two categories: non-marine insurance (arts. 2391 C.C.Q.) and marine insurance (arts. 2390 C.C.Q.; *Marine Insurance Act*, S.C. 1993, c. 22). **4°** The contract of insurance is established on the basis of an insurance application, generally presented by the future client, which, once accepted by the insurer, creates the contract (art. 2398 C.C.Q.). **5°** The requirement of good faith, formally recognized in article 6 of the *Civil Code of Québec*, imposes on the client the duty to disclose all information relevant to the evaluation of the risk, in an honest, exact and active manner (art. 2408 C.C.Q.). This requirement also imposes on the insurer an obligation to inform. **6°** A distinction must be drawn between the contract of insurance and the insurance policy, the policy being documentary evidence of the existence of the contract (art. 2399 C.C.Q.). **7°** The insurance contract is distinguished from the suretyship in that the insurer has no recourse against the insured. **8°** The codal regime respecting the insurance contract is set forth at articles 2389 to 2628 C.C.Q.
Syn. contract of insurance, insurance. **See also** aleatory contract, beneficiary[1], client[1],

contract by onerous title, contract of adhesion, good faith[1,2], insured, insurer, marine insurance, non-marine insurance, premium, suretyship.

Fr. assurance, contrat d'assurance+.

INSURANCE OF PERSONS

Contract of insurance that has for its object risks relating to the life, physical integrity or health of the insured.

Occ. Arts. 450, 463, 2392, 2415 C.C.Q.; arts. 2471, 2472, 2501 C.C.L.C.; ss. 18, 203, 285.4, *An Act respecting insurance*, R.S.Q. c. A-32; ss. 3, 208, 211, *An Act respecting the distribution of financial products and services*, R.S.Q. c. D-9.2.

Obs. 1° Insurance of persons seeks to compensate, not indemnify: the amount received by the beneficiary is pre-established and independent of the harm suffered. Certain forms of insurance of persons may nevertheless appear to be contracts of indemnity, such as the insurance bearing on the person of debtors, in which the insured capital may not exceed the amount owed by the borrower to the lender. **2°** Insurance of persons may be individual insurance or group insurance (art. 2392 C.C.Q.). **3°** There are two types of insurance of persons: life insurance, which guarantees the payment of an amount, either at the moment of death of the insured, or, if he or she is still living, at a fixed date, and health insurance, which guarantees against disability or accident. **4°** Life insurance generally aims at compensating a close one in the event of the death of the insured; in this respect, it differs from health insurance, which generally aims at compensating the insured himself or herself.

See also policy owner.

Fr. assurance de personnes.

INSURANCE POLICY

Document establishing the existence of the contract of insurance. "The ['intentional fault'] principle is fundamental to the notion of *risk* in insurance law and its 'raison d'être' is obvious. The insured is not permitted, by his own intentional act, to bring about the realization of the risk for which the insurance policy was issued" (*Goulet* v. *Transamerica Life Insurance Co. of Canada*, [2000] R.J.Q. 1066 (C.A.), M.L. Rothman, J.A.).

Occ. Arts. 2401, 2415 C.C.Q.; art. 2501 C.C.L.C.; ss. 238, 406.2, *An Act respecting insurance*, R.S.Q. c. A-32; ss. 39, 243, 414, *An Act respecting the distribution of financial products*, R.S.Q. c. D-9.2.

Obs. 1° Certain informations must be set out in the insurance policy (art. 2399 C.C.Q.). **2°** In non-marine insurance, in the case of a discrepancy between the policy and the application, article 2400 C.C.Q. provides that the latter prevails "unless the insurer has, in a separate document, indicated the particulars in respect of which there is discrepancy to the client". **3°** In group insurance, the insurer must issue the policy to the client and must give the client insurance certificates, which the client must then transmit to the participants (art. 2401 C.C.Q.).

See also client[1], insurance contract, insurer, participant.

Fr. police d'assurance.

INSURE *v.*

To guarantee against a risk by way of an insurance contract.

Occ. Arts. 2466, 2516, 2627 C.C.Q.; arts. 2566, 2606 C.C.L.C.; ss. 174.1, 174.5, *An Act respecting insurance*, R.S.Q. c. A-32; s. 8, *An Act respecting the distribution of financial products and services*, R.S.Q. c. D-9.2.

Fr. assurer.

INSURED *n.*

Person who subscribes to a contract of insurance or in respect of whom a risk is covered by a contract of insurance. "I conclude that the insured will be relieved of its duty to disclose where material facts are substantially as depicted by virtue of public character and notoriety" (*Canadian Indemnity Co.* v. *Canadian Johns-Manville Co.*, [1990] 2 S.C.R. 549, p. 594, C.D. Gonthier, J.).

Occ. Arts. 2390, 2392, 2395, 2418 C.C.Q.; arts. 2472, 2475, 2487 C.C.L.C.; art. 69 C.C.P.; ss. 238, 401, 406.1, *An Act respecting insurance*, R.S.Q. c. A-32; arts. 102, 411, 444, *An Act respecting the distribution of financial products and services*, R.S.Q. c. D-9.2.

Obs. 1° While the three terms may in fact refer to the same person, the terms *insured*, *client* and *beneficiary* must be distinguished. Life insurance best exemplifies the difference between these terms: the insured is the person whose death triggers the payment by the insurer; the client, who may or may not be the person insured, subscribes to the contract with the insurer; and the beneficiary is the person who receives the payment upon the death of the insured. **2°** In damage insurance contracts, the term *insured* generally designates the client[1] of the contract.

See also beneficiary[1], client[1], insurance contract, insurer.

Fr. assuré.

INSURER *n.*

Party to an insurance contract who undertakes, if the risk materializes, to make the agreed payment to the client or to a third party. "[...] an insurer cannot fault the insured for failing to disclose all the detailed information in its possession where the picture open and well known to a reasonably competent insurer substantially represents the facts" (*Canadian Indemnity Co.* v. *Canadian Johns-Manville Co.*, [1990] 2 S.C.R. 549, p. 594, C.D. Gonthier, J.).
Occ. Arts. 2389, 2398, 2400, 2515 C.C.Q.; arts. 2468, 2476, 2478 C.C.L.C.; arts. 69, 865.4 C.C.P.; ss. 1, 303, 406, *Insurance Act,* R.S.Q. c. A-32; ss. 8, 41, 102, *An Act respecting the distribution of financial products and services,* R.S.Q. c. D-9.2.
See also beneficiary[1], insurance contract, insured, mandatary.
Fr. assureur.

INTEGRITY OF CONSENT

Quality of consent[2] having all the features required by law.
Obs. 1° Consent must be both free and enlightened (art. 1399 C.C.Q.). **2°** The defects that may vitiate consent are error, fear and lesion (arts. 1399 to 1408 C.C.Q.).
See also consent freely given, defect of consent, enlightened consent.
Fr. intégrité du consentement.

INTENSITY OF THE OBLIGATION

Extent to which the debtor must bring about a projected outcome, as it is prescribed by law or by contract.
Obs. 1° The intensity of the obligation serves as mode of classification of obligations. Proposed by Demogue in 1926, this classification was, at first, a distinction between obligations of means and obligations of result. Some scholars, adding the obligation of warranty, now adopt a tripartite classification. **2°** Initially, the classification was applied only to contractual obligations. It is now understood to extend to legal obligations. **3°** Some have argued that, in the absence of any contractual or legal provisions, the criterion of *contingency* distinguishes obligations of means from obligations of result. **4°** The regime of the intensity of the obligation plays an important role in the determination of the burden of proof.
See also binding force of contract, civil responsibility, contingency, contract, exoneration, obligation, obligation of means, obligation of result, obligation of warranty.
Fr. intensité de l'obligation.

INTENT *n.*

Syn. intention.
Occ. Arts. 1103, 1451, 1632 C.C.Q.
Fr. intention[+], volonté[2].

INTENTION *n.*

That which, in one's conscience, forms the object of deliberation and decision and which may be also made manifest to others. *Common intention of the parties*; *intention to defraud*; *intention to contract*; *intention to harm*; *liberal intention.*
Occ. Arts. 762, 764, 1425, 1494, 1496, 1676, 1751, 1992, 2250, 2267, 2450, 2784 C.C.Q.; arts. 8, 12, 80, 937 C.C.L.C.
Obs. 1° In common parlance, intention may refer to a given gesture or action, the consequences of a given gesture or action or the reasons driving the person to act. **2°** The regime of civil liability is based, in principle, on an objective assessment of the person's conduct, rather than on a subjective intention or measure of blameworthiness based on his or her intention. In certain cases, the proof of a malicious intent can render more severe the applicable regime of civil liability. For example, a party who, in bad faith, fails to perform his or her contractual obligations may be held liable not only for the damages foreseeable at the formation of the contract, but also for all damages, including unforseeable ones, that were "an immediate and direct consequence of the non-performance" (art. 1613 C.C.Q.). A person who intentionally violates a right or freedom recognized by the *Charter of human rights and freedoms* may be held liable for punitive damages (R.S.Q. c. C-12, s. 49 para. 2). **3°** It may observed that the English text of the Civil Code uses the term *intention* on occasion as an equivalent for the French term *volonté* (arts. 9, 737, 765, 921 C.C.Q.).
Syn. intent. **See also** act by gratuitous title, cause[2], common intention, consent, contract[1], delict, fault, fraud[1], liberality[1], licitness, punitive damages, quasi-delict, will.
Fr. intention[+], volonté[2].

INTENTIONAL FAULT

Civil fault that is deliberately committed, with full knowledge of the consequences of the act. "Good morals are the basis of the prohibition codified in art. 2563 C.C.L.C. [2464 C.C.Q.], in the sense that the article expresses the legislature's condemnation of a contract that would allow an individual to benefit from his intentional fault" (*Caisse Populaire des Deux Rives* v. *Société mutuelle d'assurance contre l'incendie de la Vallée du*

Richelieu, [1990] 2 S.C.R. 995, p. 1024, C. L'Heureux-Dubé, J.).

Occ. Arts. 1471, 1474, 1613, 1706, 2464 C.C.Q.; art. 2563 C.C.L.C.

Obs. 1° Fault in all instances requires that the act or omission be voluntary. However, to commit an intentional fault, a person's will must go beyond the simple commission of an act; he or she must have intended the consequences of the act or omission. The wrongdoer must intend to cause harm or, at the very least, to act in such a way as to render the occurrence of the damage inevitable. **2°** In principle, a finding of civil liability does not depend on the intention of the wrongdoer. Intentional fault is, however, relevant in several respects. For instance, it may serve as a basis for an award of exemplary damages (s. 49 para. 2, *Charter of Human Rights and Freedoms*, R.S.Q. c. C-12); it may give rise to the liability of a person who would not have been held liable had it not been for his or her intent (arts. 1461, 1471 C.C.Q.); it may also facilitate proof of causation. In contractual matters, intentional fault precludes the wrongdoer from limiting or excluding his or her liability (art. 1474 C.C.Q.). Moreover, in insurance matters, an insurer may refuse to repair damage resulting from the intentional fault of the insured (art. 2464 C.C.Q.). **3°** Some scholars suggest that voluntary fault should be distinguished from intentional fault. According to this view, in a voluntary fault the wrongful act is consciously and wilfully committed but the realization of the damage is not sought by the wrongdoer. Others consider voluntary fault and intentional fault to be the same in cases where the injury, although not desired, is the inevitable consequence of the act or omission.

Syn. voluntary fault. **See also** abuse of right(s), contractual fault, delict, delictual fault, exemplary damages, extracontractual fault, fraud[2], gross fault, intention, non-intentional fault.

Fr. faute intentionnelle[+], faute volontaire.

INTEREST *n.*

Income produced by a sum of money over time. "The best opinion of what distinguishes interest from other payments is that interest accrues from day to day" (Claxton, *Security*, n° 16.13, p. 289).

Occ. Art. 1617 C.C.Q.; arts. 1077, 1785, 1786 C.C.L.C.; s. 3, *Interest Act*, R.S.C. 1985, c. I-15.

Obs. 1° Article 1617 C.C.Q. states that "[d]amages which result from delay in the performance of an obligation to pay a sum of money consist of interest at the agreed rate or, in the absence of any agreement, at the legal rate". **2°** Damages other than those resulting from delay in the performance of an obligation to pay a sum of money bear interest at the legal or conventional rate (art. 1618 C.C.Q.). **3°** Interest is a matter of federal jurisdiction (s. 91(19), *Constitution Act, 1867*).

See also accrue interest (to), additional indemnity[1], arrears[1,2], capital, compound interest, conventional interest rate, damages, interest rate, legal interest rate, simple interest, usurious interest rate.

Fr. intérêt.

INTEREST OWING

Syn. accrued interest.

Occ. Art. 2762 C.C.Q.; ss. 32.2(1), 32.2(2), 59(3), 65(1), 69(1), *Customs Act*, R.S.C. 1985, c. 1 (2nd Supp.).

Fr. intérêt échu.

INTEREST RATE

Percentage that allows one to determine the amount of interest produced by a sum of money for a fixed period of time. For example, an interest rate of 10% *per annum* or of 2% per month.

Occ. Arts. 1056*c* para. 2, 1078.1 C.C.L.C.

Obs. The rate of interest is fixed by the contracting parties or by law (art. 1565 C.C.Q.; s. 3, *Interest Act*, R.S.C. 1985, c. I-15).

Syn. rate of interest. **See also** conventional interest rate, legal interest rate.

Fr. taux d'intérêt.

INTERNAL PUBLIC ORDER

Domestic public order governing relations falling within the ambit of internal private law.

Obs. Internal public order is the equivalent of public order within internal law, viewed in contradistinction to international public order[1].

See also international public order[1].

Fr. ordre public interne.

INTERNAL WILL

Will that a person has formed to enter into a juridical act, considered without regard to its outward manifestation.

Syn. true will. **See also** consent[1], declared will, doctrine of the declaration of will.

Fr. volonté interne[+], volonté réelle.

INTERNATIONAL PUBLIC ORDER

1. Domestic public order governing relations falling within the ambit of private international law.

Obs. In this sense, public order may in principle be invoked to prevent the application of a foreign law designated by a Quebec conflict rule, if it is found to be irreconcilable with the legal order of the forum. Again, in the same case, it may be used to justify the direct (immediate) application of an internal rule of the forum (rule of immediate application).
See also internal public order.
Fr. ordre public international[1].

2. Public order of international origin governing relations falling within the ambit of public international law. For example, the rule regarding the binding force of treaties expressed by the maxim *pacta sunt servanda* (agreements must be honoured).
Fr. ordre public international[2].

INTERPOSED PERSON

Person who appears to be party to a juridical act, when in fact, another is party thereto.
Syn. person interposed. **See also** simulation, undisclosed mandatary.
Fr. personne interposée.

INTERPOSITION OF PERSONS

Operation, aimed at effecting simulation, that consists of substituting the person who is the real party to the juridical act with a person who appears to be a party to the act. For example, a donor, who wishes to make a gift to person incapable of receiving one, makes an apparent gift to a third person who hands over the liberality to the true beneficiary.
Obs. 1° Interposition of persons is one of the forms by which simulation may arise. **2°** Interposition of persons is used when a person wishes to contract for his or her own benefit without revealing the matter to third persons.
See also apparent act, contract of *prête-nom*, disguised act, fictitious act, interposed person, simulation.
Fr. interposition de personnes.

INTER VIVOS adv.ph. (Latin)

Between living persons. "It may be stipulated that a gift *inter vivos* may be suspended, revoked or reduced under conditions which do not depend on the will of the donor [...]" (*Daoust* v. *Lavigne*, (1941) 71 B.R. 22, p. 32, J.C. Walsh, J.).
Occ. Arts. 19, 689, 1806 C.C.Q.; arts. 754, 755, 777 C.C.L.C.
Obs. This term is used only in the English version of the Civil Code; whereas the French version uses the expression *entrevifs*.
See also act *inter vivos*, contemplation of death (in).
Fr. entre vifs[+], *inter vivos*.

INTRANSMISSIBILITY *n.*

Character of a right or of an obligation that is not susceptible of transmission.
Obs. The term *intransmissibility* is used in particular with respect to rights or obligations not susceptible of being transmitted *mortis causa*. In other cases, more precise terms such as *inalienability* and *non-assignability* are usually preferred.
See also inalienability, non-assignability, transmissibility, undisposability.
Fr. intransmissibilité.

INTRANSMISSIBLE *adj.*

Said of rights or obligations not susceptible of transmission.
Obs. 1° The intransmissible character of rights and obligations is the exception rather than the rule. However, it is generally considered that rights and obligations exclusively attached to the person are intransmissible (e.g. the right to support, recourses that belong to spouses, such as divorce proceedings or for separation as to bed and board are intransmissible). For the same reason, obligations that are *intuitu personæ* are also considered to be intransmissible. **2°** Rights that seek to protect the attributes or inherent qualities of the person, such as personality rights or human rights and freedoms, are also intransmissible. **3°** A distinction should be made between rights that, in principle, are intransmissible by reason of their nature and rights of action that arise from a violation of such rights. Rights of action are, in principle, transmissible. Thus, for example, the Civil Code provides that rights of action of the deceased for breach of personality rights are transmitted to the heirs (art. 625 para. 3 C.C.Q.).
See also inalienable, intransmissibility, non-assignable, transmissible, undisposable.
Fr. intransmissible.

INTUITU PERSONÆ CONTRACT (Latin)

Contract entered into by a party on the strength of the identity or qualities of the cocontracting party. For example, mandate, partnership, contract of employment.

Obs. 1° The obligations of the cocontracting party, in consideration of whom the *intuitu personæ* contract was entered into, can only be performed by that person. **2°** The death of the person in consideration of whom the contract was entered into terminates the *intuitu personæ* contract (arts. 2093, 2175, 2226 C.C.Q.). **3°** An *intuitu personæ* contract is, in some cases, susceptible of unilateral resiliation (arts. 2091, 2125, 2175 C.C.Q.).

See also error as to the person.

Fr. contrat *intuitu personæ*.

INTUITUS PERSONÆ *nom.ph.* (Latin)

Consideration of the person.

Fr. *intuitus personæ*.

INVALID *adj.*

Not fulfilling the conditions[4] required to produce juridical effects.

Occ. Art. 1438 C.C.Q.

See also valid.

Fr. invalide.

INVALIDATE *v.*

To render or declare invalid.

Occ. Art. 988 C.C.L.C.

See also validate.

Fr. invalider.

INVALIDITY *n.*

Status of a juridical act that does not fulfil the conditions[4] required to produce juridical effects.

Obs. 1° Juridical acts that do not respect a substantive condition (e.g. arts. 707 to 711, 1385 C.C.Q.) or a condition as to form (e.g. arts. 713, 1385 C.C.Q.) are invalid. **2°** For example, where invalidity relates to only one of the obligations contained in the act, the obligation may be annulled or deemed unwritten. In this case, the act remains valid unless it is considered to be an indivisible whole (arts. 1416, 1417, 1419, 1438 C.C.Q.).

See also annulability, inopposability, lapse, non-existence, nullity, validity.

Fr. invalidité.

INVITATION TO CONTRACT

Syn. invitation to treat.

Fr. invitation à contracter.

INVITATION TO TREAT

Invitation made to another to enter into negotiations with a view to making a contract.

Obs. A simple invitation to treat does not constitute a firm offer and, as result, does not demonstrate a willingness of its author to be bound in the case of acceptance (art. 1388 C.C.Q.).

Syn. invitation to contract. **See also** acceptance[1], letter of intention, negotiation, offer, precontractual period.

Fr. invitation à contracter.

INVOLUNTARY FAULT

Syn. non-intentional fault. "Suffice it to say that civil responsibility rests essentially on the violation of a juridical obligation, be it contractual or legal, and that basically there is no intrinsic difference between a fault, be it voluntary or involuntary, according to whether it arises from the breach of a contractual obligation or from the violation of a legal duty" (Crépeau, in *Essays on the Civil Law*, 83, p. 87)

Fr. faute involontaire, faute non intentionnelle[+].

IRRECOVERABLE *adj.*

Said of a claim that cannot be collected by reason of the debtor's inability to pay.

Obs. The accounting term *bad debt* is often encountered in this context (see, in particular, ss. 87(*i*) and 299, *Taxation Act*, R.S.Q. c. I-3). Compare with *créance irrécouvrable*, which replaced *mauvaise créance* in 1995 (s. 236, *An Act to Amend the Taxation Act and other fiscal provisions*, S.Q. 1995, c. 49).

Fr. irrécouvrable.

IRREGULAR DEPOSIT

Deposit[1] bearing on a fungible property. "An 'irregular deposit' is that in which the depositary, instead of being bound to restore the identical thing he received, is bound only to return things of the same kind and quantity. He is therefore debtor of a kind of thing and not of a thing certain as is the ordinary precarious detainer" (Planiol & Ripert, *Treatise*, vol. 2, part. 2, n° 2213, p. 277).

Fr. dépôt irrégulier.

IRRESISTIBILITY *n.*

Characteristic of an event that constitutes an insurmountable and unavoidable obstacle.

Obs. 1° Irresistibility, along with unforeseeability, are elements used to determine whether or not an event can be considered as an instance of superior force. Externality is also sometimes used as an element to be taken into account. **2°** In principle, superior force is a cause of extinction of obligations and of exemption from liability (arts. 1470, 1693 C.C.Q.).

See also damage, externality, superior force[1], unforeseeability[1].

Fr. irrésistibilité.

IRREVOCABLE *adj.*

Which cannot be revoked. *Irrevocable acceptance*; *irrevocable gifts*.

Occ. Arts. 823, 930 C.C.L.C.

Fr. irrévocable.

J

JOINT ACQUIRER

Person who acquires property with either one or several other persons.
See also acquirer.
Fr. coacquéreur.

JOINT AND SEVERAL

1. See solidary[1].
Occ. Arts. 1104, 1106, 1107 C.C.L.C.
Obs. The expression *joint and several* is used in contracts and in legislative texts (e.g. arts. 1103 to 1107, 1118, 1191 C.C.L.C.), to refer to the intention to be bound solidarily. Even though the terms *joint and several* and *solidary* are used synonymously, the union of the terms *joint* and *several* stands as a contradiction in terms. Both joint obligations and several obligations are indeed obligations that bind several debtors but, in the former case, each debtor is liable for his or her share, while in the latter case each debtor is liable for the whole. Therefore, strictly speaking, the term *joint* is incorrectly used to convey the meaning of *all together*. The terms *several* or *solidary* are sufficient to describe the effects of such an obligation. Long-standing use of the expression *joint and several* in Quebec as an equivalent for solidary may however have had the effect of giving the expression meaning independent from its use in the Common law tradition.
Fr. solidaire[1].

2. See solidary[2].
Occ. Arts. 1101, 1109, 1111 C.C.L.C.
Obs. The comments made with respect to the first sense of the expression *joint and several* apply to this sense as well.
Fr. solidaire[2].

JOINT AND SEVERAL CLAIM

See solidary personal right, joint and several[1].
Fr. [*].

JOINT AND SEVERAL DEBT

See solidary debt, joint and several[1].
Occ. Arts. 1118, 1191 C.C.L.C.
Fr. [*].

JOINT AND SEVERAL OBLIGATION

See solidary obligation, joint and several[1].
"[...] we have here a case of 'common offence or quasi-offence' of the respondent company and of the appellant resulting in a joint and several obligation on their part to persons who have sustained consequential injury (art. 1106 C.C.[L.C.]) [...]" (*R.* v. *Canada Steamship Lines Ltd.*, [1927] S.C.R. 68, p. 79, F.A. Anglin, C.J.).
Occ. Art. 1103 C.C.L.C.
Fr. [*].

JOINT CLAIM

Syn. joint personal right.
Fr. créance conjointe.

JOINT CUSTODY

Syn. cumulative custody.
Fr. garde collective, garde conjointe, garde cumulative+.

JOINT DEBT

Debt owed jointly by co-debtors.
See also joint obligation, joint personal right, solidary debt.
Fr. dette conjointe.

JOINT GIFT

Gift *inter vivos* of the same property to more than one donee, effected in a single juridical act, without the assignment of shares.
Obs. A joint gift gives rise to accretion if one of the donees fails to accept his or her share (art. 868 para. 4 C.C.L.C.).
See also conjunction.
Fr. donation conjointe.

JOINT LIABILITY

Civil liability whose reparation[1] is shared between several debtors, each of whom is held liable for their part of the debt.
Syn. joint responsibility. **See also** common fault, joint obligation, liability *in solidum*, solidarity, solidary liability.
Fr. responsabilité conjointe.

JOINTLY *adv.*

The manner in which each person may only demand or be liable for his or her share.
Obs. The expression *jointly and severally* is encountered in contracts and in certain legislative texts (arts. 1688, 1865 C.C.L.C.), to refer to the intention to be bound solidarily. The combined effect of these two adverbs is a contradiction in that *jointly and severally* evokes liability for both a share and the whole. The term *solidarily* more aptly describes the effects of the solidary obligation.
Fr. conjointement.

JOINTLY AND SEVERALLY

See solidarily.
Occ. S. 113, *Automobile Insurance Act*, R.S.Q. c. A-25; arts. 1688, 1865 C.C.L.C.
Obs. The expression *jointly and severally* is used in contracts and in legislative texts (arts. 1688, 1865 C.C.L.C.), to refer to the intention to be bound solidarily. The combined effect of these two adverbs is a contradiction in that *jointly and severally* evokes liability for both a share and the whole. The term *solidarily* more aptly describes the effects of the solidary obligation.
Fr. solidairement.

JOINT OBLIGATION

Obligation[2] involving several creditors or several debtors, each of whom is only entitled or bound to a share of the obligation.
Occ. Art. 1518 C.C.Q.
Obs. See articles 823, 2221 C.C.Q.
See also divisible obligation, joint personal right, joint debt, obligation *in solidum*, obligation with a complex modality, solidary obligation.
Fr. obligation conjointe.

JOINT PERSONAL RIGHT

Personal right held jointly by co-creditors.
Syn. joint claim. **See also** joint debt, joint obligation, solidary personal right.
Fr. créance conjointe.

JOINT RESPONSIBILITY

Syn. joint liability.
Fr. responsabilité conjointe.

JUDGE-MADE RULE

Syn. jurisprudential rule.
Fr. règle jurisprudentielle.

JUDICIAL ACTION

Syn. action.
Fr. action[+], action en justice, demande en justice.

JUDICIAL COMPENSATION

Compensation[1] resulting from a judgment that liquidates a debt. "There is judicial compensation when a debtor who is sued for the execution of a debt files a reconventional demand against the plaintiff pleading a credit in opposition to the original demand, which credit does not have or fulfill the conditions required for legal compensation" (Planiol & Ripert, *Treatise*, vol. 2, n° 597, p. 325)
Obs. Judicial compensation takes place when a debt does not meet the condition related to its liquidity. It may not make up for the absence of reciprocity, exigibility, certitude and fungibility of the debts.
See also compensation[1], conventional compensation, legal compensation.
Fr. compensation judiciaire.

JUDICIAL DAMAGES

Damages determined by judgment.
Obs. A distinction is drawn between *judicial damages* and *extrajudicial damages*.
See also extrajudicial damages.
Fr. dommages-intérêts judiciaires.

JUDICIAL DEMAND

Syn. action.
Fr. action[+], action en justice, demande en justice.

JUDICIAL DEPOSIT

Syn. judicial sequestration.
Fr. dépôt judiciaire, séquestre judiciaire[+].

JUDICIAL MANDATE

Mandate[2] conferred by judgment. For example, judicial sequestration.
Occ. Art. 445 C.C.Q.

See also conventional mandate, judicial representation, legal mandate.
Fr. mandat judiciaire.

JUDICIAL PUBLIC ORDER

Public order as determined by a court in the absence of any legislative text or when it is not clear from the language used in a legislative text whether or not a provision is imperative.
Syn. virtual public order. **See also** legislative public order.
Fr. ordre public judiciaire, ordre public virtuel⁺.

JUDICIAL REPRESENTATION

Representation in which the power to represent is granted to the representative by a judicial decision.
See also conventional representation, forced representation, judicial mandate, legal representation.
Fr. représentation judiciaire.

JUDICIAL RESOLUTION

Resolution[1] pronounced by a court.
Obs. Resolution may be pronounced by a court or it may occur as of right (art. 1605 C.C.Q.). Given that resolution occurs as of right when the debtor does not perform his or her obligation within the time allowed in the notice of default, judicial resolution is exceptional.
See also resolution (as) of right.
Fr. résolution judiciaire.

JUDICIAL SEQUESTRATION

Sequestration ordered by judicial authority. "The recourse in judicial sequestration is an interlocutory and conservatory proceeding which seeks to place into the hands of a third party property or proprietary rights directly or indirectly affected by the principal litigation" (Sarna, (1977) 23 *McGill L.J.* 508, p. 508).
Occ. Art. 1823 C.C.L.C.; title preceding art. 742 C.C.P.
Obs. 1° Judicial sequestration is a discretionary provisional remedy that the court may order, even of its own motion, if it considers it necessary for the protection of the rights of the parties (art. 742 C.C.P.). **2°** The demand for an order of sequestration is presented by motion (arts. 78, 88 C.C.P.). The petitioner must prove that he or she has an apparent right to the property at issue and that the situation is urgent. He or she must

also establish that if the sequestration is not granted the petitioner may lose his or her rights, which would cause an injury. **3°** In contrast to the *Civil Code of Lower Canada* (art. 365 C.C.L.C.), the *Civil Code of Québec* allows a legal person to be designated sequestrator to another legal person where authorized by law (art. 304 C.C.Q.). **4°** The rules related to conventional sequestration apply to judicial sequestration, as far as they are consistent, unless the court orders differently (art. 2311 C.C.Q.; art. 745 C.C.P.).
Syn. judicial deposit. **See also** conventional sequestration.
Fr. séquestre judiciaire.

JUDICIAL TERM

Suspensive term that a judge may, in certain exceptional circumstances, grant to the debtor in order to permit the debtor to perform an exigible obligation.
Obs. 1° See article 2332 C.C.Q. **2°** The granting of a judicial term does not prevent compensation (art. 1675 C.C.Q.).
Syn. delay of grace, period of grace, term of grace. **See also** conventional term, legal term, term of right.
Fr. délai de grâce, terme de grâce, terme judiciaire⁺.

JURAL *adj.*

Syn. legal[2]. *Jural concept.*
Fr. juridique[1].

JURIDICAL *adj.*

1. Syn. legal[2]. *Juridical principle.*
Occ. Arts. 1, 298, 317, 331, 357 C.C.Q.; arts. 828, 832 C.C.P.; ss. 385, 423, *An Act respecting the implementation of the reform of the Civil Code*, S.Q. 1992, c. 57.
Fr. juridique[1].

2. Syn. legal[6]. *Juridical obligation.*
Occ. Arts. 83, 138, 704, 1634, 2831 C.C.Q.; ss. 5, 141, 199, 671, *An Act respecting the implementation of the reform of the Civil code*, S.Q. 1992, c. 57.
Fr. juridique[2].

3. Syn. legal[4]. For example, a juridical regime. "One thing is certain: unless the text makes express provision to the contrary, the power to make a regulation does not include the power to make that regulation retroactive. In other words, what with respect to a statute is but a presumption, with respect to a regulation becomes a restriction: a juridical restriction whose violation entails illegality"

(Pigeon, *Drafting and Interpreting Legislation*, p. 75).
Occ. Art. 67 C.C.P.
Fr. juridique[3], légal[2+].

JURIDICAL ACT

Manifestation of intention of one or more persons in a manner and form designed to produce effects in law. For example, a contract, a putting in default, a will. "Two elements are characteristic of a juridical act: the external manifestation of intention; and its reflection in a legally recognized institution. A juridical act presumes that a person consciously marshalls a legal institution [...] so as to project legal consequences for the future" (Brierley & Macdonald (eds.), *Quebec Civil Law*, n° 141, p. 177).
Obs. 1° A juridical act may either be unilateral (e.g. a will), bilateral or multilateral (e.g. a contract). It is either by gratuitous or by onerous title. **2°** Certain terms used to designate juridical acts refer, at the same time, to the juridical act considered without regard to its material form (*negotium*) and the physical document recording it (*instrumentum*). Thus a lease may refer, on the one hand, to the abstract agreement reflecting from the meeting of minds between lessor and lessee and, on the other hand, to the deed upon which the agreement is consigned. Both of these are juridical acts.
Syn. act[1], *negotium*, title[2]. **See also** attesting deed, juridical fact[2].
Fr. acte[1], acte juridique[+], *negotium*, titre[2].

JURIDICAL CAPACITY

Syn. legal capacity.
Fr. capacité[1], capacité juridique[+], capacité légale.

JURIDICAL CAUSATION

Syn. causation[2].
Obs. The expression *juridical causation* is used as an equivalent for causation where a distinction is to be drawn between causation *per se* and material causation or cause in fact.
Fr. causalité[2+], causalité juridique, lien de causalité.

JURIDICAL CUSTODY

1. Syn. legal custody[1].
Fr. garde juridique[1].

2. Syn. custody.
Fr. garde[+], garde juridique[2].

JURIDICAL DUTY

Syn. obligation[3].
Fr. charge, dette, devoir juridique, engagement[2], obligation[3+], obligation juridique[2].

JURIDICAL FACT

1. Occurrence that is likely to entail legal consequences. For example, a contract, reckless driving causing an accident. "Many of the most important legal events in relation to status or capacity, institutions for acquiring property, and mechanisms for generating obligations thus are understood as juridical facts. Indeed, at one level, even juridical acts meet the formal definition of a juridical fact" (Brierley & Macdonald (eds.), *Quebec Civil Law*, n° 140, p. 176).
Obs. In this broad sense, a juridical fact comprises both a juridical fact[2] and a juridical act.
Syn. act[3].
Fr. acte[3], fait juridique[1+].

2. Occurrence to which the law attaches legal effects independently of the will of the persons concerned. For example, birth, death, management of the business of another, reception of a thing not due. "The category 'juridical facts' [...] comprises events, either voluntary (as in a delict) or involuntary (as in a quasi-delict), either licit (as in a quasi-contract) or illicit (as in a delict or quasi-delict), whose specific legal effects are determined not by the parties but by law" (Brierley & Macdonald (eds.), *Quebec Civil Law*, n° 406, p. 384).
Obs. Juridical facts may include natural occurrences, such as death, and the actions of a person, such as a fault causing harm.
See also juridical act, material fact.
Fr. fait juridique[2].

JURIDICAL INCAPACITY

Syn. legal incapacity.
Fr. incapacité[1], incapacité de droit, incapacité juridique[+], incapacité légale.

JURIDICAL LIABILITY *n.*

Syn. juridical responsibility.
Obs. The term *liability* is principally used to designate responsibility in civil matters.
Fr. responsabilité, responsabilité juridique[+].

JURIDICAL OBLIGATION

1. Syn. obligation[2].
Fr. obligation[2+], obligation juridique[1], obligation parfaite, obligation personnelle.

2. Syn. obligation[3].
Fr. charge, dette, devoir juridique, engagement[2], obligation[3+], obligation juridique[2].

JURIDICAL PERSON

Syn. person.
Fr. personne[+], personne juridique.

JURIDICAL PRECEPT

Syn. legal rule. "[...] the reference to the 'general principles of law' [...] draws attention to a reservoir of fundamental juridical precepts and essential legal values that transcend the Code's own formal expression and even, it may be argued, its own legal tradition" (Brierley, (1992) 42 *U.T.L.J.* 484, p. 500).
Fr. loi[3], norme juridique, précepte juridique, règle de droit[1+], règle juridique.

JURIDICAL PRINCIPLE

Syn. principle[1].
Fr. principe[1+], principe juridique.

JURIDICAL RESPONSIBILITY

Subjection of a person to an obligation to answer for certain acts, omissions or events before the law. "Lawyers, concerned only with assigning juridical responsibility, address themselves primarily to human acts or omissions and their consequences; and as a given effect may result from the co-operation of several such acts or omissions, each of them may serve as the foundation of legal responsibility, as the legal cause from one point of view" (*Canada and Gulf Terminal Railway* v. *Levesque*, [1928] S.C.R. 340, p. 348, L.P. Duff, J.).
Obs. 1° Juridical responsibility is to be contrasted with moral responsibility in that the latter, unlike juridical responsibility, obliges a person to answer for his or her acts in conscience only, without reference to legal sanctions. **2°** It is the failure to observe the pre-existing obligation of appropriate behaviour that gives rise, through the application of the principles of responsibility, to the obligation to answer for certain acts, omission or events. This obligation must be distinguished from the obligation to conduct oneself appropriately, which exists prior to the advent of the circumstances giving rise to responsibility (e.g. in civil matters, the obligation to act in such a way as to avoid causing harm to another (art. 1457 C.C.Q.)) and, in criminal law, the obligation of parents to provide the necessaries of life for their child (art. 215 Cr.C.)). **3°** Juridical responsibility encompasses both criminal and civil liability. **4°** From the Latin *respondere*: to answer.
Syn. juridical liability, legal liability[1], liability[1], responsibility. **See also** civil liability, fact, law[1], obligation[1,2].
Fr. responsabilité, responsabilité juridique[+].

JURIDICAL RULE

Syn. legal rule.
Fr. loi[3], norme juridique, précepte juridique, règle de droit[1+], règle juridique.

JURIDICAL SYSTEM

Syn. legal order.
Fr. ordre juridique[+], système de droit, système juridique.

JURIDICITY *n.*

Neol. That which is characterized as law[1].
See also legal[2].
Fr. juridicité.

JURISPRUDENCE *n.*

1. Body of decisions rendered by the courts. "[...] the profound changes in the condition of society since the Code, changes which may be summed up in the phrase 'the rise of industrialism' have added new chapters to the law, and these chapters have been added mainly by the jurisprudence. The law of commercial companies, the law of employer and workman in *la grande industrie*, the law of railways and steamships, and much of the law of insurance has grown up since the *Code Napoléon*, and is mainly the work of the judges" (Walton, *Scope and Interpretation*, p. 123). *French jurisprudence.*
Obs. 1° From the Latin *jus, juris*: law, and *prudentia*: skill, knowledge. **2°** Because the expression suggests there is an inherent authority in decided cases (i.e. that cases make law), some civilians see *case law* as inappropriate to the theory of the sources in private law, preferring expressions such as *decided cases, jurisprudence* or *established jurisprudence.*
Syn. case law[1]. **See also** custom[1], law[2], usage.
Fr. jurisprudence[1].

2. Habitual manner of settling a question of law by the courts. "[...] the *Jand'heur* jurisprudence [...] affords a truly striking illustration of the living process of interpretation of a code in a manner responding to the felt need of the times. It represents a remarkable adventure in judicial creativity, yielding an interpretation of a provision of the Code Napoleon which, as everyone agrees, the legislators of 1804 could never have imagined" (Millner, (1971) 17 *McGill L.J.* 699, p. 704). *The jurisprudence of the Court of Appeal; a reorientation of the jurisprudence; established jurisprudence; rule of jurisprudence; settled jurisprudence.*

Obs. Used in this narrow sense, *jurisprudence* refers to a proposition or a solution of law that derives from a series of decided cases, whether they originate from one or more jurisdictions. Even though it is recognized that a single decision cannot give rise to jurisprudence, some scholars argue that a single decision may, by its own persuasiveness, prompt its own spontaneous acceptance and, following the French expression, *faire jurisprudence* (i.e. establish jurisprudence). **Syn.** case law[2]. **See also** jurisprudential rule.

Fr. jurisprudence[2].

3. Science of law.

Obs. This meaning of the term *jurisprudence* is the most common in Anglo-American parlance. It is also closely related to its etymological origin: *jurisprudencia* (*jus, juris* (law) and *prudentia* (foresight, wisdom)). Since the nineteenth century, French-speaking civilian jurists have gradually abandoned this use of the term *jurisprudence*, considering it as outdated. The precise notion of *science of law* to which it refers to can be understood in a broad way, encompassing both philosophy or theory of law.

Fr. jurisprudence[3].

JURISPRUDENTIAL *adj.*

Pertaining to jurisprudence. *Jurisprudential trend; jurisprudential rule.*
Fr. jurisprudentiel.

JURISPRUDENTIAL RULE

Rule derived from jurisprudence[1].
Obs. The question of the recognition of rules with purely jurisprudential origins provoked strong controversy on the role of jurisprudence in Civil law. Even today, certain scholars adopt a formalist conception of jurisprudence, describing it as persuasive authority, while others favour a more realist or sociological description of its function, arguing that it can be the source of substantive legal rules whose binding character rests upon their sanction by the courts. The expression *jurisprudential rule* seems to rest on this latter conception of jurisprudence.

Syn. judge-made rule. **See also** jurisprudence[2].
Fr. règle jurisprudentielle.

JURISTIC *adj.*

Syn. legal[2]. *Juristic person.*
Fr. juridique[1+].

JUS n. (Latin)

1. **Syn.** law[1]. "A law student at the outset of his studies ought first to know the derivation of the word *jus*. Its derivation is from *justitia*. For, in terms of Celsus' elegant definition, the law is the art of goodness and fairness" (Ulpian, *Digest*, vol. 1, p. 1). *Jus gentium.*
Fr. droit[1+], droit objectif, *jus*[1].

2. **Syn.** right. *Jus in re.*
Fr. droit[2+], droit subjectif, *jus*[2].

JUS AD REM nom.ph. (Latin)

Personal right resulting from an obligation to give.
Obs. 1° According to certain scholars, the *jus ad rem* also applies to the personal right resulting from the obligation to deliver a determinate thing. **2°** Contrary to *jus in personam* (personal right) and *jus in re* (real right), which derive from Roman law and constitute a traditional dichotomy, the term *jus ad rem* is derived from Canon law (Ourliac & de Malafosse, *Histoire*, t. 2, n° 22, p. 51). **3°** Article 1058 C.C.L.C. specified that an obligation could have for its object to give, to do or not to do something. Article 1373 C.C.Q. does not draw a distinction between obligations to give and obligations to do. The former is generally considered as included in the latter.
See also personal right, real right.
Fr. *jus ad rem.*

JUS AD REM TRANS PERSONAM (Latin)

Personal right expressed as a relation between two persons in respect of a thing. For example, the rights in a lease of an immovable. "[...] whenever one person is in custody of a thing belonging to another, by contract (for example, a borrower, a depositary, or a mandatary with custody) or as a result of a juridical fact (for example, a *negotiorum gestor*), but does not claim a recognized real right in the thing, the situation has been characterized as that involving a jus *ad rem trans personam*" (Macdonald, (1994) 39 *McGill L.J.* 761, n° 30, p. 790).

Obs. 1° As a personal right, the *jus ad rem trans personam* does not give the holder a right in a thing as would a real right. Instead, the holder's entitlement in respect of the thing is expressed as a claim against the debtor. **2**° The *jus ad rem trans personam* is sometimes characterized as a mixed right given the difficulty of classifying adequately among real rights or personal rights.
Syn. mixed right. **See also** *jus ad rem*, personal right, real right.
Fr. droit mixte[3], *jus ad rem trans personam*[+].

JUS COGENS nom. ph. (Latin)

Syn. imperative law. "The phrase *jus cogens* refers to an open set of peremptory norms of international law which cannot be set aside by treaty or acquiescence, but only by the formation of a subsequent peremptory norm of contrary effect" (Kindred *et al.*, *International Law*, p. 165).
Fr. droit impératif[+], *jus cogens*.

JUS COMMUNE nom.ph. (Latin)

Syn. general law.
Obs. This term appears only in the English text of the Preliminary Provision of the *Civil Code of Québec*; the French text uses *le droit commun*.
Occ. Preliminary Provision of the *Civil Code of Québec*.
Fr. droit commun[1+], *jus commune*, loi générale.

JUS DISPOSITIVUM nom. ph. (Latin)

Syn. suppletive law[1].
Fr. droit supplétif[1+], *jus dispositivum*.

JUS IN PERSONAM nom.ph. (Latin)

Syn. personal right.
Fr. créance, dette active, droit de créance, droit personnel[+], *jus in personam*, obligation[4].

JUS IN RE nom.ph. (Latin)

Syn. real right. "The mode of exercise of the real right (*jus in re*) is the main feature distinguishing it from personal rights (*jura in personam*) and, in particular, the lessee's right of enjoyment of things under a contract of lease (*jus ad rem trans personam*)" (Brierley & Macdonald (eds.), *Quebec Civil Law*, n° 277, p. 286).
Obs. The plural *jura in re* is also used.
Fr. droit réel[+], *jus in re*.

JUS PUBLICUM nom.ph. (Latin)

Syn. public order. "No member of the state [...] can be allowed deliberately to imperil the *jus publicum* by flouting it in his dealings: to do so would be to place his will above the will of the community, and to dissolve the authority which is the state" (Johnson, *Maxims*, p. 88).
Fr. ordre public.

JUST *adj.*

1. In conformity with justice[1].
See also legitimate[1], equitable[1,2].
Fr. juste[1].

2. In conformity with justice[2].
Occ. Arts. 952, 1927 C.C.Q.; art. 407 C.C.L.C.; art. 9 C.C.P.
Fr. juste[2].

JUSTE TITRE (French)

Translatory title that, while vitiated, justifies the possession of a successor in title who has acted in good faith.
Obs. The *juste titre* allows the possessor in good faith who draws his or her title from a *non dominus* to claim a right over the property by way of acquisitive prescription.
Syn. justificatory title.
Fr. juste titre[?].

JUSTICE *n.*

1. Virtue seeking to preserve and promote values, such as fairness, equality, dignity and liberty, that is understood as a finality of law[1]. "Justice is a continual balancing of competing visions, plural viewpoints, shifting histories, interests, and allegiances" (Williams, *Alchemy of Race and Rights*, p. 121).
Obs. 1° For some scholars, the pursuit of justice is the fundamental goal of law[1]. **2**° Justice has been defined historically as the art of giving what is owed to each person. However, many definitions of justice are possible, depending on whether one focuses on a conception of justice that is abstract and absolute, or, alternatively, concrete and relative. **3**° A distinction is often drawn between distributive (or social) justice, which seeks to ensure the distribution of goods and honours in proportion to one's merit within a given society, from commutative (or corrective) justice, which aims to maintain or establish a formal equality in respect of intentional or unintentional exchanges between individuals. Some scholars defend an idea of contractual justice, founded upon the notion of *cor-*

rective justice, according to which each contracting party garners an advantage equivalent to what he or she brings to the contract. This notion is also said to underlie the compensatory goal of the law of civil liability. **4°** Scholars argue that the law predicated on one or another conception of justice may intervene to establish an equilibrium in contractual or extracontractual relationships by invoking, for example, good faith (art. 6 C.C.Q.), abuse of right (art. 7 C.C.Q.) or lesion caused by disproportionate prestations and exploitation of a contractual party (art. 1406 C.C.Q.).

See also equity[1], natural law[1].
Fr. justice[1].

2. Pursuit of that which can legitimately be expected from the law[1]. "There is a question of justice and injustice only where there is a plurality of individuals and some practical question concerning their situation and/or interactions vis-à-vis each other" (Finnis, *Natural Law and Natural Rights*, p.161).
Fr. justice[2].

JUSTIFICATORY TITLE

Syn. *juste titre*.
Fr. juste titre[2].

K

KEEPER *n.*

Custodian who has the custody[3] of animals and certain things.
Fr. gardien(>).

KNOWN TERM

Syn. certain term.
Fr. terme certain[+], terme connu.

L

LANDLORD *n.*

Lessor[1], in a lease of an immovable.
Occ. S. 136(1)(*f*), *Bankruptcy and Insolvency Act*, R.S.C. 1985, c. B-3.
Obs. In the *Civil Code of Québec*, the term *lessor* is used to the exclusion of landlord. This term is, however, often encountered in juridical acts and civilian legal parlance. In this context it does not refer to the doctrine of tenure inherent in the landlord-tenant relationship in the Common law tradition.
See also lessee, tenant.
Fr. bailleur[1] (>), locateur[+] (>).

LAPSE *n.*

Status of a validly formed juridical act that is deprived of effect by a later event. For example, the lapse upon divorce of gifts *mortis causa* in a contract of marriage.
Occ. Art. 964 C.C.L.C.
Obs. 1° The term is also used with respect to an offer that no longer has effect, as for example following its withdrawal or the death of the offeror. **2°** From the Latin *lapsare*, a derivative of *lapsus*: a slip, a fall.
See also invalidity, nullity.
Fr. caducité.

LATENT DEFECT

Defect in property[2] that would not be detected upon examination by a reasonable person. "There is no definition in the [Civil Code of Lower Canada] of the term 'latent defect', but it is generally accepted to refer to a 'flaw' or 'imperfection', or *vice*, as it is known in French. An abundant and sometimes conflicting jurisprudence exists on the subject in our law; however, it is generally accepted that it is left for the Court to decide in each case whether a particular defect is latent or not" (*Tellier* v. *Proulx*, [1954] C.S. 180, p. 182, H. Batshaw, J.). *Warranty against latent defects.*
Occ. Arts. 1081, 1726, 2104 C.C.Q.; art. 1524 C.C.L.C.; s. 53, *Consumer Protection Act*, R.S.Q. c. P-40.1.
Obs. 1° The notion of *latent defect* is opposed to that of *apparent defect*. In many settings,

for example, the law requires a person to warrant against latent defects, whereas, generally speaking, warranties against apparent defects are not required. Futhermore, it may be observed that the warranty against latent defects has been understood as the archetype of an obligation of warranty. **2°** The warranty against latent defects applies in the context of sale (art. 1726 C.C.Q.), exchange (art. 1798 C.C.Q.), giving in payment (art. 1800 C.C.Q.), alienation for rent (art. 1805 C.C.Q.), contract of enterprise or for services (art. 1803 C.C.Q.), and contract of partnership (art. 1828 C.C.Q.). **3°** In matters relating to sale, it is generally recognized that the warranty against latent defects rests upon five conditions: the defect has to be serious, hidden, present before the sale, unknown to the buyer at the moment of the sale and, finally, the buyer must have denounced such defect to the seller in writing within a reasonable time (arts. 1726 *et seq.* C.C.Q.).
Syn. hidden defect, redhibitory defect. **See also** apparent defect, obligation of warranty, warranty against latent defects.
Fr. défaut caché, vice caché[+], vice rédhibitoire.

LAW *n.*

1. Body of rules regulating life in society the adherence to which, where not done spontaneously, is assured by a constraint external to the individual, which constraint is most often associated with the idea of sanction. "Law, the quest of all men of good will and more especially of jurists, cannot be sought exclusively in written texts; its definition and very nature would change if it were no longer regarded as the expression of what is just, but simply as the will of those who govern" (David & Brierley, *Major Legal Systems*, pp. 103-104). *Customary law.*
Obs. 1° Legal theorists disagree as to law's defining characteristic, sometimes designated as the criterion for legality, which distinguishes law from other normative orders. For some, the criterion is seen as a matter of substance, law being defined as a body of rules intended to regulate life in society. Others fix on matters of form, such as when

169

emphasis is placed on the manner of expression of the rule of law. Alternatively, some scholars argue that the criterion is to be found in the requirement that law must be external and binding upon the subject to whom it applies. Each of these criteria has its critics; for example, in the case of the insistence upon sanction, not all legal rules are sanctioned by public authority, and some non-legal rules are subject to sanction. **2°** Such long standing debates among legal theorists would suggest that the effort to define an all-encompassing definition of law is difficult if not impossible. Positivists consider law to be either a state-sanctioned phenomenon (state-centred legal positivism) or a social phenomenon (sociological positivism). Legal pluralists recognize the existence of multiple orders of law that apply simultaneously to individuals. Jurists in the natural law tradition view law ultimately as a single, permanent and universal phenomenon that does not necessarily depend on the state, but that is rooted in nature, reason or the divine. **3°** In the positivist tradition, law and morality are considered distinctive spheres of normativity which may or may not overlap. On this view, law is comprised of rules designed to control social behaviour that are, by reason of this mode of production and their mode of enforcement, external to the person to whom they apply. Conversely rules of morality, imagined as an individual path to perfection, are often said to be internal to the subject in that, in the final analysis, the individual is answerable for them in conscience only instead of before the whole society.
Syn. *jus*[1]. **See also** justice[1,2], natural law, positive law, private law, public law.
Fr. droit[1+], droit objectif, *jus*[1].

2. Juridical act adopted by an organ of the State.
Occ. Preliminary Provision of the *Civil Code of Québec*; arts. 11, 37, 46, 299, 1257, 2659, 3080 C.C.Q.; arts. 6, 23, 300 C.C.L.C.; arts. 36, 56, 100 C.C.P.; preamble, *Charter of Human Rights and Freedoms*, R.S.Q. c. C-12.
Obs. Following this acception, the notion of *law* can be used to designate any juridical rule elaborated by an authorized State organ.
Syn. enactment.
Fr. loi[1].

3. Syn. legal rule[2]. For example, prohibitive laws.
Occ. Art. 14 C.C.L.C.
Fr. loi[3], norme juridique, précepte juridique, règle de droit[+], règle juridique.

LAWFUL *adj.*

1. Syn. licit. *In a lawful manner; lawful cause; lawful consideration.*
Occ. Arts. 2564, 2629, 2817 C.C.Q.; arts. 984, 1701, 1928, 2442 C.C.L.C.; s. 31q, *Companies Act*, R.S.Q. c. C-38.
Fr. licite.

2. Syn. legitimate[2]. *Lawful excuse; lawful expenses.*
Occ. Arts. 634, 2568, 2570 C.C.Q.; arts. 606, 666, 2379, 2268 C.C.L.C.; s. 87, *Transport Act*, R.S.Q. c. T-12.
Fr. légitime[2].

LAWFUL CAUSE

Syn. licit cause. "It is essential therefore that an obligation shall have 'a cause from which it arises', and that a contract shall have 'a lawful cause or consideration'; but it is not meant that a contract which has a lawful cause within the meaning of article 984 C.C.Q. shall be void or defective for lack of that which, under the English authorities, would constitute valuable consideration" (*Hutchison* v. *Royal Institute for the Advancement of Learning*, [1932] S.C.R. 57, p. 68, E.L. Newcombe, J.).
Fr. cause licite.

LAWFUL CONSIDERATION

Syn. licit cause.
Fr. cause licite.

LAWFULLY *adv.*

In a legal[3] manner.
Occ. Arts. 1078.1, 1216, 2179, 2390 C.C.L.C.; ss. 76, 123.31, *Companies Act*, R.S.Q. c. C-38; s. 404, *Election Act*, R.S.Q. c. E-3.3.
Obs. In a broad sense, *lawfully* refers to conformity with law[1].
See also unlawfully.
Fr. légalement.

LAWFULNESS *n.*

Syn. licitness.
Fr. licéité.

LAWFUL TITLE

Title[1] that is valid in law.
Occ. Art. 2268 C.C.L.C.
Fr. juste titre[1].

LAW OF OBLIGATIONS

Branch of private law that regulates the relationships between persons, where such relationships are represented as legal bonds.

Obs. 1° The law of obligations may be thought of as providing a code of social conduct that sets forth certain fundamental rights and duties of persons towards each other. In many respects, the rules of the law of Obligations reflect basic social values understood to be present in a given culture. For example, in Quebec these include values inherent in the law of Obligations might be thought to include individual liability for wrongdoing and debt, contractual freedom and contractual justice. **2°** The law of Obligations provides a cadre of basic concepts of private law (e.g. damage, obligation, nullity, compensation) upon which the other branches of private law (e.g. law of persons, family law) and even, in some respects, branches of public law (e.g. administrative law) depend. **3°** Drawing from the writings of Pothier, article 983 of the *Civil Code of Lower Canada* acknowledged five sources of obligations: the contract, the quasi-contract, the delict, the quasi-delict and the sole operation of law. Article 1372 of the *Civil Code of Québec* provides, by contrast, that "[a]n obligation arises from a contract or from any other act or fact to which the effects of an obligation are attached by law". **4°** In the *Civil Code of Québec*, the law of Obligations constitutes an autonomous Book five. In the *Civil Code of Lower Canada*, the title "Of Obligations" was included in Book third entitled "Of the Acquisition and Exercise of Rights of Property" ("des droits de propriété"). This arrangement was often criticized as unduly emphasizing the acquisition of ownership in the theory of obligations. **5°** Used in this sense, the word *Obligations* is generally capitalized.

Syn. obligations. **See also** civil liability, contract, duty, justice, obligation, will.

Fr. droit des obligations+, obligations.

LAW SUIT

Syn. action.

Fr. action+, action en justice, demande en justice.

LEASE *n.*

1. Contract by which a person, the *lessor*[1], undertakes to provide another, the *lessee*[1], with the enjoyment of property for a certain time and in return for rent. "[...] the essence of any lease is that the premises leased must be habitable" (*Lemcovitch* v. *Daigneault*, [1957] C.S. 178, p. 182, F.T. Collins, J.).

Occ. Arts. 1790, 1851 C.C.Q.; art. 1600 C.C.L.C.; arts. 34, 547, 684, 696.1, 954 C.C.P.; ss. 5, 28, 30.2, 33, 39, *An Act respecting the Régie du logement*, R.S.Q. c. R-8.1.

Obs. 1° The right of the lessee to enjoy the leased property (art. 1851 C.C.Q.) is a personal right, as opposed to a real right. It is the archetype of the *jus ad rem trans personam*. **2°** Under the *Civil Code of Lower Canada*, a lease could bear on movable or immovable property (whereupon it was characterized as a "lease of things"), as well as upon the work or services provided by a person (characterized as "the lease and hire of work"). Under the *Civil Code of Québec* only property can be subject to lease. The provisions relating to the lease and hire of work have been recast as a basis for the law respecting contracts of employment, contracts of enterprise, contracts for services and contracts of carriage. **3°** When a lease bears on a residential immovable, it is called *lease of a dwelling*. Leases of dwellings are governed by articles 1892 *et seq.* C.C.Q. and by the *Act respecting the Régie du logement*, R.S.Q. c. R-8.1. **4°** The codal regime respecting lease is set forth at articles 1851 to 2000 C.C.Q.

Syn. contract of lease, lease of things. **See also** lease and hire, leasing, principal lease, property[2], sub-lease.

Fr. bail[1], contrat de bail, contrat de location, contrat de louage, location[2], louage+, louage de choses.

2. Writing that records a contract of lease. *To draw up a lease*; *standard-form lease*.

Obs. Article 1895 C.C.Q. provides that within ten days of entering into the lease of a dwelling, the lessor must give the lessee a "copy of the lease" or, in the case of an oral lease, a writing that sets forth the essentials thereof.

Occ. Arts. 1893, 1903, 1905 C.C.Q.; art. 2005 C.C.L.C.

Fr. bail[2].

LEASE *v.*

1. To confer by lease. *To lease property to someone.*

Occ. Arts. 404, 1135, 1229 C.C.Q.; art. 1665.3 C.C.L.C.

Syn. rent[1].

Fr. louer[1].

2. To take under a lease. *To lease from someone.*

Occ. Art. 1384 C.C.Q.; art. 1655.2 C.C.L.C.

Syn. rent[2].

Fr. louer[2].

LEASE AND HIRE

Contract by which a person, in return for a counterprestation, undertakes to provide another, for a certain time, with either the enjoyment of a thing (*lease and hire of things*) or his or her services (*lease and hire of work* or *of services*).
Occ. Title preceding art. 1600 C.C.L.C.
Obs. Under the *Civil Code of Lower Canada*, the lease and hire could bear up on movable or immovable property (called "the lease and hire of things"), as well as upon the work or services provided by a person (called "the lease and hire of work") (arts. 1866 to 1973 C.C.Q.). In 1973 (S.Q. 1973, c. 74), a distinction was made in the Civil Code between lease of things and lease and hire of work. Since the enactment of the *Civil Code of Québec*, only property can be leased. The term *lease and hire of work* has been abandoned and its substance is carried forward as the contract of employment, the contract of enterprise, the contract for services and the contract of carriage, depending on the context.
Syn. contract of lease and hire, hire. **See also** lease[1].
Fr. louage(<).

LEASE AND HIRE OF PERSONAL SERVICE(S)

See contract of lease and hire of personal service(s). "In contracts of lease and hire of personal services, the obligations of loyalty and trust are implied conditions of the contract. Whether or not an employee is part of top management or is a key employee, he or she has an obligation of good faith and loyalty towards his or her employer" (*Matrox Electronic Systems Ltd.* v. *Gaudreau*, [1993] R.J.Q. 2449 (Sup. Ct.), p. 2466, A.D. Guthrie, J.).
Fr. [*].

LEASE (AND HIRE) OF SERVICES

See contract of lease (and hire) of services.
Fr. [*].

LEASE AND HIRE OF WORK

Contract by which a person, the *lessor of work*, undertakes, in return for remuneration, to perform work, to produce a work or to provide services for another, the *lessee of work*. "Where a property owner engages a builder and an architect to erect a house for him, it is evident that he is entering into a contract governed, as are all contracts, by rules contained in the title of *Obligations* in

the Civil Code, and in particular by that part of the title of *Lease and Hire* that governs the lease and hire of work" (Durnford, (1967) 2 R.J.T. 161, p. 165).
Occ. Art. 1665a C.C.L.C.
Obs. 1° The expression *lease and hire of work* is no longer used in the Civil Code. **2°** The lease and hire of work of the *Civil Code of Lower Canada* now corresponds to either the contract of employment, the contract of enterprise, the contract for services or the contract of carriage in the *Civil Code of Québec*, depending on context.
See also contract for (of) services, contract of carriage, contract of employment, contract of enterprise.
Fr. contrat de louage d'ouvrage, louage d'ouvrage[+].

LEASE OF THINGS

Syn. lease[1]. "Many social and economic factors have contributed to the new growth in importance of the law on lease of things in the twentieth century: once essentially limited to the realm of immoveables, it is now used in relation to property of every description [...]" (C.C.R.O., *Commentaries*, vol. II, t. 2, p. 569).
Occ. Art. 1600 C.C.L.C.
Fr. bail[1], contrat de bail, contrat de location, contrat de louage, location[2], louage[+], louage de choses.

LEASING *n.*

Contract by which a person, the *lessor*, undertakes, in return for payment, to provide financing for another, the *lessee*, by acquiring, at the request of the lessee, ownership of a movable and by placing the movable at the disposal of the lessee for a fixed term.
Occ. Arts. 1842, 2961.1 C.C.Q.; art. 1603 C.C.L.C.
Obs. 1° The lessor retains the ownership of the movable that he or she places at the disposal of the lessee. The right of ownership secures the right of the lessor to be paid. However, this right of ownership may only be set up against third parties, and in particular against the lessee's creditors, if it has been published (art. 1847 C.C.Q.). **2°** Leasing can be entered into only for the purposes of carrying on an enterprise (the French text of art. 1842 para. 3 C.C.Q.: "à des fins d'entreprise"). However, the English text of article 1842, which states "for business purposes only", might be read so as to restrict the notion of *enterprise* to undertakings that are commercial in character (compare with art. 1525 para. 3 C.C.Q.). **3°** A tripartite relationship between the seller, the lessor and the lessee

arises from the leasing contract. This is made plain in particular by the fact that the seller is bound directly toward the lessee for the conventional and legal warranties inherent in the sale (art. 1845 C.C.Q.). **4°** Leasing is useful in different contexts, including the acquisition, for a fixed period, of materials that can rapidly become obsolete. The acquisition of such property by way of outright ownership may mean a high cost, whereas a leasing arrangement may allow for a business to change equipment more often at lower cost. **5°** In practice, the expression *financial lease* or *finance lease* is sometimes used to describe a leasing contract. **6°** The codal regime respecting leasing, which is a nominate contract distinct from that of lease, is set forth at articles 1842 to 1850 C.C.Q.

Syn. contract of leasing, finance lease, financial lease, financial leasing, leasing contract. **See also** enterprise[1].
Fr. contrat de crédit-bail, crédit-bail+.

LEASING CONTRACT

Syn. leasing. "The current accepted position is that, since the adoption of the *Civil Code*, a leasing contract may no longer be characterized as a lease" (Dietze, (1999) 59 *R. du B.* 1, pp. 36-37).
Fr. contrat de crédit-bail, crédit-bail+.

LEGAL *adj.*

1. Having the nature of law[2]. *Legal rule.*
Occ. Art. 433 C.C.Q.
Fr. légal[1](<).

2. Relating to law[1]. For example, legal science, legal theory, legal counsel, legal education. "Mayrand's way of mixing materials relating to a book's legal topic and to the book's author may be thought of as an important blurring of the distinction between the law, understood as a series of propositional rules, and wider legal culture, in which those rules are produced and interpreted by its agents" (Fernandez, (2003) 53 *U. of T. L.J.* 37, pp. 62-63).
Occ. Art. 823 C.C.L.C.
Obs. In this sense, *legal* is principally opposed to *non-legal* (e.g. morality) and to facts (e.g. the opposition between legal means and non-legal means).
Syn. jural, juridical[1], juristic. **See also** legal principle, legal rule[1], legal system.
Fr. juridique[1].

3. Conforming to or permitted by law[2]. *Legal sanction.*
Occ. Art. 369 C.C.L.C.

Obs. In a broad sense, *legal* can be a synonym of *licit* to show conformity to law[1].
See also illegal[1], legitimate[1], licit.
Fr. légal[3].

4. Said of something set forth or finding its source in law[1]. "A legal person is capable of having rights and obligations (capacity for rights), performing legal acts (legal capacity) and bearing legal responsibility for legal wrongs (legal liability)" (Ruiter, *Legal Institutions*, p. 180). *Legal hypothec; legal liability; legal obligation; legal representative; legal subrogation.*
Occ. Arts. 21, 433, 1564, 1652, 2664, 2724 C.C.Q.; arts. 918, 1044, 1056, 1426 C.C.L.C.; arts. 234, 492, 559, 644 C.C.P.; s. 34, *An Act respecting the implementation of the reform of the Civil Code,* S.Q. 1992, c. 57.
Syn. juridical[3]. **See also** contractual, delictual, extracontractual, quasi-contractual, quasi-delictual.
Fr. juridique[3], légal[2+].

5. Syn. extracontractual. *Legal obligation.*
Fr. extracontractuel+, légal[4].

6. Producing one or several effects in law[1]. For example, a legal act, legal personality. "[...] the existence of two rules of law applicable to a factual situation in practice gives rise to a duality of causes in the majority of cases, because separate rules generally require different legal characterizations" (*Rocois Construction Inc.* v. *Québec Ready Mix inc.* [1990] 2 S.C.R. 440, p. 456, C.D. Gonthier, J.).
Obs. In the positivist tradition, legal obligations are contrasted with moral obligations, the latter said to exist in conscience only and not subject to the community sanction.
Syn. juridical[2]. **See also** legal custody[2], legal damages.
Fr. juridique[2].

LEGAL CAPACITY

Legal ability to hold and to exercise rights. "While the married woman was granted increased powers in 1931, then legal capacity in 1964, these reforms were above all designed to keep law's family as it 'always' had been" (Brisson & Kasirer, (1996) 23 *Man. L.J.* 406, p. 408).
Occ. Title preceding art. 985 C.C.L.C.; arts. 1002, 1919 C.C.L.C.; title of *An Act respecting the legal capacity of married women,* S.Q. 1964, c. 66 (repealed); s. 240, *Savings and Credit Unions Act,* R.S.Q. c. C-4.1; s. 69, *Canada Business Corporations Act,* R.S.C. 1985, c. C-44; s. 118(1)(c), *Bank Act,* S.C. 1991, c. 46.
Obs. 1° Legal capacity includes both capacity to enjoy rights (arts. 1, 301 C.C.Q.) and capac-

ity to exercise rights (arts. 4, 303 C.C.Q.). **2°** With respect to civil rights, every person has legal capacity. Such capacity can only be limited by express provision of law (compare, however, art. 18 C.C.L.C. with art. 1 C.C.Q., and art. 985 C.C.L.C. with art. 4 C.C.Q.). As a result, with respect to both physical and legal persons, legal capacity is the rule and incapacity the exception. **3°** In some contexts, the expression *legal capacity* is used to describe the narrower concepts of capacity to enjoy and capacity to exercise (e.g. s. 144, *An Act respecting assistance and compensation for victims of crime*, R.S.Q. c. A-13.2.1).
Syn. capacity[1], juridical capacity. **See also** aptitude, capacity to enjoy (rights), capacity to exercise (rights), civil capacity, legal incapacity, political capacity.
Fr. capacité[1], capacité juridique[+], capacité légale.

LEGAL COMPENSATION

Compensation[1] that takes place by the sole operation of law. "[...] where the creditor has transferred his claim, one is led to the conclusion that if, prior to the transfer, the claim and counter-claim were already liquid and exigible, legal compensation would have already occurred at such time and, consequently, the true amount transferred would be only the excess [...]" (Reis, (1971) 31 *R. du B.* 313, p. 314).
See also conventional compensation, judicial compensation.
Fr. compensation légale.

LEGAL CUSTODY

1. Custody that is accessory to a right. For example, the lessee of a thing.
Syn. juridical custody[1]. **See also** *de facto* custody.
Fr. garde juridique[1].

2. Syn. custody.
Fr. garde[+], garde juridique[2].

LEGAL DAMAGES

Damages fixed by provision of law.
Obs. 1° Legal damages derogate from the principle of full reparation of the harm suffered, in that the indemnity is determined by law according to pre-established criteria. The indemnity does not necessarily correspond to the harm actually suffered by the victim. **2°** Legal damages may be fixed, *inter alia*, by way of a fixed indemnity, a limitation of liability or a legal rate of interest. **3°** Examples of legal damages in the *Civil Code of Québec*

include provisions respecting deposit with an innkeeper (art. 2298 C.C.Q.), those governing carriage of property by water (art. 2074 C.C.Q.), moratory interest (art. 1617 C.C.Q.), legal interest provided at article 1618 C.C.Q., and additional indemnity (art. 1619 C.C.Q.). **4°** In a number of cases special legislation also provides fixed indemnities established in accordance with the type of harm suffered by the victim. For example, the provisions in chapter 3 of *An Act respecting industrial accidents and occupational diseases* (R.S.Q. c. A-3.001) and those in chapters 2 to 4 of the *Automobile Insurance Act* (R.S.Q. c. A-25). **5°** Other examples may be found in international conventions and treaties (e.g. art. 22, *Warsaw Convention*).
See also additional indemnity, conventional damages, full reparation, legal interest, moratory damages, predetermined damages.
Fr. dommages-intérêts légaux.

LEGAL DUTY

Syn. obligation[3].
Fr. charge, dette, devoir juridique, engagement[2], obligation[3+], obligation juridique[2].

LEGAL INCAPACITY

Condition of a person deprived by law of the capacity to enjoy or to exercise a right. "The respondent deposited monies or securities with the appellants under a supposed contract or agreement with them. Exclusively as a consequence of that contract, the appellants became entitled to hold or to deal with these monies and securities. But the contract being absolutely null on account of the legal incapacity of the respondent to act as she did, it is not susceptible of any effect; the appellants derived thereby no legal right to deal as they have done with the monies and securities [...]" (*Johnston* v. *Channel*, [1937] S.C.R. 275, pp. 280-281, T. Rinfret, J.).
Occ. Art. 599*a* C.C.L.C.; title preceding art. 818 C.C.P.; s. 141, *An Act respecting industrial accidents and occupational diseases*, R.S.Q. c. A-3.001; s. 83.27, *Automobile Insurance Act*, R.S.Q. c. A-25; s. 12, *An Act respecting health services and social services*, R.S.Q. c. S-4.2; s. 178(2), *Cree-Naskapi (of Quebec) Act*, S.C. 1984, c. 18; s. 55, *Dominion Controverted Elections Act*, R.S.C. 1985, c. C-39; s. 215(4), *Canada Elections Act*, R.S.C. 1985, c. E-2.
Obs. 1° Every person is vested with legal capacity in respect of civil rights. This capacity can only be limited by express provision of law (compare however art. 18 C.C.L.C. with art. 1 C.C.Q., and art. 985 C.C.L.C. with art. 4

C.C.Q.). Thus, with respect to both physical and legal persons, legal capacity is the rule and incapacity the exception (arts. 1, 301 C.C.Q. with respect to the enjoyment of rights; arts. 4, 303 C.C.Q. with respect to the exercise of rights). **2°** Legal incapacity is applicable to juridical acts but not to juridical facts. **3°** A distinction is drawn between incapacity to enjoy rights and incapacity to exercise them.

Syn. incapacity[1], juridical incapacity. **See also** *de facto* incapacity, general incapacity, incapacity of public order, incapacity of protection, incapacity to enjoy (rights), incapacity to exercise (rights), legal capacity, special incapacity.

Fr. incapacité[1], incapacité de droit, incapacité juridique[+], incapacité légale.

LEGAL INTEREST

See legal interest rate.
Fr. intérêt légal.

LEGAL INTEREST RATE

Interest rate fixed by law.
Obs. The legal interest rate is 5% (s. 3, *Interest Act*, R.S.C. 1985, c. I-15).
Syn. rate of legal interest. **See also** conventional interest rate.
Fr. taux d'intérêt légal.

LEGALITY

That which is characterized as legal[3]. "But, even if art. 23 were not in the Act, it would still remain true that in hearing appellant's petition, the learned trial Judge was not sitting in appeal from the decision of the Board of Inquiry. It was his duty to decide as to the legality of the detention, not as to the sufficiency of the evidence upon which the decision was based. He had no right to substitute his views for those of the Board" (*De Marigny* v. *Langlais*, [1947] B.R. 741, p. 745, P.C. Casey, J.).
Obs. In a broad sense, legality refers to what is in conformity with law[1], i.e. what is *licit*.
See also illegality[1], licitness.
Fr. légalité.

LEGAL LIABILITY *n.*

1. **Syn.** juridical responsibility. "Without prejudice, but in order to purchase his peace, defendant tendered to plaintiff and deposited in court an amount of $1,250 and costs, in full of all claims of the plaintiff. This amount of $1,250, it is said, substantially exceeds the damages actually and directly suffered by plaintiff, and the amount which would be legally recoverable if defendant were under any legal liability to him, which liability, however, despite the tender was clearly denied" (*Lister* v. *McAnulty*, [1944] S.C.R. 317, p. 320, R. Taschereau, J.).
Obs. The term *liability* is principally used to designate responsibility in civil matters.
Fr. responsabilité, responsabilité juridique[+].

2. Extracontractual liability resulting from the operation of law.
Obs. 1° Legal liability sanctions non-performance of obligations that results from the operation of law (e.g. the liability of the manufacturer for safety defects, arts. 1468, 1469 C.C.Q.). **2°** Article 1057 C.C.L.C. expressly provided that obligations could result "from the sole and direct operation of law, without the intervention of any act, and independently of the will of the person obliged or of him in whose favor the obligation is imposed".
See also contractual liability, delictual liability, extracontractual liability, legal obligation[2], quasi-contractual liability, quasi-delictual liability, strict liability.
Fr. responsabilité légale.

LEGAL MANDATE

Mandate[2] conferred by law. For example, the mandate of a tutor.
See also conventional mandate, domestic mandate, judicial mandate, legal representation.
Fr. mandat légal.

LEGAL NORM

Syn. legal rule[1,2]. "Essentially, a legal norm will be found to be sufficiently precise if it gives rise to 'legal debate'" (*Ruffo* v. *Conseil de la magistrature*, [1995] 4 S.C.R. 267, p. 330, C.-D. Gonthier, J.).
Obs. Even though some scholars distinguish legal norms from legal rules, most of the experts equate the two concepts.
Fr. loi[3], norme juridique, précepte juridique, règle de droit[1+], règle juridique.

LEGAL OBLIGATION

1. Obligation[2] arising from an act or fact to which the law[3] attaches juridical effects. "The right of action is independent of the issue of the lifting of the corporate veil. It is a direct right of action of the respondents, as third parties, against the appellant for the breach of a general legal obligation of diligence towards the respondents. The respondents have established fault, damage, and causality, and thus, as third parties, can exer-

cise a quasi-delictual recourse based on the appellant's contractual fault" (*Houle* v. *Canadian National Bank*, [1990] 3 S.C.R. 122, p. 136, C. L'Heureux-Dubé, J.).
Obs. Article 1372 C.C.Q. distinguishes between "an obligation [that] arises from a contract" and an obligation that arises from "any act or fact to which the effects of an obligation are attached by law". From this perspective, the term *legal obligation* designates any obligation not arising by contract. It could then be considered as a synonym of *extracontractual obligation*.
See also contractual obligation, extracontractual obligation, legal liability[1].
Fr. obligation légale[1].

2. Obligation[2] arising solely by operation of law[3]. For example, an alimentary obligation (art 585 C.C.Q.), the obligation arising from legal tutorship imposed upon parents (art. 192 C.C.Q.).
Obs. 1° The expression *legal obligation*, when used in this narrow sense, describes an obligation imposed by law to respond to a specific juridical situation. It arises without the parties having so intended or without the performance by them of an act or fact to which the law attaches obligations. In this sense, legal obligations are distinguished from the obligations that have as a direct source a personal act or omission to which the effects of an obligation are attached by law. **2°** Article 983 of the *Civil Code of Lower Canada* acknowledged, in accordance with the writings of Pothier, five sources of obligations: contract, quasi-contract, delict, quasi-delict and sole operation of law. This classification has not been explicitly retained in the Civil Code (art. 1372 C.C.Q.). **3°** According to article 1434 of the Civil Code, the obligations of a contract extend not only to what is expressed therein but also to what is incident to it, according to its nature and in conformity with law. These obligations, which have their source in law, are nevertheless understood to be contractual obligations (see *Bank of Montreal* v. *A.G. Quebec*, [1979] 1 S.C.R. 565, p. 572).
See also contractual obligation, legal liability[2].
Fr. obligation légale[2].

3. Obligation[3] arising solely by operation of law[3].
Fr. obligation légale[3].

LEGAL ORDER

Body of rules and institutions regulating a given group and which, considered as a whole, is understood to be composed of connected parts. For example, religious legal order.

Obs. 1° In the Western legal traditions, the concept of *legal order* is often said to imply an aspiration to coherence, even though experts disagree on the degree of coherence implicit in the notion of *legal order*. **2°** A plurality of legal orders coexist with the state-sanctioned legal order, overlapping in some spheres while remaining parallel to one another in others.
Syn. juridical system, legal system, system of law. **See also** juridical rule, law[1], legal norm, legal rule[1].
Fr. ordre juridique[+], système de droit, système juridique.

LEGAL PRINCIPLE

Syn. principle[1]. "If a party to a contract wants to make an exception to a legal principle of general application [...] he must so stipulate in the contract. The maxim *'Reus in exipiendo [sic] fit actor'* applies. The burden is on him to show that the exception was made and is applicable to the case under consideration. And the stipulation will be strictly interpreted" (*R.* v. *Canada Steamship Lines Ltd.*, [1950] S.C.R. 532, p. 574, H.G. Fauteux, J.).
Fr. principe[1+], principe juridique.

LEGAL REPRESENTATION

Representation in which the power to represent is granted to the representative by a provision of law. For example, the representation of a minor by a tutor.
See also conventional representation, forced representation, judicial representation.
Fr. représentation légale.

LEGAL REPRESENTATIVE

See successor by general title.
Occ. Arts. 21, 2288 C.C.Q.; arts. 1028, 1030 C.C.L.C.
Obs. The expression *legal representative* is sometimes used as an equivalent to *successor by general title* or *universal successor* (e.g. art. 2288 C.C.Q.; arts. 1028, 1030 C.C.L.C.). When used in this sense, the expression may be misleading in that a successor by general title is not a representative of his or her author but acts in his or her own name.
Fr. représentant légal.

LEGAL RULE

1. Rule that is part of a legal order. "Ideally, every legal rule consists in an attempt to protect or promote important social values. A legal rule, however, if strictly applied by one party, may detrimentally affect the interests of others, some of which the law considers to be of equal or perhaps even gerater importance" (Crépeau, in *Aequitas and Equity*, 583, p. 631).

Obs. 1° Despite the tendency to treat legal rules and rules of conduct as synonymous, the two concepts are not completely interchangeable. Rules of conduct are not necessarily legal rules (e.g. rules of politeness), while all legal rules are not necessarily rules of conduct (e.g. the rule establishing civil majority at art. 153 C.C.Q. or, more generally, legal definitions). **2**° Because legal rules are, for the civilian, often imagined first as legislative enactments, the legal rule is often described as general and abstract in character, even if these characteristics are not of the essence of the definition of legal rules. **3**° From Latin: *regula*, rule.

Syn. juridical precept, juridical rule, law[3], legal norm. **See also** general principles of law, legal order.

Fr. loi[3], norme juridique, précepte juridique, règle de droit[1+], règle juridique.

2. Rule that is part of positive law.

Obs. 1° Even though the concept of legal rule is often employed to refer to rules from a legislative source, not all legal rules are legislative rules. Custom can create a legal rule, as can private individuals, by way of contract, which is said to be the law of the parties. **2**° There exists a debate in doctrine as to whether jurisprudence is susceptible of creating a legal rule in the civilian tradition. Even today, certain scholars adopt a formalist conception of jurisprudence, describing it simply as a persuasive authority, while others favour a more realist or sociological description of its function, arguing that it can be the source of substantive legal rules whose binding character rests upon their sanction by the courts. **3**° A rule of law is traditionally considered to be obligatory, although it can be either imperative or suppletive. **4**° The expression *rule of law* is also used in the general theory of law to refer to the concept of law as an expression of legitimate, legal authority, notably as a safeguard against arbitrary or unjust action. In French, care should be taken to avoid confusion between *règle de droit* and *primauté du droit*.

Syn. juridical precept, juridical rule, law[3], legal norm. **See also** general principles of law, juridical order.

Fr. loi[3], norme juridique, précepte juridique, règle de droit[2+], règle juridique.

LEGAL SOLIDARITY

Solidarity established by law. For example, presumed solidarity among co-authors of a delict or a quasi-delict (art. 1526 C.C.Q.), solidarity among co-debtors of an obligation contracted for the exploitation or the service of an enterprise (art. 1525 C.C.Q.).

See also conventional solidarity.

Fr. solidarité légale.

LEGAL SUBROGATION

Subrogation arising solely by operation of law. "The principle is of significance as the Superior Court recently held that by reason of the principle of legal subrogation the debtor may have a third party repay at any time and obtain subrogation in the rights and security of the creditor repaid. The amount of repayment constitutes a new borrowing and is (usually) at a lower interest rate" (Claxton, *Security*, p. 155).

Obs. 1° Legal subrogation may be personal or real in character. **2**° Legal subrogation arises in the circumstances set forth at article 1656 C.C.Q.

See also conventional subrogation.

Fr. subrogation légale.

LEGAL SYSTEM

Syn. legal order. "In a legal system for which legislative bilingualism is the rule, the presence of two texts may [...] obscure parliamentary intention for the conscientious reader bent on considering meaning from two different perspectives. Yet whatever its merits or failings as a political symbol, the principle that each of Quebec's legislative languages enjoys equal authority does have the advantage of bringing the two texts together in a necessarily common quest for meaning" (Brisson & Kasirer, in *Civil Code of Québec* (1997) ix, p. XXXIV).

Occ. Arts. 3077, 3078 C.C.Q.

Obs. The concept of legal system is mainly used in private international law to resolve the questions of conflict of laws and conflict of jurisdictions. It is also used in comparative law in connection with the relationship between law and a given collectivity or legal tradition.

Fr. ordre juridique[+], système de droit, système juridique.

LEGAL TERM

Suspensive term established by law for the performance of certain obligations. "A legal term is a term granted or imposed by law" (Levasseur, *Obligations*, p. 39).
See also conventional term, judicial term, term of right.
Fr. terme légal.

LEGAL WARRANTY

Warranty resulting from the law. "[...] neither a manufacturer, nor generally a professional seller, can contract out of the legal warranty against latent defects or limit the liability resulting from such warranty" (*General Motors Products of Canada Ltd.* v. *Kravitz*, [1979] 1 S.C.R. 790, p. 806, Y. Pratte, J.).
Occ. Art. 1732 C.C.Q.; art. 1507 C.C.L.C.
Obs. In the contracts of sale and of lease, the warranty against latent defects is an example of a legal warranty (arts. 1726 to 1731, 1854 C.C.Q.; s. 34 *et seq.*, *Consumer Protection Act*, R.S.Q. c. P-40.1).
See also conventional warranty, obligation of warranty.
Fr. garantie légale.

LEGISLATIVE PUBLIC ORDER

Public order as determined by legislation.
Obs. Legislative public order can entail relative or absolute nullity. In a legislative text, various expressions serve to indicate whether a provision is of public order, including: *is absolutely null* (arts. 161, 541, 1823 C.C.Q.), *on pain of* (*absolute*) *nullity* (arts. 440, 1783, 1824, 2692, 2693, 2696 C.C.Q.), *notwithstanding any agreement to the contrary* (arts. 467, 1031, 2651 C.C.Q.), and *is without effect* (art. 1893 C.C.Q.).
Syn. textual public order. **See also** judicial public order.
Fr. ordre public législatif, ordre public textuel[+].

LEGITIMACY *n.*

1. Quality of that which is in conformity with justice, equity[1] or fairness. "The legitimacy of the law and the obligation to obey the law flow directly from the right of every citizen to vote" (*Sauvé* v. *Canada*, 2002 SCC 68, C.D. Gonthier, J.).
Obs. The concepts of legitimacy and legality are not synonymous. Not all that is legitimate is necessarily legal[3] and, conversely, not all that is legal[3] is necessarily legitimate. This said, the ideal of justice that informs the prevailing conception of law[1] often means that the two concepts coincide with one another.
See also illegitimacy[1], legitimate[1], licitness.
Fr. légitimité[1].

2. Quality of that which is grounded in or recognized by law[1]. "In our constitutional tradition, legality and legitimacy are linked" (*Reference re Secession of Quebec*, [1998] 2 S.C.R. 217, p. 240).
Obs. In this strict sense, legitimacy is understood to coincide with what is recognized by law[1]. This would appear to rest on a conception of law[1] that is not limited to positive law but that also extends to certain social or moral values.
See also illegitimacy[2], legality, legitimate[2].
Fr. légitimité[2].

3. Quality of that which is worthy of legal protection. "A clear majority vote in Quebec on a clear question in favour of secession would confer democratic legitimacy on the secession initiative which all of the other participants in confederation would have to recognize" (*Reference re Secession of Quebec*, [1998] 2 S.C.R. 217, p. 220).
See also legitimate[3].
Fr. légitimité[3].

LEGITIMATE *adj.*

1. In conformity with justice, equity[1] or fairness. For example, an employee may have a claim that is not founded in law but is nonetheless legitimate. *Legitimate claim*; *legitimate revendication*.
See also illegitimate[1], legal[3], licit.
Fr. légitime[1].

2. Grounded in law[1]; recognized or permitted by law[1]. *Legitimate cause*; *legitimate information*; *legitimate reason*; *legitimate succession*.
Occ. Arts. 36, 355, 837, 2230, 2261 C.C.Q.; art. 811 (3) C.C.L.C.
Obs. 1° Article 2230 C.C.Q. provides that a partnership may be dissolved by the court for a legitimate cause. **2°** The resiliation of a contract of undeclared partnership is possible for a legitimate cause, such as the failure of a partner to perform his or her obligations, or if one partner hinders the activity of others. **3°** From the Latin *legitimus*: established by law.
Syn. lawful[2]. **See also** illegitimate[2], legal[3], licit.
Fr. légitime[2].

3. Worthy of legal protection. *Legitimate interest legally protected*.
Occ. Arts. 37, 39, 1212. 2089, 3079 C.C.Q.
Fr. légitime[3].

LEND *v.*

To grant a loan.
Occ. Arts. 2316, 2691 C.C.Q.
See also borrow.
Fr. prêter.

LENDER *n.*

Person who grants a loan. "The lender is liable, in the same manner as the lender for use, for any injury resulting from defects in the property loaned (2328 [C.C.Q.]). In a loan for use where the lender knew the property had latent defects but failed to inform the borrower, he is liable for injury (2321 [C.C.Q.])" (Claxton, *Security*, n° 16.4, p. 284).
Occ. Arts. 2313, 2319, 2321, 2328, 2375 C.C.Q.; arts. 1763, 1773 C.C.L.C.
Obs. A lender who knew that the property loaned had latent defects but failed to inform the borrower is liable for any injury the latter may suffer (arts. 2321, 2328 C.C.Q.).
See also borrower, loan for use, simple loan.
Fr. prêteur.

LEONINE CLAUSE

Clause in a contract of partnership stipulating that a partner shall be excluded from sharing in the profits.
Obs. 1° According to article 2003 C.C.Q., a leonine clause in a contract of partnership is without effect. **2°** From Latin *leonine*, meaning lion.
Fr. clause léonine.

LESION *n.*

Damage suffered by a party to a juridical act that results from the formation of the act. "A more successful attempt to introduce the plea of lesion for persons of full age and capacity is found in recent consumer legislation [...] Notwithstanding this new approach to lesion in consumer matters, the initial regime codified in 1866 remains largely intact [...]" (Brierley & Macdonald (eds.), *Quebec Civil Law*, n° 448, p. 417).
Occ. Arts. 424, 472, 897, 1405, 1406, 2332 C.C.Q.
Obs. 1° The general theory of Civil law obligations distinguishes between several conceptions of lesion: objective, subjective and mixed. **2°** In principle, only contracts that are synallagmatic, commutative and by onerous title may be vitiated by lesion. **3°** Even though the rules applicable to lesion are established with respect to contractual obligations, they also apply to certain specified unilateral acts (e.g. in family matters, arts.

424, 472 C.C.Q.). **4°** Lesion only gives rise to a remedy in particular circumstances (arts. 424, 472, 897, 1405, 2332 C.C.Q.; s. 8, *Consumer Protection Act*, R.S.Q. c. P-40.1). The sanctions provided may be nullity of the contract, the reduction of the obligation (art. 1407 C.C.Q.; s. 8, *Consumer Protection Act*, R.S.Q. c. P-40.1) or the attribution of damages (art. 1407 C.C.Q.) as the case may be. However, the contract may be upheld if the defendant to an action in nullity based on lesion offers "[...] a reduction of his claim or an equitable pecuniary supplement" (art. 1408 C.C.Q.). **5°** Even though lesion and unforeseeability are related notions in that both aim to maintain the equilibrium of the contractual prestations, they are nevertheless distinguishable. Lesion must exist at the time of the formation of the contract, whereas unforeseeability arises in the context of its performance. **6°** From the Latin *læsio* (from *lædere*: to hurt): damage, injury, prejudice.
See also abuse of right(s), abusive clause, defect of consent, economic error, exploitation, good faith, mixed lesion, objective lesion, subjective lesion, unforeseeability[1].
Fr. lésion.

LESIONARY *adj.*

That which entails lesion. "[...] despite the general principle of *pacta sunt servanda*, courts have shown an increasing willingness to rewrite contracts on the basis of [...] their lesionary terms [...]" (Brierley & Macdonald (eds.), *Quebec Civil Law*, n° 151, p 192). *Lesionary contract.*
Fr. lésionnaire.

LESSEE *n.*

1. Person who is provided with the enjoyment of property by the lessor in exchange for rent. "[...] the lessee's right remains a personal right against the lessor whether he be the original lessor or a subsequent owner whose title is derived from the original lessor in one of the manners mentioned in article 1646 [C.C.L.C.]" (*General Coin Wash Leasing Inc. v. Habitat Val Orford Inc.*, [1976] 1 C.S. 107, p. 110, C.D. Gonthier, J.).
Occ. Arts. 172, 403, 1065, 1851, 1855 C.C.Q.; arts. 1600, 1606, 1617 C.C.L.C.; art. 12a C.C.P; ss. 30.2., 33, 54.7., 54.10., *An Act respecting the Régie du logement*, R.S.Q. c. R-8.1.
Obs. 1° The right of the lessee to enjoy the leased property (art. 1851 C.C.Q.) is traditionally characterized as a personal right, rather than a real right. It is the archetype of the *jus ad rem trans personam*. **2°** Lessee is

synonymous with *tenant* when used in reference to immovables, notwithstanding that, in the civil law of Quebec, the lessee has no *jus in re* or proprietary interest in the immovable. 3° Although the emphyteusis is not a lease, the English text of the Civil Code refers to the *emphyteutic lessee* (e.g. arts. 1200 *et seq.* C.C.Q.). 4° Under the *Civil Code of Lower Canada*, lessees of work were those for whose benefit other persons performed work or provided a service in exchange for remuneration. Lessees of work are equivalent to employers or clients under the *Civil Code of Québec*, in the case of contracts of employment and contracts of enterprise or for services, or to passengers, shippers or receivers in the case of contracts of carriage.
See also lease[1], lessor[1], property[2], tenant.
Fr. locataire[+], preneur[3].

2. Person who, under an alienation for rent, undertakes to pay the annuity.
Occ. Art. 1802 C.C.Q.
Fr. preneur[2].

3. Person who, under a leasing contract, takes the movable placed at his or her disposal by the lessor[2]. "In financial lease transactions it is the lessee who selects the asset, negotiates the terms and conditions of the purchase and the terms of any warranties which will apply to the same. It is the lessee who attends to all other matters which would be required of any owner purchasing such asset, save only assumption of ownership and payment of the purchase price" (Smyth, in *Meredith Lectures (1981)*, 23, p. 26).
Occ. Art. 1842 C.C.Q.
Obs. Under the contract of leasing, the lessee has the right to hold and to use the property. However, the *Civil Code of Québec* does not explicitly characterize the nature of the lessee's right as real or personal.
Fr. crédit-preneur.

LESSEE OF WORK

Person for whom the lessor of work undertakes to perform work, to produce a work or to provide services in return for remuneration.
Obs. The expression *lessee of work* is now rare. The more usual terms are *client*, in the case of contracts of enterprise or for services, *employer*, in the case of contracts of employment, and *shipper*, *consignee* or *passenger*, in the case of contracts of carriage.
See also lease and hire of work, lessor of work.
Fr. locataire d'ouvrage.

LESSOR *n.*

1. Person who undertakes to provide another, the *lessee*, with the enjoyment of property for a certain time in return for rent. "[...] the lessor must not only deliver the thing in a good state of repair in all respects. He must maintain the thing in a condition fit for the use for which it has been leased and give peaceable enjoyment of the thing during the term of the lease (Art. 1604 C.C.[L.C.])" (*Equilease Ltée* v. *Bouffard*, [1979] C.S. 191, pp. 193-194, J.B. O'Connor, J.).
Occ. Arts. 403, 1079, 1851, 1856, 1859 C.C.Q.; arts. 1600, 1604, 2005 C.C.L.C.; art. 12a C.C.P.; s. 14, *Charter of Human Rights and Freedoms*, R.S.Q. c. C-12.
Obs. 1° *Lessor* is synonymous with *landlord* when used in reference to immovables even though, in Quebec Civil law, the relationship between landlord and tenant is not understood to create a proprietary interest in the immovable comparable to landlord-tenant law in the Common law tradition. **2°** Under the *Civil Code of Lower Canada*, lessors of work were those who performed work or provided a service for remuneration. Lessors of work are equivalent today to employees, contractors, providers of services or carriers depending on whether reference is made to a contract of employment, a contract of enterprise, a contract for services or a contract of carriage.
See also landlord, lease[1], property[2].
Fr. bailleur[1], locateur[+].

2. Person who, under a leasing contract, places a movable at the disposal of the lessee[3]. "If the rights resulting from a leasing contract are registered as a lease, arguably the rights of ownership of the lessor have not been appropriately registered and will not be opposable to third parties" (Dietze, (1999) 59 *R. du B.* 1, p. 36).
Occ. Art. 1842 C.C.Q.
Obs. 1° The lessor retains the ownership of the movable that he or she places at the disposal of the lessee. However, this right of ownership may only be set up against third parties, and in particular against the lessee's creditors, if it has been published (art. 1847 C.C.Q.). **2°** The obligations of a lessor under a contract of leasing are different from those of a lessor in an ordinary lease under articles 1851 *et seq.* C.C.Q. **3°** The lessor under a leasing contract need only place property at the disposal of a lessee and need not provide the lessee with enjoyment of the property, as is the case in lease.
Fr. crédit-bailleur.

3. Person who, under an alienation for rent, transfers the ownership of an immovable in return for the payment of an annuity.
Occ. Art. 1802 C.C.Q.
See also assignee, lessee[2], seller.
Fr. bailleur[2].

4. Person who, pursuant to a contract of affreightment, places at the disposal of the charterer all or part of a means of transportation.
Occ. Arts. 2001, 2008 C.C.Q.
Obs. When the owner of the means of transportation and the lessor are the same person, the generic term *owner* is often used to designate the lessor.
Fr. fréteur.

LESSOR OF WORK

Person who undertakes to perform work, to produce a work or to provide services in return for remuneration.
Obs. The expression *lessor of work* is rare. The more current terms are *contractor*, *provider of services*, *employee* and *carrier*, depending on whether reference is made to a contract of enterprise, a contract for services, a contract of employment or a contract of carriage.
See also lease and hire of work, lessee of work.
Fr. locateur d'ouvrage.

LET *v.*

Syn. lease[1].
Fr. louer[1].

LETTER OF INTENTION

Writing by which a person expresses a desire to conclude, to modify or to resolve a contract.
Obs. 1° In general, letters of intention are used to enter into negotiations. **2°** In principle, a letter of intention does not create obligations. Therefore, it cannot be characterized as a contract or as an offer. **3°** The expression *letter of intent* is also encountered.
See also agreement in principle, gentlemen's agreement, invitation to treat, offer.
Fr. lettre d'intention.

LETTER OF UNDERSTANDING

Syn. agreement in principle.
Obs. The expression *letter of understanding* generally refers to a written document, while an agreement in principle may be expressed orally.

Fr. accord de principe+, accord préliminaire, protocole d'entente.

LIABILITY *n.*

1. Syn. juridical responsibility. "The infringement of a right guaranteed by the *Charter of Human Rights and Freedoms* [...] gives rise, under s. 49 para. 1, to an action for moral and material prejudice. Such an action is subject to civil law principles of recovery. As a result, the traditional elements of liability, namely fault, damage and causal connection, must be established" (*Aubry* v. *Éditions Vice-Versa inc.*, [1998] 1 S.C.R. 591, p. 613, C. L'Heureux-Dubé and M. Bastarache, JJ.). *Action in liability*; *exoneration from liability*; *limitation of liability clause*.
Occ. Arts. 1073, 1458, 1470 to 1472 C.C.Q.; art. 1664.4 C.C.L.C.
Obs. Depending on the context, the term *liability* may be employed to refer to the more restrictive notions of either civil liability and criminal liability.
Fr. responsabilité, responsabilité civile+.

2. Syn. obligation[3]. "The *patrimoine* is the totality of an individual's economic assets and liabilities [...] [It] is thought of in terms of a balance sheet, the assets constituting the *actif* and the liabilities the *passif*" (Nicholas, *Contract*, p. 29). *To meet one's liabilities*.
Occ. Art. 607 C.C.L.C.; s. 428(7), *Bank Act*, S.C. 1991, c. 46.
Fr. charge, dette, devoir juridique, engagement[2], obligation[3+], obligation juridique[2].

LIABILITY FOR DAMAGE CAUSED BY ANIMALS

Civil liability incurred by the owner or the custodian of an animal for the damage it has caused. "[...] when he came to vicarious liability and liability for damage caused by animals or a building, in order to remain faithful to the criterion of fault, *Domat* had to create presumptions of fault, sometimes irrebuttable presumptions, or even to place the label of 'fault' on conduct which might or might not be faulty" (Tunc, in *Int. Enc. Comp. L.*, vol. XI, p. 1-62).
Obs. Article 1466 C.C.Q provides for a presumption of liability against owners and custodians of animals, so that they can only be exonerated by proving that the damage was the result of superior force (art. 1470 C.C.Q.).
See also act of an animal, liability for damage caused by things.
Fr. responsabilité du fait des animaux.

LIABILITY FOR DAMAGE CAUSED BY ANOTHER

Civil liability incurred by a person for the damage caused by a person other than the debtor.

Obs. Liability for damage caused by another may be either contractual or extracontractual. In contractual matters, courts have recognized liability for damage caused by another by virtue of the maxim *qui facit per alium facit per se*: the contracting party is liable for the fault committed by the person whom he or she calls upon to perform the contractual obligation (*Hôpital Notre-Dame-de-l'Espérance* v. *Laurent*, [1974] C.A. 543). In extracontractual matters, articles 1459 to 1464 C.C.Q. establish the situations in which a person must answer for the behaviour of others. In light of article 1457 para. 3 C.C.Q., the question as to whether this list is exhaustive remains unanswered.

See also act of another, indirect liability, legal liability[2], liability for damage caused by things, liability of artisans, liability of curators, liability of parents, liability of schoolteachers, liability of the principal, liability of tutors, personal liability[2], strict liability, vicarious liability.

Fr. responsabilité du fait d'autrui.

LIABILITY FOR DAMAGE CAUSED BY BUILDINGS

Civil liability incurred by the owner of a building for the damage caused by its ruin.

Obs. 1° When the victim proves that the ruin was the result of lack of repairs or a defect in construction, the owner must prove the occurrence of a superior force in order to be exonerated from liability (art. 1470 C.C.Q.). **2°** Article 1467 C.C.Q. refers to immovables, whereas art. 1055 para. 3 C.C.L.C. referred to buildings.

Syn. liability for damage caused by immovables. **See also** liability for damage caused by things, ruin.

Fr. responsabilité du fait des bâtiments+, responsabilité du fait des immeubles.

LIABILITY FOR DAMAGE CAUSED BY IMMOVABLES

Syn. liability for damage caused by buildings.
Fr. responsabilité du fait des bâtiments+, responsabilité du fait des immeubles.

LIABILITY FOR DAMAGE CAUSED BY INANIMATE THINGS

Civil liability incurred by the custodian of an inanimate thing for damage caused by its autonomous act. "Mechanical beasts, albeit of another kind, were also the object of much attention in France in the first forty years of the twentieth century. Over that period, a handful of French legal scholars engaged in a vigorous and humbling debate that eventually led to the recognition of a new form of civil liability for damage caused by inanimate things" (Jutras, in *Tort Law*, 317, p. 317).

Obs. 1° Liability for damage caused by inanimate things is a specific aspect of the broader category of liability for damage caused by things, the latter extending to damage caused by animals and immovables. **2°** The fault attributed to the custodian of the thing that causes the damage is presumed. However, the custodian of a thing other than an immovable or an animal can be exonerated by proving that the damage caused by the inanimate thing is not the result of his personal fault (art. 1465 C.C.Q.). **3°** The regime for presumed liability of custodians for damage caused by inanimate things was developed through judicial interpretation of article 1054 para. 1 C.C.L.C.

See also autonomous act of a thing, liability for damage caused by things, product liability.

Fr. responsabilité du fait des choses inanimées.

LIABILITY FOR DAMAGE CAUSED BY THINGS

Civil liability incurred by a person for the damage caused by a thing by reason of the control he or she exercises over it.

Obs. 1° The codal regimes respecting liability for damage caused by things include liability for damage caused by animals, buildings and inanimate things, as well as liability resulting from safety defects in manufactured products (arts. 1465 to 1469 C.C.Q.). **2°** Liability for damage caused by animals and buildings have their origins in Roman law. At the time of the enactment of the Civil Code of Lower Canada, liability for damage caused by things was understood to be limited to those two types of liability. The owner of immovable property is still liable for the damage caused by its ruin (art. 1467 C.C.Q.). The owner and the custodian of an animal are also both liable for the damage caused by it (art. 1466 C.C.Q.). **3°** In the early part of the twentieth century courts, confronted with claims arising from frequent industrial accidents, eventually created a regime of liability for damage caused by inanimate things on the basis of article 1054 para. 1 C.C.L.C. Article 1465 C.C.Q. expressly provides that the custodian is liable for the damage resulting from the autonomous act of the thing. If it is a thing other than an immovable or an animal, he or she may be exonerated by proving absence of fault. **4°** Article 1468 C.C.Q. states that the manufacturer, the distributor and the supplier of movable property are liable for injury resulting from a safety defect in the thing.

See also act of a thing, indirect liability, liability for damage caused by animals, liability for damage caused by another, liability for damage caused by buildings, liability for damage caused by inanimate things, personal liability[2], product liability, vicarious liability.

Fr. responsabilité du fait des biens, responsabilité du fait des choses[+].

LIABILITY *IN SOLIDUM* (Latin)

Civil liability of several debtors, each of whom is held answerable to a single creditor for the entire debt, even though there is neither solidarity nor indivisibility amongst them.

Obs. 1° Obligations *in solidum* do not entail the secondary effects of solidarity, such as those relating to notice of default and interruption of prescription. **2°** In French law, the notion of an *obligation* in solidum, which is of doctrinal and jurisprudential inspiration, served in particular to fill the gap left by the absence of a provision corresponding to article 1526 C.C.Q., which establishes true solidarity among the co-authors of an extracontractual fault.

Syn. in solidum liability. **See also** common fault, joint liability, obligation *in solidum*, solidary liability.

Fr. responsabilité *in solidum*.

LIABILITY OF ARTISANS

Civil liability incurred by an artisan for the damage caused by an apprentice under his or her care or control.

Obs. The *Civil Code of Québec* does not explicitly provide for this type of liability. Under certain circumstances, however, damage caused by an apprentice can lead to liability for damages caused by agents or servants (art. 1463 C.C.Q.).

See also liability for damage caused by another.

Fr. responsabilité de l'artisan.

LIABILITY OF COMMITTENTS

Neol. Syn. liability of the principal.

Obs. The term *committent* is suggested as a more accurate rendering of the French term *commettant*, since it avoids the confusion that

principal may create with regards to the contract of agency.

Fr. responsabilité du commettant.

LIABILITY OF CURATORS

Civil liability incurred by the curator for damage caused by the person of full age under his or her custody[3].

Obs. The curator to persons of full age is liable only if he or she has committed an intentional or gross fault in exercising custody (art. 1461 C.C.Q.).

See also liability for damage caused by another.

Fr. responsabilité du curateur.

LIABILITY OF EMPLOYERS

See liability of the principal.

Obs. 1° The term *employer*, as used regarding the regime of civil liability established by article 1463 C.C.Q., has a wide meaning and does not refer to the more specialized sense in which the term is used in respect of the employment contract at articles 2085 to 2097 C.C.Q. and in various other statutes. **2°** Article 1463 C.C.Q. refers to the liability of principals as opposed to that of employers, the latter being a narrower category of principal. It is true, however, that the liability of employers is the archetype for this codal regime.

Fr. [*].

LIABILITY OF MASTERS

See liability of the principal.

Obs. The term *master* has an extended meaning similar to that of *principal* in article 1463 C.C.Q. and not the narrower, more common meaning of master, as in master and servant. Many scholars nevertheless see the term as an anachronism.

Fr. [*].

LIABILITY OF PARENTS

Civil liability incurred by the titulary of parental authority for the damage caused by the minor subject to that authority.

Obs. 1° The liability of parents is founded upon a presumption of fault. The titulary can be exonerated by proving absence of fault in the exercise of parental authority (art. 1459 C.C.Q.). **2°** A person deprived of parental authority is liable if the act or fault of the minor is related to the education he or she has given the minor (art. 1459 C.C.Q.). **3°** In 1977, the liability of the father and, in the event of his death, the mother, was replaced by the liability of the titulary of parental

authority when Quebec law replaced the concept of paternal authority in the Civil Code. The parents are not necessarily the holders of parental authority, however, so the seldom used expression *liability of the titulary of parental authority* is more precise than *liability of parents*.
Syn. liability of the titulary of parental authority. **See also** fault in the education, fault of supervision, liability for damage caused by another.
Fr. responsabilité des parents[+], responsabilité du titulaire de l'autorité parentale.

LIABILITY OF SCHOOLTEACHERS

Civil liability incurred by schoolteachers for the damage caused by the minors studying under their care.
Obs. 1° The *Civil Code of Québec* does not mention this type of liability, which was explicitly provided for by article 1054 para. 5 C.C.L.C. However, article 1460 C.C.Q. provides that the person entrusted with the custody, supervision or education of a minor is liable for the damage caused by the minor. Proof of damage by the student creates a presumption that the teacher is at fault. **2°** The regime of civil liability of schoolteachers is the same as that of parents, except that it is necessary to prove the fault of a schoolteacher acting gratuitously or for reward (art. 1460 C.C.Q.).
See also liability for damage caused by another, liability of parents.
Fr. responsabilité de l'instituteur.

LIABILITY OF THE PRINCIPAL

Civil liability incurred by a principal for damage caused by the fault of his or her agent or servant in the performance of the latter's work.
Obs. 1° To establish the liability of the principal, it is as a general rule necessary for the plaintiff to prove the following: the fault of the agent or servant, the existence of a relationship of subordination and that the agent or servant acted in the performance of the duties for which he or she is engaged. **2°** Scholars have proposed different explanations of this regime. The idea that the principal is liable because he or she profits from the activity of an agent or servant is generally agreed upon, while the doctrine of risks[1] is most often rejected, since the liability of the principal is based on the fault, not simply the activity, of the agent or servant. **3°** The liability of the principal, unlike the liability of parents, is not based on his or her personal fault; accord-

ingly, proof of absence of personal fault or superior force cannot serve as grounds for exoneration (art. 1463 C.C.Q.). The *Commentaires du ministre de la Justice* indicate that the obligation of the principal is one of warranty. **4°** Article 1463 C.C.Q. refers to the liability of the principal, not to the liability of an employer. It is nevertheless true that the liability of employers is the archetype for this regime even today. **5°** The use of the terms *principal, agent* and *servants* in article 1463 C.C.Q. as equivalents of *commettant* and *préposés* should not be taken as a reference to mandate relationships or to the Common law doctrine of agency.
Syn. liability of committents. **See also** agent and servant, liability for damage caused by another, obligation of warranty, principal[3], strict liability, subordination (relationship of).
Fr. responsabilité du commettant.

LIABILITY OF THE TITULARY OF PARENTAL AUTHORITY

Syn. liability of parents.
Obs. In 1977, the liability of the father and, in the event of his death, the mother, was replaced by the liability of the titulary of parental authority (S.Q. 1977, c. 72). Parents are not necessarily the holders of parental authority, however, so the seldom used expression *liability of the titulary of parental authority* is more precise than *liability of parents*.
Fr. responsabilité des parents[+], responsabilité du titulaire de l'autorité parentale.

LIABILITY OF TUTORS

Civil liability incurred by the tutor for damage caused by the person in his or her custody[3].
Obs. 1° The regime of liability of tutors to unemancipated minors is comparable to that of parents (art. 186 C.C.Q.). **2°** The tutor to persons of full age is liable only if he or she has committed an intentional or gross fault in exercising custody (art. 1461 C.C.Q.).
See also liability for damage caused by another.
Fr. responsabilité du tuteur.

LIABLE *adj.*

Said of a person whose juridical responsibility is established. "Both doctrine and case law emphasize that medical professionals should not be held liable for mere errors of judgment which are distinguishable from professional

fault" (*Lapointe* v. *Hôpital Le Gardeur*, [1992] 1 S.C.R. 351, p. 363, C. L'Heureux-Dubé, J.). *To be held civilly liable.*
Occ. Arts. 1457, 1458, 1466 C.C.Q.; arts. 1056, 1065, 2395 C.C.L.C.
Obs. When used as a noun, the French term *responsable* corresponds to the expression *person held liable.*
Syn. responsible. **See also** civil liability, juridical responsibility.
Fr. responsable.

LIBEL *n.*

See defamation[1].
Fr. libelle.

LIBERAL INTENTION

Intention to effect a liberality[1].
Fr. intention libérale.

LIBERALITY *n.*

1. Act by gratuitous title that entails a disposition[1]. "[...] the notion of liberality has thus been understood to signify [...] the following common elements: a juridical act (unilateral or bilateral) containing an expression of intention (an *animus donandi* or an *animus testandi*) to constitute, gratuitously, a patrimonial value in a determined or determinable person (or even to benefit some nonpersonified purpose, such as a legacy for 'charitable purposes')" (Brierley, in *Mélanges Crépeau*, 119, p. 123). *To confer a liberality.*
Occ. Arts. 622, 690, 695, 704, 1218 C.C.Q.; art. 607.7 C.C.L.C.
Obs. 1° A liberality presupposes the expression of a liberal intention resulting in the transfer, without a counterprestation, of property to the advantage of another or to a designated purpose. **2°** The main types of liberalities are the gift *inter vivos*, the gift *mortis causa* in a marriage contract and the legacy. It has been argued that the gratuitous trust, created through the constitution of a patrimony by appropriation (arts. 1260, 1262 C.C.Q.), represents a further distinct category of liberality. **3°** The notion of *act by gratuitous title* has a wider scope than that of *liberality* since it is not restricted to acts that transfer patrimonial rights. Therefore, it includes operations such as gratuitous loans and gratuitous contracts for services.
See also benevolent contract, disposition by gratuitous title, gift[1].
Fr. libéralité[1].

2. Object of a liberality[1].
Occ. Art. 691 C.C.Q.
Fr. libéralité[2].

LIBERATING *adj.*

Having the effect of releasing a person from an obligation or a thing from an encumbrance.
Syn. discharging, liberative, liberatory. **See also** liberative payment.
Fr. libératoire.

LIBERATIVE

Syn. liberating.
Fr. libératoire.

LIBERATIVE PAYMENT

Syn. liberatory payment.
Fr. paiement libératoire.

LIBERATORY

Syn. liberating.
Fr. libératoire.

LIBERATORY PAYMENT

Payment the effect of which is to discharge the debtor.
Obs. For a payment to be liberatory, it must necessarily be made in full and to the creditor or his or her representative (arts. 1557, 1561 C.C.Q.).
Syn. liberative payment.
Fr. paiement libératoire.

LICIT *adj.*

In conformity with law[1]. "It strikes one as an astounding proposition, to say the least, that what is undoubtedly licit in England under the British flag [...] should be immoral and against public order in the Province of Quebec, and that what is sanctioned by law in six of the provinces of this Dominion, should be prohibited in the seventh because of its immorality" (*Glengoil Steamship Line Co.* v. *Pilkington* (1898), 28 S.C.R. 146, pp. 155-156, R. Taschereau, J.).
Obs. 1° The term *licit* embraces conformity with law[2], public order and good morals. **2°** In connection with the *Civil Code of Lower Canada*, some scholars understood *licit* more restrictively to mean conformity with a provision of law[2] or with public order. Used in this sense, *licit* was opposed to *moral*, or in conformity with *good morals*. It may be observed that the notion of *good morals* does not appear in the *Civil Code of Québec*. **3°** When licit and illicit clauses are both present in the same contract, the sanction of nullity of the whole contract may be avoided. In the case where

illicit clauses do not bear upon an essential element of the contract, the invalid clauses may be severed from the portion that is licit.
Syn. lawful[1]. **See also** illicit, legal[3], legitimate[2], licit cause.
Fr. licite.

LICIT CAUSE

Cause[2] that is not contrary to law[3].
Syn. lawful cause, lawful consideration, licit consideration. **See also** illicit cause.
Fr. cause licite.

LICIT CONSIDERATION

Syn. licit cause.
Fr. cause licite.

LICIT DAMAGE

Damage that results from interference with a legally protected interest.
Obs. 1° In order to give rise to compensation, the damage must constitute an infringement of a licit interest. **2°** Since the terms *damage* and *injury* are synonymous, the expression *licit injury* may also be used.
See also illicit damage.
Fr. préjudice licite.

LICITNESS *n.*

Quality of that which is licit.
Syn. lawfulness. **See also** illicitness, legality, legitimacy[2].
Fr. licéité.

LICIT OBJECT

1. Juridical operation that is not contrary to law[3].
See also illicit object[1].
Fr. objet licite[1].

2. Prestation that is not contrary to law[3].
See also illicit object[2], possible object.
Fr. objet licite[2].

LIMITATION

See limitation of liability clause.
Occ. Arts. 1475, 2480 C.C.Q.
Fr. limitation.

LIMITATION OF LIABILITY CLAUSE

Clause in which the parties agree in advance to limit the debtor's liability resulting from the non-performance of an obligation. "On the whole, the more the courts have held invalid exoneration and limitation of liability clauses, the more frequent the use of the remedy of revision has become. Current judicial aversion to such clauses when inserted in certain contracts (contracts of adhesion) or by certain parties (*professionnels*) considerably enhances the significance of revision in modern law" (Legrand, (1988) 62 *Tul. L. Rev.* 963, pp. 1011-1012).
Obs. 1° Limitation of liability clauses may not limit liability arising from intentional or gross fault, or bodily or moral injury (art. 1474 C.C.Q.). **2°** Unlike a penal clause, which establishes the amount of damages as a fixed sum, a limitation of liability clause only fixes a limit with respect to damages. **3°** Limitation of liability clauses are without effect in matters relating to leases of dwellings and to the protection of consumers (art. 1900 C.C.Q.; s. 10, *Consumer Protection Act*, R.S.Q. c. P-40.1).
Syn. clause of limitation of liability, limited liability clause. **See also** exclusion (of liability) clause, exoneration clause[1], non-performance, notice of exoneration of liability, penal clause.
Fr. clause de limitation de responsabilité, clause de responsabilité atténuée, clause de responsabilité limitée, clause limitative de responsabilité+.

LIMITED LIABILITY CLAUSE

Syn. limitation of liability clause.
Fr. clause de limitation de responsabilité, clause de responsabilité atténuée, clause de responsabilité limitée, clause limitative de responsabilité+.

LIMITED PARTNER

Syn. special partner.
Fr. commanditaire.

LIMITED PARTNERSHIP

Partnership composed of general partners, who, in addition to being solidarily liable for the debts of the partnership, hold exclusive powers relating to its administration, and of special partners, who contribute to the common stock of the partnership and are liable for the common debts only up to the amount of their contribution. "The C.C.Q. expressly states that a limited partnership – presumably [...] one authorized by the constituting instrument – may make a distribution of securities to the public and issue negotiable instruments" (Claxton, (1999) 44 *McGill L.J.* 665, p. 699).

Occ. Arts. 2189, 2236 C.C.Q.; arts. 1871, 1877 C.C.L.C.; s. 2(2), *An Act respecting the legal publicity of sole proprietorships, partnerships and legal persons*, R.S.Q. c. P-45.

Obs. 1° Given the impact of the rules for limited liability on the interest of creditors of the partnership, limited partnerships must be declared to the authorities within the time period and in the manner prescribed by the *Act respecting the legal publicity of sole proprietorships, partnerships and legal persons*. In the absence of declaration, limited partnerships are deemed to be undeclared ones (arts. 2189, 2190 C.C.Q.). **2**° Although limited partnerships are not endowed with legal personality, they are similar to legal persons in many ways. In particular, they have a firm name and the power to sue in a civil action under this name (arts. 2225, 2249 C.C.Q.); they also operate as if they have a patrimony distinct from those of the partners (arts. 2199, 2208, 2221, 2249 C.C.Q.). **3**° General partners are solidarily liable for the obligations of the partnership where the property of the partnership is insufficient (art. 2246 C.C.Q.). By contrast, in general partnerships, the solidary liability of the partners arises only for obligations contracted for the service or operation of an enterprise of the partnership (art. 2221 C.C.Q.). **4**° In general, the special partners contribute property, whereas the general partners contribute to the common stock of the partnership by their knowledge, skill or labour. **5**° Specific rules respecting limited partnerships are set forth at articles 2236 to 2249 C.C.Q.

Syn. partnership *en commandite*. **See also** contract of partnership, general partner, general partnership, partner, partnership[1], special partner, undeclared partnership.

Fr. société en commandite.

LIQUID *adj.*

See liquidated claim, liquidated creance, liquidated debt, liquidation[2].

Obs. The word *liquid* also characterizes, in common language, cash that is easily and quickly obtainable or available.

Fr. liquide, liquidé.

LIQUIDATED *adj.*

See liquidated claim, liquidated creance, liquidated damages, liquidated debt, liquidation[2].

Fr. liquide, liquidé.

LIQUIDATED CLAIM

Syn. liquid claim.
Fr. créance déterminée, créance liquide[+].

LIQUIDATED CREANCE

Syn. liquid claim.
Fr. créance déterminée, créance liquide[+].

LIQUIDATED DAMAGES

Damages that have been the object of a liquidation[2].

See also compensation, contractual damages[1], conventional compensation, fixed price, liquidation[2], penal clause.

Fr. dommages-intérêts liquidés.

LIQUIDATED DEBT

Syn. liquid debt.
Fr. dette déterminée, dette liquide[+].

LIQUIDATION *n.*

1. Series of acts[1] that determine the composition and the value of one or more masses of property and fix the rights and obligations of specified persons over such masses for the purpose of the partition or division of such masses. For example, the liquidation of a succession, the liquidation of a legal person, the liquidation of a matrimonial regime.

Occ. Title preceding art. 355 C.C.Q.; arts. 364, 473, 492, 2230 C.C.Q.

See also division.

Fr. liquidation[1].

2. Process consisting in determining, precisely, the monetary value of an obligation. For example, the liquidation of damages, the judicial liquidation of a debt.

Occ. Art. 1673 C.C.Q.

Obs. Liquidation may be conventional, legal or judicial.

See also liquidated damages, quantity.

Fr. liquidation[2].

LIQUID CLAIM

Certain claim, the amount of which has been precisely fixed.

Syn. determinate claim, determinate creance, liquidated claim, liquidated creance, liquid creance. **See also** certain debt, liquid debt, liquidity.

Fr. créance déterminée, créance liquide[+].

LIQUID CREANCE

Syn. liquid claim.
Fr. créance déterminée, créance liquide[+].

LIQUID DEBT

Certain debt, the amount of which has been precisely fixed.
Obs. 1° Only certain, liquid and exigible debts whose object is a sum of money or fungible property identical in kind are open to compensation (art. 1673 C.C.Q.). **2°** Under the *Civil Code of Lower Canada*, a liquid debt was considered to be certain. That the *Civil Code of Québec* refers to both attributes at article 1673 C.C.Q. appears to suggest that a distinction may be drawn between liquid debts and certain debts, thereby detracting from the significance of the notion of *liquidity*. This view, which is difficult to reconcile with the wording of article 966 C.C.P., suggests that the notion of *liquidity* relates only to the fixed character of the monetary value of a debt. **3°** Under the C.C.L.C., *liquidated debt* was the preferred expression (e.g. art. 1188 C.C.L.C.).
Syn. determinate debt, liquidated debt. **See also** certain debt, compensation[1], liquid claim, liquidity.
Fr. dette déterminée, dette liquide[+].

LIQUIDITY *n.*

Quality of a debt or of a claim, certain in character, the amount of which has been precisely fixed.
Obs. Under the *Civil Code of Lower Canada*, liquid debts and liquid claims were considered to be certain. That the *Civil Code of Québec* refers to both attributes at article 1673 C.C.Q. appears to suggest that a distinction may be drawn between liquid claims or debts and certain debts or claims, thereby detracting from the significance of the notion of *liquidity*. This view, which is difficult to reconcile with the wording of article 966 C.C.P., suggests that the notion of *liquidity* relates only to the fixed character of the monetary value of a claim.
See also certain claim, certain debt, exigibility, liquid claim, liquid debt.
Fr. liquidité.

LITIGIOUS CREANCE

Syn. litigious personal right.
Fr. créance litigieuse.

LITIGIOUS DEBT

Syn. litigious personal right.
Fr. créance litigieuse.

LITIGIOUS PERSONAL RIGHT

Personal right whose existence or scope gives rise or may give rise to a judicial litigation.
Syn. litigious creance, litigious debt. **See also** assignment of litigious rights, litigious right, redemption of litigious rights, sale of litigious right.
Fr. créance litigieuse.

LITIGIOUS RIGHT

Right whose existence or scope gives rise or may give rise to litigation. "I cannot escape the conclusion that the respondents entirely misconceived what is incumbent on a debtor who seeks to defeat a claim of litigious rights by exercising the *retrait de droits litigieux*. The effect of the *retrait* is that the debtor assumes the bargain (*le marché*) of the buyer of the litigious right, so that the debtor is substituted for and subrogated to the buyer" (*McNaughton* v. *Irvine*, [1926] S.C.R. 8, p. 14, P.B. Mignault, J.).
Occ. Arts. 1783, 1784 C.C.Q.; arts. 1485, 1582 C.C.L.C.
Obs. Article 1782 C.C.Q. provides that a "right is litigious when it is uncertain, contested or contestable by the debtor, whether an action is pending or there is reason to presume that it will become necessary".
See also assignment of litigious rights, litigious personal right, redemption of litigious rights, sale of litigious rights.
Fr. droit litigieux.

LOAN *n.*

Real contract by which a person, the *lender*, grants to another, the *borrower*, the use of property subject to restitution after a certain time. "A loan can of course be of any property other than money; loans of commodities such as grain are common; so are loans of marketable common shares between brokers" (Claxton, *Security*, n° 16.2, p. 284).
Occ. Arts. 213, 1340, 1655, 1756, 2312 C.C.Q.; art. 1762 C.C.L.C.; ss. 450, 452(1), 458, *Bank Act*, S.C. 1991, c. 46.
Obs. 1° The two kinds of loan are loan for use and simple loan (art. 2312 C.C.Q.). When the loan bears on non-consumable property or property so considered by the parties, the contract is called a loan for use (art. 2313 C.C.Q.). However, when the lender hands over a certain quantity of money or other property that is consumed by use, the contract is called a simple loan (art. 2314 C.C.Q.). **2°** The loan for use is, by its nature, made by gratuitous title; the simple loan may be by onerous or by gratuitous title. **3°** The codal regime respecting the contract of loan is set forth at articles 2312 to 2332 C.C.Q.
Syn. contract of loan. **See also** lease[1], loan for use, real contract, simple loan.
Fr. contrat de prêt, prêt[+].

LOAN FOR CONSUMPTION

Syn. simple loan.
Occ. Arts. 1762, 1777 C.C.L.C.
Fr. *mutuum*, prêt de consommation, simple prêt[+].

LOAN FOR USE

Gratuitous loan for a determined use of non-consumable property. "The key feature distinguishing loan for use from lease is its gratuitous character (art. 1763 [C.C.L.C.]), and hence the contract stands in relation to lease exactly as gift stands in relation to sale" (Brierley & Macdonald (eds.), *Quebec Civil Law*, n° 626, p. 551).
Occ. Title preceding art. 2317 C.C.Q.; arts. 1853, 2312 C.C.Q.; art. 1763 C.C.L.C.
Obs. 1° In the loan for use, the use is generally determined by the nature of the property. It may nevertheless also be established by the parties. **2°** The parties may, by agreement, stipulate that a thing consumable by nature be considered non-consumable; the contract is then a loan for use (e.g. loan for use of stamps in circulation for display at a stamp collectors' exhibit). **3°** Loan for use entails the obligation that the borrower restore the property itself. **4°** The borrower – the only one who may use the property loaned (art. 2318 C.C.Q) –, must care for and preserve the property loaned with prudence and diligence (art. 2317 C.C.Q.). He or she is not responsible if the property is lost through the use for which it was loaned (art. 2322 C.C.Q.). **5°** Loan is distinguished from lease in that it is generally made by gratuitous title.
Syn. *commodatum*. **See also** borrower, lease[1], lender, simple loan.
Fr. commodat, prêt à usage[+].

LOAN OF MONEY

Simple loan having as its object a sum of money. "And in the case of a loan of money, the use and enjoyment of the amount lent for the time agreed upon is the consideration for the payment of the interest in addition to the amount lent" (*Rolland* v. *Caisse d'Économie Notre-Dame du Québec* (1895), 24 S.C.R. 405, p. 408, H.E. Taschereau, J.).
Occ. Arts. 2315, 2331 C.C.Q.; art. 1040c C.C.L.C.; ss. 66, 73, 74, *Consumer Protection Act*, R.S.Q. c. P-40.1.
Obs. 1° The loan of money is presumed to be made by onerous title. **2°** The rate of interest can be determined in the contract. In the absence of an agreement, the *Interest Act* applies (art. 1565 C.C.Q.; s. 3, *Interest Act*, R.S.C. 1985, c. I-15). **3°** Under the regime of the loan of money, the court may sanction lesion (art. 2332 C.C.Q.). This is an exception to the general rule that lesion between persons of full age does not vitiate consent. **4°** When the loan of money is granted by a bank, the *Bank Act* (S.C. 1991, c. 46) provides for a specific legal regime. However, when a merchant grants a loan of money to a consumer, sections 66 to 130 of the *Consumer Protection Act* (R.S.Q. c. P-40.1) relating to the contract of credit apply.
See also deposit[3], lesion, loan upon interest.
Fr. prêt d'argent.

LOAN UPON INTEREST

Loan of money stipulating a counterprestation called interest.
Occ. Title preceding art. 1785 C.C.L.C.
Obs. 1° The rate of interest can be determined in the contract. In the absence of an agreement, the rate is fixed by law (art. 1565 C.C.Q.; s. 3, *Interest Act*, R.S.C., c. I-15). **2°** The interest is owed, in principle, from the date the money is handed over to the borrower (art. 2330 C.C.Q.).
See also interest, lesion, loan of money.
Fr. prêt à intérêt.

LONGA MANU TRADITION (Latin)

Syn. symbolic tradition.
Fr. *traditio longa manu*, tradition de longue main, tradition symbolique[+].

LOSS *n.*

1. Damage consisting in an impoverishment. For example, the moral suffering following a violation of the right to reputation.
Occ. Arts. 1611, 1612 C.C.Q.; art. 1073 C.C.L.C.
Obs. 1° When civil liability is established, damage includes the loss sustained by the victim and the profit of which he has been deprived, both of which can give rise to compensatory damages (art. 1611 C.C.Q.). **2°** Traditionally, the term *loss* had a pecuniary connotation. It is nevertheless possible to claim compensation for pecuniary as well as non-pecuniary loss. **3°** The expressions *economic loss* and *pecuniary loss* are used synonymously with *material damage* and may describe both the profit deprived and the loss suffered.
Syn. *damnum emergens*. **See also** damages, loss of (a) chance, profit deprived.
Fr. *damnum emergens*, perte[+].

2. Syn. damage. "[...] the right of a fire insurance company to recover under article 1053

C.C.[L.C.] from a third party whose fault occasioned the loss for which, under its contract, it has been obliged to indemnify its assured, seems to be well recognized in the jurisprudence of the province of Quebec" (*Regent Taxi & Transport Co.* v. *Congrégation des Petits Frères de Marie*, [1929] S.C.R. 650, pp. 667-668, F.A. Anglin, C.J.).
Fr. dommage+, préjudice, tort[2].

LOSS OF AMENITIES

Moral damage consisting in a deprivation of enjoyment of life. For example, deprivation of the gratification arising from an intellectual, cultural, athletic or social activity; or the anxiety, inconveniences or frustrations arising from harm to one's person.
Fr. préjudice d'agrément.

LOSS OF A THING DUE

Destruction or disappearance of a thing that constitutes the object of a prestation.
Obs. 1° In principle, the loss of a thing due caused by a superior force frees the debtor from his or her obligation, unless he has expressly assumed such a risk (art. 1693 C.C.Q.). **2°** In bilateral contracts, the debtor whose performance is rendered impossible by a superior force cannot require his or her cocontracting party to perform the correlative obligation. Where that obligation has been performed, the rules relating to restitution apply (art. 1694 C.C.Q.). **3°** The loss of the thing may be either total or partial. Deterioration of the thing is deemed to be a form of partial loss (art. 1702 C.C.Q.).
See also doctrine of risks[1], restitution, superior force.
Fr. perte de la chose due.

LOSS OF (A) CHANCE

Deprivation of an opportunity to obtain a probable profit or to avoid probable damage. For example, the loss of a chance to obtain employment where there was a real chance of obtaining such employment on the balance of probabilities. "[...] loss of chance is a type of damage. It is the damage which results from the loss of an opportunity either to realize a benefit or to avoid an injury" (*Laferrière* v. *Lawson*, [1991] 1 S.C.R. 541, p. 559, C.D. Gonthier, J.).
Obs. 1° Compensation for loss of chance appears to call into question a number of traditional requirements of civil liability, notably the principle that damage must be certain

and that the causal relationship between fault and loss rests upon more than a mere possibility. **2°** There are a number of instances where courts have awarded damages for loss of chance, thereby treating loss of chance as certain and present damage distinct from future damage. Damage is then said to exist at the very moment the opportunity is lost if, based on a balance of probabilities, the chance was worth undertaking and could reasonably be expected to materialize. **3°** Some scholars have expressed the view that the doctrine of loss of chance should not apply in certain contexts, such as medical liability.
See also adequate causation, causation[2], damage, future damage, loss[1], present damage.
Fr. perte de (d'une) chance.

LUCRUM CESSANS nom.ph. (Latin)

Syn. profit deprived.
Obs. A distinction is drawn between *lucrum cessans* and *damnum emergens*.
Fr. gain manqué+, *lucrum cessans*, manque à gagner.

LUMP SUM

See lump sum contract, lump sum payment.
Fr. [*].

LUMP SUM CONTRACT

Syn. fixed price contract.
Fr. contrat à forfait+, marché à forfait.

LUMP SUM PAYMENT

Fulfilment of a monetary obligation by means of a single payment. "I should mention in passing that, in such an equitable distribution, the spouses may agree on various ways of dividing their assets depending on their financial situation at the time of divorce. Thus, spousal support for an unlimited time, such as that contemplated by the parties here, may well be compensatory in nature rather than simply needs based, especially when the parties do not have the resources to make a lump sum payment at the time of divorce, which may also, in some cases, confer some tax advantages. In the absence of any such mention in the agreement, the parties' intention in this regard cannot be presumed" (*L.G.* v. *G.B.*, [1995] 3 S.C.R. 370, p. 398, C. L'Heureux-Dubé, J.).
Occ. Art. 2440 C.C.Q.
See also periodic payment.
Fr. paiement unique.

M

MAINLEVÉE *n.* (French)

Attesting deed that puts an end to a seizure, an opposition or a regime of protective supervision, or that permits the cancellation of the registration of a security.
Fr. mainlevée.

MANAGEMENT OF THE AFFAIRS OF ANOTHER

Syn. management of the business of another. "There is in the management of the affairs of another a representation of interests of the master by the manager" (Planiol & Ripert, *Treatise*, vol. 2, n° 2274, p. 310).
Obs. The Civil Code uses the expression *management of the business of another* (arts. 1482 to 1490 C.C.Q.), whereas the *Civil Code of Lower Canada* also used the expression *negotiorum gestio* (arts. 1043 to 1046 C.C.L.C.), most often rendered in English as *management of affairs of another*.
Fr. gestion d'affaire(s)+, *negotiorum gestio*.

MANAGEMENT OF THE BUSINESS OF ANOTHER

Act of a person who voluntarily takes charge of the business of another without having been obliged to do so, either at the behest of the latter or by law, which gives rise to obligations.
Occ. Arts. 273, 1482, 1486, 3125 C.C.Q.
Obs. 1° Management of the business of another creates obligations between both parties similar to those between the *mandator* and the *mandatary* in a contract of mandate. **2°** Management of the business of another can arise as a result of undertaking either a juridical or a physical act. **3°** Management of the business of another has traditionally been considered a quasi-contract. The term *quasi-contract* was used at article 983 C.C.L.C. but it is not used in the Civil Code. Management of the business of another is now considered one of the "other sources of obligations" (title preceding art. 1482 C.C.Q.) reflecting the classification of the sources of obligations as stated in art. 1372 C.C.Q. **4°** The Civil Code uses the expression *management of the busi-ness of another* (arts. 1482 to 1490 C.C.Q.), whereas the *Civil Code of Lower Canada* also used the expression *negotiorum gestio* (title preceding art. 1043 C.C.L.C.). **5°** The codal regime respecting management of the business of another is set forth at articles 1482 to 1490 C.C.Q.
Syn. management of the affairs of another, *negotiorum gestio*. **See also** mandate[1], payment of a thing not due, reception of a thing not due, unjust enrichment.
Fr. gestion d'affaire(s)+, *negotiorum gestio*.

MANAGER *n.*

Person who, in the context of management of the business of another, carries out the management. "The *gérant* or manager is bound, in principle, to the same obligations as a mandatary: thus he should exercise in the management which he has undertaken the care of a prudent administrator [...]" (Planiol & Ripert, *Treatise*, vol. 2, n° 2276, p. 310).
Occ. Arts. 1482 to 1490 C.C.Q.
Syn. *negotiorum gestor*. **See also** principal[3].
Fr. gérant[1]+, *negotiorum gestor*.

MANDATARY *n.*

Person upon whom a power of representation is conferred by a mandate[1]. "The mandator cannot escape responsibility for the lawful acts of the mandatary, while the mandatary can escape responsibility if acting within the mandate" (Claxton, (1997) 42 *McGill L.J.* 797, p. 849).
Occ. Arts. 2130, 2138, 2157 C.C.Q.; art. 1701 C.C.L.C.
Obs. 1° The Civil Code imposes certain obligations upon the mandate towards the mandator in addition to the ones provided for in the contract. The mandatary is thus bound to fulfill the mandate in person, unless he or she is authorized by the mandator to appoint another person (art. 2140 C.C.Q.). The mandatary must act honestly and faithfully and avoid situations of conflict of interest (art. 2138 C.C.Q.); he or she must also inform the mandator of the stage reached in the performance of the mandate (art. 2139 C.C.Q.). **2°** Whether remunerated or not, the mandatary

is bound to act in accordance with the same standard of conduct. However, when the mandate is by gratuitous title, the court may, when assessing the extent of liability, reduce the amount of damages owed by the mandatary (art. 2148 C.C.Q.)
Syn. attorney. **See also** mandator, obligation of loyalty, person represented.
Fr. mandataire+, procureur.

MANDATE *n.*

1. Contract by which a person, the *mandator*, gives to another, the *mandatary*, the power to represent him or her for concluding or performing a juridical act. "In mandate, personal representation is the essence of the relationship [...] the rights and powers of the mandatary are limited to those of the mandator and are ultimately subject to the supervision and control of the mandator" (Claxton, (1997) 42 *McGill L.J.* 797, p. 849).
Occ. Art. 2130 C.C.Q.; art. 1701 C.C.L.C.
Obs. 1° A mandate must bear upon a juridical act but it may involve the performance of material acts that are accessory to it. **2°** In order to be valid, the mandate is generally not subject to any requirement of form. An exception is the mandate in anticipation of incapacity, which must be made by a notarial act *en minute* or in the presence of witnesses (art. 2166 C.C.Q.). **3°** The *Civil Code of Québec* is more explicit than was the *Civil Code of Lower Canada* in respect of the extent of the mandate, and provides that the powers of the mandatary extend to that which may be inferred from the powers conferred by the mandate (art. 2136 C.C.Q.). **4°** While if the word *mandate* has a very broad meaning in everyday parlance, the legal concept of mandate is to be distinguished from other agreements such as the contract for services or the contract of employment in that only the mandate confers a power of representation. A mixed contract, such as one including a mandate and a contract for services in the same act, is nevertheless possible. **5°** Mandate is either by gratuitous title or by onerous title (art. 2133 C.C.Q.). **6°** The English text of article 2130 C.C.Q. refers to the mandatary's power to represent the mandator in the "performance" of a juridical act; the French text speaks of the "accomplissement" of a juridical act, which appears to be wider in meaning in that it includes expressly the power to conclude such acts. **7°** The codal regime respecting mandate is set forth at articles 2130 to 2185 C.C.Q. **8°** From Old French *mander*: to give an order, an instruction.

Syn. contract of mandate. **See also** contract of *prête-nom*, double mandate, power of attorney[1], representation, sub-mandate.
Fr. contrat de mandat, mandat[1+].

2. Power of representation conferred on a person. "We have in this case an undisclosed mandate where the mandatary acted in his own name and in such case the mandator has no recourse against the third party unless he has been subrogated to or has had a transfer of rights from the mandatary" (*Ravitsky* v. *Ehrman*, [1969] C.S. 433, p. 434, G.S. Challies, C.J.). *To have a mandate; to give a mandate; to receive a mandate.*
Obs. A distinction is made according to the source of the power of representation between conventional mandate, judicial mandate and legal mandate.
See also domestic mandate, testamentary execution.
Fr. mandat[2].

MANDATE EXPRESSED IN GENERAL TERMS

Mandate[1] in which the powers of the mandatary are not specified.
Occ. Art. 2135 C.C.Q.
Obs. 1° A mandate expressed in general terms can be general or special, depending on whether it relates to all the affairs of the mandator or to a particular act. **2°** The mandate expressed in general terms authorizes the mandatary to perform only acts of simple administration; an express mandate is required for acts of full administration (art. 2135 C.C.Q.). Therefore, the distinction between a mandate expressed in general terms and an express mandate lies not in the number of matters entrusted to the mandatary, but in the nature of the acts with respect to each such matter the mandatary is authorized to perform. **3°** The *mandate expressed in general terms* is opposed to the *express mandate*[1].
Syn. mandate given in general terms. **See also** general mandate, special mandate.
Fr. mandat conçu en termes généraux+, mandat exprimé en termes généraux.

MANDATE GIVEN IN GENERAL TERMS

Syn. mandate expressed in general terms.
Fr. mandat conçu en termes généraux+, mandat exprimé en termes généraux.

MANDATOR *n.*

Person who, by mandate[1], confers a power of representation upon another. "As in the case of any mandate, the mandate between a manager and his client is imbued with the concept of trust. [...] This spirit of trust is reflected in the weight of the obligations that rest on the manager, which will be heavier where the mandator is vulnerable, lacks specialized knowledge, is dependent on the mandatary, and where the mandate is important" (*Laflamme* v. *Prudential-Bache Commodities Canada Ltd.*, [2000] 1 S.C.R. 638, p. 652, C.D. Gonthier, J.).
Occ. Arts. 2130, 2149, 2160 C.C.Q.; arts. 1701, 1701.1 C.C.L.C.
Obs. 1° The mandator is liable to third persons for the acts performed by the mandatary within the limits of the mandate (art. 2160 C.C.Q.). **2°** The mandator also undertakes various obligations towards the mandatary. In addition to those already provided for in the *Civil Code of Lower Canada* (giving advances and reimbursements, remuneration when the mandate is by onerous title, discharging and compensating the mandatary), the *Civil Code of Québec* provides for the obligation to cooperate with the mandatary in the fulfilment of the mandate (art. 2149 C.C.Q.).
See also duty to cooperate, mandatary, representative.
Fr. mandant.

MANUFACTURER'S LIABILITY

Liability incurred by the manufacturer of a movable thing.
Obs. 1° The expression *manufacturer's liability* is sometimes used as a synonym of *product liability*, which has a broader meaning. Manufacturer's liability remains however the archetype of the regime applicable to product liability. **2°** The word *manufacturer* has been given a liberal interpretation by the courts (e.g. the bottler of carbonated beverages has been treated as a manufacturer (*Cohen* v. *Coca-Cola Ltd.*, [1967] S.C.R. 469)). **3°** The codal regime respecting manufacturer's liability is set forth at articles 1468, 1469 and 1726 *et seq.* C.C.Q.
See also product liability.
Fr. responsabilité du fabricant[+], responsabilité du manufacturier.

MARINE INSURANCE

Contract of insurance whose object is to guarantee the insured from the risks incident to marine adventure. "Marine insurance is first and foremost a contract of maritime law. It is not an application of insurance to the maritime area. Rather, it is the other forms of insurance which are applications to other areas of principles borrowed from marine insurance" (*Triglav* v. *Terrasses Jewellers Inc.*, [1983] 1 S.C.R. 283, p. 298, J. Chouinard, J.).
Occ. Arts. 2389, 2390, 2403, 2505 C.C.Q.; arts. 2469, 2482, 2609 C.C.L.C.; s. 6, *Marine Insurance Act*, S.C. 1993, c. 22.
Obs. 1° The marine insurance regime set forth in the *Civil Code of Québec* is modelled on a United Kingdom statute of 1906 (*The Marine Insurance Act*, (1906) Edw. VII, ch. 41 (U.K.)), which is also the basis for federal law in the field. **2°** The *Civil Code of Québec* is wider in scope than the *Civil Code of Lower Canada*; marine insurance now covers risks that are not directly linked to navigation, including risks on land that are incidental to marine adventure, such as the loading of cargo, or risks connected to the building of a ship (art. 2505 C.C.Q.). **3°** The marine insurance contract is subject to the requirement of the utmost good faith (art. 2545 C.C.Q.). This requirement reflects the nature of the marine insurance contract, which is often concluded without the insurer having been able to verify personally the representations of the insured, notably because of the physical distance between them. **4°** The codal regime respecting marine insurance is set forth at articles 2505 to 2629 C.C.Q. **5°** One might question the applicability of the provisions in the Civil Code pertaining to maritime insurance since maritime law falls under federal jurisdiction as Navigation and Shipping (*Constitution Act, 1867*, s. 91(10)) and Admiralty, as defined by section 2 of the *Federal Court Act* (R.S.C. 1985, c. F-7). Thus, Canadian courts have developed federal law of general application in maritime matters.
See also non-marine insurance.
Fr. assurance maritime.

MARKETABLE QUALITY

Syn. merchantable quality.
Fr. qualité marchande.

MARKET VALUE

Syn. actual value. "The market value is normally arrived at by estimating the price at which an owner desiring but not obliged to sell would sell to a person desiring but not obliged to buy" (Challies, *Expropriation*, pp. 98-99).
Occ. Arts. 1093, 1695, 2302 C.C.Q.
Fr. valeur marchande, valeur réelle[+], valeur vénale.

MASTER *n.*

See principal[1]. "Legally, the master or the employer has no means of constraint against the domestic or the workman who refuses to work. In general, the workman does not contract any firm engagement; he quits when he wishes, save for the effect of the delay for giving notice" (Planiol & Ripert, *Treatise*, vol. 2, part. 2, n° 1844, p. 112).
Occ. Art. 1054 C.C.L.C.
Obs. The term *principal*, when used as an equivalent of the French term *committant*, is generally understood to include employers and masters.
Fr. [*].

MASTER CONTRACT

Contract whereby the parties determine the principal conditions[2] to which subsequent contracts must conform during a given period. For example, an insurance master policy.
Fr. contrat-cadre.

MASTER-SERVANT RELATIONSHIP

See subordination.
Obs. This expression, although dated, is still used in a wide sense to include all those persons referred to in article 1463 C.C.Q., but not in the narrower technical sense that master and servant had in the *Civil Code of Lower Canada*.
Fr. [*].

MATERIAL CAUSATION

Causation[1] that links an act or omission to damage, independently of the legal notion of liability.
Obs. Material causation considers as causal any factor that contributed to the realization of the damage. In this sense, it is less restrictive than causation *per se*, also called causation in law, i.e. that which is susceptible of bringing about a person's civil liability.
Syn. causation in fact. **See also** causation[2], equivalence of conditions, material cause.
Fr. causalité matérielle.

MATERIAL CAUSE

Cause[3] of the loss, considered independently of the legal notion of liability.
See also adequate cause, condition *sine qua non*, determining cause, material causation, proximate cause[1].
Fr. cause matérielle.

MATERIAL DAMAGE

Damage of a patrimonial nature.
Occ. Art. 2926 C.C.Q.; s. 201, *An Act respecting the marketing of agricultural, food and fish products*, R.S.Q. c. M-35.1.
Obs. 1° Material damage is one of the three types of injury recognized by the Civil Code along with moral and bodily damage (art. 1607 C.C.Q.). **2°** Material damage is often confused with damage to material property of a person. Material damage results not only from an infringement upon property (e.g. the destruction of an object which carries pecuniary losses), but also infringement upon a person's extrapatrimonial rights insofar as the infringement entails a pecuniary loss (e.g. bodily injury resulting in a loss of income). **3°** Most often used to establish a comparison with the Common law category of pure economic loss, the expression *pure economic loss* is not a category of damage regulated as such and does not have any specific connotation in the Civil law. The Civil law neither specifically excludes nor provides special conditions regarding the right to compensation for material damage, except with respect to its direct and certain character. **4°** A distinction is drawn between *material damage* and *moral damage*. **5°** Since the terms *damage* and *injury* are synonymous, the expression *material injury* may also be used.
Syn. corporeal damage, economic loss, pecuniary damage. **See also** bodily injury, loss[1], moral damage, personal damage, profit deprived.
Fr. perte économique, préjudice économique, préjudice matériel[+], préjudice pécuniaire.

MATERIAL FACT

Fact viewed independently of the consequences that the law may attach to it.
See also juridical fact[2].
Fr. acte matériel(<)[+], fait matériel[+].

MATERIAL IMPUTABILITY

Syn. imputability[2].
Fr. imputabilité[2+], imputabilité matérielle.

MATERIAL PROPERTY

(*Prop.*) Syn. property[2].
Fr. bien[2+], bien corporel, bien matériel, chose appropriable.

MATERIAL THING

Syn. thing[1].
Fr. chose[1+], chose corporelle, chose matérielle.

MEDIATE VICTIM

Victim suffering harm as a consequence of damage suffered by another. For example, the moral and material damage suffered by the spouse or child of the immediate victim.
Obs. Both the immediate and the mediate victim are entitled to be indemnified for the personal harm, whether material or moral, that they sustain as a result of the actionable conduct of the wrongdoer (*Hôpital Notre-Dame de l'Espérance* v. *Laurent*, [1978] 1 S.C.R. 605).
Syn. victim by ricochet. **See also** immediate victim, personal damage, ricochet damage.
Fr. victime médiate, victime par ricochet[+].

MEETING OF THE MINDS

Syn. consent[1].
Obs. The meeting of the minds is also designated by the expressions *accord of wills, agreement of wills, concurrence of wills, concordance of wills.*
Fr. accord de(s) volonté(s), consentement[1+].

MEMBER *n.*

1. Person who is part of an association.
Occ. Arts. 2186, 2268 C.C.Q.
Fr. membre[1+], sociétaire[2].

2. See partner.
Fr. membre[2].

MEMORANDUM OF UNDERSTANDING

Syn. agreement in principle.
Obs. The expression *memorandum of understanding* generally refers to a written document.
Fr. accord de principe[+], accord préliminaire, protocole d'entente.

MERCHANT *n.*

Person whose habitual or professional activity consists in carrying out acts of a commercial nature in his or her name and for his or her own profit.
Occ. Art. 2262(3) C.C.L.C.; ss. 16, 43, 96, 97, 167*a*, 182*b*, *Consumer Protection Act*, R.S.Q. c. P- 40.1.
Syn. trader. **See also** commerce[1], consumer.
Fr. commerçant.

MERCHANTABLE QUALITY

Average quality that is neither the best nor the worst. "Where [...] a fungible object is to be paid, deteriorations are at the risk of the debtor, in that the object must be at least of merchantable quality, unless the parties have otherwise provided [...]" (Brierley & Macdonald (eds.), *Quebec Civil Law*, n° 541, p. 491).
Occ. Art. 1151 C.C.L.C.
Syn. marketable quality.
Fr. qualité marchande.

MERE EXPECTANCY

Hope pertaining to a right that has not come into existence. For example, the hope that a person may entertain, before the death of the testator, of receiving a benefit under the will.
Obs. By contrast to a present right, a mere expectancy is not part of a person's patrimony and cannot be seized or protected by any judicial action.
Syn. expectancy, expectation, mere expectation, potential right. **See also** eventual right[1], present right.
Fr. droit virtuel, expectative, simple expectative[+].

MERE EXPECTATION

Syn. mere expectancy.
Fr. droit virtuel, expectative, simple expectative[+].

MINUTE n. (French)

Syn. notarial act *en minute.*
Occ. S. 36, *Notaries Act*, R.S.Q. c. N-3.
Fr. acte en minute, acte notarié en minute[+], minute.

MISE EN DEMEURE (French)

Syn. notice of default.
Fr. mise en demeure[2].

MIXED ACT

Juridical act that is civil for one party and commercial for the other. For example, the loan granted by a trader to a non-trader.
See also civil act, commercial act.
Fr. acte mixte.

MIXED CONDITION

Condition[1] that depends upon the will of a party and on that of a third person. For example, that one of the contracting parties marry a third person. "[...] nineteenth-century *doctrine* defined a mixed condition as one which was dependent on the will of one of the parties

and of a *determinate* third party" (Nicholas, *Contract*, p. 161).
Obs. The mixed condition is considered to be a type of potestative condition.
See also casual condition, potestative condition.
Fr. condition mixte.

MIXED CONTRACT

Contract of a hybrid nature consisting of several juridical transactions and presenting elements of different types of contracts, from which it derives its rules and characteristics. For example, a contract with a hotel-keeper. "It is common knowledge that a high proportion of the agreements whereby dealers sell automobiles are mixed contracts of sale and exchange" (*Garage W. Martin Ltée* v. *Industrial Acceptance Corp.*, [1970] C.A. 43, p. 44, G.H. Montgomery, J.A.).
Obs. A distinction is drawn between *mixed contracts* and *simple contracts*.
Syn. complex contract. **See also** innominate contract, simple contract.
Fr. contrat complexe+, contrat mixte.

MIXED LAW

Branch of law[1] composed of rules of both public and private law. For example, consumer law, labour law, environmental law.
Obs. While it is common to classify sectors of law as private, public or mixed law, scholars see the distinction between public law and private law as increasingly difficult to establish. Many branches of law that have traditionally been understood as private law should in fact be seen as mixed, given the presence of the State in private law relations.
Fr. droit mixte[2].

MIXED LEGAL SYSTEM

Law[1] the rules of which are derived from several legal traditions. For example, the law of Quebec, Louisiana. "[...] despite these different external factors, the mixed legal systems [...] have profound generalizable resemblances, and argue strongly for the proposition that legal history can be highly autonomous and path dependant" (Palmer, *Mixed Jurisdictions Worldwide*, p. 4).
Obs. 1° While criminal law, public law, aspects of commercial law and civil procedure in Quebec derive in many respects from legal sources from the Common law tradition, scholars generally agree that Quebec private law, as it relates to property and civil rights, originates and has developed along the lines

of the French civilian tradition. Thus, Quebec's fundamental legal categories and structures of legal thought partake of a mixed legal heritage. In addition to influences from the Common law and the Civil law, some scholars identify aboriginal law as a component of Quebec's mixed legal culture. **2°** Some scholars argue that Quebec's legal system has emerged as a mature, free-standing legal order and that its status as a mixed legal system is best understood as a matter of historical fact.
Fr. droit mixte[1].

MIXED LESION

Lesion that consists in a significant disproportion between the prestations, which disproportion results from the exploitation of one of the parties by the other.
Obs. 1° The legislature has adopted a mixed conception of lesion at article 1406 para. 1 C.C.Q. and section 8 *in limine, Consumer Protection Act* (R.S.Q. c. P-40.1). However, the regime's for the application of the principle is different given that article 1406 C.C.Q. states that the fact that there is a serious disproportion only creates a rebuttable presumption of exploitation, whereas section 8 *Consumer Protection Act* (R.S.Q. c. P-40.1) states that where the disproportion between the respective obligations of the parties is so great as it amounts to exploitation. **2°** Mixed lesion gives rise to a remedy only in certain circumstances (arts. 424, 472, 897, 2332 C.C.Q.; s. 8, *Consumer Protection Act*, R.S.Q. c. P-40.1 (*in limine*)). This solution is difficult to understand since the exploitation of a party by the other is contrary to the requirements of good faith inasmuch as it is done with the intent of injuring another (arts. 6, 7 C.C.Q.). Furthermore, art. 1375 C.C.Q. specifies that the parties shall conduct themselves in good faith at the time the obligation is created. **3°** The Civil Code Revision Office proposed to admit lesion as a defect of consent (art. 37, Bk V, *Draft Civil Code*, C.C.R.O.). That solution is adopted in German and Swiss law and by Unidroit's *Principles for International Commercial Contracts* (art. 138 *B.G.B.*; arts. 20 and 21 of the Swiss *Code des obligations*; art. 3.10 Unidroit's *Principles*).
See also abuse of right(s), exploitation, good faith, objective lesion, subjective lesion.
Fr. lésion mixte.

MIXED RIGHT

Syn. *jus ad rem transpersonam.*
Fr. droit mixte[3], *jus ad rem transpersonam+*.

MODAL *adj.*

Subject to a modality. For example, a modal contract is a contract subject to modalities.
See also conditional, pure and simple, term (with a).
Fr. modal.

MODALITY *n.*

Particular form of a juridical act, fact, or of a right or obligation. For example, undivided ownership, conditional obligation, eventual right. "[...] the Code attempts to structure every important variation on the root concept of obligation. These 'kinds' or particular forms of obligations, which are very definitional in character, are normally described as 'modalities'" (Brierley & Macdonald (eds.), *Quebec Civil Law*, n° 526, p. 479).
Occ. Title preceding art. 1497 C.C.Q.; art. 1372 C.C.Q.
Obs. 1° Modalities of obligations are divided in two categories: simple and complex (arts. 1497 to 1552 C.C.Q.). **2°** The Civil Code treats co-ownership and superficies in a Title devoted to the modalities of the right of ownership (arts. 1009 to 1118 C.C.Q.). **3°** As regards the modalities of ownership, the Civil Code uses the expression *special modes* instead of the more traditional term *modalities* (title preceding art. 1009 C.C.Q.; art. 1009 C.C.Q.).
See also modality of payment, modality of the obligation, obligation with a complex modality, obligation with a simple modality.
Fr. modalité.

MODALITY OF PAYMENT

Specified form or method for effecting payment. For example, cash payment, payment by instalments, payment with a term.
Syn. condition of payment.
Fr. condition de paiement, modalité de paiement⁺.

MODALITY OF THE OBLIGATION

Modality relating to the formation, existence, execution or extinction of an obligation.
Obs. Modalities play a role in the formation (suspensive condition), existence (resolutory condition), execution (alternative, conjunctive, divisible, facultative, indivisible, joint or solidary obligation, and suspensive term) and extinction (extinctive term) of an obligation.
See also complex obligation, pure and simple obligation.
Fr. modalité de l'obligation.

MONETARY *adj.*

See monetary clause.
Occ. Art. 590 C.C.Q.
Fr. monétaire.

MONETARY CLAUSE

Clause the purpose of which is to protect the creditor of a monetary obligation against a possible depreciation in the value of money.
Obs. 1° The principal monetary clauses are the sliding scale clause and the gold clause. **2°** This type of clause is generally found in contracts of successive performance (e.g. a lease), or in contracts where extended periods of time are granted for performance (e.g. long term loans and term sales).
Fr. clause monétaire.

MONETARY OBLIGATION

Syn. pecuniary obligation. "Several particularities govern the regime of monetary obligations, notably in relation to indexation, forfeiture of term, foreign currency, and like causes, and in relation to the greater scope for judicial revision of contracts [...]" (Brierley & Macdonald (eds.), *Quebec Civil Law*, n° 525, p. 477).
Occ. Art. 1040c C.C.L.C.
Fr. obligation de somme d'argent, obligation monétaire, obligation pécuniaire⁺.

MONTHLY PAYMENT

Amount paid monthly.
See also annuity⁴, periodic payment.
Fr. mensualité.

MORAL *adj.*

See moral damage, moral damages, moral duty, moral imputability, moral obligation, moral public order, moral responsibility.
Fr. moral.

MORAL DAMAGE

Damage of an extrapatrimonial nature. For example, the psychological injury resulting from a violation of one's right to integrity. "In regard to moral damages, the Court states that any of the three methods for calculating such damages – conceptual, personal and functional approaches as described in the *St-Ferdinand* decision – may be used to obtain the objective of full compensation for the loss sustained" (Boodman, (1999) 10 *S.C.L.R.* (2nd) 45, p. 51).
Occ. Art. 2926 C.C.Q.

Obs. 1° Moral damage is one of the three types of injury recognized by the Civil Code, the others being material damage and bodily injury (art. 1607 C.C.Q.). **2°** While moral damage is difficult to assess in monetary terms, damages awarded as a result of this type of harm are, in principle, compensatory in keeping with the *restitutio in integrum* principle. **3°** Unlike the *Civil Code of Lower Canada*, the *Civil Code of Québec* gives a more visible and central place to the human being, and this is translated into many provisions. In this spirit, the regime of compensation for moral damage, as well as that for bodily injury, comprises special rules aimed at providing a greater protection to human beings (e.g. arts. 1474, 1609 C.C.Q.). **4°** A distinction is drawn between *moral damage* and *material damage*. **5°** Given that the words *damage* and *injury* are synonymous, one may also use the expression *moral injury*.
Syn. non-pecuniary damage. **See also** æsthetic damage, bodily injury, injury to feelings, loss[1], loss of amenities, material damage, *pretium doloris*, psychological damage, *restitutio in integrum*, *solatium doloris*.
Fr. préjudice moral[+], préjudice non pécuniaire.

MORAL DAMAGES

Damages granted as compensation for moral damage.
Obs. 1° Moral damages are purely compensatory. **2°** The assessment of the *quantum* of moral damages is difficult, and courts consequently have a wide discretion. **3°** The Supreme Court of Canada, in its trilogy of cases *Andrews* v. *Grand & Toy Alberta Ltd.*, [1978] 2 S.C.R. 229, *Arnold* v. *Teno*, [1978] 2 S.C.R. 287 and *Thornton* v. *Board of School Trustees of School District No. 57 (Prince George)*, [1978] 2 S.C.R. 267, held that a court may grant moral damages by way of a lump sum, without having to specify the amounts granted with respect to each claim. **4°** Moreover, in case of complete and permanent physical incapacity, the Supreme Court of Canada, in the same trilogy of cases, has imposed a limitation of liability of $100,000, which may be increased in exceptional circumstances, and which ought to be adjusted for inflation. **5°** However, the Supreme Court of Canada, notably in cases such as *Hill* v. *Church of Scientology of Toronto*, [1995] 2 S.C.R. 1130 and *Botiuk* v. *Toronto Free Press Publications Ltd.*, [1995] 3 S.C.R. 3, has thus far refused to apply this limitation of liability to defamation suits.

See also full reparation, moral damage, nominal damages, predetermined reparation, punitive damages.
Fr. dommages-intérêts moraux.

MORAL DUTY

Syn. moral obligation.
Fr. devoir de conscience, devoir moral, obligation imparfaite, obligation morale[+].

MORAL IMPUTABILITY

Syn. imputability[1]. "The traditional principle is combatted by the authors, who would substitute for the idea of moral imputability, the simple relationship of causality as the basis of responsibility" (Planiol & Ripert, *Treatise*, vol. 2, n° 878, p. 489).
Fr. imputabilité[1+], imputabilité morale, imputabilité psychologique.

MORAL OBLIGATION

Obligation[1] binding only as a matter of conscience or honour, and which, unlike a juridical obligation, cannot be enforced by the State. For example, the duty of charity toward one's neighbour. "Silence therefore ought to be reprehensible; moreover, an obligation ought to be imposed on a *professionnel* actively to inform a *profane* of facts concerning the object of the contract that might determine the latter's consent to enter into the agreement. It was appropriate, in other words, that the moral obligation of information should be made an actionable civil obligation" (Legrand, (1991) 19 *Can. Bus. L.J.* 318, p. 332).
Obs. In law, the performance of a moral obligation constitutes a liberality rather than a payment.
Syn. duty of conscience, imperfect obligation, moral duty. **See also** juridical obligation[1], moral responsibility, natural obligation.
Fr. devoir de conscience, devoir moral, obligation imparfaite, obligation morale[+].

MORAL PUBLIC ORDER

Public order the purpose of which is the respect of good morals.
Obs. Moral public order varies over time in a given society. Contracts once considered immoral are now valid, for example, life insurance contracts and loans upon interest.
See also economic public order, good morals, political public order.
Fr. ordre public moral.

MORAL RESPONSIBILITY

Responsability of a person who has to answer for his or her acts in his or her conscience.
Obs. Moral responsibility is contrasted with juridical responsibility.
See also civil liability, juridical liability, moral obligation, penal liability.
Fr. responsabilité morale.

MORATORY *adj.*

See moratory damages.
Fr. moratoire.

MORATORY DAMAGES

Damages granted as compensation for the harm resulting from a debtor's tardiness in performing an obligation. "Damages resulting from delay in the performance of obligations – that is, moratory as opposed to compensatory damages – may also be obtained from a debtor in certain cases [...]" (Brierley & Macdonald (eds.), *Quebec Civil Law*, n° 521, p. 474).
Obs. 1° If the obligation is to pay a sum of money, moratory damages consist of interest at the agreed rate or at the legal rate (art. 1617 C.C.Q.). **2°** Moratory damages are only due and assessed as of the date of default, unless otherwise provided by law (e.g. art. 1735 C.C.Q.). **3°** Although moratory damages are compensatory in nature in that they offer compensation for the harm resulting from tardiness in the performance of the obligation, scholars have drawn a distinction between *moratory damages* and *compensatory damages*. **4°** This doctrinal distinction serves a practical purpose, particularly where the issue is to remedy the debtor's tardiness in performing a pecuniary obligation. Article 1617 C.C.Q. provides that the creditor is entitled, in such a case, to damages without having to prove that he or she has sustained any injury. **5°** From the Latin *mora*: lateness.
See also additional damages, compensatory damages, contractual damages, extracontractual damages.
Fr. dommages-intérêts moratoires.

MORTIS CAUSA *adv.ph.* (Latin)

(*Succ.*) Syn. contemplation of death (in). *Gift mortis causa.*

Occ. Arts. 386, 613, 1818,1840 C.C.Q.
Obs. The Latin term means literally *by reason of death.*
Fr. cause de mort (à)+, *mortis causa.*

MOTIVE *n.*

Syn. cause[2]. "Subjective cause is the determining motive that prompted the particular individual in question to contract" (Brierley & Macdonald (eds.), *Quebec Civil Law*, n° 439, p. 409).
Fr. cause[2+], cause concrète, cause du contrat, cause impulsive et déterminante, cause subjective, considération[2], considération principale, mobile, motif.

MULTILATERAL *adj.*

See multilateral act.
Fr. multilatéral.

MULTILATERAL ACT

Juridical act entered into by more than two parties. For example, a sale by co-owners.
Syn. plurilateral act. **See also** bilateral act, collective act, contract[1], unilateral act.
Fr. acte multilatéral+, acte plurilatéral.

MUTUAL OBLIGATION

Syn. reciprocal obligation. "[...] if, after the termination of a lease, the lessee continues in possession, and the lessor remains inactive and silent, a complete mutual obligation for continuing the lease is created by the act of occupancy of the tenant on the one side, and inaction and silence of the lessor on the other" (Litvinoff, in *Treatise*, vol. 6, n° 133, p. 216).
Occ. Art. 2394 C.C.L.C.
Fr. obligation réciproque.

MUTUUM *n.* (Latin)

Syn. simple loan.
Occ. Title preceding art. 1777 C.C.L.C.; art. 1762 C.C.L.C.
Obs. Under the *Civil Code of Lower Canada*, loan for consumption and *mutuum* were synonyms. These terms have been replaced by *simple loan* in the Civil Code.
Fr. *mutuum*, prêt de consommation, simple prêt+.

N

NAPOLEONIC CODE

See *Code Napoléon*.
Fr. [*].

NATURAL INCAPACITY

Syn. *de facto* incapacity.
Fr. inaptitude, incapacité[2], incapacité de fait, incapacité naturelle[+].

NATURAL INDIVISIBILITY

Indivisibility resulting from the very character of the object of an obligation. For example, to deliver a thing certain and determinate, to warrant a buyer against eviction.
Syn. objective indivisibility, real indivisibility, true indivisibility. **See also** conventional indivisibility, indivisibility.
Fr. indivisibilité naturelle[+], indivisibilité objective, indivisibilité réelle, indivisibilité véritable.

NATURAL JUSTICE

See general principles of law, justice[1], natural law.
Fr. justice naturelle.

NATURAL LAW

Body of precepts of an ideal law[1]. "The doctrine of Natural Law is today enjoying a revival. The adherents of positivism have themselves abandoned the myth of legislation, such as it was entertained in the nineteenth century; they now recognize the creative role of the judge [...]" (David & Brierley, *Major Legal Systems*, p. 104).
Obs. 1° Although there are numerous conceptions of natural law, doctrine of natural law generally refers to law grounded in the nature of things or to law grounded in human nature. **2°** Positive law is often set up against an ideal law generally designated as *natural law*.
See also equity[1], positive law.
Fr. droit naturel.

NATURAL OBLIGATION

Juridical obligation that is only susceptible of voluntary performance. For example, an obligation of support between brothers and sisters. "No demand may be made for forced payment of a natural obligation; yet it has been decided that a natural obligation would be considered civil in cases where the debtor acknowledged his obligation and committed himself to execute it; then, the creditor would have the right to demand payment" (C.C.R.O., *Commentaries*, vol. II, t. 2, p. 649).
Occ. Arts. 1554, 2340 C.C.Q.
Obs. 1° While a civil obligation is susceptible of compulsory execution in the case of non-performance, a natural obligation is only susceptible of voluntary performance. **2°** A natural obligation is to be distinguished from a moral obligation in that the performance of a natural obligation constitutes payment rather than a liberality. **3°** The moral obligation, unlike the natural obligation, is not classified as juridical in nature.
See also civil obligation, moral obligation.
Fr. obligation naturelle.

NECESSARY DEPOSIT

Deposit[1] that the depositor is constrained to make as a result of an accident or superior force. "The necessary deposit is that in which the depositary has not been able to choose freely the person of the depositary, because he acts under the fear of a disaster suffered, fire, flood, pillage, etc., which forced him to confide the things deposited to the hands of the first comer and with the greatest haste" (Planiol & Ripert, *Treatise*, vol. 2, part. 2, n° 2216, p. 278).
Occ. Arts. 2295, 2297 C.C.Q.; arts. 1813, 1814 C.C.L.C.
Obs. 1° The depositary is responsible for the loss of the property in the same manner as a depositary by gratuitous title (art. 2296 C.C.Q.). **2°** A deposit made in a health or social services establishment is presumed to be a necessary deposit (art. 2297 C.C.Q.).
See also simple deposit.
Fr. dépôt nécessaire.

NEGATIVE *adj.*

See negative condition.
Fr. négatif.

NEGATIVE CONDITION

Condition[1] that is fulfilled by the non-occurrence of a contemplated event. For example, if a person is not named to a particular position.
Obs. See article 1502 C.C.Q.
See also positive condition.
Fr. condition négative.

NEGLECT *n.*

Syn. negligence. "It is a familiar principle that neglect may, in law, be considered a fault only if it corresponds with a duty to act" (*Canadian National Railways Co.* v. *Lepage*, [1927] S.C.R. 575, p. 578, T. Rinfret, J.).
Occ. Art. 2075 C.C.Q.; arts. 268, 468, 1053, 1513 C.C.L.C.
Fr. faute de négligence, négligence+.

NEGLIGENCE *n.*

Non-intentional fault consisting in the failure to act with the care required of a reasonable person in order to avoid the occurrence of a foreseeable damage in given circumstances. "The crux of the matter is that, in a given case, nobody can be found negligent for having failed to foresee absolutely every possible kind of happening. The law does not require more of any man than that he should have acted in a reasonable way" (*T. Eaton Co.* v. *Moore*, [1951] S.C.R. 470, p. 475, T. Rinfret, C. J.).
Occ. Arts. 1045, 1710, 2111 C.C.L.C.
Obs. 1° Negligence and imprudence are both species of non-intentional fault that entail the same legal consequences. As such, they are often employed interchangeably. A distinction may, however, be drawn between the two notions. Negligence consists in the absence of diligence, whereas imprudence consists in the absence of prudence. It is often said of the latter that, unlike negligence, it presupposes a missed initiative. **2°** The measure of care demanded of a reasonable person used to determine whether negligence has or has not occurred requires among other things that one pay due attention to a situation, identify the precautions normally required therein and act promptly in view of avoiding the occurrence of a foreseeable injury. **3°** Unlike article 1053 C.C.L.C., article 1457 C.C.Q.

does not expressly mention negligence or neglect as an illustration of fault.
Syn. fault of negligence, neglect. **See also** civil fault, gross negligence, imprudence, non-intentional fault, obligation of diligence, obligation of means, quasi-delict, quasi delictual fault, reasonable person.
Fr. faute de négligence, négligence+.

NEGOTIATED CONTRACT

Syn. contract by negotiation.
Fr. contrat de gré à gré+, contrat de libre discussion, contrat négocié.

NEGOTIATION *n.*

Exchange between parties, written or oral, carried on with a view to contracting. *To enter negotiations.*
Obs. 1° The term is often used in the plural. **2°** The term is also used to describe exchanges between parties designed to resolve a dispute.
See also contract by negotiation, precontractual period.
Fr. pourparlers.

NEGOTIORUM GESTIO nom.ph. (Latin)

Syn. management of the business of another. "There is in *negotiorum gestio* necessarily a concept of representation for the *gestor* must have intended to manage the affairs of the proprietor" (Challies, *Unjustified Enrichment*, p. 33).
Occ. Title preceding art. 1043 C.C.L.C.
Obs. The Civil Code uses the expression *management of the business of another* (arts. 1482 to 1490 C.C.Q.), whereas the *Civil Code of Lower Canada* employed *management of the affairs of another* and *negotiorum gestio* (arts. 1043 to 1046 C.C.L.C.).
Fr. gestion d'affaire(s)+, *negotiorum gestio*.

NEGOTIORUM GESTOR nom.ph. (Latin)

Syn. manager. "[...] if the *negotiorum gestor* may recover interest on the money he advances to the owner's benefit without a putting of the owner in default, this is so not because of any particular technicality of the quasi-contract of managing the affairs of another, but because of the analogical application of a rule borrowed from a particular contract" (Litvinoff, in *Treatise*, vol. 7, Book 2, n° 254, pp. 481-482).
Fr. gérant[1]+, *negotiorum gestor*.

NEGOTIUM n. (Latin)

Syn. juridical act.
Obs. Within different juridical acts, the same term *juridical act* may denote both the juridical act considered abstractly (*negotium*) and the physical document recording it (*instrumentum*) (e.g. a deed or gift).
Fr. acte[1], acte juridique[+], *negotium*, titre[2].

NEIGHBOURHOOD DISTURBANCE

Annoyance that exceeds the limits of tolerance that neighbours owe one another. For example, the emission of pollution or of nauseating odours.
Obs. 1° Article 976 C.C.Q. provides that "[n]eighbours shall suffer the normal neighbourhood annoyances that are not beyond the limit of tolerance they owe each other, according to the nature or location of their land or local custom". **2**° The notion of *neighbourhood* is not limited to owners of contiguous property. **3**° In matters of neighbourhood disturbances, the regime of civil liability is not based on the violation of an obligation of means. **4**° Some legal scholars consider neighbourhood disturbances as a form of abuse of rights.
See also abuse of right(s).
Fr. trouble de voisinage.

NO-FAULT LIABILITY

Syn. strict liability. "Although fault-based liability remains the general rule, no-fault liability for damage caused by certain dangerous activities or circumstances is well-known" (Brunnée, in *Mélanges Crépeau*, 155, p. 192).
Obs. No-fault liability should not be confused with state-sponsored regimes that recognize a right to compensation not founded on individual liability, as is the case for the compensation of bodily injury under the *Automobile Insurance Act* (R.S.Q. c. A-25).
Fr. responsabilité absolue, responsabilité causale, responsabilité de plein droit, responsabilité objective[+], responsabilité sans faute, responsabilité stricte.

NO LIABILITY CLAUSE

1. **Syn.** exoneration clause[1].
Fr. clause de non-responsabilité[1], clause d'exonération de responsabilité[1+].

2. **Syn.** exclusion (of liability) clause.
Fr. clause de non-responsabilité[2], clause d'exclusion de responsabilité[+], clause d'exonération de responsabilité[2], clause exonératoire de responsabilité, clause exonératrice de responsabilité.

NOMINAL DAMAGES

Damages having a symbolic character awarded as compensation for harm that is considered to be insignificant.
Obs. 1° While having an inherently symbolic character, nominal damages are nevertheless awarded only in cases where the creditor has in fact suffered a loss that may be compensated, i.e. one that is direct, certain and real. **2**° The expression *token damages* is also encountered.
Syn. symbolic damages. **See also** moral damage, moral damages.
Fr. dommages-intérêts nominaux.

NOMINATE *adj.*

See nominate contract.
Fr. nommé.

NOMINATE CONTRACT

Contract that has been specifically regulated under a particular designation by the legislature. For example, mandate, sale. "The general principles of contract and the particular rules relating to a variety of nominate contracts naturally form an important part of [the *Civil Code of Lower Canada*]" (Brierley, (1987-88) 13 *Can. Bus. L.J.* 58, p. 59).
Obs. 1° In principle, the rules applicable to nominate contracts are suppletive of the general regime of contract. **2**° The expression *nominate contract* is sometimes translated in French as *contrats spéciaux* when the whole category of nominate contracts is described. **3**° A distinction is drawn between *nominate contracts* and *innominate contracts*.
Syn. special contract. **See also** innominate contract.
Fr. contrat nommé.

NOMINEE *n.*

Syn. undisclosed mandatary.
Obs. This term of Common law origin is encountered on occasion in Quebec law (see, e.g. *Victuni* v. *Minister of Revenue of the Province of Quebec*, [1980] 1 S.C.R. 580, p. 584), but the preferred terms in the Civil law are *undisclosed mandatary* or *prête-nom*.
Fr. prête-nom[1].

NON ADIMPLETI CONTRACTUS
nom.ph. (Latin)

See exception of non-performance.
Fr. *non adimpleti contractus*.

NON-ASSIGNABILITY *n.*

Attribute of a right not susceptible of assignment[1].
Obs. 1° The terms *non-assignability* and *inalienability* are not synonyms. While *inalienability* prevents, in principle, both the *inter vivos* and the *mortis causa* transfers of property, *non-assignability* prevents only the *inter vivos* transfer. Moreover, the use of the term *non-assignability* is generally associated with incorporeal property. **2°** Article 3 C.C.Q. has presented the French term *incessible* as an equivalent for the English term *inalienable*.
Syn. unassignability. **See also** assignability, inalienability, intransmissibility, undisposability.
Fr. incessibilité.

NON-ASSIGNABLE *adj.*

Not susceptible of assignment[1].
Syn. unassignable. **See also** assignable, inalienable, intransmissible, non-assignability, undisposable.
Fr. incessible.

NON-COMPETITION CLAUSE

Clause by which a party agrees to abstain from pursuing an activity similar to that engaged in by the other party. "It is quite common for employers to insist on the insertion of non-competition clauses or restrictive clauses in employment contracts in an environment characterized by the development of specialized industry, more advanced technology, more competitive markets and a greater investment in employee training" (Bonhomme, Gascon & Lepage, *Employment Contract*, p. 80).
Obs. 1° For example, non-competition clauses are found in contracts for the sale of a business and in contracts of employment. **2°** Clauses stipulating an obligation of non-competition must protect only the legitimate interests of the creditor. Such clauses must therefore be circumscribed as to time, place and activities at which they are directed. This limitation is expressly stated at article 2089 C.C.Q. regarding the contract of employment. **3°** Sometimes used as equivalents for the expression *non-competition clause*, the expressions *restrictive covenant* and *covenant in restraint of trade* belong to Common law[2] terminology.
Syn. clause not to compete. **See also** exclusivity clause, obligation of non-competition, restrictive covenant.
Fr. clause de non-concurrence.

NON-CONSENSUAL OBLIGATION

Rare Syn. extracontractual obligation.
Fr. obligation extracontractuelle.

NON-EXCLUSIVE *adj.*

See non-exclusive offer.
Fr. non exclusif.

NON-EXCLUSIVE OFFER

Offer that may be accepted by any person to whom it is addressed.
Obs. A non-exclusive offer may be made to a determinate person or to the public generally.
See also exclusive offer.
Fr. offre non exclusive.

NON-EXISTENCE *n.*

State of a juridical act that lacks an element so essential to its formation that it cannot be considered to have been formed.
Obs. 1° The notion of *non-existence* is sometimes contrasted with *absolute nullity*. Some scholars consider that certain juridical acts need not be annulled, since they never existed. Others, basing their opinion in part on articles 1416 and 1422 C.C.Q., are of the view that the appearance of validity precludes a juridical act from being considered non-existent. **2°** The notion of *non-existence* was developed principally in relation to the validity of marriage in order to circumvent the rigidity of the rule that there can be no nullity unless expressly provided by law ("pas de nullité sans texte").
Syn. inexistence. **See also** annulability, inopposability, invalidity, nullity.
Fr. inexistence.

NON-FULFILMENT *n.*

Syn. non-performance.
Fr. défaut d'exécution, inexécution+.

NON-INTENTIONAL *adj.*

See non-intentional fault.
Fr. non intentionnel.

NON-INTENTIONAL FAULT

Civil fault committed without having contemplated the consequences of one's act or omission.
Obs. In principle, a finding of civil liability does not depend on the intention of the wrongdoer. Nonetheless, the expression *non-intentional fault* is used in order to draw a dis-

tinction with *intentional fault* which, in some cases, has special legal consequences.
Syn. involuntary fault. **See also** contractual fault, extracontractual fault, imprudence, intention, intentional fault, negligence, quasidelict, quasi-delictual fault.
Fr. faute involontaire, faute non intentionnelle[+].

NON-MARINE INSURANCE

Contract of insurance whose object is to guarantee the insured from the risks that are not incident to marine adventure.
Occ. Arts. 2389, 2391, 2400, 2414 C.C.Q.; arts. 2469, 2471, 2492 C.C.L.C.
Obs. 1° Non-marine insurance is divided into insurance of persons and damage insurance (arts. 2391, 2415 to 2504 C.C.Q.). **2°** In non-marine insurance, applications are generally made on the basis of standard forms prepared by the insurers; the policy, also prepared by the insurer, completes the application. **3°** In case of discrepancy between the policy and the application, the latter prevails as the substance of the contract "unless the insurer has, in a separate document, indicated the particulars in respect of which there is discrepancy to the client" (art. 2400 C.C.Q.). **4°** This category corresponds to the French *assurance terrestre*; in English, the opposition with marine insurance undoubtedly illustrates the influence of maritime law, and in particular English law, on the field of insurance law generally.
See also damage insurance, insurance contract, insurance of persons, marine insurance.
Fr. assurance terrestre.

NON-PECUNIARY DAMAGE

Syn. moral damage. "Plaintiff's claim includes his out of pocket expenditure and losses incurred and to be incurred, an indemnity for his permanent disability and non-pecuniary damages such as pain, suffering, inconvenience and loss of enjoyment of life with which he is afflicted" (*Normandin* v. *Crevier*, [1986] 3 R.J.Q. 2495 (Sup. Ct.), p. 2508, C.A. Phelan, J.).
Obs. Given that the words *damage* and *injury* are synonymous, one may also use the expression *non-pecuniary injury*.
Fr. préjudice moral[+], préjudice non pécuniaire.

NON-PERFORMANCE *n.*

Fact of not performing an obligation. "French law starts from the proposition that compen-

sation should be given for all loss (*dommage*, *préjudice*) resulting from non-performance, but limits this proposition in all cases by the requirement that the loss should be the 'immediate and direct consequence of the non-performance' [...]" (Nicholas, *Contract*, p. 225). *The non-performance of a contract; non-performance of a mandate.*
Occ. Arts. 1079, 1475, 1918, 3127 C.C.Q.; arts. 1128 C.C.L.C.
Obs. 1° An obligation must be performed in full, properly and without delay (art. 1590 C.C.Q.). Non-performance may therefore be complete or partial. The improper performance of an obligation is equivalent to an absence of performance. **2°** Non-performance gives rise to forced specific performance or performance by equivalence. In the case of contractual obligations, non-performance may also give rise to resolution or resiliation of the contract, or reduction of the creditor's obligation (art. 1590 C.C.Q.). **3°** The written form *nonperformance* is also encountered (art. 1613 C.C.Q.).
Syn. default in performance, inexecution, non-fulfilment. **See also** comminatory clause, exception of non-performance, exclusion (of liability) clause, exoneration clause, limitation of liability clause, notice of exoneration of liability, penal clause[1], performance.
Fr. défaut d'exécution, inexécution[+].

NON-PERFORMANCE OF THE CONTRACT

See non-performance.
Fr. inexécution du contrat.

NOTARIAL ACT

Authentic act received by a notary.
Occ. Art. 1575 C.C.Q.; ss. 17, 22, 34, 50, 52, 53, *Notaries Act*, R.S.Q. c. N-3.
Obs. The notion of *notarial act* is closely associated with the codal regime related to evidence (see arts. 2803 *et seq.* C.C.Q.).
Syn. notarial deed, notarial instrument. **See also** authentic act, notarial act *en brevet*, notarial act *en minute*, private writing, semi-authentic act.
Fr. acte notarié.

NOTARIAL ACT *EN BREVET* (French)

Act received by a notary in one or several originals that he or she may deliver to the parties.
Obs. The notion of *notarial act* en brevet is closely associated with the codal regime related to evidence (see arts. 2803 *et seq.* C.C.Q.).

Syn. act *en brevet*. **See also** authentic act, notarial act *en minute*, private writing.
Fr. acte en brevet, acte notarié en brevet[+].

NOTARIAL ACT *EN MINUTE* (French)

Act received by a notary that must be deposited and conserved in his or her records to enable the delivery of authentic copies and extracts.
Occ. Arts. 423, 440, 469, 646, 1059, 1285, 1327, 1575, 1655, 1824, 2166, 2176, 2693, 2998, 3044 C.C.Q.; s. 56, *Notaries Act*, R.S.Q. c. N-3.
Obs. The notion of *notarial act* en minute is closely associated with the codal regime related to evidence (see arts. 2803 *et seq.* C.C.Q.).
Syn. act *en minute, minute*. **See also** authentic act, notarial act *en brevet*.
Fr. acte en minute, acte notarié en minute[+], minute.

NOTARIAL DEED

Syn. notarial act. "A notarial deed is a report by the notary, as set forth in it, of what he did and of what occurred in his presence" (Marler, *Real Property*, n⁰ 414, p. 181).
Occ. Arts. 660, 1209, 1979*b* C.C.L.C.
Fr. acte notarié.

NOTARIAL INSTRUMENT

Syn. notarial act. "As regards the probative value of a notarial instrument, a distinction must be made between the assertions of the notary regarding facts and formalities he had a duty to note and the assertions of the parties. As regards the first kind of assertions, no one can prove them to be false except by way of improbation" (Ducharme, in *Essays on the Civil Codes*, 75, p. 78).
Occ. Arts. 1208, 1215, 1217 C.C.L.C.
Fr. acte notarié.

NOTICE *n.*

Action of bringing a juridical act or a juridical fact to the attention of someone who may have an interest therein. "Even though we tried, at the start of this class action, to assure that as many potential members as possible be reached by the newspaper notices, when we required publication in the Concordia and McGill campus newspapers in addition to *The Gazette* and *La Presse*, we recognize that the fiction of newspaper notices coming to the attention of most or of even a substantial number of the potential members is only that,

a fiction" (*Comartin* v. *Bordet*, [1984] C.S. 584, p. 601, B.J. Greenberg, J.). *To give notice; to receive notice.*
Occ. Arts. 40, 359, 936, 1475 C.C.Q.; arts. 442*i*, 1040*a* C.C.L.C.; arts. 112, 496.1, 944 C.C.P.
Fr. notification.

NOTICE OF DEFAULT

Writing that records a putting in default. "On October 31, 1961, appellant's attorney wrote a formal notice of default to respondent alleging that Laurentian was not identifying itself properly, that it was passing itself off as the third party and was in breach of the agreement of December 19, 1960. This letter enjoined respondent to cease its contraventions and suggested that he communicate with the writer of the letter (*Cochrane* v. *Trudeau*, [1977] 2 S.C.R. 55, p. 62, J. Beetz, J.).
Occ. S. 136(c)(2), *An Act respecting the Barreau du Québec*, R.S.Q. c. B-1.
Obs. The extrajudicial demand by which a creditor puts his debtor in default must be made in writing (art. 1595 C.C.Q.).
Syn. demand letter, formal notice, *mise en demeure*. **See also** default, putting in default.
Fr. mise en demeure[2].

NOTICE OF EXONERATION OF LIABILITY

Notice by which the debtor excludes or limits, in advance, his or her liability resulting from the non-performance of an obligation.
Obs. The person against whom it is involved must be apprised of the notice at the time of formation of contract for it to be effective (art. 1475 C.C.Q.).
See also exclusion (of liability) clause, exoneration clause[1], limitation of liability clause, non-performance.
Fr. avis d'exonération de responsabilité.

NOTIFY *v.*

(*Jud. Law*) To effect notification; to give notice.
Occ. Arts. 203, 441, 1065, 1602 C.C.Q.; arts. 428, 1652.10, 2572 C.C.L.C.
Fr. notifier.

NOVATE *v.*

To effect novation. "For Quebec the rule may be laid down that the intention to novate must be expressly declared or must be evident from the act evidencing the transaction or from surrounding circumstances" (Nicholls, (1938) 16 *Can. Bar Rev.* 602, p. 615).
Fr. nover.

NOVATION *n.*

Contract whose purpose is to extinguish an obligation and to create a new obligation in its place. "The conditions required for novation are more or less implicit in the definition of novation already given. They are four: the intention to novate, a valid obligation to be extinguished and a valid new obligation that is to be substituted for it, a sufficient difference between these two obligations, and, finally, the capacity of the parties" (Nicholls, (1938) 16 *Can. Bar Rev.* 602, p. 612).
Occ. Title preceding art. 1660 C.C.Q.; arts. 1660, 1661, 1663 to 1666 C.C.Q.; art. 1169 C.C.L.C.; s. 93.12, *An Act respecting insurance*, R.S.Q. c. A-32; s. 5, *Cooperatives Act*, R.S.Q. c. C-67.2.
Obs. 1° Novation is effected by a change of creditor, of debtor or of debt (art. 1660 C.C.Q.). Some scholars characterize as *subjective novation* that which is effected by a change of creditor or debtor, and as *objective novation* that which is effected by a change of debt. **2°** The codal regime respecting novation is set forth at articles 1660 to 1666 C.C.Q. **3°** From the Latin *novatio*, from *novare*: to make new.
See also novation by change of creditor, novation by change of debt, novation by change of debtor, perfect delegation, release of obligation, subrogation.
Fr. novation.

NOVATION BY CHANGE OF CREDITOR

Novation by which a debtor is released with regard to the former creditor by becoming bound towards a new one.
See also assignment of claim(s), novation by change of debt, novation by change of debtor.
Fr. novation par changement de créancier.

NOVATION BY CHANGE OF DEBT

Novation by which the obligation of the debtor towards the creditor is replaced by another obligation, different in its object, cause or modalities.
See also consolidation of debts, giving in payment, novation by change of creditor, novation by change of debtor.
Fr. novation par changement de dette.

NOVATION BY CHANGE OF DEBTOR

Novation by which a creditor accepts a new debtor in place of the former debtor, whom he or she agrees to release. "For novation by change of debtors it is sufficient if the new debtor and the creditor intend to novate the debt, since in the terms of article 1172 [C.C.L.C.] the concurrence of the old debtor is not then required" (Nicholls, (1938) 16 *Can. Bar Rev.* 602, p. 614).
Obs. Perfect delegation effects novation by change of debtor.
See also novation by change of creditor, novation by change of debt, perfect delegation, release of obligation.
Fr. novation par changement de débiteur.

NOVATIVE *adj.*

Syn. novatory.
Fr. novatoire.

NOVATORY *adj.*

Pertaining to novation. *Novatory effect*; *novatory stipulation.*
Syn. novative. **See also** novatory intention.
Fr. novatoire.

NOVATORY INTENTION

Syn. *animus novandi.*
Fr. *animus novandi*, intention novatoire[+].

NOVUS ACTUS INTERVENIENS (Latin)

Fact that breaks the causal connection between another fact, which occurred earlier in the sequence of events, and the damage. "Even if the danger might result from the covers being lifted or falling off during the operation of the conveyer, indicating a defect in design, that is not what occurred here. The faults committed by the appellant and his father are a "new event", a *novus actus interveniens*, and were the cause of the damage as a whole suffered by the appellant" (*Dallaire* v. *Paul-Émile Martel Inc.*, [1989] 2 S.C.R. 419, p. 427, C.D. Gonthier, J.).
Obs. 1° *Novus actus interveniens* may constitute the *causa causans* (determining cause) of the damage. **2°** The fault of the victim or of a third person that occurred later in the chain of causation is not necessarily considered a *novus actus interveniens*, since there might be a plurality of causal faults.
See also adequate causation, determining cause.
Fr. *novus actus interveniens.*

NUISANCE *n.*

See abuse of right(s), neighbourhood disturbance.
Fr. nuisance.

NULL *adj.*

Tainted with nullity. *Marriage declared null; title which is null.*
Occ. Arts. 386, 1413, 1438 C.C.Q.
Obs. The term *void* is also used, although scholars see it as a Common law term.
See also invalid.
Fr. nul.

NULLITY *n.*

Retroactive termination of a juridical act that lacks a requirement necessary to its formation. For example, a gift of an immovable not in notarial form; a contract entered into as a result of fear. "Error [...] is a cause of nullity of contract, whether common to all the contracting parties or personal to one of them only, and can be proved by verbal testimony; arts. 991, 992, 1000 C.C.[L.C.]" (*R.* v. *Ogilvie* (1899), 29 S.C.R. 299, p. 324, D. Girouard, J.). *Cause of nullity; on pain of nullity; to import nullity; to entail nullity.*
Occ. Arts. 1417, 1419, 1421, 1824 C.C.Q.
Obs. 1° Juridical acts that do not respect a substantive condition (e.g. arts. 365, 707 to 711, 1385 C.C.Q.) or a condition of form (e.g. arts. 368, 713, 1385 C.C.Q.) may be annulled. **2°** A distinction is drawn between absolute nullity and relative nullity. The former sanctions acts that are contrary to the general interest, whereas the latter seeks to protect individual interests (arts. 1417 and 1419 C.C.Q.). **3°** Unless the nature of the nullity is clearly indicated in the law, the juridical act that does not meet the requirements for its formation is presumed to be relatively null (art. 1421 C.C.Q.). **4°** A declaration of nullity with respect to a juridical act has a retroactive effect and entails, in principle, the restitution of the benefits received, since the act is deemed to have never existed (arts. 1422, 1699 to 1707 C.C.Q.). **5°** Even if one of the obligations contained in a juridical act is declared null, the act nevertheless remains valid as long as it is not considered to be an indivisible whole (art. 1438 C.C.Q.).
See also absolute nullity, annulability, annulment, inopposability, invalidity, lapse, non-existence, relative nullity, rescission, resiliation[1,2], resolution[1,2], restitution, tacit nullity, textual nullity.
Fr. nullité.

NULLITY *AB INITIO*

See absolute nullity.
Fr. nullité *ab initio.*

NULLITY *PLENO JURE*

See absolute nullity.
Fr. nullité de plein droit.

O

OBJECTIVE *adj.*

See objective fault, objective indivisibility, objective liability.
Fr. objectif.

OBJECTIVE CAUSE

Syn. cause[1]. "In synallagmatic, onerous contracts, the objective cause is the correlative and reciprocal obligation of the co-contractant" (Brierley & Macdonald (eds.), *Quebec Civil Law*, n° 439, p. 410).
Fr. cause[1+], cause abstraite, cause de l'obligation, cause finale, cause objective, considération[1].

OBJECTIVE FAULT

Civil fault that a reasonable person would not have committed in similar circumstances. "French civilians have argued for an 'objective' fault in conjunction with various efforts to distance civil liability from the tar brush of blame better associated, it is said, with the kind of behaviour that results in prison terms than in damage awards" (Kasirer, (1992) 40 *Am. J. Comp. L.* 343, p. 365).
See also subjective fault.
Fr. faute objective.

OBJECTIVE INDIVISIBILITY

Syn. natural indivisibility.
Fr. indivisibilité naturelle[+], indivisibilité objective, indivisibilité réelle, indivisibilité véritable.

OBJECTIVE LESION

Lesion that consists in a significant discrepancy between contractual prestations. "The history of lesion goes back to Roman law where, in the classical period, the notion of *objective lesion* with a serious disproportion between the prestations of contracting parties (*læsio enormis*) prevailed" (Haanappel, (1982) 60 *Can. Bar Rev.* 393, p. 407).
Obs. 1° The definition of lesion at article 1406 C.C.Q. does not correspond to the notion of *objective lesion*. It appears, however, that article 1793 C.C.Q. refers to the latter concept, even though the terms *damage* and *prejudice* are used. **2**° Objective lesion reflects the notion of *lesion* as it is traditionally understood in Roman law, *Ancien droit* and French law. Except in the case of minors and persons of full age under protective supervision, this was also the conception of lesion in the *Civil Code of Lower Canada* (art. 1012 C.C.L.C.).
See also damage, mixed lesion, prejudice, subjective lesion.
Fr. lésion objective.

OBJECTIVE LIABILITY

Syn. strict liability. "From Josserand's perspective, damage caused by *any* thing, moveable or immoveable, dangerous or not, defective or not, could give rise to objective liability of the custodian" (Jutras, in *Tort Law*, 317, p. 325).
Fr. responsabilité absolue, responsabilité causale, responsabilité de plein droit, responsabilité objective[+], responsabilité sans faute, responsabilité stricte.

OBJECT NOT IN COMMERCE

Thing that cannot be the object of a juridical act of a patrimonial nature.
Obs. 1° In principle, objects not in commerce are imprescriptible, unseizable and inalienable. They may also be incorporeal. Thus, certain rights are not in commerce, such as the right to an alimentary pension or the right to a servitude, from the view point of their non-assignability or imprescriptibility. **2**° Objects not in commerce are usually classified in two categories: objects not in commerce by reason of their nature or by reason of appropriation (art. 2876 C.C.Q.). The former are not in commerce *per se*, such as the human body. This category also includes *res communes* or things in common. The latter are not in commerce for the duration of their appropriation. They include religious objects, as well as state property, such as public land, parks, ports and roads. **3**° Because they may be appropriated, things without an owner or *res nullius* are not considered objects not in

commerce. Likewise, objects with a restricted but not prohibited circulation, such as cultural property, objects affected by a stipulation of inalienability (arts. 1212 *et seq.* C.C.Q.) or movable property serving for household use (art. 401 C.C.Q.), are not considered objects not in commerce. **4°** Some dangerous objects may be excluded from commerce by legislative intervention (e.g. drugs, firearms). **5°** In principle, the sale of an object not in commerce is absolutely null.
See also object of commerce.
Fr. chose hors (du) commerce.

OBJECT OF COMMERCE

Thing that can be the object of a juridical act of a patrimonial nature.
Occ. Art. 1059 C.C.L.C.
See also object not in commerce.
Fr. chose dans le commerce.

OBJECT OF THE CONTRACT

Juridical operation envisaged by the parties at the time of the formation of the contract. For example, the sale of a car, the lease of an immovable, the loan of a tool. "The *Cour de cassation* noted that the preliminary surveys conducted by the concessionaire and handed to the building contractor before the formation of the contract had been erroneous. As a result, the contractor's consent had been vitiated with respect to the substance of the thing that formed the object of the contract" (Legrand, (1988) 62 *Tul. L. Rev.* 963, p. 974).
Occ. Arts. 1385, 1412, 1413 C.C.Q.
Obs. 1° The object is one of the four conditions of formation of contracts. The other conditions are: capacity, consent and cause (art. 1385 C.C.Q.). **2°** A contract that has an illicit object is null (art. 1413 C.C.Q.). **3°** The object of a contract is confused with the object of an obligation in the *Civil Code of Lower Canada.* Thus, while art. 982 C.C.L.C. referred to the object of an obligation, art. 984 C.C.L.C. referred to the object of a contract. Also, the paragraph following art. 990 C.C.L.C., entitled *Of the object of contracts,* referred the reader to chapter V, *Of the object of obligations.* **4°** The usefulness of the notions of *object of the contract* and *cause of the contract* has been called into question by certain scholars. They argue that the notion of *public order* is sufficient to cover the two others.
See also illicit object[1], object of the prestation, prestation.
Fr. objet du contrat.

OBJECT OF THE OBLIGATION

Syn. prestation. "Other legal consequences of non-performance of obligations of a different nature are established in article 397 [of the Civil Code of the Russian Federation]. If a debtor fails to perform its obligation to produce and transfer the object of the obligation to the creditor, or to perform defined work or render a service, the creditor shall have the right, within a reasonable time, to entrust the performance of the obligation to a third party for a reasonable price or to perform it by its own efforts" (Komarov, (1999) 44 *McGill L.J.* 357, p. 371).
Occ. Art. 1373 C.C.Q.
Fr. chose[2], objet de l'obligation, prestation[+].

OBJECT OF THE PRESTATION

That upon which a prestation bears.
Obs. 1° Rights, of whatever nature, can be objects of a prestation. **2°** According to art. 1374 C.C.Q., the object of a prestation may relate to any property, provided that it is determinate as to kind and determinable as to quantity.
See also determinable object, determinate object, object of the contract, object of the obligation.
Fr. objet de la prestation.

OBLIGATE *v.*

Syn. bind.
Occ. Arts. 1380, 1708, 1802, 2797 C.C.Q.; art. 909 C.C.L.C.
Obs. Generally used in passive form (e.g. Paul is obligated to pay on Tuesday).
Fr. engager, obliger[+].

OBLIGATION *n.*

1. Syn. duty. "[...] in its more general acceptation, the word 'obligation' means something that the law or morals command a person to do, a command that is made effective by the imposition of a sanction if the person fails to obey or comply. When given that reference, the word 'obligation' is made synonymous with the word 'duty'" (Litvinoff, in *Treatise,* vol. 5, n° 1.1, pp. 1-2). *Civil obligation; family obligation; juridical obligation; moral obligation.*
Occ. Arts. 68, 392, 522 C.C.Q.; s. 41, *Interpretation Act,* R.S.Q. c. I-16; s. 20, *Public Curator Act,* R.S.Q. c. C-81.
Obs. From the Latin *obligatio,* from *ob,* around and *ligare,* to be bound.
Fr. devoir[+], obligation[1].

2. Juridical relationship between two persons by virtue of which one of them, the *debtor*, is bound towards another, the *creditor*, to perform a prestation. "The Romanist definition [...] which understands obligations as generating a juridical link between persons that requires one of them, under compulsion of law, to act to the benefit of another, captures what for many scholars is the central feature of the law of civil obligations: legal recognition and enforcement" (Brierley & Macdonald (eds.), *Quebec Civil Law*, n° 402, pp. 378-379).

Occ. Arts. 1371, 1372, 1373 C.C.Q.

Obs. 1° An obligation may be susceptible of compulsory execution (civil obligations) or only be susceptible of voluntary performance (natural obligations). **2°** In principle, an obligation is temporary, transmissible and transferable. **3°** Drawing on the writings of Pothier, article 983 of the *Civil Code of Lower Canada* acknowledged five sources of obligations: the contract, the quasi-contract, the delict, the quasi-delict and the sole operation of law. That classification was not explicitly retained in the *Civil Code of Québec* (art. 1372 C.C.Q.). **4°** From the point of view of the creditor, the obligation is designated as a *creance* or a *claim*; from the point of view of the debtor, it is designated as a *debt*.

Syn. juridical obligation[1], perfect obligation, personal obligation. **See also** civil obligation, contract[1], delict, moral obligation, natural obligation.

Fr. obligation[2+], obligation juridique[1], obligation parfaite, obligation personnelle.

3. Obligation[2] from the point of view of the debtor. "Whether this obligation be one imposed by a law or by a contract, [...] the result, generally speaking, is the same, in the sense that the person in fault is obliged to indemnify the person aggrieved to the extent of the injury suffered" (*Ross* v. *Dunstall* (1921), 62 S.C.R. 393, p. 415, P.B. Mignault, J.). *Failure to fulfil an obligation*; *to meet one's obligation*; *to satisfy an obligation*.

Occ. Arts. 697, 1206, 1362 C.C.Q.; art. 1064 C.C.L.C.; s. 155, *Automobile Insurance Act*, R.S.Q. c. A-25; s. 11a), *Consumer Protection Act*, R.S.Q. c. P-40.1.

Syn. charge, debt[1], juridical duty, juridical obligation[2], legal duty, liability[2]. **See also** personal right.

Fr. charge, dette, devoir juridique, engagement[2], obligation[3+], obligation juridique[2].

4. Syn. personal right.

Fr. créance, dette active, droit de créance, droit personnel[+], *jus in personam*, obligation[4].

OBLIGATIONAL *adj.*

Relating to obligations, especially with reference to obligations expressly or implicitly assumed by contract. *The obligational content of a contract.*

Obs. The distinction between the terms *obligational* and *real*, especially with respect to the effects of contracts, highlights the distinction between those effects that are understood to emanate from the law of obligations and those that emanate from the law of property.

See also obligatory, real[1].

Fr. obligationnel.

OBLIGATION FOR THE DEBT

Obligation[3] owed by a co-debtor to a creditor.

Obs. 1° Obligation for the debt refers to the relationship between a creditor and co-debtors; it determines the portion of the debt that the creditor may claim from each of the debtors. Contribution to the debt refers to the relationship between co-debtors; it determines the allocation of the debt between them. **2°** These two notions are encountered in matters of solidarity and indivisibility, and with respect to usufruct (arts. 1156, 1157 C.C.Q.) and successions (art. 826 C.C.Q.).

See also contribution to the debt, indivisibility, solidarity.

Fr. obligation à la dette.

OBLIGATION IN KIND

Obligation to do or not to do, to the exclusion of the payment of a sum of money.

Obs. 1° A distinction is drawn between the obligation in kind and the pecuniary obligation, the latter bearing on the payment of a sum of money. **2°** In principle, specific performance of an obligation may not be demanded when it would have the result of physically constraining the debtor, because this is understood to be an inappropriate violation of his or her freedom (art. 1601 C.C.Q.). **3°** Superior force may be invoked to justify the non-performance of an obligation in kind, except where the debtor has guaranteed the performance of the obligation.

See also obligation not to do, obligation to do, pecuniary obligation, performance by equivalence, specific performance.

Fr. obligation en nature.

OBLIGATION *IN SOLIDUM* (Latin)

Obligation of several debtors, each of whom is liable to the creditor for the entire obligation despite the absence of solidarity and indivisibility.

Obs. 1° Examples of situations in which the obligation *in solidum* applies, subject to certain conditions, include the liability of employers for acts and omissions of employees and the obligation of support between co-debtors. **2**° Inspired by scholarly writing and jurisprudence, the concept of an obligation *in solidum* in French law has served to fill the gap left by the absence of a provision corresponding to art. 1526 C.C.Q. (art. 1106 C.C.L.C.), which establishes the solidarity among the co-authors of an extra-contractual fault. **3**° While the obligation *in solidum* does expose each debtor to liability for the whole of the debt, it does not bring about the so-called secondary effects of solidarity, such as those relating to putting in default and interruption of prescription.
Syn. imperfect solidarity, *in solidum* obligation. **See also** indivisibility, joint liability, joint obligation, liability *in solidum*, solidarity, solidary obligation.
Fr. obligation *in solidum*+, solidarité imparfaite.

OBLIGATION NOT TO COMPETE

Syn. obligation of non-competition.
Fr. obligation de non-concurrence.

OBLIGATION NOT TO DO

Obligation[3] the object of which is to refrain from doing something. For example, the non-competition clause agreed to by an employee; the non-reestablishment clause agreed to by the vendor of a business. "The debtor is in default by sole effect of law by his violation of an obligation not to do" (Kouri, (1971) 2 *R.D.U.S.* 1, p. 25).
Occ. Arts. 1597, 1603 C.C.Q.
See also obligation to do, obligation to give.
Fr. obligation de ne pas faire.

OBLIGATION OF CONFIDENTIALITY

Syn. duty of confidentiality. "It does not seem unreasonable for the obligation of confidentiality of a senior managerial officer vis-à-vis his former employer to be more onerous than that of a mere employee" (*Montour* v. *Jolicoeur*, [1988] R.J.Q. 1323 (Sup.Ct.), A.D. Guthrie, J.).
Fr. devoir de discrétion, obligation de confidentialité+.

OBLIGATION OF DILIGENCE

Syn. obligation of means. "An obligation of diligence is when a person, in the discharge of a duty, is bound to take all the care of a pru-

dent administrator" (Crépeau, in *Essays on the Civil Law*, 83, p. 96).
Fr. obligation de diligence, obligation de moyens+, obligation générale de prudence et diligence, obligation relative.

OBLIGATION OF INSTANTANEOUS PERFORMANCE

Syn. instantaneous obligation.
Fr. obligation instantanée.

OBLIGATION OF LOYALTY

Obligation for a person to act with probity and with respect towards another, taking into account the particular nature of their relationship and the bond of confidence that exists between them. "However, Quebec jurisprudence has long held that in the case of senior officers and directors a breach of the obligation of loyalty entails the responsibility to disgorge gains made as a result of that breach" (*Bank of Montreal* v. *Kuet Leong Ng*, [1989] 2 S.C.R. 429, p. 439, C.D. Gonthier, J.).
Obs. 1° The obligation of loyalty may be express (arts. 322, 1309, 2088, 2138 C.C.Q.) or implied (arts. 6, 7, 1375, 1434 C.C.Q.). **2**° The obligation of loyalty imports a duty to avoid conflicts of interest. **3**° The existence, the content and the intensity of the obligation of loyalty depends on the powers conferred to the debtor and the degree of confidence that the creditor has placed in him or her. **4**° A person may be held to an obligation of loyalty in situations which differ from the ordinary debtor-creditor relationship of obligation. For example, the administrator of the property of another shall act "in the best interest of the beneficiary or of the object pursued" (art. 1309 C.C.Q.). **5**° In the *Civil Code of Québec*, the expressions *to act with honesty and loyalty* (art. 322 C.C.Q.), *to act honestly and faithfully* (arts. 1309 and 2138 C.C.Q.) and *to act faithfully and honestly* (art. 2088 C.C.Q.) appear as equivalents to the French expression *agir avec honnêteté et loyauté*.
Syn. obligation to act faithfully. **See also** duty to cooperate, good faith, implicit obligation.
Fr. devoir de loyauté, obligation de loyauté+.

OBLIGATION OF MEANS

Obligation[3] to act with prudence and diligence. "In some cases, [one's] duty may be what is known as an 'obligation of means' (obligation de moyen). In such cases, the duty of the debtor, whether it be contractual or extra-contractual, is to take the reasonable care and attention which the 'bon père de famille' would ordinarily take so as not to cause damage to his neighbours" (Crépeau, (1962) 40 *Can. Bar Rev.* 222, pp. 223-224). **Obs. 1°** The classification based on the intensity of the obligation draws a distinction between obligations of means, obligations of result and obligations of warranty. **2°** Unless otherwise indicated, diligence and prudence are not evaluated according to subjective criteria (*in concreto*), but according to an objective standard (*in abstracto*). **3°** In order to prove the fault of the debtor, the creditor who alleges the non-performance of an obligation of means must show that the debtor did not act with the required prudence and diligence to reach the expected result or to avoid the occurence of the harm. **4°** See articles 322, 1225, 1855, 2317 C.C.Q.

Syn. general obligation of prudence and diligence, obligation of diligence, relative obligation. **See also** *culpa levis*, intensity of the obligation, obligation of result, obligation of warranty, reasonable person.

Fr. obligation de diligence, obligation de moyens+, obligation générale de prudence et diligence, obligation relative.

OBLIGATION OF NON-COMPETITION

Obligation to abstain from pursuing an activity similar to that engaged in by another.

Obs. 1° Given that obligations of non competition undermine freedom to work and freedom of commerce, clauses that create them must be designed to protect the legitimate interests of the creditor. Such clauses must therefore be directed to specific and limited restrictions of time, place and activities in order to be valid. This limitation is expressly stated at article 2089 C.C.Q. regarding the contract of employment. **2°** According to some scholars, obligations of non-competition can be created as servitudes. However, Quebec courts do not, in principle, validate servitudes that prohibit the pursuit of an economic activity on land in favour of another piece of land. Courts argue notably that such a prohibition does not confer any advantage to the land itself, but offers only a personal advantage to the creditor, who is in general the owner or the lessee of the dominant land. Following this view, the creditor of the obligation of non-competition does not therefore hold a real right. **3°** Unfair competition must be distinguished from the violation of an obligation of non-competition. Whereas unfair competition results from resorting to dishonest or unfair behaviour vis-à-vis a competitor in the pursuit of an economic activity, the obligation of non-

competition is breached from the moment the debtor undertakes the protected activity. **Syn.** obligation not to compete. **See also** non-competition clause, obligation not to do. **Fr.** obligation de non-concurrence.

OBLIGATION OF RESULT

Obligation[3] to bring about a specific and determined outcome, except in the case of a superior force preventing performance. "In the case of an obligation of result, the burden on the plaintiff is less onerous for the failure of the debtor to produce the result stipulated raises against him a prima facie case of liability from which he can only free himself by proof of a fortuitous event" (Crépeau, in *Essays on the Civil Law*, 83, p. 97).

Obs. 1° The classification based on the intensity of the obligation draws a distinction between obligations of means, obligations of result and obligations of warranty. **2°** In order to prove the fault of the debtor, the creditor who alleges the non-performance of an obligation of result must show that the debtor has failed to reach the expected result. The debtor can only be exonerated by proving the event of a superior force.

Syn. absolute obligation. **See also** intensity of the obligation, obligation of means, obligation of warranty.

Fr. obligation absolue, obligation de résultat+, obligation déterminée.

OBLIGATION OF SUCCESSIVE PERFORMANCE

Syn. continuous obligation.
Fr. obligation continue+, obligation (à exécution) successive.

OBLIGATION OF SUPPORT

1. Obligation[2] the object of which is to provide support to a person. "That does not mean that the obligation of support between ex-spouses should continue indefinitely when the marriage bond is dissolved, or that one spouse can continue to be a drag on the other indefinitely or acquire a lifetime pension as a result of the marriage, or to luxuriate in idleness at the expense of the other, to use the expressions one finds in some discussions of the subject" (*Messier* v. *Delage*, [1983] 2 S.C.R. 401, pp. 416-417, J. Chouinard, J.).

Occ. Title preceding art. 585 C.C.Q.; art. 88 C.C.Q.

Obs. 1° An obligation of support may have one of three sources: it may arise by operation of law (e.g. in the case of relatives in the direct line pursuant to art. 585 C.C.Q.); it may arise

by judicial order (e.g. in the case of corollary relief granted to a former spouse on divorce pursuant to ss. 15 and 17, *Divorce Act*, R.S.C. 1985, c. 3 (2nd Suppl.) or in the case of dissolution of a civil union (art. 521.17 C.C.Q.)), or, it may arise by juridical act (e.g. in the case of a legacy subject to a charge obliging the legatee to pay support to a person designated in the will). **2°** In some instances, such as the obligation of support between spouses during a marriage or a civil union and between relatives in the direct line, the obligation is of public order and cannot be renounced by a creditor (see *Ruel* v. *Thomas*, [1982] C.A. 357). **3°** The obligation of support between spouses and between relatives in the direct line is reciprocal and variable according to the needs and means of the parties (arts. 585, 587 C.C.Q.). Thus not only is the amount of support liable to change over time, but so may the status of creditor and debtor. **4°** In some cases, a creditor of support may have a duty to become self-sufficient so that the obligation of support will not be owed indefinitely (e.g. art. 587 C.C.Q. and s. 15.2(6)*d*), *Divorce Act*, R.S.C. 1985, c. 3 (2nd Suppl.)). **5°** The obligation of support is generally said to be a personal obligation and thus not transmissible, although a *post mortem* obligation of support is recognized in certain circumstances (arts. 684 *et seq.* C.C.Q.). **6°** In some circumstances, patrimonial rights, such as usufruct or the right of use, may be alimentary in character without necessarily corresponding to an obligation of support. This is also true of certain judicial awards, such as that of a right of use of the family residence granted to a spouse having the custody of children (art. 410 para. 3 C.C.Q.). **7°** The *Civil Code of Québec* also uses the expression *obligation to provide support* (e.g. title preceding art. 684 C.C.Q. and art. 609 C.C.Q.).
Fr. obligation alimentaire[1].

2. (*Fam.*) Obligation of support viewed from the perspective of the debtor.
Occ. Art. 88 C.C.Q.
Syn. debt for support. **See also** alimentary right.
Fr. dette alimentaire, obligation alimentaire[2+].

OBLIGATION OF WARRANTY

Obligation[3] to bring about a specific and determined outcome, even in the case of a superior force preventing performance. "In the obligation of warranty, once the creditor has proved that he is within the terms of the warranty, there is no escape whatever for the debtor" (Crépeau, in *Essays on the Civil Law*, 83, p. 97).
Occ. Art. 1731 C.C.Q.
Obs. 1° The classification based on the intensity of the obligation draws a distinction between obligations of means, obligations of result and obligations of warranty. **2°** In order to prove the fault of the debtor, the creditor who alleges the non-performance of an obligation of warranty must show that the debtor has failed to reach the expected result. In principle, the debtor cannot be exonerated by proving the event of a superior force.
See also intensity of the obligation, obligation of means, obligation of result.
Fr. obligation de garantie.

OBLIGATION *PROPTER REM* (Latin)

Syn. real obligation.
Fr. obligation *propter rem*, obligation réelle[+].

OBLIGATIONS *pl.n.*

Syn. law of obligations.
Occ. Book five of the C.C.Q.
Obs. Used in this sense, the word *Obligations* is generally capitalized.
Fr. droit des obligations[+], obligations.

OBLIGATION TO ACT FAITHFULLY

Syn. obligation of loyalty.
Obs. The expression *obligation to act in good faith* is also encountered.
Fr. devoir de loyauté, obligation de loyauté[+].

OBLIGATION TO ADVISE

Obligation to provide counsel to another in the furtherance of the latter's interest.
Obs. 1° The obligation to advise includes the obligation for the debtor to set out and evaluate in a disinterested fashion all information on which his or her advice is based. **2°** The obligation to advise arises particularly in the context of mandate such as in a brokerage contract, as well as in professional-client relationships for, among others, notaries, lawyers, physicians or architects. **3°** The obligation to advise is generally the principal obligation of contract, but it may also be an accessory obligation. For example, the obligation for a physician to provide diligent medical care carries with it the obligation to provide counsel concerning the best treatment given the circumstances.
Syn. obligation to (provide) counsel. **See also** good faith, obligation to inform.
Fr. devoir de conseil, obligation de conseil[+].

OBLIGATION TO (PROVIDE) COUNSEL

Syn. obligation to advise. "We must avoid confusing the obligation to inform, which remains a secondary obligation, with the obligation to counsel, the main obligation in many contracts, including mandates given to notaries [...]" (*Bank of Montreal* v. *Bail Ltée*, [1992] 2 S.C.R. 554, p. 587, C.D. Gonthier, J.).
Fr. devoir de conseil, obligation de conseil[+].

OBLIGATION TO DO

Obligation[3] that has as its object the performance of an act. For example, the obligation to perform some work. "When the Code of Civil Procedure was reformed in 1965, the Legislator purposely introduced the mandatory injunction, in order to provide a correlative procedural basis for enforcing the remedy of specific performance in cases of obligations to do" (Jukier, (1987) 47 *R. du B.* 47, p. 49).
Obs. Article 1058 C.C.L.C. specified that an obligation could have as an object to give, to do or not to do something. Article 1373 C.C.Q. does not explicitly draw a distinction between obligations to give and obligations to do. It is generally considered that the former are included in the latter.
See also obligation not to do, obligation to give.
Fr. obligation de faire.

OBLIGATION TO GIVE

Obligation[3] that has as its object the transfer of a real right. "Obligation to give: The verb *to give*, used in connection with the word obligation, must be understood in the technical sense of its Latin parallel *dare* (to transfer, to grant) and not in its more colloquial sense of *donare* or to give as a present [...]" (Levasseur, *Obligations*, p. 8).
Occ. Art. 1063 C.C.L.C.
Obs. 1° Article 1058 C.C.L.C. specified that an obligation could have for its object to give, to do or not to do something. Article 1373 C.C.Q. does not explicitly draw a distinction between obligations to give and obligations to do. It is generally considered that the former are included in the latter. **2°** Since, in a translatory contract, the transfer results in principle solely from an exchange of consents, the obligation to give exists in theory and for an instant only, because it is performed at the same moment it arises. However, the obligation persists when the parties have agreed to defer the transfer to a later date or when the purpose of the contract is to transfer generic things (art. 1453 C.C.Q.).

See also obligation not to do, obligation to do.
Fr. obligation de donner.

OBLIGATION TO INFORM

Obligation to reveal to another facts that the latter, in order to adjust his or her conduct, may legitimately expect to receive. "The advent of the obligation to inform is related to a certain shift that has been taking place in the civil law. While previously it was acceptable to leave it to the individual to obtain information before acting, the civil law is now more attentive to inequalities in terms of information, and imposes a positive obligation to provide information in cases where one party is in a vulnerable position as regards information [...]" (*Bank of Montreal* v. *Bail ltée*, [1992] 2 S.C.R. 554, p. 587, C.D. Gonthier, J.).
Obs. 1° At the root of the obligation to inform lies the principle of good faith (see arts. 6, 7 and 1375 C.C.Q.). This obligation is sometimes expressly provided by law, as for example in the contract of suretyship (art. 2345 C.C.Q.) and the contract of insurance (art. 2466 C.C.Q.). **2°** The obligation to inform does not extend to the information that the other party should already know or to which the other party can reasonably gain access. The obligation to inform the other party is thus balanced by the duty of the latter to obtain information. **3°** The obligation to inform exists during the formation of the contract as well as during its performance. **4°** Sometimes, the obligation to inform is an accessory obligation allowing the main obligation to be properly performed. For example, the obligation of the vendor to provide information on the use, functioning and maintenance of the property sold is considered accessory to the obligation to transfer the property.
Syn. duty to inform. **See also** fraudulent concealment, good faith, implicit obligation, obligation to advise, precontractual obligation to inform.
Fr. devoir de renseignement(s), obligation de renseigner, obligation d'information, obligation de renseignement(s)[+].

OBLIGATION WITH A COMPLEX MODALITY

Obligation[2] involving a plurality either of subjects or of objects.
Obs. 1° Alternative, conjunctive and facultative obligations involve several objects, while joint, solidary and indivisible obligations involve several subjects. **2°** The codal regime

respecting obligations with a complex modality is set forth at articles 1518 to 1552 C.C.Q.
Syn. plural obligation. **See also** alternative obligation, complex obligation, conjunctive obligation, divisible obligation, facultative obligation, indivisible obligation, joint obligation, obligation with a simple modality, solidary obligation.
Fr. obligation à modalité complexe[+], obligation plurale.

OBLIGATION WITH A MODALITY

Syn. complex obligation.
Fr. obligation à modalité, obligation complexe[+], obligation modale.

OBLIGATION WITH A SIMPLE MODALITY

Obligation[2] subject to a term[1] or a condition[1].
Obs. The codal regime respecting obligations with a simple modality is set forth at articles 1497 to 1517 C.C.Q.
See also complex obligation, conditional obligation, obligation with a complex modality, obligation with a term.
Fr. obligation à modalité simple.

OBLIGATION WITH A TERM

Obligation[2] subject to a term[1].
Occ. Title preceding art. 1508 C.C.Q.; title preceding art. 1089 C.C.L.C.
Obs. An obligation may involve one or more terms.
Syn. term obligation. **See also** complex obligation, conditional obligation.
Fr. obligation à terme.

OBLIGATORY *adj.*

Syn. binding. "[...] if the only will that man has consists in following his momentary inclinations or a fleeting assessment of his interests [...] it is necessary that the law supplement it and give agreements the obligatory force which they could not derive from the inconstancy of man [...]" (Rouhette, in *Contract Law Today*, 38, p. 42). *An obligatory formality*; *an obligatory stipulation*; *an obligatory clause*.
Occ. Art. 429 C.C.L.C.; s. 85, *An Act respecting the Régie du logement*, R.S.Q. c. R-8.1.
See also obligational.
Fr. obligatoire.

OBLIGE *v.*

Syn. bind.
Occ. Arts. 762, 1507, 1754, 1838 C.C.Q.
Fr. engager, obliger[+].

OBLIGED *adj.*

Bound by an obligation. "An obligation is a legal bond by which one person is bound towards another to [...] do, or not to do something [...] The person entitled to demand performance is called creditor; the one who is obliged to perform is called debtor" (Aubry & Rau, *Civil Law*, vol. 1, n° 296, p. 2).
Occ. Art. 627 C.C.Q.; s. 111, *Automobile Insurance Act*, R.S.Q. c. A-25.
See also discharged.
Fr. obligé.

OBLIGEE *n.*

Syn. creditor. "An obligation which [...] can be performed only by the obligor or exclusively for the benefit of the obligee-creditor [...] [is] said to have been entered into 'intuitus personæ' or in contemplation of the person of either party or of both of them. Although such obligations may be part of a party's patrimony they remain attached to the person of the obligor or the obligee [...]" (Levasseur, *Obligations*, p. 40).
Obs. The term *obligee* is commonly used in the Civil law of Louisiana. Its use is rare in Quebec legal parlance.
Fr. créancier.

OBLIGOR *n.*

Syn. debtor. "[...] a right can be said to be the 'active' component part of a patrimonial relationship in the sense that the holder of the right has the benefit of the 'action' against an obligor" (Levasseur, *Obligations*, p. 31).
Obs. The term *obligor* is commonly used in Louisiana law. The word *debtor* has a monetary connotation for Anglo-American lawyers, so the term *obligor* is sometimes preferred as an English-language equivalent to the French term *débiteur*. The use of the term is rare in Quebec legal parlance.
Fr. débiteur[+], obligé.

OBLIQUE *adj.*

See oblique action.
Occ. Art. 1629 C.C.Q.
Fr. oblique.

OBLIQUE ACTION

Action by which a creditor, who has suffered a loss as a result of the debtor's inaction, exercises one of the debtor's rights in the latter's place. "The oblique action permits a creditor to enforce a debtor's rights where he is prejudiced by his debtor's failure to do so" (Macdonald, (1986-87) 32 *McGill L.J.* 1, p. 18).

Occ. Title preceding art. 1627 C.C.Q.; art. 1629 C.C.Q.

Obs. 1° An oblique action enables the creditor to exercise the rights of his or her debtor when the latter refuses or neglects to do so. However, the creditor may not exercise rights attached exclusively to the debtor's person (art. 1627 C.C.Q.) (e.g. rights arising out of an alimentary obligation). **2°** Article 1629 C.C.Q. provides that "[t]he person against whom an oblique action is brought may set up against the creditor all the defences he could have set up against his own creditor". **3°** Since the creditor acts in the name and on behalf of the debtor, property recovered falls into the patrimony of the debtor and benefits all of his or her creditors (art. 1630 C.C.Q.). **4°** The codal regime respecting oblique actions is set forth at articles 1627 to 1630 C.C.Q. **5°** The term *subrogatory action* is sometimes used in the sense of *oblique action* although, strictly speaking, subrogation does not in fact arise in this context.

Syn. indirect action. **See also** direct action[1], Paulian action.

Fr. action indirecte, action oblique[+].

OCCASIONAL EMPLOYEE

Syn. temporary employee.
Fr. préposé occasionnel.

OCCASIONAL EMPLOYER

Syn. temporary employer.
Fr. commettant occasionnel.

OFFENCE *n.*

Rare. Syn. delict. "If a contract in itself constitutes the source of an obligation, an offence or a quasi-offence is essentially a violation of a pre-existing legal obligation such as the obligation of every person to act as a reasonable person [...]" (C.C.R.O., *Commentaries*, vol. II, t. 2, p. 560).

Occ. Arts. 983, 1007 C.C.L.C.

Obs. 1° Although the same conduct may give rise to an offence in both criminal and civil settings, the term *offence* used as a synonym for *delict* is not to be confused with the term *offence* as employed in the criminal context, where it suggests an offence against the state. **2°** The term *offence* and its synonym *delict*, which appeared at articles 983 and 1007 C.C.L.C., are no longer to be found in the Civil Code. However, as specified by s. 423 of *An Act respecting the implementation of the reform of the Civil Code* (S.Q. 1992, c. 57), the notion of *fault in the context of extra-contractual civil liability* corresponds to the notions of *offence* and *quasi-offence* in the C.C.L.C. (arts. 164, 1526, 2498 C.C.Q.). The vocabulary adopted by the Civil Code reflects the classification of the sources of obligations as stated in art. 1372 C.C.Q.

Fr. délit.

OFFER *n.*

Proposal to enter into a contract, which sets out that contract's essential elements. "[...] when the parties start a negotiation with the aim of making a contract, there must be a presumption that every precise offer which is accepted binds them, and that they are thus obliged to perform the obligation so created" (Jauffret-Spinosi, in *Contract Law Today*, 113, n° 39, p. 130). *To accept an offer.*

Occ. Arts. 1388, 1392, 1393 C.C.Q.; s. 24, *Consumer Protection Act*, R.S.Q. c. P-40.1; s. 54.7, *An Act respecting the Régie du logement*, R.S.Q. c. R-8.1; ss. 190(14), 206(1), *Canada Business Corporations Act*, R.S.C. 1985, c. C-44.

Obs. 1° An offer plays a central role in the formation of a contract. The contract is formed through the exchange of consent that is manifested by the will of the person who accepts an offer to contract with the other person (art. 1386 C.C.Q.). **2°** An offer is distinguished from a simple invitation to treat or a mere proposition to enter negotiations, which does not constitute a firm offer and, as result, does not demonstrate a willingness of its author to be bound in the case of acceptance. **3°** In consumer protection matters, an offer relating to a contract that must be evinced in writing does not bind the consumer until it has been so recorded (s. 24, *Consumer Protection Act*, R.S.Q. c. P-40.1). **4°** An offer may be made by one or more other persons whether they be one or more persons, determinate or indeterminate (art. 1390 C.C.Q.). **5°** The person formulating the offer is called the *offeror*; the person to whom the offer is made is called the *offeree.* **6°** The codal regime relating to offer and acceptance is set forth at articles 1388 *et seq.* of the *Civil Code of Québec.* The *Civil Code of Lower Canada* did not contain a comparably thorough treatment of the matter.

See also acceptance[1], agreement in principle, counter-offer, exclusive offer, express offer, implied offer, initial offer, letter of intention, non-exclusive offer, offer to a determinate person, precontractual period, promise to contract, public offer, tender, theory of reception.

Fr. offre[+], pollicitation.

OFFEREE *n.*

Person who receives an offer.
Occ. Arts. 1391, 1392, 1396 C.C.Q.
See also acceptor, offeror, promisee.
Fr. destinataire[1+], pollicité.

OFFER OF REWARD

Offer whereby the offeror proposes to pay an indemnity to any person who will render a favour or perform a good deed.
Occ. Art. 1395 C.C.Q.
Obs. The offer of reward is considered to have been accepted when a person renders the favour or performs the good deed even if he or she was not aware of the offer.
Syn. promise of reward.
Fr. offre de récompense[+], promesse de récompense.

OFFEROR *n.*

Person who makes an offer. "[...] the offer accompanied expressly or tacitly with a delay cannot be retired freely: the offeror is considered bound, provided the acceptance is made within the delay fixed" (Planiol & Ripert, *Treatise*, vol. 2, n° 981, p. 567).
Occ. Arts. 1387, 1388, 1390 C.C.Q.
Obs. The *offeror* is distinguished from the *offeree*.
See also offeree, promisor[1].
Fr. offrant[+], pollicitant.

OFFER TO A DETERMINATE PERSON

Offer made to one or more designated persons.
Obs. When the offeree indicates his or her intention to consider the offer and to reply to it within the time stated therein or within a reasonable time, it constitutes a promise to contract (art. 1396 C.C.Q.).
Syn. offer to a specified person. **See also** offer to the public, promise to contract.
Fr. offre à (une) personne déterminée.

OFFER TO AN INDETERMINATE PERSON

Syn. offer to the public.
Fr. offre à personne indéterminée, offre au public[+].

OFFER TO A SPECIFIED PERSON

Syn. offer to a determinate person.
Fr. offre à (une) personne déterminée.

OFFER TO AN UNSPECIFIED PERSON

Syn. offer to the public. "The possibility of [...] offers to the public was disputed by several writers at the beginning of the 19th century. They felt that since the offeree was not identified, an element essential to the definite nature of the offer was missing, and that an offer to an unspecified person thus could be only an offer to enter into negotiations. But these criticisms were soon abandoned" (Schlesinger, *Formation of Contracts*, p. 662).
Fr. offre à personne indéterminée, offre au public[+].

OFFER TO THE PUBLIC

Offer made to unspecified persons. For example, merchandise offered for sale in a store. "[...] a tramway company by running its cars makes an offer to the public to carry them at the ordinary rate, and the man who gets into the car or even puts his foot on the step accepts this offer" (Walton, *Obligations*, vol. 1, p. 186).
Syn. offer to an indeterminate person, offer to an unspecified person, public offer. **See also** offer to a determinate person.
Fr. offre à personne indéterminée, offre au public[+].

OMISSION *n.*

See fault of omission.
Fr. omission.

ONEROUS CONTRACT

Contract by which each party derives an advantage in exchange for that which is conferred upon the other party. For example, a contract of sale, a contract of lease and hire, an onerous deposit.
Occ. Arts. 1632 C.C.Q.
Obs. 1° Onerous contracts can be either commutative or aleatory. **2°** Onerous contracts must not be confused with bilateral contracts. A loan upon interest, for example, is considered to be an onerous contract notwithstanding its status as a unilateral contract.
Syn. contract by onerous title. **See also** aleatory contract, commutative contract, gratuitous contract.
Fr. contrat à titre onéreux[+], contrat intéressé, contrat onéreux.

ONEROUS TITLE (BY) *adj.ph.*

See by onerous title.
Fr. titre onéreux (à).

OPPOSABILITY *n.*

Characteristic of a right or of a juridical act that may be raised against third persons. For example, publication of real rights submitted to publicity allows them to be raised against third parties. "It is therefore possible to structure an arrangement using sale and reservation of ownership of the property such that it will not constitute an instalment sale as defined in article 1745 of the *Civil Code* thus avoiding any need to register for opposability and the need to follow the realization regime applicable to hypothecary creditors" (Dietze, (1999) 59 *R. du B.* 1, p. 10). *Opposability of contract.*
Occ. Art. 2942 C.C.Q.
Obs. 1° Personality rights and human rights are said to be, by their nature, opposable to all. Real rights also enjoy this characteristic. **2°** The Civil Code uses the expressions *setting up of rights* or *setting up of claims* to evoke opposability (title preceding art. 2941 C.C.Q.). It is also said of a right that is "opposable" that it may be "set up" against another. **3°** Some scholars are of the view that opposability is a Gallicism and prefer the expression *set up against another*. This latter expression is the usage preferred in the Civil Code.
See also annulability, inopposability, invalidity, non-existence, nullity, relativity of contract.
Fr. opposabilité.

OPPOSABLE *adj.*

Gall. That which can be raised against a third person. "The fact of the contract and its consequences, it is said, are 'opposable' to and by third parties, i.e. they may be invoked against third parties and by them" (Nicholas, *Contract*, p. 170).
Occ. Art. 1040*a* C.C.L.C.
See also inopposable, oppose.
Fr. opposable.

OPPOSE *v.*

Syn. set up. "A juridical act may be valid and binding between the parties to it and, yet, have no effect vis-à-vis third parties: such an act is *null* only as to those third parties in the sense that it cannot be *opposed* to them" (Levasseur, *Conventional Obligations*, pp. 52-53).
Occ. Arts. 267, 1180, 1697*b* C.C.L.C.
Obs. Some scholars see this term as Gallicism and use the expression *set up against* is sometimes used instead of *opposable*. Similarly,

not set up against is sometimes used in preference to *inopposable*, and *to set up against* in preference to the verb *oppose*.
Fr. opposer.

OPTION *n.*

Right to accept or refuse a unilateral promise to contract. "An option conveys no real rights and is not normally registered unless it be an accessory of some other contract" (*Nadeau* v. *Nadeau*, [1977] C.A. 248, p. 254, G.H. Montgomery J.). *Exercise an option; option to buy; option to purchase.*
Occ. Art. 1396 C.C.Q.
See also exercise of an option.
Fr. option.

OPTION (BETWEEN REGIMES)

Prerogative of the victim of a contractual fault to choose the regime of extracontractual liability as an alternative basis for establishing liability. "By an 'option' here is meant the possibility for A, the plaintiff, of altogether disregarding the fact that he is the creditor of a contractual duty for the breach of which he seeks compensation, and suing the defendant on the basis of a delict as if he were a complete stranger [...]" (Crépeau, in *Meredith Lectures (1964)*, 1, p. 9).
Obs. 1° In respect of the law of civil liability in the *Civil Code of Lower Canada*, the Supreme Court of Canada (*Wabasso Ltd.* v. *National Drying Machinery Co.*, [1981] 1 S.C.R. 578) allowed for option between the liability regimes in cases where the damage resulting from a contractual fault could be analyzed as an extracontractual fault. The Court thus enabled the victim to choose the regime most favourable to his or her situation. **2°** The parties to a contract may no longer avoid the rules governing contractual liability. Option between regimes, like cumulation of regimes, is prohibited (art. 1458 para. 2 C.C.Q.). **3°** The differences between the regimes are not as important as they once were, although some differences still exist (e.g. in matters of solidarity, evaluation of damages and conflict of laws). **4°** The principal argument against option between regimes of contractual and extracontractual liability is based on the idea that allowing the choice would undermine the obligatory force of contract and, as a result, impinge on the doctrine of freedom of contract.
See also contractual liability, cumulation (of regimes), extracontractual liability.
Fr. option (entre les régimes).

OPTION OF WITHDRAWAL

See withdrawal option.
Fr. dédit[1], faculté de dédit[+].

ORDINARY CREDITOR

(*Sec.*) Syn. unsecured creditor.
Fr. créancier chirographaire, créancier ordinaire[+].

ORDINARY LAW

Syn. general law.
Occ. Art. 1725 C.C.Q.
Fr. droit commun[1+], *jus commune*, loi générale.

OSTENSIBLE *adj.*

See ostensible act.
Fr. ostensible.

OSTENSIBLE ACT

Syn. apparent act.
Fr. acte apparent[+], acte ostensible, acte simulé.

OUT-OF-COURT SETTLEMENT

Syn. transaction[1].
Obs. The French expression *règlement hors cour* is used especially to designate transactions occurring once proceedings have begun. The expression *out-of-court settlement* is used more generally.
Fr. contrat de transaction, règlement hors cour, transaction[+].

P

PACT *n.*

Syn. contract[1].
Obs. 1° The term *pact* is used in its Latin form in the maxim *pacta sunt servanda* to express the notion of *the binding force of contracts*. **2°** The term is also used in public international law to designate treaties between States (e.g. the *Warsaw Pact*).
Fr. contrat[1+], convention, pacte.

PACTA SUNT SERVANDA (Latin)

See binding force of contract.
Obs. This Latin maxim means *covenants must be respected*.
Fr. *pacta sunt servanda*.

PAID *p.p.*

Wording that the creditor inscribes on a title of indebtedness in order to acknowledge that he or she has received payment of the claim.
See also acquittance[1], discharge[3], receipt[1].
Fr. acquit (pour).

PARTIAL CAUSATION

Causation[2] linking two or more facts to the damage suffered, without, however, the requirement that one of these be the exclusive cause of the damage.
See also adequate causation, contributory fault, equivalence of conditions, immediate causation, material causation.
Fr. causalité partielle.

PARTIAL INCAPACITY

Syn. special incapacity.
Fr. incapacité partielle, incapacité spéciale[+].

PARTIAL PAYMENT

Payment of a portion of a debt. "In principle, every obligation should be executed at one time; the debtor cannot force the creditor to receive partial payment" (Planiol & Ripert, *Treatise*, vol. 2, n° 432, p. 254).

Occ. Arts. 1570, 1625, 2122 C.C.Q.; ss. 60, 93, 116, *Consumer Protection Act*, R.S.Q. c. P-40.1.
Obs. Full payment is the rule for settling debts, since the creditor may not be compelled to accept partial payment of an obligation unless it is disputed in part (art. 1561 C.C.Q.).
See also full payment, indivisibility of payment.
Fr. paiement divisé, paiement fractionné, paiement partiel[+].

PARTICIPANT *n.*

Person who participates in a contract of group insurance.
Occ. Arts. 2401, 2423, 2449 C.C.Q.; arts. 2483, 2505 C.C.L.C.; ss. 406.1, 424, *An act respecting insurance*, R.S.Q. c. A-32.
Obs. 1° The client has the obligation to transmit the insurance certificate to the participant, which must have been given to the client by the insurer. If a discrepancy exists between the insurance certificate and the policy, which the participant may examine at the place of business of the client, the participant may invoke the more favourable of the two (art. 2401 C.C.Q.). **2°** The group policy may cover both the *participant*, i.e. the employee, and his or her dependents. All are insured by the group policy but the Civil Code grants rights only to the *participant*.
See also client[1], insurance contract, insurance policy.
Fr. adhérent.

PARTICULAR SUCCESSOR

Syn. successor by particular title. "Particular successors are not the heirs of their author, nor comparable to them. Consequently, the contracts which their author was able to make, as creditor or as debtor, are, in principle, a matter of indifference [...]" (Planiol & Ripert, *Treatise*, vol. 2, n° 1177, p. 668).
Fr. ayant cause à titre particulier[+], ayant cause particulier, ayant droit à titre particulier, successeur à titre particulier, successeur particulier.

PARTICULAR TITLE (BY)

See disposition by particular title, successor by particular title, transmission by (a) particular title.
Fr. titre particulier (à).

PARTNER *n.*

Party to a contract of partnership. "The contractual nature of a partnership has also as one of its consequences that the partner may associate a third person in his share in the partnership without the consent of the other persons but he may not make him a member of the partnership without their consent" (Fortin, in *Meredith Lectures (1997)*, 1, p. 6).
Occ. Arts. 839, 1696, 2198 C.C.Q.; arts. 1830, 1839 C.C.L.C.
Obs. Partners are also members of the partnership.
See also contract of partnership, general partner, limited partner, partnership[1].
Fr. associé+, sociétaire[1].

PARTNERSHIP *n.*

1. Group of persons, the *partners*, who, in a spirit of cooperation, agree to carry on an activity dedicated to the realization of a financial gain, and to which activity each person contributes property, knowledge or industry, and from which gain the partners may claim a share. "Finally, I feel it is appropriate to issue a caution against the danger of concluding too readily to the existence of tacit partnerships, for the admittedly admirable purpose of compensating for the injustice resulting from the situation in which concubines are often placed" (*Beaudoin-Daigneault* v. *Richard*, [1984] 1 S.C.R. 2, p. 17, A. Lamer, J.).
Occ. Arts. 909, 2187 C.C.Q.; arts. 1831, 1839 C.C.L.C.
Obs. 1° The *Civil Code of Québec* provides for three kinds of partnership: general partnership, limited partnership and undeclared partnership. **2°** Such partnerships are established by contract, as opposed, for example, to partnerships that take the form of joint-stock companies. The establishment of the latter requires the intervention of a public authority in accordance with a formal procedure generally provided for in a special statute, such as the *Companies Act* (R.S.Q. c. C-38) or *Canada Business Corporations Act* (R.S.C. 1985, c. C-44). **3°** Unlike partnerships that are joint-stock companies, partnerships established by contract are not endowed with juridical personality (art. 2188 C.C.Q.). **4°** Partnerships may be distinguished from undivided co-ownership insofar as partnerships reflect a "spirit of cooperation", the *affectio societatis*, i.e. an intention of the parties to participate together in a joint business endeavour. **5°** Partnerships may be distinguished from associations in that the former seek the realization of a financial gain to be shared between the members (art. 2186 C.C.Q.). **6°** In the *Civil Code of Québec*, commercial partnerships are no longer distinguished from civil ones (arts. 1863 *et seq.* C.C.L.C.). With respect to this distinction, it may be observed that the notion of *commerciality* has been replaced by the wider notion of *enterprise* in the *Civil Code of Québec* (art. 1525 para. 3 C.C.Q.).
See also association, contract of partnership, contribution (to the partnership), enterprise, general partnership, limited partnership, partner, undeclared partnership, undivided co-ownership.
Fr. société[1].

2. Syn. contract of partnership.
Fr. contrat de société+, société[2].

PARTNERSHIP AGREEMENT

Syn. contract of partnership.
Obs. The expression *partnership agreement* is often used to refer to the *instrumentum* of the contract that establishes partnership.
Fr. contrat de société.

PARTNERSHIP *EN COMMANDITE* (French)

Syn. limited partnership.
Occ. Title preceding art. 1871 C.C.L.C.
Fr. société en commandite.

PASSENGER *n.*

Person whom the carrier undertakes to take from one place to another.
Occ. Arts. 2030, 2033, 2037 C.C.Q.; arts. 1682, 2461, 2462 C.C.L.C.; s. 2(1), *Carriage by Air Act*, R.S.C. 1985, c. C-26.
See also contract for the carriage of persons, contract of carriage.
Fr. passager+, voyageur.

PASSIVE *adj.*

See passive indivisibility, passive solidarity.
Fr. passif.

PASSIVE INDIVISIBILITY

Indivisibility among debtors. "Much more common than active indivisibility, passive indivisibility must be looked upon as a secu-

rity device *naturally* or *contractually* given to an obligee by one or more obligors. Passive indivisibility vests in an obligee at least the same rights against his indivisible obligors that passive solidarity would grant him against solidary obligors" (Levasseur, *Obligations*, p. 114).
See also active indivisibility, passive solidarity.
Fr. indivisibilité passive.

PASSIVE SOLIDARITY

Solidarity among debtors. "The burdensome legal effects that passive solidarity will impose on a solidary obligor explains why the sources of solidarity are few and restrictive. No burden or risk is to be imposed on an average reasonable person unless he has agreed to assume it or unless the law has ordered it" (Levasseur, *Obligations*, p. 76).
Obs. 1° Payment made by a solidary debtor discharges the others vis-à-vis the creditor (art. 1523 C.C.Q.). **2**° Passive solidarity may be either conventional or legal (art. 1525 C.C.Q.). **3**° The codal regime respecting passive solidarity is set forth at articles 1523 to 1540 C.C.Q.
See also active solidarity, passive indivisibility.
Fr. solidarité passive.

PATENT DEFECT

Syn. apparent defect.
Fr. défaut apparent, vice apparent+.

PATRIMONIAL *adj.*

Pertaining to patrimony. "Rights having a patrimonial character are, in traditional doctrinal expositions, classed into real and personal rights" (Brierley & Macdonald (eds.), *Quebec Civil Law*, n° 134, p. 166).
Occ. Art. 192 C.C.Q.
Obs. The term *patrimonial* is also used to describe, more particularly, that which is susceptible of pecuniary evaluation.
See also patrimonial right.
Fr. patrimonial.

PATRIMONIAL RIGHT

Right which, given that it is susceptible of pecuniary evaluation, forms part of a patrimony. For example, the vendor's claim, the right of ownership. "Patrimonial rights are those that in their very essence have a monetary value. They amount, in a word, to property (or *biens*) because they are alienable or marketable, transmissible to heirs, seizable

by one's creditors, and susceptible of extinction through non-use (prescription), at least in principle" (Brierley & Macdonald (eds.), *Quebec Civil Law*, n° 127, p. 156).
Occ. Arts. 89, 382, 809 C.C.Q.
Obs. 1° As a general rule, patrimonial rights are transmissible *inter vivos* and *mortis causa*, seizable and prescriptible. **2**° Certain rights, while susceptible of giving rise to an evaluation in monetary terms when violated, are nevertheless excluded from the patrimony. This is the case, in principle, for personality rights and human rights and freedoms.
Syn. incorporeal property, incorporeal thing, property[1], *res*[2].
Fr. bien[1], bien incorporel, chose incorporelle, droit patrimonial+.

PATRIMONY *n.*

Universality of rights[1] and obligations[3] having a pecuniary value in which rights answer for obligations. "[...] it has been said that the power, the faculty of acquiring new rights is the distinctive element that gives unity to the different parts of which a patrimony is formed. This power projected upon the future is also engaged by the debtor in the obligation and not the present content of his patrimony alone" (Litvinoff, in *Treatise*, vol. 6, n° 14, p. 34).
Occ. Arts. 2, 302, 1260 C.C.Q.; art. 735.1 C.C.L.C.; s. 43, *Public Curator Act*, R.S.Q. c. C-81.
Obs. 1° The patrimony is formed of present property and obligations and has the vocation to receive future property and obligations. **2**° Certain rights, while susceptible of giving rise to an evaluation in monetary terms when violated, are nevertheless excluded from the patrimony. This is the case, in principle, for personality rights and human rights and freedoms. **3**° In the French Civilian tradition, the classical theory of the patrimony was articulated in the nineteenth century by Aubry and Rau in their celebrated *Cours de droit civil français d'après la méthode de Zachariæ*. Their work was seen as remarkable given that the theory was not explicit in the French Code Civil. They viewed the patrimony as an emanation of legal personality and characterized it as indivisible and non-transmissible *inter vivos*. The theory carries with it three corollaries: every person has a patrimony; every person has only one patrimony; a patrimony cannot exist without a person as its titulary. **4**° The theory of patrimony is one justification of the principle according to which the property of a person is the common pledge of his or her creditors (art.

2644 C.C.Q.). **5°** The *Civil Code of Québec* departs from this classical theory in that it allows that a patrimony be divided and appropriated to a purpose (art. 2 C.C.Q.). **6°** The *Civil Code of Québec* makes liberal use of the term *patrimony* in contrast with the *Civil Code of Lower Canada* in which occurrences were rare (e.g. arts. 325, 1701.1 C.C.L.C.). **7°** From the Latin *patrimonium* from *pater*: father.
See also object not in commerce, patrimonial right.
Fr. patrimoine.

PAULIAN *adj.*

See Paulian action, Paulian fraud. "In addition to the generic actions [...] the Code envisages several other similar recourses. Some of these resemble the oblique action, but the majority are Paulian in nature. Most often, these Paulian analogues are found in matrimonial or like contexts" (Brierley & Macdonald (eds.), *Quebec Civil Law*, n° 692, p. 597).
Fr. paulien.

PAULIAN ACTION

Action by which the creditor asks the court to declare inopposable to him or her injurious acts committed by the insolvent debtor in fraud of the creditor's rights.
Occ. Title preceding art. 1631 C.C.Q.; s. 93, *An Act respecting the implementation of the reform of the Civil Code*, S.Q. 1992, c. 57.
Obs. 1° Paulian actions are directed at juridical acts that render the debtor insolvent or that seek to have that effect, as well as at acts by which an insolvent debtor grants an unfair preference to another creditor (arts. 652, 1631 C.C.Q.). **2°** To be declared inopposable to third persons, the act must have been entered into with a fraudulent intent. If the act is made by gratuitous title, the act is deemed to be made with such intent (arts. 651, 1633 C.C.Q.). When the act is by onerous title, it is deemed a fraud only if the contracting party was aware of the insolvency of the debtor or knew that the act was rendering, or seeking to render, the debtor insolvent (art. 1632 C.C.Q.). Despite the text of article 2847 C.C.Q. and the use of term *deemed* at article 1632 C.C.Q., it has been decided that contrary evidence may be raised to overcome the presumption (*Banque nationale du Canada* v. *S.S. et C.B.*, [2000] R.J.Q. 658 (C.A.), p. 670, A. Forget, J.). **3°** The Paulian action must be brought within one year from the day on which the creditor had knowledge of the act that caused the damage (art. 1635 C.C.Q.). **4°** The codal regime respecting Paulian actions

is set forth at articles 1631 to 1636 C.C.Q. **5°** The English text of the Civil Code refers to the *Paulian action*, while the French text uses *action en inopposabilité*. **6°** This action is traditionally linked to the work of the Roman jurisconsult Paul (fl. c.190–c.AD 225).
Syn. action in inopposability, Paulian petition, revocatory action. **See also** oblique action, Paulian fraud.
Fr. action en inopposabilité+, action paulienne, action révocatoire.

PAULIAN FRAUD

Fraud consisting of acts committed by a debtor who, knowingly, either provokes or aggravates his or her own insolvency to the detriment of the creditors.
Obs. 1° When a creditor suffers a prejudice from a Paulian fraud, he or she may obtain a declaration that the act may not be set up against him (art. 1631 C.C.Q.). **2°** To be declared inopposable, the act must have been entered into with a fraudulent intent. If the act is by gratuitous title, the act is deemed to be made with such intent (arts. 651, 1633 C.C.Q.). When the act is by onerous title, the intention is so deemed only if the contracting party was aware of the insolvency of the debtor or knew that the act was rendering, or seeking to render, the debtor insolvent (art. 1632 C.C.Q.). Despite the text of article 2847 C.C.Q. and the use of term *deemed* at article 1632 C.C.Q., however, it has been decided that contrary evidence could be raised to overcome the presumption (*Banque nationale du Canada* v. *S.S. et C.B.*, [2000] R.J.Q. 658 (C.A.), p. 670, A. Forget, J.). **3°** The expression *Paulian fraud* is traditionally linked to the work of the Roman jurisconsult Paul (fl. c.190–c.AD 225).
See also concealment, Paulian action.
Fr. fraude paulienne.

PAULIAN PETITION

Syn. Paulian action. "The Paulian Petition can be justified by the intention on the part of the debtor to prejudice and default its future creditors. The doctrine and the jurisprudence permit this action to a creditor even posterior to the fraud" (Solomon, (1977) 37 *R. du B.* 519, p. 522).
Fr. action en inopposabilité+, action paulienne, action révocatoire.

PAY *v.*

To effect a payment. "Though the debtor may have paid in error, in this sense that he may not have known that the contract was

annulable at the time of the payment, still he did not pay a debt believing mistakenly that he owed it when he did not" (Nicholls, in *Livre-Souvenir*, 271, pp. 315-316).
Occ. Arts. 812, 1656, 2620 C.C.Q.; arts. 1118, 1140 C.C.L.C.
Syn. acquit[1], settle[1].
Fr. acquitter, payer[+], régler.

PAYABLE (ON DEMAND)

Syn. exigible.
Fr. exigible.

PAYEE *n.*

Syn. *accipiens.*
Fr. *accipiens*[+], payé, *recipiens.*

PAYER *n.*

Syn. *solvens.*
See also payee.
Fr. payeur, *solvens*[+].

PAYMENT *n.*

1. Performance of an obligation. For example, the buyer who pays the price and the vendor who delivers the thing sold both effect payment. "Every payment presupposes the existence of a debt. It is therefore normal that anyone who has paid by error without being required to do so be able to demand repayment of that money or recovery of the object of the payment" (C.C.R.O., *Commentaries*, vol. II, t. 2, p. 627). *Payment of a debt.*
Occ. Title preceding arts. 1553, 1569 C.C.Q.; arts. 1904, 2386 C.C.Q.; art. 1139 C.C.L.C.
Obs. 1° The term *payment*, in legal parlance, has a wider meaning than in ordinary usage, where it is generally used to designate the performance of an obligation to pay a sum of money (art. 1553 C.C.Q.). 2° Payment constitutes a voluntary performance of an obligation, whatever the object of that obligation may be. 3° The codal regime respecting payment is set forth at arts. 1553 to 1568 C.C.Q.
Syn. acquittance[2]. **See also** giving in payment, imputation of payment, indication of payment, indivisibility of payment, modality of payment, title of payment.
Fr. acquittement, paiement[1+], payement, règlement.

2. Act of remitting a sum of money. *Payment of interests*; *payment of an indemnity*; *payment of an annuity.*
Occ. Art. 1877 para. 5 C.C.L.C.
Fr. paiement[2], versement[+].

PAYMENT IN ADVANCE

Syn. advance payment. "From the standpoint of the lender, the so-called payment in advance reduces somewhat the risk of ultimate recovery of the principal, while exhibiting a lower rate for the same return in interest; and from the standpoint of the borrower, there is a loss of the use of the interest so deducted" (*Asconi Building* v. *Vocisano*, [1947] S.C.R. 358, p. 368, I.C. Rand, J.).
Obs. See article 1620 C.C.L.C.
Fr. paiement anticipé, paiement par anticipation[+].

PAYMENT IN CASH

Payment effected in a currency constituting legal tender.
Obs. Payment in cash is a form of cash payment[2].
Syn. cash payment[1], payment in *specie*. **See also** payment in kind[2], pecuniary obligation.
Fr. paiement en espèces.

PAYMENT IN KIND

1. Syn. specific performance.
Occ. Art. 694 para. 2 C.C.Q.
Fr. exécution directe, exécution en nature[+], paiement en nature[1].

2. Payment whose object is something other than a sum of money. For example, the delivery of a thing sold, the performance of promised work.
Occ. Art. 694 C.C.Q.
See also obligation in kind, payment in cash.
Fr. paiement en nature[2].

PAYMENT *IN SPECIE* (Latin)

Syn. payment in cash.
Fr. paiement en espèces.

PAYMENT OF A THING NOT DUE

Payment of that which is not owed. "[...] if there is bad faith on the part of one who receives payment of a thing not due, he is bound to make restitution not only of the capital, but also of the interest and fruits *from the day of the payment*" (Litvinoff, in *Treatise*, vol. 7, Book 2, n° 257, pp. 484-485).
Obs. 1° A person who makes a payment in error or to avoid harm while protesting that the payment is not due may obtain the restitution thereof (arts. 1491, 1492, 1554, 1699 to 1706 C.C.Q.). The error may bear upon the existence of the debt, the identity of the creditor or the identity of the debtor. 2° Given that

the performance of a natural obligation constitutes a valid payment, it does not give rise to restitution even though it is not susceptible of forced performance, (art. 1554 C.C.Q.).
See also management of the business of another, reception of a thing not due, recovery of a thing not due, restitution of a thing not due.
Fr. paiement de l'indu[+], paiement indu.

PAYMENT ON ACCOUNT

Syn. deposit[2]. "At first glance, there seems to be no doubt that Viger was enriched, since it obtained for the price of a vacant lot a lot improved to its specifications, without paying a cent for the levelling. It was therefore enriched by the value of the work necessary to improve the lot. The value of this enrichment greatly exceeds Giguère's claim: even if Giguère's action is maintained, Viger remains enriched by the fact that Giguère received a payment on account of $75,000 and is only suing for a balance which is less than the value of the improvements" (*Lauréat Giguère Inc.* v. *Cie. Immobilière Viger*, [1977] 2 S.C.R. 67, p. 78, J. Beetz, J.).
Occ. Ss. 150.24, 150.32, *Consumer Protection Act*, R.S.Q. c. P-40.1.
Fr. acompte.

PAYMENT WITH (A) TERM

Payment required to be made at a moment subsequent to the creation of an obligation.
See also cash payment[2], deferred payment, term[1].
Fr. paiement à terme.

PAYMENT WITH SUBROGATION

Juridical operation by which a claim paid by a third person or with money borrowed from a third person, is transferred with all its accessories to such persons. "One of the most important mechanisms of payment regulated by the Code is payment with subrogation [...]" (Brierley & Macdonald (eds.), *Quebec Civil Law*, n° 544, p. 493).
Occ. Title preceding art. 1154 C.C.L.C.
See also conventional subrogation, legal subrogation, personal subrogation.
Fr. paiement avec subrogation.

PECUNIARY *adj.*

See pecuniary obligation.
Fr. pécuniaire.

PECUNIARY DAMAGE

Syn. material damage. "[...] pecuniary damage can take the form of loss of employment, loss of clientele, general business losses, loss of income and even potential loss of future income where the defamation diminished the plaintiff's future employment opportunities" (Jukier, (1989) 49 *R. du B.* 3, p. 9).
Obs. Since the terms *damage* and *loss* are synonymous, the expression *pecuniary loss* may also be used.
Fr. perte économique, préjudice économique, préjudice matériel[+], préjudice pécuniaire.

PECUNIARY OBLIGATION

Obligation to do which consists of the payment of a sum of money. For example, the obligation of a purchaser to pay the price, of a lessee to pay the rent, or of an employer to pay a salary.
Occ. S. 127, *An Act respecting the implementation of the reform of the Civil Code*, S.Q. 1992, c. 57.
Obs. 1° A distinction is made between pecuniary obligations and obligations in kind. The latter are understood to include all obligations to do and not to do, except the payment of a sum of money. **2°** Specific performance of a pecuniary obligation is available in the event of non-performance. **3°** Delay in the performance of a pecuniary obligation gives rise to moratory damages, which consist of payment of interest on the amount due (art. 1617 C.C.Q.). **4°** Pecuniary obligations bear, in principle, on a designated amount of money (monetary nominalism), as opposed to the required number of monetary units to which correspond a given purchasing power (monetary valorism). Accordingly, pecuniary obligations are sensitive to fluctuations in the value of currency. **5°** The debtor of a pecuniary obligation may not invoke superior force to justify the non-performance of his or her obligation, since it is an obligation of warranty.
Syn. monetary obligation. **See also** obligation in kind, obligation not to do, obligation to do, performance by equivalence, specific performance.
Fr. obligation de somme d'argent, obligation monétaire, obligation pécuniaire[+].

PENAL *adj.*

See penal clause, penal liability.
Fr. pénal.

PENAL CLAUSE

1. Accessory clause in a contract that establishes in advance the amount of the indemnity to be paid, as a lump sum, in case of non-performance or delayed performance of an obligation. "The law allows two types of penal clause: those providing for liquidated damages for failure of performance and those providing a penalty for a simple delay. In the first case the creditor must choose between performance and the penalty. In the second case such a choice is not imposed upon him; the creditor can obtain both performance, or the damages substituted for it, and the penalty stipulated for the delay" (*Desrosiers and Dufour* v. *Gauthier*, [1978] 1 S.C.R. 308, p. 313, L.-P. de Grandpré, J.).
Occ. Arts. 758, 1216, 1622 to 1625, 2936 C.C.Q.; arts. 1131, 1132 C.C.L.C.
Obs. 1° The penalty may be reduced if it is abusive or if the obligation has been partially performed to the benefit of the creditor (art. 1623 C.C.Q.). In matters relating to leases of dwellings, clauses stipulating penalties in an amount exceeding the damage actually suffered are considered abusive (art. 1901 C.C.Q.). **2°** In matters relating to testamentary successions, disinheritance taking the form of a penal clause and clauses designed to prevent heirs and legatees from contesting the validity of a will are treated as null (art. 758 C.C.Q.). Article 1216 C.C.Q. provides that the penal clause "tending to prevent a person whose property is inalienable from contesting the validity of the stipulation of inalienability or from applying for authorization to transfer the property is deemed unwritten".
See also abusive clause, comminatory clause, contractual damages[2], fixed price, giving in payment clause[1], limitation of liability clause, withdrawal option.
Fr. clause de dommages-intérêts libératoires, clause d'indemnisation forfaitaire, clause pénale[1+].

2. Syn. comminatory clause.
Occ. Ss. 503, 504, *An Act respecting health services and social services*, R.S.Q. c. S-4.2; s. 3.1, *An Act respecting health services and social services for Cree Native persons*, R.S.Q. c. S-5.
Fr. clause comminatoire[+], clause pénale[2].

PENAL LIABILITY

Juridical responsibility entailing the imposition of a punishment for an act considered detrimental to society. "The damage fortuitously suffered by someone as a result of someone else's activity was left on its first bearer, because no good reason could be discovered for shifting the loss. One may wonder whether this was a justifiable policy or whether it was not the result of a confusion between moral and penal liabilities, on the one hand, and civil liability, on the other" (Tunc, in *Int. Enc. Comp. L.*, vol. XI, p. 1-112).
See also civil liability, juridical liability.
Fr. responsabilité pénale.

PENALTY *n.*

Sanction provided in a contract.
Occ. Arts. 1107, 1622, 1901 C.C.Q.; s. 8(1), *Interest Act*, R.S.C. 1985, c. I-15.
Obs. 1° The penalty is generally provided in a penal or comminatory clause, which applies when a party fails, either in whole or in part, to perform his or her obligation in a timely fashion. **2°** Penalty may be reduced by the court if it is abusive (art. 1623 C.C.Q.). In the case of lease of dwelling, the clause that provides for a penalty in an amount exceeding the value of the damage actually suffered by the lessor is abusive (art. 1901 C.C.Q.).
See also earnest, penal clause[1], penalty of withdrawal, private law penalty.
Fr. pénalité[+], peine.

PENALTY OF WITHDRAWAL

Sum of money determined by contract that must be paid by a contracting party exercising a withdrawal option.
See also earnest, stipulation as to earnest.
Fr. dédit[2].

PENDENTE CONDITIONE
adv.ph. (Latin)

Period during which the condition is pending. "The debtor is also bound, in principle, to make restitution of the fruits which he has collected *pendente conditione*" (Aubry & Rau, *Civil Law*, vol. 1, n° 302, p. 73).
See also pending condition.
Fr. *pendente conditione*.

PENDING CONDITION

Condition[1] considered at a moment in time when it is not known whether or not it will be fulfilled.
Occ. Art. 963 C.C.L.C.
Obs. The uncertainty of an obligation that turns on a pending condition ends when the condition is fulfilled or when it fails.
See also failure of the condition, fulfilment of the condition, *pendente conditione*, retroactivity of the condition.
Fr. condition pendante.

PENITUS EXTRANEUS *nom.ph.* (Latin)

Third person who is a complete stranger to a contract inasmuch as he or she did not participate in its formation, either directly or through a representative, and inasmuch as he or she is neither a successor nor a creditor of either of the parties.
Obs. 1° The *penitus extraneus* (from the Latin: a complete stranger) may be described as absolute or complete, as opposed to the successor or the creditor who, while they are third persons, nonetheless have legal relations with a contracting party. **2**° This expression is more commonly used in the plural *penitus extranei*.
Fr. *penitus extraneus*.

PENSION *n.*

Syn. annuity[2].
Fr. rente[2].

PERFECT DELEGATION

Delegation that entails the discharge of the delegator in respect of his or her creditor. "Articles 1169, 1172, and 1173 [C.C.L.C.] deal with Delegation. It will be seen that these articles envisage chiefly the situation in which A, the debtor of C, arranges for B to undertake to pay C the debt owed by A. If C accepts and discharges A completely, then there is 'perfect' Delegation, and B is C's only debtor. If, on the other hand, C is happy to accept B as an additional debtor, but refuses to discharge A, then there is 'imperfect' Delegation, and C now has two debtors, A and B. C is in a position in either case to force B to pay" (Irving, (1963) 9 *McGill L.J.* 337, p. 348).
Obs. 1° Delegation is perfect when the delegatee accepts the delegate's undertaking and discharges the delegator of his or her obligations (art. 1668 C.C.Q.). **2**° Unlike imperfect delegation, perfect delegation effects novation.
See also imperfect delegation, indication of payment.
Fr. délégation parfaite.

PERFECT OBLIGATION

Rare. Syn. obligation[2].
See also imperfect obligation.
Fr. obligation[2+], obligation juridique[1], obligation parfaite, obligation personnelle.

PERFECT REPRESENTATION

Syn. representation.

Obs. The term *perfect representation*, meaning representation in the true sense of the word, is used only in contradistinction to the term *imperfect representation*.
Fr. représentation[+], représentation immédiate, représentation parfaite.

PERFECT SOLIDARITY

Syn. solidarity.
Obs. The expression *perfect solidarity*, meaning true solidarity with all its effects, is only used in contradistinction to the expression *imperfect solidarity*, a notion which, despite some apparent similarities, is in fact distinct from solidarity. The latter is more frequently referred to as *obligation in solidum*.
Fr. corréalité, solidarité[+], solidarité parfaite, solidité.

PERFORM *v.*

To effect an obligation[3]. "[to] refuse to perform a contractual obligation is at least as blameworthy as to be guilty of some negligent act or omission in the course of its performance" (*R.* v. *Canada Steamship Lines Ltd.*, [1950] S.C.R. 532, p. 570, J.R. Cartwright, J.).
Occ. Arts. 1591, 3113 C.C.Q.; arts. 1134, 1656.3 C.C.L.C.
Syn. execute, fulfil.
Fr. exécuter.

PERFORMANCE *n.*

Act by which a debtor furnishes to the creditor the prestation owed. "[...] French law starts from the premise that what the creditor expects from an obligation is its performance in kind (*exécution en nature*) and that the law will if necessary enforce that performance (*exécution forcée*)" (Nicholas, *Contract*, p. 216). *Performance of the undertaking*; *performance of the obligation*; *performance of the prestation*.
Occ. Arts. 1383, 1694, 2345 C.C.Q.; arts. 1203, 2693 C.C.L.C.
Obs. 1° An obligation must be performed in full, properly and without delay (art. 1590 C.C.Q.). **2**° When the debtor willingly supplies the prestation due, the performance is said to be *voluntary*. It is said to be *compulsory* when it is exacted from the debtor pursuant to a court order.
Syn. execution. **See also** compulsory execution, exception of non-performance, non-performance, payment[1], voluntary performance.
Fr. exécution.

PERFORMANCE BY EQUIVALENCE

Compulsory performance of an obligation whereby the creditor is presented with a sum of money that replaces performance of the prestation in kind.

Occ. Title preceding art. 1607 C.C.Q.

Obs. 1° The term *equivalence* means that the creditor does not receive the prestation due but instead receives a sum of money designed to indemnify the loss caused by failure to perform in kind. **2**° Performance is achieved by equivalence when specific performance has the result of physically constraining the debtor, thereby violating his or her freedom (art. 1601 C.C.Q.).

See also compulsory execution, damages, indemnity, reparation by equivalence, specific performance.

Fr. exécution par équivalent.

PERFORMANCE IN KIND

Syn. specific performance.

Fr. exécution directe, exécution en nature+, paiement en nature[1].

PERFORMANCE OF THE CONTRACT

See performance.

Fr. exécution du contrat.

PERIODICAL PAYMENT

Syn. periodic payment.

Occ. Art. 2367 C.C.Q.

Fr. paiement échelonné, paiement périodique+, versements.

PERIODIC DAMAGE

Damage that occurs at regular intervals. For example, recurrent floods resulting from an inadequate sewer system.

Obs. Since the terms *damage* and *injury* are synonymous, the expression *periodic injury* may also be used.

See also continuous damage, gradual damage, recurrent damage.

Fr. préjudice périodique.

PERIODIC PAYMENT

Payment effected over a period of time, at regular intervals.

Occ. Arts. 1534, 1570, 3160 C.C.Q.

Obs. In practice, *periodic payment* is more commonly used than *arrears* to designate the payment of the dues owed to the annuitant.

Syn. instalments, periodical payment. **See also** annuity, arrears[1], lump sum payment, monthly payment.

Fr. paiement échelonné, paiement périodique+, versements.

PERIOD OF GRACE

Syn. judicial term.

Occ. Arts. 1600, 1675 C.C.Q.

Fr. délai de grâce, terme de grâce, terme judiciaire+.

PERSON *n.*

Being or entity possessing juridical personality.

Occ. Arts. 3, 4 C.C.Q.; s. 3, *Charter of Human Rights and Freedoms*, R.S.Q. c. C-12; s. 61(16), *Interpretation Act*, R.S.Q. c. I-16.

Obs. 1° Article 1 of the Civil Code provides that "[e]very human being possesses juridical personality and has the full enjoyment of civil rights". **2**° Persons are subjects of rights. They are titularies of rights and obligations. **3**° Traditionally, the notions of *person* and *thing* are used as opposites. **4**° Two types of persons are distinguished by the Civil Code: physical persons (art. 1 C.C.Q.) and legal persons (art. 298 C.C.Q.). **5**° From the Latin *persona*: actor's mask, role, character (in theater).

Syn. juridical person. **See also** patrimony, subject of rights[1,2], subject of law[1], thing[1].

Fr. personne+, personne juridique.

PERSONAL *adj.*

See personal obligation, personal right, personal subrogation.

Fr. personnel.

PERSONAL ACT OR OMISSION

Act or omission of a person causing damage that may, in some circumstances, engage the liability of that person.

See also act of another, act of a thing, personal fault, personal liability[2].

Fr. fait personnel.

PERSONAL DAMAGE

Damage suffered by the person who seeks compensation.

Obs. 1° Personal damage may be damage suffered by either a mediate or immediate victim. **2**° Since the terms *damage* and *injury* are synonymous, the expression *personal injury* may also be used.

Fr. préjudice personnel.

PERSONAL FAULT

Civil fault committed by the person causing damage.
Occ. Art. 1732 C.C.Q.
Obs. Personal liability not only results from personal acts or omissions. It may also result from the act or omission of another or from damage caused by a thing where the personal fault reflects a failure in the obligation to take proper care of a person or a thing, as the case may be.
See also individual fault, personal act or omission, personal liability[2].
Fr. faute personnelle.

PERSONAL LIABILITY

1. Civil liability for which the debtor must answer with his or her own property. For example, a trustee's personal liability for unauthorized acts. "The recent Canadian experience had been that directors of insolvent corporations, especially independent directors not having a shareholder interest in the corporation of which they were directors, tended to abandon their posts in order to avoid incurring personal liability for matters such as unpaid wages, unpaid deductions at source and other statutory liabilities" (Goldstein, in *Meredith Lectures (1998-1999)*, 253, p. 269).
Occ. Art. 3116 C.C.Q.; s. 25, *An Act respecting industrial accidents and occupational diseases*, R.S.Q. c. A-3.001; s. 60(2), *Bills of Exchange Act*, R.S.C. 1985, c. B-4.
Obs. 1° Personal liability implies that the debtor is responsible for the debt on all his or her property, whether movable and immovable (arts. 2644, 2645 C.C.Q.). **2°** Personal liability may be contractual or extracontractual. It may be the result of the fault of a person acting in his or her own name, or of a person who, while acting for another, exceeds his or her powers (e.g. art. 1320 C.C.Q.). It may also result from the act or omission of another or from the damage caused by a thing.
See also liability for damage caused by another.
Fr. responsabilité personnelle[1].

2. Civil liability resulting from the personal act or omission of the author of the damage.
See also indirect liability, liability for damage caused by another, liability for damage caused by things, vicarious liability.
Fr. responsabilité du fait des personnes, responsabilité du fait personnel, responsabilité personnelle[2+].

PERSONAL OBLIGATION

Syn. obligation[2]. "The personal obligation, being the counterpart of the personal right, refers to an obligation or a duty a person owes to another person who holds the right in personam" (Levasseur, *Obligations*, p. 27.).
Obs. The expressions *personal obligation* or *ordinary obligation* are used in distinction to *real obligation*.
See also personal right, real obligation.
Fr. obligation[2+], obligation juridique[1], obligation parfaite, obligation personnelle.

PERSONAL RIGHT

Right of a patrimonial nature that permits its holder, the *creditor*, to claim the performance of a prestation from another person, the *debtor*. "[it] is commonly asserted that in an obligation the creditor enjoys a *personal* right, since it can be exercised only against a person, the debtor, as opposed to a *real* right, which is exercised against all" (Litvinoff, in *Treatise*, vol. 5, n° 1.5, p. 9).
Occ. Arts. 1936, 2925 C.C.Q.
Obs. 1° A personal right or claim is an obligation[2] understood from the point of view of the creditor, whereas a debt is an obligation[2] understood from the point of view of the debtor. **2°** In matters relating to patrimonial rights, personal rights are traditionally distinguished from real rights. **3°** Personal rights are not to be confused with personality rights or extrapatrimonial rights exclusively attached to the person.
Syn. claim, creance, credit[2], debt[2], *jus in personam*, obligation[4]. **See also** extrapatrimonial right, *jus ad rem*, obligation[3], real right.
Fr. créance, dette active, droit de créance, droit personnel[+], *jus in personam*, obligation[4].

PERSONAL SUBROGATION

Subrogation of one creditor for another in the same obligational relationship.
Obs. 1° In the theory of obligations, personal subrogation takes the form of payment with subrogation. Article 1651 C.C.Q. provides that a "person who pays in the place of a debtor may be subrogated to the rights of the creditor. He does not have more rights than the subrogating creditor". **2°** Personal subrogation may be legal or conventional. **3°** The codal regime respecting subrogation is set forth at articles 1651 to 1659 C.C.Q.
See also benefit of subrogation, conventional subrogation, legal subrogation.
Fr. subrogation personnelle.

PERSON INTERPOSED

Syn. interposed person.
Occ. Art. 774 C.C.L.C.
Fr. personne interposée.

PERSON REPRESENTED

Person in whose name and on whose behalf another person, the representative, performs a juridical act.
Occ. Art. 3116 C.C.Q.
See also mandator, representation, representative.
Fr. représenté.

PERSON REVENDICATING

Person who sues in revendication.
Fr. revendiquant.

PHYSICAL CUSTODY

Material custody founded on the control, supervision or direction of a person, thing or animal. For example, a thief has no right to the thing stolen, although he or she has the physical custody of it.
See also custody, *de facto* custody, legal custody[1].
Fr. garde matérielle[+], garde physique.

PLURAL *adj.*

See plural obligation.
Fr. plural.

PLURAL OBLIGATION

Syn. obligation with a complex modality.
Fr. obligation à modalité complexe[+], obligation plurale.

PLURILATERAL *adj.*

See plurilateral act.
Fr. plurilatéral.

PLURILATERAL ACT

Syn. multilateral act.
Fr. acte multilatéral[+], acte plurilatéral.

POLICY HOLDER

Syn. policy owner.
Fr. preneur[1+] (>), souscripteur (>).

POLICY OWNER

Person who subscribes to an insurance of persons contract for his or her own benefit or for the benefit of another person.
Syn. policy holder. **See also** client[1], insured.
Fr. preneur[1+] (>), souscripteur (>).

POLITICAL AND MORAL PUBLIC ORDER

Syn. political public order.
Fr. ordre public politique[+], ordre public politique et moral.

POLITICAL CAPACITY

Legal capacity in respect of political rights.
Obs. 1° Political capacity falls within the province of public law, more particularly within the ambit of laws that are constitutional or quasi-constitutional in character. It is generally but not exclusively associated with the status of citizen in a given territory.
2° See ss. 21 and 22, *Charter of Human Rights and Freedoms*, R.S.Q. c. C-12 and s. 3, *Canadian Charter of Rights and Freedoms*, R.S.C. 1985, App. II, n° 44.
See also civil capacity.
Fr. capacité politique.

POLITICAL PUBLIC ORDER

Public order governing the organization of the State and the structure of society.
Obs. Political public order serves to protect the common good, and all juridical acts that contravene it are absolutely null (art. 9 C.C.Q.).
Syn. political and moral public order. **See also** economic public order, general interest, moral public order.
Fr. ordre public politique[+], ordre public politique et moral.

PORTABLE *adj.*

Said of an obligation[2] the payment of which is to be made at the domicile of the creditor.
See also portable claim, portable debt, seekable.
Fr. portable.

PORTABLE CLAIM

Claim the payment of which must be made at the domicile of the creditor.
Syn. portable creance. **See also** portable debt, seekable claim.
Fr. créance portable.

231

PORTABLE CREANCE

Syn. portable claim.
Fr. créance portable.

PORTABLE DEBT

Debt[1] the payment of which must be made at the domicile of the creditor.
Obs. 1° As a general rule, a debt is seekable, unless it relates to the sale of individualized property, in which case the payment must be made where the property was when the obligation arose. **2°** The parties may also agree to another place for payment (art. 1566 C.C.Q.), or instead designate that the debt be portable.
See also portable claim, seekable debt.
Fr. dette portable.

PORTE-FORT n. (French)

1. Syn. promise of *porte-fort*.
Fr. porte-fort[1], promesse de porte-fort[+], promesse du fait d'autrui.

2. Party in a promise of *porte-fort* who promises that a third person will bind himself or herself towards the other party. "The *porte-fort* is someone who undertakes that a third party will do something. If the third party ratifies the promise [...], the *porte-fort* is released; if the third party does not ratify, the *porte-fort* must indemnify the promise" (Nicholas, *Contract*, p. 180).
Syn. promisor[3].
Fr. porte-fort[2+], promettant[3].

POSITIVE CONDITION

Condition[1] that is fulfilled by the occurrence of a contemplated event. For example, if a certain person is named to a particular position. "We are concerned here with the necessary occurrence of a positive condition within an express term, or fixed time. If that condition fails to occur within the agreed time it is then considered that the condition can no longer occur. Under the specific circumstances, a court should have no right to extend the express term and, thereby, make it possible for the condition to occur" (Levasseur, *Obligations*, p. 59).
See also negative condition.
Fr. condition positive.

POSITIVE LAW

Body of rules, that are in force, which regulate life in society at a given time. "[...] it is open to the parties to provide for whichever positive or national substantive law, that of Quebec or otherwise, will be applicable, or to allow the arbitrators to determine which such positive law is applicable [...]" (Brierley, (1987-88) 13 *Can. Bus. L.J.* 58, p. 62).
Obs. 1° According to the classical theory of legal positivism, the category of positive law is often opposed to an ideal law generally designated as *natural law*. **2°** Positive law is also distinguished from law that might be made in the future by means of the Latin expressions *lex lata* (e.g. edicted law[2]) and *lex ferenda* (e.g. law[2] that could be edicted), respectively. **3°** Positive law is often described as emanating from a competent state authority, even though the legislator does not have a monopoly on the production of legal rules.
See also equity[1], law[1], natural law.
Fr. droit positif.

POSSIBLE DAMAGE

Future damage the occurrence of which remains uncertain.
Obs. 1° Possible damage, unlike certain damage, is not susceptible of compensation since its uncertain character means that it cannot be the object of a liquidation (art. 1611 C.C.Q.). **2°** When the threat of damage is real, the eventual victim has sufficient interest to launch an action in order to stop it from coming about (e.g. injunction, art. 751 C.C.P.). **3°** Since the terms *damage* and *injury* are synonymous, the expression *possible injury* may also be used.
Syn. eventual damage, hypothetical loss. **See also** certain damage, future damage, loss of (a) chance, present damage.
Fr. préjudice éventuel[+], préjudice hypothétique.

POSSIBLE OBJECT

Prestation that, in fact, is susceptible of performance.
See also impossible object, licit object[2].
Fr. objet possible.

POST SECURITY (FOR) *v.*

(*Sec.*) Syn. stand as surety (for).
Fr. cautionner.

POTENTIAL RIGHT

Syn. mere expectancy.
Fr. droit virtuel, expectative, simple expectative[+].

POTESTATIVE *adj.*

Quality of that which depends on the will of a person.

Syn. facultative. **See also** potestative condition, purely potestative condition, simply potestative condition.

Fr. facultatif, potestatif+.

POTESTATIVE CONDITION

Condition[1] that depends, in whole or in part, on the will of one of the contracting parties. "The obligation arising from the unilateral promise is subject to a potestative condition. It is not, however, null, because the potestative condition is on the side of the beneficiary, the obligee, and only those potestative conditions on the side of the one who binds himself, the obligor, make the obligation null" (Litvinoff, in *Treatise*, vol. 7, Book 2, n° 98, pp. 178-179).

Obs. The purely potestative condition is to be distinguished from the simply potestative condition.

Syn. facultative condition. **See also** casual condition, mixed condition, purely potestative condition, simply potestative condition.

Fr. condition facultative, condition potestative+.

POWER *n.*

1. Legal prerogative exercised on behalf of and in the interest of another. For example, the powers of representation of the mandatary, the powers of administration of the administrator of the property of others. "[...] a person, when disposing of property in the gratuitous acts envisaged, may attribute to a specified person the power to appoint the real beneficiaries of the liberality" (Brierley, (1992) 95 *R. du N.* 131, p. 148).

Occ. Arts. 1308, 2136, 2145 C.C.Q.

Obs. 1° A distinction is drawn between the power, which is exercised on behalf of and in the interest of another person, and a right, which the holder exercises on his or her own behalf and, in general, in his or her own interest. **2°** The term *power* is also used, on occasion, to describe the prerogative of the holder of the real right to exercise it on his or her own behalf. This usage is discouraged by some who would prefer to limit use of the term to the field of administration of property of others. **3°** In this sense, the term *power* is often encountered in the plural.

See also right.

Fr. pouvoir[1].

2. Authorization to act for another person, for a group of persons or a mass of property without legal personality, or for a particular purpose.

Occ. Art. 2130 C.C.Q.

Obs. 1° The administrator may be authorized to act for a group of persons or a mass of property without legal personality. In the context of the foundation in trust and the social trust, the power of the trustee bears on a patrimony by appropriation to pursue a purpose of general interest. **2°** In this sense, the term *power* is used in the singular.

See also right.

Fr. pouvoir[2].

POWER OF ATTORNEY

1. Power of representation conferred by a mandate[1].

Occ. Art. 2130 C.C.Q.

Syn. conventional mandate, procuration[1].

Fr. mandat conventionnel, procuration[1+].

2. Writing attesting the power of representation conferred by a mandate. "[...] the constant jurisprudence which imposes upon the proponents of a will the obligation to prove lucid intervals by preponderance of evidence, when a prima facie case of incapacity has been established, applies not only in cases of wills, but also in cases of execution of other instruments, as for instance powers of attorney" (*McEwen* v. *Jenkins Estate*, [1958] S.C.R. 719, p. 729, R. Taschereau, J.).

Occ. Arts. 2130, 2176 C.C.Q.; art. 1220 (5) C.C.L.C.; art. 59 C.C.P.

Syn. procuration[2].

Fr. procuration[2].

POWER OF DISCERNMENT

See discernment.

Fr. faculté de discernement.

PRE-CONTRACT *n.*

Contract which serves as preliminary to another contract. For example, a promise to contract, a contract of negotiation. "The promise of a loan, for instance, in relation to the loan itself, operates a pre-contract (*avant-contrat*) that binds the promisor to execute the loan, and that is replaced by the loan proper at the moment of execution; only then does the borrower's obligation of returning the thing commence" (Litvinoff, in *Treatise*, vol. 6, n° 123, p. 205).

Syn. *avant-contrat.* **See also** promise to contract.

Fr. avant-contrat.

PRECONTRACTUAL *adj.*

See precontractual fault, precontractual liability, precontractual period.
Obs. The term is often used with a hyphen.
Fr. précontractuel, elle.

PRECONTRACTUAL FAULT

Civil fault consisting in the violation of an obligation related to the formation of a contract. For example, the fault of a person who undertakes negotiations with a view to contracting though he or she has no intention to contract.
Obs. A precontractual fault results in extracontractual liability.
Syn. *culpa in contrahendo*[2]. **See also** precontractual liability, precontractual obligation, precontractual period.
Fr. *culpa in contrahendo*[2], faute précontractuelle+.

PRECONTRACTUAL LIABILITY

Civil liability resulting from the violation of a precontractual obligation.
Obs. Precontractual liability is extracontractual in nature.
See also precontractual fault, precontractual obligation, precontractual period.
Fr. responsabilité précontractuelle.

PRECONTRACTUAL OBLIGATION

Obligation that binds the parties during contractual negotiations. For example, the precontractual obligation to inform.
Obs. The failure to perform a precontractual obligation gives rise to the application of the extracontractual regime of civil liability (art. 1457 C.C.Q.).
See also precontractual fault, precontractual liability, precontractual obligation to inform, precontractual period.
Fr. obligation précontractuelle.

PRECONTRACTUAL OBLIGATION TO INFORM

Obligation to inform that binds the parties during contractual negotiations.
Obs. 1° At the root of the precontractual obligation to inform lies the principle of good faith (see arts. 6, 7, 1375 C.C.Q.). This precontractual obligation requires that the parties share any information of decisive importance. **2°** The precontractual obligation to inform, which is of general application, is sometimes expressly provided by law, as in loan for use (art. 2321 C.C.Q.), simple loan (art. 2328 C.C.Q.) and insurance contracts (arts. 2408 to 2410 C.C.Q.). The *Consumer Protection Act* (R.S.Q. c. P-40.1) also provides expressly for this obligation in some matters, notably in contracts of credit (art. 71, *Consumer Protection Act*, R.S.Q. c. P-40.1) and in the repair of household appliances (ss. 183 and 184, *Consumer Protection Act*, R.S.Q. c. P-40.1). **3°** Fraudulent concealment differs from the violation of a precontractual obligation to inform. In order to prove fraudulent concealment, the deceived party must demonstrate that the silence of the other party was intended to induce error, since failure to perform the precontractual obligation to inform does not require fraudulent intention.
See also fraud[2], fraudulent concealment, good faith, obligation to inform, precontractual obligation.
Fr. obligation précontractuelle de renseignement(s).

PRECONTRACTUAL PERIOD

Period of time extending from the initial proposition to contract to the moment of formation of the contract.
Obs. The initial proposition to contract may take the form of a mere invitation to treat or a true offer in the sense of article 1388 C.C.Q.
Syn. precontractual stage. **See also** precontractual fault, precontractual liability, precontractual obligation.
Fr. période précontractuelle.

PRECONTRACTUAL STAGE

Syn. precontractual period. "To ensure that there prevails a measure of rectitude at the pre-contractual stage does not entail that juridical protection be granted to naïve or foolish negotiators. Only legitimate confidence which is deserving of serious consideration must be of concern to the law" (Legrand, in *Contemporary Law*, 197, p. 200).
Fr. période précontractuelle.

PREDECESSOR (IN TITLE)

Syn. author.
Occ. Art. 2912 C.C.Q.; s. 29(1), *Industrial Design Act*, R.S.C. 1985, c. I-9.
Fr. auteur+, prédécesseur en droit, prédécesseur en titre.

PREDETERMINED REPARATION

Reparation by means of a fixed amount, which does not necessarily correspond to the damage actually sustained.

Obs. Predetermined indemnity is an exception to the principle of full reparation.
See also full reparation, penal clause.
Fr. réparation forfaitaire.

PREEMPT *v.*

To exercise the right of preemption.
Fr. préempter.

PREEMPTION *n.*

Juridical act by which a person, the *preemptor*, exercises a right to purchase property[2] in preference to any other person.
Obs. From the Latin *præ*: before, and *emptio*: purchase.
See also preemption clause, right of preemption.
Fr. préemption.

PREEMPTION CLAUSE

Clause by which the owner of property[2] undertakes to offer it to a cocontractant in preference to others in the event he or she decides to sell it.
Obs. A preemption clause is a first refusal agreement whose object is a sale.
Syn. preemptive clause. **See also** approval clause, first refusal agreement, preemption, right of preemption.
Fr. clause de préemption.

PREEMPTIVE CLAUSE

Syn. preemption clause.
Fr. clause de préemption.

PREEMPTIVE RIGHT

1. Syn. right of preemption.
Occ. Arts. 1014, 1022 C.C.Q.
Obs. This term may also be rendered *preemptive right* as in article 456 C.C.Q.
Fr. droit de préemption[1].

2. Syn. subscription right.
Occ. Art. 456 C.C.Q.; ss. 28, 49, *Canada Business Corporation Act*, R.S.C. 1985, c. C-44.
Obs. This term may also be rendered *preemptive right* as in article 456 C.C.Q.
Fr. droit de préemption[2], droit préférentiel de souscription[+].

PREEMPTOR *n.*

Neol. Person who benefits from a right of preemption.
See also preemption.
Fr. préempteur.

PREFERENCE *n.*

Syn. right of preference[2]. *Legal cause of preference*.
Occ. Arts. 2646, 2647 C.C.Q.
Fr. droit de préférence[2+], préférence.

PREJUDICE *n.*

Syn. damage. "[...] under Quebec civil law, before the claim in damages will succeed, the claimant must not only establish that a prejudice has been suffered, but also that the said debtor was in default" (Kouri, (1971) 2 *R.D.U.S.* 1, p. 3).
Occ. Arts. 294, 1338, 1631, 1965 C.C.Q.; art. 75.2 C.C.P.
Fr. dommage, préjudice[+], tort[2].

PRELIMINARY AGREEMENT

Syn. agreement in principle.
Fr. accord de principe[+], accord préliminaire, protocole d'entente.

PREMIUM *n.*

Amount that the insured must pay to the insurer under the contract of insurance. "The information insurance applicants have to declare is to be relevant to the risk against which they are insured. Insurers must demonstrate, through the use of actuarial tables, reasonable grounds for using this type of information in the calculation of a particular premium" (Lemmens, (2002) 45 *McGill L.J.* 347, p. 401.).
Occ. Arts. 2389, 2425, 2427 C.C.Q.; arts. 2468, 2516, 2519 C.C.L.C.; ss. 17, 401, 406.2, *An Act respecting insurance*, R.S.Q. c. A-32; ss. 83, 102, *An Act respecting the distribution of financial products*, R.S.Q. c. D-9.2.
Obs. The amount of the premium is set according to the level of the risk insured.
See also insurance contract, insured, insurer.
Fr. prime.

PRESENT DAMAGE

Damage that has already occurred at the time the claim for compensation is made or, at the latest, at the time the liability is assessed.
Obs. Since the terms *damage* and *injury* are synonymous, the expression *present injury* may also be used.
See also certain damage, future damage, possible damage.
Fr. préjudice actuel.

PRESENT RIGHT

Right that currently exists. For example, the right of an heir at the moment of death of the *de cujus*.

Obs. A present right can be perfect, as in the case of a definitive right, or imperfect, as in the case of an eventual right[1] and a conditional right[2].

See also definitive right, eventual right[1], mere expectancy.

Fr. droit actuel.

PRESTATION *n.*

That to which the debtor is obliged. "In relation to contract the best established use of the word [*cause*] seems to be in connection with the innominate real contracts (*do ut des*, etc.) in which the prestation on one side is represented as the cause of the obligation on the other" (Lee, (1915-16) 25 *Yale L.J.* 536, p. 538).

Occ. Arts. 1371, 1373, 1374 C.C.Q.

Obs. 1° The prestation is the object of an obligation, which may be an obligation to do or not to do (art. 1373 C.C.Q.). **2**° In bilateral contracts, the cause of the obligation of one party is the prestation of the other. For example, in a contract of lease, the obligation to provide for the peaceful enjoyment of the thing has as its cause the rent. **3**° An illicit prestation may result in the nullity of the obligation of which it is the object. It may also entail the nullity of the contract if it is its principal prestation (art. 1438 C.C.Q.). For example, a procreation or gestation agreement is null, as is its principal prestation, i.e. the obligation to bring the foetus to term (art. 541 C.C.Q.). **4**° The nature of nullity is determined by whether a general or an individual interest is protected. In the first instance, the contract is absolutely null (art. 1417 C.C.Q.), while in the second, it is relatively null (art. 1419 C.C.Q.). **5**° From the Latin *præstare*: to perform, to furnish.

Syn. object of the obligation, thing[2]. **See also** object of the contract, object of the prestation, payment[1].

Fr. chose[2], objet de l'obligation, prestation+.

PRESTATOR *n.*

Person who performs a prestation.

See also debtor.

Fr. prestataire.

PRESUMPTION *n.*

Inference that the law or court draws from a known fact for the purpose of establishing an unknown fact. For example, the presumption of good faith of article 2805 C.C.Q. "A presumption is an inference of fact which the law or the court draws from a known fact" (Ducharme, in *Essays on the Civil Codes*, 75, p. 81).

Occ. Arts. 525, 1729, 2811, 2846 C.C.Q.

Obs. 1° Generally, the recourse to presumption is used in cases which the direct proof of a litigious fact is difficult to make. The presumption allows one to infer a litigious fact from another, or many other facts, that can be proved directly. **2**° The presumption constitutes, along with written proof, oral testimony, admission and presentation of a material element of evidence, one of the five types of evidence recognized by the *Civil Code of Québec*. **3**° There are two types of presumptions: legal presumptions, which are established by law, and presumptions of fact, which are left to the discretion of the courts (art. 2849 C.C.Q.). **4**° It is provided for in article 2847 C.C.Q. that a legal presumption relating to *deemed facts* is absolute and irrebutable, whereas a legal presumption concerning *presumed facts* is simple and rebuttable by evidence on the contrary. However, despite the use of the term *deemed* at article 1632 C.C.Q., it has been decided that contrary evidence could be raised to overcome the presumption (*Banque nationale du Canada* v. *S.S. et C.B.*, [2000] R.J.Q. 658 (C.A.), p. 670, A. Forget, J.). **5**° The codal regime respecting presumptions is set forth at articles 2846 to 2849 C.C.Q.

Fr. présomption.

PRÊTE-NOM *n.* (French)

1. Syn. undisclosed mandatary. "[...] a person wishes to conceal his identity or his interest in a particular transaction. He therefore employs a *prête-nom* – a person interposed – to carry out the transaction on his behalf. The *prête-nom* usually executes a counter-letter recognizing the principal's interest" (D'Angelo, (1986) 32 *Loy. L. Rev.* 129, p. 163).

Fr. prête-nom[1].

2. Syn. contract of *prête-nom*.

Fr. contrat de prête-nom+, mandat clandestin, mandat dissimulé, prête-nom[2].

PRETIUM AFFECTIONIS
nom.ph. (Latin)

Damages granted as compensation for injury to feelings.

Obs. Translated literally, the expression *pretium affectionis* means "price of affection".

See also injury to feelings, mediate victim, *pretium doloris, solatium doloris*.

Fr. *pretium affectionis*.

PRETIUM DOLORIS *nom.ph.* (Latin)

Damages granted as compensation for pain and suffering.

Obs. 1° The action in payment of *pretium doloris* may be transmitted to one's heirs, who may therefore seek reparation for the damage sustained by the *de cujus* until the time of death (arts. 625 and 1610 C.C.Q.). **2°** Literally translated, the expression *pretium doloris* means "price of pain".

See also injury to feelings, moral damages, *pretium affectionis, solatium doloris.*

Fr. *pretium doloris.*

PRICE *n.*

Counterprestation, generally in money, for a prestation in kind furnished under an onerous contract. "The principal obligation of a buyer is to pay the price (C.C.[L.C.] 1532) [...]" (*Leo Perrault Ltée* v. *Tessier*, [1958] S.C.R. 698, p. 702, D.C. Abbott, J.). *Current price.*

Occ. Arts. 1708, 1709, 1711 C.C.Q.; art. 1472 C.C.L.C.; s. 223, *Consumer Protection Act*, R.S.Q. c. P-40.1.

Obs. 1° The price is generally a sum of money. It may also, however, be paid by way of prestation in kind such as lodging, heating, lighting or food. These prestations in kind may either be due in addition to the payment of a sum of money or they may constitute the price in and of themselves. **2°** In a contract of sale, the price must necessarily consist of a sum of money, according to the terms of article 1708 C.C.Q., otherwise the contract will be described as an *exchange*, a *giving in payment* or an *innominate contract.* **3°** For certain nominate contracts, the term *price* is replaced by more specific terms. By way of example, the price is called *rent* in a contract of lease, *remuneration* or *salary* in a contract of employment, *honorarium* or *fees* in a contract for services and *premium* or *assessment* in a contract of insurance.

See also commission, contract for (of) services, contract of carriage, contract of enterprise, freight[1,2], premium, remuneration, rent, salary, sale.

Fr. prix.

PRINCIPAL *adj.*

Character of that which, in a relation of dependence, is preponderant to another. For example, a principal real right. "What is effected is a transfer by law of the property in the accessory to the owner of the principal thing or property, a transfer based upon the fact that the two things, by the unity, constitute a new whole" (*Dulac* v. *Nadeau*, [1953] 1 S.C.R. 164, p. 183, I.C. Rand, J.).

Occ. Arts. 1134, 1545, 1892, 1940, 2336, 2344, 2356, 3074, 3121, 3139 C.C.Q.; ss. 16, 206, *Consumer Protection Act*, R.S.Q. c. P-40.1.

Obs. There is a principal obligation in every contract. For example, the obligation to advise is generally the principal obligation of a contract concluded between a notary and his or her client.

See also accessory.

Fr. principal.

PRINCIPAL *n.*

1. That which, in a relation of dependence, is preponderant to another. "Things may, without losing their individuality, exist in a relationship of coordination with other things, as is the case of the forks and spoons of a dining set, or in a relationship of subordination, as in the keys to the doors of a house. In the second relationship, the subordinate thing is called an accessory and the thing to which it is subordinate is called principal" (Yiannopoulos, in *Treatise*, vol. 2, n° 34, p. 59).

Occ. Art. 433 C.C.L.C.

Obs. 1° As a general rule, the accessory is subject to the same legal regime as the principal (*accessorium sequitur principale*). Characterization of the juridical nature of the accessory may, for example, be dictated by that of the principal (e.g. movables that are immobilized) or the accessory may be subject to the same legal rules as the principal (e.g. the obligation to deliver all the accessories of the property sold). **2°** In the relationship between accessory and principal, the very existence of the accessory may depend upon the principal (e.g. a tree that periodically produces fruit), or the principal may be serviced by the accessory (e.g. the obligation to which a hypothec is attached). **3°** From the Latin *principalis* (from *princeps*: first).

See also accessory, doctrine of accession.

Fr. principal[1].

2. Syn. capital. "The guarantor may, on default in respect of interest, enforce his hypothec for the principal in the usual way by obtaining judgment and proceeding to execution [...]" (*Corporation of the City of Three Rivers* v. *Sun Trust Co.*, [1923] S.C.R. 496, p. 498, L.P. Duff, J.).

Fr. capital+, principal[2].

3. Person who charges another person under his or her direction with the performance of a specific duty.

Occ. Art. 1463 C.C.Q.

Obs. 1° The principal is liable for the damage caused by his or her agent or servant in the performance of the latter's functions (art. 1463 C.C.Q.). **2°** The term *principal* is used in a comparable sense to the meaning given to the expression *employer and masters* in article 1054 para. 7 C.C.L.C. While the term *principal* has a distinct meaning from that usually given to the term *employer*, it is true that the employer remains the archetypical principal in connection with the law of civil liability. The status of employer depends on the existence of a contract of employment, whereas the status of principal depends on the notion of *subordination*, which may exist in the absence of a contract of employment. **3°** The use of the terms *principal, agent* and *servants* in article 1463 C.C.Q. as equivalents of *commettant* and *préposés* should not be taken as a reference to the law of mandate or to the Common law doctrine of agency.
Syn. committent. **See also** habitual employer, liability of the principal, subordination (relationship of), temporary employer.
Fr. commettant.

4. Person for whom, in the context of the management of the business of another, the management is carried out. "Broadly speaking there is a *gestion d'affaires* or a quasi-contract of *negotiorum gestio* whenever a person, *le gérant d'affaire* or the *gestor*, performs an act on behalf of and in the interest of another, *le maître de l'affaire* or the principal, without that other's authority" (Smith, (1974) 52 *Can. Bar Rev.* 1, p. 11).
Occ. Arts. 1482 to 1490 C.C.Q.
See also manager.
Fr. géré[+], maître de l'affaire.

PRINCIPAL CONSIDERATION

Syn. cause[2]. "As for the error concerning the building's failure to comply with the regulations, this cannot have been for plaintiffs a principal consideration for making the contract, as required by art. 992 C.C.[L.C.]. In fact, at the time of the sale this lack of compliance entailed no troublesome consequences or constraints for the purchasers" (*Bertrand v. Racicot*, [1979] 1 S.C.R. 441, p. 473, Y. Pratte, J.).
Occ. Art. 992 C.C.L.C.
Fr. cause[2+], cause concrète, cause du contrat, cause impulsive et déterminante, cause subjective, considération[2], considération principale, mobile, motif.

PRINCIPAL CONTRACT

Contract that exists independently of any other contract, as opposed to an accessory contract. "[...] an arbitration agreement contained in another contract is 'considered' to be an agreement separate from the other clauses of that contract such that the finding by the arbitrators that the 'principal' contract is null does not entail, by law, the nullity of the arbitration agreement itself (art. 1926.5 C.C.[L.C.])" (Brierley, (1987-88) 13 *Can. Bus. L.J.* 58, p. 62).
Occ. Arts. 2394, 3121 C.C.Q.; ss. 206, 212, *Consumer Protection Act*, R.S.Q. c. P-40.1.
See also accessory contract, principal.
Fr. contrat principal.

PRINCIPAL FRAUD

Fraud that has induced a person to bind oneself and without which he or she would never have done so.
Obs. 1° While article 993 C.C.L.C. only recognized that fraud inducing someone to enter into a contract could lead to an error vitiating consent, article 1401 C.C.Q. recognizes that fraud inducing a party to contract under more onerous terms than would otherwise have been accepted is capable of provoking an error vitiating consent. This solution, inspired by scholarly writing and jurisprudence, is based on a distinction between principal fraud – where the party would not have entered into the juridical act – and incidental fraud – where the party would have entered into the juridical act under different terms. **2°** The rights of the victim of fraud are the same, since article 1407 C.C.Q. makes no reference to the distinction between principal and incidental fraud. Therefore, all victims may demand annulment, reduction of the obligation or even claim damages.
See also incidental fraud.
Fr. dol principal.

PRINCIPAL MANDATARY

Syn. sub-mandator.
Fr. mandataire principal, sous-mandant[+].

PRINCIPAL VICTIM

Syn. immediate victim.
Fr. victime immédiate, victime initiale[+], victime principale.

PRINCIPAL REAL RIGHT

Real right which, in contrast to the accessory real right, has an autonomous existence as a patrimonial right. "[Real rights] are also sometimes termed principal real rights, in order to distinguish them from another category, that conventionally known as accessory real rights, which function as forms of security to ensure the performance of obligations" (Brierley & Macdonald (eds.), *Quebec Civil Law*, n° 278, p. 287).

Obs. 1° Within the category of real rights, a distinction is generally made between principal real rights and accessory real rights. **2°** Ownership and its dismemberments are principal real rights. They may be the object of special modalities (e.g. co-ownership, co-emphyteusis). **3°** The expression *real right* is often used to designate principal real rights (see, however, art. 2660 C.C.Q.).

See also accessory real right, real right.

Fr. droit réel principal.

PRINCIPLE *n.*

1. Basis of a legal rule. "It is a familiar principle that neglect may, in law, be considered a fault only if it corresponds with a duty to act" (*Canadian National Railways Co.* v. *Lepage*, [1927] S.C.R. 575, pp. 578-579, T. Rinfret, J.).

Syn. juridical principle, legal principle. **See also** general principles of law.

Fr. principe[1+], principe juridique.

2. Legal rule[1] considered as original, from which other rules, which are more specific, may derogate. "Consequently, those of the above-cited cases where the court refused to grant retroactive effect or recognize vested rights are also illustrations of the principle of immediate prospective application of new statutes" (Côté, *Interpretation of Legislation*, p. 133).

Obs. 1° A rule of law that contains a principle is applicable when no exception is applicable. **2°** Unlike the exception, which must be applied strictly, the principle is of general application.

Fr. principe[2].

PRINCIPLE OF THE RELATIVITY OF CONTRACT

See relativity of contract.

Fr. principe de l'effet relatif des contrats.

PRINCIPLES *pl.n.*

Body of legal rules. "The judges of Quebec, as of other civil law countries, are expected to carry the principles enunciated by the civil code to their ultimate logical consequences. Note, I say, the principles – not the principle – because the code must be construed and taken as a whole, and quite often it becomes necessary to restrict the operation of one principle in order to admit of the proper applica-

tion of another" (Anglin, (1923) 1 *Can. Bar Rev.* 33, p. 39).

Occ. Art. 429 C.C.L.C.

See also general principles of law.

Fr. principes.

PRIVATE LAW

Corpus of legal rules applicable to the relations between subjects of law when understood to be acting *qua* individuals. *Quebec private law.*

Obs. 1° It is generally accepted that private law is grounded in the protection of individual rights and interests. According to this perspective, subjects of law acting *qua* individual may be physical persons, groups and legal persons established for a private interest. **2°** The distinction between private and public law has been subject to criticism because it is often difficult to establish. It nevertheless represents a *summa divisio* of the law, which is understood to encompass all legal rules. **3°** The historical development of Quebec law, means that this distinction between public and private law also serves, among other things, to determine which corpus of general law is applicable to a given legal relationship: the civil law in private law matters, the common law in public law matters. **4°** In certain cases, rules of private law can regulate relations between individuals and legal persons in the public interest by the effect of a rule of public law (see arts. 300 and 1376 C.C.Q.). **5°** Private law is generally thought to be comprised of civil law, commercial law, and in some respects, civil procedure.

Syn. civil law[2]. **See also** civil law[1], general law, public law.

Fr. droit civil[2], droit privé[1+].

PRIVATE LAW PENALTY

Neol. Civil sanction the purpose of which is to punish the wrongdoer and to dissuade him or her from adopting a similar line of conduct. For example, punitive damages awarded in cases of extracontractual liability.

Obs. 1° The private law penalty in its various forms is to be distinguished from awards of compensatory damages, which aim, in principle, to redress the harm suffered. The private law penalty may be viewed as an exception to the principle of corrective justice which grounds the regime for full reparation for contractual and extracontractual civil liability. **2°** As an example of a private law penalty, punitive damages are only awarded in those cases provided for by law (art. 1621 C.C.Q.). For example, the victim of an illicit and intentional infringement of a right or freedom rec-

ognized by the *Charter of Human Rights and Freedoms* (R.S.Q. c. C-12, s. 49 para. 2) may petition for punitive damages. **3°** Moral damages are, in theory, of a compensatory nature. Some argue that, by reason of the difficulty of justifying them under the principle of *restitutio in integrum*, moral damages inevitably partake of a private law penalty. It should be noted, however, that in contrast to punitive damages, moral damages do not have this punitive or dissuasive function as their principal attribute. **4°** In contractual matters, the penal or comminatory clause is also referred to as a *penalty*.
See also fault[1], full reparation, moral damages, penal clause[1], penalty, punitive damages.
Fr. peine privée.

PRIVATE LAW RIGHT

Right which one subject of law acting *qua* individual may invoke against another. For example, the right of ownership, a personal right, a personality right.
Obs. A distinction may be drawn between private law rights and public law rights. Within the category of "subjective rights", the division between private law rights and public law rights is of limited practical consequence, in particular because the State itself is often holder of private law rights as they are traditionally understood. It is therefore difficult to establish an unequivocal distinction between the two categories of rights, just as it is difficult to attribute particular characteristics to each of them.
See also public law right.
Fr. droit privé[2].

PRIVATE WRITING

Writing that establishes a juridical act, signed by the interested parties, and which is drafted without the intervention of a public officer. For example, a holograph will. "Private writings that purport to establish legal rights or duties form a third category of writings that may be used in evidence" (Ducharme, in *Essays on the Civil Codes*, 75, p. 80).
Occ. Arts. 1327, 1655, 2823, 2826 C.C.Q.; arts. 776, 1221 C.C.L.C.; art. 89 C.C.P.
Obs. The notion of *private writing* is closely associated with the codal regime related to evidence (see arts. 2803 *et seq.* C.C.Q.).
Syn. act under private signature, act under private writing, deed under private writing.
See also authentic act, notarial act, semi-authentic act.
Fr. acte sous seing privé.

PROBATIVE FORM

Syn. evidentiary formality.
Fr. formalité *ad probationem*, formalité probatoire[+], forme probante, forme probatoire.

PROBATORY FORM

Syn. evidentiary formality.
Fr. formalité *ad probationem*, formalité probatoire[+], forme probante, forme probatoire.

PROBATORY FORMALITY

Syn. evidentiary formality.
Fr. formalité *ad probationem*, formalité probatoire[+], forme probante, forme probatoire.

PROCURATION *n.*

1. Syn. power of attorney[1].
Obs. From the Latin *procuratio* (from *procuratum*, supine of *procurare*: to take care of, to attend, to manage): administration, management, care.
Fr. mandat conventionnel, procuration[1+].

2. Syn. power of attorney[2]. "Many authentic acts have doubtless been executed on the faith of it by procuration not so evidenced" (*Sanscartier* v. *Robin*, (1919) 58 S.C.R. 96, p. 102, F.A. Anglin, J.).
Occ. Art. 1756 C.C.L.C.
Fr. procuration[2].

PRODUCT LIABILITY

Civil liability resulting from a safety defect in the design, manufacturing, storage or presentation of a movable thing, or from the breach of an obligation to inform. "The ambiguities and apparent contradictions in the Code's new product liability regime exemplify the difficulties of dealing satisfactorily with the complexities of modern liability while remaining consistent with codal style" (Brunnée, in *Mélanges Crépeau*, 155, p. 188).
Obs. 1° Product liability may be contractual or extracontractual. **2°** Extracontractual product liability is based on the notion of *safety defect* (art. 1469 C.C.Q.). Article 1468 C.C.Q. provides that the manufacturer, the distributor and the supplier of movable property are liable for injury resulting from a safety defect in the thing. They may be exonerated by proving that the victim knew of the defect, could have known of it, or could have foreseen the injury. They may also be exonerated by proving that they could not have known of the defect or that they accomplished their duty to inform (art. 1473

C.C.Q.). **3**° Contractual liability is based on the notion of *latent defect* (art. 1726 to 1731 C.C.Q.; s. 53, *Consumer Protection Act*, R.S.Q. c. P-40.1). The manufacturer, distributor and supplier are bound by the seller's warranty (art. 1730 C.C.Q.). **4**° In cases decided under the *Civil Code of Lower Canada*, the Supreme Court (e.g. *General Motors Products of Canada Ltd.* v. *Kravitz*, [1979] 1 S.C.R. 790) the right of a subsequent buyer to take action in contract directly against a manufacturer was recognized on the basis of the transmission of rights accessory to property. The essence of this principle is codified at articles 1442 and 1730 C.C.Q.
See also latent defect, liability for damage caused by things, manufacturer's liability, obligation to inform.
Fr. responsabilité du fait des produits.

PROFESSIONAL FAULT

Civil fault committed in the exercise of a profession. For example, the unjustified failure of an advocate to bring an action within legal delays.
Occ. S. 16, *An Act respecting health services and social services*, R.S.Q. c. S-4.2.
Obs. The source of a professional fault may be the violation of an obligation expressly set forth by the relevant code of ethics of the profession or the violation of the general obligation to act as a prudent and diligent person in the exercise of professional knowledge or in the execution of professional acts.
See also professional liability.
Fr. faute professionnelle.

PROFESSIONAL LIABILITY

Civil liability resulting from a fault committed in the exercise of a profession. For example, the liability of a surgeon who fails to observe ordinary medical procedures that a reasonable surgeon would have followed in the circumstances and thereby causes harm to a patient. "Professional liability imports the principles of ordinary civil liability. Generally, doctors have an obligation of means, and their conduct must be assessed against the conduct of a prudent and diligent doctor placed in the same circumstances" (*Lapointe* v. *Hôpital Le Gardeur*, [1992] 1 S.C.R. 351, p. 361, C. L'Heureux-Dubé, J.).
Occ. s. 174.1, *An Act respecting insurance*, R.S.Q. c. A-32; s. 46(3), *Professional Code*, R.S.Q. c. C-26; s. 56(1), *Canada Lands Surveyors Act*, S.C. 1998, c. 14.
Obs. Professional liability may be either contractual or extracontractual.
Fr. responsabilité professionnelle.

PROFIT *n.*

Enrichment of a patrimony.
Occ. Art. 1073 C.C.L.C.
See also damages, loss[1], profit deprived.
Fr. gain.

PROFIT DEPRIVED

Damage consisting in the loss of future financial gain. For example, the loss of profit following a breach of an obligation to deliver merchandise.
Obs. When civil liability is established, damage includes the loss sustained by the victim and the profit of which he or she has been deprived (art. 1611 C.C.Q.).
Syn. *lucrum cessans.* **See also** loss[1], material damage.
Fr. gain manqué[+], *lucrum cessans*, manque à gagner.

PROLONGATION *n.*

1. Syn. prorogation[1].
Fr. prolongation[1], prorogation[1+].

2. Syn. prorogation[2].
Fr. prolongation[2], prorogation[2+].

PROMISEE *n.*

Person to whom a promise is made. "A promise of sale with delivery and possession has not the effect of conveying the right of property to the promisee, when it appears from the terms of the contract that such was not the intention of the parties, but that on the contrary they meant to effect this result by a subsequent act" (*Quebec (City of)* v. *Lampson* (1918), 56 S.C.R. 288, p. 300, F.A. Anglin, J.).
Syn. beneficiary of a promise. **See also** offeree, promisor[1].
Fr. bénéficiaire d'une promesse.

PROMISE FOR ANOTHER

Juridical act the object of which is to bind a third person to one of the contracting parties. "[...] the promise for another is not binding on that other" (Levasseur, *Conventional Obligations*, p. 60).
Occ. Title preceding art. 1443 C.C.Q.
Obs. 1° The prohibition against promises for another stems from the principle of relativity of contract, according to which a contract only creates obligations for the contracting parties, and not for third persons (arts. 1440, 1443 C.C.Q.). **2**° The promise for another must not be confused with the promise of *porte-fort*. The *porte-fort* does not bind third

persons; it is the promisor under the *porte-fort* who is obliged to try to obtain the undertaking of the third person (art. 1443 C.C.Q.). **3°** The promise of *porte-fort* and the promise for another are juridical operations involving three persons, as is the stipulation for another. Unlike the other two, however, they seek to bind the third person, whereas the stipulation has the potential effect of constituting the third person creditor of an obligation.

See also promise of *porte-fort*, relativity of contract, stipulation for another, suretyship.
Fr. promesse pour autrui.

PROMISE OF FIRST OPTION

Syn. first refusal agreement.
Fr. pacte de préférence[+], promesse d'offre préalable.

PROMISE OF *PORTE-FORT* (French)

Juridical act by which one party, the *porte-fort*[2] or *promisor*[3], promises to another, the *beneficiary*, that a third person will bind himself or herself in favour of the latter.
Obs. 1° A promise of *porte-fort* binds only the person who makes it, not the third person. The latter is free to bind himself or herself toward the beneficiary or not. If the third person does so, the promisor has fulfilled the obligation toward the beneficiary; if not, the *porte-fort* will be held liable for the damage caused by the failure to perform the obligation (art. 1443 C.C.Q.). **2°** In practice, the *porte-fort* is generally a representative of the third person who, by entering into a juridical act with the beneficiary in the name of the third person, exceeds his or her powers of representation; he or she is thus making a promise to a cocontracting party that the third person will agree to ratify this act. **3°** The promise of *porte-fort* and the promise for another are juridical operations involving three persons, as is the stipulation for another. Unlike the other two, however, the stipulation has the potential effect of making the third person a creditor of an obligation.
Syn. *porte-fort*[1]. **See also** promise for another, relativity of contract, stipulation for another.
Fr. porte-fort[1], promesse de porte-fort[+], promesse du fait d'autrui.

PROMISE OF REWARD

Syn. offer of reward.
Fr. offre de récompense[+], promesse de récompense.

PROMISE OF SALE

Contract by which a person undertakes to enter into a sale. "The promise of sale is more than an offer: The offerer, besides, obliges himself to maintain it, but this obligation must be accepted by the recipient of it and the offerer notified to that effect. Otherwise, there is no contract, and hence no promise of sale" (Marler, *Real Property*, p. 194).
Occ. Arts. 1710, 1711 C.C.Q.; arts. 1477, 1478 C.C.L.C.
Obs. 1° The promise of sale is a contract that rests upon a concurrence of wills in respect of the parties' intention for property that will be sold, i.e. on the object of the eventual contract of sale, and on the price of the property. **2°** Since a promise of sale is a preliminary step toward the formation of a contract of sale, it is often characterized as a *pre-contract*. These expressions should not be understood to mean that the promise of sale is not itself a contract.
See also offer, pre-contract, promise to contract.
Fr. promesse de vente.

PROMISE TO CONTRACT

Preliminary contract by which one or both parties undertake to enter into a contract the essential terms of which are immediately determined.
Occ. Art. 1397 C.C.Q.
Obs. 1° The promise to contract differs from the offer in that it immediately constitutes a contract. **2°** When only one of the contracting parties makes an undertaking, the promise is unilateral. It is bilateral when both parties commit themselves. **3°** The promisee is entitled to damages if the promisor contracts with a third party in violation of the promise to contract. However, the contract may be set up against the promisee (art. 1397 C.C.Q.).
See also agreement in principle, bilateral promise to contract, gentlemen's agreement, letter of intention, offer, pre-contract, unilateral promise (to contract).
Fr. promesse (de contrat)[+], promesse de contracter.

PROMISE TO PURCHASE

Promise of sale, from the perspective of the promising buyer.
See also purchase.
Fr. promesse d'achat.

PROMISING BUYER

Person who, in a promise of sale, undertakes to buy.

Syn. promising purchaser. **See also** promising seller.
Fr. promettant acheteur.

PROMISING PURCHASER

Syn. promising buyer.
Fr. promettant acheteur.

PROMISING SELLER

Person who, in a promise of sale, undertakes to sell.
Syn. promising vendor. **See also** promising buyer.
Fr. promettant vendeur.

PROMISING VENDOR

Syn. promising seller.
Fr. promettant vendeur.

PROMISOR *n.*

1. Person who makes a promise. "[...] a promisor is bound to compensate the promisee for damage which the latter suffers by reason of any breach of contract for which the promisor is responsible" (Ryan, *Introduction*, pp. 66-67).
Occ. Arts. 1396, 1397, 1812, 2316 C.C.Q.
See also offeror, promisee.
Fr. promettant[1].

2. Party who, in a stipulation for another, obliges himself or herself towards the stipulator to furnish a prestation that will benefit a third person beneficiary. "If [...] the contract is deemed, from the moment of acceptance, to involve only the promisor and the third party to whose exclusive benefit it accrues, what right if any has the stipulator as a party to see to its enforcement?" (Irving, (1963) 9 *McGill L.J.* 337, p. 347).
Occ. Arts. 1444 to 1450 C.C.Q.
See also stipulation for another, stipulator, third person beneficiary.
Fr. promettant[2].

3. Syn. *porte-fort*[2]. "A promise that someone else will act or forbear must either be empty, as being impossible of fulfilment, or be construed as a promise that the promisor will ensure that the other acts or forbears" (Nicholas, *Contract*, p. 181).
Fr. porte-fort[2+], promettant[3].

PROPERTY *n.*

1. Syn. patrimonial right. "Any right having an economic worth for its titulary is, in the widest sense, property. Such rights may exist either in relation to material things and, in the classification deriving from Roman law, are then known as real rights, or in relation to other persons and then termed personal rights" (Brierley & Macdonald (eds.), *Quebec Civil Law*, n° 131, p. 161).
Occ. Arts. 899, 1261 C.C.Q.
Obs. 1° Many scholars today see the law as concerned not with things, i.e. material objects, as such, but rather with the rights pertaining to them, i.e. real rights, as well as any other asset comprised in the patrimony, such as intellectual and personal rights. Property is viewed, from this perspective, as consisting solely of rights. **2°** Property in this sense is viewed as incorporeal, but all incorporeal things are not necessarily property. Some incorporeal things, because they are devoid of pecuniary value, are classified as extrapatrimonial rights, for example, personality rights and certain human rights.
Fr. bien[1], bien incorporel, chose incorporelle, droit patrimonial[+].

2. Material thing susceptible of appropriation. "The sea, the atmosphere, the sun are things that are indispensable to terrestrial life. But they are not property because they cannot be taken over by a private person, a city or a nation" (Planiol & Ripert, *Treatise*, vol. 1, part 2, n° 2170, p. 280).
Occ. Art. 916 C.C.Q.
Obs. 1° Not all material things are property. For example, things common to all, which cannot be appropriated in totality (e.g. the ambient air) are not property. **2°** For some scholars, a thing must also have an economic or utilitarian value in order to qualify as property. **3°** The term *property* designates material things over which there exists a right of ownership. This right is often confused with the object itself, because the right is seen to extend absolute dominion over the thing. It also, however, includes material things over which lesser real rights exist, for example, an emphyteusis or a right of use.
Syn. corporeal property, material property, thing susceptible of appropriation. **See also** patrimonial right, thing[1].
Fr. bien[2+], bien corporel, bien matériel, chose appropriable.

PRO RATA adv. ph. (Latin)

Syn. rateably.
Occ. Arts. 812, 814 C.C.Q.; art. 1697*b* C.C.L.C.
Fr. marc la livre (au), par concurrence, par contribution[+], *pro rata.*

PROROGATION *n.*

1. Act of postponing the expiration of a term to a date later than that originally agreed upon. *Prorogation of a term.*
Occ. Art. 2354 C.C.Q.
Syn. extension[1], prolongation[1].
Fr. prolongation[1], prorogation[1+].

2. Act of extending the duration of a juridical situation, judicial operation or effect of a juridical act beyond the established expiration date. *Prorogation of a lease; prorogation of a mandate.*
Syn. extension[2], prolongation[2].
Fr. prolongation[2], prorogation[2+].

PROROGUE *v.*

Syn. extend.
Fr. prolonger, proroger[+].

PROVIDER OF SERVICES

Person who undertakes to provide services to another person, the *client*, in return for remuneration and without subordination.
Occ. Art. 2098 C.C.Q.
Obs. In principle, the provider of services can delegate execution of all or part of a service to a third party. In such cases, execution remains under the provider's supervision and responsibility (art. 2101 C.C.Q.).
Syn. service provider. **See also** agent and servant, client, contract for (of) services, contractor, employee, principal.
Fr. prestataire de services.

PROVISION *n.*

Expression of intent in an enactment or in a juridical act. "[...] the Crown cannot rely on its prerogatives to avoid the application of a legislative provision aimed at limiting the liability of the party who by his delict caused a damage" (*Bank of Montreal* v. *A.G. Quebec*, [1979] 1 S.C.R. 565, p. 574, Y. Pratte, J.). *Legal provision; legislative provision; regulatory provision; provision of law; provision of a will.*
Occ. Arts. 442c, 1105 C.C.L.C.; art. 2 C.C.P.; ss. 51, 52, 53, *Charter of Human Rights and Freedoms*, R.S.Q. c. C-12; ss. 41, 41.1, *Interpretation Act*, R.S.Q. c. I-16.
Obs. By extension, the term *provision* is used to designate the text containing an expression of intent.
See also condition[2].
Fr. disposition[4].

PROXIMATE CAUSATION

Causation established between the act or omission and the damage that it produces, taking into account only the cause that immediately precedes the damage. *Theory of proximate causation.*
Obs. 1° Along with the theories of adequate causation and equivalence of conditions, the theory of proximate causation is a means of determining the cause of the damage. It is often described as a theory according to which, among all the acts or omissions contributing to the occurrence of the damage, only those that immediately precede the damage in time and space are considered as being the cause of the damage. **2°** Even though this theory is occasionally invoked by the courts, it is not generally viewed as the prevailing explanation of causation.
See also adequate causation, equivalence of conditions, material causation, partial causation, proximate cause[1,2].
Fr. causalité immédiate.

PROXIMATE CAUSE

1. Doctrine of causality which holds as the real cause only the one that directly precedes the damage in the chain of events.
Obs. The expression *proximate cause* does not correspond to the Civil Code's requirement, stated at article 1607 C.C.Q., that the damage must be "an immediate and direct consequence of the debtor's default" in order for the victim to obtain compensation. The codal requirement that the damage be immediate does not necessarily designate a cause that immediately precedes the loss in time and space, without the intervention of any other cause. It refers rather to the relationship between the loss and the cause, whereby such loss must not only be the direct consequence of the act or omission, but must also be so connected that, but for the debtor's default, the loss would not have occurred. Caution should be exercised to avoid confusion between the criteria established at article 1607 C.C.Q. and the notions of *proximate cause* or *immediate cause* used by scholars as doctrines to establish causality.
Syn. *causa proxima*, immediate cause. **See also** adequate cause, determining cause, material cause, proximate causation.
Fr. *causa proxima*, cause immédiate[+].

2. Syn. determining cause. "For an event to be the cause of a damage, it is not sufficient that it merely contributes to the latter; there must be a closer connection; the event must have

been the proximate cause of the damage, so that, if it had not occurred, there would not have been even a partial loss" (*Chartier* v. *A.G. Québec*, [1979] 2 S.C.R. 474, p. 521, Y. Pratte, J.).
Fr. *causa causans*, cause déterminante[+], cause efficiente, cause génératrice.

PRUDENCE *n.*

See imprudence, obligation of means.
Fr. prudence.

PRUDENT ADMINISTRATOR

Model person who, in the performance of duties of a patrimonial character, behaves with care and diligence. "Defendant, in order to avoid liability is obliged, at the very least, to establish that he exercised the care of a prudent administrator" (*St-Lawrence Quick Service Garage Ltd.* v. *Davis*, [1956] B.R. 884, p. 887, G.R.W. Owen, J.).
Occ. Arts. 290, 490, 1045, 1064, 1617 C.C.L.C.
See also reasonable person.
Fr. bon père de famille(>), *bonus pater familias*(>), personne raisonnable(>)[+].

PSYCHOLOGICAL DAMAGE

Moral damage resulting from mental suffering. For example, the anxiety occasioned by a neurosis, psychosis or depression.
Obs. Since the terms *damage* and *harm* are synonymous, the expression *psychological harm* may also be used.
Fr. préjudice psychologique.

PSYCHOLOGICAL IMPUTABILITY

Syn. imputability[1].
Fr. imputabilité[1+], imputabilité morale, imputabilité psychologique.

PUBLICATION FORMALITY

Syn. formality as to publicity.
Occ. S. 162, *An Act respecting the implementation of the reform of the Civil Code*, S.Q. 1992, c. 57.
Fr. formalité de publicité.

PUBLIC LAW

Corpus of legal rules governing the organization and the operation of the State and its institutions, as well as their relations with individuals. "The public law of Quebec, unlike the private law, derives its principles and general content from the public law of England. By the *Treaty of Paris* in 1763 the sovereignty over New France passed from the King of France to the King of England; and automatically the law relating to the Crown, the government and the political rights of citizens, became those of an English colony" (Scott, (1956-57) 3 *McGill L.J.* 29).
Occ. Arts. 356, 399 C.C.L.C.; art. 94.1 C.C.P.
Obs. 1° It is generally accepted that public law is grounded in the protection of collective interests. **2**° The distinction between private and public law is subject to criticism because it is often difficult to establish. It nevertheless represents a *summa divisio* of the law, which is understood to encompass all legal rules. **3**° The historical development of Quebec law means that this distinction between private and public law also serves, among other things, to determine which corpus of general law is applicable to a given legal relationship: the civil law in private law matters, the common law in public law matters. **4**° In certain cases, rules of private law can regulate relations between individuals and legal persons in the public interest by the effect of a rule of public law (see arts. 300 and 1376 C.C.Q.). **5**° Constitutional and administrative law constitute the principal branches of domestic public law. Criminal law in Canada, which derives from English law, is also considered to be part of public law.
See also civil law[1], general law, private law[1], public law right.
Fr. droit public[1].

PUBLIC LAW RIGHT

Right that is consecrated by public law.
Obs. 1° A distinction is often drawn between public law rights and private law rights. However, it is difficult to establish an unequivocal distinction between the two categories of rights, just as it is difficult to attribute particular characteristics to each of them. **2**° Among public law rights, the *Charter of Human Rights and Freedoms* (R.S.Q. c. C-12) draws a distinction between political rights (ss. 21 *et seq.*), such as the right to vote and the right to exercise public functions; judicial rights (ss. 23 *et seq.*), such as the right to be tried in open court before an impartial tribunal; and economic and social rights (ss. 39 *et seq.*), such as the right to a free public education.
See also private law right.
Fr. droit public[2].

PUBLIC OFFER

Syn. offer to the public.
Fr. offre à personne indéterminée, offre au public[+].

PUBLIC ORDER

Global conception of a society expressed in its basic institutions, its general principles and its imperative norms, the purpose of which is to protect and promote the fundamental values of the community. "Governments and laws exist to maintain public order, which is the supreme law; in a word, to make communal life possible" (Johnson, *Maxims*, p. 87). *To breach public order; to respect public order; violation of public order; rules of public order.*
Occ. Arts. 8, 9, 317, 380, 757, 1411, 1413 C.C.Q.; arts. 13, 990 C.C.L.C.; arts. 99, 492 C.C.P.; s. 9.1, *Charter of Human Rights and Freedoms*, R.S.Q. c. C-12; s. 41.4, *Interpretation Act*, R.S.Q. c. I-16.
Obs. 1° Public order may be conceptualized according to its sources or its object. In terms of its sources, public order may be of national or international origin depending on whether it is articulated within a particular jurisdiction or in the international community. As for its object, public order serves to regulate either domestic or international relations. **2°** Public order may be invoked in order to have juridical acts contrary to it declared null (art. 9 C.C.Q.). **3°** Article 99 C.C.P. provides the Attorney General the right to take part *ex officio* "[i]n any action relating to the application of a provision of public order" (see also art. 492 C.C.P.). **4°** Public order may be either legislative or judicial. Moreover, scholars distinguish between political public order, economic public order and moral public order.
Syn. *jus publicum*, public order and good morals. **See also** domestic public order, economic public order, general interest, good morals, imperative law, individual interest, international public order, judicial public order, legislative public order, moral public order, nullity, political public order.
Fr. ordre public.

PUBLIC ORDER AND GOOD MORALS

Syn. public order. "The concept of public order and good morals completes the system of the civil law, supplementing the domain of the legislature and of private agreement. Furthermore, it introduces a concept of contractual limitation which is variable in content and which reflects the social standards of the era in which it is applied" (Rodgers Magnet, (1980) 40 *R. du B.* 373, p. 400).
Occ. Art. 13 C.C.L.C.
Obs. The notion *good morals* has a specific meaning when used alone, but when it is used in conjunction with the notion of *public order*, it is generally considered as a synonym of that notion.
Fr. ordre public.

PUBLIC ORDER OF DIRECTION

Economic public order, the purpose of which is to regulate the economy in the general interest of society either by restricting contractual freedom or, less frequently, by reinstating it. For example, by establishing price controls or by ensuring competition in the market place.
Obs. Juridical acts contrary to public order of direction are sanctioned with absolute nullity.
Syn. absolute public order. **See also** general interest, public order of protection.
Fr. ordre public absolu, ordre public de direction[+].

PUBLIC ORDER OF PROTECTION

Economic public order, the purpose of which is to protect the economically weaker contracting party in his or her individual interest. For example, the rules governing insurance contracts (art. 2414 C.C.Q.) or consumer contracts (ss. 8, 9, *Consumer Protection Act*, R.S.Q. c. P-40.1).
Obs. Juridical acts contrary to public order of protection are sanctioned with relative nullity.
Syn. relative public order. **See also** individual interest, public order of direction.
Fr. ordre public de protection[+], ordre public relatif.

PUBLIC POLICY

See public order. "[...] on an appeal from the Province of Quebec, the Privy Council treated public order as identical with what in England was termed public policy although it expressed the opinion that public policy was the broader of the two terms" (Challies, in *Travaux Henri Capitant*, t. 7, 645, p. 651).
Occ. Art. 6 para. 2 C.C.L.C.
Fr. ordre public.

PUNITIVE DAMAGES

Financial penalty imposed by a court in a private law context on the author of conduct viewed as reprehensible. "Quebec courts have been empowered to grant punitive or exemplary damages to defamation victims since the coming into force of s. 49 of the Quebec Charter of Human Rights and Freedoms in 1976" (Jukier, (1989) 49 *R. du B.* 3, p. 35).
Occ. Arts. 1610, 1621, 1899, 1902, 1968 C.C.Q.; art. 840 C.C.P.; s. 31, *An Act respecting collective agreement decrees*, R.S.Q. c. D-2; s. 54.10, *An Act respecting the Régie du logement*, R.S.Q. c. R-8.1; s. 45.1, *An Act respecting petroleum products and equipment*, R.S.Q. c. P-29.1.

Obs. 1° Punitive damages were not traditionally recognized in the Civil law, given that the objective to punish reprehensible conduct through legal sanction was viewed as part of the role of the criminal law. **2°** Punishment and prevention are the two leading features of punitive damages. This distinguishes punitive damages from compensatory damages, whose principal aim is to compensate the harm suffered by the victim. **3°** Article 1621 C.C.Q. limits punitive damages to cases expressly provided by law, thereby conferring upon such damage awards an exceptional character in Quebec civil law. The *Draft Civil Code* (art. 290, Bk V, C.C.R.O.) proposed extending such awards to cases of intentional or gross fault on the part of the debtor. **4°** The Supreme Court of Canada, in its trilogy of cases *Béliveau St-Jacques* v. *Fédération des employés et employées de services publics inc. (CSN)*, [1996] 2 S.C.R. 345, *Québec (Curateur public)* v. *Syndicat national des employés de l'hôpital St-Ferdinand (CSN)*, [1996] 3 S.C.R. 211 and *Augustus* v. *Gosset*, [1996] 3 S.C.R. 268, has indicated that the recourse in punitive damages available under subsection 49 (2) of the *Charter of Human Rights and Freedoms* (R.S.Q. c. C-12), is subject to the general principles of civil liability. **5°** Article 1621 C.C.Q. provides a non-limitative list of criteria to assist courts in determining the *quantum* of punitive damages, such as the gravity of the debtor's fault, his or her patrimonial situation, the extent of the reparation for which he or she is already liable to the creditor and the fact that the payment of the damages is assumed by a third person. This reaffirms the preventive character of punitive damages, considering that the *quantum* may not exceed what is considered to be sufficient to fulfil this purpose. **6°** The expressions *punitive damages* and *exemplary damages* in the Civil Code and related legislation are interchangeable. See s. 423, *An Act respecting the implementation of the reform of the Civil Code*, S.Q. 1992, c. 57.

Syn. exemplary damages. **See also** compensatory damages, damages, moral damages, private law penalty.

Fr. dommages-intérêts exemplaires, dommages-intérêts punitifs+.

PURCHASE *n.*

Sale, from the perspective of the buyer. *Agreement of purchase and sale.*

Occ. Arts. 1844, 2677 C.C.Q.; art. 1739 C.C.L.C.

See also promise to purchase, sale.

Fr. achat.

PURCHASE *v.*

Syn. buy.

Occ. Arts. 1900 C.C.Q.; art. 1664.9 C.C.L.C.

See also promise to purchase.

Fr. acheter.

PURCHASER *n.*

Syn. buyer. "In order to presume that the purchaser would not have bought, the Court must consider the motive in buying, the purpose for which the property was purchased and even the habits or status of the purchaser" (*Forget* v. *Gohier*, [1945] B.R. 437, p. 452, G. Barclay, J.).

Occ. Arts. 2786, 2790 C.C.Q.; arts. 815, 953(4), 1025 C.C.L.C.

Obs. Although the term *purchaser* does not appear in the chapter on sale, it is generally preferred to *buyer* in Book Six of the Civil Code on prior claims and hypothecs.

Fr. acheteur.

PURE AND SIMPLE *adj.ph.*

Without modality.

Occ. Arts. 1095, 1096, 1104 C.C.L.C.

Syn. unconditional[1]. **See also** modal, unconditional[2].

Fr. pur et simple.

PURE AND SIMPLE OBLIGATION

Obligation[2] that is not subject to a modality.

Obs. A pure and simple obligation is an obligation with one creditor, one debtor and one object. Because it is not subject to a modality, the pure and simple obligation gives rise to immediate performance.

Syn. simple obligation. **See also** complex obligation.

Fr. obligation pure et simple+, obligation simple.

PURE AND SIMPLE RIGHT

Right that is not qualified by a modality.

Syn. absolute right, unconditional right[1], unqualified right. **See also** conditional right, pure and simple obligation, qualified right, unconditional right[2].

Fr. droit pur et simple.

PURE ECONOMIC LOSS

See material damage.

Fr. perte purement économique.

PURELY FACULTATIVE CONDITION

Syn. purely potestative condition. "Having been given the option in clear and concise terms, the subsequent condition of a written consent is not, under the circumstances of this case, to be interpreted as a 'purely' facultative condition, but should be interpreted as one allowing the plaintiff to refuse the renewal for cause and not by caprice" (*Bernard* v. *Paquin*, [1954] B.R. 273, p. 276, G. Barclay, J.)

Fr. condition purement facultative, condition purement potestative[+].

PURELY POTESTATIVE CONDITION

Condition[1] that depends solely on the will of one of the parties. "A potestative condition in this sense, which [...] is called 'purely potestative', is one which depends for its fulfilment purely on the will of one of the parties. A promise by *B* to buy a house from *A* for 300,000 francs 'if I feel like it' is null because it is subject to a purely potestative condition on the part of the person obliged, i.e. *B*" (Nicholas, *Contract*, p. 160).

Obs. In principle, an obligation to which a purely potestative suspensive condition is attached is null if it depends solely upon the will of the debtor. In this situation, the presence of the condition suggests that the debtor does not really have the intention to be bound (art. 1500 C.C.Q.).

Syn. purely facultative condition. **See also** simply potestative condition.

Fr. condition purement facultative, condition purement potestative[+].

PUTTING IN DEFAULT

Unilateral juridical act by which a creditor enjoins the debtor to perform his obligation within a reasonable delay. "One may resume the putting in default as a measure generally required by law, by which a creditor indicates to his debtor, his desire that the latter fulfill his obligations" (Kouri, (1971) 2 *R.D.U.S.* 1, p. 5).

Occ. S. 239, *An Act respecting insurance*, R.S.Q. c. A-32; s. 136(k), *An Act respecting the Barreau du Québec*, R.S.Q. c. B-1.

Obs. 1° Putting in default formally establishes the lateness of the debtor in fulfilling his or her obligation. **2°** There are two types of putting in default: an extrajudicial notice given by the creditor to the debtor and a judicial demand filed against the debtor (arts. 1595, 1596 C.C.Q.). **3°** Despite its plain grammatical awkwardness as a nominal phrase, the expression *putting in default* is idiomatically acceptable as an equivalent for *mise en demeure* in Quebec legal parlance.

See also default, notice of default.

Fr. mise en demeure[1].

Q

QUALIFIED RIGHT

Right subject to a modality.
See also conditional right, pure and simple right, right with a term.
Fr. droit modal.

QUANTITY *n.*

Amount or part of an aliquot-share.
Occ. Art. 1374 C.C.Q.; art. 1060 C.C.L.C.
See also liquidity.
Fr. quotité.

QUANTUM (Latin)

Amount fixed by a court. For example, the *quantum* of damages, the *quantum* of a support payment. "The rule is that an appellate court should not alter the quantum of damages set by the trial judge simply because it would have awarded a different amount if it had itself been sitting at the trial level. For the quantum to be altered, an appellate court must be shown that the trial judge applied an erroneous rule of law or that the amount awarded was palpably incorrect compensation for the damage suffered" (*Laurentides Motel Ltd.* v. *Beauport (City of)*, [1989] 1 S.C.R. 705, p. 810, C. L'Heureux-Dubé, J.).
Obs. The term *quantum* is often used with respect to the assessment of damages in civil liability cases.
See also damages.
Fr. *quantum.*

QUANTUM MERUIT (Latin)

See unjust enrichment.
Obs. This Latin maxim means *as much as he deserves.*
Fr. *quantum meruit.*

QUASI-CONTRACT *n.*

Act voluntarily carried out by a person that serves to create obligations analogous to those stemming from a contract, for which that person or another is bound, even though no agreement has been entered into. "[...]

Roman law [...] did not speak of quasi-contracts but recognized that there were circumstances where the principles of justice demanded that there be an obligation. This obligation, while it could not be said to arise from a contract or a delict, arose *quasi ex contractu* as it resembled a contractual obligation" (Challies, *Unjustified Enrichment*, p. 46).
Obs. 1° The term *quasi-contract* was used at article 983 C.C.L.C. but it is not found in the Civil Code. However, the acts that give rise to quasi-contractual obligations still have legal effects, as they are now considered as "other sources of obligations". The vocabulary adopted by the Civil Code reflects the classification of the sources of obligations as stated at art. 1372 C.C.Q. **2°** The *other sources of obligations* referred to in the Civil Code include the management of the business of another (art. 1482 C.C.Q.), the reception of a thing not due (art. 1491 C.C.Q.) and unjust enrichment (art. 1493 C.C.Q.).
See also contract[1], delict, quasi-delict.
Fr. quasi-contrat.

QUASI-CONTRACTUAL *adj.*

Resulting from or relating to a quasi-contract. "To find a common denominator for what has been lumped together here, is not at all easy. In the case of quasi-contractual obligations it was probably the fact that – just as in contractual situations – some kind of negotium has taken place. Thus, the actions granted to enforce quasi-contractual obligations were all very closely modelled on specific contractual actions" (Zimmerman, *Obligations*, p. 16).
See also contractual, delictual, extracontractual, legal[4], quasi-delictual.
Fr. quasi contractuel.

QUASI-CONTRACTUAL LIABILITY

Extracontractual liability resulting from the breach of a quasi-contractual obligation. For example, the liability arising from the non-performance of duties attaching to the management of the business of another (arts. 1484 and 1489 C.C.Q.).

Obs. There are no special rules as such governing quasi-contractual liability. Consequently, the general regime of extracontractual liability will apply to regulate quasi-contractual liability.

Syn. quasi-contractual responsibility. **See also** contractual liability, delictual liability, extracontractual liability, legal liability[2], quasi-contract, quasi-delictual liability.

Fr. responsabilité quasi contractuelle.

QUASI-CONTRACTUAL OBLIGATION

Obligation[2] resulting from a quasi-contract. "Certainly these obligations, though they are laid down by express articles of the Code in which the word 'quasi-contract' does not appear, cannot be said to result from the operation of the law solely. [...] Thus, the obligation of the proprietor of the soil who has constructed buildings or works with materials which do not belong to him to pay their value, provided for by article 416 [C.C.L.C.], is a quasi-contractual obligation" (Nicholls, in *Livre-Souvenir*, 271, pp. 321-322).

See also contractual obligation, quasi-contract, quasi-contractual liability.

Fr. obligation quasi contractuelle.

QUASI-CONTRACTUAL RESPONSIBILITY

Syn. quasi-contractual liability.

Fr. responsabilité quasi contractuelle.

QUASI-DELICT *n.*

Act or omission characterized by negligence or lack of prudence, arising in an extracontractual context. "The act may constitute an offence (or delict) or a quasi-offence (or quasi-delict). These are distinguished according to the intention of their author – an offence being committed with intention to cause the damage, and a quasi-offence being due to imprudence or some other unintentional fault" (Goldenberg, *Law of Delicts*, p. 2).

Obs. The term *quasi-delict* and its synonym *quasi-offence*, used at article 1007 C.C.L.C., no longer appear in the Civil Code. However, as specified by s. 423 of *An Act respecting the implementation of the reform of the Civil Code* (S.Q. 1992, c. 57), the notion of *fault in the context of extra-contractual civil liability* corresponds to the notions of *offence* and *quasi-offence* (arts. 164, 1526, 2498 C.C.Q.). The vocabulary adopted by the Civil Code reflects the classification of the sources of obligations as stated at art. 1372 C.C.Q.

Syn. quasi-offence. **See also** contract[1], delict, delictual fault, imprudence, negli-

gence, non-intentional fault, quasi-contract, quasi-delictual liability.

Fr. quasi-délit.

QUASI-DELICTUAL *adj.*

Resulting from or relating to a quasi-delict. "Opinion seems to be divided in the Quebec courts as to the nature of this type of damages [humiliation, privation, suffering, injury to professional, social and personal reputation]. Some appear to think that such damages, in particular that resulting from injury to reputation, are necessarily delictual or quasi-delictual" (*Senez* v. *Montreal Real Estate Board*, [1980] 2 S.C.R. 555, p. 572, J. Beetz, J.).

See also contractual, delictual, extracontractual, legal[4], quasi-contractual.

Fr. quasi délictuel.

QUASI-DELICTUAL FAULT

Non-intentional fault committed in an extracontractual context.

Obs. 1° According to the classification of obligations established under article 983 C.C.L.C., offences (delicts) were opposed to quasi-offences (quasi-delicts). This distinction is not made in the *Civil Code of Québec*, which no longer uses these terms. A distinction between extracontractual fault and contractual fault now serves as the basis for the classification of obligations. Furthermore, section 423 of *An Act respecting the implementation of the reform of the Civil Code* (S.Q. 1992, c. 57) provides that the words *offences* and *quasi-offences* correspond to "fault in the context of extra-contractual civil liability". **2°** Quasi-delictual fault is most often the result of imprudence or negligence.

Syn. quasi-delictual offence. **See also** delict, delictual fault, imprudence, negligence, non-intentional fault, quasi-delict, quasi-delictual liability.

Fr. faute quasi délictuelle.

QUASI-DELICTUAL LIABILITY

Extracontractual liability arising from negligence or imprudence.

Obs. The Civil Code does not refer to quasi-delictual liability, and the term *quasi-delict* and its synonym *quasi-offence*, which appeared at article 1007 C.C.L.C., are no longer used in the Civil Code. However, as specified by s. 423 of *An Act respecting the implementation of the reform of the Civil Code* (S.Q. 1992, c. 57), the notion of *fault in the context of extra-contractual civil liability* corresponds to the notions of *offence* and *quasi-offence*.

Syn. quasi-delictual responsibility. **See also** contractual liability, delictual liability, extracontractual liability, legal liability[2], quasi-contractual liability, quasi-delict.
Fr. responsabilité quasi délictuelle.

QUASI-DELICTUAL OBLIGATION

Obligation[2] to compensate for the harm caused by a quasi-delict.
Obs. Quasi-delicts are traditionally considered to be one of the sources of obligations. However, quasi-delicts are not in themselves the general source of the obligation not to cause harm to others. It is the violation of that latter obligation that can constitute a quasi-delict. Therefore, it is preferable to characterize the obligation not to cause harm to others as *legal* rather than *quasi-delictual*.
See also delictual liability, delictual obligation, legal obligation[1], quasi-delict.
Fr. obligation quasi-délictuelle.

QUASI-DELICTUAL OFFENCE

Syn. quasi-delictual fault. "The nature of an offence may vary to a considerable extent. At one end of the spectrum, the courts in Quebec have held directors personally liable for damage caused as a result of their unauthorized, illegal or fraudulent administration. At the other end, directors have been found liable where they committed a quasi-delictual offence by acting negligently or without reasonable skill" (Smith, (1974) 34 *R. du B.* 464, p. 472).
Obs. 1° This use of the term *offence*, which is increasingly rare, has no doubt been reinforced by its use in article 1053 C.C.L.C. **2°** Used in this context, offence should not be confused with the term as it is employed in criminal law.
Fr. faute quasi-délictuelle.

QUASI-DELICTUAL RESPONSIBILITY

Syn. quasi-delictual liability.
Fr. responsabilité quasi délictuelle.

QUASI EX CONTRACTU adv.ph. (Latin)

Of quasi-contractual origin. "As examples of obligations arising *quasi ex contractu*, Justinian mentioned the 'negotiorum gestio', the obligations arising from the relationship of tutor and ward and curator and ward, the obligations arising between heir and legatee and between co-heirs, the obligations arising from common ownership where there exists no actual partnership, and the obligations arising from the receipt of money paid by mistake" (Nicholls, in *Livre-Souvenir*, 271, p. 274).
See also *ex contractu, ex delicto, ex lege,* quasi *ex delicto.*
Fr. *quasi ex contractu.*

QUASI EX DELICTO adv.ph. (Latin)

Of quasi-delictual origin.
See also *ex contractu, ex delicto, ex lege, quasi ex contractu.*
Fr. *quasi ex delicto.*

QUASI-OFFENCE *n.*

Syn. quasi-delict. "The distinction between offences and quasi-offences, or, in the French version [of the *Civil Code of Lower Canada*], between *délits* and *quasi-délits* [...] will be found first in Roman Law [...] The authors and the jurisprudence, both in France and in Quebec, have with unanimity adopted the opinion of Pothier. Pothier held that an offence was a fault that intentionally caused damage to another, a quasi-offence a fault that caused damage to another unintentionally" (Nicholls, *Offences and Quasi-Offences*, pp.15-16).
Occ. Arts. 983, 1007 C.C.L.C.
Fr. quasi-délit.

QUIT *n.*

Syn. discharge[1].
Obs. This term is commonly used in notarial practice, as in the expression *whereof quit*.
Fr. décharge[1+], quitus.

QUIT(S) *adj.*

Said of a person released from an obligation.
Fr. quitte[1].

QUITTANCE *n*

Syn. acquittance[1].
Fr. quittance[1].

R

RADICAL NULLITY

See absolute nullity.
Fr. nullité radicale.

RATEABLY *adv.*

In proportion to. For example, the proceeds from the judicial sale of an insolvent debtor's property are distributed rateably among the chirographic creditors, so that each creditor receives an amount in proportion to his or her creance (art. 2646 C.C.Q.).
Occ. Arts. 1690, 2625 C.C.Q.; arts. 749, 885, 1985 C.C.L.C.
Syn. contribution (by), *pro rata*.
Fr. marc la livre (au), par concurrence, par contribution+, *pro rata*.

RATE OF CONVENTIONAL INTEREST

Syn. conventional interest rate.
Occ. Art. 1785 C.C.L.C.
Fr. taux d'intérêt conventionnel.

RATE OF INTEREST

Syn. interest rate.
Occ. Arts. 1619, 2690 C.C.Q.; art. 1785 C.C.L.C.
Fr. taux d'intérêt.

RATE OF LEGAL INTEREST

Syn. legal interest rate.
Occ. Art. 1785 C.C.L.C.
Fr. taux d'intérêt légal.

RATIFICATION *n.*

1. Unilateral juridical act by which a represented person accepts to be bound by a juridical operation carried out on the latter's behalf by a representative who had exceeded his or her powers. "[...] the writers distinguish ratification from confirmation. They define confirmation as the waiver of an action to rescind and ratification as the approval of an act done without authority" (*Denis-Cossette* v. *Germain*, [1982] 1 S.C.R. 751, p. 796, J. Beetz, J.).

Obs. Ratification may be express or tacit.
See also confirmation, mandate[1], promise of *porte-fort*.
Fr. ratification[1].

2. Syn. confirmation.
Occ. Title preceding 2532 C.C.Q.; art. 319 C.C.Q.; arts. 1214, 1235 para. 1(2) C.C.L.C.
Obs. French scholars limit the use of the word *ratification* to the context of representation (see, however, art. 1338 *C. civ. fr.*, corresponding to art. 1423 C.C.Q.). In Quebec, this term is also used to describe the renunciation of the right to invoke relative nullity.
Fr. confirmation+, ratification[2].

RATIFY *v.*

1. To effect ratification[1]. "It is urged that this payment was subsequently ratified by the debtor and, therefore, is as binding upon him and the respondent as if made by his author ity" (*Perron* v. *Corporation du Village du Sacré-Cœur de Jésus*, [1928] S.C.R. 326, p. 328, F.A. Anglin, J.).
Occ. Arts. 319, 2533 C.C.Q.; art. 1024 C.C.P.
Fr. ratifier[1].

2. Syn. confirm. *To ratify a contract.*
See also ratification[2+].
Fr. confirmer+, ratifier[2].

REAL *adj.*

Relating to a juridical act, the formation of which depends on the handing over of a thing.
See also consensual, formalistic, real contract, real tradition, solemn.
Fr. réel.

REAL ACT

Syn. counter letter. "The revocatory action is directed towards a real act, whereas the action in declaration of simulation is directed towards a sham or an apparent act" (D'Angelo, (1986) 32 *Loy. L. Rev.* 129, p. 146).
Fr. acte réel, acte secret, acte véritable, contre-lettre+.

REAL CONTRACT

Contract which is formed by the delivery of the thing that constitutes its object. For example, a deposit (art. 2280 C.C.Q.), a loan (arts. 2313, 2314 C.C.Q.).
Obs. 1° Real contracts are formalistic contracts. **2°** The origins of the distinction between real and consensual contracts may be traced to Roman law.
See also consensual contract, formalistic act, solemn contract.
Fr. contrat réel.

REAL INDIVISIBILITY

Syn. natural indivisibility.
Fr. indivisibilité naturelle+, indivisibilité objective, indivisibilité réelle, indivisibilité véritable.

REALIZATION OF THE CONDITION

Syn. fulfilment of the condition.
Fr. accomplissement de la condition, arrivée de la condition, réalisation de la condition+.

REAL OBLIGATION

Obligation[3] to which a person is bound only by reason of his or her quality as titulary of a real right. For example, the obligation imposed upon co-owners of a common wall for its maintenance, repair and rebuilding (art. 1006 C.C.Q.); the obligation of the usufructuary to maintain the property over which he or she has a right of enjoyment (art. 1151 C.C.Q.).
Obs. 1° Real obligations arising by law are distinguished from the real obligations formed by juridical act, notably by contract. With respect to the latter, scholarly opinion tends to limit real obligations to those that have sufficient connection with the exercise of the real right considered as to its destination. **2°** When there is a transfer of the real right to which a real obligation is attached, the real obligation is also transmitted to the acquirer. **3°** The debtor of a real obligation is liable as long as he or she is the holder of the real right to which the obligation is attached. The debtor may, however, be freed therefrom in the future, particularly by abandoning the property (e.g. art. 1185 C.C.Q.). **4°** The regime for real obligations reflects preoccupations that brought about the abolition of seigneurial title in the mid-nineteenth century, in that no obligation that resembles a feudal duty may be imposed upon a person (s. 59,

An Act respecting the general abolition of feudal rights and duties, C.S.L.C. 1861, c. 41).
5° Real obligations are traditionally contrasted with personal obligations.
Syn. obligation *propter rem.* **See also** assignment of debt, obligation[2].
Fr. obligation *propter rem*, obligation réelle+.

REAL RIGHT

Right of a patrimonial nature that is exercised directly upon property. "[...] as a right assumes a person or persons by whom it is to be observed – it cannot be observed by a thing – a real right is one to be observed by all other persons; it is a right *adversus omnes* and excludes all other persons from participation in the object of the right" (Marler, *Real Property*, p. 32). *Movable real right; immovable real right; registration of real rights.*
Occ. Arts. 911, 1119, 1261, 2660 C.C.Q.; arts. 2016, 2082 C.C.L.C.; arts. 699, 715 C.C.P.; s. 51(*d*), *Cultural Property Act*, R.S.Q. c. B-4; s. 85, *Expropriation Act*, R.S.Q. c. E-24.
Obs. 1° Within the category of real rights, a distinction is generally made between principal real rights and accessory real rights. The accessory real right differs from the principal real right in that the former constitutes security that is necessarily attached to a claim for which it guarantees performance. **2°** Real rights are traditionally distinguished from personal rights within the patrimony. In addition to the classical notions of *jus in re* and *jus in personam*, other categories of patrimonial rights, such as intellectual property rights, have also emerged. **3°** Traditionally, real rights are considered to bear upon material things. One may well ask, however, whether the change of terminology in the *Civil Code of Québec* with respect to a number of institutions in property law, notably ownership, alters this assumption. According to the text of article 947 of the Civil Code, ownership now bears on *property* rather than upon *things* as it did in the former law. This might be read to suggest that real rights can bear upon incorporeal as well as corporeal property. Some scholars have suggested that this may merely reflect terminological inadvertence. It should be noted that the materialistic conception of ownership has been explicitly or implicitly retained in other instances in the Civil Code (e.g. arts. 914, 934, 939 C.C.Q.). **4°** Real rights are said to be opposable to third persons. As such, they are characterized by a right to follow and a right of preference. **5°** The classical debate as to whether a

numerus clausus of real rights is established by law has not been explicitly resolved by the *Civil Code of Québec*. However, articles 947 and 1119 C.C.Q. do not create a limitative list of such rights in definitive terms. **6**° The distinction between real and personal rights has been called into question by some scholars. Those adopting so-called "personalist" theories tend to redefine real rights as interpersonal relationships rather than relationships between persons and things. **7**° The French term *droit réel* is occasionally used in federal statutes with a definition that is broader or narrower, as the case may be, than the term as defined here (e.g. s. 2, *Federal Real Property Act*, R.S.C. 1985, c. F-8.4, where the English equivalent *interest* is proposed).
Syn. *jus in re.* **See also** *jus ad rem*, opposability, patrimonial right, real obligation, right, right of preference².
Fr. droit réel⁺, *jus in re.*

REAL SUBROGATION

Subrogation of property for other property. "Where sale and re-investment are permitted, the technique known as real subrogation (*subrogation réelle*) – the substitution of one thing for another, which thereupon takes on the legal condition of the former – finds its application" (Brierley & Macdonald (eds.), *Quebec Civil Law*, n° 133, p. 165).
Obs. 1° Depending on the context in which it operates, real subrogation may be seen as having different justifications. Scholars have advanced various theories based on universalities, on appropriation of property, as well as on value funds. **2**° Real subrogation operates *pleno jure* in a juridical universality. Thus, within the patrimony, property replacing that which has been alienated secures the obligations of the titulary as part of the common pledge of creditors (art. 2644 C.C.Q.). **3**° Real subrogation plays a specific role in a number of *de facto* universalities where the law so provides (see, in particular, in matrimonial regimes (art. 450(3) C.C.Q.), substitutions (art. 1230 C.C.Q.) and hypothecs (art. 2674 C.C.Q.)). When subrogation occurs, the substituted property takes the place of the original property within the universality (e.g. property subrogated to private property is also considered private property). **4**° Subrogation may also operate in respect of specific property, without reference to its place in a universality (e.g. in matters of insurance indemnities (art. 2497 C.C.Q.)).
See also exchange, investment, patrimony, personal subrogation, real right, subrogation.
Fr. subrogation réelle.

REAL TRADITION

Syn. actual tradition.
Fr. tradition réelle.

REAL VALUE

Syn. actual value.
Fr. valeur marchande, valeur réelle⁺, valeur vénale.

REASONABLE MAN

Syn. reasonable person.
Obs. Traditionally, the term *man* has been used in the expression *reasonable man* as a generic to mean *human being*. The expression is regarded by many as sexist and has fallen from favour. *Reasonable person* is now preferred in the literature.
Fr. bon père de famille, *bonus pater familias*, personne raisonnable⁺.

REASONABLE PERSON

Model person who, in the performance of a duty, behaves prudently and diligently. "It is necessary to determine whether the party whom it is sought to make liable behaved like a reasonable person toward the third parties, or in other words what the conduct of a reasonable contracting party would have been toward the third parties" (*Bank of Montreal* v *Bail Ltée.*, [1992] 2 S.C.R. 554, pp. 581 582, C.D. Gonthier, J.). *Reasonable person test.*
Occ. Art. 1436 C.C.Q.; art. 123 C.C.P.
Obs. 1° The notion of *reasonable person* is generally invoked as a technique for measuring the standard of behaviour required in respect of contractual or extracontractual obligations of means. Typically, it involves comparing the behaviour of the debtor to that which a reasonable person would have demonstrated in the circumstances. **2**° Traditionally, the term *man* has been used in the expression *reasonable man* as a generic to mean *human being*. The expression is regarded by many as sexist and has fallen from favour. *Reasonable person* is now preferred in the literature.
Syn. *bon père de famille, bonus pater familias*, reasonable man. **See also** obligation of means, prudent administrator.
Fr. bon père de famille, *bonus pater familias*, personne raisonnable⁺.

REBUS SIC STANTIBUS (Latin)

See unforeseeability.
Obs. This Latin maxim means *as things stand.*
Fr. *rebus sic stantibus.*

REBOUNDING DAMAGE

Syn. ricochet damage.
Obs. Since the terms *damage* and *injury* are synonymous, the expression *rebounding injury* may also be used.
Fr. préjudice par ricochet+, préjudice réfléchi.

RECEIPT *n.*

1. Writing by which the creditor acknowledges payment. "[...] the subrogating deed must either be in a notarial form, or signed by two witnesses, and the receipt given by the creditor must specify that the debt was paid with the borrowed money [...]" (Brierley & Macdonald (eds.), *Quebec Civil Law*, n° 544, p. 494).
Occ. S. 11, *Health Insurance Act*, R.S.Q. c. A-29; ss. 78, 325, 358, 362, *Code of Penal Procedure*, R.S.Q. c. C-25.1; ss. 8, 18, 20, *Deposit Act*, R.S.Q. c. D-5.
Obs. 1° Where the creditor acknowledges in the receipt that the debtor has performed the obligation completely, the receipt constitutes an acquittance. **2°** However, a receipt often only records a partial payment. This is notably the case when the contract stipulates that a monetary obligation is to be performed by instalments. With each instalment, the debtor may demand a receipt. Once the obligation is completely performed, he or she has the right to obtain an acquittance.
See also acquittance[1], paid, title of payment.
Fr. reçu[1].

2. Writing by which a person attests to having received exhibits, objects, titles or any other property[2], for deposit, in communication or after transportation. "[...] the mandate is often unilateral in form, and acceptance is often evidenced merely by the actions of the parties. The express power of attorney, the corporate resolution, and the written instructions to a stock broker are all evidenced by a unilateral writing issued by the mandator. Certain deposit receipts, consignment receipts, and commodity broker's confirmation are all examples that originate from the mandatory" (Claxton, (1999) 44 *McGill L.J.* 665, p. 690).
Occ. Art. 2285 C.C.Q.; arts. 47, 1745, 2180, 2454 C.C.L.C.; arts. 83, 146.1, 189 C.C.P.
Obs. 1° In the context of transport of goods, the bill of lading generally serves as a receipt. **2°** In commercial matters, the warehouse receipt, i.e. the receipt that indicates the warehouse where the goods have been deposited, may be negotiable.
See also bill of lading.
Fr. récépissé+, reçu[2].

3. Syn. discharge[2].
Occ. Art. 609 C.C.P.
Fr. décharge[2+], quittance[2].

RECEIVE *v.*

Syn. accept[2].
Occ. Arts. 2082, 2115 C.C.Q.
Fr. accepter[2], recevoir+.

RECEIVER *n.*

Syn. consignee.
Occ. Arts. 2030, 2041, 2061, 2084 C.C.Q.
Fr. consignataire, destinataire[2+].

RECEPTION *n.*

1. Action of receiving payment.
Obs. 1° The legal relevance of reception varies according to the regime for payment applicable in the circumstances. Where reception marks payment in full, for example, it coincides in principle with the liberation of the debtor. Where a person receives a payment in error, the payment may be the source of an obligation pursuant to the regime of the reception of a thing not due. **2°** The creditor has the obligation to receive that which is due. When the creditor refuses or neglects to receive payment, the debtor may avail himself or herself of the procedure of tender and deposit (arts. 1573 *et seq.* C.C.Q.).
See also acquittance[1], deposit[3], discharge[3], payment[2], reception of a thing not due, remittance, tender.
Fr. réception[1].

2. Syn. acceptance[3]. *Reception of the work.*
Occ. Art. 1680 C.C.L.C.
Fr. acceptation[3], réception[2+].

3. See theory of reception.
Fr. [*].

RECEPTION OF A THING NOT DUE

Reception of payment without justification giving rise to an obligation to restore it. "[T]he Code [C.C.L.C] lists two nominate quasi-contracts, relating to the voluntary management of another's business and the reception of a thing not due. Both of these existed as sources of civil obligations in Roman law and continued to be so recognized in most of the traditional legal systems extant in France up to the codification and unification of French civil law in 1804" (Fine, (1973) 19 *McGill L.J.* 453, p. 453).
Occ. Title preceding art. 1491 C.C.Q.; art. 3125 C.C.Q.

Obs. 1° A person who receives a payment that is not due may be obliged to restore it (arts. 1491, 1492, 1699 to 1706 C.C.Q.). However, there will be no restitution if the claim of the person who received the payment is prescribed or if he or she has destroyed the title or relinquished a security, unless the payment was received in good faith (art. 1491 C.C.Q.). **2°** Reception of a thing not due has traditionally been considered a quasi-contract. The term *quasi-contract* was used at article 983 C.C.L.C., but is not found in the Civil Code. Reception of a thing not due is formally classified as one of the "other sources of obligations" in the context of the classification of the sources of obligations as stated at art. 1372 C.C.Q. **3°** The codal regime respecting the reception of a thing not due is set forth at articles 1491 and 1492 C.C.Q.
See also management of the business of another, payment of a thing not due, recovery of a thing not due, restitution of a thing not due, unjust enrichment.
Fr. réception de l'indu.

RECIPIENS *n.* (Latin)

Syn. *accipiens*.
Obs. From the Latin *recipio*: to receive, to accept.
Fr. *accipiens*+, payé, *recipiens*.

RECIPROCAL, *adj*

See reciprocal obligation.
Fr. réciproque.

RECIPROCAL OBLIGATION

Obligation[2] in which the debtor is also titulary of a claim in relation to the creditor. "By examining the antecedents of the contract of employment, it becomes very clear that the failure to impose a reciprocal obligation on employers to act in good faith was not a historical accident. Victorian society merely paid lip-service to the concept of freedom of contract and to the abolition of the role of status in private law. In reality, this society prided itself not on its equality, but on its nuances of social status" (Ball, (1994) 39 *McGill L.J.* 568, p. 580).
Obs. Obligations are said to be reciprocal solely in respect of the parties to the obligational relationship, without regard to the possible connection between their respective obligations. However, in a bilateral contract, the obligations are both reciprocal and interdependent.
Syn. mutual obligation. **See also** correlative obligation.
Fr. obligation réciproque.

RECOVER *v.*

To recuperate, to obtain. "It is now settled that because funeral expenses are a charge on the estate of the deceased [art. 2002 C.C.L.C.], the near relatives specified in art. 1056 *C.C.* may only recover these expenses if they show that they had to pay them because there were not in the estate sufficient assets to cover the amount" (*Pantel* v. *Air Canada*, [1975] 1 S.C.R. 472, p. 479, L.-P. Pigeon, J.). *To recover damages; to recover the costs; to recover a thing not due.*
Occ. Arts. 1536, 2625 C.C.Q.; art. 323 C.C.P.
Obs. 1° The French-language equivalent *répéter* has a narrower meaning in that it only signifies the action of demanding and not the action of recuperating that which was demanded. **2°** From the Latin *recuperare*: to recuperate.
Fr. répéter (<).

RECOVERY *n.*

Act of recovering. "[One of the codebtors] can recover from the other only the share and portion for which, *inter se*, the other was liable [art. 1118 C.C.L.C.]. With this right of recovery [...] subrogation has nothing to do" (*R.* v. *Canada Steamship Lines Ltd.*, [1927] S.C.R. 68, p. 79, F.A. Anglin, C.J.).
Occ. Arts. 1554, 1803, 2442 C.C.Q.; s. 12, *Automobile Insurance Act*, R.S.Q. c. A-25.
See also reception of a thing not due, restitution, unjust enrichment.
Fr. répétition.

RECOVERY OF A THING NOT DUE

Recovery of that which was paid without being due.
See also payment of a thing not due, reception of a thing not due, restitution of a thing not due.
Fr. répétition de l'indu.

RECURRENT DAMAGE

Damage which occurs intermittently.
Obs. 1° Periodic damage is a recurrent damage which occurs at regular intervals. **2°** Since the terms *damage* and *injury* are synonymous, the expression *recurrent injury* may also be used.
See also continuous damage, gradual damage, periodic damage.
Fr. préjudice récurrent.

REDEEM *v.*

To effect redemption.
Fr. retraire.

REDEEMER n.

Person who exercises a right of redemption.
Obs. The redeemer who exercises a redemption in the context of a partition of a succession takes the rights, but not the obligations, of the acquirer upon the property redeemed.
Fr. retrayant.

REDEMPTION n.

Unilateral act by which a person, the redeeming party, exercises a right to substitute himself or herself in the place of the acquirer of property[1], provided the latter be reimbursed what was paid to acquire it.
Obs. See articles 710, 1582 C.C.Q.
See also redeemer, redemption of litigious rights.
Fr. retrait[2].

REDEMPTION OF LITIGIOUS RIGHTS

Redemption exercised against the acquirer of a litigious right by the person against whom the right can be invoked.
Obs. A redemption of litigious rights operates by reimbursing the acquirer the price paid for the litigious right, the interest on this price, and the costs associated with the sale (art. 1784 C.C.Q.).
See also assignment of litigious rights, litigious personal right, litigious right, right of preemption, right of redemption, sale of litigious right.
Fr. retrait litigieux.

REDHIBITORY DEFECT

Syn. latent defect.
Fr. défaut caché, vice caché[+], vice rédhibitoire.

REGIME n.

Body of rules that governs the functioning of a matter or an institution of a legal order. For example, the regime of administration of the property of another, the matrimonial regime, the regimes of contractual and extracontractual liability.
Occ. Arts. 96, 432, 3089 C.C.Q.; art. 73 C.C.L.C.
See also legal order.
Fr. régime.

RELATIONAL CONTRACT (DOCTRINE OF)

Socio-economic theory of contract, which serves to organize a framework of analysis based on economic exchanges arising in relations of subordination or cooperation, which relations are established to last over time and characterized by a spirit of confidence and loyalty. "In the relational contract, however, both the content and the source of the obligations come from the relation itself, out of slowly evolving patterns of custom and law, with only modest input from individual promise" (MacNeil, *New Social Contract*, p. 17).
Obs. 1° The concept of the relational contract and the associated relational analysis of problems in contract law seek to account for the growing importance of economic exchanges within businesses or firms (economics of organizations) as well as by way of strategic alliances or long-term relationships (economics of cooperation). **2°** This analysis of the contract stresses the importance of viewing the evolution of contracts in their social context and, therefore, represents a radical departure from the general law theory of contract, which postulates the autonomous formation of contract's obligations by the parties and the creation of a legal relationship as operating outside of its social context. **3°** From a legal perspective, relational contract embraces more than the immediate substance of the exchanged promises; considerations relevant to the relational contract include the efficiency of the economic relationship, the legitimate expectations of the parties and the social acceptability of the contract. **4°** Under the influence of the doctrine of relational contract, many contracts of successive performance requiring a sustaining cooperation between the parties are characterized as *relational contracts* (e.g. contract of employment, partnership).
Fr. contrat relationnel (théorie du).

RELATIVE EFFECT OF CONTRACT

Syn. relativity of contract.
Fr. effet relatif des contrats.

RELATIVE NULLITY

Nullity that, in the formation of a juridical act, sanctions the violation of a rule designed to protect an individual interest. For example, nullity by reason of a defect of consent. "The usual sanction for contracts that have not been validly formed is nullity [...] Although all such purported contracts are struck with nullity, some will be affected by what is labelled an absolute nullity, while others will be affected only by a relative nullity. Generally, contracts in which one party's consent is vitiated [...], those entered into by

an incapable party [...] and those that violate any other provisions characterized as being protective of public order are considered to be relatively null" (Brierley & Macdonald (eds.), *Quebec Civil Law*, n° 441, p. 411).
Occ. Art. 1420 C.C.Q.
Obs. 1° Unlike absolute nullity, relative nullity cannot be invoked by any interested person or be pronounced on the court's own motion. Relative nullity can only be raised by the person in whose interest the nullity was established and by the cocontracting party acting in good faith and having sustained injury. **2°** Relative nullity may be covered by confirmation (art. 1420 C.C.Q.).
See also absolute nullity, annulability, individual interest, rescission.
Fr. nullité relative.

RELATIVE OBLIGATION

Syn. obligation of means.
Fr. obligation de diligence, obligation de moyens+, obligation générale de prudence et diligence, obligation relative.

RELATIVE PUBLIC ORDER

Syn. public order of protection.
Fr. ordre public de protection+, ordre public relatif.

RELATIVITY OF CONTRACT

Principle according to which contracts have effect only between the contracting parties.
Obs. 1° Article 1440 C.C.Q. states the principle of the relativity of contract. Despite the fact that, as a general rule, the contract has no effect with respect to third persons, rights and obligations resulting from a contract are generally transferred to the heirs of the deceased (art. 1441 C.C.Q.); the rights of the parties to a contract pass to their successors by particular title if they are accessory to property which passes to them (art. 1442 C.C.Q.), and it is possible for contracting parties to make stipulations for the benefit of a third person (arts. 1444 to 1450 C.C.Q.). **2°** The principle of relativity of contract is based on the Roman law maxim *res inter alios acta, aliis neque nocere, neque prodesse potest*: that which is done between some persons may neither harm nor profit others. This maxim is more commonly cited in its abbreviated form *res inter alios acta*. The principle reflects the idea according to which the law considers it unjust for a person to be bound by a contractual obligation without his or her consent.

Syn. relative effect of contract. **See also** direct action[1], promise of *porte-fort*, stipulation for another.
Fr. effet relatif des contrats.

RELEASE *n.*

1. Renunciation of an advantage to which one is entitled. For example, release of solidarity (art. 1532 C.C.Q.), release of a priority or of a hypothec (art. 1691 C.C.Q.). "Release is a contractual operation whereby a creditor expressly or tacitly agrees to extinguish an obligation owed by a particular debtor [...]. The release may be total or partial [...] and may be either express or tacit [...]" (Brierley & Macdonald (eds.), *Quebec Civil Law*, n° 553, p. 500).
Occ. Title preceding art. 1687 C.C.Q.; arts. 1543, 1687, 1688, 1689, 2834 C.C.Q.; art. 1181 C.C.L.C.
Obs. 1° Release may be complete or partial, express or tacit, onerous or gratuitous (arts. 1687, 1688 C.C.Q.). **2°** The codal regime respecting release is set forth at articles 1687 to 1692 C.C.Q.
See also compensation[1], confusion, discharge[2], express release, extinction, extinctive term, impossibility of performance, novation, payment, release from solidarity, release of obligation, tacit release.
Fr. remise[2].

2. Syn. discharge[3].
Occ. Arts. 1585, 1698 C.C.Q.; art. 1202*i* C.C.L.C.
Fr. décharge[3], libération[1+].

3. Syn. discharge[5].
Fr. libération[3].

4. Attesting deed that puts an end to a seizure.
Occ. Art. 2161*h* C.C.L.C.; arts. 641.1, 658 C.C.P.
See also *mainlevée*.
Fr. mainlevée(>).

RELEASE FROM SOLIDARITY

Renunciation by the creditor of the right to demand full performance of the obligation from one of the debtors.
Obs. 1° The debtor to whom the creditor grants a release from solidarity is no longer liable for the entire debt, but rather is only liable for his or her share thereof. **2°** The creditor retains his or her right to claim for the whole debt from the debtors to whom release of solidarity was not given (art. 1532 C.C.Q.). **3°** Release from solidarity should

not be confused with release of debt. In a release of debt, the creditor renounces a part or the whole of a personal right. In a release from solidarity, the creditor of several solidary debtors does not renounce a personal right but only the benefit derived from solidarity.
See also release of obligation.
Fr. remise de solidarité.

RELEASE OF DEBT

Syn. release of obligation.
Occ. Art. 1182 C.C.L.C.
Fr. remise de dette+, remise d'une obligation.

RELEASE OF OBLIGATION

Agreement in which a creditor renounces all or part of the debt owed.
Obs. Release from solidarity should not be confused with release of debt. In a release of debt, the creditor renounces a part or the whole of a personal right. In a release from solidarity, the creditor of several solidary debtors does not renounce a personal right but only the benefit derived from solidarity.
Occ. Art. 1181 C.C.L.C.
Syn. release of debt. **See also** release from solidarity.
Fr. remise de dette+, remise d'une obligation.

RELIEVE v.

Syn. discharge. "One surety being relieved sometimes has the effect of relieving another, but that can not operate in this case where the surety was himself a party to the fault that may have relieved the other" (*Trust and Loan Co. of Canada* v. *Würtele* (1905), 35 S.C.R. 663, p. 692, J. Idington, J.).
Occ. Arts. 409, 694, 2023 C.C.Q.
Fr. libérer.

REMIT v.

To effect a remittance.
Occ. Arts. 326, 361, 1369, 2185, 2400, 2789 C.C.Q.; arts. 1202k, 1658.1, 1979c C.C.L.C.
Syn. hand over.
Fr. remettre.

REMITTANCE n.

Action of transferring to another person the detention of a property.
Occ. Arts. 1909, 2709, 2711 C.C.Q.; art. 1193 C.C.L.C.
Obs. 1° The property remitted may be a movable, as in the remittance of an object of

value to a depositary (art. 2281 C.C.Q.), or an immovable, as in the remittance of a dwelling at the termination of the lease (art. 1889 C.C.Q.). **2°** The property remitted may also be a writing, such as the original title of a negotiable instrument (art. 1568 C.C.Q.), a title of ownership (arts. 2702, 2704 C.C.Q.) or an act of procedure (art. 123 C.C.P.). **3°** The remittance of the property is essential to the formation of real contracts, such as deposits and loans. **4°** In certain cases, the remittance is equivalent to a payment and discharges the debtor (arts. 694, 813, 1562, 1564 C.C.Q.).
Syn. handing over. **See also** delivery[1,2], payment[2], real contract, removal, tradition.
Fr. remise[1].

REMOTE-PARTIES CONTRACT

Syn. contract *inter absentes*.
Occ. S. 20, *Consumer Protection Act*, R.S.Q. c. P-40.1.
Fr. contrat à distance, contrat entre absents, contrat entre non-présents+.

REMOVAL n.

Operation by which a person takes away property[2] to which he or she is entitled.
Occ. Arts. 1722, 1829, 2048, 2068 C.C.Q.
Obs. 1° The obligation to remove property arises typically in respect of translatory acts of ownership of corporeal movables, such as in sale, donation, and giving-in-payment. However, the term is also employed in other contexts, as in the contract for the carriage of goods. **2°** Expenses related to the removal are payable, in principle, by the person removing the property.
See also acceptance[3], delivery[2], remittance, tradition.
Fr. enlèvement+, retirement.

REMOVE v.

To effect a removal. "The buyer's delivery obligation to which allusion is made in articles 1495 and 1544 C.C.L.C. is to receive or remove the thing delivered by the seller" (Boodman, (1988) 67 *Can. Bar Rev.* 658, p. 661).
Syn. take delivery.
Fr. enlever+, prendre délivrance, prendre livraison, retirer[1].

REMUNERATION n.

Counterprestation having pecuniary value received in exchange for the performance of work. "The *Civil Code of Québec* refers to the

concept of 'remuneration' rather than 'wages' as is found in the *Civil Code of Lower Canada*. Therefore, except for special circumstances particular to each case, remuneration has a broader meaning than wages or salary" (Bonhomme, Gascon & Lesage, *Employment Contract*, p. 9).
Occ. Arts. 183, 1300, 2085, 2134, 2293, 2333 C.C.Q.
Obs. 1° The generic term *remuneration* is used to designate the counterprestation received for the work performed under, for example, a contract of employment, a contract of enterprise, a contract for services, a contract of carriage or a mandate. **2°** The Civil Code also speaks of remuneration in the case of a suretyship contemplated by onerous title (art. 2333 C.C.Q.). **3°** In a contract of employment, remuneration includes, among other things, the salary, the contribution of the employer to any insurance regime or retirement plan and vacation allowances. **4°** From Latin *remuneratio*, from *munus, muneris*: present, reward.
See also commission, freight[1,2], price, salary.
Fr. rémunération.

RENEWAL *n.*

Repetition of a contract of successive performance. "The legislative policy to promote stable rental accommodation has generated a new governing principle for renewal and termination of residential leases: the right to maintenance in the premises [...]" (Brierley & Macdonald (eds.), *Quebec Civil Law*, n° 620, p. 547).
Occ. Art. 1946 C.C.Q.; s. 150.2, *Consumer Protection Act*, R.S.Q. c. P-40.1; s. 160, *An Act respecting the implementation of the reform of the Civil Code*, S.Q. 1992, c. 57.
See also tacit renewal.
Fr. reconduction.

RENT *n.*

1. Price that the *lessee[1]* pays to the *lessor[1]* for the enjoyment of the property leased.
Occ. Arts. 1851, 1863, 1903, 1943 C.C.Q.; arts. 1600, 1609, 1617, 1651.2 C.C.L.C.; ss. 30.2, 39, 42, 77, 90, *An Act respecting the Régie du logement*, R.S.Q. c. R-8.1; ss. 6, 30, *Tourist Establishments Act*, R.S.Q. c. E-15.1.
Obs. The term *rent* is normally used in respect of the lease of an immovable.
See also lease[1], price, property[2].
Fr. loyer[+], prix de location.

2. Syn. annuity[1].
Occ. Arts. 704, 947 C.C.L.C.

Obs. The term *rent* is rarely used in this sense.
Fr. rente[1].

3. Syn. annuity[2]. "A rent is constituted or created principally in this way: In consideration of $100 paid by A to B, B promises to pay A $6 a year until B chooses to redeem the rent" (Marler, *Real Property*, p. 11).
Occ. Arts. 389, 1789, 1902 C.C.L.C.
Obs. While *rent* occurred in the *Civil Code of Lower Canada*, *annuity* was the preferred term in ordinary and professional parlance, even before the enactment of the *Civil Code of Québec*.
Fr. rente[2].

RENT *v.*

1. Syn. lease[1].
Fr. louer[1].

2. Syn. lease[2].
Fr. louer[2].

RENTAL *adj.*

Relating to a lease. *Rental agency, rental value*.
Occ. Art. 1853 C.C.Q; art. 1634 C.C.L.C.; ss. 36, 54.11, 112.1, *An Act respecting the Régie du logement*, R.S.Q. c. R-8.1.
Fr. locatif.

RENUNCIATION *n.*

1. Act by which the holder of a right provokes its extinction insofar as he or she is concerned. "Tacit renunciation results from unequivocal facts which necessarily imply an intention by the creditor to cancel claims on the immovable. Further, the renunciation is strictly interpreted if there is any doubt as to its scope" (*Gingras* v. *Gagnon*, [1977] 1 S.C.R. 217, p. 222, J. Beetz, J.).
Occ. Arts. 1477, 2885 C.C.Q.; arts. 1755(2), 2185 C.C.L.C.
Obs. 1° Renunciation is usually a unilateral act; it can also be bilateral, as when the consent of the other party is necessary, such as in a release of debt. **2°** Acts of renunciation may apply to both real and personal rights, as well as to means of protection or defence against claims by third parties (e.g. exception of non-performance, acquisitive prescription). They may also apply to charges of a public or family nature (e.g. tutorship). **3°** Specialized terms, such as *abandonment* and *divestment*, are used in designated circumstances.
Syn. abdication, abdicative act, act of renunciation. **See also** attributive act, constitutive

title, declaratory act, renunciatory effect, repudiation, resiliation[1,2], translatory title. **Fr.** abdication, acte abdicatif[+].

2. Act by which a person agrees not to exercise a right[2] or to give up a legal argument. For example, the renunciation of an option to purchase.
Occ. Arts. 423, 469, 641, 1006, 1110, 1191, 1296, 1477, 1691, 2175, 2501, 2936 C.C.Q.; arts. 651, 874, 1755(2), 1895, 2126, 2227, 2185 C.C.L.C.
Obs. 1° Scholars generally view renunciation as a unilateral juridical act, which may be express or tacit. It can be effected by gratuitous or onerous title. Renunciation may, for example, bear on a real right (e.g. abandonment of a servitude), a right of succession (e.g. renunciation of a succession), a right of action (e.g. discontinuance of judicial proceedings) or a benefit granted by law (e.g. renunciation of prescription). **2°** Renunciation is, in many instances, an abdicative act, i.e. an act by which the holder of a right brings about its extinction. In this respect, the rights attached to a person are not susceptible of renunciation (e.g. personality rights). However, a partial renunciation of a right attached to a person remains possible as well as the renunciation to the right of action resulting from the violation of such a right. **3°** Certain forms of renunciation are submitted to the formalities of publication (see art. 2938 C.C.Q.).
Syn. abandonment[2], waiver. **See also** abandonment[1], renunciation[1].
Fr. renonciation.

RENUNCIATIVE EFFECT

Syn. renunciatory effect.
Fr. effet abdicatif.

RENUNCIATORY EFFECT

Consequence of the extinction of a right brought about by the act of its holder. For example, following renunciation, the share of the person renouncing a succession accrues to his or her co-heirs.
Syn. abdicative effect, renunciative effect. **See also** constitutive effect, declaratory effect, extinctive effect, renunciation[1], translatory effect.
Fr. effet abdicatif.

REPAIR *v.*

To effect the reparation[1] of damage. "[...] it is settled that whereas the moment at which the loss to be compensated is determined

at the date of non-performance, the relevant moment for the calculation of damages is that of judgment, except where this will result in giving the creditor more than compensation. He may [...] have taken steps to repair the loss at some earlier time [...]" (Nicholas, *Contract*, p. 231).
Occ. Art. 1359 C.C.Q.; art. 2562 C.C.L.C.
See also indemnify.
Fr. réparer.

REPARATION *n.*

1. Act of making good a loss. *Reparation of damage.*
Occ. Arts. 1457, 1549, 1621 C.C.Q.
Obs. 1° Reparation is a central premise of the theory of civil liability. Thus, article 1457 C.C.Q. provides that the person responsible for an injury is liable for its reparation. **2°** Reparation is of two types: that which is given in kind and that which is given as equivalence, i.e. a sum of money. **3°** Generally, one refers to reparation of damage but compensation to a person.
See also performance, reparation by equivalence, reparation in kind.
Fr. réparation.

2. Syn. indemnity.
Fr. compensation[3], indemnité[+].

REPARATION BY EQUIVALENCE

Reparation[1] consisting of an indemnity equivalent to the loss sustained by the creditor.
Occ. Art. 1549 C.C.Q.
Syn. compensation[2], indemnification. **See also** damages, indemnifiable, performance by equivalence, reparation in kind.
Fr. compensation[2], indemnisation, réparation par équivalent[+].

REPARATION IN KIND

Reparation[1] by restoration to the original state. "Like its French counterpart, the regime of reparation in kind has been hampered by the traditional reluctance of judges to force the performance of an obligation when such an order would require interference with the personal liberty of the defendant. For this reason, courts have usually favoured monetary awards as the proper remedy in all cases involving obligations to do" (Brierley & Macdonald (eds.), *Quebec Civil Law*, n° 525, p. 478).
Obs. For positive obligations, reparation in kind consists of the forced performance of the obligation itself. For negative obligations, reparation in kind consists of an abstaining

from or reversing that which was done in violation of the obligation.
See also reparation by equivalence, specific performance.
Fr. réparation en nature.

REPOSSESS *v.*

To effect a repossession.
Occ. Arts. 1957, 1960 C.C.Q.; s. 81.1(1), *Bankruptcy and Insolvency Act*, R.S.C. 1985, c. B-3.
Obs. In the *Civil Code of Québec*, in the chapter on sale, the phrase *to take back* is used rather than the verb *to repossess* as the equivalent of the French verb *reprendre*.
Syn. retake possession, take back. **See also** remittance.
Fr. reprendre+, reprendre possession.

REPOSSESSION *n.*

Action by the owner to recover physical control over property detained by another, thus putting an end to the latter's detention of it.
Occ. Arts. 1960, 1968 C.C.Q.; s. 150.15, *Consumer Protection Act*, R.S.Q. c. P-40.1.
Obs. 1° Repossession takes place usually under leases of a dwelling (art. 1957 C.C.Q.) or instalment sales (art. 1748 C.C.Q.). **2°** The owner must obtain the authorization of the court if the lessee refuses to vacate the dwelling. **3°** Under an instalment sale, the exercise of the right of repossession is also subject to judicial authorization (see arts. 1749, 2778 C.C.Q. and s. 142, *Consumer Protection Act*, R.S.Q. c. P-40.1). In this context, the seller's right of repossession is comparable to a surety, which explains why repossession is subject to the rules pertaining to taking in payment (art. 1749 C.C.Q.).
Syn. retaking of possession. **See also** forced repossession, instalment sale, right of repossession.
Fr. reprise+, reprise de possession.

REPRESENT *v.*

To effect a juridical act for and in the name of another person.
Occ. Art. 290 C.C.L.C.
Fr. représenter.

REPRESENTATION *n.*

Performance by a representative of a juridical act in the name and on behalf of another, the person represented, whose patrimony is directly affected by the act. For example, the representation of a minor by the tutor, or representation of a mandator by the mandatary. "The mandator cannot escape responsibility for the lawful acts of the mandatary, while the mandatary can escape responsibility if acting within the mandate. This flows inevitably from the concept of representation" (Claxton, (1997) 42 *McGill L.J.* 797, p. 849).
Occ. Art. 4 C.C.Q.
Obs. Representation may be conventional, legal or judicial. It may be voluntary or forced.
Syn. perfect representation. **See also** mandate[1].
Fr. représentation+, représentation immédiate, représentation parfaite.

REPRESENTATIVE *n.*

Person who performs a juridical act in the name and on behalf of another, the person represented. For example, a tutor, a curator, a mandatary. "The term 'fondé de pouvoir' may identify a new form of representative who holds rights in or to property as fiduciary. The C.C.Q. names a good number of other types of representatives: the tutor, the curator, the trustee, and the mandatary holding a general mandate are some examples. All must [...] follow the rules for the administration of the property of others" (Claxton, (1999) 44 *McGill L.J.* 665, pp. 702-703).
Occ. Arts. 21,158, 276, 3116 C.C.Q.; arts. 348a, 1894, 2191 C.C.L.C.
See also mandatary, person represented, representation.
Fr. représentant.

REPUDIATE *v.*

To effect a repudiation.
Occ. Arts. 1338, 2161 C.C.Q.; arts. 866, 965 C.C.L.C.
Fr. répudier.

REPUDIATION *n.*

Renunciation of a right resulting from a liberality. For example, the renunciation of a succession. *Repudiation of a gift*; *repudiation of a legacy*.
Occ. Arts. 792, 933 para. 4 C.C.L.C.
See also renunciation[1].
Fr. répudiation.

RES n. (Latin)

1. **Syn.** thing[1].
Fr. chose[1+], chose corporelle, chose matérielle.

2. Syn. patrimonial right.
Obs. The expressions "trust res" or "res of the trust" are often encountered in the law of trusts to designate the trust property.
Fr. bien[1], bien incorporel, chose incorporelle, droit patrimonial[+].

RESCIND v.

To pronounce rescission. "They recommended that minors should not be restored for lesion if all the relevant solemnities provided by law for the alienation of their property had been carried out. This proposal, which became article 1010 C.C.L.C., followed article 1314 C.C.F. Going beyond article 1313 C.C.F., the Quebec redactors recommended that adults should *never* be able to rescind contracts on the grounds of lesion" (Cairns, (1986-87) 32 *McGill L.J.* 673, p. 683). *To rescind a contract.*
Occ. Art. 1000 C.C.L.C.
See also annul, set aside.
Fr. rescinder.

RESCISSION n.

Retroactive termination of a juridical act on the ground of lesion. "Although the Code [C.C.L.C.] indiscriminately employs the terms 'rescission' and 'nullité' [...] the remedy in effect involves the declaration of nullity, more precisely the relative nullity, of the contract together with special effects related to restitution" (Johnston, *Unfair Contracts*, p. 42). *Rescission of contract.*
Occ. Art. 751 C.C.L.C.
Obs. 1° Although the term *rescission* is traditionally reserved for nullity on the ground of lesion, the *Civil Code of Lower Canada* sometimes used it to designate relative nullity based on some other ground (art. 2258 C.C.L.C.). Conversely, the term *nullity* was also used in reference to lesion, as it is now used in the Civil Code (arts. 1001, 1002 C.C.L.C. and arts. 1407, 1408 C.C.Q.). **2°** In the *Ancien droit*, the term *rescission* was also used, to designate the nullities originating from Roman Law that could only be invoked by a person who had previously obtained a *lettre de rescision*, i.e. the King's permission. **3°** From the Latin *rescindere*: to split, to divide.
See also lesion, relative nullity, restitution.
Fr. rescision.

RESILIATE v.

1. To pronounce a resiliation[1]. "Furthermore, as in the general regime of contracts, lessees may *resiliate the contract* if they have suf-

fered a substantial prejudice because of defects in the property leased, such as when the object is unusable, or when a dwelling is not in good habitable condition or is entirely unfit for habitation" (Olivier, (1995) 40 *McGill L.J.* 187, p. 196).
Occ. Art. 1916 C.C.Q.
Obs. See article 1883 C.C.Q.
See also annul, resolve, set aside.
Fr. résilier[1].

2. To effect a resiliation[2]. *To resiliate a lease of indeterminate term; to resiliate a sale.*
Occ. Art. 2125 C.C.Q.
See also cancel.
Fr. résilier[2].

RESILIATION n.

1. Non-retroactive termination of a contract of successive performance by reason of the non-performance of an obligation by one of the parties. *Resiliation of a lease; resiliation of a contract of employment.* "The general rule is that, upon the resiliation of a lease, the lessor is always entitled to demand the payment of all rent due, and it would require very clear provisions to take away this elementary right" (*Séguin* v. *Coupal* (1940), 69 B.R. 499, p. 509, G. Barclay, J.).
Occ. Arts. 1652.10, 1655.1 C.C.L.C.
Obs. 1° Resiliation is distinct from resolution in that it terminates the contract for the future only. This stems from the very nature of a contract which has produced results that cannot be retroactively obliterated. **2°** From the Latin *resilire*: to jump back; to recoil.
See also nullity, resolution[1].
Fr. résiliation[1].

2. Non-retroactive termination of a juridical act resulting from the agreement of the parties or from the law. *Resiliation of a lease, of a contract of employment.*
Occ. Arts. 1590, 1875 C.C.Q.
Obs. Resiliation resulting from an agreement between the parties or from the unilateral decision of one party is known as *voluntary resiliation.* Resiliation by operation of law is known as *forced resiliation.*
See also bilateral resiliation, forced resiliation, revocation[1], unilateral resiliation, voluntary resiliation.
Fr. résiliation[2].

RESOLUTION n.

1. Retroactive termination of a juridical act by reason of non-performance of an obligation by one of the parties. "The right of resolution under Article 1741 of the *Civil Code* is also not available to a vendor under an instalment sale. One of the conditions for applicability of this right of resolution is that the sale is not with a term" (Dietze, (1999) 59 *R. du B.* 1, p. 17). *To obtain the resolution of a contract*; *a judgment in resolution.*

Occ. Arts. 1590, 1604, 1605 C.C.Q.

Obs. 1° Article 1590 C.C.Q. provides that the creditor is only entitled to resolution when the non-performance is unjustified. The creditor is not entitled to resolution if the default of the debtor is of minor importance (art. 1604 C.C.Q.). **2°** Resolution may be pronounced by a court or it may occur as of right (art. 1605 C.C.Q.). **3°** In principle, resolution can be distinguished from resiliation by its retroactive effect. It entails the restitution of the prestations (arts. 1606, 1699 to 1707 C.C.Q.). **4°** In general, resolution takes place only in synallagmatic contracts. **5°** From the Latin *resolutio* (from *resolvere*: to resolve): the action of untying, of loosening; dissolution.

See also annulability, exception of nonperformance, judicial resolution, resiliation[1], resolution (as) of right, resolutory clause of right, resolutory condition.

Fr. résolution[1].

2. Retroactive extinction of an obligation[2] or a right as a result of the realization of a resolutory condition.

Obs. The consequences of the realization of a resolutory condition are, in principle, resolution of right and the restitution of the prestations (art. 1507 C.C.Q.; ss. 62, 76, *Consumer Protection Act*, R.S.Q. c. P-40.1).

Fr. résolution[2].

RESOLUTION *DE JURE* (Latin)

Syn. resolution (as) of right.
Fr. résolution de plein droit.

RESOLUTION (AS) OF RIGHT

Resolution that need not be pronounced by the courts.

Obs. 1° Resolution of right results from the realization of a resolutory condition or from the non-performance of the debtor's obligation. In the latter case, resolution occurs where the debtor is in default by operation of law or where he or she has failed to perform his or her obligation within the specified time. Judicial resolution is, therefore, exceptional (arts. 1597, 1605, 1740 C.C.Q.). **2°** Article 1597 C.C.Q. sets forth the situations when the debtor is in default by operation of law. Such is the case, for example, when the performance of the obligation has become useless or when the debtor has made clear an intention not to perform the obligation.

Syn. resolution *de jure.* **See also** judicial resolution, resolutory clause of right.

Fr. résolution de plein droit.

RESOLUTIVE *adj.*

See resolutive clause, resolutive condition.
Fr. résolutoire.

RESOLUTIVE CLAUSE

Syn. resolutory clause[1]. "In commercial leases, there are often resolutive clauses which stipulate that in the event of default by the lessee, the lease terminates *ipso facto*" (Sarna, in *Meredith Lectures (1989)*, 157, p. 168).

Fr. clause de résolution, clause résolutoire[1+].

RESOLUTIVE CONDITION

Syn. resolutory condition. "[...] as a rule, a stipulation is not to be construed as a resolutive condition unless the intention to do so is expressed" (*Automotive Products Co.* v. *Insurance Co. of North America*, [1969] S.C.R. 824, p. 842, L.-P. Pigeon, J.).

Occ. Arts. 769, 1114(2) C.C.Q.; art. 1088 C.C.L.C.

Fr. condition résolutoire.

RESOLUTORY *adj.*

See resolutory clause, resolutory condition.
Fr. résolutoire.

RESOLUTORY CLAUSE

1. Clause in a juridical act providing for the resolution of the act upon the non-performance of an obligation arising therefrom.

Obs. 1° In principle, the mere default of a debtor to fulfil his or her obligations entitles the creditor to request that the contract be resolved without the requirement of a clause to this effect. In exceptional cases, this remedy is only available to the creditor where the contract so provides. Thus, in the sale of an immovable, the unpaid vendor cannot ask for resolution of the sale without a special clause to this effect (art. 1742 C.C.Q.). **2°** Resolution of right occurs when the debtor is in default by the sole operation of law or when he or she does not perform the obligation within the time allowed in the writing putting him or her in default. Judicial resolution is exceptional (arts. 1597, 1605, 1740 C.C.Q.).

Syn. clause of resolution, resolutive clause. **See also** resolutory clause of right. **Fr.** clause de résolution, clause résolutoire[1+].

2. Clause providing for a resolutory condition. **Fr.** clause résolutoire[2].

RESOLUTORY CLAUSE OF RIGHT

Resolutory clause[1] providing for the automatic resolution of the juridical act upon the non-performance of an obligation arising therefrom, within a certain lapse of time. **Obs. 1°** The creditor is not bound to take advantage of such a clause. He or she may prefer to maintain the contract and seek the remedies of compulsory execution under article 1590 C.C.Q. **2°** When a resolutory clause of right is disputed and the court finds in favour of the creditor, it will not declare the resolution but instead confirm its operation. The resolution results solely from the debtor's default. **Syn.** clause of resolution of right, express clause of resolution, express resolutory clause, stipulation of resolution upon non-performance. **See also** judicial resolution, resolution (as) of right. **Fr.** clause de résolution de plein droit, clause expresse de résolution, clause résolutoire de plein droit+, clause résolutoire expresse, pacte commissoire.

RESOLUTORY CONDITION

Condition[1] the fulfilment of which entails the retroactive extinction of a right or obligation. "[...] an obligation can be subject to a resolutory condition, as where an existing obligation can be retroactively extinguished if a predetermined event occurs. For example, in a contract that is translatory of a right in property, when the stipulated event occurs (say, the birth of children to the seller, or the bankruptcy of the purchaser), the purchaser is deemed never to have been owner, and all rights in or over the property granted by the purchaser to third parties [...] are retroactively extinguished" (Brierley & Macdonald (eds.), *Quebec Civil Law*, n° 529, p. 482). **Occ.** Arts. 1507, 1750 C.C.Q. **Obs.** Upon fulfilment of the resolutory condition, the obligation is said to disappear retroactively, of right, and is deemed never to have existed (arts. 1506, 1507 C.C.Q.). When a resolutory condition fails, the obligation becomes pure and simple. **Syn.** resolutive condition. **See also** extinctive term, resolutory clause[2], suspensive condition. **Fr.** condition résolutoire.

RESOLVE *v.*

To pronounce or effect resolution. "[...] the putting in default is of no utility if both parties desire to resolve or resiliate the contract" (Kouri, (1971) 2 *R.D.U.S.* 1, pp. 39-40). **Occ.** Art. 1606 C.C.Q. **See also** annul, cancel, resiliate[1,2], revoke, set aside. **Fr.** résoudre.

RES PERIT CREDITORI nom.ph. (Latin)

Rule according to which the loss of the thing is borne by the creditor who was prevented from performing an obligation by reason of superior force. "[...] the idea of *res perit creditori*, Roman in origin, arose from the inability of the ancient Romans to understand the correlation of performance of obligation of buyer and seller" (Wasserman, (1952) 12 *R. du B.* 366, p. 380). **Obs.** The maxim *res perit creditori* ("the thing perishes for the creditor") is used with respect to unilateral contracts. For example, if the thing perishes in the hands of a borrower or a depositary through superior force he or she is released from the obligation to remit the thing to the lender or to the depositor. **See also** doctrine of risks[1], *res perit debitori*, *res perit domino*. **Fr.** *res perit creditori*.

RES PERIT DEBITORI nom.ph. (Latin)

Rule according to which the loss of the thing is borne by the debtor who was prevented from performing an obligation by reason of superior force. **Obs. 1°** The rule *res perit debitori* ("the thing perishes for the debtor"), forming part of the doctrine of risks[1], applies to synallagmatic contracts. **2°** As an exception to the principle establishing the owner of the property as the person who assumes the risk of loss (art. 950 C.C.Q.), the risk of loss by superior force is borne, in principle, by the debtor of the obligation to deliver, regardless of whether he or she is the owner (art. 1456 C.C.Q.). **3°** The debtor, even if released from the obligation, bears the consequences of non-performance in that he or she cannot require the co-contracting party to perform the correlative obligation (art. 1694 C.C.Q.). **See also** doctrine of risks[1], *res perit creditori*, *res perit domino*. **Fr.** *res perit debitori*.

RES PERIT DOMINO nom.ph. (Latin)

Rule according to which the loss of the thing arising by reason of superior force is borne by

the owner of the thing. "As a matter of general principle, a thing perishes for its owner, *res perit domino*. Thus, if a thing is destroyed by flood or lightning, the loss is borne by the owner" (Litvinoff, in *Treatise*, vol. 7, Book 2, n° 127, p. 236).
Obs. 1° The rule *res perit domino* ("the thing perishes for the owner") is an application of the principle that the owner of property assumes the risk of loss (art. 950 C.C.Q.). **2°** Under the *Civil Code of Lower Canada*, the principle of *res perit domino* applied to synallagmatic contracts that transferred ownership. It has been replaced under the *Civil Code of Québec* by the rule *res perit debitori*, according to which the risk of loss by superior force is in principle borne by the debtor of the obligation to deliver, regardless of whether he or she is the owner (art. 1456 C.C.Q.). However, in consumer sales by instalment, the merchant assumes the risk of loss or deterioration of the property until ownership is transferred to the consumer (s. 133, *Consumer Protection Act*, R.S.Q. c. P-40.1).
See also doctrine of risks[1], *res perit creditori*, *res perit debitori*.
Fr. *res perit domino*.

RESPONSIBILITY *n.*

Syn. juridical responsibility. "The mandator cannot escape responsibility for the lawful acts of the mandatary, while the mandatary can escape responsibility if acting within the mandate. This flows inevitably from the concept of representation" (Claxton, (1997) 42 *McGill L.J.* 797, p. 849).
Obs. 1° Depending on context, the term *responsibility* may evoke the narrower and distinct notions of civil liability or criminal liability. **2°** From the Latin *respondere*: to answer.
Fr. responsabilité, responsabilité juridique[+].

RESPONSIBLE *adj.*

Syn. liable. "The general rule [...] is that a person must have been proved at fault if he is to be civilly responsible" (Nicholls, *Offences and Quasi-Offences*, p. 47).
Occ. Art. 1457 C.C.Q.; arts. 1053, 1054, 1055 C.C.L.C.
Fr. responsable.

RESTITUTIO IN INTEGRUM
nom.ph. (Latin)

Syn. full reparation. "When a plaintiff is defamed, his or her primary goal is the resto-ration of the damaged reputation. Large damage awards may indeed provide solace to the plaintiff, but it is hardly the most effective way of restoring to the plaintiff what was lost, of effecting *restitutio in integrum*" (Jukier, (1989) 49 *R. du B.* 3, p. 39).
Fr. réparation intégrale[+], *restitutio in integrum*.

RESTITUTION *n.*

Fact of returning property received without due cause. "If a thing received initially in kind cannot be restored, restitution is made by payment of the value of the thing determined according to the good or bad faith of the initial recipient" (Boodman, (1995) 6 *S. C. L. R.* 45, p. 47). *Restitution of fruits*; *restitution of the price*; *restitution of prestations*.
Occ. Title preceding art. 1699 C.C.Q.; arts. 1492, 1694, 1699 to 1701, 1838, 2265 C.C.Q.; art. 1513 C.C.L.C.; art. 470 C.C.P.; ss. 63, 64, 77, 211, *Consumer Protection Act*, R.S.Q. c. P-40.1; s. 81, *International Sale of Goods Contracts Convention Act*, S.C. 1991, c. 13.
Obs. 1° Article 1699 C.C.Q. provides for restitution where a person has received property unlawfully, by error, or under a juridical act that may not be performed by reason of superior force. Restitution also takes place following the annulment or the resolution of a juridical act. **2°** In principle, restitution is made in kind. When this is impossible or cannot be effected without serious inconvenience, restitution is made by equivalence (art. 1700 C.C.Q.). **3°** Full restitution is, in principle, the rule as is the case of restitution in kind. Restitution by equivalence may not amount to full restitution where it does not correspond to the value of the property when it was received. Where restitution would have the effect of procuring an undue advantage to one party, the court may refuse to order it or modify its scope (art. 1699 C.C.Q.). **4°** Restitution does not take place where the property has perished by superior force; the debtor must, however, assign to the creditor the indemnity he or she has received, or his or her right to an indemnity (art. 1701 C.C.Q.). **5°** A special chapter of the Civil Code (arts. 1699 to 1707 C.C.Q.) provides for the general regime relating to restitution. It may be observed that this regime is different from the Common law theory of restitution notwithstanding that, in both traditions, the general theory of restitution may be connected to the idea of unjust enrichment. **6°** From the Latin *restitutio*: a restoring.
See also nullity, reparation, resolution[1], restitution by equivalence, restitution in kind,

restitution of a thing not due, superior force[1,2].
Fr. restitution.

RESTITUTION BY EQUIVALENCE

Restitution of a sum of money equivalent to the value of the thing received.
Occ. Art. 1700 C.C.Q.
Obs. 1° Restitution by equivalence takes place where restitution in kind is impossible or cannot be effected without serious inconvenience (art. 1700 C.C.Q.). **2°** The equivalence may be fixed by taking into account the value of the property when it was received, at the time of restitution or, in some cases, at the time it was lost or alienated. The equivalence generally corresponds to the value of the property received. In cases of total loss or alienation of the property, the debtor is bound to return the lowest value, but if the restitution is due to the fault of the debtor or if the debtor is in bad faith, he or she is bound to return the highest value (art. 1701 C.C.Q.).
See also performance by equivalence, reparation in equivalence, restitution in kind.
Fr. restitution par équivalent.

RESTITUTION IN KIND

Restitution of precisely that which was received.
Occ. Arts. 1700, 2282 C.C.Q.
Obs. In principle, restitution is made in kind. Where this is impossible or cannot be effected without serious inconvenience, it is made by equivalence (art. 1700 C.C.Q.).
See also reparation in kind, restitution by equivalence, specific performance.
Fr. restitution en nature.

RESTITUTION OF A THING NOT DUE

Restitution of that which was paid without being due.
See also payment of a thing not due, reception of a thing not due, recovery of a thing not due.
Fr. restitution de l'indu.

RESTORE v.

To effect a restitution. "A successful action to recover a thing not due imposes upon the defendant a restitution obligation – an obligation to restore the thing or payment received" (Boodman, (1995) 6 *S. C. L. R.* 45, p. 47).
Occ. Arts. 1422, 1606, 1700, 1705, 1838 C.C.Q.; art. 1047 C.C.L.C.; ss. 63, 211, *Consumer Protection Act*, R.S.Q. c. P-40.1.

Obs. The verb *reimburse* is also used in the case of monetary restitution.
Fr. restituer.

RESTRICTIVE CLAUSE

Syn. restrictive covenant.
Fr. clause restrictive.

RESTRICTIVE COVENANT

Clause that results in the limitation of commerce or of a person's freedom to work. "No restrictive covenants are subject to such severe scrutiny as those in contracts of employment. The judicial policy is to protect the individual's freedom of action and his right to earn a livelihood" (Sheppard, (1963) 23 *R. du B.* 311, p. 316).
Obs. 1° Discretion clauses, non-reestablishment clauses and non-solicitation of customers clauses are examples of restrictive covenants. **2°** The notion of *restrictive covenant* is broad enough to encompass non-competition clauses as well as exclusivity clauses. In practice, however, the expressions *restrictive covenant* and *non-competition clause* are often used interchangeably. **3°** According to some scholars, the expression *restrictive covenant* should not be used in the civil law because of its different connotations in Common law[2], and instead the expressions *non-competition clause* or *exclusivity clause* are to be preferred.
Syn. restrictive clause.
Fr clause restrictive.

RETAKE POSSESSION *verb.ph.*

Syn. repossess.
Occ. Art. 1659 C.C.L.C.; ss. 138, 150.13, *Consumer Protection Act*, R.S.Q. c. P-40.1; s. 54, *An Act respecting the Régie du logement*, R.S.Q. c. R-8.1.
Obs. In the expression *retake of possession*, the words *of possession* can be considered superfluous.
Fr. reprendre+, reprendre possession.

RETAKING OF POSSESSION

Syn. repossession.
Occ. Arts. 1659.1, 1659.5 C.C.L.C.; ss. 46, 54.10, *An Act respecting the Régie du logement*, R.S.Q. c. R-8.1.
Obs. In the expression *retaking of possession*, the words *of possession* can be considered superfluous.
Fr. reprise+, reprise de possession.

RETRACT *v.*

To effect a retraction.
Syn. withdraw[1]. **See also** revoke.
Fr. retirer[2], rétracter[+].

RETRACTION *n.*

Revocation[1], with regard to an offer.
Syn. withdrawal.
Fr. rétractation[+], retrait[1].

RETROACTIVITY OF A CONDITION

Fiction by which the effects of the fulfilment or failure of a condition[1] are carried back in time. "The distinction between the effect of terms and conditions resulting from the retroactivity of the latter has been the rationale for a number of legislative interventions in hypothecary loan contracts and in consumer sales contracts" (Brierley & Macdonald (eds.), *Quebec Civil Law*, n° 533, p. 485).
Obs. The retroactivity of a condition serves to backdate the effects of the contract to the day the contract was entered into (art. 1506 C.C.Q.). Upon failure of a suspensive condition or realization of a resolutory condition, the obligation is deemed never to have existed and, by extension, the contract is treated as never having existed. Conversely, upon realization of the suspensive condition or failure of the resolutory condition, the obligation is deemed to have existed purely and simply from the day the contract was entered into. In this case, it is as if no condition had ever existed (art. 1507 C.C.Q.)
Fr. rétroactivité de la condition.

RETURNABLE *adj.*

(*Succ.*) Subject to the return of liberalities.
See also advance upon succession.
Fr. rapportable.

REVENDICATE *v.*

To seek revendication.
Occ. Arts. 953, 1714, 1741, 2919 C.C.Q.; arts. 1801, 1998(1) C.C.L.C.; arts. 597, 734 C.C.P.
Fr. revendiquer.

REVENDICATION *n.*

Action by which one seeks the restitution of a thing[1]. "It is obvious that revendication as a post-delivery remedy presupposes performance of the seller's delivery obligation" (Boodman, (1989-90) 35 *McGill L.J.* 19, p. 55).
Occ. Arts. 1714, 1741, 2919 C.C.Q.; arts. 1543, 1999, 2268 C.C.L.C.

Obs. 1° The action in revendication is used to obtain the restitution of a movable or an immovable. In principle, the right to revendicate the thing belongs to the owner (art. 953 C.C.Q.), but it is also granted to other persons by law (e.g. the liquidator of a succession (art. 777 C.C.Q.), the holder of a right of retention (art. 1593 C.C.Q.), the depositor (art. 2282 C.C.Q.) and the holder of a claim secured by a movable hypothec with delivery (art. 2706 C.C.Q.)). **2°** Revendication may be exercised in the case of a sale of property of another. The buyer in good faith of a movable may ask the revendicating proprietor for repayment of the price paid if the movable has been acquired in the ordinary course of business of an enterprise (art. 1714 C.C.Q.). **3°** In matters relating to sale, revendication usually follows the resolution of the contract. **4°** From the Latin *rei vindicatio* (from *res*: thing, and *vindicare*: to seek judicially; to reclaim as owner): action of reclaiming a thing.
See also restitution, revocation[1], sale with a term, sale of (the) property of another.
Fr. revendication.

REVERENTIAL FEAR

Fear arising out of respect for a person and out of a concern not to displease that person. "[...] the constraint resulting from reverential fear of the ascendant is tolerated only when it is 'alone,' and 'no violence has been exercised'" (Planiol & Ripert, *Treatise*, vol. 2, n° 1074, p. 614).
Occ. Art. 997 C.C.L.C.
Obs. 1° The *Civil Code of Québec* no longer refers to the notion of *reverential fear*. However, the notion of *exercise of a right or power* (e.g. art. 1403 C.C.Q.) appear to be broad enough to include it. It may be observed that only an abusive exercise of a right or power or the threat thereof vitiates consent. **2°** Under the *Civil Code of Lower Canada*, the scope of application of reverential fear as a cause of nullity was limited to fear inspired by a person's ascendants (art. 997 C.C.L.C.).
Fr. crainte révérencielle.

REVISE *v.*

To effect a revision.
Fr. réviser.

REVISION *n.*

Examination of a juridical act or legal text with a view to its modification, if need be. For example, revision of a judgment, revision of the Civil Code. "[...] the revision of the Civil

Code has been conceived of as a process of collective thinking, starting with a draft report by a Committee of experts and providing for a broad program of consultation of various kinds, both professional and general" (Crépeau, (1974) 34 *La. L. Rev.* 921, pp. 947-948).
Fr. révision.

REVISION CLAUSE

Clause by which the parties provide for the revision of the contract in specified circumstances. For example, a clause in a construction contract allowing a variation of the base price according to fluctuations in the price of building materials.
Syn. variation clause. **See also** revision of contract, unforeseeability[1].
Fr. clause de révision.

REVISION OF CONTRACT

Modification of contractual obligations.
Obs. 1° In principle, revision of contract requires the consent of the parties who, by a new agreement, modify their previous contract (art. 1439 C.C.Q.). **2°** In long-term contracts, if the parties wish to be protected against unforeseeability, they may provide for the revision of the contract by an express clause (e.g. art. 1949 C.C.Q.). **3°** Judicial revision of a contract may occur only in those exceptional cases provided by law (e.g. art. 2332 C.C.Q.; ss. 8, 272, *Consumer Protection Act*, R.S.Q. c. P-40.1).
See also revision clause, unforeseeability[1,2].
Fr. révision du contrat.

REVOCABILITY *n.*

Quality of that which is revocable.
Fr. révocabilité.

REVOCABLE *adj.*

Susceptible of revocation. "[...] their father's acceptance for himself constituted in law an acceptance of the donation to themselves. That is what art. 930 [C.C.L.C.] impliedly says, and declares to have always been the law of the province [...] And that law is consistent with the fundamental principles of donations *inter vivos*, which under pain of nullity, cannot be revocable at the donor's will. Art. 783 [C.C.L.C.]" (*Meloche* v. *Simpson* (1899), 29 S.C.R. 375, p. 389, H.E. Taschereau, J.). *Revocable gift; revocable mandate.*
Occ. Arts. 1822, 2462 C.C.Q.

See also irrevocable.
Fr. révocable.

REVOCATION *n.*

1. Non-retroactive termination of a juridical act resulting from a unilateral decision or a judicial decision. "[...] the respondents are driven to contend that this donor by himself alone had the right to revoke the substitution as long as he left the donation to his son intact, as he has virtually done. I fail to see upon what principle the consent of his son, the donee, could at all make the revocation of the substitution lawful, if it could not be lawfully made by the donor alone" (*Meloche* v. *Simpson* (1899), 29 S.C.R. 375, p. 390, H.E. Taschereau, J.). *To entail revocation; the effect of a revocation; revocation of a mandate; revocation of a will.*
Occ. Arts. 768, 1254, 2180, 2462 C.C.Q.
See also annulment, retraction.
Fr. révocation[1].

2. Syn. bilateral resiliation.
Fr. résiliation amiable, résiliation bilatérale[+], résiliation conventionnelle, révocation[2].

REVOCATORY *adj.*

Effecting revocation. *Revocatory disposition.*
See also revocatory act.
Fr. révocatoire.

REVOCATORY ACT

(*Succ.*) Juridical act effecting revocation. For example, a subsequent will.
Fr. acte révocatoire.

REVOCATORY ACTION

Syn. Paulian action.
Fr. action en inopposabilité[+], action paulienne, action révocatoire.

REVOKE *v.*

To effect revocation. "As a general rule, no doubt, a stipulation in an ordinary contract for the benefit of a third person may be revoked so long as it has not been accepted. But that can have a reasonable application only where there exists as a matter of fact such a person. Art. 1029 C.C.[L.C.]" (*Meloche* v. *Simpson* (1899), 29 S.C.R. 375, p. 387, H.E. Taschereau, J.). *To revoke a gift; to revoke a mandate; to revoke an offer; to revoke a will.*
Occ. Arts. 1253, 1439, 1446 C.C.Q.
See also cancel, retract.
Fr. révoquer.

REWARD *n.*

Indemnity[1] owed to any person who will do a favour or a good deed.
Occ. Arts. 1395, 1460 C.C.Q.
See also offer of reward.
Fr. récompense.

RICOCHET *n.*

See mediate victim, ricochet damage. "Linked to the issue of causation is the question of whether the courts should grant recovery for harm sustained by a 'ricochet victim', that is, a victim whose harm arises from someone else's damage" (Khoury, (2001) 46 *McGill L.J.* 413, p. 452).
Fr. ricochet.

RICOCHET DAMAGE

Damage suffered by one person, resulting from the damage caused to another. For example, the harm caused to a person who is deprived of the pleasures of conjugal life (*consortium*) as a result of injury inflicted upon his or her spouse.
Obs. 1° Ricochet damage is direct damage and thus susceptible to compensation when there is a causal relationship between the loss and the act or omission giving rise to liability. **2°** Since the terms *damage* and *injury* are synonymous, the expression *ricochet injury* may also be used.
Syn. rebounding damage. **See also** indirect damage, initial damage, personal damage.
Fr. préjudice par ricochet[+], préjudice réfléchi.

RIGHT *n.*

Legal prerogative that the titulary exercises in his or her own interest. For example, the right of ownership, a personal right, the right to the respect of privacy. "In French, the same word, *droit*, designates both 'law' in the general sense and 'right'. This double signification leads to the elegant distinction between *droit objectif* – i.e., law as the body of rules of conduct regulating human behaviour – and *droits subjectifs* – i.e. the 'legal rights' or the prerogatives of individuals or group of individuals that the law recognizes in relation to others or to things" (Brierley & Macdonald (eds.), *Quebec Civil Law*, n° 125, p. 155).
Occ. Arts. 3, 4, 5, 6, 7, 8, 9, 911, 1225, 1806, 2748 C.C.Q.
Obs. Used in this sense, right refers to *subjective right* as opposed to *objective right*.
Syn. *jus*[2]. **See also** abuse of rights, patrimony, person.
Fr. droit[2+], droit subjectif, *jus*[2].

RIGHT OF ACTION

Right which grounds the constitution of judicial proceedings to assert a prerogative recognized by law.
Occ. Arts. 537, 625, 929, 1637, 2880, 2926 C.C.Q.
Obs. 1° The right of action allows all relevant actors having a sufficient interest to apply to the court, for example, to settle a dispute, order a person immediately to cease an activity causing damage, confirm an agreement of separation from bed and board or homologate a holograph will. **2°** The right of action can arise from the infringement of a subjective right or from any situation for which the law gives to certain persons the capacity to act before the courts. **3°** The right of action is distinguished from the recourse to which it gives access. The recourse is the procedural vehicle by which the right of action is exercised (e.g. the action in liability, the action in nullity, the application for homologation, the application for injunction). **4°** A right of action may exist without a direct and personal interest: the right of action can, in certain cases, be exercised in the interest of another (e.g. a child who petitions the court for the institution of protective supervision for a parent; the administrator of a legal person who petitions the court on behalf of the undertaking). **5°** The right of action may, subject to certain exceptions, be assigned (art. 1637 C.C.Q.). **6°** The transaction entails the renounciation of the right of action arising from the dispute.
See also cause of action, damages, demand, litigious right, right.
Fr. droit d'action.

RIGHT OF DISCUSSION

(*Sec.*) Syn. benefit of discussion.
Fr. bénéfice de discussion[+], droit de discussion.

RIGHT OF DIVISION

(*Sec.*) Syn. benefit of division.
Fr. bénéfice de division[+], droit de division.

RIGHT OF ENJOYMENT

(*Prop.*) Syn. enjoyment. "[...] a right of enjoyment, other than the right of use and habitation (arts. 494 and 497 C.C.[L.C.]), can be assigned to others" (*Duchaine* v. *Matamajaw Salmon Club* (1919), 58 S.C.R. 222, p. 249, P.B. Mignault, J.).
Occ. Art. 1120 C.C.Q.; art. 405 C.C.L.C.
Fr. droit de jouissance, jouissance[+].

RIGHT OF FIRST REFUSAL

See right of preference[1]. "[...] a person to whom a right of first refusal has been granted by the owner of an immoveable property has no real right in the property" (*Jacol Realty Holdings Inc.* v. *Conseil d'expansion économique d'Argenteuil*, [1986] R.J.Q. 2295 (C.A.), pp. 2299-2300, M.L. Rothman, J.).
Fr. droit de premier refus.

RIGHT OF OPTION

Right conferred by law or a juridical act to exercise an option.
Occ. Title preceeding art. 630 C.C.Q.
See also option.
Fr. option.

RIGHT OF PREEMPTION

Right of a person to acquire property[2], by preference over any other person, should the property be offered for sale. "Under the *Notarial Act*, the Chamber [of Notaries] may exercise a right of preemption over certain sums to be remitted to a notary's heirs" (Macdonald, (1986-87) 32 *McGill L.J.* 1, p. 16).
Occ. S. 22, *Cultural Property Act*, R.S.Q. c. B-4; ss. 688.1, 1047, *Municipal Code of Quebec*, R.S.Q. c. C-27.1.; s. 54.8, *An Act respecting the Régie du logement*, R.S.Q. c. R-8.1.
Obs. The right of preemption may be provided by law (e.g. art. 1082 C.C.Q.) or by private agreement.
Syn. preemptive right[1]. **See also** first refusal agreement, preemption clause, preemptor, preemption, right of preference.
Fr. droit de préemption.

RIGHT OF PREFERENCE

1. Right to enter into a contract with another before anyone else. For example, the right of preemption.
Obs. The right of preference may be granted by law or provided for in a first refusal agreement.
See also first refusal agreement, right of preemption.
Fr. droit de préférence[1].

2. Right allowing a creditor to receive, by preferential attribution, any sum owed by the debtor. "But it is again in the field of real security that the right of preference, like the right to follow, produces its most important practical consequences" (Yiannopoulos, in *Treatise*, vol. 2, n° 215, p. 299).
Occ. Arts. 744, 1986 C.C.L.C.

Obs. 1° In providing that prior claims and hypothecs are the legal causes of preference, article 2647 C.C.Q introduces an exception to the general rule establishing that the patrimony of a debtor is the common pledge of his or her creditors (art. 2644 C.C.Q.). **2°** Prior claims and hypothecs carry a right of preference in favour of the creditors who are the beneficiaries of such rights (arts. 2650, 2660 C.C.Q.). Prior claims are collocated following the order fixed by law (art. 2651 C.C.Q.), whereas hypothecs are ranked according to the date of their publication (arts. 2941, 2945 C.C.Q.). **3°** Real rights are said to be characterized by a right to follow and a right of preference. Although they are not generally viewed as real rights, prior claims also confer a right of preference to their holder.
Syn. *droit de préférence*, preference. **See also** accessory real right, opposability, real right, right to follow.
Fr. droit de préférence[2+], préférence.

RIGHT OF REDEMPTION

Right that, in a contract of sale, the vendor reserves to himself or herself to take back the thing sold upon reimbursing the price paid to the buyer within an agreed upon period. "In order [...] to exercise the right of redemption, the seller must before its expiry pay or tender back whatever of the price he has received, stating his willingness to pay the necessary and useful improvements, for which, as the value is unknown, no definite amount can be offered" (Marler, *Real Property*, p. 574).
Occ. Art. 1750 C.C.Q.; arts. 1547, 1552 C.C.L.C.; s. 100, *An Act respecting the implementation of the reform of the Civil Code*, S.Q. 1992, c. 57.
Obs. 1° The period agreed upon may not exceed 5 years (art. 1753 C.C.Q.). **2°** The codal regime respecting the right of redemption is set forth at articles 1750 to 1756 of the *Civil Code of Québec*.
See also sale with right of redemption.
Fr. faculté de rachat[+], faculté de réméré.

RIGHT OF REFUSAL

Faculty given to the author of an invitation to contract to refuse its formation.
Obs. 1° Most scholars consider that an offer containing a right of refusal is not a true offer but only an invitation to negotiate. **2°** A tacit right of refusal is contained in public offers destined to form *intuitu personæ* contracts.
Fr. faculté d'agrément, réserve d'agrément[+].

RIGHT OF REPOSSESSION

Faculty enabling a person to effect a repossession.
Occ. Arts. 1749, 1969 C.C.Q.; ss. 140, 150.14, *Consumer Protection Act*, R.S.Q. c. P-40.1.
See also repossession.
Fr. droit de reprise.

RIGHT OF RETENTION

Right granted by law allowing a creditor to withhold a thing owned by his or her debtor until the debt has been paid.
Occ. Title preceding art. 1591 C.C.Q.; art. 1810 C.C.L.C.
Obs. 1° Three conditions must be satisfied in order to allow a creditor to retain a thing owned by his or her debtor: the creditor must detain the thing with the consent of the debtor; the debt must be exigible; the debt must be directly linked with the thing being withheld (art. 1592 C.C.Q.). **2°** Claims secured by a right of retention are prior claims (art. 2651(3) C.C.Q.). **3°** The holder of a right of retention is a secured creditor under the *Bank and Insolvency Act* (R.S.C. 1985, c. B-3, s. 2(1)).
Fr. droit de rétention.

RIGHT TO FOLLOW

Right that bears on property permitting the holder of the right to assert it regardless of whose hands property may be found. "General creditors, except in case of fraud, have no standing against the purchaser of an immoveable [...] In this case, the immovable no longer forms part of the debtor's patrimony and, as ordinary creditors have no right to follow, it cannot be seized" (Yiannopoulos, in *Treatise*, vol. 2, n° 215, p. 398).
Occ. Arts. 2660, 2732 C.C.Q.
Obs. 1° Real rights are said to be characterized by a right to follow and a right of preference. **2°** As the holder of an accessory real right, the hypothecary creditor loses the right to follow when the movable property that guarantees his or her claim has been alienated in the debtor's ordinary course of business (arts. 2674, 2732 C.C.Q.). **3°** Except for prior claims provided by law to the benefit of municipalities (e.g. art. 12.1 of *An Act respecting duties on transfers of immovables*, R.S.Q. c. D 15.1), prior claims do not confer a right to follow. **4°** The right to follow, because it allows its holder to assert his or her right upon property regardless of in whose hands it may be, reflects the principle that real rights may be set up against third persons.

Syn. *droit de suite*. **See also** accessory real right, opposability, real obligation, real right, real subrogation, right of preference[2].
Fr. droit de suite.

RIGHT WITH A TERM

Right subject to a term[1].
See also obligation with a term.
Fr. droit à terme.

RISK OF LOSS OF A THING

See doctrine of risks[1].
Fr. risque de la chose.

RISK OF THE CONTRACT

Loss assigned to one party when a contractual obligation cannot be performed by reason of superior force.
Obs. Risk of the contract is a feature of synallagmatic contracts.
See also doctrine of risks[1].
Fr. risque du contrat.

RUIN *n.*

Partial or total disintegration of a building or its components. "[...] the evidence clearly establishes that the damage incurred by respondent was caused by the ruin of the City's construction, that this ruin is attributable to a construction defect, and that there is a cause and effect connection between this construction defect and the damage" (*City of Quebec* v. *Picard*, [1972] S.C.R. 227, p. 232, G. Fauteux, C.J.).
Occ. Art. 1467 C.C.Q.
See also liability for damage caused by buildings.
Fr. ruine.

RULE OF CONDUCT

Rule designed to direct the behaviour of those to whom it is addressed. "*A rule of conduct* can be described as a rule which sets norms or standards of conduct, which determine the manner in which rights are exercised and responsibilities are fulfilled" (*Reference re Manitoba Language Rights*, [1992] 1 S.C.R. 212, p. 224). *Moral rule of conduct.*
Occ. Art. 1457 C.C.Q.
Obs. 1° The expression *rule of conduct* is used in art. 1457 C.C.Q. to describe the pre-existing duties that, when violated, may give rise to civil liability. **2°** A rule of conduct may either impose, forbid or permit a given course of conduct. **3°** Despite the common tendency

to treat legal rules and rules of conduct as synonymous, the two concepts are not completely interchangeable. Rules of conduct are not necessarily juridical (e.g. certain rules of politeness) and conversely, not all legal rules are necessarily rules of conduct (e.g. the rule establishing civil majority at art. 153 C.C.Q., or more generally, legal definitions).

See also legal rule[1,2].

Fr. règle de conduite.

S

SALARY *n.*

Remuneration paid by an employer to an employee.
Obs. 1° Strictly speaking, salary refers only to the sum of money periodically paid by the employer to the employee. Broadly speaking, it may be used to mean the whole remuneration paid to the employee. In addition to the base salary, it might include vacation and holiday pays as well as, in certain cases, room and board, a year-end bonus or other emoluments. **2°** Under the *Civil of Lower Canada*, the remuneration paid by a mandator to a mandatary was called *salary* (art. 1722 C.C.L.C.). The *Civil Code of Québec* now uses the term *remuneration* (art. 2134 C.C.Q.). **3°** From the Latin *salarium*: indemnity in order to buy salt.
Syn. wages. **See also** commission, price.
Fr. salaire.

SALE *n.*

Contract by which a person, the *seller*, transfers property to another, the *buyer*, for a price in money. "It is the price in money which distinguishes sale from other contracts of alienation. [...] In exchange, giving in payment and donation, there may be money, but this money is not the principal consideration of the contract" (Marler, *Real Property*, p. 254).
Occ. Arts. 1708, 1713, 1729 C.C.Q.; art. 1472 C.C.L.C.; art. 605 C.C.P.
Obs. 1° Sale is a nominate contract that is consensual, bilateral and onerous in character. The model for the contract of sale has traditionally been understood to be the transfer of ownership of corporeal property. Article 1708 par. 2 C.C.Q. also provides that a dismemberment of the right of ownership or "any other right held by the person" may be transferred by sale. **2°** The text of article 1708 para. 2 C.C.Q., by indicating that "any other right held by the person may also be tranferred by sale", might be read to suggest that that sale applies to the transfer of personal rights or claims. It may be noted, however, that the Book on obligations specifically regulates the assignment of claims (arts. 1637 to 1650 C.C.Q.). **3°** In the *Civil Code of Québec*, a distinction is expressly drawn between a sale of future property and a contract of enterprise or for services (art. 2103 C.C.Q.). Where the property furnished has more value than the work or service provided, it is a contract of sale; otherwise, it is a contract of enterprise or for services. **4°** Contracts of sale may be consumer contracts, in which case special provisions apply: arts. 1432, 1435, 1436, 1437 C.C.Q.; *Consumer Protection Act*, R.S.Q. c. P-40.1. **5°** The term *sale* is sometimes used in the plural (e.g. in the expression "sales contract"), as in the law of Louisiana, although sale is generally used in the singular in Quebec civil law parlance. **6°** The codal regime respecting sale is set forth at articles 1708 C.C.Q. to 1794 C.C.Q.
Syn. contract of sale. **See also** assignment[1], auction sale, conditional sale, consumer contract, exchange, giving in payment, instalment sale, promise of sale, purchase, sale of (the) property of another, sale with a term, sale with right of redemption, trial sale.
Fr. contrat de vente, vente[+].

SALE BY AUCTION

Syn. auction (sale).
Occ. Art. 3115 C.C.Q.
Fr. vente aux enchères.

SALE BY INSTALMENT

Syn. instalment sale.
Fr. vente à tempérament.

SALE OF AN ENTERPRISE

Sale of the whole or of a substantial part of an enterprise made outside the ordinary course of business of the seller.
Occ. Art. 2720 C.C.Q.
Obs. Although it is now repealed (s. 8, S.Q. 2002, c. 50), the *Civil Code of Québec* introduced the regime of the sale of an enterprise (arts. 1767 to 1778 C.C.Q.) by replacing that of the bulk sale, which included the sale of a stock in trade and of merchandise (art. 1569*a* to 1569*e* C.C.L.C.).
See also bulk sale, enterprise[1].
Fr. vente d'entreprise.

SALE OF CLAIMS

Assignment of claims by onerous title.
Obs. The Civil Code uses the term *assignment of claims* although *sale of claims* and *sale of debts* are also encountered in practice.
Syn. sale of creance, sale of debt.
Fr. vente de créance.

SALE OF CREANCE

Syn. sale of claims.
Fr. vente de créance.

SALE OF DEBT

Syn. sale of claims.
Occ. Art. 1570 C.C.L.C.
Obs. The word *debt* here must be taken in the sense of *debt²*.
Fr. vente de créance.

SALE OF INHERITANCE

Syn. sale of successional rights.
Fr. vente de droits successoraux⁺, vente de(s) droits successifs, vente d'hérédité.

SALE OF LITIGIOUS RIGHTS

Assignment of litigious rights by onerous title. "The provisions of the law of sale (1708) lead one to conclude that anything that can be the object of sale is property. They include the sale of an enterprise (1767 [repealed, s. 8, S.Q. 2002, c. 50]), which as a concept is an incorporeal thing and of necessity involves many rights including claims, both receivable and payable. The sale of rights of succession (1779) is expressly mentioned. The C.C.Q. also mentions the sale of litigious rights (1782), including delictual rights (1457)" (Claxton, (1997) 42 *McGill L.J.* 797, p. 843).
Occ. Title preceding art. 1782 C.C.Q.; title preceding art. 1582 C.C.L.C.
Obs. 1° In principle, the debtor is discharged upon payment to the purchaser of litigious rights of the sale price, the interest on that price and the costs (art. 1784 C.C.Q.). **2°** Judges, advocates, notaries and officers of justice may not acquire litigious rights (art. 1783 C.C.Q.). **3°** The codal regime respecting the sale of litigious rights is set forth at articles 1782 to 1784 C.C.Q.
See also assignment of litigious rights, litigious personal right, litigious right, redemption of litigious rights.
Fr. vente de droits litigieux.

SALE OF (THE) PROPERTY OF ANOTHER

Unauthorized sale of property by a person other than its owner.
Occ. Title preceding art. 1713 C.C.Q.; art. 1709 C.C.Q.
Obs. 1° When the seller represents the owner, as, for example, in the case of a mandate or an administration of the property of another, the sale is not characterized as a sale of property of another. **2°** The sale of property of another may be declared null (art. 1713 C.C.Q.). **3°** The owner whose property has been sold in contravention of his or her rights may claim the property from the buyer. The buyer in good faith of a movable may, however, ask for repayment of the price paid if the movable has been acquired in the ordinary course of business of an enterprise (art. 1714 C.C.Q.). **4°** The expression *sale of property of others* is also encountered (e.g. art. 1080 C.C.Q.).
See also revendication.
Fr. vente du bien d'autrui.

SALE OF SUCCESSIONAL RIGHTS

Assignment of rights of succession by onerous title.
Obs. 1° Unless the vendor has specified the property sold, he or she only warrants his or her quality as an heir (art. 1779 C.C.Q.). **2°** The sale of successional rights to a person who is a stranger to the succession gives the coheirs of the vendor the option to exercise a right of successional redemption (art. 848 C.C.Q.). **3°** The expression "sale of rights of succession" is also encountered (e.g. title preceding art. 1779 C.C.Q.). **4°** The codal regime respecting the sale of successional rights is set forth at articles 1779 to 1781 C.C.Q.
Syn. sale of inheritance.
Fr. vente de(s) droits successifs, vente de droits successoraux⁺, vente d'hérédité.

SALE ON APPROVAL

Syn. trial sale.
Fr. vente à l'essai.

SALE UPON TRIAL

Syn. trial sale.
Fr. vente à l'essai.

SALE WITH A TERM

Sale in which at least one of the obligations of the parties is subject to a suspensive term.
Occ. Art. 1741 C.C.Q.

Obs. When the term postpones performance of the obligation to deliver, it is a sale with future delivery. When performance of the buyer's obligation to pay the price is subject to a term, the sale is known as a sale on credit. **Syn.** term sale. **See also** conditional sale[1], instalment sale.
Fr. vente à terme.

SALE WITH OPTION TO REPURCHASE

Syn. sale with right of redemption.
Fr. vente à réméré, vente avec faculté de rachat[+].

SALE WITH RIGHT OF REDEMPTION

Sale under a resolutory condition, whereby the seller reserves the right, within an agreed period, to take back the property sold upon repayment to the buyer of the sale price. "In the case of a sale with right of redemption [...], the seller may or may not retain possession of the property, but it is the buyer who becomes proprietor" (*Nadeau* v. *Nadeau*, [1977] C.A. 248, p. 254, G.H. Montgomery, J.).
Occ. Title preceding art. 1750 C.C.Q.
Obs. 1° The expression *sale with right of redemption* is misleading in that the term *redemption* suggests that the option of the seller to take back the property is a second sale. There is in fact only one sale, which is subject to a resolutory condition (art. 1750 C.C.Q.). **2°** Sales with right of redemption may be used to secure a loan. In such a financing operation, the seller is the borrower and the buyer is the lender. Pursuant to article 1756 C.C.Q., the buyer is also deemed to be a hypothecary creditor. **3°** The period during which the right of redemption may be exercised may not exceed five years (art. 1753 C.C.Q.). **4°** The codal regime respecting the sale with right of redemption is set forth at articles 1750 to 1756 C.C.Q.
Syn. sale with option to repurchase. **See also** buyer subject to a right of redemption, conditional sale[1], resolution[2], right of redemption.
Fr. vente à réméré, vente avec faculté de rachat[+].

SCHOLARLY WRITING

Syn. doctrine.
Fr. doctrine.

SCHOLARSHIP *n*.

Syn. doctrine. "In continental civil law jurisdictions, as well as in Quebec, most theorists regard classical legal scholarship (*la doctrine*) as a 'secondary source of law'. Even though academic commentary no longer has the exalted position of the *jus respondendi* of Roman law, in contemporary civil law theory it nevertheless has the status about equal to that of precedent (*la jurisprudence*)" (Macdonald, (1985) 23 *Osgoode Hall L.J.* 573, p. 577).
Fr. doctrine.

SCHOOLTEACHERS *n*.

See liability of schoolteachers.
Fr. instituteur.

SECRET

See secret act, secret mandate.
Fr. secret.

SECRET ACT

Syn. counter letter. "The secret act can totally modify the ostensible act, not by destroying its effect, but by changing its nature" (Planiol & Ripert, *Treatise*, vol. 2, n° 1188, p. 677).
Fr. acte réel, acte secret, acte véritable, contre-lettre[+].

SECRET CONTRACT

Contract that, in an operation of simulation, constitutes the counter letter.
Occ. Art. 1451 C.C.Q.
Fr. contrat secret.

SECRET MANDATE

Syn. contract of *prête-nom*.
Fr. contrat de prête-nom[+], mandat clandestin, mandat dissimulé, prête-nom[2].

SECURE *v*.

Syn. stand as surety (for).
Occ. Art. 2246 C.C.Q.
Obs. This verb may be used for other types of security (e.g. hypothecs).
Fr. cautionner.

SECURED CREDITOR

Creditor whose claim benefits from a right of preference.
Obs. 1° Prior creditors and hypothecary creditors benefit from a right of preference. **2°** The notion of *secured creditor* may be understood differently in other contexts (e.g. s. 2(1), *Bank and Insolvency Act*, R.S.C. 1985, B-3).

See also right of preference[2], unsecured creditor.
Fr. créancier garanti.

SECURITY n.

See suretyship.
Occ. Arts. 65, 152, 525, 716 C.C.P.
Fr. [*].

SEEKABLE adj.

Said of an obligation[2] the payment of which must be made at the domicile of the debtor.
See also portable, seekable claim, seekable debt.
Fr. quérable.

SEEKABLE CLAIM

Claim the payment of which must be made at the domicile of the debtor.
Syn. seekable creance. See also portable claim, seekable debt.
Fr. créance quérable.

SEEKABLE CREANCE

Syn. seekable claim.
Fr. créance quérable.

SEEKABLE DEBT

Debt[1] the payment of which must be made at the domicile of the debtor.
Obs. 1° As a general rule, a debt is seekable unless it relates to the sale of individualized property, in which case the payment must be made where the property was when the obligation arose. 2° The parties may also agree to another place for payment (art. 1566 C.C.Q.), including the designation that the debt be portable.
See also portable debt, seekable claim.
Fr. dette quérable.

SELL v.

To enter into a sale, from the perspective of the seller.
Occ. Arts. 1709, 1713 C.C.Q.; arts. 1474, 1482 C.C.L.C.
Syn. transfer by sale. See also buy.
Fr. vendre.

SELLER n.

Person who, by contract of sale, transfers property to the buyer. "The seller who knows of a latent defect in the thing sold has the obligation to so inform his buyer [...] this is required by the most elementary honesty" (General Motors Products of Canada Ltd. v. Kravitz, [1979] 1 S.C.R. 790, p. 797, Y. Pratte, J.).
Occ. Arts. 1708, 1716, 1740 C.C.Q.; arts. 1487, 1491 C.C.L.C.
Obs. Pursuant to article 1716 C.C.Q., the seller has two principal obligations: the obligation to deliver the property and the obligation to warrant the ownership and quality of the property. However, courts acknowledge that implicit obligations for the seller may arise from the principles of the general law of contract, such as, for example, the obligation of the seller to alert the buyer as to dangers inherent in the property sold.
Syn. vendor. See also buyer, property[1].
Fr. vendeur.

SEMI-AUTHENTIC ACT

Attesting deed prepared outside Quebec, purporting to be issued by a competent public officer of another jurisdiction. For example, an original birth certificate issued by a public authority outside Quebec.
Occ. Title preceding art. 2822 C.C.Q.; arts. 89(3), 90 C.C.P.
Obs. The notion of semi-authentic act is closely associated with the codal regime related to evidence (see arts. 2803 et seq. C.C.Q.).
See also authentic act, private writing.
Fr. acte semi-authentique.

SEMI-CLANDESTINE MANDATE

See contract of prête-nom.
Fr. mandat semi-clandestin.

SENDER n.

Syn. shipper.
Fr. chargeur, expéditeur+.

SEQUESTRATE v.

To place under sequestration.
Occ. Arts. 1145, 1147 C.C.Q.; art. 465 C.C.L.C.; art. 744 C.C.P.
Fr. séquestrer.

SEQUESTRATION n.

Juridical operation by which property in dispute is placed in the hands of a person, the sequestrator, who is entrusted with its custody and who must restore it to the person who will be entitled to it when the issue is settled. "Since the court is empowered to initiate the ordering of a sequestration as well as to name the actual administrator, it is, therefore, logical that the court be further entitled to terminate the sequestration prematurely for just reason" (Sarna, (1977) 23 *McGill L.J.* 508, p. 513).

Occ. Art. 2305 C.C.Q.; arts. 1794, 1817 C.C.L.C.; art. 742 C.C.P.

Obs. 1° There are two kinds of sequestration: conventional sequestration and judicial sequestration. **2°** Notwithstanding that the object of sequestration may be movables or immovables and that it may be established by judicial authority, the *Civil Code of Québec* characterizes judicial and conventional sequestration as deposit in art. 2305 C.C.Q., under the title of nominate contracts.

See also conventional sequestration, deposit[1], judicial sequestration, simple deposit.

Fr. séquestre[1].

SEQUESTRATOR *n.*

Depositary of a sequestrated property. "Finally, the Code requires that the property be administered – that is, the sequestrator must manage the assets and may not, like a depositary, simply watch over them" (Brierley & Macdonald (eds.), *Quebec Civil Law,* n° 660, p. 577).

Occ. Arts. 2307, 2308, 2311 C.C.Q.; arts. 1821, 1827 C.C.L.C.; arts. 743, 745 C.C.P.

Obs. 1° If the sequestrator is nominated by the parties, he or she is called a conventional sequestrator (art. 2307 C.C.Q.). If a court elects the sequestrator, he or she is called a judicial sequestrator (art. 2311 C.C.Q.). **2°** The judicial sequestrator may be one of the parties to the litigation or a third party (art. 2307 C.C.Q.). **3°** The sequestrator may perform acts of simple administration of the property of others unless the parties or the court decide differently. However, when the custody or maintenance of the property entails costs that are disproportionate to its value, the sequestrator may alienate it if the parties agree or if the court gives its authorization (art. 2308 C.C.Q.). Moreover, he or she must report on his or her management (art. 2310 C.C.Q.). **4°** Under the *Bankruptcy and Insolvency Act*, the equivalent of the French term "*séquestre*" is *receiver.* The *Bankruptcy and Insolvency Act* provides for a specific regime for appointing a receiver in part XI (s. 243, *Bankruptcy and Insolvency Act,* R.S.C. 1985, c. B-3).

Fr. séquestre[2].

SERVANT *n.*

See agent and servant.

Obs. The use of the terms *principal, agent* and *servants* in article 1463 C.C.Q. as equivalents of *commettant* and *préposés* should not be taken as a reference to mandate relationships or to the Common law doctrine of agency.

Fr. [*].

SERVICE(S) *n.*

1. One's labour, art, skill or property placed at the disposal of another. "The reason for the foregoing is that an employee who is engaged in building work is not conducting building operations – he is merely furnishing his services to the owner who is himself the builder, doing the building through the arms of his men" (Durnford, (1967) 2 *R.J.T.* 161, p. 165). *Services rendered.*

Obs. 1° Broadly understood, the provision of services may be part of many types of contract, such as employment contracts, contracts of enterprise, contracts for services, loans for use and leases. **2°** The furnishing of services does not necessarily entail a contractual relationship. **3°** The *Consumer Protection Act* (R.S.Q. c. P-40.1) distinguishes between goods and services, a distinction probably borrowed from economists. For the economist, *goods* signifies owned consumer items whereas *services* pertains to all other prestations destined for consumption.

See also work.

Fr. service[1].

2. Prestation furnished in the performance of an obligation to do resulting from a contract for services. *To furnish household services; professional services.*

Obs. In this sense, the term is often used collectively as *services.*

Occ. Arts. 2098, 2100 C.C.Q.

Fr. service[2].

SERVICE PROVIDER

Syn. provider of services.

Occ. S. 117, *Consumer Protection Act,* R.S.Q. c. P-40.1.

Fr. prestataire de services.

SET ASIDE *verb.ph.*

To put an end to a juridical relationship.

Occ. Arts. 1022, 1065 C.C.L.C.

Fr. annuler(<)[+], rescinder(<)[+], résilier[1](<)[+], résoudre(<)[+].

SET-OFF *n.*

Syn. compensation[1].
Occ. Art. 2224(4) C.C.L.C.
Obs. The term *set-off* was used as a synonym for *compensation* in the *Civil Code of Lower Canada*.
Fr. compensation[1].

SET OFF *v.*

Syn. compensate.
Occ. Arts. 411(2), 1754 C.C.L.C.
Fr. compenser.

SETTLE *v.*

1. Syn. pay.
Fr. acquitter, payer[+], régler.

2. Syn. transact. "The right to settle disputes by consent, with privacy and little expense, was a natural right which the monarchy, as will have been seen, did not try to take away but for greater certainty tried to extend and in a degree to regulate" (Johnson, *Clause Compromissoire*, p. 6).
Fr. transiger.

3. Syn. dispose[2].
Fr. disposer[2].

SETTLEMENT *n.*

Syn. transaction[1]. "Once formal proceedings had progressed further, while courts still freely gave leave to parties to settle out of court, settlement may have been less likely. This was perhaps because the nature of adversarial proceedings tended to amount each side's stance towards its antagonist" (Pilarczyk, (2001) 46 *McGill L.J.* 779, p. 795).
Fr. contrat de transaction, règlement hors cour, transaction[+].

SET UP *v.*

To invoke a right or a juridical act against another. "[...] 'transfer of rentals' clauses are commonly engrafted onto deeds of hypothec [...] However it is construed, the clause can be set up against third parties only if the requirements of article 1571 or 1571c [art. 1641 C.C.Q.] are followed" (Brierley & Macdonald (eds.), *Quebec Civil Law*, n° 755, p. 637).
Occ. Arts. 1641, 2483, 2710 C.C.Q.
Obs. The expression *set up against* is sometimes used in preference to *opposable*. Similarly, *not set up against* is sometimes used in preference to *inopposable* and to *set up against* in preference to the verb *oppose*.

Syn. oppose.
Fr. opposer.

SEVERAL *adj.*

See solidary[1].
Fr. solidaire[1].

SEVERAL OBLIGATION

See solidary obligation.
Fr. obligation solidaire.

SHARED CUSTODY

Custody of a thing, the power of control, supervision or direction of which is divided so as to be exercised either regarding its activity or its structure. For example, a bottler of soft drinks must supply containers that will not explode when handled in a normal way by a distributor; thus, the bottler has custody of the structure of the thing whereas the distributor has custody of the activity of the thing.
Obs. This theory of shared custody, developed in French law and which divides the notion of *custody* into custody of the structure and custody of the activity, has been invoked in a number of Quebec judicial decisions.
See also cumulative custody, custody of the activity (of the thing), custody of the structure (of the thing), liability for damage caused by things.
Fr. garde partagée.

SHARED LIABILITY

Civil liability incurred by several persons, each of whom having contributed to cause the damage.
Occ. Art. 1478 para. 1 C.C.Q.
Obs. Liability may be shared among co-authors of the damage or between the victim and the author of the damage (art. 1478 C.C.Q.).
See also collective fault, common fault, contributory fault.
Fr. responsabilité partagée.

SHIPPER *n.*

Person who enters into a contract with a carrier in order to convey property from one place to another. "If the non-responsibility clause is not set out clearly in the contract then it cannot apply against a consignee or a shipper" (Tetley, (1979) 20 *C. de D.* 449, p. 463).
Occ. Arts. 2030, 2035, 2047, 2054, 2061 C.C.Q.; s. 4, *Bills of Lading Act*, R.S.C. 1985, c. B-5; s. 6, *Canada Transportation Act*, S.C. 1996, c. 10.

Syn. consignor, freighter, sender. **See also** consignee, contract for the carriage of goods, contract of carriage.
Fr. chargeur, expéditeur+.

SIMPLE ADMINISTRATION

Regime of administration of the property of others, the purpose of which is the protection and preservation of property[1].
Occ. Arts. 1145, 1301 C.C.Q.; s. 30, *Public Curator Act*, R.S.Q. c. C-81.
Obs. 1° Simple administration may bear on property, a mass of property, a fraction of universality, a universality or the whole patrimony. **2°** The tutor (arts. 208, 286 C.C.Q.), the liquidator of a succession (art. 802 C.C.Q.), the manager of an undivided property (art. 1029 C.C.Q.) and the sequestrator (art. 2308 C.C.Q.) are, by way of example, endowed with the powers of an administrator charged with simple administration.
See also act of administration, administration of the property of others, full administration.
Fr. simple administration.

SIMPLE CONTRACT

Contract that deals with a single juridical transaction and that is governed by its own particular rules. For example, a sale.
Obs. A distinction is drawn between a *simple contract* and a *mixed contract*.
See also mixed contract.
Fr. contrat simple.

SIMPLE DEPOSIT

Deposit[1] by gratuitous title. "Two kinds of deposits are mentioned by the Code [C.C.L.C.]: simple deposit and sequestration. Simple deposit is gratuitous and involves movables only" (Castel, *Civil Law System*, p. 136).
Occ. Arts. 1794, 1795 C.C.L.C.
Obs. 1° Under the *Civil Code of Lower Canada*, the phrase *simple deposit* was used to designate the deposit of movable property as opposed to deposit by sequestration that could also apply to immovables. The *Civil Code of Québec* does not use this phrase, since the special contract of deposit applies only to movables. **2°** In the *Civil Code of Lower Canada*, there were two types of simple deposit: voluntary deposit and necessary deposit (art. 1798 C.C.L.C.). **3°** The essence of simple deposit was its gratuitous nature; however, according to the *Civil Code of Québec*, a deposit may be by onerous title.
See also necessary deposit, sequestration.
Fr. dépôt simple.

SIMPLE INTEREST

Interest calculated on the basis of capital.
See also compound interest.
Fr. intérêt simple.

SIMPLE LOAN

Loan, the object of which is a consumable property. "Simple loan is a contract often combined with other contracts that are either nominate contracts (expressly provided for in the C.C.Q.) or contracts *sui generis* which are not provided for" (Claxton, *Security*, n° 16.1, p. 283).
Occ. Arts. 2312, 2314, 2327 C.C.Q.
Obs. 1° Simple loan is presumed to be a contract made by gratuitous title unless it is a loan of money, in which case it is presumed to be made by onerous title (art. 2315 C.C.Q.). **2°** In the case of a simple loan, the obligation of restitution entails that the borrower return property of like quantity and of the same kind and quality. **3°** Given that the simple loan bears on consumable property, the borrower becomes the owner of the property loaned. He or she therefore bears the risks of loss (art. 2327 C.C.Q.). However, the lender remains responsible for latent defects (art. 2328 C.C.Q.). **4°** The parties may, by agreement, confer the quality of non-consumability upon a thing consumable by nature; the contract is then a loan for use. This would be the case, for example, where a person lends some stamps in circulation for display at a stamp collectors' exhibition. **5°** Many special statutes, either provincial or federal, regulate the simple loan (e.g. *An Act respecting farm-loan insurance and forestry-loan insurance*, R.S.Q. c. A-29.1; *An Act respecting financial assistance for education expenses*, R.S.Q. c. A-13.3; *Canada Small Business Financing Act*, S.C. 1998, c. 36; *Farm Improvement and Marketing Cooperatives Loans Act*, R.S.C. 1985, c. 25 (3rd supp.)). **6°** In the *Civil Code of Lower Canada*, the simple loan was designated as *loan for consumption*.
Syn. loan for consumption, *mutuum*. **See also** borrower, lender, loan for use.
Fr. *mutuum*, prêt de consommation, simple prêt+.

SIMPLE OBLIGATION

Syn. pure and simple obligation.
Fr. obligation pure et simple+, obligation simple.

SIMPLY FACULTATIVE CONDITION

Syn. simply potestative condition.
Obs. The expression *simply potestative condition* is to be preferred in order to avoid confusion with the *facultative obligation*, which refers to an alternative obligation.
See also facultative condition[+], purely facultative condition.
Fr. condition simplement facultative, condition simplement potestative[+].

SIMPLY POTESTATIVE CONDITION

Condition[1] depending on the will of one of the contracting parties as well as on external circumstances beyond his or her control. "A simply potestative condition does not invalidate the obligation, whereas a purely potestative condition on the part of the debtor does. The distinction is therefore vital, but the line between a condition which depends on the will alone and one which depends on the will and an event is not sharp" (Nicholas, *Contract*, p. 162).
Obs. Since it results only partially by chance, a simply potestative condition does not entail the nullity of the obligation, because it also reflects a veritable intention to be bound.
Syn. simply facultative condition. **See also** mixed condition, purely potestative condition.
Fr. condition simplement facultative, condition simplement potestative[+].

SIMULATED

See simulated act, simulated contract.
Fr. simulé.

SIMULATED ACT

Syn. apparent act. "Ordinarily one of the parties, by means of the simulated act, proposes to deceive someone, and the simulation is thus a means of fraud" (Planiol & Ripert, *Treatise*, vol. 2, n° 1190, p. 678).
Fr. acte apparent[+], acte ostensible, acte simulé.

SIMULATED CONTRACT

Syn. apparent contract.
See also contract of *prête-nom*, counter letter, fictitious contract, simulation.
Fr. contrat simulé.

SIMULATION *n.*

Operation in which the parties conceal their true agreement behind the appearance of an ostensible act, intending for the agreement to remain secret. "Although simulation is frequently prompted or accompanied by fraud, it must not be equated with fraud and may exist in the absence of any fraudulent intent" (Le Dain, (1956) 2 *McGill L.J.* 77, p. 91).
Occ. Art. 1451 C.C.Q.
Obs. 1° In the law of obligations, simulation entails the existence of two distinct contracts: the *counter letter*, which bears upon rights and obligations between the parties, and the *apparent act*, which reflects that which the parties want third parties to believe. **2°** Simulation can arise in legitimate circumstances or it may be a means of defrauding the law. In the latter case, the counterletter is null since it is contrary to public order. **3°** The codal regime respecting simulation is set forth at articles 1451 and 1452 C.C.Q.
See also apparent act, appearance, concealed act, contract of *prête-nom*, counter letter, fictitious act, interposed person.
Fr. simulation.

SIMULTANEOUS FAULTS

Two or more civil faults committed at the same time.
Obs. Where it is not possible to establish which fault caused the damage, the authors of simultaneous faults are solidarily liable (art. 1480 C.C.Q.).
See also causal fault, collective fault, common fault, contributory fault, successive faults.
Fr. faute simultanée.

SLANDER *n.*

See defamation[1].
Fr. injure.

SLIDING *adj.*

See sliding scale clause.
Fr. mobile.

SLIDING SCALE CLAUSE

Monetary clause whereby the amount of a debt that is due is determined on the basis of fluctuations of a specified indicator.
Obs. 1° The value of a thing, a service, the cost of living index, variations in municipal or school taxes are examples of variables that, for example, may be used in sliding scale clauses. **2°** A sliding scale clause provided for in a lease may be contested where the adjustment is excessive (art. 1949 C.C.Q.).
Syn. escalator clause, indexation clause. **See also** gold clause[1,2], indexation.
Fr. clause d'échelle mobile[+], clause d'indexation, clause indexée.

SLIGHT FAULT

Syn. *culpa levis*. "This 'prudent administrator', like its counterpart the 'reasonable man', is an abstraction, and the fault such an abstract model would *not* incur is considered a 'slight fault' (*culpa levis in abstracto*)" (Litvinoff, in *Treatise*, vol. 7, Book 2, n° 183, p. 345).
Fr. *culpa levis*, faute légère+.

SOLATIUM DOLORIS nom.ph. (Latin)

See injury to feelings. "[C]ompensation for the grief and distress felt when someone close to us dies – the prejudice commonly referred to as *solatium doloris* or injury to feelings – is clearly consistent with the civil law's full recognition of moral damages" (*Augustus* v. *Gosset*, [1996] 3 S.C.R. 268, p. 286, C. L'Heureux-Dubé, J.).
Obs. 1° The term *solatium doloris* has traditionally been used to designate compensation for injury to feelings suffered as a result of the death of a loved one. Literally translated, the expression *solatium doloris* means "solace for grief" and, as such, may be used to apply to any kind of injury to feelings, whether resulting from the death of a loved one or not. **2°** Many criteria may be considered in assessing *solatium doloris*, notably the circumstances of the death, the age of the deceased and the age of the parent. **3°** The persons who may claim compensation following the death of a loved one are no longer enumerated in a limitative list, following the decision not to carry forward art. 1056 C.C.L.C. in the *Civil Code of Québec*. In theory, any person who established an injury to feelings caused by the fault of a defendant may be compensated.
See also moral damage, moral damages, *pretium affectionis*, *pretium doloris*.
Fr. *solatium doloris*.

SOLEMN *adj.*

Said of formation that depends on the observation of formalities required by law. *Solemn form*.
See also consensual, formalistic, formalistic act, real, solemn act, solemn contract.
Fr. solennel.

SOLEMN ACT

Juridical act the formation of which requires the drafting of a document according to the form prescribed by law. For example, a marriage contract (art. 440 C.C.Q.), a will (arts. 712, 713 C.C.Q.).

See also appearance, consensual act, essential formality, formalism, formalistic act, solemn contract.
Fr. acte solennel.

SOLEMN AGREEMENT

Syn. solemn contract.
Occ. Art. 1385 C.C.Q.
Fr. contrat solennel.

SOLEMN CONTRACT

Formalistic contract, the formation of which requires the drafting of a document according to the form prescribed by law. For example, marriage contracts (art. 440 C.C.Q.), instalment sales subject to the *Consumer Protection Act* (R.S.Q. c. P-40.1).
Syn. formal contract, solemn agreement, solemn covenant. **See also** consensual contract, real contract, solemn act.
Fr. contrat solennel.

SOLEMN COVENANT

Syn. solemn contract.
Fr. contrat solennel.

SOLEMN FORM

Syn. essential formality.
Occ. Art. 1414 C.C.Q.
Fr. formalité *ad solemnitatem*, formalité substantielle+, forme solennelle, solennité.

SOLEMNITY *n.*

Syn. essential formality.
Fr. formalité *ad solemnitatem*, formalité substantielle+, forme solennelle, solennité.

SOLEMNIZE *v.*

To observe the legal formalities in the formation of a solemn juridical act.
Fr. solenniser.

SOLIDARILY *adv.*

With solidarity.
Occ. Arts. 1292, 1480 C.C.Q.
Obs. The expression *jointly and severally* is sometimes used as a synonym for solidarily. The combined effect of the adverbs *jointly* and *severally* is understood by some scholars as a contradiction, in that *jointly and severally* evokes liability for both a share and the whole. It is therefore thought that solidarily is a more apt description of the effects of the solidary obligation.
Fr. solidairement.

SOLIDARITY *n.*

Characteristic of an obligation according to which, in the case of a plurality of creditors or debtors, each creditor may require full performance of the obligation and each debtor is bound for the whole obligation.
Occ. Arts. 1521, 1525, 1532, 1533, 1538, 1541 C.C.Q.
Obs. 1° Solidarity between co-creditors is called *active solidarity*, while solidarity between co-debtors is called *passive solidarity*. **2°** Solidarity is not presumed (arts. 1525, 1541 C.C.Q.). It results either from a juridical act (e.g. conventional solidarity) or by law (e.g. legal solidarity). **3°** Payment made to one of the solidary creditors discharges the debtor with regard to all the creditors (art. 1542 C.C.Q.). Payment made by a solidary debtor discharges the others toward the creditor (art. 1523 C.C.Q.). **4°** Solidarity does not pertain to the object of the obligation but rather to a plurality of titularies. The full performance of the obligation arises as a result of mutual representation between them reflecting a shared community of interest. Indivisibility, on the other hand, relates to the object of the obligation which, by reason of its nature or because of a fiction, is not susceptible of division. **5°** The codal regime respecting solidarity is set forth at articles 1523 to 1544 C.C.Q. **6°** The use of the term *correality* as a synonym of solidarity derives from Romanist terminology.
Syn. correality, perfect solidarity. **See also** indivisibility, release from solidarity, solidary obligation.
Fr. corréalité, solidarité+, solidarité parfaite, solidité.

SOLIDARY *adj.*

1. Possessing the characteristics of solidarity.
Occ. Arts. 1520, 1526, 1540 C.C.Q.
Obs. 1° The expression *joint and several* is used in contracts and in legislative texts (e.g. arts. 1103 to 1107, 1118, 1191 C.C.L.C.), to refer to the intention to be bound solidarily. Even though the terms *joint and several* and *solidary* are used synonymously, the union of the terms *joint* and *several* stands as a contradiction in terms. Both joint obligations and several obligations are indeed obligations that bind several debtors but, in the former case, each debtor is liable for his or her share, while in the latter case each debtor is liable for the whole. Therefore, strictly speaking, the term *joint* is incorrectly used to convey the meaning of *all together*. The terms *several* or

solidary are sufficient to describe the effects of such an obligation. Long-standing use of the expression *joint and several* in Quebec as an equivalent for solidary may however have had the effect of giving the expression meaning independent from its use in the Common law tradition. **2°** The term *several* is also used in this sense.
See also solidary obligation.
Fr. solidaire[1].

2. Said of a person bound by a solidary obligation.
Occ. Arts. 1370, 1529, 1690, 2902 C.C.Q.
Obs. See observations for *solidary*[1].
See also solidary debt, solidary liability.
Fr. solidaire[2].

SOLIDARY CLAIM

Syn. solidary personal right.
Occ. Arts. 1666, 2909 C.C.Q.
Fr. créance solidaire.

SOLIDARY CREANCE

Syn. solidary personal right.
Fr. créance solidaire.

SOLIDARY DEBT

Debt owed by solidary co-debtors. "Where, as it is possible, a solidary debt is contracted in the interest of only one of the co-debtors, the rules governing the latter and the other co-debtors are those governing suretyship" (Aubry & Rau, *Civil Law*, vol. 1, n° 298b, p. 33).
Occ. Arts. 1678, 2352 C.C.Q.
See also joint and several debt, joint debt, solidary obligation, solidary personal right.
Fr. dette solidaire.

SOLIDARY LIABILITY

Civil liability of several debtors, each of whom is held answerable to a single creditor for the entire debt.
Occ. S. 1036, *Taxation Act*, R.S.Q. c. I-3.
Obs. 1° Solidarity is not presumed (arts. 1525, 1541 C.C.Q.). It results either from a juridical act (conventional solidarity) or by operation of law (legal solidarity). **2°** Article 1526 C.C.Q. establishes solidarity among the co-authors of an extracontractual fault.
See also collective fault, common fault, contributory fault, joint liability, liability *in solidum*, solidary obligation, solidarity.
Fr. responsabilité solidaire.

SOLIDARY OBLIGATION

Obligation involving several creditors or several debtors, where each creditor may require performance and each debtor is bound for the whole. "In a solidary obligation, the debtors may represent each other *vis-à-vis* their creditor. Anything done by one of them is deemed to have been done by all the others" (C.C.R.O., *Commentaries*, vol. II, t. 2, p. 636).
Occ. Arts. 1526, 1623, 2900 C.C.Q.
Obs. The expression *several obligation* is also encountered.
See also indivisible obligation, joint and several obligation, joint obligation, obligation *in solidum*, obligation with a complex modality, solidarity.
Fr. obligation solidaire.

SOLIDARY PERSONAL RIGHT

Personal right held by solidary co-creditors.
Syn. solidary claim, solidary creance. **See also** joint and several claim, joint personal right, solidary debt, solidary obligation.
Fr. créance solidaire.

SOLO CONSENSU adv.ph. (Latin)

By consent alone.
See also consensualism.
Fr. *solo consensu*.

SOLVENS n. (Latin)

Person who effects payment.
Obs. From the Latin *solvere*: to pay.
Syn. payer. **See also** *accipiens*.
Fr. payeur, *solvens*+.

SPECIAL AUTHORIZATION

Syn. special power of attorney.
Occ. Art. 409 C.C.P.
Fr. procuration spéciale.

SPECIAL CONTRACT

Syn. nominate contract. "Of course all contracts are governed by the general principles of contractual obligations [...]. The significance of the distinction between special or nominate contracts and innominate contracts is that the standard incidents of special contracts are derived, in the absence of contrary intentions, from the provisions in the Code [...]" (Nicholas, *Contract*, p. 46).
Fr. contrat nommé.

SPECIAL INCAPACITY

Legal incapacity limited to juridical acts specified by law or by decision of a court.
Obs. 1° The incapacity to enjoy rights, as opposed to the incapacity to exercise rights, is always special. Examples of special incapacity to enjoy rights are the incapacity of tutors, curators and mandataries to acquire property entrusted to them (art. 1312 C.C.Q.); the incapacity of a minor to bequeath property by will (art. 708 C.C.Q.) or to give *inter vivos* (art. 1813 C.C.Q.). **2°** The incapacity to exercise rights is sometimes special. Thus, the incapacity of a simply emancipated minor is a special incapacity: he or she need only be assisted by a tutor for those acts expressly indicated in arts. 172, 173, 174 C.C.Q. Similarly, the incapacity of a person of full age under tutorship is also special: he or she need only be represented by a tutor for those acts mentioned in the judgment opening the regime of tutorship.
Syn. partial incapacity. **See also** general incapacity, incapacity to enjoy (rights), incapacity to exercise (rights).
Fr. incapacité partielle, incapacité spéciale+.

SPECIAL MANDATE

Mandate[1] relating to a particular business activity of the mandator.
Obs. 1° Article 2135 C.C.Q. expressly states that a mandate may be special. **2°** A special mandate can be expressed in general terms (e.g. to manage the use of a particular property) or it can be an express mandate (e.g. to sell a particular immovable). **3°** In certain cases, the law requires a special mandate: renunciation (art. 458 C.C.P.), acquiescence in a demand (art. 476 C.C.P.). A mandate must then be given for each such act. **4°** The *special mandate* is opposed to the *general mandate*.
See also express mandate[1], mandate expressed in general terms, special procuration.
Fr. mandat spécial.

SPECIAL PARTNER

Partner of a limited partnership who contributes to the common stock of the partnership and is liable for the debts of the partnership only up to the amount of that contribution.
Occ. Arts. 2190, 2196, 2236, 2246 C.C.Q.; art. 1872 C.C.L.C.
Obs. 1° More than one special partner may be party to a contract establishing a limited partnership. **2°** A special partner provides the partnership with capital and credit. **3°** In

principle, special partners may not perform acts relating to the administration of the limited partnership.

Syn. limited partner. **See also** contract of partnership, general partner, limited partnership, partner, partnership[1].

Fr. commanditaire.

SPECIAL POWER

Syn. special power of attorney.
Occ. Arts. 61, 629 C.C.P.
Fr. procuration spéciale.

SPECIAL POWER OF ATTORNEY

Power of attorney relating to a particular affair of the mandator.

Occ. Art. 458 C.C.P.

Obs. The *special power of attorney* is opposed to the *general power of attorney*.

Syn. special authorization, special power, special procuration. **See also** special mandate.

Fr. procuration spéciale.

SPECIAL PROCURATION

Syn. special power of attorney.
Fr. procuration spéciale.

SPECIAL TERMS

Conditions[2] that derogate from the general conditions of a standard-form contract.

See also adhesion contract, contract by negotiation, general conditions, standard form contract.

Fr. conditions particulières.

SPECIE *n.* (Latin)

Syn. cash.
Fr. argent, espèces[+], numéraire.

SPECIFIC PERFORMANCE

Performance in which the creditor receives the very prestation that is owed. "[...] under the civil law of Quebec, specific performance of contracts is the general rule, unlike the Common law approach, which favours compensation for breach by damages awards. I also agree that specific performance cannot be granted in certain cases where the personal action of the debtor of the obligation is of the essence" (*Varnet Software Corp.* v. *Varnet U.K. Ltd.*, [1994] R.J.Q. 2755 (C.A.), p. 2758, J.-L. Baudouin, J.).

Occ. Title preceding art. 1601 C.C.Q., arts. 1549, 1863 C.C.Q.; arts. 1065, 1610 C.C.L.C.

Obs. 1° Voluntary performance is generally brought about through specific performance. **2°** In the case of compulsory performance, performance is achieved by equivalence when specific performance would have the result of physically constraining the debtor and, therefore, violating his or her freedom.

Syn. payment in kind[1], performance in kind.

See also compulsory execution, *in corpore*, performance by equivalence, reparation in kind, voluntary performance.

Fr. exécution directe, exécution en nature[+], paiement en nature[1].

STANDARD CONTRACT

Syn. standard-form contract.
Occ. Ss. 107, 109, *An Act respecting occupational health and safety*, R.S.Q. c. S-2.1.
Fr. contrat type.

STANDARD-FORM CONTRACT

Written form for a contract whose content is to serve as a model for all those who wish to enter into a contract of like nature, and in which the parties need only, in most cases, complete unwritten portions in order to particularize it to their situation. For example, the standard-form lease established by regulation. "[...] in the fields of lease and hire of dwellings, insurance law and consumer law, so many codal or statutory provisions are of an imperative nature that it can be said that it is the *legislator* rather than contracting parties who drafts a standard form contract in these fields" (Haanappel, (1982) 60 *Can. Bar Rev.* 393, pp. 404-405).

Obs. 1° Adhesion contracts often take the form of standard-form contracts. **2°** The expression *boiler plate contract* is often used in informal legal parlance.

Syn. standard contract. **See also** adhesion contract, general conditions, special terms.

Fr. contrat type.

STANDARD TERM

Conventional term that is prepared in advance for general and repeated use. "Where there is agreement on the negotiated or 'accepted terms', but not on the standard terms, what does one do? The article [2.22 Unidroit *Principles*] provides, once again with the view of favouring the maintenance of the contractual bond, that the contract is formed 'on the basis of the agreed terms and of any standard terms which are common in substance [...]'" (Charpentier & Crépeau, *Unidroit Principles*, p. 21).

Obs. 1° Standard terms may be limited to one or more provisions of the contract. Common examples include standard terms for the exoneration of liability or arbitration. Standard terms that constitute a comprehensive set of provisions are usually designated by the expression *standard-form contract*. **2°** The standard terms may be prepared by the contracting party, or by a third person, or by a trade or professional association. **3°** The more colloquial lawyer's expression *boilerplate* is sometimes encountered in scholarly writings and decided cases.
See also standard-form contract.
Fr. clause type.

STAND AS SURETY (FOR) *v.ph.*

To act as surety for someone.
Syn. post security (for), secure.
Fr. cautionner.

STATE OF NECESSITY

1. Situation of urgency in which a person is justified in causing damage in order to avoid more serious harm. For example, the demolition of a house in order to prevent a fire from spreading throughout the neighborhood; a motorist hitting a parked car in order to avoid running down a pedestrian.
Obs. A state of necessity rules out a finding of fault for the person that caused the damage. However, the person responsible for the creation of the state of necessity may be held civilly liable.
See also superior force[1].
Fr. état de nécessité[1].

2. Situation brought about by especially grave circumstances that impel a person to bind himself or herself. "[...] 'state of necessity' cases, where one party, recognizing the extreme situation of need facing the other party, extorts the latter's consent, have recently been seen as types of violence even though, strictly speaking, no threat is actually made" (Brierley & Macdonald (eds.), *Quebec Civil Law*, n° 432, p. 405).
Occ. Art. 1404 C.C.Q.
Obs. 1° The recognition of a state of necessity as a vitiating factor is founded on fear as a defect of consent. **2°** In principle, consent given to a juridical act in view of being relieved from fear resulting from a state of necessity is valid. However, if the co-contracting party is not acting in good faith, article 1404 C.C.Q. declares that consent has been vitiated. **3°** Technically, the solution adopted is questionable insofar as fear based

on a state of necessity is included in the part of the Civil Code dealing with qualities and defects of consent. The solution of article 1404 C.C.Q. is based on the good or bad faith of the co-contracting party. Therefore, it is not the consent of the person who is in the state of necessity that is taken into account but the state of mind of the co-contracting party.
See also fear.
Fr. état de nécessité[2].

STATU QUO (ANTE) *nom.ph.* (Latin)

In the former state.
Fr. *statu quo (ante)*.

STATUTE *n.*

Juridical enactment adopted by a legislature which establishes one or more legal rules. "[...] it is our duty, as required by the *Interpretation Act*, to construct each statute in such manner, insofar as that is possible, 'as will ensure the attainment of its object and the carrying out of its provisions, according to their true intent, meaning and spirit'" (*Nadeau* v. *Nadeau*, [1977] C.A. 248, p. 259, F. Kaufman, J.). *To enact a statute.*
Occ. Arts. 1339(6), 2812, 2838 C.C.Q.; arts. 95, 453 C.C.P.; arts. 4, 1834 C.C.L.C.; s. 605(16), *An Act respecting the implementation of the reform of the Civil Code*, S.Q. 1992, c. 57.
Obs. 1° When defined by reference to the organ that elaborates it, a statute must be distinguished from a regulation, which is made by the executive branch of government. **2°** The definition of statute given by scholars sometimes emphasizes the origin of the statute (i.e. the statute defined as an emanation of a representative parliamentary will) or conversely its result (i.e. the statute defined as a rule or group of legal rules). Statutes are often assimilated to their physical support (i.e. to the text sanctioned by Parliament). **3°** Traditionally statutes of an imperative character are distinguished from statutes of a suppletive nature. **4°** It is said that the law *prescribes* or *provides*, rather than *stipulates*; the latter term is used primarily with regard to contracts. **5°** The expression *statute law*, used in the Anglo-American legal tradition in contrast to the Common law, is sometimes used in Quebec though without the same connotations.
See also code[1].
Fr. loi[2].

STIPULATE *v.*

1. To enunciate a provision in a juridical act.
Occ. Arts. 433, 2089 C.C.Q.; art. 779
C.C.L.C.; ss. 48, 81, *Consumer Protection Act*,
R.S.Q. c. P-40.1.
Obs. The word *stipulate* should not be used to
refer to legislative enactments.
Fr. stipuler[1].

2. To obtain an undertaking from a person.
"As a rule, any contracting parties may stipulate for the benefit of a third person as long as
1. the stipulation is contained in an otherwise
valid contract, and 2. the third person, who
need not be individually identified, is determinable at the time the stipulation is to take
effect" (Brierley & Macdonald (eds.), *Quebec
Civil Law*, n° 456, p. 422).
Occ. Art. 1617 C.C.Q.; arts. 1019, 1029, 1030
C.C.L.C.
Obs. See article 1462 C.C.Q.
Fr. stipuler[2].

STIPULATING PARTY

Party who establishes the terms of a contract,
especially of an adhesion contract.
Fr. stipulant[1].

STIPULATION *n.*

1. Syn. clause. "It is true that an attempt to
give the term 'stipulation' a legislative conno-
tation is an improper use of that term" (*Doré
v. Verdun (City of)*, [1997] 2 S.C.R. 862, p. 880,
C.D. Gonthier, J.).
Occ. Arts. 1212, 2070 C.C.Q.; arts. 813, 1510
C.C.L.C.
Fr. clause+, stipulation[1].

2. Act by which a person obtains an undertaking from another. "The will to engage toward
somebody, or to oblige somebody, is essentially a personal act; accordingly, one cannot,
in general, promise the act of another or
receive a promise (stipulation) in his name for
another" (Aubry & Rau, *Civil Law*, n° 343b,
p. 320).
Occ. Arts. 1444, 1445 C.C.Q.; art. 1029
C.C.L.C.
See also stipulation for another.
Fr. stipulation[2].

STIPULATION AS TO EARNEST

Stipulation that obliges one of the parties to
pay to the other a sum of money, *earnest*, at
the conclusion of the contract and that grants
to each party the right to withdraw from the
contract; the party who paid earnest loses it
and the party who received it pays twice the
sum received.
Obs. 1° The stipulation as to earnest is
generally encountered in contracts of sale or
promises of sale. **2**° The stipulation as to earnest may provide that the sum of money to be
remitted be more or less than double the sum
paid. In this respect, it may be observed that
the definition of earnest provided at article
1477 C.C.L.C. does not appear in the *Civil
Code of Québec*. **3**° The stipulation as to
earnest must be unequivocal, since the *Civil
Code of Québec* provides that the sum paid at
the conclusion of the contract is presumed to
be a deposit on the price, unless otherwise
stipulated in the contract (art. 1711 C.C.Q.).
4° If the right of withdrawal is not exercised,
the earnest is credited against the total price
as though it constituted a payment on account
or deposit[2].
See also deposit[2], penal clause[1], penalty
of withdrawal, promise of sale, withdrawal
option.
Fr. stipulation d'arrhes.

STIPULATION AS TO WITHDRAWAL

Syn. withdrawal clause.
Fr. clause de dédit+, stipulation de dédit.

STIPULATION FOR ANOTHER

Stipulation by which a party, the *stipulator*,
obtains from another, the *promisor*, an undertaking to perform a prestation for the benefit
of a third person, the *third person beneficiary*.
Occ. Title preceding art. 1444 C.C.Q.
Obs. 1° The stipulation for another is a dero-
gation of the principle of relativity of contracts according to which a contract only creates rights and obligations for the contracting
parties (arts. 1440, 1444 C.C.Q.). **2**° Under a
stipulation for another a direct right to the
prestation accrues to the benefit of the third
party beneficiary (art. 1444 C.C.Q.). **3**° The
stipulation for another is valid even if the
third party beneficiary does not exist or is not
determined at the time of formation of the
contract, provided he or she is determinable
at formation and will exist when the obligation is to be performed (art. 1445 C.C.Q.). **4**°
The stipulation for another is a juridical operation involving three persons, as are the
promise of *porte-fort* and the promise for
another. However, it has the potential effect
of making the third person a creditor of an
obligation, whereas the others seek to bind
the third person. **5**° The codal regime respecting stipulation for another is set forth at
articles 1444 to 1450 C.C.Q.

Syn. stipulation for the benefit of another, stipulation in favour of another. **See also** direct action[2], promise for another, promise of *porte-fort*, relativity of contract, stipulation[2]. **Fr.** stipulation pour autrui.

STIPULATION FOR THE BENEFIT OF ANOTHER

Syn. stipulation for another.
Fr. stipulation pour autrui.

STIPULATION IN FAVOUR OF ANOTHER

Syn. stipulation for another.
Fr. stipulation pour autrui.

STIPULATION OF INALIENABILITY

Clause of a juridical act, the object of which is to establish the inalienability of property.
Occ. Title preceding art. 1212 C.C.Q.; art. 1212 C.C.Q.
Obs. 1° Article 1212 of the C.C.Q. provides explicitly that a restriction upon the exercise of the right to dispose of property is only possible by gift or will. **2°** Inalienability is an exception to the general principle of free circulation of property. Consequently, the stipulation of inalienability must be temporary and justified by a serious and legitimate interest (art. 1212 C.C.Q.). **3°** In order to be set up against third persons, a stipulation of inalienability must be published in the appropriate register of movable or immovable rights (arts. 1214 and 2939 C.C.Q.). **4°** A stipulation of inalienability always entails the unseizability of property (art. 1215 C.C.Q.). **5°** The sanction of an alienation made notwithstanding a stipulation of inalienability is relative nullity (art. 1217 C.C.Q.). **6°** The court may authorize the alienation of inalienable property if the interest that had justified the stipulation has disappeared, or if a greater interest requires it (art. 1213 C.C.Q.). **7°** The codal regime respecting stipulations of inalienability is set forth at articles 1212 to 1218 C.C.Q.
See also inalienability, stipulation of unseizability.
Fr. stipulation d'inaliénabilité.

STIPULATION OF NON-LIABILITY

Syn. exclusion (of liability) clause. "The authors and the jurisprudence agree that stipulations of non-liability cannot modify the responsibility of the parties with respect to one another, unless the beneficiary has made the other party fully aware of their effect and unless the latter has consented to their inclusion in the contract" (Dessaulles, (1947) 7 *R. du B.* 147, pp. 165-166).
Fr. clause de non-responsabilité[2], clause d'exclusion de responsabilité[+], clause d'exonération de responsabilité[2], clause exonératoire de responsabilité, clause exonératrice de responsabilité.

STIPULATION OF RESOLUTION UPON NON-PERFORMANCE

Syn. resolutory clause of right.
Fr. clause de résolution de plein droit, clause expresse de résolution, clause résolutoire de plein droit[+], clause résolutoire expresse, pacte commissoire.

STIPULATION OF UNSEIZABILITY

Clause in a juridical act, the object of which is to prevent partial or total seizure of property by creditors for debt.
Occ. Art. 2649 C.C.Q.
Obs. 1° Article 2649 of the C.C.Q. provides that the stipulation of unseizability may only be made in an act by gratuitous title, that it be temporary and that it be justified by a serious and legitimate interest. **2°** Property subject to a stipulation of unseizability may be seized by creditors prior to the gift or to the opening of a legacy, with the permission of, and upon the conditions determined by the court. **3°** The donee or the legatee may explicitly or implicitly renounce conventional unseizability. The renunciation profits only the creditor in favour of whom it is stipulated. **4°** While a stipulation of inalienability always entails the unseizability of property (art. 1215 C.C.Q.), a stipulation of unseizability does not entail its inalienability.
See also stipulation of inalienability, unseizability.
Fr. stipulation d'insaisissabilité.

STIPULATOR *n.*

Person who obtains from another person an undertaking for his own benefit or that of another. "[...] not only can the stipulator claim the amount of the penalty where the promise made for the benefit of the third person is not performed; but the third person himself acquires an action to claim the object which has been stipulated for him" (Planiol & Ripert, *Treatise*, vol. 2, n° 1233, p. 703).
Occ. Arts. 1446, 1450 C.C.Q.
See also promisor[2], stipulation for another, third person beneficiary.
Fr. stipulant[2].

STOCK-IN-TRADE *n.*

Universality of movables used for the carrying on of a commerce or business.
Occ. Arts. 1569*a*, 1569*b*, 1569*c* C.C.L.C.
Obs. 1° The universality is comprised of corporeal and incorporeal things, and can also include an immovable when it is an accessory to the business. **2°** In common parlance, stock-in-trade refers to inventory or merchandise. **3°** In 1994, the legislature replaced the bulk sale, which included only the sale of a stock-in-trade and of merchandise (arts. 1569*a* to 1569*e* C.C.L.C.), by the sale of an enterprise (arts. 1767 to 1778 C.C.Q.). The articles relating to the sale of an enterprise were later repealed (s. 8, S.Q. 2002, c. 50).
Fr. fonds de commerce.

STRICT LIABILITY

Liability based exclusively on the causal link between the risk created and the damage suffered but not on the fault. For example, the liability of employers for occupational injury. "Strict liability, irrespective of fault, may be a powerful deterrent. [...] Strict liability is a means, not only of avoiding lengthy and costly discussions, but also of giving to someone an interest in doing his utmost to avoid harms" (Tunc, in *Int. Enc. Comp. L.*, vol. XI, p. 1-160).
Obs. 1° Strict liability should not be confused with no-fault regimes of compensation which establish a state-sponsored claim to compensation rather than a claim based on individual liability, as is the case for the compensation of bodily injury under the *Automobile Insurance Act* (R.S.Q. c. A-25). **2°** The term *strict liability* has a distinct meaning in criminal law, where it is used to designate public welfare or regulatory offences for which it is incumbent on the accused to demonstrate, on a balance of probabilities, that he or she used reasonable diligence to avoid the circumstances giving rise to the offence (see *R.* v. *Sault Ste-Marie*, [1978] 2 S.C.R. 1299).
Syn. absolute liability, no-fault liability, objective liability. **See also** legal liability[2], material cause, subjective liability.
Fr. responsabilité absolue, responsabilité causale, responsabilité de plein droit, responsabilité objective[+], responsabilité sans faute, responsabilité stricte.

SUB-ACQUIRER *n.*

Syn. subsequent acquirer.
Fr. acquéreur subséquent, sous-acquéreur[+], tiers acquéreur.

SUB-ACQUISITION *n.*

Syn. subsequent acquisition.
Fr. sous-acquisition.

SUBCONTRACT *n.*

Contract in which one of the contracting parties is a party to another contract, and whose object is the full or partial performance of that contract.
Occ. Art. 2013*f* C.C.L.C.
Obs. 1° A subcontract may also be described in a more precise manner, mainly when one designates the performance of a nominate contract (e.g. a sub-mandate, a sub-lease). **2°** The term may also be spelled *sub-contract*.
Fr. sous-contrat.

SUBCONTRACTING PARTY

Party to a subcontract.
Obs. The term may also be spelled *subcontracting party*.
Fr. sous-contractant.

SUBJECTIVE *adj.*

See subjective cause, subjective fault, subjective indivisibility, subjective lesion, subjective liability.
Fr. subjectif.

SUBJECTIVE CAUSE

Syn. cause[2]. "When the subjective cause of a contract is contrary to public order or good morals, the contract will be struck with nullity [...]" (Brierley & Macdonald (eds.), *Quebec Civil Law*, n° 439, p. 409).
Fr. cause[2+], cause concrète, cause du contrat, cause impulsive et déterminante, cause subjective, considération[2], considération principale, mobile, motif.

SUBJECTIVE FAULT

Civil fault whose author is aware of its reprehensible nature. "Criminal law does typically seek out a 'subjective fault' to justify the imposition of a jail term, but the subjective measure is not discernment but rather the full mental state of the accused" (Kasirer, (1992) 40 *Am. J. Comp. L.* 343, p. 362).
See also objective fault.
Fr. faute subjective.

SUBJECTIVE INDIVISIBILITY

Syn. conventional indivisibility.

Obs. Indivisibility is said to be subjective when it results from the will of the parties to a contract.
Fr. indivisibilité accidentelle, indivisibilité artificielle, indivisibilité conventionnelle+, indivisibilité de paiement, indivisibilité subjective.

SUBJECTIVE LIABILITY

Juridical responsibility based on civil fault.
Obs. Subjective liability forms the general law of civil liability.
See also contractual liability, extracontractual liability, strict liability, subjective fault.
Fr. responsabilité subjective.

SUBJECTIVE LESION

Lesion consisting in the harmful effect of a contract on one of the parties.
Obs. 1° Subjective lesion can result, in particular, from the uselessness of the contract for one of the parties or from a party's lack of means (art. 1406 para. 2 C.C.Q.; ss. 8, 9, *Consumer Protection Act*, R.S.Q. c. P-40.1). The existence of lesion then depends on an *in concreto* evaluation of the situation of the party. **2°** Subjective lesion only gives rise to a remedy for consumers, minors and persons of full age under protective supervision (art. 1406 C.C.Q.; s. 8, *Consumer Protection Act*, R.S.Q. c. P-40.1).
See also mixed lesion, objective lesion.
Fr. lésion subjective.

SUBJECT OF LAW *nom.ph.*

1. Being or entity submitted to the legal order.
Obs. The notion of *subject of law* does not correspond to the role and place of beings or entities within the framework of private law nor to their relationship with others as titularies of rights. It refers instead to the place the person holds in relation to law in the general sense and to the duty to respect rules imposed by the legal order.
Fr. sujet de droit[1].

2. See subject of rights[1,2].
Obs. The use of the expression *subject of law*, as synonymous with *subject of rights*, has developed as an equivalent for the French *sujet de droit* and is thought by some to be a Gallicism. Such use may stem from the use in French of the same word *droit* to designate both law in the general sense and right.
Fr. sujet de droit[2,3].

SUBJECT OF RIGHTS *nom.ph.*

1. Being or entity considered according to the juridical function or role it plays in a legal relationship.
Obs. 1° The notion of *subject of rights* used in this sense translates the idea of juridical agent that may be part of a legal relationship and supports both the rights and obligations that arise from such a relationship. **2°** Some scholars assimilate both notions of *subject of rights* and *person*, because all persons are subjects of rights. Traditionally, it was considered that only persons, whether physical or legal, could be subjects of rights. **3°** Certain patrimonies by appropriation are formally constituted as legal persons and, as such, they are endowed with juridical personality. Those that are not so constituted do not have juridical personality as traditionally conceived. Some scholars nevertheless see these patrimonies by appropriation, though non-personalized, as having the status of subjects of rights. **4°** The notions of *subject of rights* and *object of rights* are often contrasted in the same way as are the categories of persons and things. **5°** It is generally considered that the physical person, as subject of rights and considered as a whole, cannot itself be the object of rights. **6°** In a juridical relationship of obligations there are two or more subjects of rights: the active subject (creditor) and the passive subject (debtor). **7°** The expression *subject of law*, as equivalent to *subject of rights*, is also encountered. It has developed as an equivalent for the French *sujet de droit* and is thought by some to be a Gallicism. Such use may stem from the use in French of the same word *droit* to designate both law in the general sense and right.
Fr. sujet de droit[2].

2. Being or entity considered as having the capacity to be titulary of rights.
Obs. 1° Although the existence of a juridical relationship is implied in this notion of *subject of rights*, it emphasizes the titularity of rights as opposed to the role of the subject in such a relationship. **2°** The expression *subject of law*, as equivalent to *subject of rights*, is also encountered. It has developed as an equivalent for the French *sujet de droit* and is thought by some to be a Gallicism. Such use may stem from the use in French of the same word *droit* to designate both law in the general sense and right.
See also right.
Fr. sujet de droit[3].

SUB-MANDATARY *n.*

Person designated by a mandatary to replace him or her in the performance of a mandate[1].
Fr. sous-mandataire.

SUB-MANDATE *n.*

Contract of mandate in which a person, designated as the *sub-mandator* or *principal mandatary*, confers upon another, the *sub-mandatary*, the whole or part of a pre-existing mandate for which the former was the mandatary.
Obs. 1° See article 2142 C.C.Q. **2°** A specific prohibition from the mandator or the *intuitu personæ* nature of the mandate prevents the creation of a contract of sub-mandate. **3°** The mandator remains liable towards the third person for the acts performed by the sub-mandatary, in the same way as he or she is for the acts of the mandatary.
See also subcontract.
Fr. sous-mandat.

SUB-MANDATOR *n.*

Person who, being *mandatary*, acts as *mandator* in a contract of sub-mandate.
Obs. The sub-mandator remains liable towards the mandator for the obligations that the former has contracted with the latter, without regard to the fact that he or she was assisted by a sub-mandatary to fulfill them.
Syn. principal mandatary.
Fr. mandataire principal, sous-mandant[+].

SUBMISSION (TO ARBITRATION) *n.*

Contract by which the parties agree to submit an existing dispute to arbitration. "[T]he undertaking to arbitrate differs from the submission essentially in that the former is an agreement in contemplation of a potential dispute while the latter relates to a dispute that has arisen" (*Sport Maska Inc.* v. *Zittrer*, [1988] 1 S.C.R. 564, p. 613, C. L'Heureux-Dubé, J.).
Occ. Former art. 941 C.C.P. (1965-1986).
Obs. 1° Since the reform of the law of arbitration in 1986 (*An Act to amend the Civil Code and the Code of Civil Procedure in respect of arbitration*, S.Q. 1986, c. 73), undertakings to arbitrate and submissions are understood as different forms that can take an arbitration agreement. **2°** Undertakings to arbitrate relate to future disputes, whereas submissions relate to present disputes. **3°** The expression *enter into a submission* means to submit a dispute to arbitration.

Syn. *compromis.* **See also** arbitration agreement, undertaking to arbitrate.
Fr. compromis.

SUBORDINATION (RELATIONSHIP OF)

Juridical relationship characterized by the submission of one person to the authority of another who has the power to give orders as to duties and the manner in which they are to be performed. "A workman who causes damage while in the performance of the work for which he is employed, engages his employer's responsibility if he is in a relationship of subordination [...]" (Goldenberg, *Responsibility*, p. 71).
Obs. Relationships of subordination are often based on a contract of employment. The authority of the principal may also result from a power exercised in the absence of any contract and it is not necessary that the agent or servant be remunerated.
See also agent and servant, liability of the principal, principal[3].
Fr. lien de préposition[+], rapport de préposition.

SUBROGATE *adj.*

Syn. subrogatory.
Fr. subrogatif, subrogatoire[+].

SUBROGATE *n.*

Person substituted for another by subrogation.
Syn. subrogated party. **See also** subrogator.
Fr. subrogé.

SUBROGATE *v.*

To substitute a person or property for another by subrogation. "If the workman opts to claim under the [Workmen's Compensation] Act, the person responsible for the payment of the compensation (in this case, the City of Granby) becomes subrogated in the rights of the victim and may either personally or in the name of the workman institute action against the one responsible for the accident" (*Ouellette* v. *Duhamel*, [1950] B.R. 92, pp. 99-100, P.C. Casey, J.).
Occ. Arts. 1986, 2070 C.C.L.C.
Fr. subroger.

SUBROGATED PARTY

Syn. subrogate. "[...] the subrogated party can exercise the rights acquired from the

subrogating party, and [...] in the event that the subrogation is only for part of the rights of the subrogating party, the latter retains his claim for the rights kept by him" (*Quebec Workmen's Compensation Commission* v. *Gagnon*, [1981] 2 S.C.R. 676, p. 682, J. Chouinard, J.).
Fr. subrogé.

SUBROGATION *n.*

Replacement in a juridical relationship of one person for another or of property for other property. "[...] no notice is required for subrogation to take effect. In this subrogation differs from the assignment of a debt, in which service is required if it is to have effect against third parties [...]" (*Quebec Workmen's Compensation Commission* v. *Gagnon*, [1981] 2 S.C.R. 676, p. 686, J. Chouinard, J.).
Occ. Title preceding art. 1651 C.C.Q.; arts. 1531, 1652 to 1658 C.C.Q.; arts. 1154, 1155 C.C.L.C.; s. 83.60, *Automobile Insurance Act*, R.S.Q. c. A-25; s. 79.2, *Building Act*, R.S.Q. c. B-1.1; s. 12(2), *Farm Improvement Loans Act*, R.S.C. 1985, c. F-3; s. 12, *Fisheries Improvement Loans Act*, R.S.C. 1985, c. F-22.
Obs. 1° Personal subrogation is distinguished from real subrogation. **2°** The parties to a subrogation are known as the *subrogate* or *subrogated party* and the *subrogator*. **3°** From the Latin *subrogare*. to substitute, to elect in place of another; to subrogate.
See also conventional subrogation, legal subrogation, payment with subrogation, personal subrogation, real subrogation.
Fr. subrogation.

SUBROGATION RECEIPT

Syn. subrogatory acquittance. "We are not confronted with the case of an insurance company which, after having paid its own client, victim of an accident, [...] obtains a subrogation receipt against the tort-feasor" (*Sherwin-Williams Co. of Canada* v. *Boiler Inspection and Insurance Co. of Canada*, [1950] S.C.R. 187, p. 189, R. Taschereau, J.).
Fr. quittance subrogative, quittance subrogatoire+.

SUBROGATOR *n.*

Person who grants subrogation.
See also subrogate.
Fr. subrogeant.

SUBROGATORY *adj.*

Pertaining to subrogation. *Subrogatory acquittance.*
Syn. subrogate. **See also** subrogatory acquittance.
Fr. subrogatif, subrogatoire+.

SUBROGATORY ACQUITTANCE

Acquittance attesting to conventional subrogation.
Obs. 1° A subrogatory acquittance attests to two distinct juridical acts, a payment and a subrogation. **2°** The subrogative nature of the acquittance will not be at issue as long as the will of the creditor to subrogate the third party payer in his or her rights appears expressly in the writing (art. 1653 C.C.Q.). **3°** In practice, the term *acquittance* is often used alone to designate a subrogatory acquittance.
Syn. subrogation receipt. **See also** conventional subrogation.
Fr. quittance subrogative, quittance subrogatoire+.

SUBROGATORY ACTION

See oblique action.
Obs. The term *subrogatory action* is sometimes used in the sense of *oblique action*, although subrogation, *stricto sensu*, does not actually take place.
Fr. [*].

SUBSCRIPTION RIGHT

Right for a shareholder to subscribe, by preference, to a new issue of shares in proportion to the number already held.
Occ. Ss. 1, 52, *Securities Act*, R.S.Q. c. V-1.1.
Obs. The subscription right may be provided for in the articles of incorporation, the by-laws of the corporation or the unanimous shareholders' agreement.
Syn. preemptive right[2].
Fr. droit de préemption[2], droit préférentiel de souscription+.

SUBSEQUENT ACQUIRER

Acquirer of a patrimonial right, seen from the perspective of one of the predecessors of in title. For example, a consumer who purchases an automobile from a retailer is a subsequent acquirer in relation to the manufacturer. "In that case [*General Motors Products of Canada Ltd.* v. *Kravitz*, [1979] 1 S.C.R.

790], the court held that the warranty against latent defects, which is attached to contracts of sale by the Civil Code, is transmitted to the subsequent acquirer as an accessory to the thing sold" (Jutras, (1986-87) 12 *Can. Bus. L.J.* 295, p. 301).
Occ. Arts. 1743, 1749, 1751, 2920 C.C.Q.
Obs. The subsequent acquirer's interest may also bear on a determinable part of the patrimonial right that had been the object of the earlier acquisition.
Syn. sub-acquirer. **See also** author, subsequent acquisition, successor.
Fr. acquéreur subséquent, sous-acquéreur[+], tiers acquéreur.

SUBSEQUENT ACQUISITION

Acquisition that follows a previous one bearing on the same patrimonial right or on a determinable part therof.
Obs. In general, personal rights accessory to the property acquired by the former acquirer benefit the subsequent acquirer (see *General Motors Products of Canada Ltd.* v. *Kravitz*, [1979] 1 S.C.R. 790). This is an application of the principle that the accessory follows the principal (see art. 1442 C.C.Q.).
Syn. sub-acquisition.
Fr. sous-acquisition.

SUBSEQUENT PURCHASER

Acquirer of a thing under sale, viewed in relation to one of the predecessors of his or her author. "I think that we must acknowledge the existence of a direct remedy in warranty by a subsequent purchaser against the original seller. A claim in warranty against latent defects is not one that is personal to the purchaser in the sense that he is not entitled to it *intuitu personæ*; the purchaser is entitled to it as the owner of the thing" (*General Motors Products of Canada Ltd.* v. *Kravitz*, [1979] 1 S.C.R. 790, p. 813, Y. Pratte, J.).
Occ. Arts. 1639, 2085 C.C.L.C.
Obs. The French text of sections 53 and 54, *Consumer Protection Act* (R.S.Q. c. P-40.1) uses the term *acquéreur subséquent*, whereas the English text uses *subsequent purchaser*. These terms are not however exact synonyms as subsequent purchaser is a narrower concept than subsequent acquirer.
See also subsequent acquirer.
Fr. acquéreur subséquent(>), sous-acquéreur(>)[+], tiers acquéreur(>).

SUBSTANTIVE CONDITION

Condition[3] relative to the content or substance of an act, a fact or a situation of a juridical nature.
See also condition as to form, substantive defect.
Fr. condition de fond.

SUBSTANTIVE DEFECT

Defect in a juridical act, fact or situation which results in a failure to meet the substantive requirements of the law.
Obs. This expression is used mainly in judicial law in contradistinction to the defect of form in an act of procedure.
Syn. defect of substance.
Fr. vice de fond.

SUCCESSIVE *adj.*

See contract of successive performance.
Fr. successif.

SUCCESSIVE CONTRACT

Syn. contract of successive performance.
Fr. contrat à exécution successive[+], contrat successif.

SUCCESSIVE FAULTS

Civil faults committed one after the other.
Obs. 1° Successive faults may be committed by one or several persons. **2°** When it is not possible to identify the damage resulting from each fault, the authors of the faults are then solidarily liable (art. 1480 C.C.Q.).
See also simultaneous faults.
Fr. fautes successives.

SUCCESSIVE OBLIGATION

Syn. continuous obligation.
Fr. obligation continue[+], obligation (à exécution) successive.

SUCCESSOR *n.*

Person who holds a right or an obligation derived from another, the *author*.
Occ. Arts. 886, 926, 1023, 1062, 2097, 2679, 2912 C.C.Q; arts. 441*n*, 920 C.C.L.C.; s. 28(5)(*c*), *Status of the Artist Act*, R.S.C., c. S-19.6; s. 16(2)(a), *Telecommunications Act*, R.S.C., c. T-3.4.

Obs. A distinction is made between a universal successor, a successor by general title and a successor by particular title.

See also author, successor by general title, successor by particular title, third party, universal successor.

Fr. ayant cause+, ayant droit, successeur.

SUCCESSOR BY GENERAL TITLE

Successor called to receive an aliquot share, a universality or an aliquot share of a universality in the patrimony of his or her author's.

Occ. Arts. 2912, 2916 C.C.Q.; arts. 441n, 2268 C.C.L.C.

Obs. 1° A successor by general title generally receives the property by way of a transmission *mortis causa*. He or she may, however, receive by *inter vivos* transmission, but only by onerous title (e.g. by assignment of a universality of claims (art. 1642 C.C.Q.)). Unlike the *Civil Code of Lower Canada*, the *Civil Code of Québec* prohibits gifts by general title (art. 1823 C.C.Q.). **2°** In contractual matters, it is generally considered that the successor by general title is not a third party to the contract entered into by his or her author. Accordingly, he or she is held liable for the debts of his or her author in the same proportion as the share of property received (art. 1440 C.C.Q.). **3°** Where the successor by general title receives *mortis causa*, he is in principle bound by contracts concluded by their author (art. 1441 C.C.Q.). **4°** Scholars often include successors by general title and universal successors in the category of successors by general title. **5°** The expression *legal representative* is sometimes used as equivalent to *successor by general title* or *universal successor* (e.g. art. 2288 C.C.Q.; arts. 1028, 1030 C.C.L.C.). Used in this sense, the expression may be misleading in that the successor by general title is not a representative of the author, but acts in his or her own name. **6°** Although the terms *acquirer* and *assignee* have a narrower meaning, the expressions *acquirer by general title* and *assignee by general title* are sometimes used as equivalent to *successor by general title* where the context allows for such use.

See also successor by particular title, third person, transmission by general title, universal successor.

Fr. ayant cause à titre universel+, ayant droit à titre universel, successeur à titre universel.

SUCCESSOR BY PARTICULAR TITLE

Successor who acquires a right rather than an aliquot share, a universality or the whole of a patrimony. For example, a legatee by partic-

ular title, a purchaser. "Where an obligation is identified with the thing transferred or is the accessory thereof, the successor by particular title of the first seller is not regarded as a third party, and it is considered normal that he be automatically substituted for the previous creditor of such obligation" (*General Motors Products of Canada Ltd.* v. *Kravitz*, [1979] 1 S.C.R. 790, p. 809, Y. Pratte, J.).

Occ. Arts. 1442, 2912 C.C.Q.; arts. 441n, 2198, 2200 C.C.L.C.; s. 83, *An Act respecting the implementation of the reform of the Civil Code*, S.Q. 1992, c. 57.

Obs. 1° Successors by particular title may receive rights either by *inter vivos* or *mortis causa* transmission, by onerous or by gratuitous title. **2°** In principle, successors by particular title are considered third parties to contracts entered into by their authors. Accordingly, they only receive rights from their author and the transmission of such rights does not entail transmission of obligations to which their author was held. However, there are a number of exceptions to this principle, notably in cases of assignment of contract (e.g. art. 1937 C.C.Q., in matters of residential leases; art. 2097 C.C.Q., in matters of contracts of employment). **3°** The *Civil Code of Québec* provides that "[t]he rights of the parties to a contract pass to their successors by particular title if they are accessory to property which passes to them or are directly related to it" (art. 1442 C.C.Q.). **4°** Although the terms *acquirer* and *assignee* have a narrower meaning, the expressions *acquirer by particular title* and *assignee by particular title* are sometimes used as equivalent to *successor by particular title*.

Syn. particular successor. **See also** successor by general title, third person, transmission by (a) particular title, universal successor.

Fr. ayant cause à titre particulier+, ayant cause particulier, ayant droit à titre particulier, successeur à titre particulier, successeur particulier.

SUCCESSOR BY UNIVERSAL TITLE

Syn. universal successor.

Occ. Arts. 2912, 2916 C.C.Q.

Fr. ayant cause universel+, ayant droit universel, successeur universel.

SUI GENERIS adj.ph. (Latin)

Possessed of unique qualities barring inclusion in any known category. *Sui generis right.*

See also innominate contract.

Fr. *sui generis.*

SUI GENERIS CONTRACT (Latin)

Syn. innominate contract.
Fr. contrat innommé+, contrat *sui generis*.

SUIT *n.*

Syn. action.
Fr. action+, action en justice, demande en justice.

SUPEREMINENT PRINCIPLES OF LAW

Syn. general principles of law. "'General principles of law' or [...] super-eminent principles [...] are the foundational concepts of Codal rules that apply them or derogate from them [...]" (Brierley, (1992) 42 *U.T.L.J.* 484, p. 500).
Obs. 1° The expression is generally used in the plural, but the singular form of the expression is also encountered. **2°** In French law, *general principles*, from which statutes may derogate are often distinguished from *supereminent principles*, which have a supra-legislative effect.
See also fundamental principles of law.
Fr. principes fondamentaux du droit, principes généraux du droit+.

SUPERIOR FORCE

1. Unforeseeable and irresistible event rendering the performance of an obligation impossible. "[...] there is only a fine distinction between the statement that one acted reasonably and carefully in the light of all the circumstances (absence of fault) and the statement that the damage was caused by an external event (superior force) that could not be reasonably foreseen, and against which no reasonable precautions could or should be taken" (Brierley & Macdonald (eds.), *Quebec Civil Law*, n° 480, p. 443).
Occ. Arts. 1470, 1693, 1804, 2464 C.C.Q.; art. 17(24) C.C.L.C.
Obs. 1° Superior force is, in principle, a cause of extinction of obligations and of exemption from liability (arts. 1470, 1693 C.C.Q.). **2°** In addition to being unforeseeable and irresistible, some scholars consider that superior force must also be external to the conduct of the person raising the defence. A strike, an equipment failure or an automobile accident resulting from the state of health of the driver (s. 108, *Automobile Insurance Act*, R.S.Q. c. A-25), for example, would not be considered as external events insofar as their occurrence is connected to the conduct of one of the parties to the obligation.

Syn. *force majeure*[1]. **See also** act of state, doctrine of risks[1], external cause, fortuitous event, impossibility of performance, state of necessity[1], unforeseeability[1].
Fr. force majeure[1].

2. Superior force[1] resulting from a natural cause.
Obs. The term *superior force* is used in opposition to *fortuitous event*, the latter resulting from the act or omission of a person.
Syn. *force majeure*[2].
Fr. force majeure[2].

SUPPLETIVE LAW

1. Law[1] from which one may derogate by private agreement. For example, the matrimonial regime established by law (art. 432 C.C.Q.), the intestate regime of succession (art. 613 C.C.Q.). "The intrinsic structure of the law on inheritance is provided in the portion of the Code that appears to be primarily devoted to the law on abintestate successions [...]. These provisions do, indeed, serve as the general or suppletive law in the absence or inefficacity of a will" (Brierley & Macdonald (eds.), *Quebec Civil Law*, n° 338, p. 334).
Obs. 1° The law of contract is, as a general rule, suppletive law, given the overarching principle of freedom of contract. It is, however, impossible to derogate from the rules of public order (art. 9 C.C.Q.). **2°** Special rules for certain contracts may also complement or depart from the general rules applicable to all contracts (art. 1377 C.C.Q.).
Syn. *jus dispositivum*. **See also** imperative law.
Fr. droit supplétif[1+], *jus dispositivum*.

2. See Common law[1]. "In principle, the civil code is at the centre of the *ius commune* in Quebec and functions as the implicit, general, residual, suppletive law in Quebec" (Macdonald, in *Mélanges Crépeau*, 579, p. 596).
Fr. droit supplétif[2].

SURETY *n.*

Person who undertakes towards a creditor to perform the obligation of the debtor in the event the latter fails to do so. "A surety can bind himself without the consent of the debtor [...]" (Claxton, *Security*, p. 303). *To act as surety, to become a surety* (art. 2349 C.C.Q.).
Occ. Arts. 1643, 2333, 2387, 2625, 2766, 2899 C.C.Q.; art. 1929 C.C.L.C.; art. 526 C.C.P.
Obs. 1° As a general rule, the surety must meet two requirements: he or she must be

domiciled in Canada and must maintain sufficient property in Quebec to satisfy the obligation (art. 2337 C.C.Q.). **2°** The surety may, as a general rule, invoke the benefit of discussion: when sued for payment, he or she may demand that the creditor seize and sell the principal debtor's property first (arts. 2347, 2348 C.C.Q.). **3°** A surety who binds himself or herself solidarily with the principal debtor loses the benefit of discussion and, when there is more than one surety, the benefit of division (art. 2352 C.C.Q.).
Syn. guarantor. **See also** benefit of discussion, benefit of division, cosurety, solidarity, suretyship.
Fr. caution[1+], fidéjusseur.

SURETYSHIP *n.*

Contract by which a person, the *surety*, undertakes towards a creditor to perform the obligation of the debtor in the event the latter fails to do so. "A surety may have legitimate reasons for not disclosing the suretyship to his heirs. This may be the price of family harmony" (*National Bank of Canada* v. *Soucisse*, [1981] 2 S.C.R. 339, p. 358, J. Beetz, J.).
Occ. Art. 2333 C.C.Q.; art. 1929 C.C.L.C.
Obs. 1° While suretyship is a contract, in principle, the obligation to provide surety may be legal or judicial in origin (art. 2334 C.C.Q.). **2°** The contract of suretyship may be gratuitous or onerous. **3°** In principle, suretyship is a personal security that engages the whole patrimony of the surety as a guarantee against the risk of the debtor's insolvency. However, when specified property of the surety guarantees the debt it is considered to be a real security. **4°** Suretyship gives to the surety a benefit of division and a benefit of discussion, unless he or she has renounced these benefits or has bound himself or herself solidarily with the principal debtor (arts. 2347, 2349, 2352 C.C.Q.). **5°** Following the principle established in *National Bank of Canada* v. *Soucisse* ([1981] 2 S.C.R. 339), article 2345 C.C.Q. imposes upon the creditor an obligation to provide certain information to the surety. This rule is completed by article 2355 C.C.Q., which prevents the surety from renouncing his or her right to information in advance. **6°** The expression *security for costs* in the law of procedure is commonly used as an English equivalent for *cautionnement pour frais*. This may explain why in the English text of the *Code of Civil Procedure* the term *security*, which generally has a wider scope than *suretyship*, is used as the equivalent of the French term *cautionnement* (arts. 152, 525, 716 C.C.P.). **7°** The codal regime

respecting suretyship is set forth at articles 2333 to 2366 C.C.Q.
Syn. contract of suretyship. **See also** benefit of discussion, benefit of division, promise of *porte-fort*, solidarity.
Fr. caution[2], cautionnement[+], contrat de cautionnement.

SUSPENSIVE *adj.*

See suspensive condition, suspensive effect, suspensive term.
Fr. suspensif.

SUSPENSIVE CONDITION

Condition[1], whose fulfilment entails the retroactive creation of a right or obligation.
Occ. Arts. 750, 1744, 1507 C.C.Q.; arts. 1087, 1089 C.C.L.C.
Obs. The fulfilment of a suspensive condition has the effect of making the obligation pure and simple retroactively to the day the juridical act was entered into (art. 1506 C.C.Q.). If the suspensive condition fails to come about, the obligation is deemed never to have existed (art. 1507 C.C.Q.).
Syn. suspensory condition. **See also** eventual right[1], resolutory condition, suspensive term.
Fr. condition suspensive.

SUSPENSIVE EFFECT

Effect of a suspensive condition or term, which results in the postponement of the creation or of the exigibility of a right or obligation.
Obs. The suspensive condition delays the creation of the right or obligation, whereas the suspensive term only delays its exigibility.
Fr. effet suspensif.

SUSPENSIVE TERM

Term[1] upon which depends the exigibility of a right or obligation[2]. "In the matter of obligations, two kinds of suspensive terms are distinguished. When the term is established by contract or by the law, it is called 'term of right'; when it is conceded to the debtor by the tribunal, it is called 'term or delay of grace.' These two kinds of terms differ among themselves not only in their source, but also in their effects, and in the causes for their termination" (Planiol & Ripert, *Treatise*, vol. 2, n° 348, p. 206).
Occ. Art. 1508 C.C.Q.
Obs. Suspensive terms are not to be confused with suspensive conditions. The latter suspends the inception of a right, whereas the

former only suspends its exigibility and does not affect its existence.
See also extinctive term, forfeiture of (the) term, suspensive condition.
Fr. terme suspensif.

SUSPENSORY CONDITION

Syn. suspensive condition. "The obligation to cover depends on a suspensory condition, like the principal obligations the performance of which it guarantees, but the surety is nonetheless bound once he has undertaken his obligation, subject to fulfilment of the condition and provided there is no prior revocation" (*Banque Nationale* v. *Soucisse*, [1981] 2 S.C.R. 339, p. 348, J. Beetz, J.).
Fr. condition suspensive.

SYMBOLIC DAMAGES

Syn. nominal damages.
Fr. dommages-intérêts nominaux.

SYMBOLIC TRADITION

Tradition carried out by the handing over of an object that represents the thing to be delivered. For example, the key to the premises where the thing is located.
Syn. *longa manu* tradition. **See also** actual tradition, fictitious tradition, handing over, tradition by interversion of title.
Fr. *traditio longa manu*, tradition de longue main, tradition symbolique⁺.

SYNALLAGMATIC *adj.*

Obliging reciprocally two or more persons towards each other.

Occ. Arts. 1378, 1380, 1591 C.C.Q.
Obs. From the Greek *sunallagmatikos*, from *sunallagma*: covenant, contract (root *sunallatein*: to exchange, to reconcile).
Syn. bilateral.
Fr. synallagmatique⁺, bilatéral.

SYNALLAGMATIC CONTRACT

Syn. bilateral contract. "[..] the law is well settled in Quebec that in a synallagmatic contract the party to such contract who is himself in default cannot claim damages from the other party for breach of the contract" (*Leo Perrault Ltée* v. *Tessier*, [1958] S.C.R. 698, p. 702, D.C. Abbott, J.).
Occ. Art. 1591 C.C.Q.
Fr. contrat bilatéral, contrat synallagmatique⁺.

SYNALLAGMATIC PROMISE (TO CONTRACT)

Syn. bilateral promise to contract.
Fr. promesse bilatérale (de contrat), promesse synallagmatique (de contrat)⁺.

SYNALLAGMATIC PROMISE OF SALE

Syn. bilateral promise of sale.
Fr. promesse bilatérale de vente⁺, promesse synallagmatique de vente.

SYSTEM OF LAW

Syn. legal order.
Fr. ordre juridique⁺, système de droit, système juridique.

T

TACIT ACCEPTANCE

Acceptance[1] inferred from conduct indicating an intent to accept. "[...] the sending of goods ordered, the doing of work by request, getting into a tramcar, the finding and returning of a lost article for which a reward has been offered, are illustrations of tacit acceptance" (Walton, *Obligations*, vol. 1, p. 196).
Occ. Art. 650 C.C.L.C.
See also acceptance[1], express acceptance.
Fr. acceptation tacite.

TACIT CONSENT

Consent made known by conduct from which the will to enter into a juridical act can be inferred. "[...] is 'silence' a form of consent? The principle is that silence is not tantamount to consent. However, under certain circumstances, silence will be considered tacit consent" (Levasseur, *Conventional Obligations*, p. 31).
Obs. Mere silence does not imply consent. The law and particular circumstances, such as usage or prior business relations, may give that effect to silence (art. 1394 C.C.Q.). The parties may also decide that silence will have this effect.
Syn. implicit consent, implied consent, tacit manifestation of intent, tacit manifestation of will. **See also** express consent.
Fr. consentement implicite, consentement tacite+, manifestation de volonté tacite.

TACIT MANDATE

Mandate[1] that exists even though the will of the mandator or of the mandatary is not expressed explicitly, in written or oral form.
Obs. 1° Even though the Civil Code expressly provides only for the tacit acceptance of the mandatary, decided cases have also recognized the tacit consent of the mandator. In both instances, the consent is not expressed, but may be inferred from the acts and even from the silence of either party. **2°** *Tacit mandate* is opposed to *express mandate*[2].

See also apparent mandate, implicit consent, tacit consent.
Fr. mandat tacite.

TACIT MANIFESTATION OF INTENT

Syn. tacit consent.
Fr. consentement implicite, consentement tacite+, manifestation de volonté tacite.

TACIT MANIFESTATION OF WILL

Syn. tacit consent.
Obs. See article 1386 C.C.Q.
Fr. consentement implicite, consentement tacite+, manifestation de volonté tacite

TACIT NULLITY

Nullity not expressly provided for by a text of law, but resulting from the interpretation of rules establishing the necessary requirements for the formation of an act.
Obs. It is generally recognized that the rule stating that there can be no nullity except where expressly provided by law is limited to questions that relate to the public interest (e.g. marriage). However, tacit nullity may also arise in circumstances where a juridical act does not conform to a legal rule, even if that rule does not provide for nullity in the case of its violation.
See also textual nullity.
Fr. nullité tacite, nullité virtuelle+.

TACIT OFFER

Syn. implied offer.
Obs. Some scholars distinguish *implied offers* from *tacit offers*, limiting the former to offers manifested by actions and the latter to offers evinced by silence or inaction.
Fr. offre implicite, offre tacite+.

TACIT RELEASE

Release[1] resulting from conduct that indicates an intention to renounce a right.
Obs. Article 1688 C.C.Q. states that release may be express or tacit.
Fr. remise tacite.

TACIT RENEWAL

Renewal of a contract of successive performance resulting from the fact that the parties continue to perform after the expiration of the agreed term. "We can see that the legislature chose the rule of tacit renewal for an indeterminate period, which does not prevent the contracting parties from being bound by a series of fixed term contracts as long as there is not a tacit renewal of the contract" (Bonhomme, Gascon & Lesage, *Employment contract*, p. 27).
Occ. Arts. 579, 1667 C.C.L.C.
Obs. 1° The law expressly provides for tacit renewal of a lease of an immovable (art. 1879 C.C.Q.) and of a contract of employment (art. 2090 C.C.Q.). In other contracts of successive performance, it may result where stipulated in the contract. **2°** Compare with the legal regime respecting the renewal of residential leases at articles 1941 *et seq.* C.C.Q.
Fr. tacite reconduction.

TAKE BACK *verb.ph.*

Syn. repossess.
Occ. Arts. 1748, 1754 C.C.Q.; arts. 1546, 1555, 1773 C.C.L.C.
Obs. In the *Civil Code of Québec*, under the chapter of sale, the expression *to take back* is used rather than the verb *to repossess* as equivalent to the French verb *reprendre*.
Fr. reprendre[+], reprendre possession.

TAKE DELIVERY

Syn. remove.
Occ. Arts. 1734, 2047 C.C.Q.
Fr. enlever[+], prendre délivrance, prendre livraison, retirer[1].

TECHNOLOGY-BASED DOCUMENT

Document recorded on one or several media based on information technology.
Occ. Arts. 2837, 2841 C.C.Q.; art. 89(4) C.C.P.; ss. 3, 4, 5, 12, 38, *An Act to establish a legal framework of information technologies*, S.Q. 2001, c. 32.
Obs. 1° A technology-based document may rely upon different media using information technology, whether it be electronic, magnetic, optical, wireless or other (S.Q. 2001, c. 32, s. 1(2)). **2°** In 2001 (S.Q. 2001, c. 32), the notion of *computerized records*, previously used in the Civil Code, was replaced by *technology-based document*. While the use of the former expression was reserved to juridical acts recorded on a computer, the latter includes any intelligible information, whether it is made up of words, sounds or images inscribed on any technological medium. **3°** In the *Canada Evidence Act* (R.S.C. 1985, c. C-5, s. 31.8), and the *Personal Information Protection and Electronic Documents Act* (S.C. 2000, c. 5, s. 31(1)) one encounters the expression *electronic document* rather than *technology-based document*.
Syn. electronic document. **See also** attesting deed, electronic contract.
Fr. document électronique, document technologique[+].

TEMPORARY EMPLOYEE

Agent or servant who is under the authority of a principal for a limited period of time.
Syn. occasional employee. **See also** agent or servant, habitual employee, liability of the principal, temporary employer.
Fr. préposé occasionnel.

TEMPORARY EMPLOYER

Principal who has a person under his or her authority for a limited period of time.
Syn. occasional employer. **See also** habitual employer, liability of the principal, principal[3], temporary employee.
Fr. commettant occasionnel.

TENANT *n.*

Lessee[1] in a contract of lease of an immovable.
Occ. Former art. 1635 C.C.L.C. (1866-1973).
Obs. In the *Civil Code of Québec*, the term *lessee* is used to the exclusion of tenant. This term is, however, often encountered in juridical acts and civilian legal practice. In this context it does not refer to the doctrine of tenure inherent in the landlord-tenant relationship in the Common law tradition.
See also landlord, lessor[1].
Fr. locataire(>)[+], preneur[3](>).

TENDER *n.*

Operation whereby a debtor presents his or her creditor with the thing owed at the time and place where it is payable and demands to receive payment. *Tender and deposit.*
Occ. Title preceding art. 1573 C.C.Q.; arts. 1577, 2534 C.C.Q.; art. 189 C.C.P.; ss. 18, 20, *Deposit Act*, R.S.Q. c. D-5.
Obs. 1° When it has been declared valid by a court, tender is equivalent to a payment that frees the debtor from the day the offer is made (art. 1588 C.C.Q.). However, in order for a tender to have this effect on a monetary debt, it must be accompanied by a deposit of the sum owed (art. 1574 C.C.Q.). **2°** The codal

regime respecting tender and deposit is set forth at articles 1573 to 1589 C.C.Q.
Syn. actual tender. **See also** deposit[3].
Fr. offre réelle.

TENDER AND DEPOSIT

See tender, deposit[3]. "[T]he classic case of tender and deposit [is] where a creditor refuses to accept payment from his debtor for whatever reason, in consequence of which the sum in dispute is deposited into court. Funds so deposited, at least, so long as there has been no acceptance by the creditor are deemed not to have left the patrimony of the debtor, and hence do not consitute 'payment'" (*9010-6816 Québec inc. (Re)*, [1999] Q.J. No. 1138 (Sup. Ct.), para. 19, I.J. Halperin, J.).
Occ. Art. 1589 C.C.Q.; title preceding art. 1162 C.C.L.C.
Fr. offres et consignation.

TERM *n*.

1. Future and certain event upon which depends either the exigibility or the extinction of a right or obligation. For example, a debt payable on the death of the creditor, a debt payable in three months, a lease made for two years. "[...] the obligor is not automatically in default from the mere arrival of the term. When the term allowed for performance arrives it has no other effect than turning the obligation subject to the term into one pure and simple, that is, one immediately exigible" (Litvinoff, in *Treatise*, vol. 7, Book 2, n° 177, p. 332). *Arrival of the term*; *expiration of the term*; *beneficiary of the term*.
Occ. Arts. 1508, 1511 to 1517 C.C.Q.; art. 1089 C.C.L.C.
Obs. 1° Terms, like conditions, are modalities of the obligation. However, while terms affect the exigibility or extinction of the obligation, conditions affect its existence (arts. 1497, 1508 C.C.Q.). In addition, where a term is characterized by the certainty of its eventuality, the advent of a condition is uncertain. **2°** Article 1510 C.C.Q. states that "[i]f an event that was considered certain does not occur, the obligation is exigible from the day on which the event normally should have occurred". **3°** In principle, the term is for the benefit of the debtor, but in certain circumstances, it may also be for the benefit of the creditor or for both parties (art. 1511 C.C.Q.). **4°** Suspensive terms are distinguished from extinctive terms (arts. 1508, 1517 C.C.Q.). **5°** The codal regime respecting terms is set forth at articles 1508 to 1517 C.C.Q.
See also certain term, condition[1], conventional term, expiration, extinctive term, for-feiture of the term, judicial term, legal term, modality of the obligation, suspensive term, term of right, uncertain term.
Fr. terme.

2. **Syn.** condition[2]. "But whilst there has been a diminution of the actual freedom of both parties to decide the terms of their contract, the principle of freedom of contract is still fully accepted [...]" (Ryan, *Introduction*, p. 39). *Terms and conditions of the contract.*
Occ. Arts. 411, 694, 1118 C.C.Q.; ss.107, 144, 150.13, *Consumer Protection Act*, R.S.Q. c. P-40.1.
Fr. condition[2].

TERMINATION *n*.

Syn. extinction.
Occ. Title preceding art. 1208 C.C.Q.; art. 1116 C.C.Q.
Fr. extinction.

TERM OBLIGATION

Syn. obligation with a term.
Fr. obligation à terme.

TERM OF GRACE

Syn. judicial term.
Fr. délai de grâce, terme de grâce, terme judiciaire[+].

TERM OF RIGHT

Term[1] to which the beneficiary lays claim as a matter of right and not as a matter of grace. "The term of right is in general established by contract. Ordinarily the contract from which the term is derived is express, and there is good reason for this: it is important to fix its duration by establishing a definite date. However, the contractual term can be tacit: that happens when the obligation is of such a nature that it cannot be exercised immediately, either because of the distance, or because it involves the accomplishment of work [...]" (Planiol & Ripert, *Treatise*, vol. 2, n° 349, p. 206).
Obs. In general, a term of right is simply called a *term*, since its opposite, *judicial term* or *term of grace*, is infrequently encountered.
See also conventional term, judicial term, legal term.
Fr. terme de droit.

TERM SALE

Syn. sale with a term.
Occ. Art. 1745 C.C.Q.
Fr. vente à terme.

TERM (WITH A) *prep.ph.*

Depending on the arrival of a term[1] for exigibility or extinction. "From a functional point of view, retroactivity is perhaps the key feature that distinguishes the effect of a conditional obligation from that of an obligation with a term" (Brierley & Macdonald (eds.), *Quebec Civil Law*, n° 533, p. 484).
Occ. Arts. 1513, 1906 C.C.Q.; art. 1090 C.C.L.C.
See also conditional, modal, obligation with (a) term, payment with (a) term.
Fr. terme (à).

TEXTUAL NULLITY

Nullity expressly provided for by a text of law.
Obs. See articles 161, 440, 541, 1824, 2692 C.C.Q.
Syn. express nullity. **See also** tacit nullity.
Fr. nullité expresse, nullité textuelle+.

TEXTUAL PUBLIC ORDER

Syn. legislative public order.
Fr. ordre public législatif, ordre public textuel+.

THEORY OF APPEARANCE

Doctrine according to which the simple outward appearance of a situation that does not conform to reality is sufficient to produce legal effects in order to protect a third party of good faith who has been misled by the appearance.
Obs. 1° The theory of appearance was initially a judicial invention. Civil law scholars generally agree that the theory applies to a broad range of sectors of law, including the law of persons and the family (e.g. apparent capacity, apparent marriage) as well as property law (e.g. appearance of ownership). The legislature has expressly provided for the theory in several sectors of law, such as the apparent mandate (art. 2163 C.C.Q.), the apparent creditor (art. 1559 C.C.Q.), or the apparent heir (art. 101 C.C.Q.). **2°** Application of this theory rests on two requirements: a material element, i.e. the apparent fact, and an intellectual element, i.e. the erroneous belief of a third person in good faith. In respect of this latter requirement, courts seek to determine if there exists, for the third person, reasonable grounds for believing in the apparent situation. **3°** Justified by the need for security of transactions and by the desire to protect third persons in good faith, the theory of appearance may be, in some circumstances, an exception to the consensualist principle of the binding force of contracts, as well as an exception to the rule according to which one cannot give more rights than he or she has. This exceptional character of the theory of appearance may explain why it is interpreted restrictively, in particular that its application is often said to depend on a clear text. **4°** The person who invokes application of the theory bears the burden of proof.
See also appearance of right.
Fr. théorie de l'apparence.

THEORY OF DECLARATION

Theory according to which the contract *inter absentes* is formed when and where the offeree manifests his or her acceptance.
Obs. 1° According to this theory, it is sufficient for the offeree to manifest his or her intention for the contract to be validly formed (e.g. by signing a letter). Because of its inherent evidentiary difficulties, this theory has generally been shunned by legislatures, scholarly commentators and courts. **2°** Article 1387 C.C.Q. provides that the contract is formed when and where the offeror receives acceptance.
See also theory of expedition, theory of information, theory of reception.
Fr. théorie de la déclaration.

THEORY OF EXPEDITION

Theory according to which the contract *inter absentes* is formed when and where the offeree entrusts the acceptance to an intermediary charged with its delivery. "[...] according to the theory of expedition, the contract is not complete until the acceptance has [...] been put in a course of transmission to the offeree" (Walton, *Obligations*, vol. 1, p. 200).
Obs. 1° Prior to the adoption of the *Civil Code of Québec*, the courts often applied the theory of expedition when offer and acceptance were exchanged by the same means of communication, when the means of communication where different, they usually applied the theory of reception. However, article 1387 C.C.Q. provides that the contract is formed when and where the offeror receives acceptance, regardless of the means of communication used. **2°** This theory is based on the transmission of the acceptance to an intermediary, not to a mandatary.
See also theory of declaration, theory of information, theory of reception.
Fr. théorie de l'émission, théorie de l'expédition+.

THEORY OF INFORMATION

Theory according to which the contract *inter absentes* is formed when and where the offeror takes cognizance of the acceptance.
Obs. 1° Even though it may be thought of as one of the logical consequences of consensualism, this theory has not been retained in the *Civil Code of Québec* because of the evidentiary difficulties and potential for fraud to which it may give rise. Article 1387 C.C.Q. provides that the contract is formed when and where the offeror receives acceptance. **2°** Some scholars consider the theory of information to be a broad category grouping together the theory of reception and the theory of information.
See also theory of declaration, theory of expedition, theory of reception.
Fr. théorie de l'information.

THEORY OF RECEPTION

Theory according to which the contract *inter absentes* is formed when and where the acceptance by the offeree reaches the offeror.
Obs. 1° As the contract is formed when and where the offeror receives acceptance, regardless of the means of communication used (art. 1387 C.C.Q.). **2°** The parties may stipulate that the formation of the contract is suspended until the moment when the acceptor receives acknowledgment of receipt or confirmation by the offeror of the reception of his or her acceptance. Such clauses are frequently used in electronic contracts. **3°** Article 1387 C.C.Q. does not modify the rules relative to mandate. Where acceptance is communicated to the offeror's mandatary, the contract is formed when and where the mandatary receives the acceptance, since he or she represents the mandator (art. 2130 C.C.Q.).
See also acceptation[1], theory of declaration, theory of expedition, theory of information.
Fr. théorie de la réception.

THEORY OF THE AUTONOMY OF WILL

See autonomy of will.
Fr. théorie de l'autonomie de la volonté.

THING *n.*

1. Material object. "[...] the law is well settled that a person who has a thing under his care may be relieved of responsibility for damages caused by it by showing that he was unable by reasonable means to prevent the damage [...]"
(*M. & W. Cloaks Ltd.* v. *Cooperberg*, [1959] S.C.R. 785, p. 786, P. Kerwin, C.J.).
Occ. Arts. 913, 914 C.C.Q.
Syn. corporeal thing, material thing, *res*[1].
See also patrimonial right, property[2].
Fr. chose[1+], chose corporelle, chose matérielle.

2. Syn. prestation.
Occ. Arts. 1093, 1139 C.C.L.C.
Fr. chose[2], objet de l'obligation, prestation[+].

THING NOT DUE

That which one is not owed. "Although these actions [in nullity based on art. 33 C.C.P.] also sought reimbursement of the taxes and assessments wrongly paid, the trial judge expressed the view that they were not strictly speaking actions to recover things not due, based on arts. 1047 *et seq.* of the *Civil Code* [arts. 1491, 1492 C.C.Q.], because the monies paid were paid in accordance with the valuation and collection rolls in force" (*Abel Skiver Farm Corp.* v. *Ste-Foy (Town of)*, [1983] 1 S.C.R. 403, pp. 415-416, J. Beetz, J.).
Occ. Title preceding art. 1491 C.C.Q.; art. 3125 C.C.Q.
See also payment of a thing not due, reception of a thing not due, restitution of a thing not due, unjust enrichment.
Fr. indu.

THING SUSCEPTIBLE OF APPROPRIATION

Syn. property[2].
Fr. bien[2+], bien corporel, bien matériel, chose appropriable.

THIRD PARTY

Person extraneous to a contract. "It is well established that an act which constitutes contractual fault as against another contracting party may also constitute delictual or quasi delictual fault as against a third party, and so be a basis for an action under arts. 1053 *et seq.* of the *Civil Code* [*of Lower Canada*]" (*Parrot* v. *Thompson*, [1984] 1 S.C.R. 57, p. 58, J. Chouinard, J.).
Occ. Arts. 9, 1730 C.C.L.C.
Obs. A *third party* to a contract is sometimes referred to as a *stranger to the contract*.
See also *penitus extraneus*, relative effect of contract, third person, warranty against acts of third persons.
Fr. tiers(>).

THIRD PARTY BENEFICIARY

Syn. third person beneficiary.
Fr. tiers bénéficiaire.

THIRD PERSON

Person extraneous to a juridical relationship.
"Claims for services as against persons are
the paradigmatic personal (or relative) rights
in that they cannot be set up against third
persons" (Macdonald, (1994) 39 *McGill L.J.*
761, n° 36, p. 798).
Occ. Arts. 1440, 1455, 2941 C.C.Q.; arts.
1023, 1027 C.C.L.C.
Obs. 1° Persons that are not parties to a contract and that are not successors by particular
title are considered as absolute third persons.
Are often set up against each other true third
persons, or *penitus extranei*, who are complete strangers to a contract, and the successor or the creditor who, while they are third
persons, nonetheless maintain a legal relation with a contracting party. **2°** The relativity of contract is a principle according to
which the effect of the contract does not
extend to third persons (art. 1440 C.C.Q.),
also called *penitu extranei*. However, if a
party dies, his of her heirs will not be considered as a third person, even though they are
not parties to the initial contract (art. 1441
C.C.Q.). In the same manner, successors by
particular title will not be considered as third
persons in respect to the rights that "are
accessory to property which passes to them or
are directly related to it" (art. 1442 C.C.Q.).
3° It is generally said that third persons must
take into consideration the juridical situation
created by the contract. For example, third
persons who voluntarily contribute to the
violation of a contract may be held extra-
contractually liable for the damage they
cause. **4°** The expression *third party* is confined to persons extraneous to a contract.
See also *penitus extraneus*, third party, warranty against acts of third persons.
Fr. tiers.

THIRD PERSON BENEFICIARY

Person to whose advantage the promisor[2], in
a stipulation for another, binds himself or
herself towards the stipulator. "The third
person beneficiary of the stipulation has an
action against the promisor to obtain performance of the promise, as if he had himself
stipulated" (Planiol & Ripert, *Treatise*, vol. 2,
n° 1260, p. 714).
Occ. Arts. 1444, 1449, 1450, 1496 C.C.Q.
Syn. third party beneficiary. **See also** promisor[2], stipulation for another, stipulator.
Fr. tiers bénéficiaire.

THREAT *n.*

Manifestation of an intention to harm ano-
ther, the result of which is to inspire fear.
Occ. Art. 1402 C.C.Q.
Obs. Fear provoked by threats can vitiate
consent (arts. 1402, 1403 C.C.Q.).
See also defect of consent, fear, state of
necessity[2], violence.
Fr. menace.

TITLE *n.*

1. Legal basis of a right, possession or detention. For example, a juridical act, the law.
"This simply means that if the possessor is
holding the property under a title, the latter
will be examined, and if it discloses, for example, that the possession is precarious (such as
that of a tenant under a lease), the possessor
will not be able to avail himself of prescription" (Durnford, (1964-65) 67 *R. du N.* 559,
p. 560). *Precarious title; interverted title.*
Occ. Arts. 928, 932, 2914 C.C.Q.; arts. 2208,
2242 C.C.L.C.
See also *juste titre*, lawful title, tradition by
interversion of title.
Fr. titre[1].

2. Syn. juridical act. "Writings drawn up to
serve as proof do not bear a special name
in French. They are called sometimes *acts*,
sometimes *titles:* but those two expressions
are ambiguous, and apply to the juridical act
established by the writing, as well as the written proof itself" (Planiol & Ripert, *Treatise*,
vol. 2, n° 56, p. 43).
Occ. Arts. 932, 1181 C.C.Q.; art. 2254 C.C.L.C.
Fr. acte[1], acte juridique[+], *negotium*, titre[2].

3. Syn. attesting deed. *Title search.*
Occ. Arts. 1689, 2833, 2834 C.C.Q.
Fr. acte[2], acte instrumentaire[+], *instrumen-
tum*, titre[3].

TITLE OF CLAIM

Syn. title of indebtedness.
Fr. titre de créance.

TITLE OF INDEBTEDNESS

Deed attesting to a personal right.
Occ. Arts. 2688, 2692, 3014 C.C.Q.
Obs. Bearer instruments and promissory
notes are examples of titles of indebtedness.
Rules concerning assignment of claims
attested by bearer instrument are set forth in
articles 1647 *et seq.* C.C.Q.
Syn. title of claim. **See also** attesting deed,
personal right.
Fr. titre de créance.

TITLE OF PAYMENT

Deed attesting to a payment.
See also acquittance[1], attesting deed, discharge[1], receipt[1].
Fr. titre de paiement.

TORT *n.*

1. See delict.
Obs. Given the fact that the Common law regime for nominate torts has no analogue in the modern civil law, it has been suggested that *torts* is an inappropriate borrowing from the Common law, notwithstanding its connection to Old French.
Fr. [*].

2. See extracontractual liability. "It is true that the CIVILIAN jurists do not have exactly the concept of a tort. They speak rather in terms of 'liability'" (Tunc, in *Int. Enc. Comp. L.*, vol. XI, p. 1-12).
Occ. S. 3, *Crown Liability and Proceedings Act*, R.S.C. 1985, c. C-50.
Obs. 1° This term is borrowed from the Common law to designate the field of extracontractual liability. **2°** In this sense, the term is often used in the plural.
Fr. responsabilité extracontractuelle.

TOTAL INCAPACITY

Syn. general incapacity.
Fr. incapacité générale+, incapacité totale.

TRADER *n.*

Syn. merchant.
Occ. Arts. 1005, 1489, 2268 para. 3 C.C.L.C.
Fr. commerçant.

TRADITION *n.*

Delivery[1] of a material thing that is the object of an obligation to give. "[...] sale does no longer consider tradition, a juridical act, as effecting the transfer of ownership, but only as a simple delivery, a material act, not having any other effect than to transfer possession" (Planiol & Ripert, *Treatise*, vol. 2, n° 1448, p. 815).
Obs. 1° Tradition may constitute either a mode of performance of an obligation to deliver (art. 1717 C.C.Q.) or a condition for the formation of a contract. **2°** Tradition accompanied by a promise of sale is equivalent to a sale (art. 1710 C.C.Q.). Likewise, tradition and consent of the parties are sufficient for the formation of a contract of gift of movables (art. 1824 C.C.Q.). **3°** The term *tradi-*

tion sometimes refers more broadly to the delivery of a material thing necessary for the formation of real contracts, as in a deposit or a loan (arts. 2280, 2313, 2314 C.C.Q.). **4°** Tradition does not necessarily entail material delivery of a thing in a physical sense: it may be fictitious or symbolic. **5°** From the Latin *traditio*: a surrender, delivery, transmission.
See also actual tradition, fictitious tradition, handing over, real contract, removal, symbolic tradition.
Fr. tradition.

TRADITION BY INTERVERSION OF TITLE

Tradition carried out by the modification of the title of the person already holding the thing. For example, in the case of a lessee who purchases from the lessor a movable previously rented from the latter.
Syn. *brevi manu* tradition. **See also** actual tradition, fictitious tradition, symbolic tradition.
Fr. *traditio brevi manu*, tradition de brève main, tradition par interversion de titre+.

TRANSACT *v.*

To effect a transaction.
Occ. Art. 212 C.C.Q.; arts. 307, 1925 C.C.L.C.; art. 394 C.C.P.
Syn. settle[2].
Fr. transiger.

TRANSACTION *n.*

1. Contract by which the parties prevent a future contestation or put an end to proceedings already commenced by means of mutual concessions or reservations. "Transaction has the effect of *res judicata* between the parties and is the equivalent of a judgment. The interruption of prescription will not go beyond the date of a transaction, any more than the date of a final judgment" (*Jumbo Motors Express Ltd.* v. *François Nolin Ltée*, [1985] 1 S.C.R. 423, p. 435, J. Chouinard, J.).
Occ. Arts. 2504, 2631, 2896, 2968 C.C.Q.; arts. 307, 747, 1918, 2604 C.C.L.C.; art. 1025 C.C.P.
Obs. 1° A transaction has the effect of *res judicata* between the parties; however, the transaction is not subject to compulsory execution until it is homologated (art. 2633 C.C.Q.). **2°** A transaction that bears on the status or the capacity of a person or that touches any matter of public order is forbidden (art. 2632 C.C.Q.). **3°** A transaction is distinguished from an arbitration agreement in that it settles the parties' dispute, whereas

an arbitration agreement is a contract by which the parties submit a dispute to an arbitrator, to the exclusion of the courts (art. 2638 C.C.Q.). **4°** The codal regime respecting transactions is set forth at articles 2631 to 2637 C.C.Q.
Syn. contract of transaction, out-of-court settlement, settlement. **See also** confirmation, novation, ratification[2].
Fr. contrat de transaction, règlement hors cour, transaction[+].

2. **Syn.** contract[1]. "A owes money to B, and B, who is in need of cash, sells his debt against A to C by the civil law transaction known as sale of a debt" (Nicholls, (1938) 16 *Can. Bar Rev.* 602, p. 607).
Occ. Art. 1695 C.C.Q.
Obs. In common parlance, the term *transaction* is also used to designate any type of agreement, in particular, a commercial or a stock-market operation (see art. 1695 C.C.Q.).
Fr. contrat[1+], convention, pacte.

3. Series of contracts agreed to in respect of the same economic venture. *Commercial transaction; complex legal transaction.*
Obs. In principle, the contracts that are part of a transaction are considered as facts and, as such, may be used in the interpretation of any contract forming part of the whole.
Fr. ensemble contractuel.

TRANSFER *n.*

Transmission of a right. "Even the most restrictive theory accepts the transfer of rights that are identified with the thing or accessories thereto" (*General Motors Products of Canada Ltd.* v. *Kravitz*, [1979] 1 S.C.R. 790, p. 809, Y. Pratte, J.).
Occ. Arts. 1212, 1453, 1807, 2756 C.C.Q.
Obs. The term *transfer* is used more particularly with respect to transmission of rights *inter vivos.*
Syn. conveyance[2].
Fr. transfert[+], translation.

TRANSFER *v.*

To carry out a transfer. "The first of the two principal obligations of the seller is to deliver the thing sold (art. 1491 C.C.L.C.) – that is, to transfer the thing into the power and possession of the buyer (art. 1492 C.C.L.C.)" (Brierley & Macdonald (eds.), *Quebec Civil Law*, n° 581, p. 520).
Occ. Arts. 419, 1454, 1826 C.C.Q.; arts. 1022, 1492 C.C.L.C.
Syn. convey[2].
Fr. transférer.

TRANSFER BY SALE

Syn. sell.
Fr. vendre.

TRANSFER OF CLAIM

Syn. assignment of claim(s).
Fr. cession de créance[+], cession-transport, transport-cession, transport de créance.

TRANSFER OF DEBT

Syn. assignment of claim(s). "[...] while the general transfer of debts is perfected between the assignor and assignee by completion of authentic title or delivery of title under private signature, the assigned debtor as a third party is not bound to make payment to the assignee unless and until he has been served with a copy or extract of the assignment or has accepted it" (Miller & Sarna, (1981) 59 *Can. Bar Rev.* 638, p. 641).
Occ. Art. 1651.7 C.C.L.C.
Obs. Articles 1174 and 1571*a* of the *Civil Code of Lower Canada* use the term *debt* to designate a claim.
Fr. cession de créance[+], cession-transport, transport-cession, transport de créance.

TRANSLATORY *adj.*

See translatory effect, translatory title.
Fr. translatif.

TRANSLATORY ACT

Juridical act, the purpose of which is to transfer a right from one titulary to another.
Obs. 1° A translatory act transfers a right from one patrimony to another. **2°** Whereas constitutive acts create new rights, translatory acts transfer existing rights. **3°** See article 1433 C.C.Q.
See also attributive act, constitutive act, declaratory act, renunciation[1], translatory contract, translatory effect.
Fr. acte translatif.

TRANSLATORY ACT OF OWNERSHIP

Translatory title, the purpose of which is to transfer the right of ownership from one titulary to another. For example, a sale, a giving in payment.
Obs. 1° In the context of translatory acts of ownership, delivery transfers neither the ownership nor the possession of the property, since both have been transferred, in principle, upon the conclusion of the contract (art. 1453

C.C.Q.). **2°** This expression is encountered most often in matters relating to prescription.
See also contract translatory of ownership.
Fr. acte translatif de propriété.

TRANSLATORY CONTRACT

Contract whose object is to transfer a right from one contracting party to another. For example, a sale, a gift. "The problem of risk in translatory contracts is [...] only a small part of the larger question of impossibility as an excuse for non-performance" (Brierley & Macdonald (eds.), *Quebec Civil Law*, n° 462, p. 427).
Obs. The translatory effect of contracts is expressly stated at arts. 1433 and 1453 C.C.Q. These articles are in apparent contradiction with the definition of a contract at article 1378 C.C.Q., which characterizes contracts as instruments for the creation of obligations.
See also contract[1], translatory title.
Fr. contrat translatif.

TRANSLATORY EFFECT

Effect of that which transfers a right from one titulary to another. For example, the transfer of ownership resulting from a contract of sale.
Obs. The translatory effect of contracts is expressly stated at art. 1433 C.C.Q. This article is in apparent contradiction with the definition of a contract (art. 1378 C.C.Q.) which, by characterizing contracts as instruments for the creation of obligations, excludes numerous contracts from its scope.
See also constitutive effect, declaratory effect, extinctive effect, renunciatory effect, translatory title.
Fr. effet translatif.

TRANSLATORY TITLE

Title[1], the legal basis of which is a translatory act. For example, a title based on sale.
Occ. Arts. 2206, 2251 C.C.L.C.
Fr. titre translatif.

TRANSLATORY TITLE OF OWNERSHIP

Title[1] of ownership, the legal basis of which is a translatory act. For example, a title[1] of ownership based on sale.
Obs. This expression is encountered most often in matters relating to prescription.
See also contract translatory of ownership, *juste titre*.
Fr. titre translatif de propriété.

TRANSMISSIBILITY *n.*

Character of a right or obligation susceptible of transmission. *Transmissibility of rights of action.*
Obs. The term *transmissibility* is used particularly with respect to rights or obligations transmitted *mortis causa*. In other cases, more precise terms such as *alienability* and *assignability* are preferred.
See also assignability, intransmissibility.
Fr. transmissibilité.

TRANSMISSIBLE *adj.*

Said of rights or obligations susceptible of transmission. "The right of the legal representatives of a deceased person to take up the *instance* on a suit instituted by him, even where the right to obtain the principal object of such suit was not transmissible or transmitted to them, was fully recognized by Pigeau [...] under the old law and seems to be generally, though not unanimously, acknowledged, by the commentators under the Code Napoléon" (*Wilson* v. *Giroux* (1902), 21 C.S. 56, pp. 63-64, C.J. Doherty, J.).
Obs. 1° Rights and obligations are, in principle, transmissible unless the law declares them intransmissible or unless intransmissibility results from their nature or their particular purpose (e.g. personality rights and human rights and freedoms are in principle intransmissible). **2°** On the regime for transmissibility in contract, see articles 1441, 1442 C.C.Q. and article 1030 C.C.L.C. **3°** In principle, the right of a creditor to damages is fully transmissible, with the exception of claims arising from breach of personality rights which can be transmitted only to heirs (art. 1610 C.C.Q.) **4°** The term *transmissible* is used especially with respect to rights or obligations susceptible of being transmitted *mortis causa*. In other cases, more precise terms such as *alienable* and *assignable* are preferred.
See also assignable, intransmissible.
Fr. transmissible.

TRANSMISSION *n.*

Operation by which rights or obligations pass from one person or patrimony to another. "The Quebec civil code [C.C.L.C.] moreover distinguishes between the transmission and the property transmitted, the term succession being supplied to either (Art. 596 C.C.[L.C.]) and there is no doubt in my mind that they are entirely distinguishable" (*Barthe* v. *Alleyn-Sharples* (1920), 60 S.C.R. 1, p. 34, P.B. Mignault, J.).

Occ. Arts. 2938, 2998 para. 2 C.C.Q.; arts. 596, 2098 C.C.L.C.; s. 103(1)(*b*), *Cooperative Credit Associations Act*, S.C. 1991, c. 48; s. 96(1)(*b*), *Bank Act*, S.C. 1991, c. 46.

Obs. 1° Transmission may be voluntary or may result from the operation of law. It may take place *inter vivos* or *mortis causa* and may be made by gratuitous or onerous title. It may also be universal, by general title or by particular title. **2°** In its most general sense, transmission is similar to a disposition². These notions are however distinct in that transmission may bear on rights or obligations whereas a disposition² may only involve rights. **3°** The person transmitting the right or obligation is called the *author* or *predecessor in title*; the beneficiary of the transmission is called the *successor*.

See also assignment¹, disposition², mutation, transfer, transmission by general title, transmission by particular title, universal transmission.

Fr. transmission.

TRANSMISSION BY (A) PARTICULAR TITLE

Transmission of a right² rather than an aliquot share, a universality or the whole of a patrimony. "In transmissions, by a particular title, the acquirer is not held personally for the debts, to any extent or for any fraction" (Planiol & Ripert, *Treatise*, vol. 1, n° 2558, p. 510).

Obs. 1° Transmission by particular title may take place *inter vivos* or *mortis causa* and may be made by gratuitous or onerous title. **2°** It is generally considered that transmission by particular title takes place with respect to rights and that transmission of such rights does not entail transmission of the author's obligations (e.g. in the case of the sale of a car, the buyer will not be held responsible for the debts the vendor may have contracted in order to finance the initial purchase of the car). However, there are a number of exceptions to this principle, notably in cases of assignment of contract (e.g. art. 1937 C.C.Q., in matters of residential leases; art. 2097 C.C.Q., in matters of contracts of employment). **3°** The *Civil Code of Québec* provides that "[t]he rights of the parties to a contract pass to their successors by particular title if they are accessory to property which passes to them or are directly related to it" (art. 1442 C.C.Q.). **4°** For an application of transmission by particular title in respect of legacies, see article 734 C.C.Q.

See also assignment of debt, delegation, relativity of contract, successor by particular title, transmission by general title, universal transmission.

Fr. transmission à titre particulier.

TRANSMISSION BY GENERAL TITLE

Transmission of an aliquot share of a patrimony, a universality, or an aliquot share of a universality of such patrimony.

Obs. 1° Transmission by general title applies to rights and obligations to which the author was held, in the same proportion as the share received. **2°** Transmission by general title generally occurs *mortis causa*. It may however arise *inter vivos*, but only by onerous title (e.g. by assignment of a universality of claims (art. 1642 C.C.Q.)). Unlike the *Civil Code of Lower Canada*, the *Civil Code of Québec* prohibits gifts by general title (art. 1823 C.C.Q.). **3°** Article 733 C.C.Q. gives a limitative list of universalities that may be the object of a legacy by general title. According to some scholars, this list is of general application. **4°** In contractual matters, see articles 1440, 1441 C.C.Q.

See also disposition by general title, gift by general title, relativity of contract, successor by general title, transmission by (a) particular title, universal transmission.

Fr. transmission à titre universel.

TRANSPORT *n.*

1. Syn. carriage¹.
Occ. Art. 2590 C.C.L.C.
Fr. transport¹.

2. Syn. contract of carriage.
Fr. contrat de transport⁺, transport².

TRANSPORT *v.*

Syn. carry.
Occ. Art. 1577 C.C.Q.
Fr. transporter¹.

TRANSPORTATION *n.*

Syn. carriage¹.
Occ. Arts. 1165, 1678 C.C.L.C.
Fr. transport¹.

TRANSPORT OF GOODS

See carriage of goods.
Fr. [*].

TRANSPORT OF MERCHANDISE

See carriage of goods.
Fr. [*].

TRANSPORT OF PERSONS

See carriage of persons.
Fr. [*].

TRANSPORT OF PROPERTY

See carriage of goods.
Fr. [*].

TRIAL SALE

Sale subject to the condition that the trial of the property will demonstrate that it possesses the characteristics necessary for the use for which it will be put by the buyer.
Occ. Title preceding art. 1744 C.C.Q.
Obs. 1° The condition upon which the obligation of the buyer in a trial sale depends must not be purely potestative (art. 1500 C.C.Q.). Thus, if an examination reveals that the property possesses the requisite characteristics, the condition is fulfilled and the sale is perfected. In this sense, the expression *sale on approval*, which is sometimes used as synonym for *trial sale*, may be misleading. **2°** The fulfilment of the condition has a retroactive effect and the buyer becomes owner as of the day the contract was entered into (art. 1506 C.C.Q.). **3°** Article 1744 C.C.Q. provides that the trial sale is presumed to have been made under a suspensive condition. The parties may, however, agree to a trial sale under resolutory condition.
Syn. sale on approval, sale upon trial.
Fr. vente à l'essai.

TRUE *adj.*

See true act, true indivisibility, true will.
Fr. véritable.

TRUE ACT

Syn. counter letter.
Fr. acte réel, acte secret, acte véritable, contre-lettre+.

TRUE INDIVISIBILITY

Syn. natural indivisibility.
Fr. indivisibilité naturelle+, indivisibilité objective, indivisibilité réelle, indivisibilité véritable.

TRUE WILL

Syn. internal will. "Second, the courts may, by way of 'interpretation' of the contract, rightly invoke the parties' intention to ascertain the genuine content of an absent or inadequately-expressed will. By shedding light on the parties' true will, the courts again remain loyal to one of the central tenets of the will theory" (Legrand, (1989) 34 *McGill L.J.* 908, p. 916).
Fr. volonté interne+, volonté réelle.

U

UBERRIMA FIDES (Latin)

See good faith[1,2].
Fr. *uberrima fides.*

UNABLE *adj.*

Syn. incapable[2].
Occ. Arts. 26, 272 C.C.Q.; art. 97 C.C.P.; s. 28, *Public Curator Act*, R.S.Q. c. C-81.
Obs. This term is also used in a broader sense to refer to the situation of a person who cannot express his or her will or to act for any reason (e.g. arts. 398, 549 C.C.Q.).
Fr. inapte[+], incapable[2].

UNASSIGNABILITY *n.*

Syn. non-assignability.
Fr. incessibilité.

UNASSIGNABLE *adj.*

Syn. non-assignable.
Fr. incessible.

UNAVAILABILITY *n.*

Attribute of property that is not susceptible of immediate use or delivery. "The only explanation offered for the delay in effecting repairs [...] was the unavailability of parts [...] The Court concludes that Plaintiff was deprived of the object leased because the manufacturer and the dealer failed to make replacement parts available to the parties concerned within a reasonable delay" (*Comitini* v. *GMAC Leaseco Ltd.*, [1993] Q.J. n° 879 (Sup. Ct.), par. 19 (QL), J. Gomery, J.).
Fr. indisponibilité[2].

UNAVAILABLE *adj.*

Not susceptible of immediate use or delivery.
Fr. indisponible[2].

UNCERTAIN *adj.*

See uncertain creance, uncertain debt, uncertain term.
Fr. incertain.

UNCERTAIN CLAIM

Creance the existence or validity of which may reasonably be disputed. For example, litigious claims.
Syn. uncertain creance. **See also** certain claim, certain debt, exigible claim, liquid claim, litigious personal right, litigious right, suspensive condition.
Fr. créance incertaine.

UNCERTAIN CREANCE

Syn. uncertain claim.
Fr. créance incertaine.

UNCERTAIN DEBT

Debt[1] the existence or validity of which may reasonably be disputed.
Obs. Litigious debts are uncertain in character.
See also certain claim, certain debt, exigible debt, litigious personal right, litigious right, suspensive condition, uncertain claim.
Fr. dette incertaine.

UNCERTAIN TERM

Syn. unspecified term. "A term is said to be uncertain only when the period of time preceding the occurrence of the definite event or term is not fixed but is determinable either by the intent of the parties or by the occurrence of a future and certain event. [...] As an example of an uncertain term, although a certain event, we could select the time of death of a person: thus, Gaius could agree to pay Paul upon Modestinus' death. The reference to Modestinus' death would be an uncertain term" (Levasseur, *Obligations*, p. 37).
Obs. Most scholars prefer to speak of an *unspecified term*.
See also certain term.
Fr. terme incertain[+], terme inconnu, terme indéterminé.

UNCONDITIONAL *adj.*

1. Syn. pure and simple.
Fr. pur et simple.

2. Without condition[1].
See also pure and simple.
Fr. pur et simple(>).

UNCONDITIONAL RIGHT

1. Syn. pure and simple right.
Fr. droit pur et simple.

2. Right to which no condition is attached.
See also conditional right, pure and simple right.
Fr. droit pur et simple(>).

UNDECLARED PARTNERSHIP

Partnership which is established by an express contract or results from an overt act indicating the intention of the partners to carry on business together.
Occ. Arts. 2189, 2197, 2250 C.C.Q.
Obs. 1° Undeclared partnerships are not subject to the requirements of *An Act respecting the legal publicity of sole proprietorships, partnerships and legal persons* (R.S.Q. c. P-45). **2°** Like general and limited partnerships, undeclared partnerships are not endowed with juridical personality. Compared to general and limited partnerships, undeclared partnerships may be said to enjoy even fewer of the attributes of juridical personality. While they may have a name, for example, undeclared partnerships may not sue in a civil action under that name and, in respect of third persons, each partner remains owner of the property he or she furnished to the partnership (art. 2252 C.C.Q.). **3°** Undeclared partnerships may be distinguished from undivided co-ownership insofar as they reflect a "spirit of cooperation", the *affectio societatis*, i.e. an intention of the parties to be partners to a joint business. **4°** Undeclared partnership is similar to the anonymous partnership of the *Civil Code of Lower Canada* (art. 1870 C.C.L.C.). **5°** Specific rules relating to undeclared partnerships are set forth at articles 2250 to 2266 C.C.Q.
See also contract of partnership, general partnership, limited partnership, partner, partnership[1].
Fr. société en participation.

UNDERTAKING *n.*

Obligation[3] that the debtor assumes by a juridical act. *Contractual undertaking.*
Occ. Arts. 1458 para. 1, 1574 para. 2, 2352 C.C.Q.; s. 314, *Consumer Protection Act*, R.S.Q. c. P-40.1; s. 23, *Public Curator Act*, R.S.Q. c. C-81.

Syn. commitment, engagement. **See also** unilateral undertaking (of will).
Fr. engagement[1].

UNDERTAKING BY UNILATERAL WILL

See unilateral undertaking (of will).
Fr. engagement par volonté unilatérale.

UNDERTAKING TO ARBITRATE

Clause[1] by which the parties agree in advance to submit to arbitration any dispute that may arise between them with regard to a contract or a business relationship. "A complete undertaking to arbitrate, described variously as true, real or formal, is that by which the parties undertake in advance to submit to arbitration any disputes which may arise regarding their contract, and which specifies that the award made will be final and binding on the parties" (*Zodiac International Productions Inc.* v. *Polish People's Republic*, [1983] 1 S.C.R. 529, p. 533, J. Chouinard, J.).
Obs. 1° The undertakings to arbitrate (often referred to in English by the French term *clause compromissoire*) is considered to be a distinct agreement from the principal agreement within which it is incorporated. Consequently, the nullity of the principal agreement does not entail the nullity of the undertaking to arbitrate (art. 2642 C.C.Q.). **2°** Since the reform of the law of arbitration in 1986 (*An Act to amend the Civil Code and the Code of Civil Procedure in respect of arbitration*, S.Q. 1986, c. 73), only complete arbitration clauses are valid. Such clauses meet the requirements of the definition of the arbitration agreement insofar as they attest the common will of the parties to submit the dispute to arbitration, to the exclusion of the courts. **3°** Prior to the reform of the law of arbitration in 1986, undertakings to arbitrate took one of two forms: the pre-judicial arbitration clause or the complete arbitration clause. In the pre-judicial arbitration clause, the parties provided for preliminary arbitration before bringing the dispute before the courts. This kind of clause was rendered invalid by the reform of 1986. In the complete arbitration clause, the parties agree never to bring the case before the courts. After much debate concerning the proper scope of former article 951 C.C.P., the Supreme Court decided in favour of the validity of this clause (*Zodiak International* v. *Polish People's Republic*, [1983] 1 S.C.R. 529).

See also arbitration agreement, submission (to arbitration).
Fr. clause compromissoire⁺, clause d'arbitrage.

UNDETERMINED TERM

Syn. unspecified term.
Obs. Most scholars prefer to speak of an *unspecified term*.
Fr. terme incertain⁺, terme inconnu, terme indéterminé.

UNDISCLOSED MANDATARY

Mandatary who, in dealing with third parties on behalf of the mandator, does not reveal his or her capacity as mandatary but allows others to believe that he or she is acting on his or her own behalf.
Obs. The mandatary acting in his or her name is liable to third persons, subject to any rights such persons may have against the mandator (art. 2157 C.C.Q.).
Syn. nominee, *prête-nom*[1]. **See also** contract of *prête-nom*, imperfect representation, interposed person.
Fr. prête-nom[1].

UNDISPOSABILITY *n.*

Neol. Attribute of property not susceptible of disposition by the effect of law or a juridical act.
Obs. While some scholars consider that inalienability has the same effects as undisponibility – inalienability often seen as suppressing the entire right to dispose of property – these two notions are different. *Undisponibility*, which precludes the disposal of property, is a broader term than *inalienability*, which only forbids its alienation; the latter term leaves the possibility of the material disposal of the thing. Moreover, undisponibility is often associated with rights attached to a person (e.g. the right to a name).
See also inalienability, intransmissibility, non-assignability.
Fr. indisponibilité[1].

UNDISPOSABLE *adj.*

Neol. Not susceptible of disposition by the effect of law or a juridical act.
See also inalienable, intransmissible, non-assignable, undisposability.
Fr. indisponible[1].

UNFORESEEABILITY *n.*

1. Characteristic of an event that a reasonable person would not normally have anticipated.
Obs. 1° Unforeseeability, along with irresistibility, is an element used to determine whether or not an event can be considered as a case of superior force with respect to the law of civil liability. Externality is also sometimes considered to be an element that must be taken into account. **2°** Superior force is a cause of extinction of obligations and of exemption from liability (arts. 1470, 1693 C.C.Q.).
See also damage, externality, foreseeability, irresistibility, superior force[1], unforeseeseable damage, unforeseen damage.
Fr. imprévisibilité.

2. Change of circumstances that one of the parties could not foresee at the time of formation of the contract and that has the effect of rendering its performance more onerous. "[...] the strictness of the judicial attitude toward unforeseeability has more recently been tempered by a rather flexible application of the criteria for determining when performance has become impossible due to a superior force" (Brierley & Macdonald (eds.), *Quebec Civil Law*, n° 449, p. 418).
Obs. 1° If the parties seek protection against unforeseeability, particularly in long-term contracts, they may, by an express clause, provide for the revision of the contract. In the absence of such a clause, unforeseeability does not give rise, in principle, to a remedy in Quebec law. According to the principle of the binding character of the contract, parties must perform their obligations even in cases of unforeseeability (art. 1439 C.C.Q.). **2°** Unforeseeability renders the performance of the contract more onerous, whereas superior force makes it impossible. **3°** While unforeseeability and lesion are related notions, both aimed at protecting an equilibrium of contractual prestations, they may nevertheless be distinguished. Lesion must exist at the time of the formation of the contract, whereas unforeseeability arises in the context of its performance. **4°** The Civil Code Revision Office proposed to permit the revision of a contract when unforeseeable circumstances entailed excessive damage (art. 75, Bk V, *Draft Civil Code*, C.C.R.O.). This solution has been adopted in Unidroit's *Principles for International Commercial Contracts* (arts. 6.2.2, 6.2.3 Unidroit's *Principles*). German and Swiss law have also adopted this same solution, but base the revision of the contract on the notion of *good faith* (art. 242

Bürgerliches Gesetzbuch; art. 2 Swiss *Code des obligations*).
Syn. *imprévision.* **See also** lesion, revision clause, revision of contract, superior force[1].
Fr. imprévision.

UNFORESEEABLE *adj.*

See unforeseeable damage.
Fr. imprévisible.

UNFORESEEABLE DAMAGE

Damage resulting from non-performance of an obligation that a prudent and diligent debtor would not normally have been able to foresee.
Obs. Since the terms *damage* and *injury* are synonymous, the expression *unforeseeable injury* may also be used.
See also foreseeable damage, foreseen damage, non-performance, unforeseen damage.
Fr. préjudice imprévisible.

UNFORESEEN *adj.*

See unforeseen damage.
Fr. imprévu.

UNFORESEEN DAMAGE

Damage resulting from the non-performance of an obligation that the debtor had not foreseen.
Obs. Since the terms *damage* and *injury* are synonymous, the expression *unforeseen injury* may also be used.
See also foreseeable damage, foreseen damage, non-performance, unforeseeable damage.
Fr. préjudice imprévu.

UNILATERAL *adj.*

See unilateral act, unilateral contract, unilateral promise (to contract), unilateral promise of sale, unilateral resiliation, unilateral undertaking (of will).
Fr. unilatéral.

UNILATERAL ACT

Juridical act that originates from a single author. For example, a will (art. 704 C.C.Q.), a confirmation of a contract that is null (art. 1423 C.C.Q.), a decision of a deliberative assembly, a renunciation of succession (art. 646 C.C.Q.). "To show that the impoverishment of the donor and the enrichment of the donee are devoid of cause, one must establish the absence of a desire by the donor (the person impoverished) to benefit the donee by a unilateral act" (Fine, (1973) 19 *McGill L.J.* 453, p. 468).
Obs. 1° A unilateral act may be individual; it can also be collective when it is jointly undertaken by a group of persons pursuing a common interest. **2°** A unilateral act resulting from the will of only one person should not be confused with a unilateral contract, which reflects a concurrence of wills of two or more persons even though only one party incurs obligations (art. 1378 C.C.Q.). Moreover, a unilateral act should not be confused with a unilateral undertaking. Although the unilateral act gives rise to juridical effects, it does not create an obligation in and of itself.
See also bilateral act, collective act, doctrine of undertaking by unilateral will, individual act, multilateral act, offer, unilateral contract, unilateral undertaking (of will).
Fr. acte unilatéral.

UNILATERAL CONTRACT

Contract creating an obligation for only one party. For example, a gift, a loan. "A juridical act is said to be 'unilateral' when it is the product of a single will. [...] In that sense the unilateral act is opposed to the contract, which is an accord of wills. A contract is therefore never a unilateral act, as to the number of wills necessary to produce it; if one speaks of unilateral contracts, one employs the word in another sense, one refers then not to its formation, but to its effects" (Planiol & Ripert, *Treatise*, vol. 2, n° 948, p. 549).
Occ. Arts. 1378, 1380 C.C.Q.
See also bilateral contract, unilateral act, unilateral undertaking (of will).
Fr. contrat unilatéral.

UNILATERAL PROMISE (TO CONTRACT)

Promise to contract in which a person undertakes to enter into a specific contract at a later date, provided the beneficiary of the promise still desires it. "[...] as distinguished from an offer, a unilateral promise to contract is already a contract in itself; it requires the consent of the two parties and gives rise to a firm obligation on the part of the promisor, an obligation correlative to a right that the beneficiary may assign [...]" (Litvinoff, in *Treatise*, vol. 7, Book 2, n° 98, p. 177).
Obs. 1° The promisee agrees to consider the transaction that has been proposed to him or her, without being bound immediately. Thus, the promisee has an option. **2°** Acceptance of a unilateral promise creates either the proposed contract or a bilateral promise (art.

1396 C.C.Q.). **3**° A unilateral promise to contract differs from an offer in that it immediately creates a contract that is said to be unilateral, but only one of the parties is obliged. Nevertheless, it may not be considered the equivalent of a unilateral undertaking since its formation depends on the promisee's acceptance.
See also bilateral promise to contract, offer, option.
Fr. promesse unilatérale (de contrat).

UNILATERAL PROMISE OF SALE

Unilateral promise to enter into a contract of sale. "Unilateral promises of sale are recognized [...] as valid contracts whereby one party obligates himself towards the other to make an actual sale when the beneficiary or obligee requires that the promise be fulfilled" (Litvinoff, in *Treatise*, vol. 7, Book 2, n° 101, p. 184).
See also bilateral promise of sale, option, unilateral promise (to contract).
Fr. promesse unilatérale de vente.

UNILATERAL RESILIATION

Voluntary resiliation resulting from the decision of one of the parties to a juridical act.
Obs. In certain circumstances, the law allows a party to terminate the contract without obtaining the consent of the other contracting parties. Such is the case, for example, in respect of a contract of employment with an indeterminate term (art. 2091 C.C.Q.), a lease for an indeterminate period (art. 1885 C.C.Q.), a mandate (art. 2175 C.C.Q.), or a contract of undeclared partnership (art. 2260 C.C.Q.).
See also bilateral resiliation.
Fr. résiliation unilatérale.

UNILATERAL UNDERTAKING (OF WILL)

Unilateral act imposing an obligation[3] on the person creating it.
Obs. 1° Whereas a contract is a bilateral or even a multilateral act reflecting a meeting of the minds of the parties, a unilateral undertaking of will, like a unilateral act, results from the sole will of its author. **2**° According to some scholars, a unilateral expression of will is sufficient to create an obligation. Given the principle enunciated at article 1372 C.C.Q. that law and contract are the only sources of obligations, the prevailing view is that unilateral undertakings are not recognized as sources of obligations in themselves.

See also doctrine of undertaking by unilateral will, offer, unilateral act, unilateral contract.
Fr. engagement unilatéral (de volonté).

UNIVERSAL DISPOSITION

Disposition[2] of the whole of a patrimony in favour of a person or a purpose of private or social utility of the whole of a patrimony.
Obs. 1° A universal disposition may benefit more than one person or purpose at once. **2**° For example, trusts allow the disposal of the whole of a patrimony in favour of purposes of private or social utility (arts. 1266, 1269, 1270 C.C.Q.). **3**° A distinction is drawn between universal dispositions, dispositions by general title and dispositions by particular title.
See also universal transmission.
Fr. disposition universelle.

UNIVERSAL SUCCESSOR

Successor called to receive the entirety of the author's patrimony. For example, legal heirs, universal legatees.
Obs. 1° Where the author of the universal successor is a physical person, the universal successor may only acquire rights *mortis causa*, as this is the only way of transmitting the patrimony of a person in its entirety. **2**° Where the author of the universal successor is not a physical person, the successor does not receive *mortis causa* but for different reasons (e.g. termination of a trust (arts. 1296 to 1298 C.C.Q.); merger of companies (ss. 123.120, *Companies Act*, R.S.Q. c. C-38)). **3**° In contractual matters, the universal successor is not a third party to contracts entered into by his or her author and is in principle bound by such contracts (arts. 1440, 1441 C.C.Q.). **4**° Scholars often include *successors by general title* and *universal successors* in the same category of *successors by general title*. **5**° The expression *legal representative* is sometimes used as equivalent to *successor by general title* or *universal successor* (e.g. art. 2288 C.C.Q.; arts. 1028, 1030 C.C.L.C.). Used in this sense, the expression may be misleading, in that the universal successor is not a representative of the author but acts in his or her own name. **6**° Although the term *assignee* has a narrower meaning, the expression *assignee by universal title* is sometimes used as equivalent to *universal successor*, where the context allows.
Syn. successor by universal title. **See also** successor by general title, successor by particular title, universal transmission.
Fr. ayant cause universel+, ayant droit universel, successeur universel.

UNIVERSAL TRANSMISSION

Transmission of an entire patrimony. "In universal transmissions, the acquirer or his successor are held for the debts and obligations of their author" (Planiol & Ripert, *Treatise*, vol. 1, n° 2558, p. 510).
Obs. 1° Universal transmission bears upon the author's rights as well as his or her obligations. **2°** It is generally said that a universal transmission can only take place *mortis causa*, in that the patrimony of a person can only be transmitted, in its entirety, *mortis causa*. However, where the author of the transmission is not a physical person, the universal transmission may be effected for different reasons (e.g. termination of a trust (arts. 1296 to 1298 C.C.Q.); merger of companies (s. 123.120, *Companies Act*, R.S.Q. c. C-38)). **3°** See, in contractual matters, articles 1440, 1441 C.C.Q. **4°** See, in matters relating to successions, article 732 C.C.Q.
See also relativity of contract, transmission by general title, transmission by (a) particular title, universal disposition, universal gift, universal successor.
Fr. transmission universelle.

UNJUST ENRICHMENT

Patrimonial advantage, acquired at the expense of another, which, because it is without legal justification, gives rise to an obligation to indemnify the person impoverished. "[...] this Court's decision in *Cie Immobilière Viger Ltée* v. *Lauréat Giguère Inc.* [...] confirmed that the theory of unjust enrichment has been incorporated into the civil law" (*Lapierre* v. *A.G. Quebec*, [1985] 1 S.C.R. 241, p. 251, J. Chouinard, J.).
Occ. Title preceding art. 1493 C.C.Q.; art. 3125 C.C.Q.
Obs. 1° The theory of unjust enrichment is based on the principle that it is unfair for a person to be enriched without justification at the expense of another. **2°** Article 1494 C.C.Q. provides that the enrichment is justified when it "results from the performance of an obligation, from the failure of the person impoverished to exercise a right [...], or from an act performed by the person impoverished for a personal and exclusive interest or at his own risk and peril, or with a constant liberal intention". **3°** Unjust enrichment gives rise to an indemnity corresponding to the lesser of either the enrichment or the impoverishment (art. 1493 C.C.Q.). The indemnity is, in principle, assessed on the day of the demand (art. 1495 C.C.Q.). **4°** The codal regime respecting unjust enrichment is set forth in a chapter of the Civil Code entitled "Certain Other Sources of Obligations" (arts. 1493 to 1496 C.C.Q.).
Syn. unjustified enrichment. **See also** equity[1], management of the business of another, reception of a thing not due.
Fr. enrichissement injustifié[+], enrichissement sans cause.

UNJUSTIFIED ENRICHMENT

Syn. unjust enrichment. "In Quebec, both before and after promulgation of the *Civil Code* [*of Lower Canada*], case law implicitly but effectively applied the theory of unjustified enrichment [...]. It was especially after the 1930s, however, that a number of writers made a systematic analysis of the theory of unjustified enrichment, at the same time as many decisions in the trial and appeal courts attempted to define the scope of the conditions for its application [...]" (*Cie Immobilière Viger* v. *Lauréat Giguère Inc.*, [1977] 2 S.C.R. 67, p. 76, J. Beetz, J.).
Fr. enrichissement injustifié[+], enrichissement sans cause.

UNLAWFUL *adj.*

1. **Syn.** illicit. "In order to receive punitive damages under the second paragraph of section 49 of the Quebec Charter, the victim must have suffered an unlawful interference with a right guaranteed by the Charter" (Des Rosiers & Langevin, *Representing Victims of Sexual and Spousal Abuse*, n° 319, p. 182). *In an unlawful manner.*
Occ. Arts. 1499, 2555, 2564 C.C.Q.; arts. 989, 990, 1892(8), 2610 C.C.L.C.; art. 36 C.C.P.; s. 49, *Charter of Human Rights and Freedoms*, R.S.Q. c. C-12; s. 231, *Companies Act*, R.S.Q. c. C-38.
Fr. illégal[2], illicite[+].

2. **Syn.** illegitimate[2].
Fr. illégitime[2].

UNLAWFUL CAUSE

Syn. illicit cause.
Fr. cause illégale, cause illicite[+], considération illégale.

UNLAWFUL CONDITION

Syn. illicit condition.
Fr. condition illégale, condition illicite[+].

UNLAWFUL CONSIDERATION

Syn. illicit cause.
Occ. Art. 989 C.C.L.C.
Fr. cause illégale, cause illicite[+], considération illégale.

UNLAWFULLY *adv.*

In an unlawful[1] manner.
Occ. Arts. 1650, 1699 C.C.Q.; s. 382, *Election Act*, R.S.Q. c. E-3.3; s. 60, *An Act respecting the lands in the domain of the state*, R.S.Q. c. T-8.1.
Obs. In a broad sense, unlawfully may be used to refer to a lack of conformity to law[1].
See also lawfully.
Fr. illégalement.

UNQUALIFIED RIGHT

Syn. pure and simple right.
Fr. droit pur et simple.

UNSECURED CREDITOR

Creditor whose claim does not benefit from a right of preference.
Obs. Prior creditors and hypothecary creditors benefit from a right of preference.
Syn. chirographic creditor, ordinary creditor.
See also right of preference[2], secured creditor.
Fr. créancier chirographaire, créancier ordinaire[+].

UNSEIZABILITY *n.*

Attribute of property, the seizure of which by creditors for debt is totally or partially forbidden. "[...] if we examine the situations in which the law provides for unseizability, the desire to protect claims for support in the broad sense seems to prevail. The objective is often to prevent seizures in the hands of third parties, that is, seizures at source" (*Poulin* v. *Serge Morency et associés*, [1999] 3 S.C.R. 351, p. 368, C. Gonthier, J.).
Occ. Arts. 2393, 2649 C.C.Q.
Obs. 1° Unseizability is an exception to the principle that all property of a person is seizable, principle that is a corollary of the rule that provides that the property of a debtor is the common pledge of his or her creditors (art. 2644 C.C.Q.). One should however note that unseizability is the general rule for the State's property (art. 916 C.C.Q.). **2°** Unseizability can flow from the nature of property (e.g. servitudes), from the will of a person (e.g. stipulations of inalienability) or from the law (e.g. judicially awarded support (art. 553 C.C.P.)). **3°** Unseizability is either relative or absolute. Relative unseizability, enumerated at articles 2648 C.C.Q. and 552 C.C.P., are let to the debtor's choice, who may, or may not, invoke it at the time of seizure. Contrarily, absolute unseizability, enumerated at articles 553 to 553.2 C.C.P., prohibits

the seizure of property without the need for the debtor to invoke it.
Syn. exemption from seizure. **See also** inalienability, stipulation of unseizability.
Fr. insaisissabilité.

UNSEIZABLE *adj.*

Not able to be seized. "We have texts of law setting out cases in which immoveables form part of the public domain as opposed to immoveables which are privately owned. As part of the public domain such exceptional immoveables are unseizable, imprescriptible and not subject to privileges" (*Alain Lavoie Ltée* v. *Léo Lisi Ltée*, (1981) C.A. 292 at 294, G.R.W. Owen J.).
Occ. Arts. 1215, 2377, 2444 C.C.Q.; art. 2561 C.C.L.C.; art. 83.28, *Automobile Insurance Act*, R.S.Q. c. A-25.
Syn. exempt from seizure. **See also** unseizability.
Fr. insaisissable.

UNSPECIFIED

See unspecified term.
Fr. inconnu.

UNSPECIFIED TERM

Term[1] whose date of arrival is not specified at the time of the inception of a right or obligation[2]. For example, at the death of a specified person.
Syn. uncertain term, undetermined term.
See also certain term.
Fr. terme incertain[+], terme inconnu, terme indéterminé.

USAGE *n.*

Established practice generally followed in a given milieu, to which law attaches certain effects. "[c]ustom may be a usage local to some part, canton or district of a country where a contract is made [...] Usages of trade are local as well as general, and are known, or presumed to be known, in any locality, to or by every one in any particular trade or business to which they are applicable" (Johnson, *Conflict of Laws*, pp. 640-641). *Usage of trade*.
Occ. Arts. 1139, 1300, 1338, 1394, 1426, 1434, 1457, 1765, 1874 C.C.Q.; arts. 21, 455, 1016, 1024 C.C.L.C.
Obs. 1° The distinction between *custom* and *usage* is difficult to delineate precisely, and the terms are sometimes used interchangeably even though they are not strictly speaking synonyms (e.g. arts. 976, 2004, 2526 C.C.Q. where the terms *custom* and *custom-*

ary are used as equivalents of the French term *usage*). **2°** Usage can develop in a given locality (e.g. usage of the place (1139 C.C.Q.)), a given profession (e.g. generally recognized accounting practices (art. 1345 C.C.Q.)) or in a particular trade (*lex mercatoria* or law merchant). For these reasons, the terms *local usage, professional usage, commercial usage* or *usage of trade* are encountered. **3°** In contract, and more commonly in business or employment law, usage plays an important role as it can help define a juridical relationship between parties. Usage may also serve as an aid when interpreting a contract (art. 1426 C.C.Q.).
See also custom[1], jurisprudence[1], law[2].
Fr. usage.

USURIOUS *adj.*

See usurious interest rate, usury.
Fr. usuraire.

USURIOUS CONTRACT

See usury.
Fr. contrat usuraire.

USURIOUS INTEREST

See usurious interest rate.
Fr. intérêt usuraire.

USURIOUS INTEREST RATE

Excessive interest rate. "[...] the basic purpose of the statute [s. 347 Cr.C.] [...] is to prohibit the imposition of usurious interest rates" (*Degelder Construction Co.* v. *Dancorp Developments Ltd.*, [1998] 3 S.C.R. 90, p. 106, J.C. Major, J.).
Obs. While the terms *usury* and *usurious interest rate* are not used in the Civil Code or in statutes, the law intervenes in situations where the interest rate is excessive. For example, in matters concerning loans of money, the borrower, suffering lesion, may obtain the annulment of the contract, the reduction of his or her obligations, or the revision of the terms and conditions of performance (art. 2332 C.C.Q.). Certain statutes also establish maximum interest rates (*Small Loans Act*, R.S.C. 1970, c. S-11; *Pawnbrokers Act*, R.S.C. 1970, c. P-5), and a contractual stipulation providing for an interest rate above 60 percent constitutes a criminal offence (s. 347, *Criminal Code*, R.S.C. 1985, c. C-46).
See also conventional interest rate, lesion, usury.
Fr. taux d'intérêt usuraire.

USURIOUS LOAN

Loan of money imposing an excessive interest rate upon the borrower.
See also usury.
Fr. prêt usuraire.

USURY *n.*

Excessive interest resulting from a loan. "The Deuteronomic commandment on usury [...] has had a fateful career. Its checkered fortunes over a twenty-five-hundred-year span in Orient and Occident disclose an unexplored episode in the tangled history of 'transvaluations of values' which culminated in the spirit of capitalism" (Nelson, *Usury*, p. XIX).
Obs. 1° Historically, Roman law allowed the charging of interest on loans in certain circumstances. Although earlier medieval theologies condemned any lending of money at interest, in the thirteenth century a distinction was drawn between acceptable and excessive interest, the latter being censored as luxury. **2°** The term usury is also used to designate the fact of charging interest at an excessive rate. **3°** From the Latin *usura* (from *usus*: use): profit, interest.
See also usurious interest rate.
Fr. usure.

V

VALID *adj.*

Fulfilling the conditions[4] required to produce legal effects.
Occ. Arts. 1556 to 1560 C.C.Q.; art. 1488 C.C.L.C.
See also invalid, null.
Fr. valable, valide[+].

VALIDATE *v.*

To render or to declare valid.
Obs. When a person renounces his or her right to ask for the annulment of a juridical act that is tainted with relative nullity, the terms *confirm* or *ratify*[2] are used rather than *validate*.
See also confirm, invalidate.
Fr. valider.

VALIDATION *n.*

Act of validating; the result of such an act.
See also confirmation.
Fr. validation.

VALIDITY *n.*

Characteristic of a juridical act that satisfies the conditions[4] necessary to produce its effects in law. "It is not essential to the validity of a payment that it should be made in cash; its equivalent may be accepted; any form or mode of payment may satisfy the debtor and creditor, either by bills, notes, transfer of credits, novations, compensation, *dation en paiement*, or otherwise. But no matter how made, it must have the effect of extinguishing the debt" (*R.* v. *Ogilvie* (1899), 29 S.C.R. 299, pp. 337-338, D. Girouard, J.). *Condition of validity; validity of a contract.*
Occ. Arts. 984, 2135 C.C.L.C.
Obs. The validity of juridical acts depends, in principle, on respect of conditions of substance (e.g. arts. 707 to 711, 1385 C.C.Q.) and conditions as to form (e.g. arts. 713, 1385 C.C.Q.).
See also invalidity, inopposability, lapse, nullity.
Fr. validité.

VALIDLY *adv.*

In a manner which produces juridical effects. "[...] the substantive requirements for validly formed contractual obligations are elaborated in detail. They reflect the root conception of contract as a bilateral juridical act that is, an explicit agreement between two or more parties" (Brierley & Macdonald (eds.), *Quebec Civil Law*, n° 424, p. 400).
Occ. Arts. 776, 2023 C.C.L.C.
Fr. valablement[+], validement.

VALUABLE CONSIDERATION

See counterprestation.
Occ. Art. 1901 C.C.L.C.
Obs. Used in this sense, *consideration* corresponds to the Common law notion of *consideration*. However, in the civil law, *consideration* is more generally understood as a synonym for *cause*. Hence, to use it as an equivalent of the notion of *counterprestation* may be viewed as an inappropriate borrowing from the Common law.
Fr. considération valable.

VALUE *n.*

See actual value, error as to value, market value, real value, value debt.
Fr. valeur.

VALUE DEBT

Debt bearing on an economic value that is only converted into money at the time of payment.
Obs. 1° The economic value of the debt is generally linked to the value of material property. Therefore, the value debt is to be distinguished from the indexable debt, which has for object a sum of money and which fluctuates according to one or more economic indexes. **2°** The debtor of a value debt bears the risk of monetary devaluation or inflation.
See also obligation in kind, pecuniary obligation.
Fr. dette de valeur.

VARIATION CLAUSE

Syn. revision clause.
Fr. clause de révision.

VENDOR n.

Syn. seller. "The vendor impliedly guarantees the purchaser against any interference by the vendor and those claiming under him with his quiet enjoyment of the property, and against eviction by third parties" (Ryan, *Introduction*, p. 93).
Occ. Arts. 1206, 2948 C.C.Q.; art. 2000 C.C.L.C.
Fr. vendeur.

VICARIOUS LIABILITY

Civil liability incurred by a person for the damage caused by the fault of another person in those cases specified by law. "[...] vicarious liability and strict liability usually fulfill a function of loss distribution since they are usually borne by large enterprises, or persons who normally take out liability insurance" (Tunc, in *Int. Enc. Comp. L.*, vol. XI, p. 1-180).
Obs. 1° This term is sometimes used to designate the different sources of liability arising from the act or omission of others under articles 1459 to 1464 C.C.Q., though, strictly speaking, only the liability of the principal amounts to a true regime of vicarious liability. **2°** The English language civilian usage of this term is not necessarily co-extensive with the term as it is employed in the Common law[2]. **3°** Since the terms *liability* and *responsibility* are synonymous, *vicarious responsibility* may also be used.
Syn. vicarious responsibility. **See also** act of another, indirect liability, legal liability[2], liability for damage caused by another, liability for damage caused by things, liability of the principal, personal liability[1], strict liability.
Fr. responsabilité du fait d'autrui(>).

VICARIOUS RESPONSIBILITY

Syn. vicarious liability.
Fr. responsabilité du fait d'autrui(>).

VICTIM n.

Person who sustains damage or suffers an injury.
Occ. Arts. 1473, 3126 C.C.Q.; art. 397(2) C.C.P.
See also fault of the victim, immediate victim, juridical responsibility, mediate victim.
Fr. victime.

VICTIM BY RICOCHET

Syn. mediate victim.
Fr. victime médiate, victime par ricochet[+].

VINCULUM JURIS (Latin)

See obligation[2].
Obs. Emperor Justinian commenced his analysis of the law of Obligations in the *Institutes* with a definition: *Obligatio est iuris vinculum, quo necessitate adstringimur alicuius solvendæ rei secundum nostra civitatis iura* (Inst.3.13) [An obligation is a legal tie which binds us to the necessity of making some performance in accordance with the laws of our state (Peter Birks, trans.)]. This definition of the obligation based on the metaphor of the "legal bond" or "legal tie" remains widely influential.
Fr. *vinculum juris*.

VIOLENCE n.

Physical constraint illegally provoking fear. "[...] the ambit of violence, like that of fraud, has been expanding in recent years. It now seems to encompass even cases of economic violence in contracts entered into by parties of unequal bargaining power" (Brierley & Macdonald (eds.), *Quebec Civil Law*, n° 432, p. 405).
Occ. Art. 1402 C.C.Q.
Obs. Fear provoked by violence vitiates consent (art. 1402 C.C.Q.).
See also defect of consent, fear, state of necessity[2], threat.
Fr. violence.

VIRTUAL PUBLIC ORDER

Syn. judicial public order.
Fr. ordre public judiciaire, ordre public virtuel[+].

VOID adj.

See null.
Occ. Arts. 762, 1080 C.C.L.C.
Fr. nul.

VOID v.

See annul.
Fr. annuler.

VOIDABLE adj.

See annullable.
Occ. Arts. 803, 1214 C.C.L.C.

Obs. Some scholars see it as a Common law term.
Fr. annulable.

VOLUNTARY FAULT

Syn. intentional fault.
Obs. 1° Voluntariness is used to suggest intention rather than that the person is simply conscious of engaging in wrongful conduct. **2°** Some scholars suggest that voluntary fault should be distinguished from intentional fault; according to this view, in a voluntary fault, the wrongful act is consciously and wilfully committed but the damage is not sought by the wrongdoer. Others consider that voluntary fault and intentional fault are the same where the injury, although not desired, is the inevitable consequence of the act or omission.
Fr. faute intentionnelle⁺, faute volontaire.

VOLUNTARY PERFORMANCE

Act of the debtor who, by his own will, supplies the prestation due.
See also compulsory execution, payment[1], specific performance.
Fr. exécution volontaire.

VOLUNTARY REPRESENTATION

Representation in which the representative's power to represent is based on the volition of the person represented. For example, the mandate.
Obs. *Voluntary representation* is opposed to *forced representation*.
See also conventional representation.
Fr. représentation volontaire.

VOLUNTARY RESILIATION

Resiliation resulting from the agreement of the parties or from the unilateral decision of one of them.
Obs. 1° As in the case of contractual formation, the termination of a contract requires a meeting of minds (*bilateral resiliation*) (art. 1439 C.C.Q.). However, in exceptional cases, the law allows a single party to terminate the contract (*unilateral resiliation*) (arts. 1885, 2091, 2125, 2175, 2260 C.C.Q.). **2°** Certain juridical acts, such as marriage, are not susceptible of voluntary resiliation.
See also bilateral resiliation, forced resiliation, unilateral resiliation.
Fr. résiliation volontaire.

W

WAGER *n.*

Syn. wagering contract.
Occ. S. 11, *An Act respecting the Régie des alcools, des courses et des jeux*, R.S.Q. c. R-6.1.
Fr. contrat de pari⁺, pari.

WAGERING *n.*

Syn. wagering contract.
Occ. Arts. 2512, 2541 C.C.Q.
Fr. contrat de pari⁺, pari.

WAGERING CONTRACT

Aleatory contract by which parties undertake to remit a sum of money or a specific thing to another party whose opinion, in respect of a given fact, is found to be correct.
Occ. Arts. 2512, 2629 C.C.Q.
Obs. 1° In general, a wagering contract involves a divergence of opinions between the parties. An exception to this regards bookmakers whose business consists of taking all bets respecting some future event whatever may be the opinion of the cocontracting party. In Canada, such business is, in principle, illegal (s. 201(1), *Criminal Code*, R.S.C. 1985, c. C-46). **2°** A gaming contract is valid where it is expressly authorized by law in particular, if it bears on "lawful activities and games requiring only skill or bodily exercises on the part of the parties, unless the amount at stake is immoderate according to the circumstances and in view of the condition and means of the parties" (art. 2629 C.C.Q.). **3°** When the gaming contract is unauthorized, the obligation that results from it is not susceptible to compulsory execution. However, if the losing party voluntarily pays the debt, what has been paid cannot legally be reclaimed, except if the claimant is a minor or a protected person of full age or a major not endowed with reason (art. 2630 C.C.Q.). **4°** The legal regimes governing gaming and wagering contracts are the same. However, these contracts are distinguished in practice. In wagering contracts, the party whose opinion in respect of a given fact is found to be correct has the right to be paid. This fact, although it may bear on a past, present or future event, is beyond the control of the parties. In contrast, in gaming contracts parties take part in the event that makes the payment due. **5°** The codal regime respecting gaming contracts is set forth at articles 2629 and 2630 C.C.Q.
Syn. bet, betting, wager, wagering. **See also** contingency¹, gambling debt, gaming contract, natural obligation.
Fr. contrat de pari⁺, pari.

WAGES *pl.n.*

Syn. salary.
Fr. salaire.

WAIVER *n.*

(*Prop.*) Syn. renunciation².
Fr. renonciation.

WARRANT *v.*

To be held to a warranty.
Occ. Arts. 1716, 1723, 1727, 1854, 2120 C.C.Q.; arts. 1508, 1522 C.C.L.C.
Fr. garantir.

WARRANTEE *n.*

(*Sec.*) Person to whom a warranty is owed.
Fr. garanti.

WARRANTOR *n.*

Person who owes a warranty. "It may be said here, that the architect and contractor are not, under article 1688 [C.C.L.C.], *insurers* of the stability of the building, whatever happens or whatever the cause of loss. They are warrantors, only within the intent of the article. Their warranty is against a perishing due to their oversight, negligence, want of skill and judgment, failure to use all *known and available tests and means* to assure stability" (Johnson, *Responsibility of Architects, Engineers and Builders*, p. 43).
Occ. Arts. 889, 1657, 1698, 1724, 2066 C.C.Q.; arts. 748, 1202*i* C.C.L.C.; art. 220 C.C.P.
Fr. garant.

WARRANTY *n.*

Obligation[3] imposed upon a person, the *warrantor*, in favour of another, the *warrantee*, to ensure the peaceful and useful enjoyment of the rights that the former has transferred to the latter. "The warranty obligation, which is essentially the complement to or corollary of the delivery obligation, has in turn two objectives: warranty against eviction and warranty against latent defects" (*General Motors Products of Canada Ltd.* v. *Kravitz*, [1979] 1 S.C.R. 790, p. 796, Y. Pratte, J.).
Occ. Arts. 890, 2412, C.C.Q.; arts. 796, 1491, 1506, 1531 C.C.L.C.
Obs. 1° The Civil Code deals with warranties principally in the title on sale; articles 1716 to 1735 C.C.Q., which govern the warranty owed by the vendor to the buyer, constitute the general law in this area. Warranties also exist in other instances. For example, the warranty owed by the assignor of a personal right to the assignee (art. 1576 C.C.Q.), by the lessor to the lessee (art. 1854 C.C.Q.), by the partners to the partnership (art. 2199 C.C.Q.), by the copartitioners to each other (arts. 889, 891 C.C.Q.). **2°** A vendor must ensure that the buyer will have the peaceful possession of the thing sold (*warranty against eviction*). The vendor must also give him or her the useful possession of the thing (*warranty against latent defects*). **3°** Legal warranty is distinguished from conventional warranty.
See also conventional warranty, legal warranty, obligation of warranty, warranty clause.
Fr. garantie.

WARRANTY AGAINST ACTS OF THIRD PERSONS

Warranty against eviction according to which the warrantor is legally bound to defend the warrantee against any disturbances in law caused by a third person and to compensate the warrantee if he or she is evicted.
Obs. 1° Warranty against acts of third persons exists, not only in the contract of sale (arts. 1723 *et seq.* C.C.Q.) but also in the contract of lease (art. 1859 C.C.Q.), in partition (art. 889 C.C.Q.) and in the assignment of a personal right (art. 1639 C.C.Q.). **2°** This warranty, which exists as of right, may be replaced by a conventional warranty. **3°** A warranty of this nature only covers warranty against disturbances in law and not against disturbances in fact.
See also warranty against personal acts.
Fr. garantie du fait des tiers.

WARRANTY AGAINST LATENT DEFECTS

Obligation[3] of the warrantor to give the warrantee useful possession, that is to say, to provide the latter with a thing free of latent defects that would considerably diminish or eliminate its usefulness. "[...] to deny the transfer of the claim in warranty against latent defects to the sub-purchaser of the thing would be [...] inconsistent with the principles of the Code. Also, such an approach to the law of obligations would be too individualistic and ill-suited to present-day realities" (*General Motors Products of Canada Ltd.* v. *Kravitz*, [1979] 1 S.C.L.C. 790, p. 813, Y. Pratte, J.).
Obs. 1° The warranty against latent defects forms part of the contracts of sale (arts. 1726 to 1731 C.C.Q.) and of lease (art. 1854 C.C.Q.). **2°** Such warranty, which exists as of right, may be replaced by a conventional warranty (e.g. arts. 1732, 1733 C.C.Q.). **3°** In matters relating to sale, it is generally said that the warranty against latent defects rests upon five conditions: the defect must be severe and hidden, it must be present before the sale, it must be unknown to the buyer at the moment of the sale and, finally, the buyer must have notified the seller of the defect in writing within a reasonable time (arts. 1726 *et seq.* C.C.Q.).
See also warranty.
Fr. garanties des défauts cachés, garantie des vices cachés+.

WARRANTY AGAINST PERSONAL ACTS

Warranty against eviction according to which the warrantor is legally bound not to do anything which might disturb the warrantee in his or her use and enjoyment of the thing.
Occ. Art. 1509 C.C.L.C.
Obs. 1° Article 1732 C.C.Q. provides for a warranty against personal acts in sale; the warranty is also recognized in lease[1] and in gifts. **2°** This warranty is of the essence of the contract of sale. Article 1732 C.C.Q. implicitly prohibits any stipulations excluding it, giving to the warranty against personal acts an imperative character. **3°** This warranty covers disturbances arising both in law and in fact.
See also warranty against acts of third persons.
Fr. garantie du fait personnel.

WARRANTY CLAUSE

Clause in a contract whereby the parties set forth the extent of a warranty.
Obs. See articles 1639, 1716, 1732 and 1733 C.C.Q.
See also clause excluding warranty, conventional warranty, legal warranty, obligation of warranty.
Fr. clause de garantie.

WARRANTY OF PAYMENT

Conventional warranty whereby an assignor guarantees, in favour of the assignee, the solvency of the debtor when the claim assigned falls due. "When the seller sells *with warranty of payment, garantie de fournir et faire valoir*, he undertakes to furnish and make good to the transferee whatever portion of the debt he may not succeed in obtaining from the debtor and his sureties, if any, after discussion of their property and the securities held for the debt, provided the transferee has not by his own act impaired these securities or acted negligently in the preservation or enforcement of his rights" (Marler, *Real Property*, n° 612, p. 289).
Occ. Art. 1988 C.C.L.C.
Obs. 1° Warranty of payment binds an assignor only up to the amount paid by the assignee. **2°** Unless the assignment by onerous title has been made at the risk of the assignee, the assignor guarantees the existence of the claim and that it is owed to him or her, even if the assignment is made without warranty (art. 1639 C.C.Q.). **3°** Warranty of payment is a more onerous obligation in its effects than simple warranty of solvency. In the latter instance, the assignor answers only for the solvency of the debtor at the time of assignment (art. 1640 C.C.Q.).
Syn. guarantee of payment. **See also** assignment of creance, warranty of payment clause.
Fr. garantie de fournir et faire valoir.

WARRANTY OF PAYMENT CLAUSE

Clause in an assignment of claims providing a warranty of payment.
Syn. clause of *fournir et faire valoir*, guarantee of payment clause. **See also** warranty of payment.
Fr. clause de fournir et faire valoir.

WILL *n.*

1. Ability of the person to choose freely to act or to abstain from acting and, notably, to move towards the accomplishment of the action or abstention or, more generally, of the intended outcome. "In Germany the role of the will in the formation of contractual obligations has been the object of numerous studies known in France through the works of Saleilles" (Planiol & Ripert, *Treatise*, vol. 2, n° 945, p. 546). *Autonomy of the will.*
Obs. 1° *Will* in this sense is sometimes referred to as a capacity to formulate intention. **2°** The conduct of a person having this ability is sometimes said to reflect human agency.
See also *de facto* capacity, discernment, legal capacity.
Fr. volonté[1].

2. Syn. intention. *The last will of the testator; the will to live together.*
Occ. Arts. 258, 444, 553, 1386, 1423, 1446, 1649 C.C.Q.
Obs. The expressions *the last wishes of the deceased* or *the expression of his or her last wishes* are used to designate the intentional measures taken by a person during the course of his or her life with the view that the wishes will be executed after his or her death (arts. 714, 717, 722 C.C.Q.).
Fr. intention[+], volonté[2].

WITHDRAW *v.*

1. Syn. retract. *To withdraw an offer.*
Fr. retirer[2], rétracter[+].

2. To repudiate a contract unilaterally.
Occ. Art. 1785 C.C.Q.
See also withdrawal clause, withdrawal option.
Fr. dédire (se).

WITHDRAWAL *n.*

Syn. retraction.
Fr. rétractation[+], retrait[1].

WITHDRAWAL CLAUSE

Clause conferring a withdrawal option.
Syn. forfeit clause, stipulation as to withdrawal. **See also** stipulation as to earnest, withdrawal option.
Fr. clause de dédit[+], stipulation de dédit.

WITHDRAWAL OPTION

Option to repudiate a contract unilaterally.
Obs. 1° Withdrawal options are provided for by law (arts. 1914, 1915 C.C.Q.; ss. 59, 73, *Consumer Protection Act*, R.S.Q. c. P-40.1) or by agreement between the contracting parties. **2°** The exercise of a withdrawal option may be subject to the payment of an indem-

nity by the contracting party invoking it (e.g. a sale with earnest). **3°** The principle of irrevocability of gifts precludes the donor from providing for a withdrawal option in his or her favour.
See also stipulation as to earnest, withdrawal clause.
Fr. dédit[1], faculté de dédit[+].

WORK *n.*

Human activity intended to produce wealth or to provide services. "The obligation to execute the work is an employee's first obligation" (Aust & Charette, *Employment Contract*, p. 99).
Occ. Arts. 2088, 2098 C.C.Q.; art. 1694 C.C.L.C.; s. 19, *Charter of Human Rights and Freedoms*, R.S.Q. c. C-12.
Obs. Work is performed not only by employees but also by persons engaged in relations other than that of employment. For example, independent contractors, providers of services, directors of corporations and mandataries also perform work, as do volunteer workers and spouses who work in the home.
See also contract for (of) services, contract of employment, contract of enterprise, service(s)[1].
Fr. ouvrage, travail[1+].

WORK *v.*

To perform work.
Fr. travailler.

WORK CONTRACT

Syn. contract of employment.
Occ. Art. 1661.4 C.C.L.C.
Fr. contrat d'emploi, contrat de louage de services[1], contrat de louage de service(s) personel(s), contrat de travail[+], contrat individuel de travail, louage de service(s) personel(s).

WORKMAN *n.*

Physical person who performs manual tasks. "Before the master or employer is responsible for the damage caused by his servant or workman it must be shown that the damage was caused in the performance of the work for which he was employed" (Nicholls, *Offences and Quasi-Offences*, p. 69).
Occ. Arts. 2123, 2726 C.C.Q.; arts. 1054 para. 7, 2013a C.C.L.C.; s. 4(1)(a), *Competition Act*, R.S.C. 1985, c. C-34; s. 2., *Fair Wages and Hours of Labour Act*, R.S.C. 1985, c. L-4.

Obs. 1° The notion of *workman* reflects a nineteenth-century reality, a time where the distinction drawn between blue-collar workers and white-collar workers played a determinating role in the way work was organized. This distinction is now superseded. **2°** When the workman performs his or her tasks under the direction or control of another person, he or she is an employee. If, on the contrary, the workman performs the work autonomously, he or she is an independent contractor or a subcontractor. **3°** The workman who has taken part as an employee in the construction or renovation of an immovable and has not been paid, benefits from the right of a legal hypothec on that immovable (art. 2726 C.C.Q.). This legal hypothec replaces the workman's privilege (arts. 2013 and 2013d C.C.L.C.).
See also contract of employment, contract of enterprise.
Fr. ouvrier.

WRONG *n.*

1. Syn. fault[1]. "There may be no right definition of wrong, and the disagreement between partisans of the French and the local schools as to what fault means is instructive mostly as a lesson in the perils of legal transplanting within a legal tradition" (Kasirer, (1992) 40 *Am.J.Comp.L.* 343, p. 359).
Occ. Former art. 208 C.C.L.C.
Fr. faute[1+], tort[1].

2. Syn. damage. "If a child after birth has no right of action for pre-natal injuries, we have a wrong inflicted for which there is no remedy [...] it is but natural justice that a child, if born alive and viable, should be allowed to maintain an action in the courts for injuries wrongfully committed upon its person while in the womb of its mother" (*Montreal Tramways Co.* v. *Léveillé*, [1933] S.C.R. 456, p. 464, J.H. Lamont, J.).
Fr. dommage, préjudice[+], tort[2].

WRONGDOER *n.*

Person who has committed a fault. "With respect to the amount of damages due for compensation, there is a general principle which implies that full compensation is necessary. Hence, all damages caused by the non-performance or improper performance of an obligation must be compensated, regardless of the nature of the fault or property status of the wrongdoer" (Komarov, (1999) 44 *McGill L.J.* 357, p. 361).
Fr. fautif.

WRONGFUL *adj.*

Constituting a fault. "The occurrence of harm, caused by a wrongful action or event for which the defendant is accountable, is at the root of all claims in civil liability" (Brierley & Macdonald (eds.), *Quebec Civil Law*, n° 470, p. 434). *Wrongful act*; *wrongful exercise of a right*; *wrongful behaviour*.
Occ. Arts. 1462, 1480 C.C.Q.
See also at fault.
Fr. fautif[2].

French / English
LEXICON

OBLIGATIONS

A

ABANDON	abandonment[1]
ABDICATIF, IVE	abdicative
ABDICATION	abdication, abdicative act, act of renunciation, renunciation[1+]
ABSOLU, UE	absolute
ABUS DE(S) DROIT(S)	abuse of right(s)
ABUSIF, IVE	abusive
ACCEPTANT, ANTE	acceptor
ACCEPTATION[1]	acceptance[1]
ACCEPTATION[2]	acceptance[2]
ACCEPTATION[3]	acceptance[3+], reception[2]
ACCEPTATION DE(S) RISQUE(S)	assumption of risk(s)
ACCEPTATION EXPRESSE	express acceptance
ACCEPTATION TACITE	tacit acceptance
ACCEPTER[1]	accept[1]
ACCEPTER[2]	accept[2+], receive
ACCESSOIRE *adj.*	accessory
ACCESSOIRE *n.*	accessory
ACCIDENTEL, ELLE	accidental
ACCIPIENS	*accipiens*[+], payee, *recipiens*
ACCOMPLISSEMENT DE LA CONDITION	accomplishment of the condition, fulfilment of the condition[+], realization of the condition
ACCORD DE PRINCIPE	agreement in principle[+], letter of understanding, memorandum of understanding, preliminary agreement
ACCORD DE(S) VOLONTÉ(S)	meeting of the minds, consent[1+]
ACCORD PRÉLIMINAIRE	agreement in principle[+], letter of understanding, memorandum of understanding, preliminary agreement
ACHAT	purchase
ACHETER	buy[+], purchase
ACHETEUR, EUSE	buyer[+], purchaser
ACHETEUR À RÉMÉRÉ	buyer subject to right of redemption
ACOMPTE	deposit[2+], payment on account
ACQUÉREUR	acquirer
ACQUÉREUR SUBSÉQUENT	sub-acquirer, subsequent acquirer[+]
ACQUÉRIR[1]	acquire[1]
ACQUÉRIR[2]	acquire[2]
ACQUISITION[1]	acquisition[1]

ACQUISITION[2]	acquisition[2]
ACQUIT (POUR)	paid
ACQUITTEMENT	acquittance[2], payment[1+]
ACQUITTER	acquit[1], pay[+], settle[1]
ACTE[1]	act[1], juridical act[+], *negotium*, title[2]
ACTE[2]	act[2], *acte*, attesting deed[+], deed[1], *instrumentum*, title[3]
ACTE[3]	act[3], juridical fact[1+]
ACTE ABDICATIF	abdication, abdicative act, act of renunciation, renunciation[1+]
ACTE APPARENT	apparent act[+], ostensible act, simulated act
ACTE À TITRE GRATUIT	act by gratuitous title
ACTE À TITRE ONÉREUX	act by onerous title
ACTE ATTRIBUTIF	attributive act
ACTE AUTHENTIQUE	authentic act[+,] authentic deed, authentic document, authentic instrument, authentic writing
ACTE BILATÉRAL	bilateral act
ACTE CIVIL	civil act
ACTE COLLECTIF	collective act
ACTE CONSENSUEL	consensual act
ACTE CONSERVATOIRE	act of conservation, conservatory act[+]
ACTE CONSTITUTIF	constituting act, constitutive act[+]
ACTE D'ADMINISTRATION	act of administration
ACTE D'ALIÉNATION	act of alienation
ACTE DÉCLARATIF	declaratory act
ACTE DE COMMERCE	commercial act
ACTE DE CONSERVATION	act of conservation, conservatory act[+]
ACTE DE DISPOSITION	act of disposition
ACTE DÉGUISÉ	concealed act[+], disguised act
ACTE DE PLEINE ADMINISTRATION	act of full administration
ACTE DE PURE ADMINISTRATION	act of mere administration[+], act of simple administration[2]
ACTE DE SIMPLE ADMINISTRATION[1]	act of simple administration[1]
ACTE DE SIMPLE ADMINISTRATION[2]	act of mere administration[+], act of simple administration[2]
ACTE EN BREVET	act *en brevet*, notarial act *en brevet*[+]
ACTE EN MINUTE	act *en minute*, *minute*, notarial act *en minute*[+]
ACTE ENTRE VIFS	act *inter vivos*
ACTE FICTIF	fictitious act
ACTE FORMALISTE	formalistic act
ACTE INDIVIDUEL	individual act
ACTE INSTRUMENTAIRE	act[2], *acte*, attesting deed[+], deed[1], *instrumentum*, title[3]
ACTE JURIDIQUE	act[1], juridical act[+], *negotium*, title[2]

ACTE MATÉRIEL	material fact(>)
ACTE MIXTE	mixed act
ACTE MULTILATÉRAL	multilateral act+, plurilateral act
ACTE NOTARIÉ	notarial act+, notarial deed, notarial instrument
ACTE NOTARIÉ EN BREVET	act *en brevet*, notarial act *en brevet*
ACTE NOTARIÉ EN MINUTE	act *en minute*, *minute*, notarial act *en minute*+
ACTE OSTENSIBLE	apparent act+, ostensible act, simulated act
ACTE PLURILATÉRAL	multilateral act+, plurilateral act
ACTE RÉEL	counter letter+, real act, secret act, true act
ACTE RÉVOCATOIRE	revocatory act
ACTE SECRET	counter letter+, real act, secret act, true act
ACTE SEMI-AUTHENTIQUE	semi-authentic act
ACTE SIMULÉ	apparent act+, ostensible act, simulated act
ACTE SOLENNEL	solemn act
ACTE SOUS SEING PRIVÉ	act under private signature, act under private writing, deed under private writing, private writing+
ACTE TRANSLATIF	translatory act
ACTE TRANSLATIF DE PROPRIÉTÉ	translatory act of ownership
ACTE UNILATÉRAL	unilateral act
ACTE VÉRITABLE	counter letter+, real act, secret act, true act
ACTIF, IVE	active
ACTION	action+, judicial action, judicial demand, law suit, suit
ACTION DIRECTE[1]	direct action[1]
ACTION DIRECTE[2]	direct action[2]
ACTION DIRECTE[3]	direct action[3]
ACTION EN INOPPOSABILITÉ	action in inopposability, Paulian action+, Paulian petition, revocatory action
ACTION EN JUSTICE	action+, judicial action, judicial demand, law suit, suit
ACTION INDIRECTE	indirect action, oblique action+
ACTION OBLIQUE	indirect action, oblique action+
ACTION PAULIENNE	action in inopposability, Paulian action+, Paulian petition, revocatory action
ACTION RÉVOCATOIRE	action in inopposability, Paulian action+, Paulian petition, revocatory action
ADHÉRENT, ENTE[1]	adhering party
ADHÉRENT, ENTE[2]	participant
ADHÉSION	adhesion
ADMINISTRATEUR DU BIEN D'AUTRUI	administrator of the property of another, administrator of the property of others+
ADMINISTRATION DU BIEN D'AUTRUI	administration of the property of another, administration of the property of others+
AD SOLEMNITATEM	*ad solemnitatem*+, *ad validitatem*

AD VALIDITATEM	*ad solemnitatem*+, *ad validitatem*
AFFRANCHI, IE	discharged+, freed
AFFRÈTEMENT	affreightment, contract of affreightment+
AFFRÉTER	affreight, charter+
AFFRÉTEUR	charterer
AGRÉER	assent
AGRÉMENT[1]	acceptance[1]
AGRÉMENT[2]	consent[3]
AGRÉMENT[3]	assent
AGRÉMENT[4]	[*]
ALÉA[1]	contingency[1]
ALÉA[2]	contingency[2]
ALÉAS DE LA VIE	contingencies of life
ALÉATOIRE	aleatory
ALIÉNABILITÉ	alienability
ALIÉNABLE	alienable
ALIÉNATAIRE	alienee
ALIÉNATEUR, TRICE	alienator
ALIÉNATION	alienation
ALIÉNER	alienate
ALTERNATIF, IVE	alternative
ANATOCISME	anatocism
ANIMUS	*animus*
ANIMUS NOVANDI	*animus novandi*+, novatory intention
ANNUITÉ	annuity[4]
ANNULABILITÉ	annulability
ANNULABLE	annullable
ANNULATION	annulment
ANNULER	annul
ANTICIPÉ, ÉE	in advance
APPARENCE	appearance
APPARENCE DE DROIT	appearance of right+, colour of right
APPARENT, ENTE	apparent
APPORT (EN SOCIÉTÉ)	contribution (to the partnership)
APTE	able, capable[2]+
APTITUDE	ability, aptitude, capacity[2], capacity of fact, competence, competency, *de facto* capacity+
ARBITRAGE	arbitration
ARBITRE	arbitrator
ARBITRER	arbitrate[2]
ARGENT	cash+, *specie*
ARRÉRAGER (S')	[*]
ARRÉRAGES[1]	arrears[1], periodic payment+(>)

ARRÉRAGES[2]	accumulated debt, arrears[2+]
ARRHES	earnest
ARRIÉRÉ, ÉE	arrears (in)
ARRIÉRÉ	accumulated debt, arrears[2+]
ARRIÉRER	[*]
ARRIVÉE DE LA CONDITION	accomplishment of the condition, fulfilment of the condition[+], realization of the condition
ARRIVÉE DU TERME	arrival of the term, expiration[+], expiration of the term, expiry of the term
ASSOCIATION	association
ASSOCIÉ, ÉE	partner
ASSURANCE	contract of insurance, insurance, insurance contract[+]
ASSURANCE DE DOMMAGES	damage insurance
ASSURANCE DE PERSONNES	insurance of persons
ASSURANCE MARITIME	marine insurance
ASSURANCE TERRESTRE	non-marine insurance
ASSURÉ, ÉE	insured
ASSURER	insure
ASSUREUR	insurer
À TERME	[*]
À TITRE GRATUIT	by gratuitous title
À TITRE ONÉREUX	by onerous title
ATTRIBUTIF, IVE	attributive
AUTEUR, EURE	author[+], predecessor (in title)
AUTONOMIE DE LA VOLONTÉ (THÉORIE DE L')	autonomy of the will (theory of the)
AVANT-CONTRAT	*avant-contrat*, pre-contract[+]
AVÈNEMENT DU TERME	arrival of the term, expiration[+], expiration of the term, expiry of the term
AVIS D'EXONÉRATION DE RESPONSABILITÉ	notice of exoneration of liability
AYANT CAUSE	successor
AYANT CAUSE À TITRE PARTICULIER	particular successor, successor by particular title[+]
AYANT CAUSE À TITRE UNIVERSEL	successor by general title
AYANT CAUSE PARTICULIER	particular successor, successor by particular title[+]
AYANT CAUSE UNIVERSEL	successor by universal title, universal successor[+]
AYANT DROIT	successor
AYANT DROIT À TITRE PARTICULIER	particular successor, successor by particular title[+]
AYANT DROIT À TITRE UNIVERSEL	successor by general title
AYANT DROIT UNIVERSEL	successor by universal title, universal successor[+]

B

BAIL¹	contract of lease, lease¹⁺, lease of things
BAIL²	lease²
BAIL À RENTE	alienation for rent
BAILLEUR, ERESSE¹	lessor¹⁺
BAILLEUR, ERESSE²	lessor³
BÉNÉFICE DE CESSION D'ACTIONS	benefit of subrogation
BÉNÉFICE DE DISCUSSION	benefit of discussion⁺, right of discussion
BÉNÉFICE DE DIVISION	benefit of division⁺, right of division
BÉNÉFICE DE SUBROGATION	benefit of subrogation
BÉNÉFICIAIRE¹	beneficiary¹
BÉNÉFICIAIRE²	beneficiary²
BÉNÉFICIAIRE D'UNE PROMESSE	beneficiary of a promise, promisee⁺
BIEN¹	incorporeal property, incorporeal thing, patrimonial right⁺, property¹, *res*²
BIEN²	corporeal property, material property, property²⁺, thing susceptible of appropriation
BIEN À VENIR	future property⁺, future thing
BIEN CORPOREL	corporeal property, material property, property²⁺, thing susceptible of appropriation
BIEN DANS LE COMMERCE	[*]
BIEN HORS (DU) COMMERCE	[*]
BIEN INCORPOREL	incorporeal property, incorporeal thing, patrimonial right⁺, property¹, *res*²
BIEN MATÉRIEL	corporeal property, material property, property²⁺, thing susceptible of appropriation
BILATÉRAL, ALE	bilateral, synallagmatic⁺
BONA FIDES	*bona fides*
BON DOL	*dolus bonus*
BONNE FOI¹	fair dealing, good faith¹⁺
BONNE FOI²	good faith²
BONNES MŒURS	good morals
BON PÈRE DE FAMILLE	*bon père de famille*, *bonus pater familias*, reasonable man, reasonable person⁺
BONUS PATER FAMILIAS	*bon père de famille*, *bonus pater familias*, reasonable man, reasonable person⁺

C

CADUCITÉ	lapse
CANCELLATION	[*]
CAPABLE[1]	capable[1]
CAPABLE[2]	able, capable[2+]
CAPACITÉ[1]	capacity[1], juridical capacity, legal capacity[+]
CAPACITÉ[2]	ability, aptitude, capacity[2], capacity of fact, competence, competency, *de facto* capacity[+]
CAPACITÉ CIVILE	civil capacity
CAPACITÉ D'ACQUISITION	capacity to acquire (rights), capacity to enjoy (rights)[+]
CAPACITÉ DE DISCERNEMENT	capacity of discernment
CAPACITÉ DE FAIT	ability, aptitude, capacity[2], capacity of fact, competence, competency, *de facto* capacity[+]
CAPACITÉ DE JOUISSANCE	capacity to acquire (rights), capacity to enjoy (rights)[+]
CAPACITÉ D'EXERCICE	capacity to exercise (rights)
CAPACITÉ JURIDIQUE	capacity[1], juridical capacity, legal capacity[+]
CAPACITÉ LÉGALE	capacity[1], juridical capacity, legal capacity[+]
CAPACITÉ NATURELLE	ability, aptitude, capacity[2], capacity of fact, competence, competency, *de facto* capacity[+]
CAPACITÉ POLITIQUE	political capacity
CAPITAL	capital[+], capital sum, principal[2]
CAS FORTUIT	fortuitous event
CASUEL, ELLE	casual
CAUSA CAUSANS	*causa causans*, determining cause[+], efficient cause, proximate cause[2]
CAUSALITÉ[1]	causality[1], causation[1+]
CAUSALITÉ[2]	causality[2], causal relation, causation[2+], causation in law, juridical causation
CAUSALITÉ ADÉQUATE	adequate causation
CAUSALITÉ IMMÉDIATE	proximate causation
CAUSALITÉ JURIDIQUE	causality[2], causal relation, causation[2+], causation in law, juridical causation
CAUSALITÉ MATÉRIELLE	causation in fact, material causation[+]
CAUSALITÉ PARTIELLE	partial causation
CAUSA PROXIMA	*causa proxima*, immediate cause, proximate cause[1+]
CAUSA SINE QUA NON	*causa sine qua non*, cause *sine qua non*, condition *sine qua non*[+]
CAUSE[1]	abstract cause, cause[1+], cause of the obligation, consideration[1], final cause, objective cause

CAUSE[2]	cause[2+], cause of the contract, concrete cause, consideration[2], motive, principal consideration, subjective cause
CAUSE[3]	cause[3]
CAUSE ABSTRAITE	abstract cause, cause[1+], cause of the obligation, consideration[1], final cause, objective cause
CAUSE ADÉQUATE	adequate cause
CAUSE CONCRÈTE	cause[2+], cause of the contract, concrete cause, consideration[2], motive, principal consideration, subjective cause
CAUSE D'ACTION	cause of action
CAUSE DE L'OBLIGATION	abstract cause, cause[1+], cause of the obligation, consideration[1], final cause, objective cause
CAUSE DE MORT (À)	contemplation of death (in)[+], *mortis causa*
CAUSE DÉTERMINANTE	*causa causans*, determining cause[+], efficient cause, proximate cause[2]
CAUSE DU CONTRAT	cause[2+], cause of the contract, concrete cause, consideration2, motive, principal consideration, subjective cause
CAUSE EFFICIENTE	*causa causans*, determining cause[+], efficient cause, proximate cause[2]
CAUSE ÉTRANGÈRE	external cause
CAUSE FAUSSE	false cause
CAUSE FINALE	abstract cause, cause[1+], cause of the obligation, consideration[1], final cause, objective cause
CAUSE GÉNÉRATRICE	*causa causans*, determining cause[+], efficient cause, proximate cause[2]
CAUSE ILLÉGALE	illegal cause, illicit cause[+], illicit consideration, unlawful cause, unlawful consideration
CAUSE ILLICITE	illegal cause, illicit cause[+], illicit consideration, unlawful cause, unlawful consideration
CAUSE IMMÉDIATE	*causa proxima*, immediate cause, proximate cause[1+]
CAUSE IMMORALE	immoral cause
CAUSE IMPULSIVE ET DÉTERMINANTE	cause[2+], cause of the contract, concrete cause, consideration[2], motive, principal consideration, subjective cause
CAUSE LICITE	lawful cause, lawful consideration, licit cause[+], licit consideration
CAUSE MATÉRIELLE	material cause
CAUSE OBJECTIVE	abstract cause, cause[1+], cause of the obligation, consideration[1], final cause, objective cause
CAUSE *SINE QUA NON*	*causa sine qua non*, cause *sine qua non*, condition *sine qua non*[+]
CAUSE SUBJECTIVE	cause[2+], cause of the contract, concrete cause, consideration[2], motive, principal consideration, subjective cause
CAUTION[1]	guarantor, surety[+]
CAUTION[2]	contract of suretyship, suretyship[+]

CAUTIONNEMENT	contract of suretyship, suretyship[+]
CAUTIONNER	post security (for), secure, stand as surety (for)[+]
CÉDANT, ANTE	assignor
CÉDÉ, ÉE	assigned debtor
CÉDER	assign[+], cede
CESSIBILITÉ	assignability
CESSIBLE	assignable
CESSION	assignment[+], cession, conveyance[3]
CESSION DE CONTRAT	assignment of contract
CESSION DE CRÉANCE	assignment of claim(s)[+], assignment of creance, transfer of claim, transfer of debt
CESSION DE DETTE	assignment of debt
CESSION DE(S) DROITS HÉRÉDITAIRES	assignment of hereditary rights, assignment of inheritance, assignment of rights of inheritance, assignment of rights of succession, assignment of successional rights[+]
CESSION DE DROITS LITIGIEUX	assignment of litigious rights
CESSION DE(S) DROITS SUCCESSIFS	assignment of hereditary rights, assignment of inheritance, assignment of rights of inheritance, assignment of rights of succession, assignment of successional rights[+]
CESSION D'HÉRÉDITÉ	assignment of hereditary rights, assignment of inheritance, assignment of rights of inheritance, assignment of rights of succession, assignment of successional rights[+]
CESSIONNAIRE	assignee
CESSION-TRANSPORT	assignment of claim(s)[+], assignment of creance, transfer of claim, transfer of debt
CHARGE	charge, debt[1], juridical duty, juridical obligation[2], legal duty, liability[2], obligation[3+]
CHARGEUR, EURE	consignor, freighter, sender, shipper[+]
CHOSE[1]	corporeal thing, material thing, res[1], thing[1+]
CHOSE[2]	object of the obligation, prestation[+], thing[2]
CHOSE APPROPRIABLE	corporeal property, material property, property[2+], thing susceptible of appropriation
CHOSE CORPORELLE	corporeal thing, material thing, res[1], thing[1+]
CHOSE DANS LE COMMERCE	object of commerce
CHOSE FUTURE	future property[+], future thing
CHOSE HORS (DU) COMMERCE	object not in commerce
CHOSE INCORPORELLE	incorporeal property, incorporeal thing, patrimonial right[+], property[1], res
CHOSE MATÉRIELLE	corporeal thing, material thing, res[1], thing[1+]
CIVIL	civil
CLAUSE	clause[+], stipulation[1]
CLAUSE ABUSIVE	abusive clause
CLAUSE COMMINATOIRE	comminatory clause[+], penal clause[2]
CLAUSE COMPROMISSOIRE	*clause compromissoire*, undertaking to arbitrate[+]

CLAUSE D'AGRÉMENT	approval clause
CLAUSE D'ARBITRAGE	arbitration clause
CLAUSE D'ÉCHELLE MOBILE	escalator clause, indexation clause, sliding scale clause[+]
CLAUSE DE DATION EN PAIEMENT	clause of *dation en paiement*, clause of giving in payment, *dation en paiement* clause, giving in payment clause[+]
CLAUSE DE DÉDIT	forfeit clause, stipulation as to withdrawal, withdrawal clause[+]
CLAUSE DE DOMMAGES-INTÉRÊTS LIBÉRATOIRES	penal clause[1]
CLAUSE DE FOURNIR ET FAIRE VALOIR	clause of *fournir et faire valoir,* guarantee of payment clause, warranty of payment clause[+]
CLAUSE DE GARANTIE	warranty clause
CLAUSE DE LIMITATION DE RESPONSABILITÉ	clause of limitation of liability, limitation of liability clause[+], limited liability clause
CLAUSE DE NON-CONCURRENCE	clause not to compete, non-competition clause[+]
CLAUSE DE NON-GARANTIE	clause excluding warranty
CLAUSE DE NON-RESPONSABILITÉ[1]	exoneration clause[1+], exoneration of liability clause, no liability clause[1]
CLAUSE DE NON-RESPONSABILITÉ[2]	exclusion (of liability) clause[+], exemption clause, exoneration clause[2], no liability clause[2], stipulation of non-liability
CLAUSE DE PRÉEMPTION	preemption clause[+], preemptive clause
CLAUSE DE PREMIER REFUS	first refusal clause
CLAUSE DE RÉSOLUTION	clause of resolution, resolutive clause, resolutory clause[1+]
CLAUSE DE RÉSOLUTION DE PLEIN DROIT	clause of resolution of right, express clause of resolution, express resolutory clause, resolutory clause of right[+], stipulation of resolution upon non-performance
CLAUSE DE RESPONSABILITÉ ATTÉNUÉE	clause of limitation of liability, limitation of liability clause[+], limited liability clause
CLAUSE DE RESPONSABILITÉ LIMITÉE	clause of limitation of liability, limitation of liability clause[+], limited liability clause
CLAUSE DE RÉVISION	revision clause[+], variation clause
CLAUSE DE STYLE[1]	*clause de style*
CLAUSE DE STYLE[2]	customary clause
CLAUSE D'EXCLUSION DE RESPONSABILITÉ	exclusion (of liability) clause[+], exemption clause, exoneration clause[2], no liability clause[2], stipulation of non-liability
CLAUSE D'EXCLUSIVITÉ	exclusivity clause
CLAUSE D'EXONÉRATION DE RESPONSABILITÉ[1]	exoneration clause[1+], exoneration of liability clause, no liability clause[1]
CLAUSE D'EXONÉRATION DE RESPONSABILITÉ[2]	exclusion (of liability) clause[+], exemption clause, exoneration clause[2], no liability clause[1], stipulation of non-liability
CLAUSE D'INDEMNISATION FORFAITAIRE	penal clause[1]

CLAUSE D'INDEXATION	escalator clause, indexation clause, sliding scale clause[+]
CLAUSE ÉLUSIVE DE RESPONSABILITÉ	exclusion (of liability) clause[+], exemption clause, exoneration clause[2], no liability clause[2], stipulation of non-liability
CLAUSE EXONÉRATOIRE DE RESPONSABILITÉ	exclusion (of liability) clause[+], exemption clause, exoneration clause[2], no liability clause[2], stipulation of non-liability
CLAUSE EXONÉRATRICE DE RESPONSABILITÉ	exclusion (of liability) clause[+], exemption clause, exoneration clause[2], no liability clause[2], stipulation of non-liability
CLAUSE EXPRESSE DE RÉSOLUTION	clause of resolution of right, express clause of resolution, express resolutory clause, resolutory clause of right[+], stipulation of resolution upon non-performance
CLAUSE EXTERNE	external clause
CLAUSE ILLISIBLE	illegible clause
CLAUSE INDEXÉE	escalator clause, indexation clause, sliding scale clause[+]
CLAUSE LÉONINE	leonine clause
CLAUSE LIMITATIVE DE RESPONSABILITÉ	clause of limitation of liability, limitation of liability clause[+], limited liability clause
CLAUSE MONÉTAIRE	monetary clause
CLAUSE OR	gold clause[1]
CLAUSE PÉNALE[1]	penal clause[1]
CLAUSE PÉNALE[2]	comminatory clause[+], penal clause[2]
CLAUSE RÉSOLUTOIRE[1]	clause of resolution, resolutive clause, resolutory clause[1+]
CLAUSE RÉSOLUTOIRE[2]	resolutory clause[2]
CLAUSE RÉSOLUTOIRE DE PLEIN DROIT	clause of resolution of right, express clause of resolution, express resolutory clause, resolutory clause of right[+], stipulation of resolution upon non-performance
CLAUSE RÉSOLUTOIRE EXPRESSE	clause of resolution of right, express clause of resolution, express resolutory clause, resolutory clause of right[+], stipulation of resolution upon non-performance
CLAUSE RESTRICTIVE	restrictive clause, restrictive covenant[+]
CLAUSE RESTRICTIVE DE COMMERCE	clause in restraint of trade
CLAUSE TYPE	standard term
CLAUSE VALEUR OR	gold clause[2]
CLIENT, ENTE	client[2]
COACQUÉREUR, ÉRESSE	joint acquirer
COAUTEUR, EURE	coauthor
CO-CAUTION	cosurety
COCONTRACTANT, ANTE	cocontracting party
COCRÉANCIER, IÈRE	co-creditor
CODE[1]	code[1]

CODE²	code²
CODE³	code³
CODE⁴	code⁴
CODÉBITEUR, TRICE	co-debtor
CODE CIVIL	civil code
CODE CIVIL DU BAS CANADA	*Civil Code of Lower Canada*
CODE CIVIL DU QUÉBEC¹	*Civil Code of Québec¹*
CODE CIVIL DU QUÉBEC²	*Civil Code of Québec²*
CODE NAPOLÉON	*Code Napoléon*
COFIDÉJUSSEUR, EURE	cosurety
COLLECTIF, IVE	collective
COMMANDITAIRE	limited partner, special partner⁺
COMMANDITÉ, ÉE	general partner
COMMERÇANT, ANTE	merchant⁺, trader
COMMERCE¹	commerce¹
COMMERCE²	commerce²
COMMERCIAL, ALE	commercial
COMMERCIALITÉ	commerciality
COMMETTANT, ANTE	committent, principal³⁺
COMMETTANT HABITUEL	habitual employer
COMMETTANT OCCASIONNEL	occasional employer, temporary employer⁺
COMMISSION	commission
COMMODANT, ANTE	lender(>)
COMMODAT	*commodatum*, loan for use⁺
COMMODATAIRE	borrower(>)
COMMON LAW¹	common law²
COMMON LAW²	common law³
COMMON LAW³	common law⁴
COMMUNE INTENTION	common intention
COMPENSABLE	compensable
COMPENSATION¹	compensation¹⁺, set-off
COMPENSATION²	compensation², indemnification, reparation by equivalence⁺
COMPENSATION³	compensation⁴, indemnity⁺, reparation²
COMPENSATION CONVENTIONNELLE	contractual compensation, conventional compensation⁺
COMPENSATION JUDICIAIRE	judicial compensation
COMPENSATION LÉGALE	legal compensation
COMPENSATOIRE	compensatory
COMPENSER	compensate⁺, set-off
COMPLEXE	complex
COMPOSÉ, ÉE	compound
COMPROMETTRE	arbitrate¹

COMPROMIS	*compromis*, submission (to arbitration)+
COMPTANT (AU)	cash (in)
CONCURRENCE (PAR)	[*]
CONDITION[1]	condition[1]
CONDITION[2]	condition[2+], term[2]
CONDITION[3]	condition[3]
CONDITION ACCOMPLIE	accomplished condition, fulfilled condition+
CONDITION CASUELLE	casual condition
CONDITION DÉFAILLIE	failed condition
CONDITION DE FOND	substantive condition
CONDITION DE FORME	condition as to form
CONDITION DE PAIEMENT	condition of payment, modality of payment+
CONDITION FACULTATIVE	facultative condition, potestative condition+
CONDITION ILLÉGALE	illegal condition, illicit condition+, unlawful condition
CONDITION ILLICITE	illegal condition, illicit condition+, unlawful condition
CONDITION IMMORALE	immoral condition
CONDITION IMPOSSIBLE	impossible condition
CONDITION MIXTE	mixed condition
CONDITION NÉGATIVE	negative condition
CONDITIONNEL, ELLE	conditional
CONDITION PENDANTE	pending condition
CONDITION POSITIVE	positive condition
CONDITION POTESTATIVE	facultative condition, potestative condition+
CONDITION PUREMENT FACULTATIVE	purely facultative condition, purely potestative condition+
CONDITION PUREMENT POTESTATIVE	purely facultative condition, purely potestative condition+
CONDITION RÉSOLUTOIRE	resolutive condition, resolutory condition+
CONDITIONS GÉNÉRALES	general conditions
CONDITION SIMPLEMENT FACULTATIVE	simply facultative condition, simply potestative condition+
CONDITION SIMPLEMENT POTESTATIVE	simply facultative condition, simply potestative condition+
CONDITION *SINE QUA NON*	*causa sine qua non*, cause *sine qua non*, condition *sine qua non*+
CONDITIONS PARTICULIÈRES	special terms
CONDITION SUSPENSIVE	suspensive condition+, suspensory condition
CONFIRMATION	confirmation+, ratification[2]
CONFIRMER	confirm+, ratify[2]
CONFUSION	confusion
CONJOINTEMENT	jointly

CONJOINTEMENT ET SOLIDAIREMENT	solidarily
CONJONCTION	conjunction
CONNAISSEMENT	bill of lading
CONSENSUALISME	consensualism
CONSENSUEL, ELLE	consensual
CONSENTEMENT[1]	meeting of the minds, consent[1+]
CONSENTEMENT[2]	consent[2]
CONSENTEMENT[3]	consent[3]
CONSENTEMENT ÉCLAIRÉ	enlightened consent[+], informed consent
CONSENTEMENT EXPLICITE	explicit consent, express consent[+], express manifestation of intent, express manifestation of will
CONSENTEMENT EXPRÈS	explicit consent, express consent[+], express manifestation of intent, express manifestation of will
CONSENTEMENT IMPLICITE	implicit consent, implied consent, tacit consent[+], tacit manifestation of intent, tacit manifestation of will
CONSENTEMENT LIBRE	consent freely given
CONSENTEMENT TACITE	implicit consent, implied consent, tacit consent[+], tacit manifestation of intent, tacit manifestation of will
CONSENTIR	consent
CONSIDÉRATION[1]	abstract cause, cause[1+], cause of the obligation, consideration[1], final cause, objective cause
CONSIDÉRATION[2]	cause[2+], cause of the contract, concrete cause, consideration[2], motive, principal consideration, subjective cause
CONSIDÉRATION[3]	consideration[3]
CONSIDÉRATION ILLÉGALE	illegal cause, illicit cause[+], illicit consideration, unlawful cause, unlawful consideration
CONSIDÉRATION PRINCIPALE	cause[2+], cause of the contract, concrete cause, consideration[2], motive, principal consideration, subjective cause
CONSIDÉRATION VALABLE	valuable consideration
CONSIGNATAIRE	addressee, consignee[+], receiver
CONSIGNATION	consignment, deposit[3+]
CONSIGNER	consign, deposit[2+]
CONSOLIDATION DE DETTES	consolidation of debts[+], consolidation of indebtedness
CONSOMMATEUR, TRICE	consumer
CONSOMMATION	consumption
CONSTITUTIF, IVE	constitutive
CONTINU, UE	continuous
CONTRACTANT, ANTE	contracting party
CONTRACTER[1]	contract[1]
CONTRACTER[2]	contract[2]
CONTRACTEUR, EURE	[*]

CONTRACTUEL, ELLE	contractual[+], conventional
CONTRAT[1]	agreement[1], contract[1+], covenant, pact, transaction[2]
CONTRAT[2]	agreement[2], contract[2+], deed[2]
CONTRAT ACCESSOIRE	accessory contract
CONTRAT À DISTANCE	contract between absents, contract *inter absentes*[+], remote-parties contract
CONTRAT À DURÉE DÉTERMINÉE	contract with a determinate term
CONTRAT À DURÉE INDÉTERMINÉE	contract with an indeterminate term
CONTRAT À EXÉCUTION INSTANTANÉE	contract of instantaneous execution, contract of instantaneous performance[+], instantaneous contract
CONTRAT À EXÉCUTION SUCCESSIVE	contract of successive execution, contract of successive performance[+], successive contract
CONTRAT À FORFAIT	fixed price contract[+], lump sum contract
CONTRAT ALÉATOIRE	aleatory contract
CONTRAT APPARENT	apparent contract
CONTRAT À TITRE GRATUIT	contract by gratuitous title, gratuitous contract[+]
CONTRAT À TITRE ONÉREUX	contract by onerous title, onerous contract[+]
CONTRAT BILATÉRAL	bilateral contract[+], synallagmatic contract
CONTRAT-CADRE	master contract
CONTRAT COLLECTIF	collective contract
CONTRAT COMMUTATIF	commutative contract
CONTRAT COMPLEXE	complex contract, mixed contract[+]
CONTRAT CONSENSUEL	consensual contract
CONTRAT D'ADHÉSION	adhesion contract[+], contract of adhesion
CONTRAT D'AFFRÈTEMENT	contract of affreightment[+], affreightment
CONTRAT D'ALIÉNATION	contract of alienation
CONTRAT D'ASSOCIATION	contract of association
CONTRAT D'ASSURANCE	contract of insurance, insurance, insurance contract[+]
CONTRAT DE BAIL	contract of lease, lease[1+], lease of things
CONTRAT DE BÉNÉVOLAT	benevolent contract
CONTRAT DE BIENFAISANCE	benevolent contract
CONTRAT DE CAUTIONNEMENT	contract of suretyship, suretyship[+]
CONTRAT D'ÉCHANGE	barter, exchange[+]
CONTRAT DE CONSOMMATION	consumer contract
CONTRAT DE CRÉDIT	contract of credit[+], credit contract
CONTRAT DE CRÉDIT-BAIL	contract of leasing, finance lease, financial lease, financial leasing, leasing[+], leasing contract
CONTRAT DE DÉPÔT	contract of deposit, deposit[1+]
CONTRAT DE DONATION	contract of gift, donation, gift[1+]
CONTRAT DE GRÉ À GRÉ	contract by mutual agreement, contract by negotiation[+], contract *de gré à gré*, negotiated contract
CONTRAT DE JEU	gaming contract

CONTRAT DE LIBRE DISCUSSION	contract by mutual agreement, contract by negotiation[+], contract *de gré à gré*, negotiated contract
CONTRAT DE LOCATION	contract of lease, lease[1+], lease of things
CONTRAT DE LOUAGE	contract of lease, lease[1+], lease of things
CONTRAT DE LOUAGE DE SERVICES[1]	contract of employment[+], contract of lease and hire of personal service(s), contract of lease (and hire) of services[1], employment contract, individual contract of employment, work contract
CONTRAT DE LOUAGE DE SERVICES[2]	contract for (of) services[+], contract of lease (and hire) of services[2], contract of service(s),
CONTRAT DE LOUAGE DE SERVICE(S) PERSONNEL(S)	contract of employment[+], contract of lease and hire of personal service(s), contract of lease (and hire) of services[1], employment contract, individual contract of employment, work contract
CONTRAT DE LOUAGE D'OUVRAGE	lease and hire of work
CONTRAT DE MANDAT	contract of mandate, mandate[1+]
CONTRAT D'EMPLOI	contract of employment[+], contract of lease and hire of personal service(s), contract of lease (and hire) of services[1], employment contract, individual contract of employment, work contract
CONTRAT D'ENTREPRISE	contract for work, contract of enterprise[+]
CONTRAT DE PARI	bet, betting, wager, wagering, wagering contract[+]
CONTRAT DE PRÊT	contract of loan, loan[+]
CONTRAT DE PRÊTE-NOM	agreement to act as nominee, clandestine mandate, contract of *prête-nom*[+], *prête-nom*[2], secret mandate
CONTRAT DE RENTE	annuity[3], annuity contract[+]
CONTRAT DE SERVICE(S)	contract for (of) services[+], contract of lease (and hire) of services[2], contract of service(s)
CONTRAT DÉSINTÉRESSÉ	benevolent contract
CONTRAT DE SOCIÉTÉ	contract of partnership[+], partnership[2], partnership agreement
CONTRAT DE TRANSACTION	contract of transaction, out-of-court settlement, settlement, transaction[+]
CONTRAT DE TRANSPORT	carriage[2], contract of carriage[+], contract of transport, contract of transportation, transport[2]
CONTRAT DE TRANSPORT DE BIENS	contract for the carriage of goods[+], contract for the carriage of property
CONTRAT DE TRANSPORT DE PERSONNES	contract for the carriage of persons
CONTRAT DE TRAVAIL	contract of employment[+], contract of lease and hire of personal service(s), contract of lease (and hire) of services[1], employment contract, individual contract of employment, work contract
CONTRAT DE VENTE	contract of sale, sale[+]
CONTRAT ÉLECTRONIQUE	electronic contract
CONTRAT ENTRE ABSENTS	contract between absents, contract *inter absentes*[+], remote-parties contract
CONTRAT ENTRE NON-PRÉSENTS	contract between absents, contract *inter absentes*[+], remote-parties contract

CONTRAT ENTRE PRÉSENTS	contract between persons present
CONTRAT FICTIF	fictitious contract
CONTRAT FORMALISTE	formalistic contract
CONTRAT INDIVIDUEL	individual contract
CONTRAT INDIVIDUEL DE TRAVAIL	contract of employment[+], contract of lease and hire of personal service(s), contract of lease (and hire) of services[1], employment contract, individual contract of employment, work contract
CONTRAT INNOMMÉ	innominate contract[+], *sui generis* contract
CONTRAT INSTANTANÉ	contract of instantaneous execution, contract of instantaneous performance[+], instantaneous contract
CONTRAT INTÉRESSÉ	contract by onerous title[+], onerous contract
CONTRAT *INTUITU PERSONÆ*	*intuitu personæ* contract
CONTRAT MIXTE	complex contract, mixed contract[+]
CONTRAT NÉGOCIÉ	contract by mutual agreement, contract by negotiation[+], contract *de gré à gré*, negotiated contract
CONTRAT NOMMÉ	nominate contract[+], special contract
CONTRAT ONÉREUX	contract by onerous title, onerous contract[+]
CONTRAT PAR CORRESPONDANCE	contract by correspondence
CONTRAT PAR TÉLÉPHONE	contract by telephone
CONTRAT PRINCIPAL	principal contract
CONTRAT RÉEL	real contract
CONTRAT RELATIONNEL (THÉORIE DU)	relational contract (doctrine of)
CONTRAT SECRET	secret contract
CONTRAT SIMPLE	simple contract
CONTRAT SIMULÉ	simulated contract
CONTRAT SOLENNEL	formal contract, solemn agreement, solemn contract[+], solemn covenant
CONTRATS SPÉCIAUX	nominate contract[+], special contract
CONTRAT SUCCESSIF	contract of successive execution, contract of successive performance[+], successive contract
CONTRAT *SUI GENERIS*	innominate contract[+], *sui generis* contract
CONTRAT SYNALLAGMATIQUE	bilateral contract[+], synallagmatic contract
CONTRAT SYNALLAGMATIQUE IMPARFAIT	imperfect bilateral contract[+], imperfect synallagmatic contract
CONTRAT TRANSLATIF	translatory contract
CONTRAT TRANSLATIF DE PROPRIÉTÉ	contract translatory of ownership
CONTRAT TYPE	standard contract, standard-form contract[+]
CONTRAT UNILATÉRAL	unilateral contract
CONTRAT USURAIRE	usurious contract
CONTRE-LETTRE	counter letter[+], real act, secret act, true act
CONTRE-OFFRE	counter-offer[+], counter-proposal
CONTREPARTIE	counterprestation

CONTRE-PRESTATION ou CONTREPRESTATION	counterprestation
CONTRE-PROPOSITION	counter-offer+, counter-proposal
CONTRIBUTION À LA DETTE	contribution to the debt(s)
CONVENTION	agreement[1], contract[1+], covenant, pact, transaction[2]
CONVENTION D'ANATOCISME	anatocism agreement, compound interest contract+, contract of capitalization of interest
CONVENTION D'ARBITRAGE	arbitration agreement+, contract of arbitration
CONVENTION D'ARRHES	agreement for earnest
CONVENTIONNEL, ELLE	contractual+, conventional
COOBLIGÉ, ÉE	co-debtor
CORRÉALITÉ	correality, perfect solidarity, solidarity+
CORRÉLATION	correlation
COUTUME[1]	custom[1]
COUTUME[2]	custom[2+], customary law[1]
CRAINTE	fear
CRAINTE RÉVÉRENCIELLE	reverential fear
CRÉANCE	claim, creance, credit[2], debt[2], *jus in personam*, obligation[4], personal right+
CRÉANCE ALIMENTAIRE	alimentary claim, alimentary creance, alimentary right+, claim for support
CRÉANCE CERTAINE	certain claim+, certain creance
CRÉANCE CONJOINTE	joint claim, joint personal right+
CRÉANCE DÉTERMINÉE	determinate claim, determinate creance, liquidated claim, liquidated creance, liquid claim+, liquid creance
CRÉANCE DIVISIBLE	divisible claim+, divisible creance
CRÉANCE EXIGIBLE	demandable claim, demandable creance, exigible claim+, exigible creance
CRÉANCE INCERTAINE	uncertain claim+, uncertain creance
CRÉANCE INDIVISIBLE	indivisible claim+, indivisible creance
CRÉANCE LIQUIDE	determinate claim, determinate creance, liquidated claim, liquidated creance, liquid claim+, liquid creance
CRÉANCE LITIGIEUSE	litigious creance, litigious debt, litigious personal right+
CRÉANCE PORTABLE	portable claim+, portable creance
CRÉANCE QUÉRABLE	seekable claim+, seekable creance
CRÉANCE SOLIDAIRE	solidary claim, solidary creance, solidary personal right+
CRÉANCIER, IÈRE	creditor+, obligee
CRÉANCIER ALIMENTAIRE	creditor of support
CRÉANCIER CHIROGRAPHAIRE	chirographic creditor, ordinary creditor, unsecured creditor+
CRÉANCIER D'ALIMENTS	creditor of support

CRÉANCIER GARANTI	secured creditor
CRÉANCIER ORDINAIRE	chirographic creditor, ordinary creditor, unsecured creditor[+]
CRÉDIRENTIER, IÈRE	annuitant
CRÉDIT	credit[1]
CRÉDIT À LA CONSOMMATION	consumer credit
CRÉDIT-BAIL	contract of leasing, finance lease, financial lease, financial leasing, leasing[+], leasing contract
CRÉDIT-BAILLEUR, ERESSE	lessor[2]
CRÉDIT-PRENEUR, EUSE	lessee[3]
CULPA IN COMMITTENDO	*culpa in committendo, culpa in faciendo,* fault of commission[+]
CULPA IN CONTRAHENDO[1]	*culpa in contrahendo[1]*
CULPA IN CONTRAHENDO[2]	*culpa in contrahendo[2],* precontractual fault[+]
CULPA IN FACIENDO	*culpa in committendo, culpa in faciendo,* fault of commission[+]
CULPA IN NON FACIENDO	*culpa in non faciendo, culpa in omittendo,* fault of omission[+]
CULPA IN OMITTENDO	*culpa in non faciendo, culpa in omittendo,* fault of omission[+]
CULPA LATA ou *LATA CULPA*	*culpa lata,* gross fault[+]
CULPA LEVIS ou *LEVIS CULPA*	*culpa levis*
CULPA LEVISSIMA ou *LEVISSIMA CULPA*	*culpa levissima*
CUMUL (DES RÉGIMES)	cumulation (of regimes)[+], *cumul* (of regimes)

D

DAMNUM EMERGENS	*damnum emergens,* loss[1+]
DATION	dation
DATION EN PAIEMENT	*dation en paiement,* giving in payment[+]
DÉBIRENTIER, IÈRE	debtor of an annuity[+], debtor of the rent
DÉBITEUR, TRICE	debtor[+], obligor
DÉBITEUR ALIMENTAIRE	alimentary debtor, debtor of support[+]
DÉBITEUR CÉDÉ	assigned debtor
DÉBITEUR D'ALIMENTS	debtor of support
DÉBOURSÉ[1]	expenditure[1], expense[1+]
DÉBOURSÉ[2]	expenditure[2], expense[2+]
DÉCHARGE[1]	discharge[1+], quit
DÉCHARGE[2]	discharge[2+], receipt[3]
DÉCHARGE[3]	discharge[3+], release[2]
DÉCHÉANCE	forfeiture
DÉCHÉANCE DU TERME	forfeiture of (the) term

DÉCLARATIF, IVE	declaratory
DÉCLARATION DE VOLONTÉ	declaration of will
DÉDIRE (SE)	withdraw[2]
DÉDIT[1]	withdrawal option
DÉDIT[2]	penalty of withdrawal
DÉFAILLANCE DE LA CONDITION	failure of the condition
DÉFAILLIR	fail
DÉFAUT	default
DÉFAUT APPARENT	apparent defect
DÉFAUT CACHÉ	hidden defect, latent defect[+], redhibitory defect
DÉFAUT DE FORME	defect of form[+], formal defect
DÉFAUT D'EXÉCUTION	default in performance, inexecution, non-fulfilment, non-performance[+]
DÉGUISÉ, ÉE	disguised
DÉLAI DE GRÂCE	delay of grace, judicial term[+], period of grace, term of grace
DÉLÉGANT, ANTE	delegator
DÉLÉGATAIRE	delegatee
DÉLÉGATION	delegation
DÉLÉGATION IMPARFAITE	imperfect delegation
DÉLÉGATION PARFAITE	perfect delegation
DÉLÉGUÉ, ÉE	delegate
DÉLÉGUER	delegate
DÉLICTUEL, ELLE	delictual
DÉLIT	delict[+], offence
DÉLIVRANCE[1]	delivery[1]
DÉLIVRANCE[2]	[*]
DÉLIVRER	deliver[1]
DEMANDE EN JUSTICE	action[+], judicial action, judicial demand, law suit, suit
DEMEURE	default
DÉPENSE[1]	expenditure[1], expense[1+]
DÉPENSE[2]	expenditure[2], expense[2+]
DÉPOSANT, ANTE	depositor
DÉPOSER	deposit[1]
DÉPOSITAIRE	depositary
DÉPÔT[1]	contract of deposit, deposit[1+]
DÉPÔT[2]	[*]
DÉPÔT HÔTELIER	deposit with an innkeeper
DÉPÔT IRRÉGULIER	irregular deposit
DÉPÔT JUDICIAIRE	judicial deposit, judicial sequestration[+]
DÉPÔT NÉCESSAIRE	necessary deposit
DÉPÔT SIMPLE	simple deposit

DESTINATAIRE[1]	offeree
DESTINATAIRE[2]	addressee, consignee[+], receiver
DETTE	charge, debt[1], juridical duty, juridical obligation[2], legal duty, liability[2], obligation[3+]
DETTE ACTIVE	claim, creance, credit[2], debt[2], *jus in personam*, obligation[4], personal right[+]
DETTE ALIMENTAIRE	debt for support, obligation of support[2+]
DETTE CERTAINE	certain debt
DETTE CONJOINTE	joint debt
DETTE DE JEU (OU DE PARI)	gambling debt
DETTE DÉTERMINÉE	determinate debt, liquid debt[+], liquidated debt
DETTE DE VALEUR	value debt
DETTE DIVISIBLE	divisible debt
DETTE ÉCHUE	expired debt, debt fallen due[+]
DETTE EXIGIBLE	debt payable (on demand), demandable debt, exigible debt[+]
DETTE INCERTAINE	uncertain debt
DETTE INDIVISIBLE	indivisible debt
DETTE LIQUIDE	determinate debt, liquid debt[+], liquidated debt
DETTE PORTABLE	portable debt
DETTE QUÉRABLE	seekable debt
DETTE SOLIDAIRE	solidary debt
DEVOIR	duty[+], obligation[1]
DEVOIR DE COLLABORATION	duty to collaborate, duty to cooperate[+]
DEVOIR DE CONSCIENCE	duty of conscience, imperfect obligation, moral duty, moral obligation[+]
DEVOIR DE CONSEIL	obligation to advise[+], obligation to (provide) counsel
DEVOIR DE DISCRÉTION	duty of confidentiality[+], obligation of confidentiality
DEVOIR DE LOYAUTÉ	obligation of loyalty[+], obligation to act faithfully
DEVOIR DE RENSEIGNEMENT(S)	duty to inform, obligation to inform[+]
DEVOIR JURIDIQUE	charge, debt[1], juridical duty, juridical obligation[2], legal duty, liability[2], obligation[3+]
DEVOIR MORAL	duty of conscience, imperfect obligation, moral duty, moral obligation[+]
DIFFAMATION[1]	defamation[1]
DIFFAMATION[2]	defamation[2]
DIFFÉRER	defer
DILIGENCE	diligence
DISCERNEMENT	discernment
DISCUSSION	discussion
DISCUTER	discuss
DISPOSER[1]	dispose[1]
DISPOSER[2]	dispose[2+], settle[3]

351

DISPOSITION[1]	disposal[1], disposition[1+]
DISPOSITION[2]	disposal[2], disposition[2+]
DISPOSITION[3]	disposal[3], disposition[3+]
DISPOSITION[4]	provision
DISPOSITION À CAUSE DE MORT	disposition in contemplation of death, disposition *mortis causa*[+]
DISPOSITION À TITRE GRATUIT	disposition by gratuitous title
DISPOSITION À TITRE ONÉREUX	disposition by onerous title
DISPOSITION À TITRE PARTICULIER	disposition by particular title
DISPOSITION À TITRE UNIVERSEL	disposition by general title
DISPOSITION ENTRE VIFS	disposition *inter vivos*
DISPOSITION *INTER VIVOS*	disposition *inter vivos*
DISPOSITION JURIDIQUE	disposition (of property) by juridical act
DISPOSITION MATÉRIELLE	disposition (of property) by material act
DISPOSITION *MORTIS CAUSA*	disposition in contemplation of death, disposition *mortis causa*[+]
DISPOSITION PHYSIQUE	disposition (of property) by material act
DISPOSITION UNIVERSELLE	universal disposition
DIVISIBILITÉ[1]	divisibility[1]
DIVISIBILITÉ[2]	divisibility[2]
DIVISIBLE	divisible
DIVISION	division
DOCTRINE[1]	doctrine[1]
DOCTRINE[2]	doctrine[2]
DOCUMENT ÉLECTRONIQUE	electronic document, technology-based document[+]
DOCUMENT TECHNOLOGIQUE	electronic document, technology-based document[+]
DOL[1]	*dolus malus,* fraud[1+]
DOL[2]	fraud[2]
DOLI CAPAX	*doli capax*
DOL INCIDENT	incidental fraud
DOLOSIF, IVE	[*]
DOL PRINCIPAL	principal fraud
DOLUS BONUS	*dolus bonus*
DOLUS MALUS	*dolus malus,* fraud[1+]
DOMMAGE	damage[+], harm, injury, loss[2], prejudice, wrong[2]
DOMMAGES	damages
DOMMAGES ET INTÉRÊTS	damages
DOMMAGES-INTÉRÊTS	damages
DOMMAGES-INTÉRÊTS ADDITIONNELS[1]	additional damages[1+], additional indemnity[2]
DOMMAGES-INTÉRÊTS ADDITIONNELS[2]	additional damages[2]
DOMMAGES-INTÉRÊTS COMPENSATOIRES[1]	compensatory damages[1]

DOMMAGES-INTÉRÊTS COMPENSATOIRES[2]	compensatory damages[2]
DOMMAGES-INTÉRÊTS CONTRACTUELS[1]	contractual damages[2]
DOMMAGES-INTÉRÊTS CONTRACTUELS[2]	[*]
DOMMAGES-INTÉRÊTS CONVENTIONNELS	contractual damages[1], conventional damages[+]
DOMMAGES-INTÉRÊTS EXEMPLAIRES	exemplary damages, punitive damages[+]
DOMMAGES-INTÉRÊTS EXTRACONTRACTUELS	extra-contractual damages
DOMMAGES-INTÉRÊTS EXTRAJUDICIAIRES	extrajudicial damages
DOMMAGES-INTÉRÊTS JUDICIAIRES	judicial damages
DOMMAGES-INTÉRÊTS LÉGAUX	legal damages
DOMMAGES-INTÉRÊTS LIQUIDÉS	liquidated damages
DOMMAGES-INTÉRÊTS MORATOIRES	moratory damages
DOMMAGES-INTÉRÊTS MORAUX	moral damages
DOMMAGES-INTÉRÊTS NOMINAUX	nominal damages[+], symbolic damages
DOMMAGES-INTÉRÊTS PUNITIFS	exemplary damages, punitive damages[+]
DON[1]	contract of gift, donation, gift[1+]
DON[2]	gift[2]
DONATAIRE	donee
DONATEUR, TRICE	donor
DONATION	contract of gift, donation, gift[1+]
DONATION CONJOINTE	joint gift
DON MANUEL	don manuel
DONNER[1]	give[1]
DONNER[2]	give[2]
DONNEUR D'OUVRAGE	client[2]
DOUBLE MANDAT	double mandate
DOUÉ DE RAISON	endowed with reason
DROIT[1]	*jus*[1], law[1+]
DROIT[2]	*jus*[2], right[+]
DROIT ACTUEL	present right
DROIT ALIMENTAIRE	alimentary claim, alimentary creance, alimentary right[+], claim for support
DROIT APPARENT	apparent right
DROIT À TERME	right with a term
DROIT CIVIL[1]	civil law[1]
DROIT CIVIL[2]	civil law[2], private law[+]
DROIT CIVIL[3]	civil law[3]
DROIT COMMUN[1]	common law[1], *droit commun*, general law[+], ordinary law, *jus commune*

DROIT COMMUN[2]	[*]
DROIT CONDITIONNEL	conditional right
DROIT COUTUMIER[1]	custom[2+], customary law
DROIT COUTUMIER[2]	common law[2]
DROIT D'ACTION	right of action
DROIT DE CRÉANCE	claim, creance, credit[2], debt[2], *jus in personam*, obligation[4], personal right[+]
DROIT DE DISCUSSION	benefit of discussion[+], right of discussion
DROIT DE DIVISION	benefit of division[+], right of division
DROIT DÉFINITIF	definitive right[+]
DROIT DE JOUISSANCE	enjoyment[+], right of enjoyment
DROIT DE PRÉEMPTION[1]	preemptive right[1], right of preemption[+]
DROIT DE PRÉEMPTION[2]	preemptive right[2], subscription right[+]
DROIT DE PRÉFÉRENCE[1]	right of preference[1]
DROIT DE PRÉFÉRENCE[2]	*droit de préférence*, preference, right of preference[2+]
DROIT DE PREMIER REFUS	right of first refusal
DROIT DE REPRISE	right of repossession
DROIT DE RÉTENTION	right of retention
DROIT DES OBLIGATIONS	law of obligations[+], obligations
DROIT DE SUITE	*droit de suite*, right to follow[+]
DROIT DISPONIBLE	disponible right
DROIT D'OPTION	right of option
DROIT ÉVENTUEL[1]	eventual right[1]
DROIT ÉVENTUEL[2]	contingent right[1], eventual right[2+]
DROIT EXTRAPATRIMONIAL	extrapatrimonial right.
DROIT FONDAMENTAL	fundamental right
DROIT HORS (DU) COMMERCE	[*]
DROIT IMPÉRATIF	imperative law[+], *jus cogens*
DROIT LITIGIEUX	litigious right
DROIT MIXTE[1]	mixed legal system
DROIT MIXTE[2]	mixed law
DROIT MIXTE[3]	*jus ad rem trans personam*[+], mixed right
DROIT MODAL	qualified right
DROIT NATUREL	natural law
DROIT OBJECTIF	*jus*[1], law[1+]
DROIT PATRIMONIAL	incorporeal property, incorporeal thing, patrimonial right[+], property[1], *res*[2]
DROIT PERSONNEL	claim, creance, credit[2], debt[2], *jus in personam*, obligation[4], personal right[+]
DROIT POSITIF	positive law
DROIT PRÉFÉRENTIEL DE SOUSCRIPTION	preemptive right[2], subscription right[+]
DROIT PRIVÉ[1]	civil law[2], private law[+]

DROIT PRIVÉ[2]	private law right
DROIT PUBLIC[1]	public law
DROIT PUBLIC[2]	public law right
DROIT PUR ET SIMPLE	absolute right, pure and simple right[+], unconditional right[1], unqualified right
DROIT RÉEL	*jus in re*, real right[+]
DROIT RÉEL ACCESSOIRE	accessory real right
DROIT RÉEL DE GARANTIE	accessory real right
DROIT RÉEL PRINCIPAL	principal real right
DROIT SUBJECTIF	*jus*[2], right[+]
DROIT SUPPLÉTIF[1]	*jus dispositivum*, suppletive law[1+]
DROIT SUPPLÉTIF[2]	suppletive law[2]
DROIT VIRTUEL	expectancy, expectation, mere expectancy[+], mere expectation, potential right

E

ÉCHANGE	barter, exchange[+]
ÉCHANGER	barter, exchange[+]
ÉCHÉANCE	arrival of the term, expiration[+], expiration of the term, expiry of the term
ÉCHÉANCE DU TERME	arrival of the term, expiration[+], expiration of the term, expiry of the term
ÉCHOIR	expire (to)
ÉCONOMIQUE	economic
EFFET ABDICATIF	abdicative effect, renunciative effect, renunciatory effect[+]
EFFET CONSTITUTIF	constitutive effect
EFFET DÉCLARATIF	declaratory effect
EFFET EXTINCTIF	extinctive effect
EFFET RELATIF DES CONTRATS	relative effect of contract, relativity of contract[+]
EFFET SUSPENSIF	suspensive effect
EFFET TRANSLATIF	translatory effect
EMPLOYÉ, ÉE	employee[1]
EMPLOYEUR, EURE	employer[1]
EMPRUNT	contract of loan(>), loan(>)[+]
EMPRUNTER	borrow
EMPRUNTEUR, EUSE	borrower
ENGAGEMENT[1]	commitment, engagement, undertaking[+]
ENGAGEMENT[2]	charge, debt[1], juridical duty, juridical obligation[2], legal duty, liability[2], obligation[3+]
ENGAGEMENT D'HONNEUR	gentlemen's agreement, honour-only agreement[+]

ENGAGEMENT PAR VOLONTÉ UNILATÉRALE	undertaking by unilateral will
ENGAGEMENT UNILATÉRAL (DE VOLONTÉ)	unilateral undertaking (of will)
ENGAGER	bind+, obligate, oblige
ENLÈVEMENT	removal
ENLEVER	remove+, take delivery
ENRICHISSEMENT INJUSTIFIÉ	unjust enrichment+, unjustified enrichment
ENRICHISSEMENT SANS CAUSE	unjust enrichment+, unjustified enrichment
ENSEMBLE CONTRACTUEL	transaction[3]
ENTENTE	bargain
ENTREPRENEUR, EUSE	contractor
ENTREPRISE[1]	entreprise[1]
ENTREPRISE[2]	entreprise[2]
ENTRE VIFS	*inter vivos*
ÉQUIPOLLENT, ENTE	equipollent
ÉQUIPOLLER (À)	[*]
ÉQUITABLE[1]	equitable[1](>)
ÉQUITABLE[2]	equitable[2]+(>), fair(>)
ÉQUITÉ	equity[1]
EQUITY	Equity[2]
ÉQUIVALENCE DES CONDITIONS	equivalence of conditions
ERGA OMNES	*erga omnes*
ERREUR	error
ERREUR DE DROIT	error of law
ERREUR DE FAIT	error of fact
ERREUR DE FORME	clerical error+, error of form, error as to (of) form
ERREUR ÉCONOMIQUE	economic error+, error as to value
ERREUR INEXCUSABLE	inexcusable error
ERREUR MATÉRIELLE	clerical error+, error of form, error as to (of) form
ERREUR-OBSTACLE	absolute error
ERREUR SUR LA CONSIDÉRATION PRINCIPALE	error as to a principal consideration
ERREUR SUR LA PERSONNE	error as to the person
ERREUR SUR LA SUBSTANCE	error as to substance
ERREUR SUR LA VALEUR	error as to value
ERREUR-VICE DU CONSENTEMENT	error constituting a defect of consent
ESCOMPTE	discount
ESPÈCES	cash+, *specie*
ESTHÉTIQUE	[*]
ÉTAT DE NÉCESSITÉ[1]	state of necessity[1]
ÉTAT DE NÉCESSITÉ[2]	state of necessity[2]
EX BONA FIDE	*ex bona fide*

EXCEPTION D'INEXÉCUTION	exception of non-performance[+], *exceptio non adimpleti contractus*
EXCEPTIO NON ADIMPLETI CONTRACTUS	exception of non-performance[+], *exceptio non adimpleti contractus*
EX CONTRACTU	*ex contractu*
EX DELICTO	*ex delicto*
EXÉCUTER	execute, perform[+]
EXÉCUTION	execution, performance[+]
EXÉCUTION DIRECTE	payment in kind[1], performance in kind, specific performance[+]
EXÉCUTION DU CONTRAT	performance of the contract
EXÉCUTION EN NATURE	payment in kind[1], performance in kind, specific performance[+]
EXÉCUTION FORCÉE	compulsory execution
EXÉCUTION PAR ÉQUIVALENT	performance by equivalence
EXÉCUTION SPÉCIFIQUE	specific performance
EXÉCUTION VOLONTAIRE	voluntary performance
EXÉCUTOIRE	executory
EXIGIBILITÉ	exigibility
EXIGIBLE	exigible[+], demandable, payable (on demand)
EX LEGE	*ex lege*
EXONÉRATION	exoneration
EXONÉRER	exonerate
EXPECTATIVE	expectancy, expectation, mere expectancy[+], mere expectation, potential right
EXPÉDITEUR, TRICE	consignor, freighter, sender, shipper[+]
EXPLOITATION	exploitation
EXTÉRIORITÉ	externality
EXTINCTION	extinction[+], termination
EXTRACONTRACTUEL, ELLE	extracontractual[+], legal[5]
EXTRAPATRIOMIAL, ALE	extrapatrimonial

F

FACULTATIF, IVE	facultative, potestative[+]
FACULTÉ D'AGRÉMENT	right of refusal
FACULTÉ DE DÉDIT	withdrawal option
FACULTÉ DE DISCERNEMENT	power of discernment
FACULTÉ DE RACHAT	right of redemption
FACULTÉ DE RÉMÉRÉ	right of redemption
FAIT	fact(<)
FAIT AUTONOME DE LA CHOSE	autonomous act of a thing

FAIT D'AUTRUI	act of another
FAIT DE LA CHOSE	act of a thing
FAIT DE L'ANIMAL	act of an animal
FAIT DES BIENS	act of a thing
FAIT DES CHOSES INANIMÉES	[*]
FAIT DES PRODUITS	[*]
FAIT DU BÂTIMENT	[*]
FAIT DU PRINCE	act of state[+], *fait du prince*
FAIT JURIDIQUE[1]	act[3], juridical fact[1+]
FAIT JURIDIQUE[2]	juridical fact[2]
FAIT MATÉRIEL	material fact
FAIT PERSONNEL	personal act or omission
FAUSSE CAUSE	false cause
FAUTE[1]	fault[1+], wrong[1]
FAUTE[2]	civil fault[+], fault[2]
FAUTE CAUSALE	causal fault
FAUTE CIVILE	civil fault[+], fault[2]
FAUTE COLLECTIVE	collective fault
FAUTE COMMUNE	common fault[+], common offence
FAUTE CONTRACTUELLE	contractual fault
FAUTE CONTRIBUTOIRE	contributory fault
FAUTE D'ABSTENTION	*culpa in non faciendo, culpa in omittendo*, fault of omission[+]
FAUTE D'ACTION	*culpa in committendo, culpa in faciendo*, fault of commission[+]
FAUTE DANS LA GARDE	custodial fault
FAUTE DANS LA SURVEILLANCE	fault of supervision
FAUTE DANS L'ÉDUCATION	fault in the education
FAUTE DE COMMISSION	*culpa in committendo, culpa in faciendo*, fault of commission[+]
FAUTE DE LA VICTIME	fault of the victim
FAUTE DÉLICTUELLE	delictual fault
FAUTE DE NÉGLIGENCE	fault of negligence, negligence[+], neglect
FAUTE D'IMPRUDENCE	fault of imprudence, imprudence[+]
FAUTE DOLOSIVE	fraud[2]
FAUTE D'OMISSION	*culpa in non faciendo, culpa in omittendo*, fault of omission[+]
FAUTE EXCLUSIVE	exclusive fault
FAUTE EXTRACONTRACTUELLE	extracontractual fault
FAUTE INDIVIDUELLE	individual fault
FAUTE INTENTIONNELLE	intentional fault[+], voluntary fault
FAUTE INVOLONTAIRE	involuntary fault, non-intentional fault[+]
FAUTE LÉGÈRE	*culpa levis*[+], slight fault
FAUTE LOURDE	*culpa lata*, gross fault[+]

FAUTE NON DOLOSIVE	[*]
FAUTE NON INTENTIONNELLE	involuntary fault, non-intentional fault+
FAUTE OBJECTIVE	objective fault
FAUTE PERSONNELLE	personal fault
FAUTE PRÉCONTRACTUELLE	*culpa in contrahendo*², precontractual fault+
FAUTE PROFESSIONNELLE	professional fault
FAUTE QUASI DÉLICTUELLE	quasi-delictual fault+, quasi-delictual offense
FAUTE SIMULTANÉE	simultaneous fault
FAUTES SUCCESSIVES	successive faults
FAUTE SUBJECTIVE	subjective fault
FAUTE TRÈS LÉGÈRE	*culpa levissima*
FAUTE VOLONTAIRE	intentional fault+, voluntary fault
FAUTIF, IVE¹ *adj.*	at fault
FAUTIF, IVE² *adj.*	wrongful
FAUTIF, IVE *n.*	wrongdoer
FAUX, FAUSSE	false
FICTIF, IVE	fictitious
FIDÉJUSSEUR, EURE	guarantor, surety+
FONDS DE COMMERCE	stock-in-trade
FORCE EXÉCUTOIRE	executory effect
FORCE MAJEURE¹	*force majeure*¹, superior force¹+
FORCE MAJEURE²	*force majeure*², superior force²+
FORCE OBLIGATOIRE DU CONTRAT	binding force of contract
FORFAIT	fixed price
FORFAITAIRE	[*]
FORMALISME	formalism
FORMALISTE	formalistic
FORMALITÉ	form¹, formality+
FORMALITÉ *AD HABILITATEM*	enabling form, formality *ad habilitatem*+
FORMALITÉ *AD PROBATIONEM*	evidentiary form, evidentiary formality+, formality *ad probationem*, probative form, probatory form, probatory formality
FORMALITÉ *AD SOLEMNITATEM*	essential formality+, formality *ad solemnitatem*, solemn form, solemnity
FORMALITÉ DE PUBLICITÉ	formality as to publicity+, formality of publication, publication formality
FORMALITÉ HABILITANTE	enabling form, formality *ad habilitatem*+
FORMALITÉ PROBATOIRE	evidentiary form, evidentiary formality+, formality *ad probationem*, probative form, probatory form, probatory formality
FORMALITÉ SUBSTANTIELLE	essential formality+, formality *ad solemnitatem*, solemn form, solemnity
FORME¹	form¹, formality+
FORME²	form²
FORME HABILITANTE	enabling form, formality *ad habilitatem*+

FORME PROBANTE	evidentiary form, evidentiary formality[+], formality *ad probationem*, probative form, probatory form, probatory formality
FORME PROBATOIRE	evidentiary form, evidentiary formality[+], formality *ad probationem*, probative form, probatory form, probatory formality
FORME SOLENNELLE	essential formality[+], formality *ad solemnitatem*, solemn form, solemnity
FOURNIR ET FAIRE VALOIR	*fournir et faire valoir*
FRANC ET QUITTE	*franc et quitte*, free and clear[+]
FRAUDE[1]	*dolus malus*, fraud[1+]
FRAUDE[2]	fraud[2]
FRAUDE PAULIENNE	paulian fraud
FRAUDER	defraud
FRAUDULEUX, EUSE	fraudulent
FRAUDULEUSEMENT	fraudulently
FRET[1]	freight[1]
FRET[2]	freight[2]
FRET[3]	freight[3]
FRÉTEUR	lessor[4]

G

GAGE COMMUN DES CRÉANCIERS	common pledge of creditors
GAIN	profit
GAIN MANQUÉ	*lucrum cessans*, profit deprived[+]
GARANT	warrantor
GARANTI, IE *n.* et *adj.*	warrantee
GARANTIE *n.f.*	warranty
GARANTIE CONTRACTUELLE	conventional warranty
GARANTIE CONVENTIONNELLE	conventional warranty
GARANTIE DE FOURNIR ET FAIRE VALOIR	guarantee of payment, warranty of payment[+]
GARANTIE DES DÉFAUTS CACHÉS	warranty against latent defects
GARANTIE DES VICES CACHÉS	warranty against latent defects
GARANTIE DU FAIT DES TIERS	warranty against acts of third persons
GARANTIE DU FAIT PERSONNEL	warranty against personal acts
GARANTIE LÉGALE	legal warranty
GARANTIR	warrant
GARDE	care, custody[+], juridical custody[2], legal custody[2]
GARDE ALTERNATIVE	alternate custody
GARDE COLLECTIVE	collective custody, cumulative custody[+], joint custody

GARDE CONJOINTE	collective custody, cumulative custody[+], joint custody
GARDE CUMULATIVE	collective custody, cumulative custody[+], joint custody
GARDE DE FAIT	custody *de facto*, custody in fact, *de facto* custody[+]
GARDE DE (LA) STRUCTURE	custody of the structure (of the thing)[+], *garde de la structure*
GARDE DU COMPORTEMENT	custody of the activity (of the thing)[+], *garde du comportement*
GARDE JURIDIQUE[1]	juridical custody[1], legal custody[1+]
GARDE JURIDIQUE[2]	care, custody[+], juridical custody[2], legal custody[2]
GARDE MATÉRIELLE	physical custody
GARDE PARTAGÉE	shared custody
GARDE PHYSIQUE	physical custody
GARDIEN, IENNE	custodian[+], guardian
GÉRANT, ANTE[1]	manager[+], *negotiorum gestor*
GÉRANT, ANTE[2]	general partner
GÉRÉ, ÉE	principal[4]
GESTION D'AFFAIRE(S)	management of the affairs of another, management of the business of another[+], *negotiorum gestio*
GRÉ À GRÉ (DE)	*gré à gré (de)*

H

HABILITER[1]	habilitate[1]
HABILITER[2]	habilitate[2]

I

ILLÉGAL, ALE[1]	illegal[1]
ILLÉGAL, ALE[2]	illegal[2], illicit[+], unlawful[1]
ILLÉGALEMENT	unlawfully
ILLÉGALITÉ[1]	illegality[1]
ILLÉGALITÉ[2]	illegality[2], illicitness[+]
ILLÉGITIME[1]	illegitimate[1]
ILLÉGITIME[2]	illegitimate[2+], unlawful[2]
ILLÉGITIME[3]	illegitimate[3]
ILLÉGITIMITÉ[1]	illegitimacy[1]
ILLÉGITIMITÉ[2]	illegitimacy[2]

ILLÉGITIMITÉ[3]	illegimacy[3]
ILLICÉITÉ	illegality[2], illicitness[+]
ILLICITE	illegal[2], illicit[+], unlawful[1]
IMPARFAIT, AITE	imperfect
IMPOSSIBILITÉ D'EXÉCUTION	impossibility of performance
IMPOSSIBLE	impossible
IMPRÉVISIBILITÉ	unforeseeability[1]
IMPRÉVISIBLE	unforeseeable
IMPRÉVISION	*imprévision*, unforeseeability[2+]
IMPRÉVU, UE	unforeseen
IMPRUDENCE	fault of imprudence, imprudence[+]
IMPRUDENT, ENTE	imprudent
IMPUTABILITÉ[1]	imputability[1+], moral imputability, psychological imputability
IMPUTABILITÉ[2]	imputability[2+], material imputability
IMPUTABILITÉ MATÉRIELLE	imputability[2+], material imputability
IMPUTABILITÉ MORALE	imputability[1+], moral imputability, psychological imputability
IMPUTABILITÉ PSYCHOLOGIQUE	imputability[1+], moral imputability, psychological imputability
IMPUTABLE[1]	imputable[1]
IMPUTABLE[2]	imputable[2]
IMPUTATION DES PAIEMENTS	imputation of payment
IMPUTER[1]	impute[1]
IMPUTER[2]	impute[2]
IMPUTER[3]	impute[3]
IN ABSTRACTO	*in abstracto*
INALIÉNABILITÉ	inalienability
INALIÉNABLE	inalienable
INAPTE	incapable[2+], unable
INAPTITUDE	*de facto* incapacity[+], factual incapacity, inability, incapacity[2], natural incapacity
INCAPABLE[1]	incapable[1+], incapable person[1+]
INCAPABLE[2]	incapable[2+], unable
INCAPACITÉ[1]	incapacity[1], juridical incapacity, legal incapacity[+]
INCAPACITÉ[2]	*de facto* incapacity[+], factual incapacity, inability, incapacity[2], natural incapacity
INCAPACITÉ D'ACQUISITION	incapacity to acquire (rights), incapacity to enjoy (rights)[+]
INCAPACITÉ DE DÉFIANCE	incapacity of public order
INCAPACITÉ DE DROIT	incapacity[1], juridical incapacity, legal incapacity[+]
INCAPACITÉ DE FAIT	*de facto* incapacity[+], factual incapacity, inability, incapacity[2], natural incapacity
INCAPACITÉ DE JOUISSANCE	incapacity to acquire (rights), incapacity to enjoy (rights)[+]

INCAPACITÉ DE PROTECTION	incapacity of protection
INCAPACITÉ D'EXERCICE	incapacity to exercise (rights)
INCAPACITÉ D'ORDRE PUBLIC	incapacity of public order
INCAPACITÉ GÉNÉRALE	general incapacity[+], total incapacity
INCAPACITÉ JURIDIQUE	incapacity[1], juridical incapacity, legal incapacity[+]
INCAPACITÉ LÉGALE	incapacity[1], juridical incapacity, legal incapacity[+]
INCAPACITÉ NATURELLE	*de facto* incapacity[+], factual incapacity, inability, incapacity[2], natural incapacity
INCAPACITÉ PARTIELLE	partial incapacity, special incapacity[+]
INCAPACITÉ SPÉCIALE	partial incapacity, special incapacity[+]
INCAPACITÉ TOTALE	general incapacity[+], total incapacity
INCERTAIN, AINE	uncertain
INCESSIBILITÉ	non-assignability[+], unassignability
INCESSIBLE	non-assignable[+], unassignable
IN CONCRETO	*in concreto*
INCONNU, UE	unspecified
IN CORPORE	*in corpore*
INDEMNISABLE	indemnifiable
INDEMNISATION	compensation[2], indemnification, reparation by equivalence[+]
INDEMNISER	indemnify
INDEMNITAIRE	indemnificatory
INDEMNITÉ	compensation[4], indemnity[+], reparation[2]
INDEMNITÉ ADDITIONNELLE[1]	additional indemnity[1]
INDEMNITÉ ADDITIONNELLE[2]	additional damages[1+], additional indemnity[2]
INDEXATION	indexation
INDEXER	index
INDICATION DE PAIEMENT	indication of payment
INDIRECT	indirect
INDISPONIBILITÉ[1]	undisposability
INDISPONIBILITÉ[2]	unavailability
INDISPONIBLE[1]	undisposable
INDISPONIBLE[2]	unavailable
INDIVISIBILITÉ	indivisibility
INDIVISIBILITÉ ACCIDENTELLE	accidental indivisibility, artificial indivisibility, contractual indivisibility, conventional indivisibility[+], subjective indivisibility
INDIVISIBILITÉ ACTIVE	active indivisibility
INDIVISIBILITÉ ARTIFICIELLE	accidental indivisibility, artificial indivisibility, contractual indivisibility, conventional indivisibility[+], subjective indivisibility
INDIVISIBILITÉ CONVENTIONNELLE	accidental indivisibility, artificial indivisibility, contractual indivisibility, conventional indivisibility[+], subjective indivisibility

INDIVISIBILITÉ DE PAIEMENT	accidental indivisibility, artificial indivisibility, contractual indivisibility, conventional indivisibility[+], subjective indivisibility
INDIVISIBILITÉ DU PAIEMENT	indivisibility of payment
INDIVISIBILITÉ NATURELLE	natural indivisibility[+], objective indivisibility, real indivisibility, true indivisibility
INDIVISIBILITÉ OBJECTIVE	natural indivisibility[+], objective indivisibility, real indivisibility, true indivisibility
INDIVISIBILITÉ PASSIVE	passive indivisibility
INDIVISIBILITÉ RÉELLE	natural indivisibility[+], objective indivisibility, real indivisibility, true indivisibility
INDIVISIBILITÉ SUBJECTIVE	accidental indivisibility, artificial indivisibility, contractual indivisibility, conventional indivisibility[+], subjective indivisibility
INDIVISIBILITÉ VÉRITABLE	natural indivisibility[+], objective indivisibility, real indivisibility, true indivisibility
INDIVISIBLE	indivisible
INDU, UE	[*]
INDU	thing not due
INEXÉCUTION	default in performance, inexecution, non-fulfilment, non-performance[+]
INEXÉCUTION DU CONTRAT	non-performance of the contract
INEXISTENCE	inexistence, non-existence[+]
INGRATITUDE	ingratitude
IN INTEGRUM	*in integrum*
INITIAL, ALE	initial
INJURE	slander
INNOMMÉ, ÉE ou INNOMÉ, ÉE	innominate
INOPPOSABILITÉ	inopposability
INOPPOSABLE	inopposable
INSAISISSABILITÉ	exemption from seizure, unseizability[+]
INSAISISSABLE	unseizable[+], exempt from seizure
IN SOLIDUM	*in solidum*
INSTITUTEUR, TRICE	schoolteachers
INSTITUTION D'HÉRITIER	appointment of (an) heir
INSTRUMENTUM	act[2], *acte*, attesting deed[+], deed[1], *instrumentum*, title[2]
INTÉGRAL, ALE	full
INTÉGRITÉ DU CONSENTEMENT	integrity of consent
INTENSITÉ DE L'OBLIGATION	intensity of the obligation
INTENTION	intent, intention[+], will
INTENTION COMMUNE	common intention
INTENTION LIBÉRALE	liberal intention
INTENTION NOVATOIRE	*animus novandi*[+], novatory intention
INTÉRÊT	interest

INTÉRÊT À ÉCHOIR	accrue interest (to)
INTÉRÊT COMPOSÉ	compound interest
INTÉRÊT CONVENTIONNEL	conventional interest
INTÉRÊT ÉCHU	accrued interest[+], interest owing
INTÉRÊT GÉNÉRAL	general interest
INTÉRÊT LÉGAL	legal interest
INTÉRÊT PARTICULIER	individual interest
INTÉRÊT SIMPLE	simple interest
INTÉRÊT USURAIRE	usurious interest
INTERPOSITION DE PERSONNES	interposition of persons
INTER VIVOS	inter vivos
INTRANSMISSIBILITÉ	intransmissibility
INTRANSMISSIBLE	intransmissible
INTUITUS PERSONÆ	*intuitus personæ*
INVALIDE	invalid
INVALIDER	invalidate
INVALIDITÉ	invalidity
INVITATION À CONTRACTER	invitation to contract, invitation to treat[+]
IRRÉCOUVRABLE	irrecoverable
IRRÉSISTIBILITÉ	irresistibility
IRRESPONSABLE *adj.*	[*]
IRRESPONSABLE *n.*	non-responsible
IRRÉVOCABLE	irrevocable

J

JEU	gaming contract
JOUIR	enjoy
JOUISSANCE	enjoyment[+], right of enjoyment
JURIDICITÉ	juridicity
JURIDIQUE *n.m.*	[*]
JURIDIQUE[1] *adj.*	jural, juridical[1], juristic, legal[2+]
JURIDIQUE[2] *adj.*	juridical[2], legal[6+]
JURIDIQUE[3] *adj.*	juridical[3], legal[4+]
JURISPRUDENCE[1]	jurisprudence[1+], case law[1]
JURISPRUDENCE[2]	jurisprudence[2+], case law[2]
JURISPRUDENCE[3]	jurisprudence[3]
JURISPRUDENTIEL, IELLE	jurisprudential
JUS[1]	*jus[1]*, law[1+]
JUS[2]	*jus[2]*, right[+]

JUS AD REM	*jus ad rem*
JUS AD REM TRANS PERSONAM	*jus ad rem trans personam*+, mixed right
JUS COGENS	imperative law+, *jus cogens*
JUS COMMUNE	common law[1], *droit commun*, general law+, ordinary law, *jus commune*
JUS DISPOSITIVUM	*jus dispositivum*, suppletive law[1]+
JUS IN PERSONAM	claim, creance, credit[2], debt[2], *jus in personam*, obligation[4], personal right+
JUS IN RE	*jus in re*, real right+
JUSTE[1]	just[1]
JUSTE[2]	just[2]
JUSTE TITRE[1]	lawful title
JUSTE TITRE[2]	*juste titre*+, justificatory title
JUSTICE[1]	justice[1]
JUSTICE[2]	justice[2]
JUSTICE COMMUTATIVE	corrective justice
JUSTICE CORRECTIVE	corrective justice
JUSTICE DISTRIBUTIVE	distributive justice
JUSTICE NATURELLE	natural justice<

L

LEASING	[*]
LÉGAL, ALE[1]	legal[1](>)
LÉGAL, ALE[2]	juridical[3], legal[4]+
LÉGAL, ALE[3]	legal[3]
LÉGAL, ALE[4]	extracontractual+, legal[5]
LÉGALEMENT	lawfully
LÉGALITÉ	legality
LÉGITIME[1]	legitimate[1]
LÉGITIME[2]	illégitime[2], légal[3]
LÉGITIME[3]	legitimate[3]
LÉGITIMITÉ[1]	legitimacy[1]
LÉGITIMITÉ[2]	legitimacy[2]
LÉGITIMITÉ[3]	legitimate[3]
LÉSER	[*]
LÉSION	lesion
LÉSION MIXTE	mixed lesion
LÉSIONNAIRE	lesionary
LÉSION OBJECTIVE	objective lesion
LÉSION SUBJECTIVE	subjective lesion

LETTRE D'INTENTION	letter of intention
LEVÉE D'OPTION	exercise of an option
LEVER UNE OPTION	exercise of an option
LIBELLE	libel
LIBÉRALITÉ[1]	liberality[1]
LIBÉRALITÉ[2]	liberality[2]
LIBÉRATION[1]	discharge[3+], release[2]
LIBÉRATION[2]	discharge[4]
LIBÉRATION[3]	discharge[5+], release[3]
LIBÉRATION DU DÉBITEUR	discharge of the debtor
LIBÉRATOIRE	discharging, liberating[+], liberative, liberatory
LIBÉRÉ, ÉE	discharged[+], freed
LIBÉRER	discharge[+], relieve
LIBERTÉ CONTRACTUELLE	contractual freedom, freedom of contract[+]
LICÉITÉ	lawfulness, licitness[+]
LICITE	lawful[1], licit[+]
LIEN CAUSAL	[*]
LIEN DE CAUSALITÉ	causality[2], causal relation, causation[2+], causation in law, juridical causation
LIEN DE PRÉPOSITION	subordination (relationship of)
LIMITATIF, IVE	limiting
LIMITATION	limitation
LIQUIDATION[1]	liquidation[1]
LIQUIDATION[2]	liquidation[2]
LIQUIDE	liquid, liquidated
LIQUIDÉ, ÉE	liquidated
LIQUIDITÉ	liquidity
LIVRAISON	delivery[2]
LIVRER	deliver[2]
LOCATAIRE	lessee[1]
LOCATAIRE D'OUVRAGE	lessee of work
LOCATEUR, TRICE	lessor[1]
LOCATEUR D'OUVRAGE	lessor of work
LOCATIF, IVE	rental
LOCATION[1]	[*]
LOCATION[2]	contract of lease, lease[1+], lease of things
LOI[1]	law [2]
LOI[2]	statute
LOI[3]	juridical precept, juridical rule, law[3], legal norm, legal rule[+]
LOI GÉNÉRALE	common law[1], *droit commun*, general law[+], *jus commune*, ordinary law
LOUAGE	contract of lease, lease[1+], lease of things

LOUAGE DE CHOSES	contract of lease, lease[1+], lease of things
LOUAGE DE SERVICES	[*]
LOUAGE DE SERVICE(S) PERSONNEL(S)	[*]
LOUAGE D'OUVRAGE	lease and hire of work
LOUER[1]	lease[1+], rent[1]
LOUER[2]	lease[2+], rent[2]
LOYER	rent[1]
LUCRUM CESSANS	*lucrum cessans*, profit deprived[+]

M

MAINLEVÉE	*mainlevée*[+], release[4](<)
MAÎTRE DE L'AFFAIRE	principal[3]
MAÎTRE DE L'OUVRAGE	client[2]
MANDANT, ANTE	mandator
MANDAT[1]	contract of mandate, mandate[1+]
MANDAT[2]	mandate[2]
MANDAT *AD LITEM*	*ad litem* mandate
MANDATAIRE	attorney, mandatary[+]
MANDATAIRE PRINCIPAL	principal mandatary, sub-mandator[+]
MANDAT APPARENT	apparent mandate
MANDAT CLANDESTIN	agreement to act as nominee, clandestine mandate, contract of *prête-nom*[+], *prête-nom*[2], secret mandate
MANDAT CONÇU EN TERMES GÉNÉRAUX	mandate expressed in general terms[+], mandate given in general terms
MANDAT CONVENTIONNEL	conventional mandate, power of attorney[1+], procuration[1]
MANDAT DISSIMULÉ	agreement to act as nominee, clandestine mandate, contract of *prête-nom*[+], *prête-nom*[2], secret mandate
MANDAT DOUBLE	double mandate
MANDAT EXPRÈS[1]	express mandate[1]
MANDAT EXPRÈS[2]	express mandate[2]
MANDAT EXPRIMÉ EN TERMES GÉNÉRAUX	mandate expressed in general terms[+], mandate given in general terms
MANDAT GÉNÉRAL	general mandate
MANDAT JUDICIAIRE	judicial mandate
MANDAT LÉGAL	legal mandate
MANDAT SEMI-CLANDESTIN	semi-clandestine mandate
MANDAT SPÉCIAL	special mandate

MANDAT TACITE	tacit mandate
MANIFESTATION DE VOLONTÉ EXPRESSE	explicit consent, express consent[+], express manifestation of intent, express manifestation of will
MANIFESTATION DE VOLONTÉ TACITE	implicit consent, implied consent, tacit consent[+], tacit manifestation of intent, tacit manifestation of will
MANŒUVRE DOLOSIVE	fraudulent artifices
MANŒUVRE FRAUDULEUSE	fraudulent artifices
MANQUE À GAGNER	*lucrum cessans*, profit deprived[+]
MARCHÉ À FORFAIT	fixed price contract[+], lump sum contract
MARC LA LIVRE (AU)	contribution (by), *pro rata*, rateably[+]
MAUVAISE FOI[1]	bad faith[1]
MAUVAISE FOI[2]	bad faith[2]
MEMBRE[1]	member[1]
MEMBRE[2]	member[2]
MENACE	threat
MENSUALITÉ	monthly payment
MINUTE	act *en minute*, notarial act *en minute*[+], *minute*
MISE COMMUNE	contribution (to the partnership)
MISE EN DEMEURE[1]	putting in default
MISE EN DEMEURE[2]	demand letter, formal notice, *mise en demeure*, notice of default[+]
MISE SOCIALE	contribution (to the partnership)
MOBILE *adj.*	sliding
MOBILE *n.m.*	cause[2+], cause of the contract, concrete cause, consideration[2], motive, principal consideration, subjective cause
MODAL, ALE	modal
MODALITÉ	modality
MODALITÉ DE L'OBLIGATION	modality of the obligation
MODALITÉ DE PAIEMENT	condition of payment, modality of payment[+]
MONÉTAIRE	monetary
MORAL, ALE	moral
MORATOIRE	moratory
MORTIS CAUSA	contemplation of death (in)[+], *mortis causa*
MOTIF	cause[2+], cause of the contract, concrete cause, consideration[2], motive, principal consideration, subjective cause
MULTILATÉRAL, ALE	multilateral
MUTATION	conveyance[2](>), transfer(>)[+]
MUTUUM	loan for consumption, *mutuum*, simple loan[+]

N

NÉGATIF, IVE	negative
NÉGLIGENCE	fault of negligence, negligence+, neglect
NÉGLIGENCE GROSSIÈRE	gross negligence
NÉGOCIATION	[*]
NEGOTIORUM GESTIO	management of the affairs of another, management of the business of another+, *negotiorum gestio*
NEGOTIORUM GESTOR	manager+, *negotiorum gestor*
NEGOTIUM	act[1], juridical act+, *negotium,* title[2]
NOMMÉ, ÉE	nominate
NON ADIMPLETI CONTRACTUS	*non adimpleti contractus*
NON EXCLUSIF, IVE	non-exclusive
NON INTENTIONNEL, ELLE	non-intentional
NON RESPONSABLE	[*]
NON-RESPONSABLE	[*]
NORME JURIDIQUE	juridical precept, juridical rule, law[3], legal norm, legal rule+
NOTIFICATION	notice
NOTIFIER	notify
NOVATION	novation
NOVATION PAR CHANGEMENT DE CRÉANCIER	novation by change of creditor
NOVATION PAR CHANGEMENT DE DÉBITEUR	novation by change of debtor
NOVATION PAR CHANGEMENT DE DETTE	novation by change of debt
NOVATOIRE	novative, novatory+
NOVER	novate
NOVUS ACTUS INTERVENIENS	*novus actus interveniens*
NUISANCE	nuisance
NUL, NULLE	null
NULLITÉ	nullity
NULLITÉ *AB INITIO*	nullity *ab initio*
NULLITÉ ABSOLUE	absolute nullity
NULLITÉ DE PLEIN DROIT	nullity *pleno jure*
NULLITÉ EXPRESSE	express nullity, textual nullity+
NULLITÉ RADICALE	radical nullity
NULLITÉ RELATIVE	relative nullity
NULLITÉ TACITE	tacit nullity
NULLITÉ TEXTUELLE	express nullity, textual nullity+

NULLITÉ VIRTUELLE	tacit nullity
NUMÉRAIRE	cash[+], *specie*

O

OBJECTIF, IVE	objective
OBJET DE LA PRESTATION	object of the prestation
OBJET DE L'OBLIGATION	object of the obligation, prestation[+], thing[2]
OBJET DÉTERMINABLE	determinable object
OBJET DÉTERMINÉ	determinate object
OBJET DU CONTRAT	object of the contract
OBJET ILLICITE[1]	illicit object[1]
OBJET ILLICITE[2]	illicit object[2]
OBJET IMPOSSIBLE	impossible object
OBJET LICITE[1]	licit object[1]
OBJET LICITE[2]	licit object[2]
OBJET POSSIBLE	possible object
OBLIGATION[1]	duty[+], obligation[1]
OBLIGATION[2]	juridical obligation[1], obligation[2+], perfect obligation, personal obligation
OBLIGATION[3]	charge, debt[1], juridical duty, juridical obligation[2], legal duty, liability[2], obligation[3+]
OBLIGATION[4]	claim, creance, credit[2], debt[2], *jus in personam,* obligation[4], personal right[+]
OBLIGATION ABSOLUE	absolute obligation, obligation of result[+]
OBLIGATION À LA DETTE	obligation for the debt
OBLIGATION ALIMENTAIRE[1]	obligation of support[1]
OBLIGATION ALIMENTAIRE[2]	debt for support, obligation of support[2+]
OBLIGATION ALTERNATIVE	alternative obligation
OBLIGATION À MODALITÉ	complex obligation[+], obligation with a modality
OBLIGATION À MODALITÉ COMPLEXE	obligation with a complex modality[+], plural obligation
OBLIGATION À MODALITÉ SIMPLE	obligation with a simple modality
OBLIGATION À TERME	obligation with a term[+], term obligation
OBLIGATION CIVILE	civil obligation
OBLIGATION COMPLEXE	complex obligation[+], obligation with a modality
OBLIGATION CONDITIONNELLE	conditional obligation
OBLIGATION CONJOINTE	joint obligation
OBLIGATION CONJONCTIVE	conjunctive obligation
OBLIGATION CONTINUE	continuous obligation[+], obligation of successive performance, successive obligation
OBLIGATION CONTRACTUELLE	contractual obligation[+], conventional obligation

OBLIGATION CORRÉLATIVE	correlative obligation
OBLIGATION DE COLLABORATION	duty to collaborate, duty to cooperate[+]
OBLIGATION DE CONFIDENTIALITÉ	duty of confidentiality[+], obligation of confidentiality
OBLIGATION DE CONSEIL	obligation to advise[+], obligation to (provide) counsel
OBLIGATION DE COOPÉRATION	duty to collaborate, duty to cooperate[+]
OBLIGATION DE DILIGENCE	general obligation of prudence and diligence, obligation of diligence, obligation of means[+], relative obligation
OBLIGATION DE DONNER	obligation to give
OBLIGATION DE FAIRE	obligation to do
OBLIGATION DE GARANTIE	obligation of warranty
OBLIGATION DÉLICTUELLE	delictual obligation
OBLIGATION DE LOYAUTÉ	obligation of loyalty[+], obligation to act faithfully
OBLIGATION DE MOYENS	general obligation of prudence and diligence, obligation of diligence, obligation of means[+], relative obligation
OBLIGATION DE NE PAS FAIRE	obligation not to do
OBLIGATION DE NON-CONCURRENCE	obligation of non-competition[+], obligation not to compete
OBLIGATION DE RENSEIGNEMENT(S)	duty to inform, obligation to inform[+]
OBLIGATION DE RENSEIGNER	duty to inform, obligation to inform[+]
OBLIGATION DE RÉSULTAT	absolute obligation, obligation of result[+]
OBLIGATION DE SOMME D'ARGENT	monetary obligation, pecuniary obligation[+]
OBLIGATION DÉTERMINÉE	absolute obligation, obligation of result[+]
OBLIGATION D'INFORMATION	duty to inform, obligation to inform[+]
OBLIGATION DIVISIBLE	divisible obligation
OBLIGATION EN NATURE	obligation in kind
OBLIGATION EXPRESSE	express obligation
OBLIGATION EXTRA-CONTRACTUELLE	extracontractual obligation[+], non-consensual obligation
OBLIGATION FACULTATIVE	facultative obligation
OBLIGATION GÉNÉRALE DE PRUDENCE ET DILIGENCE	general obligation of prudence and diligence, obligation of diligence, obligation of means[+], relative obligation
OBLIGATION IMPARFAITE	duty of conscience, imperfect obligation, moral duty, moral obligation[+]
OBLIGATION IMPLICITE	implicit obligation[+], implied obligation
OBLIGATION INDIVISIBLE	indivisible obligation
OBLIGATION *IN SOLIDUM*	imperfect solidarity, *in solidum* obligation, obligation *in solidum*[+]
OBLIGATION INSTANTANÉE	instantaneous obligation[+], obligation of instantaneous performance
OBLIGATION JURIDIQUE[1]	juridical obligation[1], obligation[2+], perfect obligation, personal obligation

OBLIGATION JURIDIQUE[2]	charge, debt[1], juridical duty, juridical obligation[2], legal duty, liability[2], obligation[3+]
OBLIGATION LÉGALE[1]	legal obligation[1]
OBLIGATION LÉGALE[2]	legal obligation[2]
OBLIGATION LÉGALE[3]	legal obligation[3]
OBLIGATION MODALE	complex obligation[+], obligation with a modality
OBLIGATION MONÉTAIRE	monetary obligation, pecuniary obligation[+]
OBLIGATION MORALE	duty of conscience, imperfect obligation, moral duty, moral obligation[+]
OBLIGATION NATURELLE	natural obligation
OBLIGATIONNEL, ELLE	obligational
OBLIGATION PARFAITE	juridical obligation[1], obligation[2+], perfect obligation, personal obligation
OBLIGATION PÉCUNIAIRE	monetary obligation, pecuniary obligation[+]
OBLIGATION PERSONNELLE	juridical obligation[1], obligation[2+], perfect obligation, personal obligation
OBLIGATION PLURALE	obligation with a complex modality[+], plural obligation
OBLIGATION PRÉCONTRACTUELLE	precontractual obligation
OBLIGATION PRÉCONTRACTUELLE DE RENSEIGNEMENT(S)	precontractual obligation to inform
OBLIGATION *PROPTER REM*	obligation *propter rem*, real obligation[+]
OBLIGATION PURE ET SIMPLE	pure and simple obligation[+], simple obligation
OBLIGATION QUASI CONTRACTUELLE	quasi-contractual obligation
OBLIGATION QUASI DÉLICTUELLE	quasi-delictual obligation
OBLIGATION RÉCIPROQUE	mutual obligation, reciprocal obligation[+]
OBLIGATION RÉELLE	obligation *propter rem*, real obligation[+]
OBLIGATION RELATIVE	general obligation of prudence and diligence, obligation of diligence, obligation of means[+], relative obligation
OBLIGATIONS	law of obligations[+], obligations
OBLIGATION SIMPLE	pure and simple obligation[+], simple obligation
OBLIGATION SOLIDAIRE	solidary obligation
OBLIGATION SOUS CONDITION	conditional obligation
OBLIGATION (À EXÉCUTION) SUCCESSIVE	continuous obligation[+], obligation of successive performance, successive obligation
OBLIGATOIRE	binding[+], obligatory
OBLIGÉ, ÉE *adj.*	obliged
OBLIGÉ, ÉE *n.*	debtor[+], obligor
OBLIGER	bind[+], obligate, oblige
OBLIQUE	oblique
OFFRANT, ANTE	offeror
OFFRE	offer

OFFRE À (UNE) PERSONNE DÉTERMINÉE	offer to a determinate person[+], offer to a specified person
OFFRE À PERSONNE INDÉTERMINÉE	offer to an indeterminate person, offer to an unspecified person, offer to the public[+], public offer
OFFRE AU PUBLIC	offer to an indeterminate person, offer to an unspecified person, offer to the public[+], public offer
OFFRE DE RÉCOMPENSE	offer of reward[+], promise of reward
OFFRE EXCLUSIVE	exclusive offer
OFFRE EXPRESSE	express offer
OFFRE IMPLICITE	implied offer[+], tacit offer
OFFRE INITIALE	initial offer
OFFRE NON EXCLUSIVE	non-exclusive offer
OFFRE RÉELLE	actual tender, tender[+]
OFFRES ET CONSIGNATION	tender and deposit
OFFRE TACITE	implied offer[+], tacit offer
OMISSION	omission
OPPOSABILITÉ	opposability
OPPOSABLE	opposable
OPPOSER	oppose, set up[+]
OPTION	option
OPTION (ENTRE LES RÉGIMES)	option (between regimes)
OR	gold
ORDRE JURIDIQUE	juridical system, legal order[+], legal system, system of law
ORDRE PUBLIC	*jus publicum*, public order[+], public order and good morals
ORDRE PUBLIC ABSOLU	absolute public order, public order of direction[+]
ORDRE PUBLIC DE DIRECTION	absolute public order, public order of direction[+]
ORDRE PUBLIC DE PROTECTION	public order of protection[+], relative public order
ORDRE PUBLIC ÉCONOMIQUE	economic and social public order, economic public order[+]
ORDRE PUBLIC ÉCONOMIQUE ET SOCIAL	economic and social public order, economic public order[+]
ORDRE PUBLIC INTERNATIONAL[1]	international public order[1]
ORDRE PUBLIC INTERNATIONAL[2]	international public order[2]
ORDRE PUBLIC INTERNE	internal public order
ORDRE PUBLIC JUDICIAIRE	judicial public order[+], virtual public order
ORDRE PUBLIC LÉGISLATIF	legislative public order[+], textual public order
ORDRE PUBLIC MORAL	moral public order
ORDRE PUBLIC NATIONAL	domestic public order
ORDRE PUBLIC POLITIQUE	political and moral public order, political public order[+]
ORDRE PUBLIC POLITIQUE ET MORAL	political and moral public order, political public order[+]

ORDRE PUBLIC RELATIF	public order of protection[+], relative public order
ORDRE PUBLIC TEXTUEL	legislative public order[+], textual public order
ORDRE PUBLIC VIRTUEL	judicial public order[+], virtual public order
OSTENSIBLE	ostensible
OUVRAGE	work
OUVRIER, IÈRE *n.*	workman

P

PACTA SUNT SERVANDA	*pacta sunt servanda*
PACTE	agreement[1], contract[1+], covenant[1], pact, transaction[2]
PACTE COMMISSOIRE	clause of resolution of right, express clause of resolution, express resolutory clause, resolutory clause of right[+], stipulation of resolution upon non-performance
PACTE DE PRÉFÉRENCE	first refusal agreement[+], promise of first option
PAIEMENT[1]	acquittance[2], payment[1+]
PAIEMENT[2]	payment[2]
PAIEMENT ANTICIPÉ	advance payment[+], payment in advance
PAIEMENT À TERME	payment with (a) term
PAIEMENT AVEC SUBROGATION	payment with subrogation
PAIEMENT (AU) COMPTANT	cash payment[2]
PAIEMENT DE L'INDU	payment of a thing not due
PAIEMENT DIFFÉRÉ	deferred payment
PAIEMENT DIVISÉ	partial payment
PAIEMENT ÉCHELONNÉ	instalments, periodical payment, periodic payment[+]
PAIEMENT EN ESPÈCES	cash payment[1], payment in cash[+], payment in *specie*
PAIEMENT EN NATURE[1]	payment in kind[1], performance in kind, specific performance[+]
PAIEMENT EN NATURE[2]	payment in kind[2]
PAIEMENT FRACTIONNÉ	partial payment
PAIEMENT INDU	payment of a thing not due
PAIEMENT INTÉGRAL	full payment
PAIEMENT LIBÉRATOIRE	liberative payment, liberatory payment[+]
PAIEMENT PAR ANTICIPATION	advance payment[+], payment in advance
PAIEMENT PARTIEL	partial payment
PAIEMENT PÉRIODIQUE	instalments, periodical payment, periodic payment[+]
PAIEMENT UNIQUE	lump sum payment
PAR CONCURRENCE	contribution (by), *pro rata*, rateably[+]

PAR CONTRIBUTION	contribution (by), *pro rata*, rateably[+]
PARI	bet, betting, wager, wagering, wagering contract[+]
PARTIE CONTRACTANTE	contracting party
PASSAGER, ÈRE	passenger
PATRIMOINE	patrimony
PATRIMONIAL	patrimonial
PAULIEN, IENNE	paulian
PAYÉ, ÉE	accipiens[+], payee, *recipiens*
PAYEMENT	acquittance[2], payment[1+]
PAYER	acquit[1], pay[+], settle[1]
PAYEUR, EUSE	payer, *solvens*[+]
PÉCUNIAIRE	pecuniary
PEINE	penalty
PEINE PRIVÉE	private law penalty
PÉNAL, ALE	penal
PÉNALITÉ	pénalité
PENDENTE CONDITIONE	*pendente conditione*
PENITUS EXTRANEUS	*penitus extraneus*
PÉRIODE PRÉCONTRACTUELLE	precontractual period[+], precontractual stage
PERSONNE	juridical person, person[+]
PERSONNE INTERPOSÉE	interposed person[+], person interposed
PERSONNE JURIDIQUE	juridical person, person[1+]
PERSONNEL, ELLE	personal
PERSONNE RAISONNABLE	*bon père de famille, bonus pater familias,* reasonable man, reasonable person[+]
PERTE	*damnum emergens,* loss[1+]
PERTE DE (D'UNE) CHANCE	loss of (a) chance
PERTE DE LA CHOSE DUE	loss of a thing due
PERTE ÉCONOMIQUE	corporeal damage, economic loss, material damage[+], pecuniary damage
PERTE PUREMENT ÉCONOMIQUE	pure economic loss
PLEINE ADMINISTRATION	full administration
PLURAL, ALE	plural
PLURILATÉRAL, ALE	plurilateral
POLICE D'ASSURANCE	insurance policy
POLLICITANT, ANTE	offeror
POLLICITATION	offer
POLLICITÉ, ÉE	offeree
PORTABLE	portable
PORTE-FORT[1]	*porte-fort*[1], promise of *porte-fort*[+]
PORTE-FORT[2]	porte-fort[2+], promisor[3]
POTESTATIF, IVE	facultative, potestative[+]
POURPARLERS	negotiation

POUVOIR[1]	power[1]
POUVOIR[2]	power[2]
PRÉCEPTE JURIDIQUE	juridical precept, juridical rule, law[3], legal norm, legal rule[+]
PRÉCONTRACTUEL, ELLE	precontractual
PRÉDÉCESSEUR EN DROIT	author[1+], predecessor (in title)
PRÉDÉCESSEUR EN TITRE	author[1+], predecessor (in title)
PRÉEMPTER	preempt
PRÉEMPTEUR, EUSE	preemptor
PRÉEMPTION	preemption
PRÉFÉRENCE	*droit de préférence*, preference, right of preference[2+]
PRÉJUDICE	damage[+], harm, injury, loss[2], prejudice, wrong[2]
PRÉJUDICE ACTUEL	present damage
PRÉJUDICE CERTAIN	actual damage, certain damage[+]
PRÉJUDICE COLLECTIF	collective injury
PRÉJUDICE CONTINU	continuous damage
PRÉJUDICE CORPOREL	bodily injury[+], corporal damage
PRÉJUDICE D'AFFECTION	injury to feelings
PRÉJUDICE D'AGRÉMENT	loss of amenities
PRÉJUDICE DIRECT	direct damage
PRÉJUDICE ÉCONOMIQUE	corporeal damage, economic loss, material damage[+], pecuniary damage
PRÉJUDICE ESTHÉTIQUE	aesthetic damage
PRÉJUDICE ÉVENTUEL	eventual damage, hypothetical loss, possible damage[+]
PRÉJUDICE FUTUR	future damage
PRÉJUDICE GRADUEL	gradual damage
PRÉJUDICE HYPOTHÉTIQUE	eventual damage, hypothetical loss, possible damage[+]
PRÉJUDICE ILLICITE	illicit damage
PRÉJUDICE IMPRÉVISIBLE	inexécution, préjudice imprévu, préjudice prévisible, préjudice prévu
PRÉJUDICE IMPRÉVU	unforeseen damage
PRÉJUDICE INDIRECT	indirect damage
PRÉJUDICE INITIAL	initial damage
PRÉJUDICE LICITE	licit damage
PRÉJUDICE MATÉRIEL	corporeal damage, economic loss, material damage[+], pecuniary damage
PRÉJUDICE MORAL	moral damage[+], non-pecuniary damage
PRÉJUDICE NON PÉCUNIAIRE	moral damage[+], non-pecuniary damage
PRÉJUDICE PAR RICOCHET	rebounding damage, ricochet damage[+]
PRÉJUDICE PÉCUNIAIRE	corporeal damage, economic loss, material damage[+], pecuniary damage
PRÉJUDICE PÉRIODIQUE	periodic damage

PRÉJUDICE PERSONNEL	personal damage
PRÉJUDICE PRÉVISIBLE	foreseeable damage
PRÉJUDICE PRÉVU	foreseen damage
PRÉJUDICE PROGRESSIF	gradual damage
PRÉJUDICE PSYCHOLOGIQUE	psychological damage
PRÉJUDICE RÉCURRENT	recurrent damage
PRÉJUDICE RÉEL	actual damage, certain damage+
PRÉJUDICE RÉFLÉCHI	rebounding damage, ricochet damage+
PRENDRE DÉLIVRANCE	remove+, take delivery
PRENDRE LIVRAISON	remove+, take delivery
PRENEUR, EUSE[1]	client[1]+, applicant, policy holder (<), policy owner+ (<)
PRENEUR, EUSE[2]	lessee[2]
PRENEUR, EUSE[3]	lessee[1]+, tenant (<)
PRÉPOSÉ, ÉE	agent, agent and servant+
PRÉPOSÉ HABITUEL	habitual employee
PRÉPOSÉ OCCASIONNEL	occasional employee, temporary employee+
PRÉSOMPTION	presumption
PRESTATAIRE	prestator
PRESTATAIRE DE SERVICES	provider of services+, service provider
PRESTATION	object of the obligation, prestation+, thing[2]
PRESTER	[*]
PRÊT	contract of loan, loan+
PRÊT À INTÉRÊT	loan upon interest
PRÊT À USAGE	*commodatum*, loan for use+
PRÊT D'ARGENT	loan of money
PRÊT DE CONSOMMATION	loan for consumption, *mutuum*, simple loan+
PRÊTE-NOM[1]	nominee, *prête-nom*[1], undisclosed mandatary+
PRÊTE-NOM[2]	agreement to act as nominee, clandestine mandate, contract of *prête-nom*+, *prête-nom*[2], secret mandate
PRÊTER	lend
PRÊTEUR, EUSE	lender
PRETIUM AFFECTIONIS	*pretium affectionis*
PRETIUM DOLORIS	*pretium doloris*
PRÊT USURAIRE	usurious loan
PRÉVISIBILITÉ	foreseeability
PRÉVISIBLE	foreseeable
PRÉVU, UE	foreseen
PRIME	premium
PRINCIPAL, ALE	principal
PRINCIPAL[1]	principal[1]
PRINCIPAL[2]	capital+, capital sum, principal[2]

PRINCIPE[1]	juridical principle, legal principle, principle[1+]
PRINCIPE[2]	principle[2]
PRINCIPE DE LA RELATIVITÉ DES CONTRATS	principle of the relativity of contract
PRINCIPE DE L'EFFET RELATIF DES CONTRATS	principle of the relativity of contract
PRINCIPE JURIDIQUE	juridical principle, legal principle, principle[1+]
PRINCIPES	principles
PRINCIPES FONDAMENTAUX DU DROIT	general principles of law[+], fundamental principles of law, supereminent principles of law
PRINCIPES GÉNÉRAUX DU DROIT	fundamental principles of law, general principles of law[+], supereminent principles of law
PRIX	price
PRIX DE LOCATION	rent[1]
PROCURATION[1]	conventional mandate, power of attorney[1+], procuration[1]
PROCURATION[2]	power of attorney[2+], procuration[2]
PROCURATION GÉNÉRALE	general authorization, general power, general power of attorney[+], general procuration
PROCURATION SPÉCIALE	special authorization, special power, special power of attorney[+], special procuration
PROCUREUR, EURE	attorney, mandatary[+]
PROLONGATION[1]	extension[1], prolongation[1], prorogation[1+]
PROLONGATION[2]	extension[2], prolongation[2], prorogation[2+]
PROLONGER	extend[+], prorogue
PROMESSE (DE CONTRAT)	promise to contract
PROMESSE BILATÉRALE (DE CONTRAT)	bilateral promise (to contract)[+], synallagmatic promise (to contract)
PROMESSE BILATÉRALE DE VENTE	bilateral promise of sale[+], synallagmatic promise of sale
PROMESSE D'ACHAT	promise to purchase
PROMESSE DE CONTRACTER	promise to contract
PROMESSE DE PORTE-FORT	*porte-fort*[1], promise of *porte-fort*[+]
PROMESSE DE RÉCOMPENSE	offer of reward[+], promise of reward
PROMESSE DE VENTE	promise of sale
PROMESSE D'OFFRE PRÉALABLE	first refusal agreement[+], promise of first option
PROMESSE DU FAIT D'AUTRUI	*porte-fort*[1], promise of *porte-fort*[+]
PROMESSE POUR AUTRUI	promise for another
PROMESSE SYNALLAGMATIQUE (DE CONTRAT)	bilateral promise (to contract)[+], synallagmatic promise (to contract)
PROMESSE SYNALLAGMATIQUE DE VENTE	bilateral promise of sale[+], synallagmatic promise of sale
PROMESSE UNILATÉRALE (DE CONTRAT)	unilateral promise (to contract)
PROMESSE UNILATÉRALE DE VENTE	unilateral promise of sale
PROMETTANT, ANTE[1]	promisor[1]

PROMETTANT, ANTE[2]	promisor[2]
PROMETTANT, ANTE[3]	*porte-fort*[2+], promisor[3]
PROMETTANT ACHETEUR	promising buyer[+], promising purchaser
PROMETTANT VENDEUR	promising seller[+], promising vendor
PRO RATA	contribution (by), *pro rata*, rateably[+]
PROROGATION[1]	extension[1], prolongation[1], prorogation[1+]
PROROGATION[2]	extension[2], prolongation[2], prorogation[2+]
PROROGER	extend[+], prorogue
PROTOCOLE D'ENTENTE	agreement in principle[+], letter of understanding, memorandum of understanding, preliminary agreement
PRUDENCE	prudence
PUR ET SIMPLE	pure and simple[+], unconditional[1]

Q

QUALITÉ MARCHANDE	marketable quality, merchantable quality[+]
QUANTUM	*quantum*
QUANTUM MERUIT	*quantum meruit*
QUASI CONTRACTUEL, ELLE	quasi-contractual
QUASI-CONTRAT	quasi-contract
QUASI DÉLICTUEL, ELLE	quasi-delictual
QUASI-DÉLIT	quasi-delict[+], quasi-offence
QUASI EX CONTRACTU	*quasi ex contractu*
QUASI EX DELICTO	*quasi ex delicto*
QUÉRABLE	seekable
QUITTANCE[1]	acquittance[1+], discharge[6], quittance
QUITTANCE[2]	discharge[2+], receipt[3]
QUITTANCER	acquit[2]
QUITTANCE SUBROGATIVE	subrogation receipt, subrogatory acquittance[+]
QUITTANCE SUBROGATOIRE	subrogation receipt, subrogatory acquittance[+]
QUITTE[1]	quit(s)
QUITTE[2]	clear
QUITUS	discharge[1+], quit
QUOTITÉ	quantity

R

RAPPORT DE CAUSALITÉ	[*]

RAPPORT DE PRÉPOSITION	subordination (relationship of)
RATIFICATION[1]	ratification[1]
RATIFICATION[2]	confirmation[+], ratification[2]
RATIFIER[1]	ratify[1]
RATIFIER[2]	confirm[+], ratify[2]
RÉALISATION DE LA CONDITION	accomplishment of the condition, fulfilment of the condition[+], realization of the condition
REBUS SIC STANTIBUS	*rebus sic stantibus*
RÉCÉPISSÉ	receipt[2]
RÉCEPTION[1]	reception[1]
RÉCEPTION[2]	acceptance[3+], reception[2]
RÉCEPTION[3]	[*]
RÉCEPTION DE L'INDU	reception of a thing not due
RECEVOIR	accept[2+], receive
RECIPIENS	*accipiens*[+], payee, *recipiens*
RÉCIPROQUE	reciprocal
RÉCOMPENSE	reward
RECONDUCTION	renewal
RECONNAISSANCE DE DETTE	acknowledgment of debt
REÇU[1]	receipt[1]
REÇU[2]	receipt[2]
REDDITION DE COMPTE	accounting
REDEVANCE	dues
RÉEL, ELLE	real
RÉGIME	regime
RÈGLE *CONTRA PROFERENTEM*	*contra proferentem* rule
RÈGLE DE CONDUITE	rule of conduct
RÈGLE DE DROIT[1]	juridical precept, juridical rule, law[3], legal norm, legal rule[1+]
RÈGLE DE DROIT[2]	juridical precept, juridical rule, law[3], legal norm, legal rule[2+]
RÈGLE JURIDIQUE	juridical precept, juridical rule, law[3], legal norm, legal rule[+]
RÈGLE JURISPRUDENTIELLE	jurisprudential rule[+], judge-made rule
RÈGLEMENT	acquittance[2], payment[1+]
RÈGLEMENT HORS COUR	contract of transaction, out-of-court settlement, settlement, transaction[1+]
RÉGLER	acquit[1], pay[+], settle[1]
RELATION CAUSALE	[*]
RELATIVITÉ DES CONTRATS	[*]
REMETTRE	hand over, remit[+]
REMISE[1]	handing over, remittance[+]
REMISE[2]	release[1]
REMISE DE DETTE	release of debt, release of obligation[+]

REMISE DE SOLIDARITÉ	release from solidarity
REMISE D'UNE OBLIGATION	release of debt, release of obligation[+]
REMISE EXPRESSE	express release
REMISE TACITE	tacit release
RÉMUNÉRATION	remuneration
RENONCIATION	abandonment[2], renunciation[2+]
RENTE[1]	annuity[1+], rent[2]
RENTE[2]	annuity[2+], pension, rent[3]
RENTE[3]	annuity[3], annuity contract[+]
RÉPARATION	reparation[1]
RÉPARATION EN NATURE	reparation in kind
RÉPARATION FORFAITAIRE	predetermined reparation
RÉPARATION INTÉGRALE	full reparation[+], *restitutio in integrum*
RÉPARATION PAR ÉQUIVALENT	compensation[2], indemnification, reparation by equivalence[+]
RÉPARER	repair
RÉPÉTER	recover
RÉPÉTITION	recovery
RÉPÉTITION DE L'INDU	recovery of a thing not due
REPRENDRE	repossess[+], retake possession, take back
REPRENDRE POSSESSION	repossess[+], retake possession, take back
REPRÉSENTANT, ANTE	representative
REPRÉSENTANT LÉGAL	legal representative
REPRÉSENTATION	perfect representation, representation[+]
REPRÉSENTATION CONTRACTUELLE	contractual representation, conventional representation[+]
REPRÉSENTATION CONVENTIONNELLE	contractual representation, conventional representation[+]
REPRÉSENTATION FORCÉE	forced representation
REPRÉSENTATION IMMÉDIATE	perfect representation, representation[+]
REPRÉSENTATION IMPARFAITE	imperfect representation
REPRÉSENTATION JUDICIAIRE	judicial representation
REPRÉSENTATION LÉGALE	legal representation
REPRÉSENTATION MÉDIATE	imperfect representation
REPRÉSENTATION PARFAITE	perfect representation, representation[+]
REPRÉSENTATION VOLONTAIRE	voluntary representation
REPRÉSENTÉ, ÉE	person represented
REPRÉSENTER	represent
REPRISE	repossession[+], retaking of possession
REPRISE DE DETTE	assumption of debt
REPRISE DE POSSESSION	repossession[+], retaking of possession
REPRISE FORCÉE	forced repossession
RÉPUDIATION	repudiation

RÉPUDIER	repudiate
RESCINDABLE	[*]
RESCINDER	rescind+, set aside(>)
RESCISION	rescission
RÉSERVE D'AGRÉMENT	right of refusal
RÉSILIABLE	[*]
RÉSILIATION¹	resiliation¹
RÉSILIATION²	resiliation²
RÉSILIATION AMIABLE	amicable resiliation, bilateral resiliation+, conventional resiliation, revocation²
RÉSILIATION BILATÉRALE	amicable resiliation, bilateral resiliation+, conventional resiliation, revocation²
RÉSILIATION CONVENTIONNELLE	amicable resiliation, bilateral resiliation+, conventional resiliation, revocation²
RÉSILIATION FORCÉE	forced resiliation
RÉSILIATION UNILATÉRALE	unilateral resiliation
RÉSILIATION VOLONTAIRE	voluntary resiliation
RÉSILIER¹	resiliate¹+, set aside(>)
RÉSILIER²	cancel+(>), resiliate²+
RÉSOLUBLE	[*]
RÉSOLUTION¹	resolution¹
RÉSOLUTION²	resolution²
RÉSOLUTION DE PLEIN DROIT	resolution (as) of right+, resolution *de jure*
RÉSOLUTION JUDICIAIRE	judicial resolution
RÉSOLUTOIRE	resolutive, resolutory
RÉSOUDRE	cancel+(>), resolve+, set aside(>)
RES PERIT CREDITORI	*res perit creditori*
RES PERIT DEBITORI	*res perit debitori*
RES PERIT DOMINO	*res perit domino*
RESPONSABILITÉ	juridical liability, juridical responsibility+, legal liability¹, liability¹, responsibility
RESPONSABILITÉ ABSOLUE	absolute liability, no-fault liability, objective liability, strict liability+
RESPONSABILITÉ CAUSALE	absolute liability, no-fault liability, objective liability, strict liability
RESPONSABILITÉ CIVILE	civil liability+, civil responsibility
RESPONSABILITÉ COLLECTIVE	collective liability
RESPONSABILITÉ CONJOINTE	joint liability+, joint responsibility
RESPONSABILITÉ CONTRACTUELLE	contractual liability+, contractual responsibility
RESPONSABILITÉ DE L'ARTISAN	liability of artisans
RESPONSABILITÉ DÉLICTUELLE	delictual liability+, delictual responsibility
RESPONSABILITÉ DE L'INSTITUTEUR	liability of schoolteachers
RESPONSABILITÉ DE PLEIN DROIT	absolute liability, no-fault liability, objective liability, strict liability+

RESPONSABILITÉ DES PARENTS	liability of parents[+], liability of the titulary of parental authority
RESPONSABILITÉ DU COMMETTANT	liability of committents, liability of the principal[+]
RESPONSABILITÉ DU CURATEUR	liability of curators
RESPONSABILITÉ DU FABRICANT	manufacturer's liability
RESPONSABILITÉ DU FAIT D'AUTRUI	liability for damage caused by another[+], vicarious liability(<), vicarious responsibility(<)
RESPONSABILITÉ DU FAIT DES ANIMAUX	liability for damage caused by animals
RESPONSABILITÉ DU FAIT DES BÂTIMENTS	liability for damage caused by buildings[+], liability for damage caused by immovables
RESPONSABILITÉ DU FAIT DES BIENS	liability for damage caused by things
RESPONSABILITÉ DU FAIT DES CHOSES	liability for damage caused by things
RESPONSABILITÉ DU FAIT DES CHOSES INANIMÉES	liability for damage caused by inanimate things
RESPONSABILITÉ DU FAIT DES IMMEUBLES	liability for damage caused by buildings[+], liability for damage caused by immovables
RESPONSABILITÉ DU FAIT DES PERSONNES	personal liability[2]
RESPONSABILITÉ DU FAIT DES PRODUITS	product liability
RESPONSABILITÉ DU FAIT PERSONNEL	personal liability[2]
RESPONSABILITÉ DU MANUFACTURIER	manufacturer's liability
RESPONSABILITÉ DU TITULAIRE DE L'AUTORITÉ PARENTALE	liability of parents[+], liability of the titulary of parental authority
RESPONSABILITÉ DU TUTEUR	liability of tutors
RESPONSABILITÉ EXTRACONTRACTUELLE	extracontractual liability
RESPONSABILITÉ INDIRECTE	indirect liability[+], indirect responsibility
RESPONSABILITÉ *IN SOLIDUM*	*in solidum* liability, liability *in solidum*[+]
RESPONSABILITÉ JURIDIQUE	juridical liability, juridical responsibility[+], legal liability[1], liability[1], responsibility
RESPONSABILITÉ LÉGALE	legal liability[2]
RESPONSABILITÉ MORALE	moral responsibility
RESPONSABILITÉ OBJECTIVE	absolute liability, no-fault liability, objective liability, strict liability[+]
RESPONSABILITÉ PARTAGÉE	shared liability
RESPONSABILITÉ PÉNALE	penal liability
RESPONSABILITÉ PERSONNELLE[1]	personal liability[1]
RESPONSABILITÉ PERSONNELLE[2]	personal liability[2]
RESPONSABILITÉ PRÉCONTRACTUELLE	precontractual liability
RESPONSABILITÉ PROFESSIONNELLE	professional liability

RESPONSABILITÉ QUASI CONTRACTUELLE	quasi-contractual liability+, quasi-contractual responsibility
RESPONSABILITÉ QUASI DÉLICTUELLE	quasi-delictual liability+, quasi-delictual responsibility
RESPONSABILITÉ SANS FAUTE	absolute liability, no-fault liability, objective liability, strict liability+
RESPONSABILITÉ SOLIDAIRE	solidary liability
RESPONSABILITÉ STRICTE	absolute liability, no-fault liability, objective liability, strict liability+
RESPONSABILITÉ SUBJECTIVE	subjective liability
RESPONSABLE	liable+, responsible
RESTITUER	restore
RESTITUTIO IN INTEGRUM	full reparation+, *restitutio in integrum*
RESTITUTION	restitution
RESTITUTION DE L'INDU	restitution of a thing not due
RESTITUTION EN NATURE	restitution in kind
RESTITUTION PAR ÉQUIVALENT	restitution by equivalence
RÉTICENCE	concealment
RÉTICENCE DOLOSIVE	deceitful concealment, fraudulent concealment+
RÉTICENCE FRAUDULEUSE	deceitful concealment, fraudulent concealment+
RETIREMENT	removal
RETIRER[1]	remove+, take delivery
RETIRER[2]	retract+, withdraw[1]
RÉTRACTATION	retraction+, withdrawal
RÉTRACTER	retract+, withdraw[1]
RETRAIRE	redeem
RETRAIT[1]	retraction+, withdrawal
RETRAIT[2]	redemption
RETRAIT LITIGIEUX	redemption of litigious rights
RETRAYANT, ANTE	redeemer
RETRAYÉ, ÉE	[*]
RÉTROACTIVITÉ DE LA CONDITION	retroactivity of a condition
REVENDICATION	revendication
REVENDIQUANT, ANTE	person revendicating
REVENDIQUER	revendicate
RÉVISER	revise
RÉVISION	revision
RÉVISION DU CONTRAT	revision of contract
RÉVOCABILITÉ	revocability
RÉVOCABLE	revocable
RÉVOCATION[1]	revocation[1]
RÉVOCATION[2]	amicable resiliation, bilateral resiliation+, conventional resiliation, revocation[2]
RÉVOCATOIRE	revocatory

RÉVOQUER	revoke
RICOCHET	ricochet
RISQUE DU CONTRAT	risk of the contract
RUINE	ruin

S

SALAIRE	salary+, wages
SALARIÉ, ÉE *adj.*	[*]
SALARIÉ, ÉE *n.*	employee[1]
SECRET, ÈTE	secret
SÉQUESTRE[1]	sequestration
SÉQUESTRE[2]	sequestrator
SÉQUESTRE CONVENTIONNEL	conventional sequestration
SÉQUESTRE JUDICIAIRE	judicial deposit, judicial sequestration+
SÉQUESTRER	sequestrate
SERVICE[1]	service(s)[1]
SERVICE[2]	service(s)[2]
SIMPLE ADMINISTRATION	simple administration
SIMPLE EXPECTATIVE	expectancy, expectation, mere expectancy+, mere expectation, potential right
SIMPLE PRÊT	loan for consumption, *mutuum*, simple loan+
SIMULATION	simulation
SIMULÉ, ÉE	simulated
SOCIÉTAIRE[1]	partner
SOCIÉTAIRE[2]	member[1]
SOCIÉTÉ[1]	partnership[1]
SOCIÉTÉ[2]	contract of partnership+, partnership[2], partnership agreement
SOCIÉTÉ ANONYME	anonymous partnership
SOCIÉTÉ CIVILE	civil partnership
SOCIÉTÉ COMMERCIALE	commercial partnership
SOCIÉTÉ EN COMMANDITE	limited partnership+, partnership *en commandite*
SOCIÉTÉ EN NOM COLLECTIF	general partnership
SOCIÉTÉ EN PARTICIPATION	undeclared partnership
SOLATIUM DOLORIS	*solatium doloris*
SOLENNEL, ELLE	solemn
SOLENNISER	solemnize
SOLENNITÉ	essential formality+, formality *ad solemnitatem*, solemn form, solemnity
SOLIDAIRE[1]	solidary[1]

SOLIDAIRE[2]	solidary[2]
SOLIDAIREMENT	solidarily
SOLIDARITÉ	correality, perfect solidarity, solidarity[+]
SOLIDARITÉ ACTIVE	active solidarity
SOLIDARITÉ CONTRACTUELLE	contractual solidarity, conventional solidarity[+]
SOLIDARITÉ CONVENTIONNELLE	contractual solidarity, conventional solidarity[+]
SOLIDARITÉ IMPARFAITE	imperfect solidarity[+], *in solidum* obligation, obligation *in solidum*
SOLIDARITÉ LÉGALE	legal solidarity
SOLIDARITÉ PARFAITE	correality, perfect solidarity, solidarity[+]
SOLIDARITÉ PASSIVE	passive solidarity
SOLIDITÉ	correality, perfect solidarity, solidarity[+]
SOLO CONSENSU	*solo consensu*
SOLVENS	payer, *solvens*[+]
SOULTE	balance
SOUS-ACQUÉREUR, ÉRESSE	sub-acquirer, subsequent acquirer[+]
SOUS-ACQUISITION	sub-acquisition, subsequent acquisition[+]
SOUS-CONTRACTANT, ANTE	subcontracting party
SOUS-CONTRAT	subcontract
SOUSCRIPTEUR, TRICE	applicant, client[1+], policy holder (<), policy owner[+] (<)
SOUS-MANDANT, ANTE	principal mandatary, sub-mandator[+]
SOUS-MANDAT	sub-mandate
SOUS-MANDATAIRE	sub-mandatary
STATU QUO (ANTE)	*statu quo (ante)*
STIPULANT, ANTE[1]	stipulating party
STIPULANT, ANTE[2]	stipulator
STIPULATION[1]	clause[+], stipulation[1]
STIPULATION[2]	stipulation[2]
STIPULATION D'ARRHES	stipulation as to earnest
STIPULATION DE DÉDIT	forfeit clause, stipulation as to withdrawal, withdrawal clause[+]
STIPULATION D'INALIÉNABILITÉ	stipulation of inalienability
STIPULATION D'INSAISISSABILITÉ	stipulation of inseizability
STIPULATION POUR AUTRUI	stipulation for another[+], stipulation for the benefit of another, stipulation in favour of another
STIPULER[1]	stipulate[1]
STIPULER[2]	stipulate[2]
SUBJECTIF, IVE	subjective
SUBROGATIF, IVE	subrogate, subrogatory[+]
SUBROGATION	subrogation
SUBROGATION CONVENTIONNELLE	contractual subrogation, conventional subrogation[+]
SUBROGATION LÉGALE	legal subrogation

SUBROGATION PERSONNELLE	personal subrogation
SUBROGATION RÉELLE	real subrogation
SUBROGATOIRE	subrogate, subrogatory[+]
SUBROGÉ, ÉE	subrogate[+], subrogated party
SUBROGEANT, ANTE	subrogator
SUBROGER	subrogate
SUCCESSEUR, EURE	successor
SUCCESSEUR À TITRE PARTICULIER	particular successor, successor by particular title[+]
SUCCESSEUR À TITRE UNIVERSEL	successor by general title
SUCCESSEUR PARTICULIER	particular successor, successor by particular title[+]
SUCCESSEUR UNIVERSEL	successor by universal title, universal successor[+]
SUCCESSIF, IVE	successive
SUI GENERIS	*sui generis*
SUJET DE DROIT[1]	subject of law[1]
SUJET DE DROIT[2]	subject of rights[1]
SUJET DE DROIT[3]	subject of rights[2]
SUJET DU DROIT	subject of law[1]
SUSPENSIF, IVE	suspensive
SYNALLAGMATIQUE	bilateral, synallagmatic[+]
SYSTÈME DE DROIT	juridical system, legal order[+], legal system, system of law
SYSTÈME JURIDIQUE	juridical system, legal order[+], legal system, system of law

T

TACITE RECONDUCTION	tacit renewal
TAUX DE CRÉDIT	credit rate
TAUX D'INCAPACITÉ	incapacity rate
TAUX D'INTÉRÊT	interest rate[+], rate of interest
TAUX D'INTÉRÊT CONVENTIONNEL	conventional interest rate[+], rate of conventional interest
TAUX D'INTÉRÊT LÉGAL	legal interest rate[+], rate of legal interest
TAUX D'INTÉRÊT USURAIRE	usurious interest rate
TERME	term[1]
TERME (À)	term (with a)
TERME CERTAIN	certain term[+], determinate term, fixed term, known term
TERME CONNU	certain term[+], determinate term, fixed term, known term
TERME CONTRACTUEL	contractual term, conventional term[+]
TERME CONVENTIONNEL	contractual term, conventional term[+]

TERME DE DROIT	term of right
TERME DE GRÂCE	delay of grace, judicial term[+], period of grace, term of grace
TERME EXTINCTIF	extinctive term
TERME INCERTAIN	uncertain term, undetermined term, unspecified term[+]
TERME INCONNU	uncertain term, undetermined term, unspecified term[+]
TERME INDÉTERMINÉ	uncertain term, undetermined term, unspecified term[+]
TERME JUDICIAIRE	delay of grace, judicial term[+], period of grace, term of grace
TERME LÉGAL	legal term
TERME SUSPENSIF	suspensive term
THÉORIE DE LA CAUSALITÉ ADÉQUATE	doctrine of adequate causation
THÉORIE DE LA CAUSALITÉ IMMÉDIATE	doctrine of proximate cause
THÉORIE DE LA CAUSALITÉ PARTIELLE	doctrine of partial causation
THÉORIE DE LA *CAUSA PROXIMA*	doctrine of *causa proxima*
THÉORIE DE LA DÉCLARATION	theory of declaration
THÉORIE DE LA DÉCLARATION DE VOLONTÉ	doctrine of the declaration of will
THÉORIE DE L'APPARENCE	theory of appearance
THÉORIE DE LA RÉCEPTION	theory of reception
THÉORIE DE L'AUTONOMIE DE LA VOLONTÉ	theory of the autonomy of will
THÉORIE DE LA VOLONTÉ RÉELLE	doctrine of the internal will
THÉORIE DE L'ÉMISSION	theory of expedition
THÉORIE DE L'ENGAGEMENT PAR VOLONTÉ UNILATÉRALE	doctrine of undertaking by unilateral will
THÉORIE DE L'ENGAGEMENT UNILATÉRAL	doctrine of unilateral undertaking
THÉORIE DE L'ÉQUIVALENCE DES CONDITIONS	doctrine of the equivalence of conditions
THÉORIE DE L'EXPÉDITION	theory of expedition
THÉORIE DE L'IMPRÉVISION	doctrine of unforseen circumstances
THÉORIE DE L'INFORMATION	theory of infor mation
THÉORIE DES RISQUES[1,2]	doctrine of risks[1,2]
THÉORIE DU CONTRAT RELATIONNEL	doctrine of relational contract
TIERS	third party(<)[+], third person[+]
TIERS ACQUÉREUR	sub-acquirer, subsequent acquirer[+]
TIERS BÉNÉFICIAIRE	third party beneficiary, third person beneficiary[+]
TITRE[1]	title[1]
TITRE[2]	act[1], juridical act[+], *negotium*, title[2]

TITRE[3]	act[2], *acte*, attesting deed[+], deed[1], *instrumentum*, title[3]
TITRE CONSTITUTIF	constitutive title
TITRE DE CRÉANCE	title of indebtedness
TITRE DE PAIEMENT	title of payment
TITRE ONÉREUX (À)	onerous title (by)
TITRE TRANSLATIF	translatory title
TITRE TRANSLATIF DE PROPRIÉTÉ	translatory title of ownership
TITRE UNIVERSEL (À)	general title (by)
TORT[1]	fault[1+], wrong[1]
TORT[2]	damage[+], harm, injury, loss[2], prejudice, wrong[2]
TRADITIO BREVI MANU	*brevi manu* tradition, tradition by interversion of title[+]
TRADITIO LONGA MANU	*longa manu* tradition, symbolic tradition[+]
TRADITION	tradition
TRADITION ACTUELLE	actual tradition[+], effective tradition, real tradition
TRADITION DE BRÈVE MAIN	*brevi manu* tradition, tradition by interversion of title[+]
TRADITION DE LONGUE MAIN	*longa manu* tradition, symbolic tradition[+]
TRADITION FEINTE	feigned tradition, fictitious tradition[+]
TRADITION FICTIVE	feigned tradition, fictitious tradition[+]
TRADITION PAR INTERVERSION DE TITRE	*brevi manu* tradition, tradition by interversion of title[+]
TRADITION RÉELLE	actual tradition[+], effective tradition, real tradition
TRADITION SYMBOLIQUE	*longa manu* tradition, symbolic tradition[+]
TRANSACTION	contract of transaction, out-of-court settlement, settlement, transaction[1+]
TRANSFÉRER	convey[2], transfer[+]
TRANSFERT	conveyance[2], transfer[+]
TRANSIGER	settle[2], transact[+]
TRANSLATIF, IVE	translatory
TRANSLATION	conveyance[2], transfer[+]
TRANSMISSIBILITÉ	transmissibility
TRANSMISSIBLE	transmissible
TRANSMISSION	transmission
TRANSMISSION À TITRE PARTICULIER	transmission by (a) particular title
TRANSMISSION À TITRE UNIVERSEL	transmission by general title
TRANSMISSION UNIVERSELLE	universal transmission
TRANSPORT[1]	carriage[1+], conveyance[1], transport[1], transportation
TRANSPORT[2]	carriage[2], contract of carriage[+], contract of transport, contract of transportation, transport[2]
TRANSPORT[3]	assignment[+], cession, conveyance[3]

TRANSPORT-CESSION	assignment of claim(s)+, assignment of creance, transfer of claim, transfer of debt
TRANSPORT DE BIENS	carriage of goods+, carriage of merchandise, carriage of property
TRANSPORT DE CHOSES	carriage of goods+, carriage of merchandise, carriage of property
TRANSPORT DE CRÉANCE	assignment of claim(s)+, assignment of creance, transfer of claim, transfer of debt
TRANSPORT DE DETTE	assignment of debt
TRANSPORT DE MARCHANDISES	carriage of goods+, carriage of merchandise, carriage of property
TRANSPORT DE PERSONNES	carriage of persons
TRANSPORTER[1]	carry+, convey[1], transport
TRANSPORTER[2]	assign+, cede
TRANSPORTEUR, EUSE	carrier
TRAVAIL	work
TRAVAILLER	work
TROC	barter, exchange+
TROQUER	barter, exchange+
TROUBLE DE DROIT	disturbance of law
TROUBLE DE FAIT	disturbance of fact
TROUBLE DE VOISINAGE	neighbourhood disturbance

U

UBERRIMA FIDES	*uberrima fides*
UNILATÉRAL, ALE	unilateral
USAGE	usage
USURAIRE	usurious
USURE	usury

V

VALABLE	valid
VALABLEMENT	validly
VALEUR	value
VALEUR ACTUELLE	actual value+, market value, real value
VALEUR MARCHANDE	actual value+, market value, real value
VALEUR RÉELLE	actual value+, market value, real value
VALEUR VÉNALE	actual value+, market value, real value

VALIDATION	validation
VALIDE	valid
VALIDEMENT	validly
VALIDER	validate
VALIDITÉ	validity
VENDEUR, EUSE	seller[+], vendor
VENDRE	sell[+], transfer by sale
VENTE	contract of sale, sale[+]
VENTE À L'ESSAI	sale on approval, sale upon trial, trial sale[+]
VENTE À RÉMÉRÉ	sale with option to repurchase, sale with right of redemption[+]
VENTE À TEMPÉRAMENT	conditional contract of sale, conditional sale[2], conditional sales contract, instalment sale[+], sale by instalment
VENTE À TERME	sale with a term[+], term sale
VENTE AUX ENCHÈRES	auction sale[+], sale by auction
VENTE AVEC FACULTÉ DE RACHAT	sale with option to repurchase, sale with right of redemption[+]
VENTE CONDITIONNELLE[1]	conditional sale[1]
VENTE CONDITIONNELLE[2]	[*]
VENTE DE CRÉANCE	sale of claims[+], sale of creance, sale of debt
VENTE DE DROITS LITIGIEUX	sale of litigious rights
VENTE DE(S) DROITS SUCCESSIFS	sale of inheritance, sale of successional rights[+]
VENTE DE DROITS SUCCESSORAUX	sale of inheritance, sale of successional rights[+]
VENTE D'ENTREPRISE	sale of an enterprise
VENTE D'HÉRÉDITÉ	sale of inheritance, sale of successional rights[+]
VENTE DU BIEN D'AUTRUI	sale of (the) property of another
VENTE EN BLOC	bulk sale
VÉRITABLE	true
VERSEMENT	payment[2]
VERSEMENTS	instalments, periodical payment, periodic payment[+]
VICE APPARENT	apparent defect[+], patent defect
VICE CACHÉ	hidden defect, latent defect[+], redhibitory defect
VICE DE FOND	defect of substance, substantive defect[+]
VICE DE FORME	defect of form[+], formal defect
VICE DU CONSENTEMENT	defect of consent
VICE RÉDHIBITOIRE	hidden defect, latent defect[+], redhibitory defect
VICTIME	victim
VICTIME IMMÉDIATE	immediate victim[+], initial victim, principal victim
VICTIME INITIALE	immediate victim[+], initial victim, principal victim
VICTIME MÉDIATE	mediate victim[+], victim by ricochet
VICTIME PAR RICOCHET	mediate victim[+], victim by ricochet
VICTIME PRINCIPALE	immediate victim[+], initial victim, principal victim

VINCULUM JURIS	*vinculum juris*
VIOLENCE	violence
VOITURIER, IÈRE	carrier
VOLONTÉ[1]	will[1]
VOLONTÉ[2]	intent, intention[2], will[2]
VOLONTÉ DÉCLARÉE	declared will[+], externalized will
VOLONTÉ EXTERNE	declared will[+], externalized will
VOLONTÉ INTERNE	internal will[+], true will
VOLONTÉ RÉELLE	internal will[+], true will
VOYAGEUR, EUSE	passenger

LIST OF AUTHORS AND PUBLICATIONS
QUOTED IN ABBREVIATED FORM

Anglin, (1923) 1 *Can. Bar Rev.* 33

J. Anglin, "Some Differences Between the Law of Quebec and the Law as Administered in the Other Provinces of Canada" (1923) 1 *Can. Bar Rev.* 33.

Athanassidis, (1985) 5 *R.E.J.* 267

M. Athanassidis, "Sources of Disciplinary Power: An Analysis of the Employment Contract" (1985) 5 *R.E.J.* 267.

Aubry & Rau, *Civil Law*, vol. 4

C. Aubry & C. Rau, *Obligations, Cours de droit civil français*, vol. 4, 6th ed. (by Bartin) trans. by Louisiana State Law Institute (St. Paul, Minnesota: West Publishing Co., 1965).

Aust & Charette, *Employment Contract*

E.A. Aust & L. Charette, *The Employment Contract*, 2nd ed. (Cowansville, Québec: Éditions Yvon Blais, 1993).

Ball, (1994) 39 *McGill L.J.* 568

S.R. Ball, "Bad Faith Discharge" (1994) 39 *McGill L.J.* 568.

Baudouin, in *Essays on the Civil Law*, 151

J.-L. Baudouin, "Theory of Imprevision and Judicial Intervention to Change a Contract" in J. Dainow, ed., *Essays on the Civil Law of Obligations* (Baton Rouge: Louisiana State University Press, 1969) 151.

Baudouin, in *Civil Law*, 169

J.-L. Baudouin, "Delicts under the Quebec Civil Code" in E. McWhinney, ed., *Canadian Jurisprudence: The Civil Law and Common Law in Canada* (Toronto: Carswell, 1958) 169.

Benedek, (1998) 32 *R.J.T.* 607

D. Benedek, "Non-Pecuniary Damages: Defined, Assessed and Capped" (1998) 32 *R.J.T.* 607.

Bernard *et al.*, (1992) 11 *Can. J. Fam. L.* 57

C. Bernard, R. Ward & B.M. Knoppers, "'Best Interests of the Child' Exposed: A Portrait of Quebec Custody and Protection Law" (1992) 11 *Can. J. Fam. L.* 57.

Bissett-Johnson, (1978) 24 *McGill L.J.* 316

A. Bissett-Johnson, "Damages for Personal Injuries – The Supreme Court Speaks" (1978) 24 *McGill L.J.* 316.

Blumenstein, in *Meredith Lectures (1964)*, 57

J.H. Blumenstein, "Special Cases of Contractual Damages" in *Meredith Memorial Lectures (1964)* (Montréal: Wilson & Lafleur, 1964) 57.

Bonhomme *et al.*, *Employment Contract*

R. Bonhomme, C. Gascon & L. Lesage, *The Employment Contract under the Civil Code of Québec* (Cowansville, Québec: Éditions Yvon Blais, 1994).

Boodman, (1999) 10 *S.C.L.R.* (2d) 45

M. Boodman, "Developments in Civil Law: The 1997-98 Term" (1999) 10 *S.C.L.R.* (2d) 45.

Boodman, in *Mélanges Crépeau*, 75

M. Boodman, "The Conditional Sale: de quoi s'agit-il?" in *Mélanges Paul-André Crépeau* (Cowansville, Québec: Éditions Yvon Blais, 1997) 75.

Boodman, (1995) 6 *S.C.L.R.* 45

M. Boodman, "Municipal Taxes, the Civil Codes, Comity and Tragedy" (1995) 6 *S.C.L.R.* 45.

Boodman, (1989-90) 35 *McGill L.J.* 19

M. Boodman, "The Seller's Revendication Remedy as a Fossil" (1989-90) 35 *McGill L.J.* 19.

Boodman, (1988) 67 *Can. Bar Rev.* 658

M. Boodman, "The Right of Retention of the Seller of Moveables in Quebec" (1988) 67 *Can. Bar Rev.* 658.

Boodman, (1987) 47 *R. du B.* 871

M. Boodman, "The Prepaying Buyer of Corporeal Moveables in Quebec" (1987) 47 *R. du B.* 871.

Bridge, in *Recovery of Damages*, 67

M.G. Bridge, "Recovery of Damages for Loss of Future Earnings: Personal Injury Claims by Immediate Victims" in M.G. Bridge, P.-A. Crépeau & P.P.C. Haanappel, eds., *Recovery of Damages for Loss of Future Earnings: Canadian and Comparative Studies / L'évaluation du préjudice en cas de perte de gains : Études canadiennes et comparatives* (Montréal: Q.R.C.P.C.L., 1987) 67.

Bridge *et al.*, (1999) 44 *McGill L.J.* 567

M. Bridge, R.A. Macdonald, R.L. Simmonds & C. Walsh, "Formalism, Functionalism, and Understanding the Law of Secured Transactions" (1999) 44 *McGill L.J.* 567.

Brien, in *Meredith Lectures (1983-84)*, 1

J. Brien, "Responsibility of Architects and Engineers: Where Do We Stand?" in *Meredith Memorial Lectures (1983-84)* (Don Mills, Ontario: Richard De Boo, 1985) 1.

Brierley, in *Mélanges Crépeau*, 119

J.E.C. Brierley, "The Gratuitous Trust: A New Liberality in Quebec Law" in *Mélanges Paul-André Crépeau* (Cowansville, Québec: Éditions Yvon Blais, 1997) 119.

Brierley, in *Droit québécois et droit français*, 383

J.E.C. Brierley, "The New Quebec Law of Trusts: The Adaptation of Common Law Thought to Civil Law Concepts" in H.P. Glenn, ed., *Droit québécois et droit français : communauté, autonomie, concordance* (Cowansville, Québec: Éditions Yvon Blais, 1993) 383.

Brierley, (1992) 95 *R. du N.* 131

J.E.C. Brierley, "Power of Appointment in Quebec Civil Law (première partie)" (1992) 95 *R. du N.* 131.

Brierley, (1992) 42 *U.T.L.J.* 484

J.E.C. Brierley, "The Renewals of Quebec's Distinct Legal Culture: The New *Civil Code of Québec*" (1992) 42 *U.T.L.J.* 484.

Brierley, (1990) 69 *Can. Bar Rev.* 364

J.E.C. Brierley, "Wills – General Powers of Appointment in Wills – Bare Powers and Trust Powers – Ontario and Quebec Compared: *Re Nicholls*; *Royal Trust* v. *Brodie*" (1990) 69 *Can. Bar Rev.* 364.

Brierley, (1987-88) 13 *Can. Bus. L.J.* 58

J.E.C. Brierley, "Quebec's New (1986) Arbitration Law" (1987-88) 13 *Can. Bus. L.J.* 58.

Brierley, in *Canadian Family Law*, vol. 2, 795

J.E.C. Brierley, "Husband and Wife in the Law of Quebec: A 1970 Conspectus" in D. Mendes da Costa, ed., *Studies in Canadian Family Law*, vol. 2 (Toronto: Butterworths, 1972) 795.

Brierley, (1970) 30 *R. du B.* 473

J.E.C. Brierley, "Aspects of the Promise to Arbitrate in the Law of Quebec" (1970) 30 *R. du B.* 473.

Brierley, (1968) 14 *McGill L.J.* 521

J.E.C. Brierley, "Quebec's Civil Law Codification: Viewed and Reviewed" (1968) 14 *McGill L.J.* 521.

Brierley & Macdonald (eds.), *Quebec Civil Law*

J.E.C. Brierley & R.A. Macdonald, eds., *Quebec Civil Law: An Introduction to Quebec Private Law* (Toronto: Emond Montgomery, 1993).

Brisson & Kasirer, in *Civil Code of Québec* (1997) ix

J.-M. Brisson & N. Kasirer, "Preface" in *Civil Code of Québec. A Critical Edition / Code civil du Québec. Édition critique* (Cowansville, Québec: Éditions Yvon Blais / Q.R.C.P.C.L., 1997) ix.

Brisson & Kasirer, (1996) 23 *Man. L.J.* 406

J.-M. Brisson & N. Kasirer, "The Married Woman in Ascendance, the Mother Country in Retreat: From Legal Colonialism to Legal Nationalism in Quebec Matrimonial Law Reform, 1866-1991" (1996) 23 *Man. L.J.* 406.

Brossard, (1955) 5 *Thémis* 239

A. Brossard, "Four Lectures on The Law of Torts in Quebec" (1955) 5 *Thémis* 239.

Brossard, (1945) 23 *Can. Bar Rev.* 1

A. Brossard, "A Synopsis of Torts in Quebec and a Parallel Between Some Provisions of the Common Law and the Code" (1945) 23 *Can. Bar Rev.* 1.

Brunnée, in *Mélanges Crépeau*, 155

J. Brunnée, "From a 'Black Hole' into a Greener Future? Comparative Perspectives on Environnemental Liability Law in Quebec and its Reform" in *Mélanges Paul-André Crépeau* (Cowansville, Québec: Éditions Yvon Blais, 1997) 155.

C.C.R.O., *Commentaries*, vol. II, t. 2

Civil Code Revision Office, *Report on the Québec Civil Code,* vol. II, t. 2, *Commentaries* (Québec: Éditeur officiel du Québec, [1978] 1978).

C.C.R.O., *Matrimonial Regimes*

Civil Code Revision Office, *Report on Matrimonial Regimes* (Québec: Éditeur officiel du Québec, 1968).

Cairns, (1986-87) 32 *McGill L.J.* 673

J.W. Cairns, "Employment in the Civil Code of Lower Canada: Tradition and Political Economy in Legal Classification and Reform" (1986-87) 32 *McGill L.J.* 673.

Cantin Cumyn, (1994) 3 *J. Int'l. Tr. & Corp. Pl.* 69

M. Cantin Cumyn, "The Trust in a Civilian Context: The Quebec Case" (1994) 3 *J. Int'l. Tr. & Corp. Pl.* 69.

Caron & Brierley, (1980) 25 *McGill L.J.* 421

Y. Caron & J.E.C. Brierley, "The Trust in Quebec" (1980) 25 *McGill L.J.* 421.

Castel, *Civil Law System*

J.G. Castel, *The Civil Law System of the Province of Quebec* (Toronto: Butterworths, 1962).

Challies, *Unjustified Enrichment*

G.S. Challies, *The Doctrine of Unjustified Enrichment in the Law of the Province of Quebec* (Montréal: Wilson & Lafleur, 1970).

Challies, *Expropriation*

G.S. Challies, *The Law of Expropriation* (Montréal: Wilson & Lafleur, 1963).

Challies, in *Travaux Henri Capitant*, t. 7, 645

G.S. Challies, "What are Public Order and Good Morals?" in *Travaux de l'Association Henri Capitant pour la culture juridique française*, t. 7 (Montréal: Eugène Doucet limitée, 1956) 645.

Challies, (1952) 3 *Thémis* 77

G.S. Challies, "Good Morals" (1952) 3 *Thémis* 77.

Charlap, in *Livre-Souvenir*, 417

G. Charlap, "The Contract of Employment" in *Livre-Souvenir des journées du droit civil français* (Montréal: Le Barreau de Montréal, 1936) 417.

Charles, *Assessment of Damages*

W.H.R. Charles, *Charles Handbook on Assessment of Damages in Personal Injury Cases*, 2nd ed. (Toronto: Carswell, 1990).

Charpentier & Crépeau, *Unidroit Principles*

É. Charpentier & P.-A. Crépeau, *The Unidroit Principles and the Civil Code of Québec: Shared Values? / Les Principes d'Unidroit et le Code civil du Québec : valeurs partagées?* (Scarborough, Ontario: Carswell, 1998).

Claxton, (1999) 44 *McGill L.J* 665

J.B. Claxton, "The *Fondé de pouvoir* for Holders of Secured Indebtedness: Article 2692 Revisited – A Critical Examination" (1999) 44 *McGill L.J.* 665.

Claxton, (1997) 42 *McGill L.J.* 797

J.B. Claxton, "'The Corporate Trust Deed in Quebec Law': Article 2692 of the Civil Code of Québec" (1997) 42 *McGill L.J.* 797.

Claxton, *Security*

J.B. Claxton, *Security on Property and the Rights of Secured Creditors under the Civil Code of Québec* (Cowansville, Québec: Yvon Blais, 1994).

Connell-Thouez, in *Family Law*, 27

K. Connell-Thouez, "Matrimonial Property Regimes in Quebec Before and After the Reform of 1981: Adapting Traditional Institutions to Modern Reality" in K. Connell-Thouez & B.M. Knoppers, eds., *Contemporary Trends in Family Law: A National Perspective* (Toronto: Carswell, 1984) 27.

Côté, *Interpretation of Legislation*

P.-A. Côté, *The Interpretation of Legislation in Canada*, 3rd ed. (Scarborough, Ontario: Carswell, 2000).

Cranley Glass, (1997) 20 *Int'l J.L. & Psychiatry* 5

K. Cranley Glass, "Refining Definitions and Devising Instruments: Two Decades of Assessing Mental Competence" (1997) 20 *Int'l J.L. & Psychiatry* 5.

Crépeau, in *Aequitas and Equity*, 583

P.-A. Crépeau, "Abuse of Rights in the Civil Law of Quebec", in A.M. Rabello, ed., *Aequitas and Equity: Equity in Civil Law and Mixed Jurisdictions* (Jerusalem: The Hebrew University of Jerusalem, 1997) 583.

Crépeau, in *Civil Codes* (1993) xi

P.-A. Crépeau, "Preface" in P.-A. Crépeau, ed., *The Civil Codes. A Critical Edition, 1993 / Les Codes civils. Édition critique, 1993* (Cowansville, Québec: Éditions Yvon Blais, 1994) xi.

Crépeau, in *Draft*, vol. I, xxiii

P.-A. Crépeau, "Foreword" in Civil Code Revision Office, *Report on the Québec Civil Code,* vol. I: *Draft Civil Code* (Québec: Éditeur officiel du Québec, [1978] 1977) xxiii.

Crépeau, (1974) 34 *La. L. Rev.* 921

P.-A. Crépeau, "Civil Code Revision in Quebec" (1974) 34 *La. L. Rev.* 921.

Crépeau, in *Essays on the Civil Law*, 83

P.-A. Crépeau, "Civil Responsibility: A Contribution Towards a Rediscovery of Contractual Liability" in J. Dainow, ed., *Essays on the Civil law of Obligations* (Baton Rouge: Louisiana State University Press, 1969) 83.

Crépeau, in *Meredith Lectures (1964)*, 1

P.-A. Crépeau, "General Rules Concerning Contractual and Delictual Damages" in *Meredith Memorial Lectures (1964)* (Montréal: Wilson & Lafleur, 1964) 1.

Crépeau, (1962) 40 *Can. Bar Rev.* 222

P.-A. Crépeau, "Liability for Damage Caused by Things: From the Civil Law Point of View" (1962) 40 *Can. Bar Rev.* 222.

Crothers, (1985) 26 *C. de D.* 881

J.D. Crothers, "*Faute lourde* and the Perfectly Drafted Exclusion Clause: A 'Civil' Response to a 'Common' Problem with Special Reference to Contracts for the Provision of Security Services" (1985) 26 *C. de D.* 881.

Currie, *Public International Law*

J. Currie, *Public International Law* (Toronto: Irvin Law Inc., 2001).

D'Angelo, (1986) 32 *Loy. L. Rev.* 129

L. D'Angelo, "Simulation" (1986) 32 *Loy. L. Rev.* 129.

Danson, (1998) 43 *McGill L.J.* 25

J. Danson, "Compelled Production of Medical Reports" (1998) 43 *McGill L.J.* 25.

David & Brierley, *Major Legal Systems*

R. David, *Major Legal Systems in the World Today: an Introduction to the Comparative Study of Law*, transl. and adapt. by J.E.C. Brierley, 3rd ed. (London: Stevens, 1985).

Deschamps, in *Reform of the Civil Code*, 3

M. Deschamps, "Deposit/Loan" in "Marine Insurance, Carriage by Water, Affreightment, Deposit, Loan, Surety ship, Gaming and Wagering, Transaction, Arbitration Agreements, Insurance and Annuities" in *Reform of the Civil Code*, vol. 3-B, 1993, 3.

Des Rosiers & Langevin, *Representing Victims of Sexual and Spousal Abuse*

N. Des Rosiers & L. Langevin, *Representing Victims of Sexual and Spousal Abuse* (Toronto: Irwin Law Inc., 2002).

Dessaulles, (1947) 7 *R. du B.* 147

P. Dessaulles, "Clauses of Non-liability" (1947) 7 *R. du B.* 147.

Dietze, (1999) 59 *R. du B.* 1

S H. Dietze, "Recent Developments in Secured Financing by Way of Instalment Sale, Leasing and Lease" (1999) 59 *R. du B.* 1.

Ducharme, in *Essays on the Civil Codes*, 75

L. Ducharme, "The Rules of Evidence in Civil and Commercial Matters in Quebec Law" in R.A. Landry & E. Caparros, eds., *Essays on the Civil Codes of Québec and St. Lucia* (Ottawa: University of Ottawa Press, 1984) 75.

Ducharme, in *Reform of the Civil Code*

L. Ducharme "The New Law of Civil Evidence in the Civil Code of Québec" in "Evidence, Prescription, Transitional Law" in *Reform of the Civil Code*, vol. 5-A, 1993.

Durnford, (1964-65) 67 *R. du N.* 559

J.W. Durnford, "Prescription as a Mode of Acquisition of Immoveable Property" (1964-1965) 67 *R. du N.* 559.

Durnford, (1967) 2 *R.J.T.* 161

J.W. Durnford, "The Liability of the Builder, Architect and Engineer for Perishing and Other Defects in Construction" (1967) 2 *R.J.T.* 161.

Fernandez, (2003) 53 *U. of T. L.J.* 37

A. Fernandez, "Albert Mayrand's Private Law Library: An Investigation of the Person, the Law of Persons, and 'Legal Personality' in a Collection of Law Books", (2003) 53 *U. of T. L.J.* 37.

Fine, (1973) 19 *McGill L.J.* 453

J.D. Fine, "Cause in the Quebec Law of Enrichment Without Cause" (1973) 19 *McGill L.J.* 453.

Finnis, *Natural Law and Natural Rights*

J. Finnis, *Natural Law and Natural Rights* (New York: Oxford University Press, 1980).

Fortin, in *Meredith Lectures (1997)*

G. Fortin, "Qu'est ce qu'une société?/ What is a Partnership?" in "Les sociétés, les fiducies et les entités hybrides en droit commercial contemporain/ Contemporary Utilisation of Non-Corporate Vehicles of Commerce" in *Meredith Memorial Lectures* (1997).

Freedman, (2000) 28 *Man. L.J.* 1

B.J. Freedman, "Electronic Contracts Under Canadian Law – A Practical Guide" (2000) 28 *Man. L.J.* 1.

Garant, in *Canadian Charter*, 331

P. Garant, "Fundamental Rights and Fundamental Justice" in G.-A. Beaudoin & E. Ratushny, eds., *The Canadian Charter of Rights and Freedoms*, 2nd ed. (Toronto: Carswell, 1989) 331.

Glendon, *Transformation of Family Law*

M.A. Glendon, *The Transformation of Family Law: State, Law and the Family in the United States and Western Europe* (Chicago: University of Chicago Press, 1989).

Glenn, (1974) 52 *Can. Bar Rev.* 297

H.P. Glenn, "Civil Responsibility – Right to Privacy in Quebec – Recent Cases" (1974) 52 *Can. Bar Rev.* 297.

Gliserman, (1972) 32 *R. du B.* 498

I. Gliserman, "Fraudulent Preferences in Bankrupt Estates in Quebec and Prescription" (1972) 32 *R. du B.* 498.

Goldenberg, *Law of Delicts*

H.C. Goldenberg, *The Law of Delicts Under the Civil Code of Québec* (Montréal: Wilson & Lafleur, 1935).

Goldenberg, *Responsibility*

H.C. Goldenberg, *The Responsibility for Offences and Quasi-Offences under the Civil code of Lower Canada* (Montréal: McGill University, 1932).

Goldstein, in *Meredith Lectures (1998-1999)*, 253

Y. Goldstein, "The Impact of the Civil Law on Bankruptcy and Insolvency Practice in Quebec *or* Whose Bankruptcy Act is it Anyway?" in *Meredith Memorial Lectures (1998-1999)* (Montréal: McGill University) 253.

Gonthier, (2000) 45 *McGill L.J.* 567

C.D. Gonthier, "Liberty, Equality, Fraternity: The Forgotten Leg of the Trilogy, or Fraternity: The Unspoken Third Pillar of Democracy" (2000) 45 *McGill L.J.* 567.

Gow, (1967) 13 *McGill L.J.* 245

J.J. Gow, "Conveyance of the Title on the Sale of Corporeal Moveables" (1967) 13 *McGill L.J.* 245.

Haanappel, (1982) 60 *Can. Bar. Rev.* 393

P.P.C. Haanappel, "Contract Law Reform in Quebec" (1982) 60 *Can. Bar Rev.* 393.

Hall, (1945) 23 *Can. Bar Rev.* 831

A.R. Hall, "Cause or Consideration" (1945) 23 *Can. Bar Rev.* 831.

Hanigsberg, (1991) 23 *Ottawa L.R.* 35

J.E. Hanigsberg, "Power and Procreation: State Interference in Pregnancy" (1991) 23 *Ottawa L.R.* 35.

Hauser, (1959) 33 *Tul. L. Rev.* 307

R. Hauser, "Breach of Contracts Damages During Inflation" (1959) 33 *Tul. L. Rev.* 307.

Hendy, (1988) 3 *C.F.L.Q.* 185

D.M. Hendy, "The Effects of Quebec Marriage Contracts on the Division of Property at the Time of Divorce in Quebec and Ontario" (1988) 3 *C.F.L.Q.* 185.

Hoffman, (1974) 20 *McGill L.J.* 124

C. Hoffman, "Comments. Acceleration Clauses and Article 1040b C.C." (1974) 20 *McGill L.J.* 124.

Hogue, *Common Law*

A.R. Hogue, *Origins of the Common Law* (Indianapolis: Liberty Fund, 1985).

Irving, (1963) 9 *McGill L.J.* 337

C.P. Irving, "Article 1029 C.C.: Stipulation for a Third Party Notes on the Jurisprudence of Quebec" (1963) 9 *McGill L.J.* 337.

Jauffret-Spinosi, in *Contract Law Today,* 113

C. Jauffret-Spinosi, "The Domain of Contract" in D. Harris & D. Tallon, eds., *Contract Law Today* (Oxford: Clarendon Press, 1989) 113.

Johnson, *Conflict of Laws*

W.S. Johnson, *Conflict of Laws,* 2nd ed. (Montréal: Wilson & Lafleur, 1962).

Johnson, *Responsibility of Architects, Engineers and Builders*

W.S. Johnson, *The Joint and Several Responsibility of Architects, Engineers and Builders* (Montréal: Wilson & Lafleur, 1955).

Johnson, *Clause Compromissoire*

W. S. Johnson, *The Clause Compromissoire: Its Validity in Quebec* (Montréal: W.S. Johnson, 1945).

Johnson, *Maxims*

W.S. Johnson, *Maxims of the Civil Law: Essays in the Evolution of Law* (Montréal: Wilson & Lafleur, 1929).

Johnston, in *Roman Law of Property*, 153

D. Johnston, "Successive Rights and Successful Remedies: Life Interests in Roman Law" in P. Birks, ed., *New Perspectives in the Roman Law of Property* (Oxford: Clarendon Press, 1989) 153.

Johnston, *Unfair Contracts*

R.S. Johnston, *Unfair Contracts: An Analysis of Regimes of Legal Protection in Canada* (Montréal: LL.M. Thesis, Faculty of Law, McGill University, 1979).

Jones, (1993) 38 *McGill L.J.* 394

D.K. Jones, "Retrospective on the Future: Brain Death and Evolving Legal Regimes for Tissue Replacement Technology" (1993) 38 *McGill L.J.* 394.

Jordan, (1968) 14 *McGill L.J.* 209

F.J.E. Jordan, "The Federal Divorce Act (1968) and the Constitution" (1968) 14 *McGill L.J.* 209.

Jukier, (1989) 49 *R. du B.* 3

R. Jukier, "Non-Pecuniary Damages in Defamation Cases" (1989) 49 *R. du B.* 3.

Jukier, (1987) 47 *R. du B.* 47

R. Jukier, "The Emergence of Specific Performance as a Major Remedy in Quebec Law" (1987) 47 *R. du B.* 47.

Jutras, in *Tort Law*, 317

D. Jutras, "Louis and the Mechanical Beast or Josserand's Contribution to Objective Liability in France" in I. Englard, ed., *The Philosophy of Tort Law* (North York: Captus University Publications, 1993) 317.

Jutras, (1986-87) 12 *Can. Bus. L.J.* 295

D. Jutras, "Civil Law and Pure Economic Loss: What Are We Missing?" (1986-87) 12 *Can. Bus. L.J.* 295.

Kahn, (1959-60) 6 *McGill L.J.* 98

A. Kahn, "Contracts by Correspondence" (1959-60) 6 *McGill L.J.* 98.

Kasirer, (1996) 99 *R. du N.* 3

N. Kasirer, "The 'Judicial Will' Architecturally Considered" (1996) 99 *R. du N.* 3.

Kasirer, (1992) 40 *Am. J. Comp. L.* 343

N. Kasirer, "The *infans* as *bon père de famille*: 'Objectively Wrongful Conduct' in the Civil Law Tradition" (1992) 40 *Am. J. Comp. L.* 343.

Kasirer, (1990) 35 *McGill L.J.* 841

N. Kasirer, "Canada's Criminal Law Codification Viewed and Reviewed" (1990) *35 McGill L.J.* 841.

Kauffman, (1997) 57 *R. du B.* 589

D.H. Kauffman, "New Legal Warranties Under Quebec Construction Law" (1997) 57 *R. du B.* 589.

Khoury, (2001) 46 *McGill L.J.* 413

L. Khoury, "The Liability of Auditors beyond Their Clients: A Comparative Study" (2001) 46 *McGill L.J.* 413.

Kindred *et al.*, *International Law*

H.M. Kindred, A.L.C. De Mestral, T.L. McDorman, K. Mickelson, R. Provost, L.C. Reif & S.A. Williams, *International Law, Chiefly as Interpreted and Applied in Canada*, 6th ed. (Toronto: Emond Montgomery, 2000).

Kolish, (1986-87) 32 *McGill L.J.* 602

E. Kolish, "Imprisonment for Debt in Lower Canada, 1791-1840" (1986-87) 32 *McGill L.J.* 602.

Komarov, (1999) 44 *McGill L.J.* 357

S.K. Komarov, "The Civil Code of the Russian Federation: General Provisions on Liability for the Violation of Obligations" (1999) 44 *McGill L.J.* 357.

Kouri, (2001) 32 *R.D.U.S.* 213

R.P. Kouri, "From Presumptions of Fact to Presumptions of Causation: Reflections on the Perils of Judge-Made Rules in Quebec Medical Malpractice Law" (2001) 32 *R.D.U.S.* 213.

Kouri, (1991) 22 *R.D.U.S.* 77

R.P. Kouri, "The Law Governing Human Experimentation in Quebec" (1991) 22 *R.D.U.S.* 77.

Kouri, (1984) 9 *Jus Medicum* 71

R.P. Kouri, "The Legal Status of the Unborn Child in Quebec Law: A New Perspective" (1984) 9 *Jus Medicum* 71.

Kouri, (1971) 2 *R.D.U.S.* 1

R.P. Kouri, "The Putting in Default" (1971) 2 *R.D.U.S.* 1.

Kouri, (1970) 1 *R.D.U.S.* 77

R.P. Kouri, "The Bequest of Human Organs for Purposes of Homotransplantation" (1970) 1 *R.D.U.S.* 77.

Landry, in _Essays on the Civil Law_, 115

R. Landry, "The Revocatory Action in the Québec Civil Code: General Principles" in J. Dainow, ed., _Essays on the Civil Law_ (Baton Rouge: Louisiana State University Press, 1969) 115.

Lawson, _Negligence_

F.H. Lawson, _Negligence in the Civil Law_ (Oxford: Clarendon Press, 1962).

Le Dain, (1957) 4 _McGill L.J._ 219

G.E. Le Dain, "The Real Estate Broker", (1957) 4 _McGill L.J._ 219.

Le Dain, (1956) 2 _McGill L.J._ 77

G.E. Le Dain, "Security Upon Moveable Property in the Province of Quebec" (1956) 2 _McGill L.J._ 77.

Le Dain, (1952-55) 1 _McGill L.J._ 237

G.E. Le Dain, "The Transfer of Property and Risk in the Sale of Fungibles" (1954-55) 1 _McGill L.J._ 237.

Lee, (1915-16) 25 _Yale L.J._ 536

R. Lee, "Cause and Consideration in the Quebec Civil Code" (1915-16) 25 _Yale L.J._ 536.

Legrand, (1991) 19 _Can. Bus. L.J._ 318

P. Legrand jr., "Information in Formation of Contracts: A Civilian Perspective" (1991) 19 _Can. Bus. L.J._ 318.

Legrand, in _Contemporary Law_, 197

P. Legrand jr., "Pre-contractual Relations in Quebec Law: Towards a Theoretical Framework" in _Contemporary Law / Droit contemporain_, Congrès international de droit comparé (Montréal: Yvon Blais, 1990) 197.

Legrand, (1989) 34 _McGill L.J._ 908

P. Legrand jr., "The Case for Judicial Revision of Contracts in French Law (and Beyond)" (1989) 34 _McGill L.J._ 908.

Legrand, (1988) 62 _Tul. L. Rev._ 963

P. Legrand jr., "Judicial Revision of Contracts in French Law: A Case-Study" (1988) 62 _Tul. L. Rev._ 963.

Lemann, (1954) 29 _Tul. L. Rev._ 22

T.B. Lemann, "Some Aspects of Simulation in France and Louisiana" (1954) 29 _Tul. L. Rev._ 22.

Lemmens, (2002) 45 _McGill L.J._ 347

T. Lemmens, "Selective Justice, Genetic Discrimination and Insurance: Should We Single Out Genes in our Laws?" (2000) 45 _McGill L.J._ 347.

Levasseur, *Obligations*

A.A. Levasseur, *Louisiana Law of Obligations in General: A Précis* (Austin, Texas: Butterworth Legal Publishers, 1988).

Levasseur, *Conventional Obligations*

A.A. Levasseur, *Précis in Conventional Obligations – A Civil Code Analysis* (Charlottesville: The Michie Company, Law Publishers, 1980).

Litvinoff, in *Treatise,* **vol. 5**

S. Litvinoff, in *Louisiana Civil Law Treatise*, vol. 5, 2nd ed. (St. Paul, Minn.: West Publishing Co., 2001).

Litvinoff, in *Treatise,* **vol. 6**

S. Litvinoff, in *Louisiana Civil Law Treatise*, vol. 6 (St. Paul, Minn.: West Publishing Co., 1969).

Litvinoff, in *Treatise,* **vol. 7, Book 2**

S. Litvinoff, in *Louisiana Civil Law Treatise*, vol. 7, Book 2 (St. Paul, Minn.: West Publishing Co., 1975).

Luntz, *Assessment of Damages*

H. Luntz, *Assessment of Damages for Personal Injury and Death* (Toronto: Butterworth, 1974).

Macdonald, in *Meredith Lectures (1997)*

R.A. Macdonald, "The Security Trust: Basic Principles" in *Meredith Memorial Lectures (1997)* (Montréal: McGill University, 1997).

Macdonald, in *Mélanges Crépeau,* **579**

R.A. Macdonald, "Encoding *Canadian* Civil Law" in *Mélanges Paul-André Crépeau* (Cowansville, Québec: Éditions Yvon Blais, 1997) 579.

Macdonald, (1997) 42 *McGill L.J.* **119**

R.A. Macdonald, "Legal Bilingualism" (1997) 42 *McGill L.J.* 119.

Macdonald, (1994) 39 *McGill L.J.* **761**

R.A. Macdonald, "Reconceiving the Symbols of Property: Universalities Interests and Other Heresies" (1994) 39 *McGill L.J.* 761.

Macdonald, (1986-87) 32 *McGill L.J.* **1**

R.A. Macdonald, "Enforcing Rights in Corporeal Moveables: Revendication and its Surrogates" (1986-87) 32 *McGill L.J.* 1.

Macdonald, (1986) 31 *McGill L.J.* **573**

R.A. Macdonald, "Enforcing Rights in Corporeal Moveables: Revendication and its Surrogates" (1986) 31 *McGill L.J.* 573.

Macdonald, (1985) 23 *Osgoode Hall L.J.* 573

R.A. Macdonald, "Understanding Civil Law Scholarship in Quebec" (1985) 23 *Osgoode Hall L.J.* 573.

MacNeil, *New Social Contract*

I.R. MacNeil, *The New Social Contract: An Inquiry into Modern Contractual Relations* (New Haven and London: Yale University Press, 1980).

Manwaring, (1993) 25 *Ottawa L.R.* 235

J. A. Manwaring, "Unconscionability: Contested Values, Competing Theories and Choice of Rule of Law" (1993) 25 *Ottawa L.R.* 235.

Marler, in *Meredith Lectures (1960)*, 1

J. de M. Marler, "The Planning and Drafting of Wills" in *Meredith Memorial Lectures (1960)* (Montréal: Wilson Lafleur, 1961) 1.

Marler, *Real Property*

W. de M. Marler & G.C. Marler, *The Law of Real Property: Quebec* (Toronto: Burroughs and Co., 1932).

Massey & Stern, (1996) 56 *La. L. Rev.* 743

D.C. Massey & M.A. Stern, "Punitive Damages and the Louisiana Constitution: Don't Leave Home Without It" (1996) 56 *La. L. Rev.* 743.

Mayrand, (1974) 34 *La. L. Rev.* 993

A. Mayrand, "Abuse of Rights in France and Quebec" (1974) 34 *La. L. Rev.* 993.

Mendes Da Costa, (1969) 7 *Osgoode Hall L.J.* 111

D. Mendes Da Costa, "The Divorce Act, 1968 and Grounds for Divorce Based upon Matrimonial Fault" (1969) 7 *Osgoode Hall L.J.* 111.

Meredith, (1948) 26 *Can. Bar Rev.* 95

W.C.J. Meredith, "Delicts and Quasi-Delicts: 1923-1947" (1948) 26 *Can. Bar Rev.* 95.

Michaud, (1984) 15 *R.G.D.* 293

A. Michaud, "Mitigation of Damage in the Context of Remedies for Breach of Contract" (1984) 15 *R.G.D.* 293.

Miller & Sarna, (1981) 59 *Can. Bar Rev.* 638

L. Miller & L. Sarna, "Assignment of Book Debts: Protection of Third Parties in Quebec" (1981) 59 *Can. Bar Rev.* 638.

Millner, (1971) 17 *McGill L.J.* 699

M.A. Millner, "'Autonomous Acts of Things' in Quebec Law – Legal Adventurism versus Legal Conservatism" (1971) 17 *McGill L.J.* 699.

Morgan, (1999) 44 *McGill L.J.* 849

C. Morgan, "Employer Monitoring of Employee Electronic Mail and Internet Use" (1999) 44 *McGill L.J.* 849.

Nelson, *Usury*

B. Nelson, *The Idea of Usury : From Tribal Brotherhood to Universal Otherhood* (Chicago: University of Chicago Press, 1969).

Newman, (1952) 30 *Can. Bar Rev.* 1042

H. Newman, "Case and Comment. Wills – Effect of a General Revocatory Clause – 'Revoking Any and All Former Wills Made by Me'" (1952) 30 *Can. Bar Rev.* 1042.

Newman, (1952) 30 *Can. Bar Rev.* 662

H. Newman, "The Doctrine of Cause and Consideration in the Civil Law" (1952) 30 *Can. Bar Rev.* 662.

Nicholas, *Contract*

B. Nicholas, *The French Law of Contract*, 2nd ed. (New York: Oxford University Press, 1992).

Nicholls, (1948) 26 *Can. Bar Rev.* 590

G.V.V. Nicholls, "Wills Made in the Form Derived from the Laws of England – Essential Formalities – Articles 851 and 855 of the Quebec Civil Code" (1948) 26 *Can. Bar Rev.* 590.

Nicholls, (1938) 16 *Can. Bar. Rev.* 602

G.V.V. Nicholls, "The Bills of Exchange Act and Novation in the Province of Quebec" (1938) 16 *Can. Bar Rev.* 602.

Nicholls, *Offences and Quasi-Offences*

G.V.V. Nicholls, *The Responsibility for Offences and Quasi-Offences Under the Law of Quebec* (Toronto: Carswell, 1938).

Nicholls, in *Livre-Souvenir*, 271

G.V.V. Nicholls, "The Doctrine of the Quasi-Contract in the Province of Quebec: its Debt to the Code Napoléon and its Development" in *Livre-Souvenir des journées du droit civil français* (Montréal: Le Barreau de Montréal, 1936) 271.

Olivier, (1995) 40 *McGill L.J.* 187

A. Olivier, "Fitness for Purpose in the Contract Law of Lease under the Civil Code of Québec" (1995) 40 *McGill L.J.* 187.

Ourliac & de Malafosse, *Histoire*, t. 2

P. Ourliac & J. de Malafosse, *Histoire du droit privé*, t. 2, *Les biens* (Paris: P.U.F., 1971).

Palmer, *Mixed Jurisdictions Worldwide*

V.V. Palmer, ed., *Mixed Jurisdictions Worldwide: the Third Legal Family* (Cambridge, U.K.; New York: Cambridge University Press, 2001).

Paterson, (1980) 40 *R. du B.* 816

A.K. Paterson, "Informed Consent: The Scope of the Doctor's Duty to Disclose" (1980) 40 *R. du B.* 816.

Payne, *Divorce*

J.D. Payne, *Payne on Divorce*, 4th ed. (Scarborough, Ont.: Carswell, 1996).

Payne, (1989) 20 *R.G.D.* 477

J.D. Payne, "Further Reflections on Spousal and Child Support After Pelech, Caron and Richardson" (1989) 20 *R.G.D.* 477.

Pierre, (1997) 28 *R.G.D.* 235

B. Pierre, "Classification of Property and Conceptions of Ownership in Civil and Common Law" (1997) 28 *R.G.D.* 235.

Pigeon, *Drafting and Interpreting Legislation*

L.-P. Pigeon, *Drafting and Interpreting Legislation* (Toronto: Carswell, 1988).

Pilarczyk, (2001) 46 *McGill L.J.* 779

I.C. Pilarczyk, "The Law of Servants and the Servants of Law: Enforcing Master's Rights in Montréal, 1830-1845" (2001) 46 *McGill L.J.* 779.

Planiol & Ripert, *Treatise*, vol. 1

M. Planiol & G. Ripert, *Treatise on the Civil Law*, 12th ed., vol. 1, transl. by Louisiana State Law Institute (Baton Rouge: Louisiana State Law Institute, 1959).

Planiol & Ripert, *Treatise*, vol. 2

M. Planiol & G. Ripert, *Treatise on the Civil Law*, 11th ed., vol. 2, transl. by Louisiana State Law Institute (Baton Rouge: Louisiana State Law Institute, 1959).

Pound, (1970) 16 *McGill L.J.* 312

R.W. Pound, "Selected Under the Quebec Law of Conditional Sale" (1970) 16 *McGill L.J.* 312.

Reis, (1971) 31 *R. du B.* 313

B. Reis, "Effect of Transfer and Bankruptcy on the Possibility of Compensation" (1971) 31 *R. du B.* 313.

Rodgers Magnet, (1980) 40 *R. du B.* 373

S. Rodgers Magnet, "The Right to Emergency Medical Assistance in the Province of Quebec" (1980) 40 *R. du B.* 373.

Rosenberg, (1960-61) 7 *McGill L.J.* 2

G.A. Rosenberg, "The Notion of Good Faith in the Civil Law of Quebec" (1960-61) 7 *McGill L.J.* 2.

Rouhette, in *Contract Law Today*, 38

G. Rouhette, "The Obligatory Force of Contract in French Law" in D. Harris & D. Tallon, eds., *Contract Law Today* (Oxford: Clarendon Press, 1989) 38.

Ruiter, *Legal Institutions*

D.W.P. Ruiter, *Legal Institutions* (London: Kluwer Academic Publishers, Law and Philosophy Library, 2001).

Ryan, *Introduction*

K.W. Ryan, *An Introduction to the Civil Law* (Sydney: The Law Book Co. of Australia Pty Ltd., 1962).

Sarna, in *Meredith Lectures (1989)*, 157

L. Sarna, "Recourses of Lessors Against Defaulting Tenants in Commercial Leases" in *Meredith Memorial Lectures (1989)* (Cowansville, Québec: Éditions Yvon Blais, 1989) 157.

Sarna, (1978) 56 *Can. Bar Rev.* 626

L. Sarna, "Assignments of Book Accounts, Assignor's Warranties and Standing to Sue" (1978) 56 *Can. Bar Rev.* 626.

Sarna, (1977) 23 *McGill L.J.* 508

L. Sarna, "Aspects of the Law of Judicial Sequestration in Quebec" (1977) 23 *McGill L.J.* 508.

Schlesinger, *Formation of Contracts*

R.B. Schlesinger, ed., *Formation of Contracts : A Study of the Common Core of Legal Systems* (Dobbs Ferry, N.Y.: Oceana Pub. Inc., 1968).

Scott, (1956-57) 3 *McGill L.J.* 29

F.R. Scott, "Areas of Conflict in the Field of Public Law and Policy" (1956-57) 3 *McGill L.J.* 29.

Scott, in *Livre-Souvenir*, 177

F.R. Scott, "The Law of Successions in the Quebec and in the French Civil Codes" in *Livre-Souvenir des journées du droit civil français* (Montréal: Le Barreau de Montréal, 1936) 177.

Scrutton, *Affreightment*

T.E. Scrutton, *The Contract of Affreightment as Expressed in Charter-Parties and Bills of Lading* (London: Sweet & Maxwell, 1998).

Sheppard, (1963) 23 *R. du B.* 311

C.-A. Sheppard, "The Enforcement of Restrictive Covenants in Quebec Law" (1963) 23 *R. du B.* 311.

Smith, (1974) 34 *R. du B.* 464

J. Smith, "The Duties of Care and Skill of Corporate Executives in the Company Law of the Province of Quebec" (1974) 34 *R. du B.* 464.

Smith, (1974) 52 *Can. Bar Rev.* 1

J. Smith, "The Protection of Third Parties Contracting with Companies in Quebec" (1974) 52 *Can. Bar Rev.* 1.

Smith, (1973) 33 *R. du B.* 253

J. Smith, "Liability of Corporate Executive for Illegal Profits in the Company Law of the Province of Quebec" (1973) 33 *R. du B.* 253.

Smyth, (1956-57) 3 *McGill L.J.* 171

J.C. Smyth, "Seizin in the Quebec Law of Successions" (1956-57) 3 *McGill L.J.* 171.

Smyth, in *Meredith Lectures (1981)*, 23

K. Smyth, "Financial Leasing: Some of its Characteristics, Advantages and Pitfalls" in *Meredith Memorial Lectures (1981)* (Don Mills, Ont.: Richard De Boo, 1982) 23.

Solomon, (1977) 37 *R. du B.* 519

N.H. Solomon, "Faillite" (1977) 37 *R. du B.* 519.

Tetley, in *Int. Enc. Comp. L.*, vol. XII, c. 4

W. Tetley, "Maritime Transportation", in *Int. Enc. Comp. L.*, vol. XII, *Law of Transport*, c. 4 (2001).

Tetley, (1994) 39 *McGill L.J.* 303

W. Tetley, "Evasion/Fraude à la loi" (1994) 39 *McGill L.J.* 303.

Tetley, (1987) 47 *R. du B.* 237

W. Tetley, "Set-off, Recoupment, Compensation and Counterclaim" (1987) 47 *R. du B.* 237.

Tetley, (1979) 20 *C. de D.* 449

W. Tetley, "The Himalaya Clause, 'Stipulation pour autrui', Non-Responsibility Clauses and Gross Negligence under the Civil Code" (1979) 20 *C. de D.* 449.

Tetley, (1977) 23 *McGill L.J.* 668

W. Tetley, "Letters of Indemnity: Should they be tolerated?" (1977) 23 *McGill L.J.* 668.

Thomas, *Roman Law*

P.-J. Thomas, *Introduction to Roman Law* (Deventer: Kluwer Law & Taxation Pub., 1986).

Tunc, in *Int. Enc. Comp. L.*, vol. XI

A. Tunc, "Introduction" in *Int. Enc. Comp. L.*, vol. XI, *Torts* (1983).

Turgeon, in *Matrimonial Property Law*, vol. 2, 139

H. Turgeon, "Matrimonial Property Law in the Province of Quebec" in W. Friedman, ed., *Matrimonial Property Law*, vol. 2 (Toronto: Carswell, 1955) 139.

Ulpian, *Digest*, vol. 1

Ulpian, in T. Mommsen, P. Krueger, & A. Watson, eds., *The Digest of Justinian*, vol. 1 (Philadelphia: University of Pennsylvania Press, 1985).

Van Zyl, *Roman Private Law*

D.H. Van Zyl, *History and Principles of Roman Private Law* (Durban, Pretoria: Butterworths, 1983).

Waddams, in *Meredith Lectures (1979)*, 63

S.M. Waddams, "Sections 8 to 10 of the Quebec Consumer Protection Act: A Common Law View" in *Meredith Memorial Lectures (1979)* (Toronto: Richard De Boo, 1979) 63.

Walton, *Obligations*, vol. 1

F.P. Walton, *The Egyptian Law of Obligations: A Comparative Study with Reference to the French and English Law*, vol. 1 (London: Stevens and Sons Ltd., 1920).

Walton, *Scope and Interpretation*

F.P. Walton, *The Scope and Interpretation of the Civil Code of Lower Canada* (Montréal: Wilson & Lafleur, 1907).

Wasserman, (1952) 12 *R. du B.* 366

G. Wasserman, "Impossibility of Performance in the Civil Law of Quebec" (1952) 12 *R. du B.* 366.

Waters, *Law of Trusts*

D.W.M. Waters, *Law of Trusts in Canada*, 2nd ed. (Toronto: Carswell, 1984).

Watt, (1947) 7 *R. du B.* 226

A.M. Watt, "The Doctrine of Common Fault" (1947) 7 *R. du B.* 226.

Weber, (1960) 20 *R. du B.* 526

S.W. Weber, "Critique des arrêts: The Liability of a Builder to Purchaser or Subsequent Acquirer under Article 1688 C.C." (1960) 20 *R. du B.* 526.

Weinstein, (1974) 9 *R.J.T.* 383

S. Weinstein, "Medical and Hospital Responsibility in Quebec and the Use of the Contractual Regime in 1974" (1974) 9 *R.J.T.* 383.

Wilhelmson, (1992) 37 *McGill L.J.* 995

M. Wilhelmson, "The Nature of the Quebec Partnership: Moral Person, Organized Indivision or Autonomous Patrimony?" (1992) 37 *McGill L.J.* 995.

Williams, *Alchemy of Race and Rights*

P. Williams, *The Alchemy of Race and Rights: The Diary of a Law Professor* (Cambridge: Harvard University Press, 1991).

Willis, in *Meredith Lectures (1965)*, 23

R.H. Willis, "The Incapacity of Mental Illness" in *Meredith Memorial Lectures (1965)* (Montréal: Wilson & Lafleur, 1965) 23.

Yiannopoulos, *Treatise*, vol. 2

A.N. Yiannopoulos, *Louisiana Civil Law Treatise*, vol. 2, 3rd ed. (St. Paul, Minn.: West Publishing, 1991).

Zimmerman, *Obligations*

R. Zimmerman, *The Law of Obligations, Roman Foundations of the Civilian Tradition* (Cape Town, South Africa: Juta & Co., 1990).